# FINANCIAL MARKETS AND SERVICES



**E. Gordon**
***M.Com., M.Phil.***

*Former Professor and Head,*
*Dept. of Commerce,*
*A.N.J.A. College, Sivakasi.*

**Dr. K. Natarajan**
***M.Com., M.Phil., Ph.D.***

*Former Principal,*
*S.V.N. College, Madurai*
*&*
*Former Director, Management Studies,*
*Sri Kaliswari College, Sivakasi.*

Himalaya Publishing House

ISO 9001:2015 CERTIFIED

| | | | | | |
|---|---|---|---|---|---|
| **First Edition** | : | **1999** | **Reprint** | : | **2013** |
| **Reprint** | : | **2001** | **Ninth Revised Edition** | : | **2014** |
| **Second Revised Edition** | : | **2003** | **Tenth Revised Edition** | : | **2016** |
| **Third Revised Edition** | : | **2006** | **Reprint** | : | **2017** |
| **Fourth Revised Edition** | : | **2007** | **Eleventh Revised Edition** | : | **2018** |
| **Fifth Revised Edition** | : | **2008** | **Reprint** | : | **2019, 2020** |
| **Sixth Revised Edition** | : | **2010** | **Reprint** | : | **2021, 2022** |
| **Seventh Revised Edition** | : | **2011** | **Twelfth Revised Edition** | : | **2023** |
| **Eighth Revised Edition** | : | **2012** | **Reprint** | : | **2024** |

**Published by** : Mrs. Meena Pandey
for **HIMALAYA PUBLISHING HOUSE PVT. LTD.,**
"Ramdoot", Dr. Bhalerao Marg, Girgaon, Mumbai - 400 004.
**Phone:** 022-23860170, 23863863; **Fax:** 022-23877178
**E-mail:** himpub@bharatmail.co.in; **Website:** www.himpub.com

**Branch Offices** :

**New Delhi** : "Pooja Apartments", 4-B, Murari Lal Street, Ansari Road, Darya Ganj, New Delhi - 110 002. Phone: 011-23270392, 23278631; Fax: 011-23256286

**Nagpur** : Kundanlal Chandak Industrial Estate, Ghat Road, Nagpur - 440 018. Phone: 0712-2721215, 2721216

**Bengaluru** : Plot No. 91-33, 2nd Main Road, Seshadripuram, Behind Nataraja Theatre, Bengaluru - 560 020. Phone: 080-41138821; Mobile: 09379847017, 09379847005

**Hyderabad** : No. 3-4-184, Lingampally, Besides Raghavendra Swamy Matham, Kachiguda, Hyderabad - 500 027. Phone: 040-27560041, 27550139

**Chennai** : No. 34/44, Motilal Street, T. Nagar, Chennai - 600 017. Mobile: 09380460419

**Pune** : "Laksha" Apartment, First Floor, No. 527, Mehunpura, Shaniwarpeth (Near Prabhat Theatre), Pune - 411 030. Phone: 020-24496323, 24496333; Mobile: 09370579333

**Cuttack** : Plot No 5F-755/4, Sector-9, CDA Markat Nagar, Cuttack - 753 014, Odisha. Mobile: 09338746007

**Kolkata** : 3, S.M. Bose Road, Near Gate No. 5, Agarpara Railway Station, North 24 Parganas, West Bengal - 700109. Mobile: 09674536325

**DTP by** : Sudhakar Shetty

**Printed at** : Geetanjali Press Pvt. Ltd., Nagpur on behalf of HPH.

# PREFACE TO THE TWELFTH REVISED EDITION

It is with immense pleasure we present this Twelfth Edition in the hands of our esteemed readers. Healthy and regulated financial markets are very vital for mobilising capital by maintaining the confidence of the investors, issuers and intermediaries. Many developments have taken place in the financial sector in recent times in tune with new technological developments, introduction of new products, growth of financial markets and global integration. In order to keep pace with the changing economic environment and ever increasing demands of various market participants, the regulatory bodies have been taking all measures to facilitate easy and transparent capital mobilisation by ensuring adequate investor protection. SEBI has launched Unified Payment Interface payment option to retail investors. It has introduced new listing norms for the start-ups. It has also laid down strict norms for credit rating agencies so that ratings may be based on current and future risks rather than on historical data. The Union Budget 2019-20 has paved way for the launching of 'Social Stock Exchange'. All these recent developments have been duly covered in this edition. It is a restructured, revised and updated version of the previous edition. It is hoped that the present edition will meet fully the requirements of both categories of readers, practical and academic.

We are greatly indebted to all over well-wishers for their constant encouragement and valuable suggestions. Our publishers particularly Mrs. Meena Pandey, Shri Neeraj Pandey, Shri K.N. Pandey, Shri Anuj Pandey, Mrs. Nimisha and all other members of the Himalaya Publishing House Pvt. Ltd. deserve special thanks for their wholehearted support and cooperation in bringing out this edition elegantly and in time.

Critical comments and constructive suggestions for the improvement of this book are most welcome and will be greatly appreciated.

*Sivakasi* **E. Gordon**

*January, 2023* **K. Natarajan**

# PREFACE TO THE FIRST EDITION

Consequent upon the restructuring of commerce and management curricula by many Universities and autonomous colleges, many new subjects on thrust areas have recently been introduced. One such broad area is the **FINANCIAL SECTOR** which comprises of financial markets, financial institutions and financial services.

Financial markets have been increasingly influenced in recent times by financial innovations in terms of products and instruments, adoption of modern technologies, opening up of the market to the global economy, streamlining of the regulatory framework and so on. Similarly, many innovative financial products are introduced to cater to the varied requirements of both corporate and individual customers. In the aftermath of this changing financial scenario, students of commerce and management are badly in need of a suitable textbook covering all these aspects incorporating the latest developments in the respective fields.

Realising the imperative need to bring out a suitable book on **'Financial Markets and Services'** tailored to meet the specific requirements of students of many universities, a modest attempt has been made to present this edition in the hands of the academic community. The speciality of this volume is that all matters are presented in a lucid manner and in simple language, notwithstanding the technical nature of the subject. All latest developments have been covered, and above all, it is most student-friendly. We are confident that this book will serve as a beacon light to the student community who pursue higher education in the discipline of commerce and management.

For the convenience of students, the present work is divided into two sections — Section A dealing with financial markets and Section B dealing with financial services. This book owes its consummation to various distinguished personalities who have expressed their views on this subject in different books, journals, magazines and papers.

We are greatly indebted to all our well-wishers for their constant encouragement and valuable suggestions. Our publishers deserve special thanks for their wholehearted support and cooperation in bringing out this edition elegantly and in time.

Critical comments and constructive suggestions for the improvement of this book are most welcome and will be greatly appreciated.

We wish to express thanks to Mr. K. Sivadasan, Area Representative and members of Himalaya Publishing House Pvt. Ltd. for their wholehearted cooperation.

**E. Gordon**
**K. Natarajan**

# CONTENTS

## SECTION A: FINANCIAL MARKETS



## SECTION B: FINANCIAL SERVICES

# DETAILED CONTENTS

## SECTION A: FINANCIAL MARKETS

# SECTION - A

# FINANCIAL MARKETS

1. The Financial System in India
2. Money Market
3. New Issue Market
4. Secondary Market
5. Securities and Exchange Board of India
6. Investors' Protection
7. OTCEI, NSE and BSE
8. Depository System

1

# THE FINANCIAL SYSTEM IN INDIA

The economic development of any country depends upon the existence of a well organised financial system. It is the financial system which supplies the necessary financial inputs for the production of goods and services which in turn promote the well-being and standard of living of the people of a country. Thus, the 'financial system' is a broader term which brings under its fold the financial markets and the financial institutions which support the system. The major assets traded in the financial system are money and monetary assets. The responsibility of the financial system is to mobilise the savings in the form of money and monetary assets and invest them to productive ventures. An efficient functioning of the financial system facilitates the free flow of funds to more productive activities and thus promotes investment. Thus, the financial system provides the intermediation between savers and investors and promotes faster economic development.

## FUNCTIONS OF THE FINANCIAL SYSTEM

### 1. Provision of liquidity

The major function of the financial system is the provision of money and monetary assets for the production of goods and services. There should not be any shortage of money for productive ventures. In financial language, the money and monetary assets are referred to as liquidity. The term liquidity refers to cash or money and other assets which can be converted into cash readily without loss of value and time. Hence, all activities in a financial system are related to liquidity — either provision of liquidity or trading in liquidity. In fact, in India the RBI has been vested with the monopoly power of issuing coins and currency notes. Commercial banks can also create cash (deposit) in the form of 'credit creation' and other financial institutions also deal in monetary assets. Over supply of money is also dangerous to the economy. In India, the RBI is the leader of the financial system and hence it has to control the money supply and creation of credit by banks and regulate all the financial institutions in the country in the best interest of the nation. It has to shoulder the responsibility of developing a sound financial system by strengthening the institutional structure and by promoting savings and investment in the country.

### 2. Mobilisation of savings

Another important activity of the financial system is to mobilise savings and channelise them into productive activities. The financial system should offer appropriate incentives to attract savings and make them available for more productive ventures. Thus, the financial system facilitates the transformation of savings into investment and consumption. The financial intermediaries have to play a dominant role in this activity.

### 3. Size transformation function

Generally, the savings of millions of small investors are in the nature of a small unit of capital which cannot find any fruitful avenue for investment unless it is transformed into a perceptible size of credit unit. Banks and other financial intermediaries perform this size transformation function by collecting deposits from a vast majority of small customers and giving them as loan of a sizeable quantity. Thus, this size transformation function is considered to be one of the very important functions of the financial system.

### 4. Maturity transformation function

Another function of the financial system is the maturity transformation function. The financial intermediaries accept deposits from public in different maturities according to their liquidity preference and lend them to the borrowers in different maturities according to their need and promote the economic activities of a country.

### 5. Risk transformation function

Most of the small investors are risk-averse with their small holding of savings. So, they hesitate to invest directly in stock market. On the other hand, the financial intermediaries collect the savings from individual savers and distribute them over different investment units with their high knowledge and expertise. Thus, the risks of individual investors get distributed. This risk transformation function promotes industrial development. Moreover, various risk mitigating tools are available in the financial system like hedging, insurance, use of derivatives, etc.

## FINANCIAL CONCEPTS

An understanding of the financial system requires an understanding of the following important concepts:

(*i*) Financial assets.

(*ii*) Financial intermediaries.

(*iii*) Financial markets.

(*iv*) Financial rates of return.

(*v*) Financial instruments.

## FINANCIAL ASSETS

In any financial transaction, there should be a creation or transfer of financial asset. Hence, the basic product of any financial system is the financial asset. A financial asset is one which is used for production or consumption or for further creation of assets. For instance, A, buys equity shares and these shares are financial assets since they earn income in future.

In this context, one must know the distinction between financial assets and physical assets. Unlike financial assets, physical assets are not useful for further production of goods or for earning income. For example, X purchases land and buildings, or gold and silver. These are physical assets since they cannot be used for further production. Many physical assets are useful for consumption only.

It is interesting to note that the objective of investment decides the nature of the asset. For instance, if a building is bought for residence purposes, it becomes a physical asset. If the same is bought for hiring, it becomes a financial asset.

### Classification of financial assets

Financial assets can be classified differently under different circumstances. One such classification is:

(*i*) Marketable assets

(*ii*) Non-marketable assets

#### ❖ Marketable assets

Marketable assets are those which can be easily transferred from one person to another without much hindrance. Examples: Shares of Listed Companies, Government Securities, Bonds of Public Sector Undertakings, etc.

#### ❖ Non-marketable assets

On the other hand, if the assets cannot be transferred easily, they come under this category. Examples: Bank Deposits, Provident Funds, Pension Funds, National Savings Certificates, Insurance Policies, etc. This classification is shown in the following Chart 1.1.

**CHART 1.1**

**FINANCIAL ASSETS**

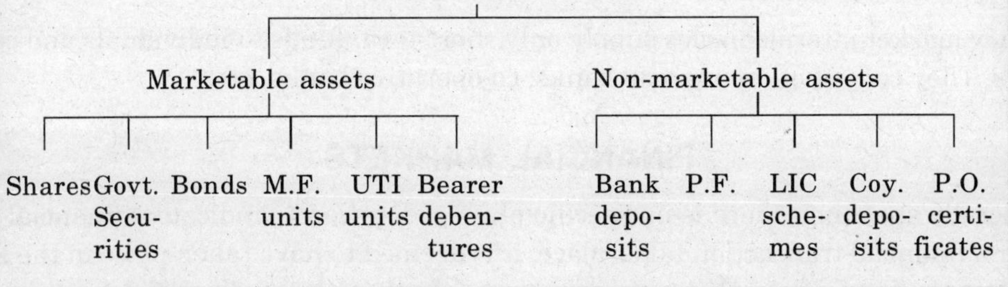

### ❖ Cash asset

In India, all coins and currency notes are issued by the RBI and the Ministry of Finance, Government of India. Besides, commercial banks can also create money by means of creating credit. When loans are sanctioned, liquid cash is not granted. Instead, an account is opened in the borrower's name and a deposit is created. It is also a kind of money asset.

### ❖ Debt asset

Debt asset is issued by a variety of organisations for the purpose of raising their debt capital. Debt capital entails a fixed repayment schedule with regard to interest and principal. There are different ways of raising debt capital. Example: issue of debentures, raising of term loans, working capital advance, etc.

### ❖ Stock asset

Stock is issued by business organisations for the purpose of raising their fixed capital. There are two types of stock — namely equity and preference. Equity shareholders are the real owners of the business and they enjoy the fruits of ownership and at the same time they bear the risks as well. Preference shareholders, on the other hand get a fixed rate of dividend (as in the case of debt asset) and at the same time they retain some characteristics of equity.

## FINANCIAL INTERMEDIARIES

The term financial intermediary includes all kinds of organisations which intermediate and facilitate financial transactions of both individuals and corporate customers. Thus, it refers to all kinds of financial institutions and investing institutions which facilitate financial transactions in financial markets. They may be in the organised sector or in the unorganised sector as shown in Chart 1.2 displayed in page 8. They may also be classified into two:

(*i*) Capital market intermediaries.

(*ii*) Money market intermediaries.

### ❖ Capital market intermediaries

These intermediaries mainly provide long-term funds to individuals and corporate customers. They consist of term lending institutions like financial corporations and investing institutions like LIC.

### ❖ Money market intermediaries

Money market intermediaries supply only short-term funds to individuals and corporate customers. They consist of commercial banks, co-operative banks, etc.

## FINANCIAL MARKETS

Generally speaking, there is no specific place or location to indicate a financial market. Wherever a financial transaction takes place, it is deemed to have taken place in the financial market. Hence, financial markets are pervasive in nature since, financial transactions are themselves very pervasive throughout the economic system. For instance, issue of equity shares, granting of loan by term lending institutions, deposit of money into a bank, purchase of debentures, sale of shares and so on.

However, financial markets can be referred to as those centres and arrangements which facilitate buying and selling of financial assets, claims and services. Sometimes, we do find the existence of a specific place or location for a financial market as in the case of stock exchange.

## Classification of financial markets

The classification of financial markets in India is shown in Chart 1.3 displayed in page 9.

### ❖ Unorganised markets

In these markets, there are a number of moneylenders, indigenous bankers, traders, etc., who lend money to the public. Indigenous bankers also collect deposits from the public. There are also private finance companies, chit funds, etc., whose activities are not controlled by the RBI. Recently, the RBI has taken steps to bring private finance companies and chit funds under its strict control by issuing Non-Banking Financial companies (Reserve Bank) Directions, 1998. The RBI has already taken some steps to bring the unorganised sector under the organised fold. They have not been successful. The regulations concerning their financial dealings are still inadequate and their financial instruments have not been standardised.

### ❖ Organised markets

In the organised markets, there are standardised rules and regulations governing their financial dealings. There is also a high degree of institutionalisation and instrumentalisation. These markets are subject to strict supervision and control by the RBI or other regulatory bodies.

These organised markets can be further classified into two. They are:

(*i*) Capital market.

(*ii*) Money market.

### ❖ Capital market

The capital market is a market for financial assets which have a long or indefinite maturity. Generally, it deals with long-term securities which have a maturity period of above one year. Capital market may be further divided into three namely:

(*i*) Industrial securities market.

(*ii*) Government securities market, and

(*iii*) Long-term loans market.

#### (i) Industrial securities market

As the very name implies, it is a market for industrial securities namely: (*i*) Equity shares or ordinary shares, (*ii*) Preference shares, and (*iii*) Debentures or bonds. It is a market where industrial concerns raise their capital or debt by issuing appropriate instruments. It can be further subdivided into two. They are:

(*i*) Primary market or New issue market.

(*ii*) Secondary market or Stock exchange.

**CHART 1.2**

**FINANCIAL INTERMEDIARIES IN INDIA**

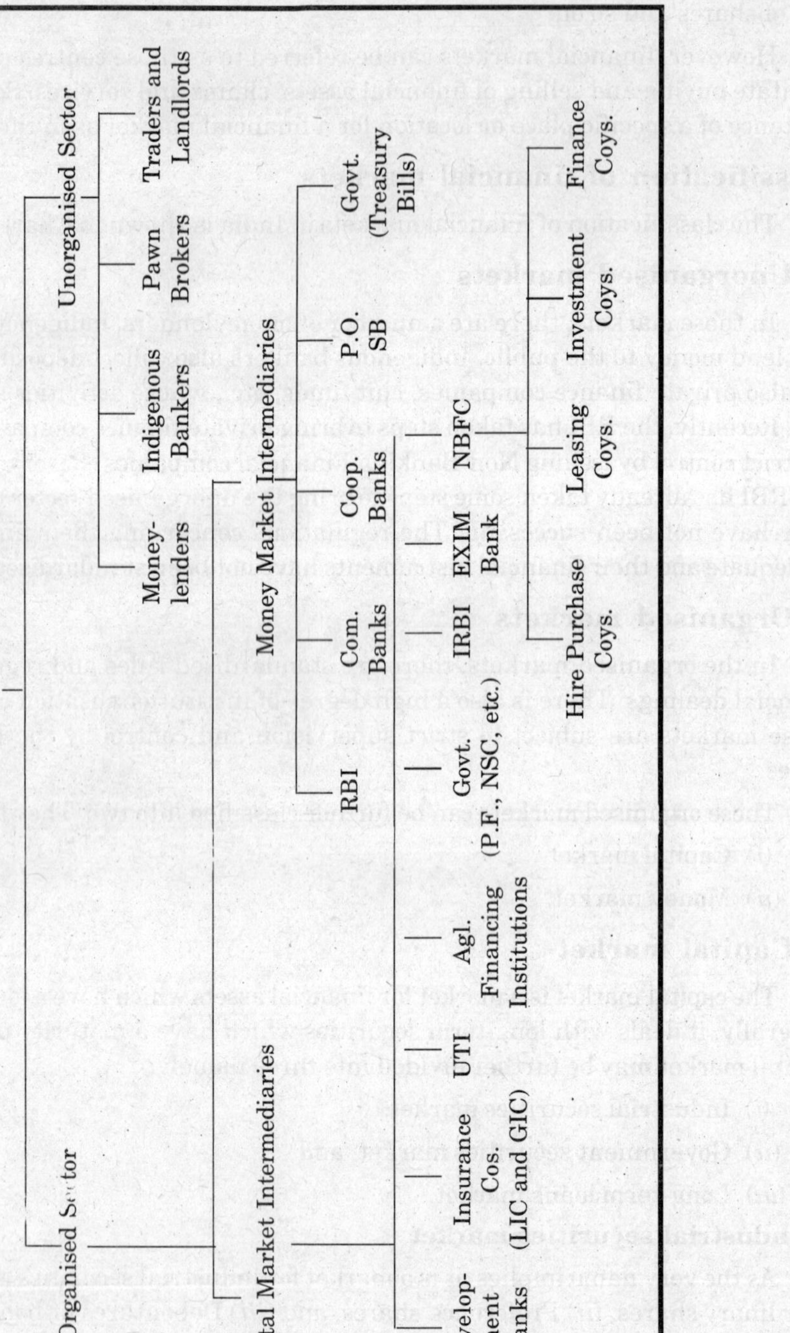

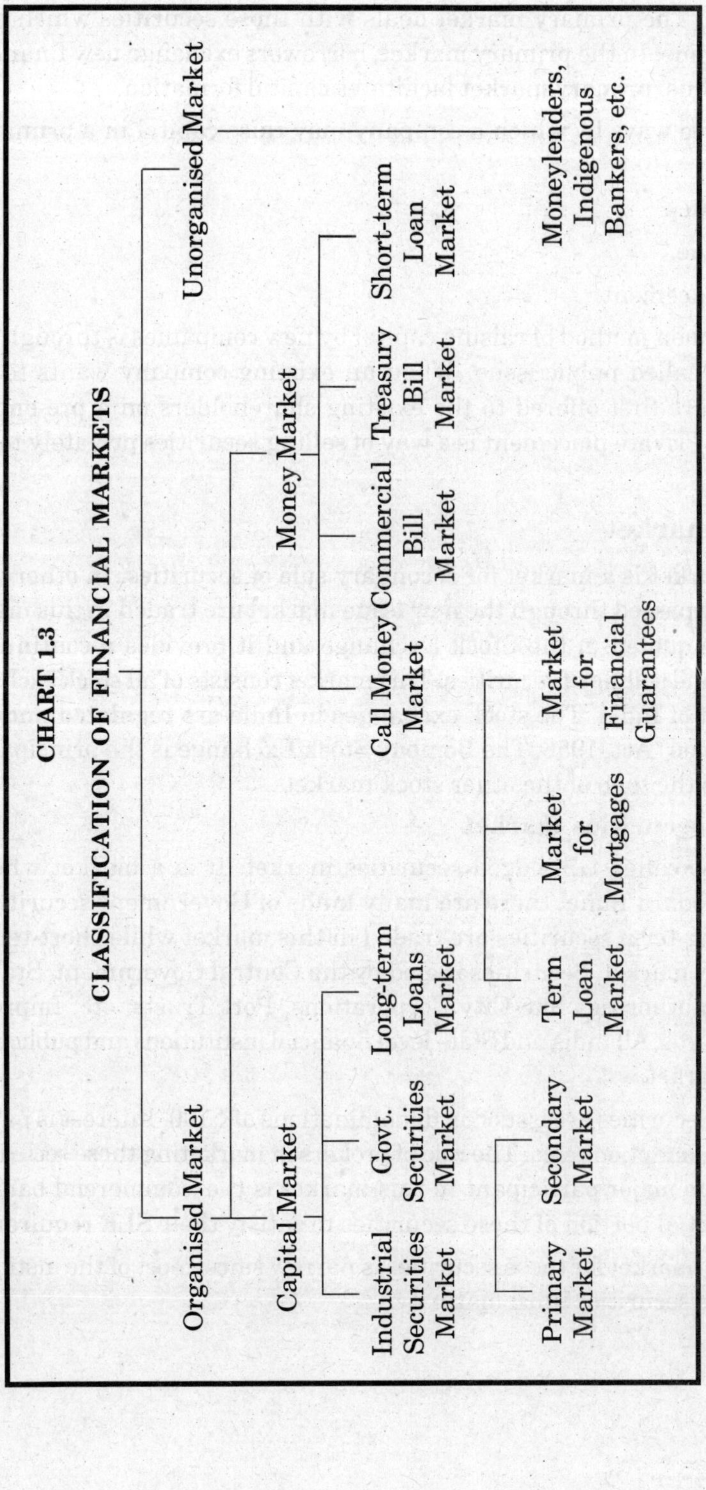


CHART 1.3

CLASSIFICATION OF FINANCIAL MARKETS

### ❖ Primary market

Primary market is a market for new issues or new financial claims. Hence, it is also called New Issue Market. The primary market deals with those securities which are issued to the public for the first time. In the primary market, borrowers exchange new financial securities for long-term funds. Thus, primary market facilitates capital formation.

There are three ways by which a company may raise capital in a primary market. They are:

(*i*) Public issue.

(*ii*) Rights issue.

(*iii*) Private placement.

The most common method of raising capital by new companies is through sale of securities to the public. It is called public issue. When an existing company wants to raise additional capital, securities are first offered to the existing shareholders on a pre-emptive basis. It is called rights issue. Private placement is a way of selling securities privately to a small group of investors.

### ❖ Secondary market

Secondary market is a market for secondary sale of securities. In other words, securities which have already passed through the new issue market are traded in this market. Generally, such securities are quoted in the Stock Exchange and it provides a continuous and regular market for buying and selling of securities. This market consists of all stock exchanges recognised by the Government of India. The stock exchanges in India are regulated under the Securities Contracts (Regulation) Act, 1956. The Bombay Stock Exchange is the principal stock exchange in India which sets the tone of the other stock markets.

**(ii) Government securities market**

It is otherwise called Gilt-edged securities market. It is a market where Government Securities are traded. In India, there are many kinds of Government securities — short-term and long-term. Long-term securities are traded in this market while short-term securities are traded in the money market. Securities issued by the Central Government, State Governments, Semi-government authorities like City Corporations, Port Trusts, etc. Improvement Trusts, State Electricity Boards, All India and State level financial institutions and public sector enterprises are dealt in this market.

Government Securities are issued in denominations of ₹ 100. Interest is payable half-yearly and they carry tax exemptions also. The role of brokers in marketing these securities is practically very limited and the major participant in this market is the 'commercial banks' because they hold a very substantial portion of these securities to satisfy their SLR requirements.

The secondary market for these securities is narrow since, most of the institutional investors tend to retain these securities until maturity.

The Government Securities are in many forms. These are generally:

(*i*) Stock certificates or inscribed stock.

(*ii*) Promissory notes.

(*iii*) Bearer bonds which can be discounted.

Government Securities are sold through the Public Debt Office of the RBI while Treasury Bills (short-term securities) are sold through auctions.

Government Securities offer a good source of raising inexpensive finance for the Government exchequer and the interest on these securities influences the prices and yields in this market. Hence, this market also plays a vital role in monetary management.

## ❖ STRIPS – Separate Trading of Registered Interest and Principal of Securities

With a view to improving liquidity and widening the investor base of the Government Securities market, stripping and reconstitution of Government Securities have been permitted under the Government Securities Act, 2006. Stripping is nothing but the process of separating a standard coupon leaving bond into its constituent interest and principal components. For example, stripping a 15-year security would yield 30 coupon securities (generally coupon payments are made on Jan 2 and July 2) maturing on the respective coupon dates and one principal security representing the principal amount maturing on the redemption date of the 15-year security. All the 30 coupon securities and the principal security would thereafter become zero coupon bonds. The reverse of stripping in called reconstitution. That is, when all the coupon STRIPS and the principal STRIPS are reassembled into the original Government Security, it is called reconstitution.

The special feature of STRIPS is that the coupon STRIPS of the same date, though from different stocks are exchangeable since they are identical by their maturity dates. STRIPS provide additional instruments to institutional investors for their asset-liability management. Again, STRIPS have zero investment risk (discounted instruments with no periodic interest payment). Stripping/Reconstitution can be done at the option of the holder at any time from the date of issues of a Government Security till its maturity. The minimum amount of securities that needs to the submitted for Stripping/Reconstitution will be ₹ 1 crore (face value) and multiples thereof.

## ❖ R. Gandhi Committee's Recommendations

To enhance liquidity in the Government Securities market and Interest Rate Derivatives market, the following measures have been taken on the recommendations of the above Committee:

(*i*) The auction bid timing has been reduced from 120 minutes to 90 minutes.

(*ii*) The settlement cycle of the primary auction for T-Bills has been changed from $T_2$ to $T_1$ basis.

(*iii*) Buyback/switching of Government securities has been introduced for ₹ 500 billion.

(*iv*) The investment limit for FIIs will be gradually raised to US $ 30 billion.

(*v*) Inflation-indexed bonds have been launched.

**(iii) Long-term loans market**

Development banks and commercial banks play a significant role in this market by supplying long-term loans to corporate customers. Long-term loans market may further be classified into:

(*i*) Term loans market.

(*ii*) Mortgages market.

(*iii*) Financial guarantees market.

## ❖ Term loans market

In India, many industrial financing institutions have been created by the Government both at the national and regional levels to supply long-term and medium-term loans to corporate customers directly as well as indirectly. These development banks dominate the industrial finance in India. Institutions like IRBI, IFCI, and other state financial corporations come under this category. These institutions meet the growing and varied long-term financial requirements of industries by supplying long-term loans. They also help in identifying investment opportunities, encourage new entrepreneurs and support modernisation efforts.

## ❖ Mortgages market

The mortgages market refers to those centres which supply mortgage loan mainly to individual customers. A mortgage loan is a loan against the security of immovable property like real estate. The transfer of interest in a specific immovable property to secure a loan is called mortgage. This mortgage may be equitable mortgage or legal one. Again, it may be a first charge or second charge. Equitable mortgage is created by a mere deposit of title deeds to properties as security, whereas in the case of a legal mortgage the title in the property is legally transferred to the lender by the borrower. Legal mortgage is less risky.

Similarly, in the first charge, the mortgager transfers his interest in the specific property to the mortgagee as security. When the property in question is already mortgaged once to another creditor, it becomes a second charge when it is subsequently mortgaged to somebody else. The mortgagee can also further transfer his interest in the mortgaged property to another. In such a case, it is called a sub-mortgage.

The mortgage market may have primary market as well as secondary market. The primary market consists of original extension of credit and secondary market has sales and resales of existing mortgages at prevailing prices.

In India, residential mortgages are the most common ones. The Housing and Urban Development Corporation (HUDCO) and the LIC play a dominant role in financing residential projects. Besides, the Land Development Banks provide cheap mortgage loans for the development of lands, purchase of equipment, etc. These development banks raise finance through the sale of debentures which are treated as trustee securities.

## ❖ Financial guarantees market

A guarantee Market is a centre where finance is provided against the guarantee of a reputed person in the financial circle. Guarantee is a contract to discharge the liability of a third party in case of his default. Guarantee acts as a security from the creditor's point of view. In case the borrower fails to repay the loan, the liability falls on the shoulders of the guarantor. Hence, the guarantor must be known to both the borrower and the lender and he must have the means to discharge his liability.

Though there are many types of guarantees, the common forms are: (*i*) Performance guarantee, and (*ii*) Financial guarantee. Performance guarantees cover the payment of earnest money, retention money, advance payments, non-completion of contracts, etc. On the other hand, financial guarantees cover only financial contracts.

In India, the market for financial guarantees is well organised. The financial guarantees in India relate to:

(*i*) Deferred payments for imports and exports.

(*ii*) Medium and long-term loans raised abroad.

(*iii*) Loans advanced by banks and other financial institutions.

These guarantees are provided mainly by commercial banks, development banks, Governments, both Central and States and other specialised guarantee institutions like ECGC (Export Credit Guarantee Corporation) and DICGC (Deposit Insurance and Credit Guarantee Corporation). This guarantee financial service is available to both individual and corporate customers. For a smooth functioning of any financial system, this guarantee service is absolutely essential.

## IMPORTANCE OF CAPITAL MARKET

Absence of capital market acts as a deterrent factor to capital formation and economic growth. Resources would remain idle if finances are not funneled through the capital market. The importance of capital market can be briefly summarised as follows:

(*i*) The capital market serves as an important source for the productive use of the economy's savings. It mobilises the savings of the people for further investment and thus, avoids their wastage in unproductive uses.

(*ii*) It provides incentives to saving and facilitates capital formation by offering suitable rates of interest as the price of capital.

(*iii*) It provides an avenue for investors, particularly the household sector to invest in financial assets which are more productive than physical assets.

(*iv*) It facilitates increase in production and productivity in the economy and thus, enhances the economic welfare of the society. Thus, it facilitates 'the movement of stream of command over capital to the point of highest yield' towards those who can apply them productively and profitably to enhance the national income in the aggregate.

(*v*) The operations of different institutions in the capital market induce economic growth. They give quantitative and qualitative directions to the flow of funds and bring about rational allocation of scarce resources.

(*vi*) A healthy capital market consisting of expert intermediaries promotes stability in values of securities representing capital funds.

(*vii*) Moreover, it serves as an important source for technological upgradation in the industrial sector by utilising the funds invested by the public.

Thus, a capital market serves as an important link between those who save and those who aspire to invest their savings.

## MONEY MARKET

Money market is a market for dealing with financial assets and securities which have a maturity period of up to one year. In other words, it is a market for purely short-term funds. The money market may be subdivided into four. They are:

(*i*) Call money market.

(*ii*) Commercial bills market.

(*iii*) Treasury bills market.

(*iv*) Short-term loan market.

### ❖ Call money market

The call money market is a market for extremely short period loans say one day to fourteen days. So, it is highly liquid. The loans are repayable on demand at the option of either the lender or the borrower. In India, call money markets are associated with the presence of stock exchanges and hence, they are located in major industrial towns like Mumbai, Kolkata, Chennai, Delhi, Ahmedabad, etc. The special feature of this market is that the interest rate varies from day-to-day and even from hour-to-hour and centre-to-centre. It is very sensitive to changes in demand and supply of call loans.

### ❖ Commercial bills market

It is a market for bills of exchange arising out of genuine trade transactions. In the case of credit sale, the seller may draw a bill of exchange on the buyer. The buyer accepts such a bill, promising to pay at a later date the amount specified in the bill. The seller need not wait until the due date of the bill. Instead, he can get immediate payment by discounting the bill.

In India, the bill market is underdeveloped. The RBI has taken many steps to develop a sound bill market. The RBI has enlarged the list of participants in the bill market. The Discount and Finance House of India was set up in 1988 to promote secondary market in bills. In spite of all these, the growth of the bill market is slow in India. There are no specialised agencies for discounting bills. The commercial banks play a significant role in this market.

### ❖ Treasury bills market

It is a market for treasury bills which have 'short-term' maturity. A treasury bill is a promissory note or a finance bill issued by the Government. It is highly liquid because its repayment is guaranteed by the Government. It is an important instrument for short-term borrowing of the Government. There are two types of treasury bills namely: (*i*) Ordinary or Regular and (*ii*) *ad hoc* treasury bills popularly known as '*ad hocs*'.

Ordinary treasury bills are issued to the public, banks and other financial institutions with a view to raising resources for the Central Government to meet its short-term financial needs.

*Ad hoc* treasury bills are issued in favour of the RBI only. They are not sold through tender or auction. They can be purchased by the RBI only. *Ad hocs* are not marketable in India but holders of these bills can sell them back to RBI. Treasury bills have a maturity period of 91 days or 182 days or 364 days only. Financial intermediaries can park their temporary surpluses in these instruments and earn income.

### ❖ Short-term loan market

It is a market where short-term loans are given to corporate customers for meeting their working capital requirements. Commercial banks play a significant role in this market. Commercial banks provide short-term loans in the form of cash credit and overdraft. Overdraft facility is mainly given to business people, whereas cash credit is given to industrialists. Overdraft is purely a temporary accommodation and it is given in the current account itself. But, cash credit is for a period of one year and it is sanctioned in a separate account.

## FOREIGN EXCHANGE MARKET

The term foreign exchange refers to the process of converting home currencies into foreign currencies and *vice versa.* According to Dr. Paul Einzing, 'Foreign exchange is the system or process of converting one national currency into another, and of transferring money from one country to another'.

The market where foreign exchange transactions take place is called a foreign exchange market. It does not refer to a marketplace in the physical sense of the term. In fact, it consists of a number of dealers, banks and brokers engaged in the business of buying and selling foreign exchange. It also includes the central bank of each country and the treasury authorities who enter into this market as controlling authorities. Those engaged in the foreign exchange business are controlled by the Foreign Exchange Maintenance Act (FEMA).

### ❖ Functions

The most important functions of this market are:

(*i*) To make necessary arrangements to transfer purchasing power from one country to another.

(*ii*) To provide adequate credit facilities for the promotion of foreign trade.

(*iii*) To cover foreign exchange risks by providing hedging facilities.

In India, the foreign exchange business has a three-tiered structure consisting of:

(*i*) Trading between banks and their commercial customers.

(*ii*) Trading between banks through authorised brokers.

(*iii*) Trading with banks abroad.

Brokers play a significant role in the foreign exchange market in India. Apart from authorised dealers, the RBI has permitted licensed hotels and individuals (known as Authorised Money Changers) to deal in foreign exchange business. The FEMA helps to smoothen the flow of foreign currency and to prevent any misuse of foreign exchange which is a scarce commodity.

## FINANCIAL RATES OF RETURN

Most households in India still prefer to invest on physical assets like land, buildings, gold, silver, etc. But, studies have shown that investment in financial assets like equities in capital market fetches more return than investments on gold. It is imperative that one should have some basic knowledge about the rate of return on financial assets also.

The return on Government Securities and bonds are comparatively less than on corporate securities due to lower risk involved therein. The Government and the RBI determine the interest rates on Government Securities. Thus, the interest rates are administered and controlled. The peculiar feature of the interest rate structure is that the interest rates do not reflect the free market forces. They do not reflect the scarcity value of capital in the country also. Most of these rates are fixed on an ad hoc basis depending upon the credit and monetary policy of the Government.

Generally, the interest rate policy of the Government is designed to achieve the following:

(*i*) To enable the Government to borrow comparatively at cheaper rate.

(*ii*) To ensure stability in the macroeconomic system.

(*iii*) To support certain sectors through preferential lending rates.

(*iv*) To mobilise substantial savings in the economy.

The interest rate structure for bank deposits and bank credits is also influenced by the RBI. Normally, interest is a reward for risk undertaken through investment and at the same time it is a return for abstaining from consumption. The interest rate structure should allocate scarce capital between alternative uses. Unfortunately, in India the administered interest rate policy of the Government fails to perform the role of allocating scarce resources between alternative uses.

### ❖ Recent trends

With a view to bring the interest rates nearer to the free market rates, the Government has taken the following steps:

(*i*) The interest rates on company deposits are freed.

(*ii*) The interest rates on 364 days Treasury Bills are determined by auctions and they are expected to reflect the free market rates.

(*iii*) The coupon rates on Government loans have been revised upwards so as to be market-oriented.

(*iv*) The interest rates on debentures are allowed to be fixed by companies depending upon the market rates.

(*v*) The maximum rates of interest payable on bank deposits (fixed) are freed for all deposits.

Thus, all attempts are being taken to adopt a realistic interest rate policy so as to give a positive return in real terms adjusted for inflation. The proper functioning of any financial system requires a good interest rate structure.

## FINANCIAL INSTRUMENTS

Financial instruments refer to those documents which represent financial claims on assets. As discussed earlier, financial asset refers to a claim to the repayment of a certain sum of money at the end of a specified period together with interest or dividend. Examples: Bill of Exchange, Promissory Note, Treasury Bill, Government Bond, Deposit Receipt, Share, Debenture, etc. The innovative instruments introduced in India have been discussed later in the chapter 'Financial Services'.

Financial instruments can also be called financial securities. Financial securities can be classified into:

(*i*) Primary or direct securities.

(*ii*) Secondary or indirect securities.

### ❖ Primary securities

These are securities directly issued by the ultimate investors to the ultimate savers, *e.g.*, shares and debentures issued directly to the public.

### ❖ Secondary securities

These are securities issued by some intermediaries called financial intermediaries to the ultimate savers, *e.g.*, Unit Trust of India and Mutual Funds issue securities in the form of units to the public and the money pooled is invested in companies.

Again these securities may be classified on the basis of duration as follows:

(*i*) Short-term securities.

(*ii*) Medium-term securities.

(*iii*) Long-term securities.

Short-term securities are those which mature within a period of one year, *e.g.*, Bill of Exchange, Treasury Bill, etc. Medium-term securities are those which have a maturity period ranging between one to five years, *e.g.*, Debentures maturing within a period of five years. Long-term securities are those which have a maturity period of more than five years, *e.g.*, Government Bonds maturing after ten years.

### ❖ Characteristic features of financial instruments

Generally speaking, financial instruments possess the following characteristic features:

(*i*) Most of the instruments can be easily transferred from one hand to another without many cumbersome formalities.

(*ii*) They have a ready market, *i.e.*, they can be bought and sold frequently and thus, trading in these securities is made possible.

(*iii*) They possess liquidity, *i.e.*, some instruments can be converted into cash readily. For instance, a bill of exchange can be converted into cash readily by means of discounting and rediscounting.

(*iv*) Most of the securities possess security value, *i.e.*, they can be given as security for the purpose of raising loans.

(*v*) Some securities enjoy tax status, *i.e.*, investments in these securities are exempted from Income Tax, Wealth Tax, etc., subject to certain limits, *e.g.*, Public Sector Tax Free Bonds, Magnum Tax Saving Certificates.

(*vi*) They carry risk in the sense that there is uncertainty with regard to payment of principal or interest or dividend as the case may be.

(*vii*) These instruments facilitate futures trading so as to cover risks due to price fluctuations, interest rate fluctuations, etc.

(*viii*) These instruments involve less handling costs since expenses involved in buying and selling these securities are generally much less.

(*ix*) The return on these instruments is directly in proportion to the risk undertaken.

(*x*) These instruments may be short-term or medium-term or long-term depending upon the maturity period of these instruments.

## DEVELOPMENT OF FINANCIAL SYSTEM IN INDIA

Some serious attention was paid to the development of a sound financial system in India only after the launching of the planning era in the country. At the time of Independence in 1947, there was no strong financial institutional mechanism in the country. There was absence of issuing institutions and non-participation of intermediary financial institutions. The industrial sector also had no access to the savings of the community. The capital market was very primitive and shy. The private as well as the unorganised sector played a key role in the provision of 'liquidity'. On the whole, chaotic conditions prevailed in the system.

With the adoption of the theory of mixed economy, the development of the financial system took a different turn so as to fulfil the socio-economic and political objectives. The Government started creating new financial institutions to supply finance both for agricultural and industrial development and it also progressively started nationalising some important financial institutions so that the flow of finance might be in the right direction.

### ❖ Nationalisation of Financial Institutions

As stated earlier, the RBI is the leader of the financial system. But, it was established as a private institution in 1935. It was nationalised in 1948. It was followed by the nationalisation of the Imperial Bank of India in 1956 by renaming it as State Bank of India. In the same year, 245 Life Insurance Companies were brought under Government control by merging all of them into a single corporation called Life Insurance Corporation of India. Another significant development in our financial system was the nationalisation of 14 major commercial banks in 1969. Again, six banks were nationalised in 1980. This process was then extended to General Insurance Companies which were reorganised under the name of General Insurance Corporation of India. Thus, the important financial institutions were brought under public control.

### ❖ Starting of Unit Trust of India

Another landmark in the history of development of our financial system is the establishment of new financial institutions to strengthen our system and to supply institutional credit to industries.

The Unit Trust of India was established in 1964 as a public sector institution to collect the savings of the people and make them available for productive ventures. It is the oldest and largest mutual fund in India. It is governed by its own statutes and regulations. However, since 1994, the schemes of UTI have to be approved by the SEBI. It has introduced a number of open-ended and close-ended schemes. It also provides repurchase facility of units of the various income schemes after a minimum lock-in period of one year. Some of the unit schemes of UTI are linked with stock exchanges. Its investment is confined to both corporate and non-corporate sectors. In recent years, it has established the following subsidiaries:

(*i*) The UTI Bank Ltd. in April 1994.

(*ii*) The UTI Investor Service Ltd. to act as UTI's own Registrar and Transfer Agency.

(*iii*) The UTI Security Exchange Ltd.

## ❖ Establishment of Development Banks

Many development banks were started not only to extend credit facilities to financial institutions but also to render advisory services. These banks are multipurpose institutions which provide medium and long-term credit to industrial undertakings, discover investment projects, undertake the preparation of project reports, provide technical advice and managerial services and assist in the management of industrial units. These institutions are intended to develop backward regions as well as small and new entrepreneurs.

The Industrial Finance Corporation of India (IFCI) was set up in 1948 with the object of 'making medium and long-term credits more readily available to industrial concerns in India, particularly under circumstances where normal banking accommodation is inappropriate or recourse to capital issue method is impracticable'. At the regional level, State Financial Corporations were established under the State Financial Corporation Act, 1951 with a view of providing medium and long-term finance to medium and small industries. It was followed by the establishment of the Industrial Credit and Investment Corporation of India (ICICI) in 1955 to develop large and medium industries in private sector, on the initiative of the World Bank. It adopted a more dynamic and modern approach in industrial financing. Subsequently, the Government of India set up the Refinance Corporation of India (RCI) in 1958 with a view of providing refinance facilities to banks against term loans granted by them to medium and small units. Later on, it was merged with the Industrial Development Bank of India.

The Industrial Development Bank of India (IDBI) was established on July 1, 1964 as a wholly-owned subsidiary of the RBI. The ownership of IDBI was then transferred to the Central Government with effect from February 16, 1976. The IDBI was the apex institution in the area of development banking and as such it had to coordinate the activities of all the other financial institutions. However, it has been converted into a commercial bank and so it has lost the status of a development bank now. At the State level, the State Industrial Development Corporations (SIDCO)/State Industrial Investment Corporations were created to meet the financial requirements of the States and to promote regional development.

In 1971, the IDBI and LIC jointly set up the Industrial Reconstruction Corporation of India (IRCI) with the main objective of reconstruction and rehabilitation of sick industrial undertakings. The IRCI was converted into a statutory corporation in March 1985 and renamed as the Industrial Reconstruction Bank of India (IRBI). In 1997, the IRBI has to be completely restructured since it itself has become sick due to financing of sick industries. Now, it is converted into a limited company with a new name of Industrial Investment Bank of India (IIBI). Its objective is to finance only expansion, diversification, modernisation, etc., of industries and thus it has become a development bank.

The Small Industries Development Bank of India (SIDBI) was set up as a wholly-owned subsidiary of IDBI. It commenced operations on April 2, 1990. The SIDBI has taken over the responsibility of administrating the Small Industries Development Fund and the National Equity Fund.

## ❖ Institution for Financing Agriculture

In 1963, the RBI set up the Agricultural Refinance and Development Corporation (ARDC) to provide refinance support to banks to finance major development projects such as minor irrigation, farm mechanisation, land development, horticulture, dairy development, etc. However, in July 1982, the National Bank for Agriculture and Rural Development (NABARD) was established and the ARDC was merged with it. The whole sphere of agricultural finance has been handed over to NABARD. The functions of the Agricultural Credit Department and Rural Planning and Credit Cell of the RBI have been taken over by NABARD.

## ❖ Institution for Foreign Trade

The Export and Import Bank of India (EXIM Bank) was set up on January 1, 1982 to take over the operations of International Finance wing of the IDBI. Its main objective is to provide financial assistance to exporters and importers. It functions as the principal financial institution for coordinating the working of other institutions engaged in financing of foreign trade. It also provides refinance facilities to other financial institutions against their export-import financing activities.

## ❖ Institution for Housing Finance

The National Housing Bank (NHB) has been set up on July 9, 1988 as an apex institution to mobilise resources for the housing sector and to promote housing finance institutions both at regional and local levels. It provides refinance facilities to housing finance institutions and scheduled banks. It also provides guarantee and underwriting facilities to housing finance institutions. Again, it coordinates the working of all agencies connected with housing.

## ❖ Stock Holding Corporation of India Ltd. (SHCIL)

In 1987 another institution, *viz.*, Stock Holding Corporation of India Ltd. was set up to tone up the stock and capital markets in India. Its main objective is to provide quick share transfer facilities, clearing services, depository services, support services, management information services and development services to investors both individuals and corporates. The SHCIL was set up by seven All India financial institutions, *viz.*, IDBI, IFCI, ICICI, LIC, GIC, UTI and IRBI.

## ❖ Mutual Funds Industry

Mutual funds refer to the funds raised by financial service companies by pooling the savings of the public and investing them in a diversified portfolio. They provide investment avenues for small investors who cannot participate in the equities of big companies. Mutual funds have been floated by some public sector banks, LIC, GIC and recently by private sector also.

## ❖ Venture Capital Institutions

Venture capital is another method of financing in the form of equity participation. A venture capitalist finances a project based on the potentialities of a new innovative project. Much thrust is given to new ideas or technological innovations. Indeed, it is a long-term risk capital to finance high technology projects. The IDBI venture capital fund was set up in 1986. The IFCI has started a subsidiary to finance venture capital, *viz.*, The Risk Capital and Technology Finance Corporation (RCTC). Likewise, the ICICI and the UTI have jointly set up the Technology Development and Information Company of India Limited (TDICI) in 1988 to provide venture capital. Similarly, many State Financial Corporations and commercial banks have started subsidiaries to provide venture capital. The Indus Venture Capital Fund and the Credit Capital Venture Fund Limited come under the private sector.

## ❖ Credit Rating Agencies

Of late, many credit rating agencies have been established to help investors to make a decision of their investment in various instruments and to protect them from risky ventures. At the same time, it has the effect of improving the competitiveness of the companies so that one can excel the other. Credit rating is now mandatory for all debt instruments. Similarly, for accepting deposits, non-banking companies have to compulsorily go for credit rating. Some of the important credit rating agencies established are:

(*i*) Credit Rating and Information Services of India Ltd. (CRISIL).

(*ii*) Investment Information and Credit Rating Agency of India Ltd. (ICRA).

(*iii*) Credit Analysis and Research Ltd. (CARE).

The rating is confined to fixed deposits, debentures, preference shares and short-term instruments like commercial paper. The rating of equity shares will come into effect soon. The establishment of various credit rating agencies will go a long way in stabilising the financial system in India by supplying vital credit information about corporate customers.

## ❖ Multiplicity of Financial Instruments

The expansion in size and number of financial institutions has consequently led to a considerable increase in the financial instruments also. New instruments have been introduced in the form of innovative schemes of LIC, UTI, Banks, Post Office Savings Bank Accounts, Shares and debentures of different varieties, Public Sector Bonds, National Savings Scheme, National Savings Certificates, Provident Funds, Relief Bonds, Indira Vikas Patra, etc. Thus, different types of instruments are available in the financial system so as to meet the diversified requirements of varied investors and thereby making the system more healthy and vibrant.

## ❖ Legislative Support

The Indian financial system has been well supported by suitable legislative measures taken by the Government then and there for its proper growth and smooth functioning. Though there are many enactments, some of them are very important. The Indian Companies Act was passed in 1956 with a view of regulating the functioning of companies from birth to death. It mainly aims at giving more protection to investors since there is a diversity of ownership and management in companies. It was a follow-up to the Capital Issues Control Act passed in 1947. Again, in 1956, the Securities Contracts (Regulation) Act was passed to prevent undesirable transactions in securities. It mainly regulates the business of trading in the stock exchanges. This act permitted only recognised stock exchanges to function.

To ensure the proper functioning of the economic system and to prevent concentration of economic power in the hands of a few, the Monopolies and Restrictive Trade Practices Act was passed in 1970. In 1973, the Foreign Exchange Regulations Act was enacted to regulate the foreign exchange dealings and to control Indian investments abroad and *vice versa*.

The Capital Issues Control Act was replaced by setting up of the Securities Exchange Board of India. Its main objective is to protect the interest of investors by suitably regulating the dealings in the stock market and money market so as to achieve efficient and fair trading in these markets. When the Government adopted the New Economic Policy, many of these acts were amended so as to remove many unwanted controls. Banks and financial institutions have been permitted to become members of the stock market in India. They have been permitted to float mutual funds, undertake leasing business, carry-out factoring services, etc.

Besides the above, the Indian Contract Act, The Negotiable Instruments Act, The Law of Limitation Act, The Banking Regulations Act, The Stamp Act, etc., deserve a special mention. When the financial system grows, the necessity of regulating it also grows side-by-side by means of bringing suitable legislations. These legislative measures have reorganised the Indian financing system to a greater extent and have restored confidence in the minds of the investing public as well.

However, to avoid overlap in certain key areas between SEBl and other bodies such as Company Law Board, RBI, etc., it is necessary to classify the respective jurisdictions. At present, the jurisdiction is divided between the RBI (money market, repos, debt market, etc.) and SEBI. It would be advisable to consolidate the securities laws into one comprehensive legislation on the lines of the British Financial Services and Market Act, 2000.

### ❖ Financial Sector Legislative Reforms Commission (FSLRC)

The Central Government has very recently constituted the Financial Sector Legislative Reforms Commission (FSLRC) under the chairmanship of former Justice B.N. Srikrishna to rewrite and harmonise the various financial sector legislations, rules and regulations. There are over 60 acts and multiple rules and regulations and many of them have become archaic. Moreover, a large number of amendments made in these acts over time have increased the ambiguity and complexity of the system.

## FINANCIAL MARKETS REGULATION DEPARTMENT (FMRD)

The FMRD was set up on November 3, 2014 with a view to regulating, developing and overseeing the financial markets operating in India in an integrated manner. It also aims at strengthening the financial market infrastructure and market surveillance in line with global standards. For this purpose, it has to find out ways and means to make market access norms easier for all participants in addition to expanding the menu of financial products and services across all segments of financial markets including derivatives markets. Further, it has to leverage the market analytics and surveillance mechanism for appropriate policy inputs. It is expected that this department will take necessary measures to make the financial markets more efficient and transparent.

## FINANCIAL SYSTEM AND ECONOMIC DEVELOPMENT

The financial system plays a significant role in the process of economic development of a country. The financial system comprises of a network of commercial banks. Non-banking companies, development banks and other financial and investment institutions offer a variety of financial products and services to suit to the varied requirements of different categories of people. Since they function in a fairly developed capital and money markets, they play a crucial role in spurring economic growth in the following ways:

(i) **Mobilising savings:** The financial system mobilises the savings of the people by offering appropriate incentives and by deepening and widening the financial structure. In other words, the financial system creates varieties of forms of savings so that savings can take place according to the varying asset preferences of different classes of savers. In the absence of the financial system, all savings would remain idle in the hands of the savers and they would not have flown into productive ventures.

(ii) **Promoting investments:** For the economic growth of any nation, investment is absolutely essential. This investment has to flow from the financial system. In fact, the level of investment determines the increase in output of goods and services and incomes in the country. The financial system collects the savings and channels them into investment which contributes positively towards economic development.

(iii) **Encouraging investment in financial assets:** The dynamic role of the financial system in the economic development is that it encourages savings to flow into financial assets (money and monetary assets) as against physical assets (land, gold and other goods and services). The investments in physical assets are speculative and would breed inflation. On the other hand, investment in financial assets are non-inflationary in nature and would aid growth in the economy. The larger the proportion of the financial assets, the greater is the scope for economic growth in the long run.

(iv) **Allocating savings on the basis of national priorities:** Above all, the financial system allocates the savings in a more efficient manner so that the scarce capital may be more efficiently utilised among the various alternative investments. In other words, it gives preference to certain sectors, from the social and economic point of view, on the basis of national priorities.

(v) **Creating credit:** Large financial resources are needed for the economic development of a nation. These resources are supplied by the financial system not only in the form of liquid cash but also in the form of 'created money' or 'deposit money' by creating credit and thereby making available large resources to finance trade, production, distribution, etc. Thus, it accelerates economic growth by facilitating the transactions of trade, production and distribution on a large-scale.

(vi) **Providing a spectrum of financial assets:** The financial system provides a spectrum of financial assets so as to meet the varied requirements and preferences of households. Thus, it enables them to choose their asset portfolios in such a way as to achieve a preferred mix of return, liquidity and risk. Thus, it contributes to the economic development of a country.

(vii) **Financing trade, industry and agriculture:** All the financial institutions operating in a financial system take all efforts to ensure that no worthwhile project — be it in trade or agriculture or industry — suffers due to lack of funds. Thus, they promote industrial and agricultural development which have a greater say on the economic development of a country.

(viii) **Encouraging entrepreneurial talents:** The financial institutions encourage the managerial and entrepreneurial talents in the economy by promoting the spirit of enterprise and risk-taking capacity. They also furnish the necessary technical consultancy services to the entrepreneurs so that they may succeed in their innovative ventures.

(ix) **Providing financial services:** Sophistication and innovations have started appearing in the arena of financial intermediations as well. The financial institutions play a very dynamic role in the economic development of a country not only as a provider of finance, but also as a departmental store of finance by offering varieties of innovative financial products and services to meet the ever-increasing demands of their clients both corporates and individuals.

(x) **Developing backward areas:** The integral policy of the national development plans of every country concentrates on the development of relatively less developed areas called backward areas. The financial institutions provide a package of services, infrastructure and incentives conducive to a healthy growth of industries in such backward areas and thus, they contribute for the uniform development of all regions in a country.

## WEAKNESSES OF INDIAN FINANCIAL SYSTEM

After the introduction of planning, rapid industrialisation has taken place. It has in turn led to the growth of the corporate sector and the Government sector. In order to meet the growing requirements of the Government and the industries, many innovative financial instruments have been introduced. Besides, there has been a mushroom growth of financial intermediaries to meet the ever-growing financial requirements of different types of customers. Hence, the Indian financial system is more developed and integrated today than what it was 50 years ago. Yet, it suffers from some weaknesses as listed below:

(i) **Lack of coordination between different financial institutions:** There are a large number of financial intermediaries. Most of the vital financial institutions are owned by the Government. At the same time, the Government is also the controlling authority of these institutions. In these circumstances, the problem of coordination arises. As there is multiplicity of institutions in the Indian financial system, there is lack of coordination in the working of these institutions.

(ii) **Monopolistic market structures:** In India, some financial institutions are so large that they have created a monopolistic market structures in the financial system. For instance, a major share of life insurance business is in the hands of LIC. The UTI has more or less monopolised the mutual fund industry. The weakness of this large structure is that it could lead to inefficiency in their working or mismanagement or lack of effort in mobilising savings of the public and so on. Ultimately, it would retard the development of the financial system of the country itself.

(iii) **Dominance of development banks in industrial financing:** The development banks constitute the backbone of the Indian financial system occupying an important place in the capital market. The industrial financing today in India is largely through the financial institutions created by the Government both at the national and regional levels. These development banks act as distributive agencies only, since, they derive most of their funds from their sponsors. As such, they fail to mobilise the savings of the public. This would be a serious bottleneck which stands in the way of the growth of an efficient financial system in the country. For industries abroad, institutional finance has been a result of institutionalisation of personal savings through media like banks, LIC, pension and provident funds, Unit Trusts and so on. But they play a less significant role in Indian financial system, as far as industrial financing is concerned. However, in recent times attempts are being made to raise funds from the public through the issue of bonds, units, debentures and so on. It will go a long way in forging a link between the normal channels of savings and the distributing mechanism.

(iv) **Inactive and erratic capital market:** The important function of any capital market is to promote economic development through mobilisation of savings and their distribution to productive ventures. As far as industrial finance in India is concerned, corporate customers are able to raise their financial resources through development banks. So, they need not go to the capital market. Moreover, they don't resort to capital market since it is very erratic and inactive. Investors too prefer investments in physical assets to investments in financial assets. The weakness of the capital market is a serious problem in our financial system.

(v) **Imprudent financial practice:** The dominance of development banks has developed imprudent financial practice among corporate customers. The development banks provide most of the funds in the form of term loans. So, there is a preponderance of debt in the financial structure of corporate enterprises. This predominance of debt capital has made the capital structure of the borrowing concerns uneven and lopsided. To make matters worse, when corporate enterprises face any financial crisis, these financial institutions permit a greater use of debt than is warranted. It is against the traditional concept of a sound capital structure.

However, in recent times, all efforts have been taken to activate the capital market. Integration is also taking place between different financial institutions. For instance, the Unit Linked Insurance Schemes of the UTI are being offered to the public in collaboration with the LIC. Similarly, the refinance and rediscounting facilities are provided by the IDBI aim at integration. Thus, the Indian financial system has become a developed one.

The Structure of Indian Financial System is displayed in the following Chart 1.4.

**CHART 1.4**

**THE STRUCTURE OF INDIAN FINANCIAL SYSTEM**

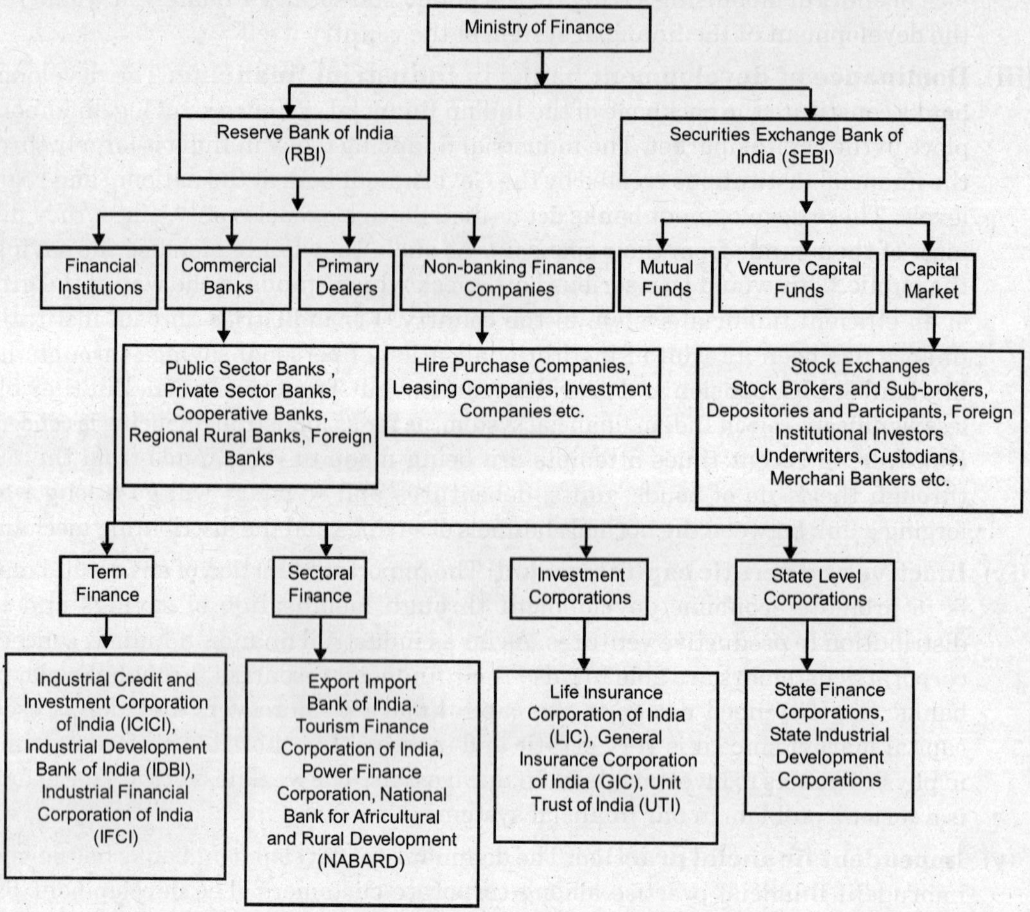


***Source:*** The Indian Banker.

## QUESTIONS

## I. Objective type questions:

### A. Fill in the blanks:

1. __________ assets are mostly useful for consumption.
2. The market for new issues is called __________ market.
3. Loan against the security of immovable property is called __________ loan.
4. __________ guarantee cover the payment of earnest money, retention money and advance payments.
5. The SHCIL was set up in the year __________.

[**Key:** 1. Physical, 2. Primary, 3. Mortgage, 4. Performance, 5. 1987]

## B. Choose the best answer from the following:

1. The following one is a financial asset:

   (*a*) Gold (*b*) Silver

   (c) Share (*d*) Land

2. Which one of the following is a cash asset?

   (*a*) Deposit created out of loans (*b*) Share

   (*c*) Bond (*d*) Post office certificate

3. The component of a capital market is:

   (*a*) Treasury bill market (*b*) Government securities market

   (*c*) Commercial bill market (*d*) (*a*) and (*b*) together

4. The money market instrument is:

   (*a*) Bond (*b*) Debenture

   (*c*) Stock certificate (*d*) Certificate of deposit

5. Government Bond is a:

   (*a*) Short-term security (*b*) Long-term security

   (*c*) Medium-term security (*d*) Either short-term or long-term security

[**Key:** 1. (*c*), 2. (*a*), 3. (*b*), 4. (*d*), 5. (*b*)]

## C. State whether the following statements are TRUE or FALSE:

1. Building bought for hiring is a financial asset.
2. LIC is primarily a money market intermediary.
3. Companies can raise capital in a primary market only through Rights Issue.
4. The most liquid financial market is the call money market.
5. A promissory note issued by the Government is called Treasury Bill.

[**Key:** 1. True, 2. False, 3. False, 4. True, 5. True]

## II. Short answer type questions:

1. Distinguish between a physical asset and a financial asset.
2. Classify financial assets giving examples.
3. What is a money market?
4. What is a capital market?
5. Distinguish between a primary market and a secondary market.
6. What is performance guarantee?
7. State the functions of a foreign exchange market.
8. What do you mean by indirect securities? Give an example.
9. What is venture capital financing?
10. What is STRIPS?

## III. Answer the following in a paragraph:

1. What is a capital market? What are its major constituents?
2. Write a brief note on the financial guarantees market operating in India.
3. What are financial instruments? What are their characteristic features?
4. What legislative measures have been taken by the Government to support the Indian financial system?
5. Classify financial assets and bring out their features.
6. Distinguish between stripping and reconstitution.

## IV. Essay type questions:

1. Classify the various financial intermediaries functioning in the Indian financial system and bring out their features.
2. Show the classification of Indian financial markets in the form of a chart and explain the features of each market.
3. What do you mean by financial rate of return? What are the basic objectives of the interest rate policy of the Government and what steps have been taken by the Government in this direction?
4. Trace out the development of the financial system in India.
5. "In spite of suitable legislative measures, the Indian financial system remains weak". Comment.
6. Discuss the role of the financial system in the economic development of a country.

# 2 MONEY MARKET

Money market is a market for short-term loans or financial assets. It is a market for the lending and borrowing of short-term funds. As the name implies, it does not actually deal in cash or money. But it actually deals with near substitutes for money or near money like trade bills, promissory notes and Government papers drawn for a short period not exceeding one year. These short-term instruments can be converted into cash readily without any loss and at low transaction cost.

Money market is the centre for dealing mainly in short-term money assets. It meets the short-term requirements of borrowers and provides liquidity or cash to lenders. It is the place where short-term surplus funds at the disposal of financial institutions and individuals are borrowed by individuals, institutions and also the Government.

The money market does not refer to a particular place where short-term funds are dealt with. It includes all individuals, institutions and intermediaries dealing with short-term funds. The transactions between borrowers, lenders and middlemen take place through telephone, telegraph, mail and agents. No personal contact or presence of the two parties is essential for negotiations in a money market. However, a geographical name may be given to a money market according to its location. For example, the London money market operates from Lambard Street and the New York money market operates from Wall Street. But, they attract funds from all over the world to be lent to borrowers from all over the globe. Similarly, the Mumbai money market is the centre for short-term loanable funds of not only Mumbai, but also the whole of India.

## DEFINITION

According to Crowther, 'The money market is the collective name given to the various firms and institutions that deal in the various grades of near money'.

The RBI defines the money market as, 'a market for short-term financial assets that are close substitutes for money, facilitates the exchange of money for new financial claims in the primary market as also for financial claims, already issued, in the secondary market'.

## MONEY MARKET VS. CAPITAL MARKET

In this context, it is imperative that one should know the distinction between a money market and a capital market. The distinction is briefly shown in the following table:

| *Money Market* | *Capital Market* |
|---|---|
| (*i*) It is a market for short-term loanable funds for a period of not exceeding one year. | (*i*) It is a market for long-term funds exceeding a period one year. |
| (*ii*) This market supplies funds for financing current business operations, working capital require-ments of industries and short period requirements of the Government. | (*ii*) This market supplies funds for financing the fixed capital requirements of trade and commerce as well as the long-term requirements of the Government. |
| (*iii*) The instruments that are dealt in a money market are bills of exchange, treasury bills, com-mercial papers, certificate of deposit, etc. | (*iii*) This market deals in instruments like shares, debentures, Government bonds, etc. |
| (*iv*) Each single money market instru-ment is of large amount. A TB is of minimum for one lakh. Each CD or CP is for a minimum of ₹ 25 lakh. | (*iv*) Each single capital market instru-ment is of small amount. Each share value is ₹ 10. Each debenture value is ₹ 100. |
| (*v*) The Central bank and Commercial banks are the major institutions in the money market. | (*v*) Development banks and insurance companies play a dominant role in the capital market. |
| (*vi*) Money market instruments generally do not have secondary markets. | (*vi*) Capital market instruments gene-rally have secondary markets. |
| (*vii*) Transactions mostly take place over-the-phone and there is no formal place. | (*vii*) Transactions take place at a formal place, *viz.*, stock exchange. |
| (*viii*) Transactions have to be conducted without the help of brokers. | (*viii*) Transactions have to be conducted only through authorised dealers. |

## FEATURES OF A MONEY MARKET

The following are the general features of a money market:

(*i*) It is a market purely for short-term funds or financial assets called near money.

(*ii*) It deals with financial assets having a maturity period up to one year only.

(*iii*) It deals with only those assets which can be converted into cash readily without loss and with minimum transaction cost.

(*iv*) Generally, transactions take place through phone, *i.e.*, oral communication. Relevant documents and written communications can be exchanged subsequently. There is no formal place like stock exchange as in the case of a capital market.

(*v*) Transactions have to be conducted without the help of brokers.

(*vi*) It is not a single homogeneous market. It comprises of several submarkets, each specialising in a particular type of financing, *e.g.*, Call money market, Acceptance market, Bill market and so on.

(*vii*) The components of a money market are the Central Bank, Commercial Banks, Non-banking financial companies, discount houses and acceptance houses. Commercial banks generally play a dominant role in this market.

## ❖ Objectives

The following are the important objectives of a money market:

(*i*) To provide a parking place to employ short-term surplus funds.

(*ii*) To provide room for overcoming short-term deficits.

(*iii*) To enable the central bank to influence and regulate liquidity in the economy through its intervention in this market.

(*iv*) To provide a reasonable access to users of short-term funds to meet their requirements quickly, adequately and at reasonable costs.

## CHARACTERISTIC FEATURES OF A DEVELOPED MONEY MARKET

In order to fulfil the above objectives, the money market should be fully developed and efficient. In every country of the world, some type of money market exists. Some of them are highly developed while others are not well developed. Prof. S.N. Sen has described certain essential features of a developed money market. They are as follows:

**(i) Highly organised banking system:** The commercial banks are the nerve centre of the whole money market. They are the principal suppliers of short-term funds. Their policies regarding loans and advances have greater impact on the entire money market. The commercial banks serve as vital link between the central bank and the various segments of the money market. Consequently, a well developed money market and a highly organised banking system co-exist. In an underdeveloped money market, the commercial banking system is not fully developed.

**(ii) Presence of a central bank:** The central bank acts as the banker's bank. It keeps their cash reserves and provides them financial accommodation in difficulties by discounting their eligible securities. In other words, it enables the commercial banks and other institutions to convert their assets into cash in times of financial crisis. Through its open market operations, the central bank absorbs surplus cash during off-seasons and provides additional liquidity in the busy seasons. Thus, the central bank is the leader, guide and controller of the money market. In an underdeveloped money market, the central bank is in its infancy and not in a position to influence and control the money market.

**(iii) Availability of proper credit instruments:** It is necessary for the existence of a developed money market a continuous availability of readily acceptable negotiable securities such as bills of exchange, treasury bills, etc. in the market. There should be a number of dealers in the money market to transact in these securities. Availability of negotiable securities and the presence of dealers and brokers in large numbers to transact in these securities are needed for the existence of a developed money market. There is absence of adequate and proper credit instruments as well as dealers to deal in these instruments in an underdeveloped money market.

(iv) **Existence of sub-markets:** The number of sub-markets determines the development of a money market. The larger the number of sub-markets, the broader and more developed will be the structure of money market. The several sub-markets together make a coherent money market. In an underdeveloped money market, the various sub-markets, particularly the bill market, are absent. Even if sub-markets exist, there is no co-ordination between them. Consequently, different money rates prevail in the sub-markets and they remain unconnected with one another.

(v) **Ample resources:** There must be availability of sufficient funds to finance transactions in the sub-markets. These funds may come from within the country and also from foreign countries. The London, New York and Paris money markets attract funds from all over the world. The underdeveloped money markets are starved of funds.

(vi) **Existence of secondary market:** There should be an active secondary market in these instruments.

(vii) **Demand and supply of funds:** There should be a large demand and supply of short-term funds. It presupposes the existence of a large domestic and foreign trade. Besides, it should have adequate amount of liquidity in the form of large amounts maturing within a short period.

### ❖ Other factors

Besides the above, other factors also contribute to the development of a money market. Rapid industrial development leading to the emergence of stock exchanges, large volume of international trade leading to the system of bills of exchange, political stability, favourable conditions for foreign investment, price stabilisation, etc. are the other factors that facilitate the development of money market in the country.

London money market is a highly developed money market because it satisfies all requirements of a developed money market.

If any one or more of these factors are absent, then the money market is called an underdeveloped one.

## IMPORTANCE OF MONEY MARKET

A developed money market plays an important role in the financial system of a country by supplying short-term funds adequately and quickly to trade and industry. The money market is an integral part of a country's economy. Therefore, a developed money market is highly indispensable for the rapid development of the economy. A developed money market helps the smooth functioning of the financial system in any economy in the following ways:

(i) **Development of trade and industry:** Money market is an important source of financing trade and industry. The money market, through discounting operations and commercial papers, finances the short-term working capital requirements of trade and industry and facilitates the development of industry and trade both — national and international.

**(ii) Development of capital market:** The short-term rates of interest and the conditions that prevail in the money market influence the long-term interest as well as the resource mobilisation in capital market. Hence, the development of capital market depends upon the existence of a developed money market.

**(iii) Smooth functioning of commercial banks:** The money market provides the commercial banks with facilities for temporarily employing their surplus funds in easily realisable assets.

The banks can get back the funds quickly, in times of need, by resorting to the money market. The commercial banks gain immensely by economising their cash balances in hand and at the same time meeting the demand for large withdrawal of their depositors. It also enables commercial banks to meet their statutory requirements of Cash Reserve Ratio (CRR) and Statutory Liquidity Ratio (SLR) by utilising the money market mechanism.

**(iv) Effective central bank control:** A developed money market helps the effective functioning of a central bank. It facilitates effective implementation of the monetary policy of a central bank. The central bank, through the money market, pumps new money into the economy in slump and siphons it off in boom. The central bank, thus, regulates the flow of money so as to promote economic growth with stability.

**(v) Formulation of suitable monetary policy:** Conditions prevailing in a money market serve as a true indicator of the monetary state of an economy. Hence, it serves as a guide to the Government in formulating and revising the monetary policy then and there depending upon the monetary conditions prevailing in the market.

**(vi) Non-inflationary source of finance to government:** A developed money market helps the Government to raise short-term funds through the treasury bills floated in the market. In the absence of a developed money market, the Government would be forced to print and issue more money or borrow from the central bank. Both ways would lead to an increase in prices and the consequent inflationary trend in the economy.

## COMPOSITION OF MONEY MARKET

As stated earlier, the money market is not a single homogeneous market. It consists of a number of sub-markets which collectively constitute the money market. There should be competition within each sub-market as well as between different sub-markets. The following are the main sub-markets of a money market:

(*i*) Call money market.

(*ii*) Commercial bills market or discount market.

(*iii*) Acceptance market.

(*iv*) Treasury bill market.

## CALL MONEY MARKET

The call money market refers to the market for extremely short period loans, say one day to fourteen days. These loans are repayable on demand at the option of either the lender or the borrower. As stated earlier, these loans are given to brokers and dealers in stock exchange. Similarly, banks with 'surplus funds' lend to other banks with 'deficit funds' in the call money market. Thus, it provides an equilibrating mechanism for evening out short-term surpluses and deficits. Moreover, commercial banks can quickly borrow from the call market to meet their statutory liquidity requirements. They can also maximise their profits easily by investing their surplus funds in the call market during the period when call rates are high and volatile.

### ❖ Operations in call market

Borrowers and lenders in a call market contact each other over telephone. Hence, it is basically over-the-telephone market. After negotiations over the phone, the borrowers and lenders arrive at a deal specifying the amount of loan and the rate of interest. After the deal is over, the lender issues FBL cheque in favour of the borrower. The borrower in turn issues call money borrowing receipt. When the loan is repaid with interest, the lender returns the duly discharged receipt.

Instead of negotiating the deal directly, it can be routed through the Discount and Finance House of India (DFHI). The borrowers and lenders inform the DFHI about their fund requirement and availability at a specified rate of interest. Once the deal is confirmed, the Deal Settlement Advice is exchanged. In case the DFHI borrows, it issues a call deposit receipt to the lender and receives RBI cheque for the money borrowed. The reverse is taking place in the case of lendings by the DFHI. The duly discharged call deposit receipt is surrendered at the time of settlement. Call loans can be renewed up to a maximum period of 14 days only and such renewals are recorded on the back of the deposit receipt by the borrower.

### ❖ Call loan market transactions and participants

In India, call loans are given for the following purposes:

(*i*) To commercial banks to meet large payments, and large remittances, to maintain liquidity with the RBI and so on.

(*ii*) To the stock brokers and speculators to deal in stock exchanges and bullion markets.

(*iii*) To the bill market for meeting matured bills.

(*iv*) To the Discount and Finance House of India and the Securities Trading Corporation of India to activate the call market.

(*v*) To individuals of very high status for trade purposes to save interest on OD or cash credit.

The participants in this market can be classified into two categories, *viz.*:

(*i*) Those permitted to act as both lenders and borrowers of call loans.

(*ii*) Those permitted to act only as lenders in the market.

The first category includes all Commercial banks, Cooperative banks, DFHI and STCI. In the second category, LIC, UTI, GIC, IDBI, NABARD, Specified mutual funds, etc. are included. They can only lend and they cannot borrow in the call market.

## Advantages

In India, commercial banks play a dominant role in the call loan market. They used to borrow and lend among themselves and such loans are called inter-bank loans. They are very popular in India. So, many advantages are available to commercial banks. They are as follows:

(i) **High liquidity:** Money lent in a call market can be called back at any time when needed. So, it is highly liquid. It enables commercial banks to meet large sudden payments and remittances by making a call on the market.

(ii) **High profitability:** Banks can earn high profits by lending their surplus funds to the call market when call rates are high and volatile. It offers a profitable parking place for employing the surplus funds of banks temporarily.

(iii) **Maintenance of SLR:** Call market enables commercial banks to maintain their statutory reserve requirements. Generally, banks borrow on a large-scale every reporting Friday to meet their SLR requirements. In the absence of call market, banks have to maintain idle cash to meet their reserve requirements. It will tell upon their profitability.

(iv) **Safe and cheap:** Though call loans are not secured, they are safe since the participants have a strong financial standing. It is cheap in the sense brokers have been prohibited from operating in the call market. Hence, banks need not pay brokerage on call money transactions.

(v) **Assistance to central bank operations:** Call money market is the most sensitive part of any financial system. Changes in demand and supply of funds are quickly reflected in call money rates and it gives an indication to the central bank to adopt an appropriate monetary policy. Moreover, the existence of an efficient call market helps the central bank to carry-out its open market operations effectively and successfully.

## Drawbacks

The call market in India suffers from the following drawbacks:

(i) **Uneven development:** The call money market in India is confined to only big industrial and commercial centres like Mumbai, Kolkata, Chennai, Delhi, Bengaluru and Ahmedabad. Generally, call markets are associated with stock exchanges. Hence, the market is not evenly developed.

(ii) **Lack of integration:** The call markets in different centres are not fully integrated. Besides, a large number of local call markets exist without any integration.

(iii) **Volatility in call money rates:** Another drawback is the volatile nature of the call money rates. Call rates vary to a greater extent in different centres in different seasons on different days within a fortnight. The rates vary between 12 per cent and 85 per cent. One cannot believe 85 per cent being charged on call loans.

## COMMERCIAL BILLS MARKET OR DISCOUNT MARKET

A commercial bill is one which arises out of a genuine trade transaction, *i.e.*, credit transaction. As soon as goods are sold on credit, the seller draws a bill on the buyer for the amount due. The buyer accepts it immediately agreeing to pay the amount mentioned therein after a certain specified date. Thus, a bill of exchange contains a written order from the creditor to the debtor, to pay a certain sum, to a certain person, after a certain period. A bill of exchange is a 'self-liquidating' paper and negotiable. It is drawn always for a short period ranging between 3 months and 6 months.

### ❖ Definition

Section 5 of the Negotiable Instruments Act defines a bill of exchange as follows:

'An instrument in writing containing an unconditional order, signed by the maker, directing a certain person to pay a certain sum of money only to, or to the order of a certain person or to the bearer of the instrument'.

### ❖ Types of bills

Many types of bills are in circulation in a bill market. They can be broadly classified as follows:

(*i*) Demand and usance bills.
(*ii*) Clean bills and documentary bills.
(*iii*) Inland and foreign bills.
(*iv*) Export bills and import bills.
(*v*) Indigenous bills.
(*vi*) Accommodation bills and supply bills.

**(i) Demand and usance bills**

Demand bills are otherwise called sight bills. These bills are payable immediately as soon as they are presented to the drawee. No time of payment is specified and hence they are payable at sight.

Usance bills are called time bills. These bills are payable immediately after the expiry of time period mentioned in the bills. The period varies according to the established trade custom or usage prevailing in the country.

**(ii) Clean bills and documentary bills**

When bills have to be accompanied by documents of title to goods like Railway receipt, Lorry receipt, Bill of Lading, etc., the bills are called documentary bills. These bills can be further classified into D/A bills and D/P bills. In the case of D/A bills, the documents accompanying bills have to be delivered to the drawee immediately after his acceptance of the bill. Thus, a D/A bill becomes a clean bill immediately after acceptance. Generally, D/A bills are drawn on parties who have a good financial standing.

On the other hand, the documents have to be handed over to the drawee only against payment in the case of D/P bills. The documents will be retained by the banker till the payment of such bills. When bills are drawn without accompanying any document, they are called clean bills. In such a case, documents will be directly sent to the drawee.

**(iii) Inland and foreign bills**

Inland bills are those drawn upon a person resident in India and are payable in India. Foreign bills are drawn outside India and they may be payable either in India or outside India. They may be drawn upon a person resident in India also. Foreign bills have their origin outside India. They also include bills drawn in India but made payable outside India.

**(iv) Export bills and import bills**

Export bills are those drawn by Indian exporters on importers outside India and import bills are drawn on Indian importers in India by exporters outside India.

**(v) Indigenous bills**

Indigenous bills are those drawn and accepted according to native custom or usage of trade. These bills are popular among indigenous bankers only. In India, they are called 'hundis'. The hundis are known by various names such as 'Shahjog', 'Namjog', 'Jokhani', 'Termainjog', 'Darshani', 'Dhanijog' and so on.

**(vi) Accommodation bills and supply bills**

If bills do not arise out of genuine trade transactions, they are called accommodation bills. They are known as 'kite bills' or 'wind bills'. Two parties draw bills on each other purely for the purpose of mutual financial accommodation. These bills are discounted with bankers and the proceeds are shared among themselves. On the due dates, they are paid.

Supply bills are those drawn by suppliers or contractors on the Government departments for the goods supplied by them. These bills are neither accepted by the departments nor accompanied by documents of title to goods. So, they are not considered as negotiable instruments. These bills are useful only for the purpose of getting advances from commercial banks by creating a charge on these bills.

## ❖ Operations in bill market

From the operations point of view, the bill market can be classified into two, *viz.:*

(*i*) Discount market.

(*ii*) Acceptance market.

**(i) Discount market**

Discount market refers to the market where short-term genuine trade bills are discounted by financial intermediaries like commercial banks. When credit sales are effected, the seller draws a bill on the buyer who accepts it promising to pay the specified sum at the specified period. The seller has to wait until the maturity of the bill for getting payment. But, the presence of a bill market enables him to get payment immediately. The seller can ensure payment immediately by discounting the bill with some financial intermediary by paying a small amount of money called 'Discount rate'. On the date of maturity, the intermediary claims the amount of the bill from the person who has accepted the bill.

In some countries, there are some financial intermediaries who specialise in the field of discounting. For instance, in London Money Market there are specialised institutions called

Discount Houses which specialise only in the field of discounting bills. Such institutions are conspicuously absent in India. Hence, commercial banks in India have to undertake the work of discounting. However, the DFHI has been established to activate this market.

**(ii) Acceptance market**

The acceptance market refers to the market where short-term genuine trade bills are accepted by financial intermediaries. All trade bills cannot be discounted easily because the parties to the bills may not be financially sound. In case such bills are accepted by financial intermediaries like banks, the bills earn a good name and reputation and such bills can be readily discounted anywhere. In London, there are specialist firms called acceptance houses which accept bills drawn by traders and impart greater marketability to such bills. However, their importance has declined in recent times. In India, there are no acceptance houses. The commercial banks undertake the acceptance business to some extent.

## ❖ Advantages or Importance

Commercial bill market is an important source of short-term funds for trade and industry. It provides liquidity and activates the money market. In India, commercial banks play a significant role in this market due to the following advantages:

(i) **Liquidity:** Bills are highly liquid assets. In times of necessity, bills can be converted into cash readily by rediscounting them with the central bank.

(ii) **Self-liquidating and negotiable asset:** Bills are self-liquidating in character since they have a fixed tenure. Moreover, they are negotiable instruments and hence they can be transferred freely by a mere delivery or by endorsement and delivery.

(iii) **Certainty of payment:** Bills are drawn and accepted by business people. Generally, businesspeople are used to keep their words and the use of bills imposes a strict financial discipline on them. Hence, bills would be honoured on the due date.

(iv) **Ideal investment:** Bills are for periods not exceeding 6 months. They represent advances for a definite period. This enables financial institutions to invest their surplus funds profitably by selecting bills of different maturities. For instance, commercial banks can invest their funds on bills in such a way that the maturity of these bills may coincide with the maturity of their fixed deposits.

(v) **Simple legal remedy:** In case the bills are dishonoured, the legal remedy is simple. Such dishonoured bills have to be simply noted and protested and the whole amount should be debited to the customer's accounts.

(vi) **High and quick yield:** The financial institutions earn a high and quick yield. The discount is deducted at the time of discounting itself, whereas in the case of other loans and advances, interest is payable only when it is due. The discount rate is also comparatively high.

(vii) **Central bank control:** The central bank can easily influence the money market by manipulating the bank rate or the rediscounting rate. Suitable monetary policy can be taken by adjusting the bank rate depending upon the monetary conditions prevailing in the market.

## ❖ Drawbacks

In spite of these merits, the bill market has not been well developed in India. The reasons for the slow growth are the following:

(i) **Absence of bill culture:** Businesspeople in India prefer OD and cash credit to bill financing. Therefore, banks usually accept bills for the conversion of cash credits and overdrafts of their customers. Hence, bills are not popular.

(ii) **Absence of rediscounting among banks:** There is no practice of rediscounting of bills among banks who need funds and those who have surplus funds. In order to enlarge the rediscounting facility, the RBI has permitted financial institutions like LIC, UTI, GIC and ICICI to rediscount genuine eligible trade bills of commercial banks. Even then, bill financing is not popular.

(iii) **Stamp duty:** Stamp duty discourages the use of bills. Moreover, stamp papers of required denomination are not available.

(iv) **Absence of secondary market:** There is no active secondary market for bills. Rediscounting facility is available in important centres and that too it is restricted to the apex level financial institutions. Hence, the size of the bill market has been curtailed to a large extent.

(v) **Difficulty in ascertaining genuine trade bills:** The financial institutions have to verify the bills so as to ascertain whether they are genuine trade bills and not accommodation bills. For this purpose, invoices have to be scrutinised carefully. It involves additional work.

(vi) **Limited foreign trade:** In many developed countries, bill markets have been established mainly for financing foreign trade. Unfortunately, in India, foreign trade as a percentage to national income remains small and it is reflected in the bill market also.

(vii) **Absence of acceptance services:** There are no discount houses or acceptance houses in India. Hence, specialised services are not available in the field of discounting or acceptance.

(viii) **Attitude of banks:** Banks are shy of rediscounting bills even with the central bank. They have a tendency to hold the bills till maturity and hence it affects the velocity of circulation of bills. Again, banks prefer to purchase bills instead of discounting them.

# BILL MARKET SCHEME

A well organised bill market is essential for the smooth working of the credit system, progress of commercial banking as well as linking up the various credit agencies effectively to the central bank of a country. Realising its importance, the Central Banking Enquiry Committee emphasised the need for developing a bill market in India as early as 1931. But, it did not develop even after the establishment of the Reserve Bank due to several reasons.

In January 1952, for the first time, the Reserve Bank introduced a Bill Market Scheme.

Under Section 17(4) of the Reserve Bank of India Act, the bank undertook to make advances to scheduled banks against the security of usance promissory notes or trade bills having a maturity of 90 days and bearing two signatures, of which one will be that of a scheduled bank.

This facility was originally restricted to banks having deposits of more than ₹ 10 crores. The minimum value of each bill was fixed at ₹ 1 lakh and the minimum amount of advance was ₹ 25 lakhs for a bank. The scheme was introduced on an experimental basis for a period of 4 years. Later on the recommendations of the Shroff Committee, the scheme was extended to all scheduled banks. The minimum amount of each bill was reduced to ₹ 50,000 and the minimum limit of advance for a bank was reduced to ₹ 10 lakhs.

In 1957, on the recommendations of the Export Promotion Committee, the Reserve Bank of India, extended the scheme to include export bills in order to enable scheduled banks to provide finance to exports on a liberal scale. The extension of the bill market scheme to export bills has been continued further year-after-year.

### ❖ New Bill Market Scheme 1970

The 1952 Bill Market Scheme remained a partial success. It was criticised that it did not develop a good bill market in India. The scheme appears to be a device for extending credit for banks during busy seasons. It is not based on genuine trade bills but on the conversion of loans and advances by scheduled banks into usance bills.

The Deheja Committee set in motion the introduction of a new bill market. The report brought out the abuses of cash credit system and suggested the use of bill financing and for the supervision of the end-use of funds lent by commercial banks.

A study group was appointed by the Reserve Bank in February 1970, under the chairmanship of Shri M. Narasimham to go into the question of enlarging the use of the bill of exchange as an instrument for providing credit and creation of a bill market in India. The group submitted the report in June 1970. Following its recommendations, the Reserve Bank announced a new bill market scheme under Section 17(2)(a) of the Reserve Bank of India Act in November 1970.

(*i*) All eligible scheduled banks are eligible to offer bills of exchange for rediscount.

(*ii*) The bills of exchange should be a genuine trade bill and should have arisen out of the sale of goods. Accommodation bills are not eligible for this purpose.

(*iii*) The bill should not have a maturity time of more than 120 days and when it is offered to the Reserve Bank for rediscount its maturity should not exceed 90 days.

(*iv*) The bill should have at least two good signatures, one of which should be that of a licensed scheduled bank.

(*v*) The minimum amount of bill should be ₹ 5,000 and on one occasion, the value of bill offered for rediscount should not be less than ₹ 50,000.

In 1971, the Reserve Bank simplified the procedure for rediscounting the bills. To avoid delays and reduce the work involved in physically delivering and redelivering the bills to and from the bank, it was decided to dispense with the actual lodgement of bills, each of the face value of ₹ 2 lakhs and below.

The minimum amount of a bill eligible for rediscount with the bank was reduced to ₹ 1,000. The facility which was available only in Mumbai, Kolkata, Chennai and New Delhi, was extended to Kanpur and Bengaluru.

In April 1972, the bills drawn on and accepted by the Industrial Credit and Investment Corporation of India Limited on behalf of the purchasers were covered by the scheme provided they are presented to the Reserve Bank by an eligible scheduled bank.

In 1973, the minimum value of a bill for the purpose of actual lodgement with the Reserve Bank was raised from ₹ 2 lakhs to ₹ 10 lakhs.

The New Bill Market Scheme has opened vistas of development of a full-fledged bill market in India. Certain criticisms are levelled against the working of the scheme. The unorganised money market has not been drawn within its fold. Most of the bills presented for rediscount relate to trade and not agriculture. The period of the bill admitted under the scheme is inadequate. The procedure followed for determining the eligibility of the bank for the purpose of rediscounting is far from satisfactory.

The Reserve Bank has been making constant efforts for the orderly development of a bill market. However, it will take a long time to have a bill market of the type found in advanced countries.

## TREASURY BILL MARKET

Just like commercial bills which represent commercial debt, treasury bills represent short-term borrowings of the Government. Treasury bill market refers to the market where treasury bills are bought and sold. Treasury bills are very popular and enjoy a higher degree of liquidity since they are issued by the Government.

### ❖ Meaning and features

A treasury bill is nothing but a promissory note issued by the Government under discount for a specified period stated therein. The Government promises to pay the specified amount mentioned therein to the bearer of the instrument on the due date. The period does not exceed a period of one year. It is purely a finance bill since it does not arise out of any trade transaction. It does not require any 'grading' or 'endorsement' or 'acceptance' since it is a claim against the Government.

Treasury bills are issued only by the RBI on behalf of the Government. Treasury bills are issued for meeting temporary Government deficits. The treasury bill rate or the rate of discount is fixed by the RBI from time-to-time. It is the lowest one in the entire structure of interest rates in the country because of short-term maturity and high degree of liquidity and security.

### ❖ Types of treasury bills

In India, there are two types of treasury bills, *viz.*, (*i*) Ordinary or regular and (*ii*) *'Ad hoc'* known as *'ad hocs'*. Ordinary treasury bills are issued to the public and other financial institutions for meeting the short-term financial requirements of the Central Government. These bills are freely marketable and they can be bought and sold at any time and they have secondary market also.

On the other hand, *'Ad hocs'* are always issued in favour of the RBI only. They are not sold through tender or auction. They are purchased by the RBI and the RBI is authorised to issue currency notes against them. They are not marketable in India. However, the holders of these bills can always sell them back to the RBI. *Ad hocs* serve the Government in the following ways:

(*i*) They replenish cash balances of the Central Government. Just like State Governments get advance (ways and means advances) from the RBI, the Central Government can raise finance through these ad hocs.

(*ii*) They also provide an investment medium for investing the temporary surpluses of State Governments, Semi-government departments and foreign central banks.

On the basis of periodicity, treasury bills may be classified into three. They are:

(*i*) 91 days treasury bills,

(*ii*) 182 days treasury bills, and

(*iii*) 364 days treasury bills.

Ninety-one days treasury bills are issued at a fixed discount rate of 4 per cent as well as through auctions. 364 days treasury bills do not carry any fixed rate. The discount rate on these bills are quoted in auction by the participants and accepted by the authorities. Such a rate is called cut-off rate. In the same way, the rate is fixed for 91 days treasury bills sold through auction. 91 days treasury bills (tap basis) can be rediscounted with the RBI at any time after 14 days of their purchase. Before 14 days, a penal rate is charged.

## ❖ Operations and participants

The RBI holds 91 days Treasury Bills (TBs) and they are issued on tap basis throughout the week. However, 364 days TBs are sold through auction which is conducted once in a fortnight. The date of auction and the last date of submission of tenders are notified by the RBI through a press release. Investors can submit more than one bid also. On the next working day of the date of auction, the accepted bids with the prices are displayed. The successful bidders have to collect letters of acceptance from the RBI and deposit the same along with a cheque for the amount due on RBI within 24 hours of the announcement of auction results.

Institutional investors like commercial banks, DFHI, STCI, etc., maintain a Subsidiary General Ledger (SGL) account with the RBI. Purchases and sales of TBs are automatically recorded in this account. Investors who do not have SGL account can purchase and sell TBs through DFHI. The DFHI does this function on behalf of investors with the help of SGL transfer forms. The DFHI is actively participating in the auctions of TBs. It is playing a significant role in the secondary market also by quoting daily buying and selling rates. It also gives buyback and sellback facilities for periods up to 14 days at an agreed rate of interest to institutional investors. The establishment of the DFHI has imparted greater liquidity in the TB market.

The participants in this market are the following:

(*i*) RBI and SBI.

(*ii*) Commercial banks.

(*iii*) State Governments.

(*iv*) DFHI.

(*v*) STCI.

(*vi*) Financial institutions like LIC, GIC, UTI, IDBI, ICICI, IFCI, NABARD, etc.

(*vii*) Corporate customers.

(*viii*) Public.

Though many participants are there, in actual practice, this market is in the hands of the banking sector. It accounts for nearly 90 per cent of the annual sale of TBs.

## ❖ Importance or Merits

(i) **Safety:** Investments in TBs are highly safe since the payment of interest and repayment of principal are assured by the Government. They carry zero default risk since they are issued by the RBI for and on behalf of the Central Government.

(ii) **Liquidity:** Investments in TBs are also highly liquid because they can be converted into cash at any time at the option of the investors. The DFHI announces daily buying and selling rates for TBs. They can be discounted with the RBI and further refinance facility is available from the RBI against TBs. Hence, there is a ready market for TBs.

(iii) **Ideal short-term investment:** Idle cash can be profitably invested for a very short period in TBs. TBs are available on tap throughout the week at specified rates. Financial institutions can employ their surplus funds on any day. The yield on TBs is also assured.

(iv) **Ideal fund management:** TBs are available on tap as well as through periodical auctions. They are also available in the secondary market. Fund managers of financial institutions build-up a portfolio of TBs in such a way that the dates of maturities of TBs may be matched with the dates of payment of their liabilities like deposits of short-term maturities. Thus, TBs help financial managers to manage the funds effectively and profitably.

(v) **Statutory liquidity requirement:** As per the RBI directives, commercial banks have to maintain SLR (Statutory Liquidity Ratio) and for measuring this ratio investments in TBs are taken into account. TBs are eligible securities for SLR purposes. Moreover, to maintain CRR (Cash Reserve Ratio). TBs are very helpful. They can be readily converted into cash and thereby CRR can be maintained.

(vi) **Source of short-term funds:** The Government can raise short-term funds for meeting its temporary budget deficits through the issue of TBs. It is a source of cheap finance to the Government since the discount rates are very low.

(vii) **Non-inflationary monetary tool:** TBs enable the Central Government to support its monetary policy in the economy. For instance, excess liquidity, if any, in the economy can be absorbed through the issue of TBs. Moreover, TBs are subscribed by investors other than the RBI. Hence, they cannot be monetised and their issue does not lead to any inflationary pressure at all.

(viii) **Hedging facility:** TBs can be used as a hedge against heavy interest rate fluctuations in the call loan market. When the call rates are very high, money can be raised quickly against TBs and invested in the call money market and *vice versa*. TBs can be used in ready forward transactions.

## ❖ Defects

(i) **Poor yield:** The yield from TBs is the lowest. Long-term Government securities fetch more interest and hence subscriptions for TBs are on the decline in recent times.

(ii) **Absence of competitive bids:** Though TBs are sold through auction in order to ensure market rates for the investors, in actual practice, competitive bids are conspicuously absent. The RBI is compelled to accept these non-competitive bids. Hence, adequate return is not available. It makes TBs unpopular.

(iii) **Absence of active trading:** Generally, the investors hold TBs till maturity and they do not come for circulation. Hence, active trading in TBs is adversely affected.

# MONEY MARKET INSTRUMENTS

A variety of instruments are available in a developed money market. In India, till 1986, only a few instruments were available. They were:

(*i*) Treasury bills in the treasury market.

(*ii*) Money at call and short notice in the call loan market.

(*iii*) Commercial bills, and promissory notes in the bill market.

Now, in addition to the above, the following new instruments are available:

(*i*) Commercial papers.

(*ii*) Certificate of Deposit.

(*iii*) Inter-bank participation certificates.

(*iv*) Repo Instruments.

The new instruments are discussed below:

# COMMERCIAL PAPERS

## ❖ Introduction

During the 1980s, a wave of financial liberalisation and innovation in financial instruments swept across the world. A basic feature of the many innovations is the trend towards securitisation, *i.e.*, raising money direct from the investors in the form of negotiable securities as a substitute for bank credit. The companies found it cheaper to borrow directly from public by way of short-term paper. The cost of fund is cheaper for the companies as it involved lower information and transaction cost. This also suits the interest of many investors as it provides them with a wide spectrum of financial instruments to choose from and in placing their funds at reasonably high rates of return. Commercial paper is a new instrument used for financing working capital requirements of corporate enterprises.

## ❖ What is a commercial paper?

A commercial paper is an unsecured promissory note issued with a fixed maturity by a company approved by RBI, negotiable by endorsement and delivery, issued in bearer form and issued at such discount on the face value as may be determined by the issuing company.

## ❖ Participants

**Issuers**

All private sector company, public sector units, non-banking company, etc.

**Investors**

Individuals, banks, corporates and also NRIs. Usually banks, large corporate bodies and public sector units with investible funds participate in CP market.

## ❖ Features of commercial paper

1. Commercial paper is a short-term money market instrument comprising usance promissory note with a fixed maturity.
2. It is a certificate evidencing an unsecured corporate debt of short-term maturity.
3. Commercial paper is issued at a discount to face value basis but it can also be issued in interest-bearing form.
4. The issuer promises to pay the buyer some fixed amount on some future period but pledges no assets, only his liquidity and established earning power, to guarantee that promise.
5. Commercial paper can be issued directly by a company to investors or through banks/ merchant bankers.

## ❖ Advantages of commercial paper

(i) **Simplicity:** The advantage of commercial paper lies in its simplicity. It involves hardly any documentation between the issuer and investor.

(ii) **Flexibility:** The issuer can issue commercial paper with the maturities tailored to match the cash flow of the company.

(iii) **Diversification:** A well rated company can diversify its source of finance from banks to short-term money markets at somewhat cheaper cost.

(iv) **Easy to raise long-term capital:** The companies which are able to raise funds through commercial paper become better known in the financial world and are thereby placed in a more favourable position for raising such long-term capital as they may, from time-to-time, require. Thus, there is an in-built incentive for companies to remain financially strong.

(v) **High returns:** The commercial paper provides investors with higher returns than they could get from the banking system.

(vi) **Movement of funds:** Commercial paper facilitates securitisation of loans resulting in creation of a secondary market for the paper and efficient movement of funds providing cash surplus to cash deficit entities.

## ❖ Commercial paper market in other countries

The roots of commercial paper can be traced way back to the early nineteenth century when the firms in the USA began selling open market paper as a substitute for bank loan needed for short-term requirements but it developed only in 1920s. The development of consumer finance companies in the 1920s and the high cost of bank credit resulting from the incidence of compulsory reserve requirements in the 1960s contributed to the popularity of commercial paper in the USA. Today, the US commercial paper market is the largest in the world. The outstanding amount at the end of 1990 in the US commercial paper market stood at $ 557.8 billion. The commercial paper issues in the US are exempted from Security Exchange Commission registration and from requirement of issue of prospectus so long as proceeds are used to finance current transactions and the paper's maturity is less than 270 days.

Most of the commercial paper market in Europe is modelled on the lines of the US market. In UK, the Sterling Commercial Paper Market was launched in May 1986. In UK, the borrower must be listed on the stock exchange and he must have met assets of at least $ 50 million. However, rating by credit agencies is not required. The maturities of commercial paper must be between 7 and 364 days. The commercial paper is exempted from stamp duty.

In France, commercial papers were thought of as a flexible alternative to bank loans. The commercial paper was introduced in December 1985. Commercial paper can be issued only by non-bank French companies and subsidiaries of foreign companies. The papers are in bearer form. It can be either issued by dealers or placed directly. The maturity ranges from ten days to seven years. Rating by credit agencies is essential. To protect investors, law contains fairly extensive disclosure requirements and requires publication of regular financial statements by issuers. The outstanding amount at the end of 1990 in France commercial paper market was $ 31 billion.

The Canadian commercial paper market was launched in 1950s. The commercial paper is generally used for terms of 30 days to 365 days although terms such as overnight are available. The commercial paper issued by Canadian companies is normally secured by pledge of assets. The outstanding amount at the end of 1990 in the Canadian market was $ 26.8 billion.

In Japan, the Yen commercial paper market was opened in November 1987. The commercial paper issues carry maturities from two weeks to nine months. Japan stands second in the commercial paper market in the world with an outstanding amount of $ 117.3 billion in 1990.

In 1980s, many other countries launched commercial paper market, notably Sweden (early 1980s), Spain (1982), Hong Kong (1982), Singapore (1984) and Norway (1984).

## ❖ Commercial Paper in India

In India, on the recommendations of the Vaghul Working Group, the RBI announced on 27th March, 1989 that commercial paper will be introduced soon in Indian money market. The recommendations of the Vaghul Working Group on introduction of commercial paper in Indian money market are as follows:

1. There is a need to have limited introduction of commercial paper. It should be carefully planned and the eligibility criteria for the issuer should be sufficiently rigorous to ensure that the commercial paper market develops on healthy lines.
2. Initially, access to the commercial paper market should be restricted to rated companies having a net worth of ₹ 5 crores and above with good dividend payment record.
3. The commercial paper market should function within the overall discipline of CAS. The RBI would have to administer the entry on the market, the amount of each issue and the total quantum that can be raised in a year.

4. No restriction be placed on the participants in the commercial paper market except by way of minimum size of the note. The size of any single issue should not be less than ₹ 1 crore and the size of each lot should not be less than ₹ 5 lakhs.
5. Commercial paper should be excluded from the stipulations on unsecured advances in the case of banks.
6. Commercial paper would not be tied to any specific transaction and the maturity period may be 7 days and above but not exceeding six months, backed up if necessary by a revolving underwriting facility of less than three years.
7. The issuing company should have a net worth of not less than ₹ 5 crores, a debt-equity ratio of not more than 1.5, a current ratio of more than 1.33, a debt servicing ratio closer to 2, and be listed on the stock exchange.
8. The interest rate on commercial paper would be market-dominated and the paper could be issued at a discount to face value or could be interest-bearing.
9. Commercial paper should not be subject to stamp duty at the time of issue as well as at the time of transfer by endorsement and delivery.

On the recommendations of the Vaghul Working Group, detailed guidelines were issued by the RBI in December 1989, through non-banking companies (Acceptance of Deposits through Commercial Paper) Direction, 1989 and finally the commercial papers were introduced in India from 1st January, 1990.

## ❖ RBI Guidelines on Commercial Paper Issue

The important guidelines are:

1. A company can issue commercial paper only if it has:
   (*i*) A tangible net worth of not less than ₹ 10 crores as per the latest balance sheet;
   (*ii*) Minimum current ratio of 1.33 : 1;
   (*iii*) A fund-based working capital limit of ₹ 25 crores or more;
   (*iv*) A debt servicing ratio closer to 2;
   (*v*) The company is listed on a stock exchange;
   (*vi*) Subject to CAS discipline;
   (*vii*) It is classified under Health Code No. 1 by the financing banks;
   (*viii*) The issuing company would need to obtain P1 from CRISIL.
2. Commercial paper shall be issued in ₹ 5 lakhs and multiples there of but the minimum amount to be invested by a single investor shall be ₹ 1 crore.
3. The commercial paper shall be issued for a minimum maturity period of 7 days and the maximum period of one year from the date of issue. There will be no grace period on maturity.
4. The aggregate amount shall not exceed 20 per cent of the issuer's fund-based working capital.
5. The commercial paper is issued in the form of usance promissory notes, negotiable by endorsement and delivery. The rate of discount could be freely determined by the

issuing company. The issuing company has to bear all flotation cost, including stamp duty, dealers' fee and credit rating agency fee.

6. The issue of commercial paper cannot be underwritten or co-opted in any manner. However, commercial banks can provide standby facility for redemption of the paper on the maturity date.
7. Investment in commercial paper can be made by any person or banks or corporate bodies registered or incorporated in India and unincorporated bodies too. Non-Resident Indians can invest in commercial paper on non-repatriation basis.
8. The companies issuing commercial paper would be required to ensure that the relevant provisions of the various statutes such as Companies Act, 1956, the IT Act, 1961 and the Negotiable Instruments Act, 1981 are complied with.

## ❖ Procedure and timeframe for issue of commercial paper

1. Application to RBI through financing bank or leader of consortium bank for working capital facilities together with a certificate from credit rating agency.
2. RBI to communicate in writing their decision on the amount of commercial paper to be issued to the leader bank.
3. Issue of commercial paper to be completed within 2 weeks from the date of approval of RBI through private placement.
4. The issue may be spread over 2 weeks on different dates but all such commercial papers shall bear the same maturity date.
5. Issuing company to advise RBI through the bank/leader of the bank, the amount of actual issue of commercial paper within 3 days of completion of the issue.

## ❖ Implications of commercial paper

The issue of commercial paper is an important step in disintermediation bringing a large number of borrowers as well as investors in touch with each other, without the intervention of the banking system as financial intermediary. The borrowers can get at least 20 per cent of their working capital requirements directly from market at rates which may be more advantageous than borrowing through a bank. The first-class borrowers have the prestige of joining the elitist commercial paper club with the approval of CRISIL, the banking system and the RBI. However, RBI has presently stipulated that the working capital limits of the banks will be reduced to the extent of issue of commercial paper. Industrialists have already made a plea that the issue of commercial paper should be outside the scheme of bank finance and other guidelines such as recommendation of banks and approval of RBI should be waived. RBI has not accepted the plea at present as commercial paper is a unsecured borrowing and not related to a trade transaction. The main aim of the RBI is to ensure that commercial paper develops a sound money market instrument. So, in the initial stages emphasis should be on the quality rather than quantity.

### ❖ Implications on bank

The impact of issue of commercial paper on commercial banks would be of two dimensions. One is that the banks themselves can invest in commercial paper and show this as short-term investment. The second aspect is that the banks are likely to lose interest on working capital loan which has been hitherto lent to the companies, which have, now started borrowing through commercial paper.

Further, the larger companies might avail of the cheap funds available in the market during the slack season worsening the bank's surplus fund position, but come to the banking system for borrowing during the busy season when funds are costly. This would mean the banks are the losers with a clear impact on profitability.

However, the banks stand to gain by charging higher interest rate on reinstated portion especially if it is done during busy season and by way of service charges for providing standby facilities and issuing and paying commission. Further, when large borrowers are able to borrow directly from the market, banks will correspondingly be freed from the pressure on resources.

### ❖ Impact on the economy

The process of disintermediation is taking place in the free economies all over the world. With the introduction of CP, financial disintermediation has been gaining momentum in the Indian economy. If CPs are allowed to free play, large companies as well as banks would learn to operate in a competitive atmosphere with more efficiency. This would result in greater excellence in the services of banks as well as management of finance by companies.

### ❖ Recent trends

(*i*) Call/put options are not permitted in CPs.

(*ii*) Credit Rating for issuance of CPs can be obtained from any one of the SEBI registered credit rating agencies.

(*iii*) The settlement cycle for OTC trades in CPs shall be either T + 0 or T + 1 basis.

(*iv*) The OTC trades in CPs shall be settled through either National Securities Clearing Corporation Ltd. or Indian Clearing Corporation Ltd. or MCX–CCL.

(*v*) Buyback of CPs by the issuers shall be through the secondary market at the prevailing market price.

(*vi*) Dematerialisation facility has been extended to commercial papers also.

### ❖ Future of commercial paper in India

Corporate enterprises requiring burgeoning funds to meet their expanding needs find it easier and cheaper to raise funds from market by issuing commercial paper. Further, it provides greater degree of flexibility in business finance to the issuing company inasmuch as it can decide the quantum of CP and its maturity on the basis of its future cash flows. CPs have made a good start. The outstanding amount of CPs stood at ₹ 3,913.3 billion at the end of May, 2017.

However, the secondary market is virtually non-existent. Only commercial banks pick up these papers and hold till maturity. No secondary market is allowed to develop on any significant scale. Further, trading is cumbersome as procedural requirements are onerous. The stamp duty payable by banks subscribing to commercial paper from the primary market is lower than which is charged to non-banking entities like primary dealer, corporates and non-banking finance companies. As a result, the entities prefer to buy CPs from banks instead of directly subscribing to them. The structural rigidities such as rating requirements, timing of issue, terms of issue, maturity range, denominational range and interest rate stand in the way of developing commercial paper market. The removal of stringent conditions and imposing of such regulatory measures justifiable to issuers, investors and dealers will improve the potentiality of CP as a source of corporate financing.

## CERTIFICATE OF DEPOSIT (CD)

Certificate of Deposits are short-term deposit instruments issued by banks and financial institutions to raise large sums of money.

CDs are issued in the form of usance promissory notes. They are negotiable and are in marketable form bearing specific face value and maturity. The CDs are transferable from one party to another. Due to their negotiable nature, they are also known as negotiable certificate of deposit.

### ❖ Issuers

The issuers of certificate of deposits are commercial banks, financial institutions, etc.

### ❖ Subscribers

CDs are available for subscription by individuals, corporations, trusts, associations and NRIs.

### ❖ Features of certificate of deposit

1. Document of title to time deposit.
2. Unsecured negotiable pronotes.
3. Freely transferable by endorsement and delivery.
4. Issued at discount to face value.
5. Repayable on a fixed date without grace days.
6. Subject to stamp duty like the usance promissory notes.

The banks in the USA in 1960s introduced CDs which are freely negotiable and marketable any time before maturity. The CDs were issued by big banks in the USA in units of $ 1 million at face value bearing fixed interest with a maturity generally ranging from 1 to 6 months. Banks sold CDs direct to investors or through dealers who subsequently traded this instrument in secondary market. The American banks issued for the first time dollar CDs in London in 1966. The Bank of England gave permission to around 40 banks to make CD issue.

The feasibility of introducing CDs in India was examined by the Tambe Working Group in 1982 which did not, however, favour the introduction of this instrument. The matter was again studied in 1987 by the Vaghul Working Group on the Money Market. The Vaghul Group recognised that CP would be attractive both to the banker and investor in that the bank is not required to encash the deposit prematurely while the investor can liquify the instrument before its maturity in the secondary market.

On the recommendations of the Vaghul Committee, the RBI formulated a scheme in June 1989 permitting scheduled commercial banks (excluding RRBs) to issue CDs. In terms of the scheme, CDs can be issued by scheduled commercial banks at a discount on face value and the discount rates are market-determined. The RBI has issued detailed guidelines for the issue of CDs and, with the changes introduced subsequently, the scheme for CDs has been liberalised.

## ❖ RBI guidelines

1. The denomination of CDs could be in multiples of ₹ 5 lakhs subject to a minimum size of an issue to a single investor being ₹ 25 lakhs. The CDs above ₹ 25 lakhs will be in multiples of ₹ 5 lakhs. The amount relates to face value (not maturity value) of CDs issued.
2. The CDs are short-term deposit instruments with maturity period ranging from 3 months to one year. The banks can issue at their discretion, the CDs for any number of months/days beyond the minimum usance period of three months and within the maximum usance of one year.
3. CDs can be issued to individuals, corporations, companies, trust funds, associations, etc. Non-Resident Indians (NRIs) can also subscribe to CDs but only on a non-repartiation basis.
4. CDs are freely transferable by endorsement and delivery but only after 45 days of the date of issue to the primary investor. As such, the maturity period of CDs available in the market can be anywhere between 1 day and 320 days.
5. They are issued in the form of usance promissory notes payable on a fixed date without days of grace. CDs are subject to payment of stamp duty like the usance promissory notes.
6. Banks have to maintain CRR and SLR on the issue price of CDs and report them as deposits to the RBI. Banks are neither permitted to grant loans against CDs nor to buy them back prematurely.
7. From October 17, 1992, the limit for issue of CDs by scheduled commercial banks (excluding Regional Rural Banks) has been raised from 7 per cent to 10 per cent of the fortnightly aggregate deposits in 1989-90. The ceilings on outstanding of CDs at any point of time are prescribed by the Reserve Bank of India for each bank. Banks are advised by the RBI to ensure that the individual bankwise limits prescribed for issue of CDs are not exceeded at any time.
8. Three financial institutions, *viz.*, Industrial Development Bank of India, Industrial Credit and Investment Corporation of India and Industrial Finance Corporation of India, were permitted to issue CDs with a maturity period of more than one year up to three years with an initial aggregate limit of ₹ 1,000 crores (enhanced to ₹ 1,350 crores in May 1992). Effective from July 29, 1992, the Industrial Reconstruction Bank of India has also been permitted to issue CDs up to a limit of ₹ 100 crores.
9. The minimum credit rating for CD shall be $A_3$ (investment grade).

## ❖ Advantages

1. Certificate of deposits are the most convenient instruments to depositors as they enable their short-term surpluses to earn higher return.
2. CDs also offer maximum liquidity as they are transferable by endorsement and delivery. The holder can resell his certificate to another.
3. From the point of view of issuing bank, it is a vehicle to raise resources in times of need and improve their lending capacity. The CDs are fixed term deposits which cannot be withdrawn until the redemption date.
4. This is an ideal instrument for banks with short-term surplus funds to invest at attractive rates.

## ❖ Impediments

The scheme of CDs has been in operation for almost six years now. It is yet to gain ground and its usage is confined only to a few corporations and banks. The number of issuing banks has been 51 in March 1992-93 and the amount outstanding has been ₹ 9,803 crores. The number of issuing banks and the amount outstanding have declined to 48 and ₹ 5,571 crores respectively. The reasons for the slow growth are the following:

### 1. Stamp duty

The CDs are subject to stamp duty applicable to usance pronotes. Besides, the cost involved which is anywhere between 0.5 per cent and 1 per cent p.a. which makes the CDs less attractive, there are practical problems such as non-availability of stamps of required denomination, the time involved in getting the CDs stamped due to procedural delays at the stamp office, etc.

There is, therefore, an immediate need for revamping stamp duty on CDs if this instrument is to become popular.

### 2. Development of secondary market

There is a need for developing an active and liquid secondary market for CDs. The Discount and Finance House of India Ltd. (DFHI) has been designated to trade in the CDs in the secondary market.

In spite of DFHI intending to trade in CDs for which it is publishing its daily discount rates in the press and also individually approaching the issuing banks, the secondary market in this instrument has yet to gather momentum. Some of the inhibiting factors in this regard are as follows:

(*i*) Since CD holders have received highly attractive returns on their holdings, they are reluctant to disinvest them for a better trade-off;

(*ii*) CD holders particularly those outside Mumbai, may not be aware of the trading in CDs by DFHI and its dealing procedure;

(*iii*) Banks are not investing in CDs since this instrument has no fiscal advantage nor does the holding bank has the benefit of netting off the holding as an eligible asset from its DTL;

(*iv*) Some banks have reportedly not yet issued the proper scrips to CD holders;

(*v*) Limited size of the primary market and holdings confined to a few holders at selected centres are the other reasons.

The following steps can be taken to activate the secondary market:

(*a*) DFHI may intensify its efforts in making banks and through them the CD holders, aware of its trading in CDs and its dealing procedure.

(*b*) Banks may advise their CD holders about the opportunities for disinvesting their holdings for a better trade-off.

(*c*) Once some merchant banks create money market funds after obtaining the RBI's approval, they will be able to actively trade in money market instruments including CDs and commercial paper.

(*d*) Banks/merchant banks offering investment services to their clients may create trading opportunities in CDs.

(*e*) RBI may examine selective relaxation of the ceiling on CDs outstanding for individual banks and reduction in the minimum size of the deposit to broadbase the CD holders, in order to improve the size of the primary market, which will hopefully provide a fillip to the secondary market.

(*f*) In order to eliminate the hassle of moving CDs from up-country centres to Mumbai to facilitate trading with DFHI, the issuing banks may hold the CDs in safe custody duly discharged by the CD holders at their respective Mumbai branches which could handle the sale transactions on behalf of and as and when desired by their clients, with DFHI by tendering the CDs, to DFHI, and also, if required, pay the proceeds of CDs on maturity to the holders on behalf of the issuing branches. In due course, RBI may consider permitting banks to act as depository agencies in CDs on behalf of investors dispensing with the issue of actual certificates so that sales and purchases of CDs are effected through internal book-keeping in banks, thus obviating the need for physical movement of certificates.

(*g*) In order that the banks have some incentive to invest in CDs, these holdings may be permitted as an eligible asset for netting off from their respective DTL. In some countries like Singapore and Malaysia, CDs below 1 year are even treated as an eligible asset to a specified extent, for the purpose of SLR. As a result, banks at these centres actively invest in CDs and also trade in the secondary market.

### 3. Lock-in period

The minimum lock-in period of 45 days is yet another problem.

Removal of this stipulation may go a long way in popularising CD scheme. The outstanding amount of Certificate of Deposit stood at ₹ 1,723.1 billion as on May 31, 2017.

## INTER-BANK PARTICIPATION CERTIFICATE

The Governor of the Reserve Bank of India while dealing with credit policy measures in October 1988, had informed the bank Chiefs about a proposal to authorise banks to fund their short-term needs from within the system through issuance of inter-bank participations. This announcement by the RBI was in line with the recommendations made by the Working Group on the money market. Inter-bank participation certificate provides them an additional instrument for even out short-term liquidity within the perimeter of the banking system, particularly at times when there are imbalances affecting the maturity mix of assets in bankers' books.

Since then the regular guidelines applicable to inter-bank participations have been brought out by the RBI, the salient features thereof may be briefly set out as given hereafter:

(*i*) The objective is to provide a certain element of liquidity to the portfolio of banks particularly in the credit segment support of funds to tide over, situations arising from lags in the funds flow of the borrowers.

(*ii*) The scheme is confined to scheduled commercial banks only and the period of participation is restricted to minimum 91 days and maximum 180 days.

(*iii*) Participations permitted are of two types namely with and without risk to the lender. The without risk type of participation is confined to a tenure of 90 days only.

(*iv*) Originally a ceiling interest rate of 12.5 per cent per annum was prescribed for the lent funds under 'without risk' participation and this was removed later on along with removal of ceilings of inter-bank call rate and the interest rate for rediscounting of bills.

(*v*) Banks are permitted to issue participations under the "with risk" nomenclature for the advance classified under Health Code-1 status and the aggregate amount of such participations in any account should not exceed 40 per cent of the outstandings in the account at the time of issue.

(*vi*) The distinction between 'with risk' and 'without risk' sharing arrangements in so far as the borrower bank is concerned, is that under 'with risk' participation the issuing bank will reduce the amount of the participation from the advances outstanding while the participating bank will show the participation as part of its advances, whereas under the 'without risk' sharing arrangement the issuing bank will show the participation as a borrowing while the participating bank will show it as advances to banks. In the latter case, the participation is treated as part of the net demand and time liabilities and net bank balances for purposes of statutory reserve requirements.

## ❖ Advantages of the scheme

(*i*) The scheme benefits the issuing and participating banks to the extent that it provides access to funds against advances comparatively with less cumbersome procedure than through regular consortium tie-up.

(*ii*) It also facilitates banks having surplus funds on their hands to build up and earn more on their assets over a certain period than with the earlier time-consuming and procedurally complicated tie-ups with other banks. At the same time, those banks who are in need of funds can take advantage of the market if they have an overlent position for a short while.

### ❖ Suggestions

(*i*) The scheme may be enlarged so as to admit term lending financial institutions and organisations like LIC, UTI and GIC as participants. In that case, the market may turn out to be more broad-based and competitive.

(*ii*) The scheme may incorporate provisions for redemption earlier than due date.

(*iii*) It may be stipulated that the rate of interest on lending to the issuing bank should not exceed 0.5 per cent the interest rate at which the issuing bank has lent to its borrower.

(*iv*) A second tier transferability may be permitted to create more appeal for the scheme.

(*v*) There can be also a provision to extend the tenure of participation beyond the present permitted time limits by another 30 days if the lender and borrower banks so agree.

## REPO INSTRUMENTS

Repo stands for repurchase. Under Repo transaction, the borrower parts with securities to the lender with an agreement to repurchase them at the end of the fixed period at a specified price. At the end of the period, the borrower will repurchase the securities at the predetermined price. The difference between the purchase price and the original price is the cost for the borrower. This cost of borrowing is called 'Repo Rate' which is little cheaper than pure borrowing.

A transaction is called a Repo when viewed from the perspective of the seller of the securities and Reverse Repo when described from the point of view of the suppliers of funds. Thus, whether a given agreement is termed a Repo or Reverse Repo depends largely on which party initiated the transaction.

Repo transactions are conducted in the money market to manipulate short-term interest rate and manage liquidity levels. In India, Repos are normally conducted for a period of 3 days. The eligible securities for the purpose are decided by RBI. These securities are usually government promissory notes, treasury bills and public sector bonds.

When the RBI announces a fixed rate Repo, for certain number of days/period it conveys its intention to market at the desirable level of short-term interest rate. When RBI conducts 'Repos', the short-term interest rate in the money market may not go below the RBI Repo rate. If the interest is lower in other markets such as foreign exchange market, treasury bills market, holders of funds may go for Repos with RBI. Thus, Repo transactions ensure stability in short-term interest rates in the money market. In case, the RBI wants to inject fresh funds in the market, it will conduct 'Reverse Repo' transactions with primary dealers against Government securities.

## STRUCTURE OF INDIAN MONEY MARKET

The structure of Indian money market is displayed in the Chart 2.1.

As shown in the chart, the Indian money market is highly disintegrated and unorganised. There are two sectors, *viz.*, organised and unorganised. In between these two, there exists the cooperative sector. The cooperative sector is also subject to strict control and supervision and hence it can very well be included under the organised sector.

**CHART 2.1**

**INDIAN MONEY MARKET**

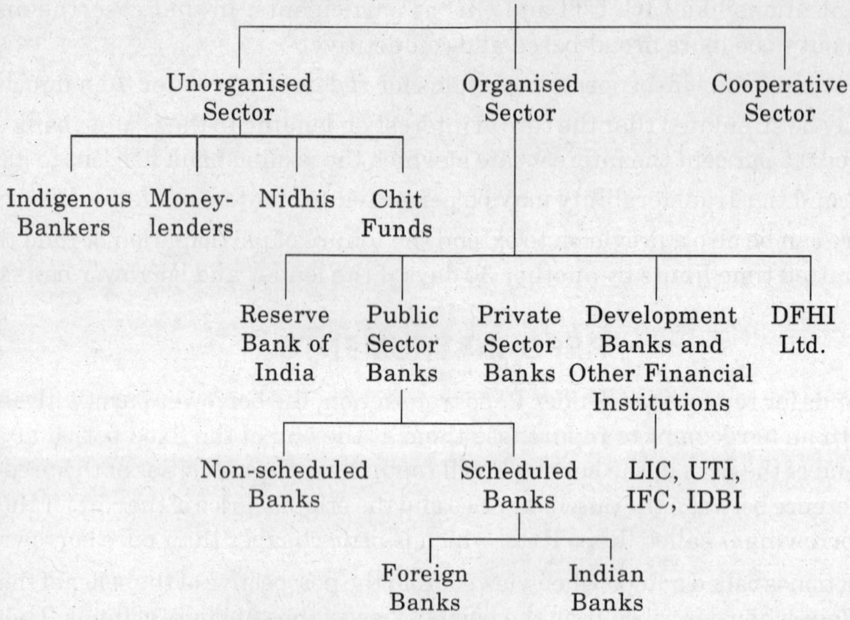


In the organised sector, the RBI, public sector banks, private sector banks, development banks and other financial institutions play a dominant role. The RBI is the nerve centre of the monetary system of our country and it is the leader of the Indian money market. Commercial banks form the nucleus of the Indian money market. At the same time, the unorganised sector exists side by side with the organised sector. This sector remains outside the purview of the RBI even today. It makes the Indian money market an underdeveloped one.

## FEATURES OR DEFICIENCIES OF INDIAN MONEY MARKET

The features or the deficiencies of the Indian money market are the following:

**(i) Existence of Unorganised Sector:** The Indian money market consists of organised and unorganised sectors. The organised sector comprises of the Reserve Bank, the State Bank of India and its subsidiaries, private sector banks and foreign banks. Life Insurance Corporation of India, Unit Trust of India, Industrial Finance Corporation, State Financial Corporations also participate in the operations of the money market as lenders. The unorganised sector comprises of indigenous bankers. A substantially higher rate of interest prevails in the unorganised market. The indigenous banks follow their own rules of banking and finance. Many attempts were made by RBI to bring the indigenous bankers under its direct control. These efforts have not been successful. They have not accepted the conditions prescribed by RBI. The indigenous bankers are now slowly coming under the organised banking system by availing of the rediscounting facilities from RBI.

(ii) **Absence of integration:** The Indian money market was divided into several sections with each section being loosely connected with other sections. The organised banking system and the unorganised banking system did not have any contact between them remaining completely aloof from each other. With the setting up of the Reserve Bank of India and the passing of the Banking Regulations Act, 1949, the conditions have improved. The RBI effectively controls the affairs of the organised sector and it has become an important part of the Indian money market.

(iii) **Diversity in money rates of interest:** There exists wide diversity in the money rates of interest in the money market. The immobility of funds from one section to another contributes to the diversity in interest rates. At present, the wide divergence does not exist. The different rates of interest get adjusted to the changes in the bank rate. Still, the situation cannot be said to be identical with that found in the developed money market. Moreover, the money rates of interest also differ between different regions or centres. This leads to fluctuations in security prices. This is due to the difficulty of making cheap and quick remittance of funds from one financial centre to the others. The Reserve Bank of India has rationalised the system of remittance of funds between different parts of the country so as to equalise the money rates throughout the country.

(iv) **Seasonal stringency of funds:** The demand for money in Indian money market is of seasonal in nature. During the busy season from October to April, money is needed for financing the marketing of agricultural products, seasonal industries such as sugar, gur, etc., and to some extent coal. From the end of April, the demand for money begins to decrease till the end of October. Consequently, the money rates fluctuate from one period to another. RBI attempts to lessen the fluctuation in money rates by increasing the money supply during busy season and withdrawing the same during lean season.

(v) **Absence of bill market:** The bill market in Indian money market is in its infancy. The market for Government and semi-government securities is narrow. The investors in government securities are limited to institutional investors comprising RBI, LIC, commercial banks, etc. Transactions in the inter-bank call money market constitute the core of the Indian money market. The commercial banks had substantial recourse to RBI for financial accommodation. The market for bill of exchange and treasury bills is little developed. The Reserve Bank of India has taken steps to develop genuine bill market in India.

(vi) **No contact with foreign money markets:** The Indian money market is an insular one with little contact with money market in other countries. There is large movement of capital between money markets in Western countries. The Indian money market does not attract any foreign funds as developed money markets do.

(vii) **Limited instruments:** The supply of money market instruments like bills, TBs, etc. is very limited and inadequate considering the varied requirements of short-term funds. In fact, in a developed money market, there should be well diversified mix of money market instruments so as to meet the varied requirements of borrowers and lenders.

(viii) **Limited secondary market:** The secondary market is very limited in the case of money market instruments. Practically speaking, it is restricted to rediscounting of commercial and treasury bills. In India, people generally prefer cash credit and OD to bill financing. Hence, the primary market is also limited. Similarly, due to low yield, the market for TBs is also restricted. In India, banks have a tendency to hold these bills till maturity, thus preventing an active trade in these bills.

(ix) **Limited participants:** Again, the participants in the Indian money market are also limited. Entry into the market is strictly regulated. In fact, there are a larger number of borrowers but a few lenders. Hence, the market is not very active, broad and vibrant.

## RECENT DEVELOPMENTS

In recent years, the money market is undergoing structural changes in India. Many steps have been taken to transform the restricted and narrow market to an active and broad market. Some important measures adopted in this direction are the following:

**(i) Integration of unorganised sector with the organised sector**

The process of integration of the unorganised money market with the organised sector has already started. This is being done by means of bringing the institutions in the unorganised sector within the orbit of control and regulation exercised by the RBI. These institutions are now slowly coming under the organised sector by subjecting themselves to the control of RBI and availing of the rediscounting facilities from the RBI.

Again, at present, commercial banks have been asked to extend their network of branches in rural areas and this has enlarged the 'monetised sector' in the economy by restricting the activities of the unorganised sector.

**(ii) Widening of call money market**

In recent times, many steps have been taken to widen the call market. LIC, GIC, IDBI, UTI, specified mutual funds have been permitted to enter into this market as lenders only. The DFHI and STCI have been permitted to operate both as lenders and borrowers. This increase in the number of participants has definitely widened the call market making it more active.

**(iii) Introduction of innovative instruments**

New innovations have been introduced in the structure and instrument traded in the money market. 182 days treasury bills have been introduced since November 1986 on the recommendations of Chakraborty Committee. Again 364 days TBs with higher yields have been introduced from April 1992. These bills are sold through periodical auctions at varying rates of interest so as to enable the investors to get market rates of interest.

Moreover, new instruments such as certificate of deposit, commercial paper and inter-bank participation certificate have been introduced and necessary guidelines have been issued for their operation. Thus, all attempts have been taken to provide a well diversified mix of money market instruments so as to make the market very active.

Recently, schemes for the development of secondary market in commercial paper and for trading in CDs and PCs have been initiated by the RBI.

**(iv) Offering of market rates of interest**

In order to popularise money market instruments, the ceiling on interest rate has been abolished. Call money rate, bill discounting rate, inter-bank rate, etc. have been freed from May 1, 1989. TBs are issued through auction so as to fetch market rates of interest. Thus, today Indian money market offers full scope for the play of market forces in determining the rates of interest.

**(v) Promotion of bill culture**

All attempts are being taken to discourage cash credit and OD system of financing and to popularise bill financing. Exemption from stamp duty is given on rediscounting of derivative usance promissory notes arising out of genuine trade bill transactions with a view to promoting bill culture in the country.

**(vi) Entry of Money Market Mutual Funds (MMMFs)**

Certain private sector mutual funds and subsidiaries of commercial banks have been recently permitted to deal in money market instruments. This has been done with a view to expanding the money market and also for developing secondary market for money market instruments. These funds can invest in money market instruments. They can also lend to call market. Frequent realisation of interest and redemption of fund at short notice are the special features of this fund.

**(vii) Setting up of credit rating agencies**

The Credit Rating Information Services of India Ltd. (CRISIL) provides credit ratings for raising funds through money market instruments like commercial papers. Of late, credit information agencies like Investment Information and Credit Rating Agency of India (IICRA), Credit Analysis and Research Limited (CARE), etc. have been established to provide credit information through financial analysis of leading companies and industrial sectors. All these measures have strengthened the Indian money market by paving way for safe and liquid short-term investments.

**(viii) Adoption of suitable monetary policy**

In recent times, the RBI is adopting a more realistic and appropriate monetary policy so as to increase the resources in the money market and make it more active than before. For instance, the CRR has been brought down from 15 per cent in 1995 to 12 per cent in July 1996. Again it was brought down to 4 per cent in April 2019 and 3% in April 2021. These successive reductions have helped to increase the resources available in the money market.

**(ix) Establishment of DFHI**

The Discount and Finance House of India was established in 1988 to activate the money market and to promote a secondary market in all money market. It deals in all money market instruments as market maker. In view of its importance, it has been discussed in detail subsequently.

**(x) Setting up of Securities Trading Corporation of India Ltd. (STCI)**

The RBI has set up the STCI in May 1994 with an authorised capital of ₹ 500 crores. Its main objective is to provide a secondary market in government securities. As far as money market is concerned, its operations are mostly confined to treasury bills and money at call and short notice. The STCI has enlarged the treasury bill market and the call market and provided an active secondary market for treasury bills.

**(xi) Introduction of Non-Cumulative Debentures (NCDs)**

The RBI has issued directions regulating the issue of NCDs of maturity up to one year which are money market instruments. NCDs cannot be issued for maturity less than 90 days and cannot have call/put options that are exercisable within 90 days from the date of issue.

In view of these recent developments, the money market in India can no longer be called an underdeveloped one. In terms of organised relationship and specialisation of functions, the Indian money market is considered a developed one.

## DISCOUNT AND FINANCE HOUSE OF INDIA (DFHI)

The Discount and Finance House of India (DFHI) has been set up as a specialised money market institution with the objective of providing liquidity to money market instruments and to develop a secondary market.

The working group on money market suggested the setting up of DFHI in 1987. In pursuance of the recommendations of the working group, the Reserve Bank set up jointly with public sector banks and financial institutions, the Discount and Finance House of India Limited. The DFHI was incorporated under the Indian Companies Act, 1956 and commenced its operations in April 1988.

It is a joint-stock company and is jointly owned by RBI, the public sector banks and the all India financial institutions which have contributed its paid-up capital of ₹ 150 crores. The main objective of establishing DFHI has been to strengthen the short-term money market and make short-term resources available to the institutions. It shall generate the bill culture and bill discipline amongst the banks, financial institutions and the Central and State Government undertakings. In addition, refinance facility with the RBI and a line of credit of ₹ 100 crores from public sector banks on a consortium basis are the main sources of its funds. The option of borrowing in the call money market and on short-term basis is also open to the DFHI. However, the total amount of credit that the DFHI can borrow either from RBI or from its consortium lenders is limited to ten times its net worth.

### Functions

The main functions of DFHI are as follows:

1. To discount, rediscount, buy, sell, underwrite or acquire and sell marketable securities and negotiable instruments including treasury bills, trade bills, bills of exchange, promissory notes, commercial bills and commercial papers.
2. To undertake buyback arrangements in trade and treasury bills as well as securities of local authorities, public sector institutions, Government and commercial and non-commercial houses.
3. To carry on business as a lender, borrower, broker or as a broking house in the inter-bank call money market.
4. To promote and support company funds, trusts and such other organisations for the development of short-term money market.
5. To advise Governments, banks, financial institutions or business houses in evolving schemes for growth, development and expansion of the money market.

Although the DFHI is empowered to undertake a wide range of business, it will, in its initial stages deal mainly with the 182 days treasury bills and selectively repurchase and resell the bills only from/to banks for short period up to 14 days at predetermined prices. As regards short-term commercial bills, the aim of the DFHI is to provide liquidity to commercial bills which have already been rediscounted by banks and financial institutions, thus giving them access to liquid funds.

The operations of DFHI are aimed at imparting greater flexibility to banks in their fund management. Corporate bodies and other institutions will also find it attractive to invest their short-term surplus funds in treasury bills and secondary market will be created by the presence of DFHI.

The DFHI participates in the call, notice and term markets as a borrower and as a lender. It also purchases and sells treasury bills at the auctions, commercial bills, commercial papers and certificate of deposits. All transactions are done through exchange of cheques drawn on the RBI to facilitate same day settlement.

## ❖ Call, notice and term money

In order to provide some flexibility in the money market, the DFHI has been allowed with effect from July 28, 1988 to participate in the call and notice money market both as a lender and as a borrower. The DFHI borrows in markets for lending as also to fund its other assets such as treasury bills and commercial bills. It also lends funds realised through the sale of money market assets. The minimum amount of transaction is generally ₹ 1 crore. However, in respect of cooperative banks, the minimum amount per transaction is ₹ 50 lakhs for dealings in notice and term money. The DFHI has been effectively pooling the lenders' supplies to meet the borrowers' requirements. Despite a commendable performance, the market share of DFHI in the call money operations is still negligible.

## ❖ Treasury bills

The DFHI's operations in 182 days treasury bills are aimed at imparting greater flexibility to banks in their funds management. When the inter-bank call money market is tight, banks holding 182 days TBs have an advantage in raising funds at lower cost against the collateral of these bills, through the DFHI. When the conditions are easy in the call money market, banks having surplus funds can enter into buying arrangements in 182 days TBs with the DFHI for comparatively better returns. With its dealing in 182 days TBs, the DFHI has been playing a vital role in developing a secondary market for these bills.

Besides sale and purchase of 182 days treasury bills on outright basis, the DFHI also provides repo facility (selling TBs with an assurance to buy them back or buying bills with an assurance of selling back to the holder after a fixed duration) to banks, select financial institutions and public sector undertakings, up to a period of 14 days at negotiated interest rates. For banks, 'repo' facility provides the flexibility for maintenance of Cash Reserve Ratio and Statutory Liquidity Requirements.

## ❖ Commercial bills

With a view of providing liquidity to commercial bills discounted by scheduled commercial banks, the DFHI provides rediscounting facilities to banks through purchase of Derivative

Usance Promissory Notes (DPNs) drawn in favour of the DFHI by banks. The DPNs are then sold by them to investors such as financial institutions, approved State Cooperative Banks and Urban Cooperative Banks duly endorsed in their favour. In case the investors are in need of funds, they can sell these DPNs to the DFHI at quoted bid rediscount rates. On maturity, the holder will have to present the DPN duly discharged to the drawer (bank) for the payment of maturity proceeds. The DFHI daily quotes its bid and offer rediscount rates. The DPNs are generally drawn for a minimum amount of ₹ 50 lakhs for the usance period of 15 to 90 days.

### ❖ Performance

Now, the DFHI has grown into an effective organisation. It is playing a vital role in call money market, government securities and bills market. Its resources form about 10 to 15 per cent of the total money market funds. However, the operations of the DFHI is subject to a number of constraints such as paucity of funds, competition from primary dealers, weak inter-bank transactions, presence of few large players in the market and too much dependence on the RBI. Despite the limitations, the DFHI is making concerned efforts to expand its operations to provide additional liquidity in the market.

## QUESTIONS

### I. Objective type questions:

#### A. Fill in the blanks:

1. The market for extremely short period loans is called __________.
2. __________ are drawn by contractors on the government departments for the goods supplied to them.
3. The bill which does not require any acceptance is called __________.
4. __________ has been set up mainly to provide a secondary market in government securities.
5. The Discount and Finance House of India was set up in the year __________

[**Key:** 1. Call money market, 2. Supply bills, 3. Treasury bill, 4. STCI, 5. 1987]

#### B. Choose the best answer from the following:

1. The market for short-term loans is known as:

   (*a*) Call money market (*b*) Treasury bill market

   (*c*) Money market (*d*) Acceptance market

2. Bills drawn and accepted payable after three months are called:

   (*a*) Indigenous bills (*b*) Usance bills

   (*c*) Clean bills (*d*) Supply bills

3. The market which helps commercial banks to maintain their SLR requirements is:

   (*a*) Call loan market (*b*) Discount market

   (*c*) Acceptance market (*d*) Commercial bill market

4. The certificate which evidences an unsecured corporate debt of short-term maturity is:
   (*a*) Short-term loan certificate (*b*) Certificate of deposit
   (*c*) Inter-bank participation certificate (*d*) Commercial paper
5. The major player in the Indian money market is:
   (*a*) Cooperative banks (*b*) Indigenous banks
   (*c*) Commercial banks (*d*) Reserve Bank of India

[**Key:** 1. (*c*), 2. (*b*), 3. (*a*), 4. (*d*), 5. (*c*)]

## C. State whether the following statements are TRUE or FALSE:

1. Money market supplies funds for financing working capital requirements of industries.
2. 'Ad hoc' treasury bills are always issued in favour of the RBI only.
3. LIC and UTI can act as both lenders and borrowers of call loans in India.
4. 91 days treasury bills do not carry any fixed rate of discount.
5. Certificate of deposit can be issued only by commercial banks.

[**Key:** 1. True, 2. True, 3. False, 4. False, 5. False]

## II. Short answer type questions:

1. Define a money market.
2. State the objectives of a money market.
3. What is a call money market?
4. Who are the participants in a call loan market?
5. Distinguish between a discount market and acceptance market.
6. What is a commercial paper?
7. What do you know about certificate of deposit?
8. Who are the participants in the unorganised money market in India?
9. State the objectives of the Discount and Finance House of India.
10. Explain CRISIL.
11. What is non-cumulative debenture?

## III. Answer the following in a paragraph:

1. Distinguish between a money market and a capital market.
2. Bring out the features of a money market.
3. Discuss the importance of a commercial bill market.
4. State the causes for the unpopularity of bill market in India.
5. What are the merits of a treasury bill market?
6. State the steps taken by the RBI to promote the bill market in India.
7. What are the functions of the Discount and Finance House of India?

## IV. Essay type questions:

1. Discuss the features of a developed money market and bring out its importance.
2. Discuss the various components of a money market and bring out their features.
3. List down the various money market instruments and state their features in brief.
4. Give the structure of the Indian money market and point out its deficiencies.
5. What steps have been taken in recent years to make the Indian money market a developed one?

# 3 NEW ISSUE MARKET

## MEANING

The industrial securities market in India consists of new issue market and stock exchange. The new issue market deals with the new securities which were not previously available to the investing public, *i.e.*, the securities that are offered to the investing public for the first time. The market, therefore, makes available a new block of securities for public subscription. In other words, new issue market deals with raising of fresh capital by companies either for cash or for consideration other than cash.

The new issue market encompasses all institutions dealing in fresh claim. These claims may be in the form of equity shares, preference shares, debentures, rights issues, deposits, etc. All financial institutions which contribute, underwrite and directly subscribe to the securities are part of new issue market.

## STOCK EXCHANGE

The stock exchange is a market for old securities, *i.e.*, those which have been already issued and listed on a stock exchange. These securities are purchased and sold continuously among investors without the involvement of companies. Stock exchange provides not only free transferability of shares but also makes continuous evaluation of securities traded in the market.

## DISTINCTION BETWEEN NEW ISSUE MARKET AND STOCK EXCHANGE

The distinction between the new issue market and the stock exchange can be made on three grounds.

(*i*) Functional difference.

(*ii*) Organisational difference.

(*iii*) Nature of contribution to industrial finance.

### (i) Functional difference

The new issue market deals with new securities which are issued for the first time for public subscription. The stock exchange provides a ready market for buying and selling of old securities.

### (ii) Organisational difference

The stock exchanges have physical existence and are located in particular geographical areas. The stock exchange is a place, where dealers of security meet regularly at appointed time announced by the market. It is a well established organisation with rules and regulations for a smooth conduct of the business. The members are supplied with information about companies and daily changes in prices of stocks.

The new issue market enjoys neither any tangible form nor any administrative organisational set-up nor is subject to any centralised control and administration for the execution of the business. It renders service to the lenders and borrowers of funds at the time of any particular operation and the services are taken up entirely by banks, brokers and underwriters.

### (iii) Nature of contribution to industrial finance

The new issue market provides the issuing company with funds for starting a new enterprise or for either expansion or diversification of an existing one by making a direct link between companies which require funds and the investing public. So, the contribution of new issue market is direct. The role of stock exchange in providing capital is indirect as it provides marketability to the shares.

## RELATIONSHIP BETWEEN NEW ISSUE MARKET AND STOCK EXCHANGE

Despite the above-mentioned differences, the new issue market and stock exchange are inseparably connected and work in conjunction with each other.

The new issues first placed in the new issue market can be disposed of subsequently in the stock exchange. The stock exchange provides the mechanism for regular and continuous purchase and sale of securities. This facility is of immense utility to potential investors who are assured that they will be able to dispose of the allotment of shares at any time. Thus, the two markets are complementary in nature.

Both the markets are connected to each other even at the time of new issue. The companies which make new issue apply for listing of shares on a recognised stock exchange. Listing of shares adds prestige to the firm and widens the market for the investors. The companies which want stock exchange listing have to comply with statutory rules and regulations of the stock exchange to ensure fair dealing in them. The stock exchanges, thus, exercise considerable control over the organisation of new issues.

The new issue market and stock market are economically an integral part of a single market, *i.e.*, industrial securities market. Both are susceptible to the common influence of the environmental conditions such as political stability, economic conditions, monetary policy of the central bank and the fiscal policy of the government. The two markets act and react upon each other in the same direction. When the stock prices go up in the market, the new issues increase and when the stock prices show a downward trend the new issues decline. The new issue market also depends on the stock exchange to find out price movements and general economic outlook and to forecast the climate for the success of new issues.

## FUNCTIONS OF NEW ISSUE MARKET

The main function of a new issue market is to facilitate transfer of resources from savers to the users. The savers are individuals, commercial banks, insurance companies, etc. The users are public limited companies and the government. The new issue market plays an important role of mobilising the funds from the savers and transferring them to borrowers for productive purposes, an important requisite of economic growth. It is not only a platform for raising finance to establish new enterprises but also for expansion/diversification/modernisation of existing units. On this basis, the new issue market can be classified as:

1. Market where firms go to the public for the first time through Initial Public Offering (IPO).
2. Market where firms which are already trading raise additional capital through Seasoned Equity Offering (SEO).

The main functions of a new issue market can be divided into a triple service functions:

1. Origination.
2. Underwriting.
3. Distribution.

### ❖ Origination

Origination refers to the work of investigation, analysis and processing of new project proposals. Origination starts before an issue is actually floated in the market. There are two aspects in this function:

(*i*) A careful study of the technical, economic and financial viability to ensure soundness of the project. This is a preliminary investigation undertaken by the sponsors of the issue.

(*ii*) Advisory services which improve the quality of capital issues and ensure its success.

The advisory services include:

(*a*) Type of Issue. This refers to the kind of securities to be issued whether equity share, preference share, debenture or convertible debenture.

(*b*) Magnitude of issue.

(*c*) Time of floating an issue.

(*d*) Pricing of an issue — whether shares are to be issued at par or at premium.

(*e*) Methods of issue.

(*f*) Technique of selling the securities.

The function of origination is done by merchant bankers who may be commercial banks, all India financial institutions or private firms. Initially, this service was provided by specialised division of commercial banks. At present, financial institutions and private firms also perform this service. Though this service is highly important, the success of the issue depends, to a large extent, on the efficiency of the market.

The origination itself does not guarantee the success of the issue. Underwriting, a specialised service, is required in this regard.

## ❖ Underwriting

Underwriting is an agreement, whereby the underwriter promises to subscribe to a specified number of shares or debentures or a specified amount of stock in the event of public not subscribing to the issue. If the issue is fully subscribed, then there is no liability for the underwriter. If a part of share issues remains unsold, the underwriter will buy the shares. Thus, underwriting is a guarantee for the marketability of shares.

## ❖ Methods of underwriting

An underwriting agreement may take any of the following three forms:

(i) **Standing behind the issue:** Under this method, the underwriter guarantees the sale of a specified number of shares within a specified period. If the public do not subscribe to the specified amount of issue, the underwriter buys the balance in the issue.

(ii) **Outright purchase:** The underwriter, in this method, makes outright purchase of shares and resells them to the investors.

(iii) **Consortium method:** Underwriting is jointly done by a group of underwriters in this method. The underwriters form a syndicate for this purpose. This method is adopted for large issues.

## ❖ Advantages of underwriting

Underwriting assumes great significance as it offers the following advantages to the issuing company.

1. The issuing company is relieved from the risk of finding buyers for the issue offered to the public. The company is assured of raising adequate capital.
2. The company is assured of getting the minimum subscription within the stipulated time, a statutory obligation to be fulfilled by the issuing company.
3. Underwriters undertake the burden of highly specialised function of distributing securities.
4. They provide expert advice with regard to timing of security issue, the pricing of issue, the size and type of securities to be issued, etc.
5. Public confidence on the issue is enhanced when underwriting is done by reputed underwriters.

The underwriters in India may be classified into two categories:

(*i*) Institutional underwriters.

(*ii*) Non-institutional underwriters.

The institutional underwriters are: (*a*) Life Insurance Corporation of India (LIC), (*b*) Unit Trust of India (UTI), (*c*) Industrial Development Bank of India (IDBI), (*d*) Industrial Credit and Investment Corporation of India (ICICI), and (*e*) Commercial Banks and General Insurance Companies. The pattern of underwriting of the above institutional underwriters differ vastly in India. LIC and UTI have purchased industrial securities from the new issue market with a view to holding them on their own portfolio. They have a preference for underwriting shares in large and well established firms. The development banks have given special attention to the issues in backward states and industries in the priority list. The thrust of the development banks is also towards small and new issues which do not have adequate support from other institutions. General insurance companies have shown preference in underwriting the securities of fairly new issues.

The non-institutional underwriters are brokers. They guarantee shares only with a view to earning commission from the company floating the issue. They are known to off-load the shares later to make a profit. The brokers work with profit motive in underwriting industrial securities. After the elimination of forward trading, stock exchange brokers have begun to take an underwriting business. The percentage of securities underwritten to the total private capital issue varies between 72 per cent and 97 per cent.

### ❖ Distribution

Distribution is the function of sale of securities to ultimate investors. This service is performed by brokers and agents who maintain a regular and direct contact with the ultimate investors.

## METHODS OF FLOATING NEW ISSUES

The various methods which are used in the floatation of securities in the new issue market are:

(*i*) Public issues.
(*ii*) Offer for sale.
(*iii*) Placement.
(*iv*) Rights issues.

### ❖ Public issues

Under this method, the issuing company directly offers to the general public/institutions a fixed number of shares at a stated price through a document called prospectus. This is the most common method followed by joint stock companies to raise capital through the issue of securities. The prospectus must state the following:

1. Name of the company.
2. Address of the registered office of the company.
3. Existing and proposed activities.
4. Location of the industry.
5. Names of directors.

6. Authorised and proposed issue capital to the public.
7. Dates of opening and closing the subscription list.
8. Minimum subscription.
9. Names of brokers/underwriters/bankers/managers and registrars to the issue.
10. A statement by the company that it will apply to stock exchange for quotations of its shares.

According to the Companies Act, 1956, every application form must be accompanied by a prospectus. Now, it is no longer necessary to furnish a copy of the prospectus along with every application form as per the Companies Amendment Act, 1988. Now, an abridged prospectus, is being annexed to every share application form.

### Merits of issue through prospectus

1. Sale through prospectus has the advantage of inviting a large section of the investing public through advertisement.
2. It is a direct method and no intermediaries are involved in it.
3. Shares, under this method, are allotted to a large section of investors on a non-discriminatory basis. This procedure helps in wide dispersion of shares and to avoid concentration of wealth in few hands.

### Demerits

1. It is an expensive method. The company has to incur expenses on printing of prospectus, advertisement, bank's commission, underwriting commission, legal charges, stamp duty, listing fee and registration charges.
2. This method is suitable only for large issues.

## ❖ Offer for sale

The method of offer of sale consists in outright sale of securities through the intermediary of issue houses or share brokers. In other words, the shares are not offered to the public directly. This method consists of two stages: The first stage is a direct sale by the issuing company to the issue house and brokers at an agreed price. In the second stage, the intermediaries resell the above securities to the ultimate investors. The issue houses or stock brokers purchase the securities at a negotiated price and resell at a higher price. The difference in the purchase and sale price is called turn or spread. It is otherwise called Bought Out Deals (BOD).

Let us take a simple example. X, a small company has a turnover of ₹ 2 crores a year. It requires additional funding of ₹ 8 crores to expand its capacity. The merchant banker sees potential business for the company. He asks the promoters of the company to sell 8 lakh shares of its capital to it. The company gets ₹ 8 crores to expand its business. The merchant banker/ issue house is now holding 80 per cent of the company's entire capital. In 12 month's time the company expanded its operations marketed its products successfully and earned sufficient profit. Now, the issue house decides to off-load the 80 per cent capital to the public at a premium of ₹ 30 per share. In a period of 18 months, the merchant bank/issue house has earned a profit of ₹ 2.4 crores.

## Advantages

Bought out deal enables an issuer with good project to obtain funds with a minimum cost without the fear of undersubscription. The intermediary, *i.e.*, merchant bankers/issue houses get higher return than the conventional merchant banking services.

Indbank Merchant Banking had gone in for a buyout agreement with Madhya Pradesh based distillery to buy shares worth ₹ 2.5 crores each at ₹ 60. After six months, the shares were sold at ₹ 71.50 per share with a assured return of 38.33 per cent for the sponsor.

The advantage of this method is that the company is relieved from the problem of printing and advertisement of prospectus and making allotment of shares. Offer for sale is not common in India. This method is used generally in two instances:

(*i*) Offer by a foreign company of a part of it to Indian investors.

(*ii*) Promoters diluting their stake to comply with requirements of stock exchange at the time of listing of shares.

## ❖ New Provision

To accommodate more companies under offer for sale mechanism, now SEBI has permitted promoters or large investors in companies with a market capitalisation of ₹ 1,000 crores and above, to opt for this route in case they want to dilute their stakes in listed companies. Hindustan Copper, BGR Energy and SAIL have tapped this market through this route.

## ❖ Placement

Under this method, the issue houses or brokers buy the securities outright with the intention of placing them with their clients afterwards. Here, the brokers act as almost wholesalers selling them in retail to the public. The brokers would make profit in the process of reselling to the public. The issue houses or brokers maintain their own list of clients and through customer contact sell the securities. There is no need for a formal prospectus as well as underwriting agreement.

Placement has the following advantages:

1. Timing of issue is important for successful floatation of shares. In a depressed market conditions when the issues are not likely to get public response through prospectus, placement method is a useful method of floatation of shares.
2. This method is suitable when small companies issue their shares.
3. It avoids delays involved in public issue and it also reduces the expenses involved in public issue.
4. There are no entry barriers for a company to access the private placement market. This route is also available to unlisted and closely held public companies.
5. A private placement deal can be successfully executed much faster than a public offering. The procedural formalities for a private placement are minimal. A private placement deal can be successfully closed in 4 to 6 weeks.
6. There is greater flexibility in the working out the terms of the issue. The issues deal with only a few institutional investors and hence renegotiating the terms of issue is easy.

7. This method is also suitable to first generation entrepreneurs who are less known to the public which makes the public issue less successful.
8. The issue expenses in case of private placement is low. The absence of several statutory and non-statutory expenses associated with underwriting, brokerage, printing, promotion, etc., makes the transaction cost of private placement approximately to 2 per cent of the total cost of issue.

The main disadvantage of this method is that the securities are not widely distributed to the large section of investors. A selected group of small investors are able to buy a large number of shares and get majority holding in a company.

This method of private placement is used to a limited extent in India. The promoters sell the shares to their friends, relatives and well-wishers to get minimum subscription which is a precondition for issue of shares to the public.

## ❖ Rights issue

Rights issue is a method of raising funds in the market by an existing company.

A right means an option to buy certain securities at a certain privileged price within a certain specified period. Shares, so offered to the existing shareholders are called rights shares.

Rights shares are offered to the existing shareholders in a particular proportion to their existing share ownership. The ratio in which the new shares or debentures are offered to the existing share capital would depend upon the requirement of capital. The rights themselves are transferable and saleable in the market.

Section 81 of the Companies Act deals with rights issue. According to this section, where a company increases its subscribed capital by the issue of new shares either after two years of its formation or after one year of its first issue of share whichever is earlier, these have to be first offered to the existing shareholders with the right to reserve them in favour of a nominee.

A company issuing rights is required to send a circular to all existing shareholders. The circular should provide information on how additional funds would be used and their effect on the earning capacity of the company. The company should normally give a time limit of at least one month to two months to shareholders to exercise their rights. If the rights are not fully taken up, the balance is to be equitably distributed among the applicants for additional shares. Any balance still left over may be disposed of in the market in a way which is most beneficial to the company.

### Advantages

1. The cost of issue is minimum. There is no underwriting, brokerage, advertising and printing of prospectus expenses.
2. It ensures equitable distribution of shares to all existing shareholders and so control of company remains undisturbed as proportionate ownership in the company remains the same.
3. It prevents the directors from issuing new shares in their own name or to their relatives at a lower price and get controlling right.

## ❖ Auction based offer-for-sale

The SEBI has introduced a new 'Auction based offer-for-sale' method to allow promoters in leading listed companies to off-load small trenches of their shares through a fast-tracked offer made via the stock exchanges. Under this method, the issuer has to simply auction shares at different prices subject to a floor, with the flexibility to allocate additional shares to investors placing higher bids. It does not require any reservation for retail investors, tedious process of preparing a red-herring prospectors, fixing a price brand mandatory for public offers and hiring investment bankers which are normal under book-building route. It is very much preferable to other options such as getting these companies to buyback only the shares of the government or draining them of their cash hoard through hefty dividend payouts. This new method can be quickly executed at minimal cost, while allowing limited opportunity for speculation in the secondary market.

**Distinction between 'public offer and offer for sale conventional method vs. Auction method (offer-for-sale on stock exchanges)**

The conventional method, *i.e.*, follow on public offer is different from 'offer-for-sale on stock exchange' or 'auction method' in the following ways:

| *Sl. No.* | *Follow-on public offer* | *Offer-for-sale on stock exchange* |
|---|---|---|
| 1. | One has to comply with an elaborate process with lot of documentations. | The process is very simple requiring less than one week and the duration of offer for sale will not exceed one trading day. |
| 2. | It requires filling of the requisite number of independent directors with the regulators. | No such filings is required. |
| 3. | There is overhand of extra liquidity into the market through FPO. | Since the process is very short there is no overhand, no hammering of shares in the secondary market. |
| 4. | Allotment is made at one price on proportionate basis. | Allotment is made on price priority or at one proportionate basis. |
| 5. | Institutional investors cannot get huge chunk of shares despite their willingness. | A minimum of 25 per cent is reserved for mutual funds, insurance companies. One fund or an insurance company may get the entire 25 per cent. |

## ❖ Institutional Placement Programme (IPP)

IPP is yet another method authorised by SEBI recently to access the capital market. Companies including Government companies will be able to place up to 10 per cent of their equity with institutional investors. This IPP route will obviate the need for a government company to undertake a block deal or a follow-on-offer-for-sale to meet the listing guidelines.

## GENERAL GUIDELINES FOR NEW ISSUE

All issues by a new company have to be made at par and for existing companies the issue price should be justified as per Malegam Committee's recommendations which are as follows:

The issue price should be justified by:

(*i*) The Earnings Per Share (EPS) for the last three years and comparison of pre-issue price to earnings ratio to the Price to Earnings (P/E) of the industry.

(*ii*) The latest Net Asset Value (NAV).

(*iii*) The minimum return on increased net worth to maintain pre-issue EPS. A company may also raise funds from the international markets by issuing Global Depository Receipts (GDRs) and American Depository Receipts (ADRs).

The SEBI does not play any role in price fixation. In fact, the issuers in consultation with the merchant bankers will decide the price. However, they are required to give full disclosures of the parameters which they had considered while deciding the issue price. In actual practice, there are two types of issue pricing namely:

(*i*) In the first type, the company and the lead manager fix the price which is called fixed price.

(*ii*) In the second type, the company and the lead manager stipulate a floor price or a price band and leave it to market forces to determine the final price which is called book building price.

## PRINCIPAL STEPS OF A PUBLIC ISSUE

Public issue, as already stated, refers to the issue of new shares to the public. The new shares/debentures may be offered either directly to the public through a prospectus (offer document) or indirectly through an offer for sale involving financial intermediaries or issuing houses.

The main steps involved in public issue are the following:

**(i) Draft prospectus**

A draft prospectus is prepared giving all details as mentioned earlier. Any company or a listed company making a public issue or a rights issue of value of more than ₹ 50 lakhs has to file a draft offer document with SEBI for its observation. The company can proceed further only after getting observations from the SEBI. The company has to open its issue within three months from the date of SEBI's observation letter.

**(ii) Fulfillment of Entry Norms (ENs)**

The SEBI has laid down certain parameters for accessing the primary market. If a company fulfils these parameters (entry norms), then only it can enter into the primary market. The entry norms are:

- The company should have net tangible assets of at least ₹ 3 crores for three full years.
- It should have distributable profits in at least three years.
- It should possess net worth of at least ₹ 1 crore in three years.

- If it has to change its name, at least 50 per cent revenue for the preceding one year should be from the new activity.
- The issue size should not exceed 5 times the pre-issue net worth.

To ensure that genuine companies do not suffer due to the rigidity of those parameters, The SEBI has laid down two more alternative routes for accessing the primary market.

### ❖ Entry Norm II (EN II)

The Entry Norm II is as follows:

- If the issue is through book-building route, at least 50 per cent of the issue should be allotted to Qualified Institutional Buyers (QIBs).
- The minimum post-issue face value capital shall be ₹ 10 crores or there shall be a compulsory market-making for at least two years.

### ❖ Entry Norm III (EN III)

If a company cannot satisfy the requirements laid down under Entry Norm II, it can enter into the primary market through EN III route:

The EN III requires the following:

1. The company should have at least 1,000 prospective allottees.
2. The project should be appraised and participated to the extent of 15 per cent by financial institutions and scheduled commercial banks of which at least 10 per cent comes from the appraisers.
3. The minimum post-issue face value capital shall be ₹ 10 crores or there shall be a compulsory market-making for at least 2 years.

The above entry norms are not applicable to private and public sector banks, listed companies' rights issue and an infrastructure company whose project has been appraised by a financial institution or a bank and not less than 5 per cent of the project cost is financed by these institutions.

**(iii) Appointment of underwriters**

Underwriters are appointed to shoulder the liability and subscribe to the shortfall in case the issue is undersubscribed. For this commitment, they are entitled to get a maximum commission of 2.5 per cent on the amount undertaken.

**(iv) Appointment of bankers**

Generally, the company nominates its own banker to act as collecting agent. The bankers along with their branch network act as collecting agencies and process the funds procured during the public issue.

**(v) Initiating allotment procedure**

The next step is that the registrars process the application forms, tabulate the amounts collected during the issue and initiate the allotment procedures. The allotment procedure can be initiated only when the issue is subscribed to the minimum level.

**(vi) Brokers to the issue**

Then, recognised members of the stock exchanges are appointed as brokers to the issue for marketing the issue. They are eligible for a maximum brokerage of 1.5 per cent.

**(vii) Filing of documents**

The draft prospectus, along with the copies of the agreements entered into with the lead manager, underwriters, bankers, registrars and brokers to the issue have to be filed with the Registrar of Companies of the State where the registered office of the company is located.

**(viii) Printing of prospectus and application forms**

After filing the above documents, the prospectus and application forms are printed and dispatched to all merchant bankers, underwriters and brokers to the issue.

**(ix) Listing the issue**

It is essential to send a letter to the stock exchange concerned where the issue is proposed to be listed giving all necessary details and stating the intention of getting the shares listed on the stock exchange. The initial listing application has to be sent with a fee of ₹ 7,500.

**(x) Publication in newspapers**

The next step is to publish an abridged version of the prospectus and the issues commencing and closing dates in major English dailies and vernacular newspapers.

**(xi) Allotment of shares**

After the close of the public issue all application forms are scrutinised, tabulated and then shares are allotted against those applications received.

**(xii) Underwriter's liability**

In case, the issue is not fully subscribed, then the liability for the subscription to the extent of undersubscription falls on the shoulders of underwriters who have to subscribe to the shortfall.

**(xiii) Optional listing**

The shares, after having been allotted, have to be listed compulsorily in the Regional Stock Exchange and optionally at other stock exchanges.

## ❖ Central Listing Authority (CLA)

A Central Listing Authority has been set up and its functions have been detailed under Regulation 8 of SEBI (Central Listing Authority) Regulations, 2003.

The main functions of CLA are:

- Processing applications for letter precedent to listing from applicants.
- Making recommendations to the SEBI on issues pertaining to the protection of the interest of investors in securities.
- Making suggestions for the development and regulation of the securities market including listing agreements, listing conditions and disclosures to be made in offer documents.
- Undertaking any other functions as may be delegated to it by the SEBI.

## ❖ Grading of IPO mandatory

SEBI has made grading of all IPOs mandatory for which draft documents are filed with it after April 2007. It shall be mandatory to obtain grading from at least one credit rating agency.

The issues shall be required to disclose all the grades obtained by it in the prospectus, abridged prospectus, issue advertisements and all other places where the issuer is advertising for the IPO.

## PRINCIPAL STEPS OF PRIVATE PLACEMENT

Private placement may be done in respect of equity shares, preference shares, bonds and debentures. Generally, the private placement of bonds and debentures is very popular. The private placement involves the following steps for a debt instrument.

**(i) Terms and conditions**

The terms and conditions of the issue like the value of the instrument, maturity period, yield rate, issue and redemption details, etc. should be clearly laid down and the instrument should be structured accordingly.

**(ii) Credit rating**

It is mandatory to obtain credit rating from a recognised credit rating agency who will evaluate the various aspects concerned with the instrument and give proper rating.

**(iii) Confidential Information Memorandum (CIM)**

Just like the offer document in the case of shares, this document contains all details about the company and the instrument. An investor can have a thorough knowledge about the issue by going through this document.

**(iv) Trustees to the issue**

The next step is to appoint trustees to the issue to protect the interest of investors. Generally, banks or other financial institutions may be appointed as trustees.

**(v) Pre-launching formality**

Just one or two days before the launching date, the CIM is sent to the prospective investors inviting them to subscribe to the issue.

**(vi) Pricing the issue**

Sometimes, pre-marketing campaign may be conducted by the Issue Houses to ascertain the investors towards private placement and the probable prices. Since book-building method is adopted by many companies, this campaign is not generally resorted to.

**(vii) Post-issue steps**

After the closing of the issue expires, a decision is taken on allotment and the certificates are issued. Oversubscriptions are refunded. The details of the issue are sent to the stock exchange concerned where it is likely to be listed.

The above steps are followed for shares also except the fact that the terms and conditions of issue, its modalities, etc. are decided by the shareholders at their meeting and there is no need to appoint trustees.

## PRINCIPAL STEPS INVOLVED IN THE CASE OF OFFER-FOR-SALE

In the case of offer-for-sale, generally merchant bankers play a dominant role by acting as a conduit through which a company routes its shares to the public. There may be promoters or sponsors also who may off-load the shares by offering them to the public at an appropriate time. The steps involved are:

(i) **Agreement:** The first step is to enter into an agreement with the merchant banker or sponsor group laying down the terms and conditions of the issue.

(ii) **Registration:** The agreement has to be registered with the stock exchange concerned.

(iii) **Default:** If any default is committed by the sponsor, it will be referred to an arbitration committee set up by the stock exchange.

(iv) **Off-loading:** The sponsor can off-load his position provided the promoter's post-issue holding will not be less than 20 per cent with a three-year lock-in period.

(v) **Market-maker:** The sponsor should agree to act as a market-maker for the companies' share for 18 months and should also identify another market-maker for such compulsory market-making. These two market-makers should hold up to 5 per cent of the equity offered to the public between themselves.

## SEBI's GUIDELINES FOR IPOs

The SEBI has been issuing guidelines from time-to-time with regard to IPOs so as to protect the interest of investors and also to promote a healthy capital market in the country. Some of the important guidelines pertaining to IPOs are:

1. All allotments have to be made within 30 days of the closure of the public issue and 42 days in the case of a rights issue.
2. The set offer to the general public has to be at least 25 per cent of the total issue size for listing on a stock exchange. For listing an IPO on the NSE:
   (*a*) The paid-up capital should be ₹ 20 crores.
   (*b*) The issuing company should have a track record of profitability.
   (*c*) The project should be appraised by a financial institution or a commercial bank or category I Merchant Banker.
3. In case an issue exceeds more than ₹ 100 crores, the issue is allowed to place the whole issue through book-building.
4. A minimum of 50 per cent of the net offer to the public has to be reserved for investors applying for less than 1,000 shares.
5. All listing formalities for a public issue have to be completed within 70 days from the date of closure of the subscription list.
6. There should be at least 5 investors for every ₹ 1 lakh of equity offered.
7. The PAN or GIR number should be compulsory quoted in the application where the monetary value of investment is ₹ 50,000 or above.

8. The subscription list for public issues shall be kept open for at least 3 working days and not more than 10 working days.
9. SEBI has launched Unified Payments Interface (UPI) as an alternative payment option for retail investors for buying shares in a public issue from January 1, 2019. It will reduce the listing time for an IPO to three days from the existing six at present due to the avoidance of any manual intervention.

### ❖ Other methods

Issue of bonus shares, offer to the employees, offer to the creditors and offer to the customers are other methods of issuing securities.

1. **Issue of bonus shares:** (Refer Chapter 5).
2. **Offer to the employees:** The issue of shares may be offered to employees. This helps to promote better industrial relations and higher productivity. Public sector organisations and joint sector organisations offer shares to their employees.
3. **Offer to the creditors:** At the time of reorganisation of capital, creditors may be asked to buy shares in full settlement of their loans or advances.
4. **Offer to the customers:** Public utility undertakings offer shares to their customers. Shareholding by customers give them a say in the affairs and functioning of the concern.

## INSTRUMENTS OF ISSUE

Traditionally, equity shares and preference shares are issued by companies as ownership capital and debentures and bonds as debt capital. Recently, new instruments to meet the varied needs of investors in terms of security, rate of return, marketability and appreciation in value are being issued by the companies.

The important new instruments and their characteristics are explained below.

### (i) Secured Premium Notes (SPN) with detachable warrants

Secured Premium Notes are issued along with a detachable warrant. The warrants attached to it ensure the holders right to apply and get equity shares after a notified period provided the SPN is fully paid-up.

The SPN is issued at a nominal value and does not carry any interest.

The SPN is redeemed by repayment in several instalments at a premium over the face value. The premium amount is distributed equally over the period of maturity of the instrument.

There is a lock-in period for SPN during which no interest will be paid for the invested amount.

The instrument is secured by a mortgage of all immovable properties of the company.

The investor can dispose of the SPN on allotment at a premium if the shares of the issuing company commands a high premium in the market.

The conversion of detachable warrant into equity shares will have to be done within the time limit given by the company.

**(ii) Equity shares with detachable warrants**

In this instrument, along with fully paid-up equity shares, detachable warrants are issued which entitle the warrant holder to apply for a specified number of shares at a determined price. Detachable warrants are registered separately with the stock exchange and traded separately.

**(iii) Preference shares with warrants**

This instrument shall carry a certain number of warrants entitling the holder to apply for equity shares 'at premium' at any time in one or more stages between the third and fifth year from the date of allotment. From the date of allotment, the preference shares with warrants should not be transferred or sold for a period of three years.

**(iv) Non-convertible debentures with detachable equity warrants**

The holder of the instrument is given an option to buy a specified number of shares from the company at a predetermined price with a definite time-frame. There is a specific lock-in period after which the holder can exercise his option to apply for equity shares.

**(v) Fully convertible cumulative preference shares**

This instrument has two parts — A and B. Part A is convertible into equity shares automatically on the date of allotment without application by the allottee. Part B will be redeemed at par/converted into equity after a lock-in period, at the option of the investors.

**(vi) Zero interest fully convertible debentures (FCDs)**

No interest will be paid to the holders of this instrument till the lock-in period. After a notified period, this debenture will be automatically and compulsorily converted into shares. Before the conversion of FCDs into equity, if the company issues rights, it would be available to the holders in the proportion decided by the company.

**(vii) Fully Convertible Debentures (FCDs) with interest**

This instrument carries no interest for a specified period. After this period, option is given to apply for equities at premium for which no additional amount is payable. However, interest on FCDs is payable at a determined rate from the date of first conversion to second/final conversion and equity will be issued in lieu of it interest amount.

**(viii) Zero interest partly Convertible Debentures (PCDs) with detachable and separately tradable warrants**

This partly convertible debenture has two parts — A and B. Part A is convertible into equity shares at a fixed amount on the date of allotment. Part B is non-convertible and redeemed at par at the end of a specific period. Part B will also carry a detachable and separately tradable warrant. It also gives an option to the holder to receive equity share for every warrant.

**(ix) Zero interest bonds**

Zero interest bonds are sold at a discount from their eventual maturity value and bear no interest. In India, zero interest convertible bonds are issued by companies. These bonds do not carry any interest till the date of conversion and are converted into equity shares at par or premium on the expiry of a fixed period.

**(x) Deep discount bonds**

These bonds are sold at a large discount to their nominal value. There is no interest payments on these bonds and the investors get return as accretion to the par value of the instrument over its life.

The Industrial Development Bank of India issued in February 1996 Deep Discount Bonds. Each bond having a face value of ₹ 2,00,000 was issued at a discounted price of ₹ 53,000 with a maturity period of 25 years. The Industrial Finance of India issued Deep Discount Bonds of ₹ 2,500 and promised ₹ 1,00,000 after 25 years. The Small Industrial Bank of India also issued similar type of bonds.

**(xi) Option bonds**

Option bonds may be cumulative or non-cumulative as per the option of the holder of the bonds. In case of cumulative bonds, interest is accumulated and is payable on maturity only. In case of non-cumulative bonds, the interest is paid periodically. The option is to be exercised by the investor at the time of investment. The Industrial Development Bank of India issued option bonds in January 1992.

**(xii) Bonds with warrants**

A warrant allows the holder to buy a number of equity shares at a pre-specified price in future. The warrants are usually attached to debentures or preference shares issued by companies as sweeteners to make issues more attractive. Essar Gujarat, Ranbaxy and Reliance have issued bonds with equity warrants.

**(xiii) Indian Depository Receipt (IDR)**

An IDR in nothing but a document representing underlying shares of a foreign company denominated in Indian currency. In other words, when a foreign company wants to raise capital from Indian investors, it issues IDRs. It is just the opposite of GDR (Global Depository Receipt). A GDR is used when an Indian company decides to raise money in the capital markets of a foreign country. For instance, the Tata Steel raised $ 500 million through GDR which was listed on the London stock exchange. Each GDR represented one share in Tata Steel. Each GDR was priced at $ 7.644 during the issue and now it is trading at $ 14.5.

An IDR will be listed on Indian stock exchanges — the BSE, NSE, etc.; and one can trade in IRDs just like regular shares. An IDR holder is one of the owners of a foreign company and he is entitled to dividends, rights issue, etc. that the company gives. The Standard Chartered Bank is the first company to make use of IDRs to raise capital in India.

## ❖ IDR vs. Share

An IDR is different from a share in the following ways:

(*i*) A share is a direct holding in a company whereas an IDR is a representation of share in an indirect way.

(*ii*) Multiple IDRs may be required to hold a single share.

(*iii*) Shareholders are automatically entitled to certain rights while such rights have to be specifically set out for IDR holders.

(*iv*) IDRs may be converted into shares subject to certain restrictions.

(*v*) Taxation rules are different for shares and IDRs. For instance, IDRs are not exempted from long-term capital gains like shares.

### ❖ Advantages

The following are the merits of investing in IDRs:

(*i*) One can invest in a foreign company without any background at the trading laws and practices of that country.

(*ii*) One is free to invest without any limits on individual overseas investments.

(*iii*) Since IDRs are denominated in rupees, they are free from risks on forex fluctuations.

(*iv*) IDR provides an opportunity to diversify one's investment portfolio by investing in foreign companies.

### ❖ Restrictions

(*i*) Generally, an IDR holder cannot redeem the IDR into a share for at least one year from the issue date.

(*ii*) After conversion, it has to be held for a maximum of 30 days, after which it can be liquidated.

**(xiv) Inflation-indexed Bonds (IIBs)**

Inflation-indexed Bonds are those bonds where the return increases along with inflation in the economy. It guarantees a real return to the investors. It has been designed primarily to hedge investors against inflation risk of an investment. If the principal amount alone is indexed to inflation and not the coupon, it is called capital indexed bonds.

### ❖ Features of IIBs in India

(*i*) Initially, its maturity period is 10 years.

(*ii*) Inflation protection is available for both bond and coupon.

(*iii*) The coupon rate will be fixed for entire duration of the bond.

(*iv*) Periodic coupon payments will be paid on adjusted principal on the basis of the inflation rate (India's WPI).

(*v*) Interest will be paid half-yearly.

(*vi*) The investment limit is from ₹ 10,000 to ₹ 2 crores.

(*vii*) The adjusted principal or the face value whichever is higher will be paid on maturity.

(*viii*) It will be available for trading in the secondary market also.

Besides the above, the Abid Hussain Committee has recommended the issue of the following instruments:

(*i*) Floating rate notes
(*ii*) Clip and strip bonds
(*iii*) Dual convertible bonds
(*iv*) Index rate notes
(*v*) Stepped coupon bonds
(*vi*) Dual option warrants
(*vii*) Extendable notes
(*viii*) Level pay floating rate notes
(*ix*) Commodity bonds
(*x*) Industrial revenue bonds.

The Pherwani Study Group has recommended the following new instruments:

1. Participating preference share
2. Participating debenture
3. Convertible debenture with options
4. Third party convertible debenture
5. Convertible debentures redeemable at premium
6. Debt for equity swap

**(xv) Blue Bonds**

Those securities which are issued for various blue economy related activities including oceanic resource mining and sustainable fishing are called Blue Bonds.

## PLAYERS IN THE NEW ISSUE MARKET

There are many players in the new issue market. The important of them are the following:

1. Merchant bankers.
2. Registrars.
3. Collecting and coordinating bankers.
4. Underwriters and brokers.
5. Printers, advertising agencies and mailing agencies.

### 1. Merchant bankers

They are the issue managers, lead managers, co-managers and are responsible to the company and SEBI. Their functions and working are described in a separate chapter.

### 2. Registrars to the issue

Registrars are an important category of intermediaries who undertake all activities connected with new issue management. They are appointed by the company in consultation with the merchant bankers to the issue. Registrars have a major role, next to merchant bankers, in respect of servicing of investors.

The role of registrar in the pre-issue, during the currency of issue, pre-allotment, allotment and post-allotment are described below:

### ❖ Role of registrar in pre-issue

1. Suggest draft application form to the merchant bankers.
2. Help in identifying the collection centres. The choice of collection centre and of collecting banker is critical to the success of the issue.
3. Assist in opening collection accounts with banks and lay down procedure for operation of these accounts.
4. Send instructions to collecting branches, for collection of application along with cheques, drafts, stock invest separately and remittance of funds.

5. Workout modalities to receive the collection figures on a regular basis until the subscription list is closed.

### ❖ During the currency of issue

1. Receive the collection figures everyday.
2. Tabulate and classify the collection data on the basis of the standard proforma of slabs of shares applied for.
3. Keep the merchant bankers and the company informed of the progress of total subscriptions.
4. Inform the stock exchange about the closure of issue.

### ❖ Pre-allotment work

1. Get all application forms from the collecting bankers and sort out valid and invalid application forms.
2. The valid applications are to be categorised and grouped as cash, draft and stock invest applications.
3. Reclassify the valid applications eligible for allotment.
4. Prepare the list with inverted numbers and then approach the regional stock exchange for finalising the basis of allotment, in the event of oversubscription.
5. Finalise the allotment as per the basis approved by the stock exchange.
6. Tally the final list approved for allotment and rejections with the in-house control numbers and correct mistakes, if any.

### ❖ Allotment work

The most important work of a registrar is allotment of shares. The system of proportional allotment was adopted for new issues in 1993. A new quota system was approved by SEBI in April 1995. According to the new system 50 per cent of quota is for small investors and another, 50 per cent for other categories. The small investors include all applicants up to 1,000 shares. It has also been revised recently.

### ❖ Post-allotment work

1. Get the letters of allotment and refund orders printed ready for despatch. They have to be mailed on or before 70 days from the closing date of subscription. For any delay, get the permission of the Registrar of Companies and the relevant regional stock exchange.
2. Submit all statements to the company for their final approval.
3. Arrange to pay the brokerage and underwriting commission and submit their relevant statements.
4. Assist the company in getting the allotted shares listed on the stock exchange.

### ❖ Qualifications for registrars to the issue

To be appointed as Registrar to the Issue, registration with SEBI is essential. The criteria adopted by SEBI for registration are the competency and expertise, quality of manpower, their track record, adequacy of infrastructure such as computers, storage space, etc. and capital adequacy. A net worth of ₹ 6 lakhs is essential for Registrars. SEBI has laid down a code of conduct for their observance. They have to maintain proper books of accounts and registers for a period of three years.

### 3. Collecting and coordinating bankers

Collecting bankers collect the subscriptions in cash, cheques, stock invest, etc.

Coordinating bankers collect information on subscriptions and co-ordinate the collection work. They monitor the work and inform it to the registrars and merchant bankers.

Collecting banker and coordinating banker may be the same bank or different banks.

### 4. Underwriters and brokers

The functions and role of underwriters are explained separately.

Brokers along with the network of sub-brokers market the new issues. They send their own circulars and applications to the clients and do follow-up work to market the securities.

**5. Printers, advertising agencies and mailing agencies** are other organisations involved in the new issue market operations.

## RECENT TRENDS IN NEW ISSUE MARKET

Economic liberalisation, privatisation, foreign private participation, disinvestment in public sector and regulatory changes have provided a new impetus to the capital market.

Table 3.1 shows the resources mobilised from the primary market during 2020-21 and 2021-22.

**TABLE 3.1: MOBILISATION OF RESOURCES FROM THE PRIMARY MARKET**

*(Amount in ₹ Crore)*

| *Item* | *2020-21* | | *2021-22 (P)* | |
|---|---|---|---|---|
| | *Number* | *Amount* | *Number* | *Amount* |
| 1 | 2 | 3 | 4 | 5 |
| **I. Primary Market** | | | | |
| **A. Public and Rights Issues** | | | | |
| **1. Private Sector [(a) + (b)]** | **90** | **1,07,867.9** | **192** | **1,50,483.6** |
| (*a*) Financial | 26 | 31,395.9 | 36 | 24,477.4 |
| (*b*) Non-financial | 64 | 76,472.0 | 156 | 1,26,006.3 |
| **2. Public Sector [(a) + (b) + (c)]** | **5** | **12,485.2** | .... | .... |
| (*a*) Public Sector Undertakings | 2 | 1,262.9 | .... | .... |
| (*b*) Government Companies | ... | .... | ... | ... |
| (*c*) Banks/Financial Institutions | 3 | 11,222.3 | .... | .... |
| **3. Total [(1 + 2, (i) + (ii), (a) + (b)]** | **95** | **1,20,353.1** | **192** | **1,50,483.6** |
| *Instrument Type* | | | | |
| (*i*) Equity | 78 | 1,10,118.3 | 164 | 1,38,894.2 |
| (*ii*) Debt | 17 | 10,234.8 | 28 | 11,589.4 |
| *Issuer Type* | | | | |
| (*a*) IPOs | 55 | 31,029.7 | 120 | 1,12,552.5 |
| (*b*) Listed | 40 | 89,323.4 | 72 | 37,931.2 |
| **B. Euro Issues (ADRs and GDRs)** | ... | ... | .... | .... |
| **C. Private Placement** | | | | |
| **1. Private Sector [(a) + (b)]** | **1,778** | **4,39,420.8** | **1,323** | **4,09,475.1** |
| (*a*) Financial | 1,481 | 2,82,705.3 | 1,055 | 3,01,948.8 |
| (*b*) Non-financial | 297 | 1,56,715.5 | 268 | 1,07,526.3 |
| **2. Public Sector [(a) + (b)]** | **264** | **3,91,768.9** | **158** | **2,17,723.1** |
| (*a*) Financial | 174 | 2,61,055.9 | 110 | 1,63,336.2 |
| (*b*) Non-financial | 90 | 1,30,713.0 | 48 | 54,386.9 |
| **3. Total [(1 + 2, (i) + (ii)]** | **2,042** | **8,31,189.7** | **1,481** | **6,27,198.2** |
| (*i*) Equity | 30 | 74,738.4 | 29 | 31,438.5 |
| (*ii*) Debt | 2,012 | 7,56,451.2 | 1,452 | 5,95,759.8 |
| **D. Qualified Institutional Placement** | **31** | **82,423.6** | **29** | **31,438.5** |
| **E. Mutual Funds Mobilisation (Net)#** | .... | **2,14,743.0** | .... | **2,46,729.6** |
| 1. Private Sector | .... | 1,42,377.9 | .... | 1,48,286.9 |
| 2. Public Sector | .... | 72,365.1 | .... | 98,442.7 |

.... Nil

# Net of redemptions

***Source:*** RBI Annual Report, 2022.

## PERFORMANCE OF THE PRIMARY MARKET DURING 2019-20 AND 2020-21

### ❖ Performance during 2019-20

The primary segment of the equity market witnessed significant activity during 2019-20. Resource mobilisation through initial public offers (IPOs), follow-on public offers (FPOs) and rights issues has increased more than four-fold to ₹ 76,382 crores during 2019-20. Of these, ₹ 21,323 core were mobilised through 60 IPO/FPO issues, out of which 46 issues amounting to ₹ 495 crores were listed on the Small and Medium Enterprises (SME) platform of the BSE and the NSE. Resource mobilisation through rights issues amounted to ₹ 55,059 crores mostly by telecom companies. Resource mobilisation through qualified institutional placement (QIP) also increased sharply to ₹ 51,216 crores in 2019-20 from ₹10,289 crores in 2018-19.

### ❖ Performance during 2020-21

The primary segment of the equity market witnessed increased activity during 2020-21. Resource mobilisation through initial public offers (IPOs), follow-on public offers (FPOs) and right issues has increased by 43.1 per cent to ₹ 1.1 lakh crores during 2020-21 from ₹ 76,965 crores in the previous year. Of these, ₹ 46,060 crores were mobilised through 57 IPO/FPO issues, out of which 27 issues amounting to ₹ 246 crores were listed on the small and medium enterprises (SME) platform of the BSE and the NSE. Resource mobilisation through right issues increased to ₹ 64,059 crores during 2020-21 from ₹ 55,642 crores in the previous year. However, resource mobilisation through preferential allotment and qualified institutional placement (QIP) has decreased to ₹ 1.2 lakh crores during 2020-21, as against ₹ 2.3 lakh crores during the previous year.

### ❖ 100 Per cent application money for QIBs

The SEBI has made it mandatory for all Qualified Institutional Buyers (QIBs) to pay 100 per cent of the application money while bidding for public issues. So far, they have to pay only 10 per cent of the application amount as margin, whereas High Net worth Individuals (HNIs) and retail inventors have to pay 100 per cent of application money in all primary market issuances. This new norm will come into force from 1st May, 2010 onwards this is a welcoming move since it would avoid inflated demand in public issues by QIBs and provide a common level playing field to all investors. This step would also help reduce the time gap between the dates of issues closure and listing of issues. In fact, SEBI is aiming to have a period of one week (T+8) by the end of this year. However, SEBI has reduced the listing time from the present 22 days to 12 days after IPO and this has come into effect from May 1st, 2010 onwards.

### ❖ ASBA route to apply for IPOs

The SEBI has introduced a new facility, *viz.*, Application Supported by Block Amount (ASBA) route to apply for IPOs from Sept. 2008 onwards. The ASBA allows subscribers to public issues to have their application money blocked in a special account in a bank so that they have to pay only upon allotment of shares. The banks offering ASBA are called Self-Certified Syndicate Banks (SCSBs). It is a good way for banks to mobilise deposits and at the same time it is a simple, smart and safe way of making an application. But the response to this new route from the retail investors seems to be poor. According to Prime Database, on an average the 18 IPOs of 2009 could get only 13.35 per cent of applications of retail investors through the ASBA route. This facility is available to Qualified Institutional Buyers and also to High Net Worth Individuals. It is extended to Rights Issue also.

The SEBI has made ASBA facility mandatory for all non-retail investors like High Net Worth Individuals (HNIs) and institutional investors investing in public and rights issues. This has come into effect from May 2, 2011 onwards.

### ❖ French auction method

The Government has decided to adopt French Auction method for public offers of public sector undertakings. The proposed French Auction method differs from the existing Dutch Auction method in many ways. Under the Dutch Auction method, investors have to bid within the price band fixed by the issuing company. Finally, shares would be allotted proportionately at a uniform price to the allottees. But, under French Auction route, there will be no upper limit to bid price and the highest bidder will secure the largest share of allotments. In other words, the highest bidders, in the descending order, will get preference in allotment based on the price bids they have placed for the shares. This is an alternative book-building model. A complete freedom is given to lid above a certain floor price and allotment takes place on price-priority basis and that too at differential prices. The basic principle involved is higher the bid, higher the allocation. This method has a distinct advantage of better price discovery through keen competition among investors. It is being tried for the institutional portion of the issue.

### ❖ Mandatory listing and grading of IPO

Listing has been made mandatory for all IPOs so that only genuine companies can tap the capital market. The unlisted companies must get listed in at least one stock exchange having nationwide terminals. Similarly, grading of IPO has been made mandatory after April 2007. The IPO should be graded at least by one credit rating agency so that the proposed investors could easily be aware of the investment opportunities in the company.

### ❖ Income tax permanent account number

With effect from July 2, 2007, the Income Tax Permanent Number (PAN) has been made the sole identification number for all participants transacting in the securities market, irrespective of the amount of transaction.

## ANCHOR INVESTORS

The anchor investors are nothing but the main investors to an issue. According to the SEBI's recent recommendations, only banks and public financial institutions could be anchor investors in bourses. The Bimal Jalan Committee has recommended a minimum ₹ 1,000 crores net worth for these anchor investors. Moreover, they should be identified in the application itself while seeking permission by any entity. The maximum number of anchor investors in a public issue has been fixed at ₹ 25 up to ₹ 250 crores. Now, there can be ten additional investors for every additional allocation of ₹ 250 crores subject to a minimum allotment of ₹ 5 crores per anchor investor.

## CROWD FUNDING

When a project is entirely financed by a group of individuals instead of by professional bodies like banks, venture capitalists and Angel investors, it is referred to as Crowed Funding. It is an appealing choice of funding for start-ups.

## MAJOR REFORMS IN THE PRIMARY MARKET (2012-13)

(*i*) The eligibility conditions for initial IPOs have been revised as stated below:

(*a*) The issuers company should be profitable for at least three out of the preceding five years with a minimum average pre-tax operating profit of ₹ 15 crores.

(or)

(*b*) The issuer shall undertake to allot at least 75 per cent of the net offer to the Qualified Institutional Buyers.

(*ii*) For further public offers and rights issues through fast track route by well established companies, the minimum level of average market capitalisation is ₹ 3,000 crores instead of ₹ 5,000 crores insisted earlier.

(*iii*) The minimum promoters' contribution in IPOs shall be at least 20 per cent of the post-issue capital. In case, it is less than the stipulated amount, the Alternative Investment Funds (AIFs) may be utilised subject to a maximum of 10 per cent of the post-issue capital.

(*iv*) Any changes up to 20 per cent in the amount proposed to be raised can be done without the necessity of filing any document with the SEBI.

(*v*) The SEBI's framework for rejection of Draft offer documents has been prepared and clearly displayed for the benefit of issuers.

(*vi*) For pricing the Qualified Institutions Placements (QIPs), a maximum discount of 5 per cent has been permitted to the price calculated as per SEBI regulations and subject to approval by shareholders. Moreover, they are permitted to invest in the primary as well as secondary market.

(*vii*) The minimum allotment to Retail individual investors shall be at least the minimum application size which has been raised to ₹ 10,000 – ₹ 15,000 as against ₹ 5,000 – ₹ 7,000 prescribed earlier. This is to encourage wider retail participation.

(*viii*) No withdrawal or lowering the size of bids shall be permitted for non-retail investors at any stage.

(*ix*) The disclosure of financial information should be at least 5 days prior to issue opening instead of 2 days stipulated earlier.

(*x*) It is mandatory to include Business Responsibility Report as a part of Annual Report with a focus on the environmental, social and governance issues.

(*xi*) It is mandatory to obtain authentication on SCORES (SEBI's Online Complaints Redressal System) for getting the equity shares listed on stock exchanges.

(*xii*) e-IPOs, *i.e.*, electronic initial public offers have been introduced.

## MAJOR REFORMS DURING 2014-15

(*i*) New dilution norms have been laid down by SEBI to encourage many companies including first-generation and new-age companies to go for listing and thereby to revitalise the primary market. The new requirement is that the minimum dilution to the public in an IPO shall be 25 per cent or ₹ 400 crores whichever is lower, with a need to get to 25 per cent dilution in three years.

(*ii*) The minimum public shareholding in PSUs has been fixed at par with private sector companies. It requires all listed PSUs to maintain a 25 per cent minimum public shareholding as against 10 per cent previously. This stipulation has to be achieved within a period of three years. This move will further deepen liquidity in the market.

(*iii*) SEBI has further expanded the Offer For Sale (OFS) mechanism to the top 200 companies as against the present level of 100 companies. It has also reserved a minimum 10 per cent of the issue size to the retail investors who bid for amounts less than ₹ 2 lakhs. This will encourage more retail participation in OFS.

(*iv*) SEBI has decided to increase the anchor investor's bucket to 60 per cent from the current requirement of 30 per cent.

(*v*) SEBI has further permitted bonus shares held for more than a year to be offered for sale in an IPO provided such bonus shares were issued out of free reserves or share premium.

(*vi*) Recently, SEBI has authorised municipal authorities to issue debt securities under SEBI (Issue and Listing of Debt Securities by Municipality) Regulations, 2015. This move will widen the debt market.

Thus, SEBI has unveiled a number of measures to revitalise and boost the primary market.

## MAJOR REFORMS DURING 2015-16

(i) To facilitate more issuers to raise capital through the 'Fast Track' route, the market capitalisation requirements of the public shareholding of the issuer has been reduced from ₹ 3,000 crores to ₹ 1,000 crores in the case of further public offers and ₹ 250 crores in the case of rights issue.

(ii) Public issue of equity shares to any company, or its promoter or its directors who are in the list of defaulters has been completely prohibited.

(iii) The time period for listing of securities has been reduced from $T_{12}$ to $T_6$.

(iv) The SEBI has introduced an elaborate framework for giving an exit opportunity to shareholders in the case of any change in objects by issuers in accordance with the Companies Act, 2013.

## MAJOR REFORMS DURING 2019-20

### ❖ IPO share allotments

Investors are classified into different categories. Each category has to follow its own set of rules while investing in Initial Public Offerings (IPOs). Non-banking financial institutions (NBFCs) now come under 'Qualified Institutional Buyers' (QIBs). Until now, banks and insurance companies alone were classified as QIBs. Only those registered NBFCs with the RBI and with a net worth of over ₹ 500 crores can be classified as QIBs.

### ❖ Usage of IPO proceeds

Now, SEBI has the power to regulate how companies make use of the money they raise through IPO over ₹ 100 crores instead of ₹ 500 crores earlier.

### ❖ Instant redemption

The shareholder can now buy and sell liquid funds instantly. However, this is only for amounts up to ₹ 50,000 on a per-day basis. The shareholder can use his e-wallets to buy liquid funds up to ₹ 50,000 per year.

## ADVANTAGES OF PRIMARY MARKET

Absence of primary market acts as a deterrent factor to capital formation and economic growth. The importance of primary market can be studied under the following headings:

(i) **Avenue for investment:** A primary market provides good avenues for investments in financial assets which are more productive than physical assets. Most of the investors, particularly the household sector prefers this avenue since it is convenient and more profitable.

(ii) **Mobilisation of savings:** A well developed primary market offers adequate incentives in the form of interest or dividend that may allure investors from all walks of the society to invest savings in the primary market.

(iii) **Channelising savings for productive use:** The primary market helps to mobilise the small and scattered savings and augment the availability of investible funds. These funds are utilised for productive purposes and thus, the wastage in unproductive uses is avoided.

(iv) **Source of large supply of funds:** The rapid development of any country requires the growth of large-scale industries which need huge capital. The huge amount of funds required for these industries cannot be provided by few persons. But huge money can be raised in a primary market by floating new shares in the market.

(v) **Rapid industrial growth:** The primary market facilitates increase in production and productivity in the economy by means of establishing many new companies and thereby promoting rapid industrial growth in a country.

(vi) **Source for expansions and technological upgradation:** The primary market also serves as an important source for raising money for expansion of industries as well as for their technological upgradation.

## ❖ Disadvantages

The following are the reasons for the poor performance of the primary market.

(i) **Possibility for deceiving investors:** There is ample scope for attracting investors by giving misleading informations. The issuing companies are often tempted to present a rosy picture about the prospective projects. They make exaggerated claims about their prospects as well as oversubscription. As a result, innocent investors are affected.

(ii) **No fixed norms for project appraisal:** There is no adequate institutional arrangement for the appraisal of the projects to be undertaken by the new companies. Again, there are no fixed norms for getting the appraisals approved by designated institutions. Hence, poor investors have no scope to ascertain the actual profitability of a project.

(iii) **Lack of post-issue seriousness:** Moreover, there is no seriousness among most of the investors to check the performance of the company after the issue. Once the issue is subscribed, their duty is over.

(iv) **Ineffective role of merchant bankers:** The merchant bankers do not pay adequate attention to the technical, managerial and feasibility aspects while appraising the project proposals. In fact, they do not seem to play a development role as a result of which the small investors are duped by the companies.

(v) **Delay in the allotment process:** There is inordinate delay in receiving allotment letters, share certificates, refund orders, etc. If shares are not allotted, the investor suffers loss of interest. There is delay in effecting transfer of shares. All these factors tend to affect the small investors who hesitate to approach a primary market for investing their funds.

(vi) **Poor mobilisation of savings:** The new issue market is not able to mobilise adequate savings from the public. It is estimated that only 5 per cent to 10 per cent of financial savings of the household sector go to the primary market.

(vii) **Hesitancy to invest in shares:** Generally, there is a tendency on the part of the investors to prefer fixed income bearing securities like preference shares and debentures. They hesitate to invest in equity shares since they do not fetch any fixed income. This risk aversion factor stands in the way of development of a healthy primary market.

Over the years, SEBI and government have come up with a series of regulatory measures to give a boost to new issue market. A recent inspection of 24 merchant bankers exposed blatant falsehood in the issue of prospectus regarding status of project and financials. The SEBI has debarred 64 merchant bankers from undertaking any fresh activity. In September 1997, SEBI brought about some changes in SEBI (Merchant Bankers) Rules and Regulations, 1992. Accordingly, only corporate bodies will be allowed to function as merchant bankers. Multiple categories of merchant bankers shall be abolished and there will be just one entity, *viz.*, Merchant Banker. The merchant bankers will be prohibited from carrying out fund-based activity other than those related exclusively to the capital market.

## SUGGESTIONS

An expert panel of SEBI has favoured mandatory one-year market making for all new issues.

Besides the above regulatory measures, the following suggestions are made for a better performance of the New Issue Market.

(*i*) The merchant bankers or the lead managers should own full responsibility for disclosures and projections about the company. The certificate from them should not be taken at the last word at any stage.

(*ii*) Setting up of merchant bankers developed on the pattern of issue houses in UK would be advisable. Their main advantage would be skill and expertise which would have a statutory effect on the quality of new issues as well as standard and efficiency of the market itself.

## QUESTIONS

### I. Objective type questions:

### A. Fill in the blanks:

1. New Issue Market deals with __________ securities.
2. Public issue involves no __________.
3. Rights shares are offered to __________ shareholders.
4. To be appointed as Registrar, registration with __________ is essential.
5. __________ is the suitable method where small companies issue shares.

[**Key:** 1. New, 2. Intermediaries, 3. Existing, 4. SEBI, 5. Placement.]

### B. State whether the following are TRUE or FALSE:

1. New Issue Market encompasses all institutions dealing in fresh issue.
2. Offer of sale is a common method in India.
3. Zero interest bonds are sold at discount.
4. Underwriting is a guarantee for marketability of shares.
5. Offer for sale and follow on offer are one and the same.

[**Key:** 1. True, 2. False, 3. True, 4. True, 5. False.]

### II. Short answer type questions:

1. Distinguish between new issue market and stock exchange.
2. What are the advantages of underwriting?
3. What do you mean by public issues?
4. Write a note on Secured Premium Note.
5. What is origination?
6. Distinguish between Auction-based offer for sale and Follow on offer.

7. Describe the different methods of floating new issues.
8. Analyse the principal steps involved in the public issue of shares.
9. Who are the players in the new issue market? Discuss their functions.
10. What is Inflation Indexed Bond? State its main features.
11. Distinguish between Inflation Indexed Bond and Capital Indexed Bond.
12. What is instant redemption?
13. What do you mean by Crowd Funding?
14. What is the advantage of Unified Payments Interface?

## III. Essay type questions:

1. Write an essay on the functions of New Issue Market.
2. Examine the recent trends in the primary market in India.
3. Explain the term 'New Issue Market'. How does it differ from the secondary market? Are they connected to each other?
4. Explain the various new instruments introduced in the new issue market.
5. Discuss the role of different players in the new issue market.

# 4 SECONDARY MARKET

## INTRODUCTION

The market where existing securities are traded is referred to as the secondary market or stock market. In a stock market, purchases and sales of securities whether of Government or Semi-Government bodies or other public bodies and also shares and debentures issued by joint-stock companies are effected. The securities of Government are traded in the stock market as a separate component, called gilt-edged market. Government securities are traded outside the trading wing in the form of over-the-counter sales or purchases. Another component of the stock market deals with trading in shares and debentures of limited companies.

Stock exchanges are the important ingredient of the capital market. They are the citadel of capital and fortress of finance. They are the theatres of trading in securities and as such they assist and control the buying and selling of securities. Thus, according to Husband and Dockeray, *'Securities or stock exchanges are privately organised markets which are used to facilitate trading in securities'*. However, at present, stock exchanges need not necessarily be privately organised ones.

As per the Securities Contracts Regulation Act, 1956, a stock exchange has been defined as follows: *'It is an association, organisation or body of individuals whether incorporated or not, established for the purpose of assisting, regulating and controlling business in buying, selling and dealing in securities'*. In brief, stock exchanges constitute a market where securities issued by the Central and State Governments, public bodies and joint-stock companies are traded.

## FUNCTIONS/SERVICES OF STOCK EXCHANGES

The stock market occupies a pivotal position in the financial system. It performs several economic functions and renders invaluable services to the investors, companies, and to the economy as a whole. They may be summarised as follows:

(i) **Liquidity and marketability of securities:** Stock exchanges provide liquidity to securities since securities can be converted into cash at any time according to the discretion of the investor by selling them at the listed prices. They facilitate buying and selling of securities at listed prices by providing continuous marketability to the investors in respect of securities they hold or intend to hold. Thus, they create a ready outlet for dealing in securities.

(ii) **Safety of funds:** Stock exchanges ensure safety of funds invested because they have to function under strict rules and regulations and the bye-laws are meant to ensure safety of investible funds. Overtrading, illegitimate speculation, etc. are prevented through carefully designed set of rules. This would strengthen the investor's confidence and promote larger investment.

(iii) **Supply of long-term funds:** The securities traded in the stock market are negotiable and transferable in character and as such they can be transferred with minimum of formalities from one hand to another. So, when a security is transacted, one investor is substituted by another, but the company is assured of long-term availability of funds.

(iv) **Flow of capital to profitable ventures:** The profitability and popularity of companies are reflected in stock prices. The prices quoted indicate the relative profitability and performance of companies. Funds tend to be attracted towards securities of profitable companies and this facilitates the flow of capital into profitable channels. In the words of Husband and Dockeray, 'Stock exchanges function like a traffic signal, indicating a green light when certain fields offer the necessary inducement to attract capital and blazing a red light when the outlook for new investment is not attractive'.

(v) **Motivation for improved performance:** The performance of a company is reflected on the prices quoted in the stock market. These prices are more visible in the eyes of the public. Stock market provides room for this price quotation for those securities listed by it. This public exposure makes a company conscious of its status in the market and it acts as a motivation to improve its performance further.

(vi) **Promotion of investment:** Stock exchanges mobilise the savings of the public and promote investment through capital formation. But for these stock exchanges, surplus funds available with individuals and institutions would not have gone for productive and remunerative ventures.

(vii) **Reflection of business cycle:** The changing business conditions in the economy are immediately reflected on the stock exchanges. Booms and depressions can be identified through the dealings on the stock exchanges and suitable monetary and fiscal policies can be taken by the government. Thus, a stock market portrays the prevailing economic situation instantly to all concerned so that suitable actions can be taken.

(viii) **Marketing of new issues:** If the new issues are listed, they are readily acceptable to the public, since listing presupposes their evaluation by concerned stock exchange authorities. Public response to such new issues would be relatively high. Thus, a stock market helps in the marketing of new issues also.

**(ix) Miscellaneous services:** Stock exchange supplies securities of different kinds with different maturities and yields. It enables the investors to diversify their risks by a wider portfolio of investment. It also inculcates saving habits among the community and paves the way for capital formation. It guides the investors in choosing securities by supplying the daily quotation of listed securities and by disclosing the trends of dealings on the stock exchange. It enables companies and the Government to raise resources by providing a ready market for their securities.

## RECOGNITION OF STOCK EXCHANGES — PROCEDURE

The stock exchanges in India have to be recognised by the Central Government under SCRA and SEBI and they have to comply with the provisions of the SCRA and SEBI and also the bye-laws and regulations duly approved by the Government.

Any stock exchange which needs recognition under SEBI Act has to submit an application in the prescribed manner to the Central Government. This application must be accompanied by the following documents:

(*i*) A copy of the bye-laws of the stock exchange for its operation.

(*ii*) A copy of the rules relating to its constitution, governing body, powers and duties of the office-bearers, the admission procedure, etc.

### ❖ Grant of recognition

Recognition will be granted by the Central Government provided the following conditions are fulfilled:

(*i*) The rules and bye-laws of the stock exchange applying for registration must ensure fair dealing and protect the interest of investors.

(*ii*) The stock exchange concerned must be willing to comply with any other conditions that may be imposed by the Government from time-to-time.

(*iii*) The grant of recognition must be in the interest of trade as well as in the public interest.

While granting recognition, the Central Government may prescribe conditions regarding the qualifications for membership, the method of entering into contracts, the representation of the Central Government on the stock exchange and the maintenance of accounts and their audit.

### ❖ Renewal of recognition

If any stock exchange intends to renew its recognition, it must once again make an application to the Central Government in the aforesaid manner three months before the expiry of the period of recognition.

### ❖ Withdrawal of recognition

The Central Government may withdraw the recognition granted to any stock exchange at any time if it opines that the recognition granted is against the interest of trade or public interest. While doing so, it must give sufficient opportunity to the governing body of the stock exchange to explain its position. However, such a withdrawal will have no effect on the contracts entered into before the date of withdrawal.

## ORGANISATION OF STOCK EXCHANGES IN INDIA

The first organised stock exchange in India was started in Bombay in 1875 with the formation of the 'Native Share and Stock Broker's Association'. Thus, the Bombay Stock Exchange is the oldest one in the country. With the growth of joint-stock companies, the stock exchanges also made a steady growth.

However, many of the old stock exchanges established on a regional basis have decided to exit. As per SEBI's order passed in 2012, every stock exchange must have a minimum net worth of ₹ 100 crores and an annual trading volume of ₹ 1,000 crores. Many of them found it is difficult to achieve this target within the stipulated period of two years and hence they have preferred the 'exit' route. As on March 31, 2016, 17 regional stock exchanges have been granted exit by SEBI. Now, we have the following stock exchanges functioning in India as on March 31, 2016:

- Ahmedabad Stock Exchange Ltd. — Permanent
- Bombay Stock Exchange Ltd. — Permanent
- Calcutta Stock Exchange Ltd. — Permanent
- Metropolitan Stock Exchange of India Ltd. (Renewal of recognition granted) — Permanent
- National Stock Exchange of India Ltd. — Permanent

### ❖ Demutualisation of stock exchanges

The transition process of an exchange from a 'mutually-owned' association to a company 'owned by shareholders' is called demutualisation.

In other words, transforming the legal structure, of an exchange from a mutual form to a business corporation form is referred to as demutualisation.

In a mutual exchange, the three functions of ownership, management and trading are interlinked into a single group. It means that the broker members of the exchange are the owners as well as traders on the exchange and further they themselves manage the exchange. These three functions are segregated from one another after demutualisation. The demutualised stock exchanges in India are:

(*i*) The National Stock Exchange (NSE).

(*ii*) Over The Counter Exchange of India (OTCEI).

### ❖ Corporatisation of stock exchanges

The process of converting the organisational structure of the stock exchange from a non-corporate structure to a corporate structure is called Corporatisation of stock exchanges. As stated earlier, some of the stock exchanges were established as 'Association of persons' in India like BSE, ASE and MPSE. Corporatisation of these exchanges is the process of converting them into incorporated companies.

## ❖ Listing of stock exchanges

Recently, the SEBI has permitted stock exchanges and depositories to list in order to ensure greater transparency and accountability. However, stock exchanges are not permitted to list on themselves. They have to be operational for at least three years to list. The other conditions to be fulfilled for listing are:

- The minimum net worth for exchanges and depositories should be ₹ 100 crores.
- The clearing corporations should have a minimum net worth of ₹ 300 crores.
- Clearing houses are not eligible for listing.
- No single investor can hold more than five per cent in exchanges.
- However, institutional investors are allowed to hold up to 15 per cent stake.
- The public shall hold 51 per cent in exchanges.
- Exchanges and depositories may list if they address conflict of interest between business and regulatory functions.
- Exchanges should similarly transfer one-fifth of their profits to their investor protection fund.
- Non-operational stock exchanges may voluntarily exit.

## ❖ Management

The recognised stock exchanges are managed by 'Governing Boards'. The governing boards consists of elected member directors from stock broker members, public representatives and government nominees nominated by the SEBI. The Government has also powers to nominate Presidents and Vice-presidents of stock exchanges and to approve the appointment of the Chief Executive and public representatives. The major stock exchanges are managed by the Chief Executive Director and the smaller stock exchanges are under the control of a Secretary.

The governing Boards have wide powers such as:

(*i*) Selection of office bearers and setting up of committees like Listing Committee, Arbitration Committee, Defaulter's Committee, etc.,

(*ii*) Admission and expulsion of members,

(*iii*) Management of the properties and finances of the exchange,

(*iv*) Framing and interpretation of rules, bye-laws, etc. for the regulation of stock exchange,

(*v*) Adjudication of disputes among members or outsiders,

(*vi*) Management of the affairs of the exchange in the best interest of the investors and public interest.

## ❖ Membership

To become a member of a recognised stock exchange, a person must possess the following qualifications:

(*i*) He should be a citizen of India.

(*ii*) He should not be less than 21 years of age.

(*iii*) He should not have been adjudged bankrupt or insolvent.

(*iv*) He should not have been convicted for an offence involving fraud or dishonesty.

(*v*) He should not be engaged in any other business except dealing in securities.

(*vi*) He should not have been expelled by any other stock exchange or declared a defaulter by any other stock exchange.

Apart from individuals, a company is also eligible to become a member provided it satisfies the conditions imposed by the stock exchange concerned.

## LISTING OF SECURITIES

Listing of securities means that the securities are admitted for trading on a recognised stock exchange. Transactions in the securities of any company cannot be conducted on stock exchanges unless they are listed by them. Hence, listing is the basis of stock exchange operations. It is the green signal given to selected securities to get the trading privileges of the stock exchange concerned. Securities become eligible for trading only through listing.

Listing is compulsory for those companies which intend to offer shares/debentures to the public for subscription by means of issuing a prospectus. Moreover, the SEBI insists on listing for granting permission to a new issue by a public limited company. Again, financial institutions do insist on listing for underwriting new issues. Thus, listing becomes an unavoidable one today.

The companies which have got their shares/debentures listed in one or more recognised stock exchanges must submit themselves to the various regulatory measures of the stock exchange concerned as well as the SEBI. They must maintain necessary books, documents, etc., and disclose any information which the stock exchange may call for.

### ❖ Group A, group B and group C shares (BSE)

The listed shares are generally divided into two categories namely:

(*i*) Group A shares (Specified shares or cleared securities).

(*ii*) Group B shares (Non-specified shares or non-cleared securities).

Group A shares represent large and well established companies having a broad investor base. These shares are actively traded. Naturally, these shares attract a lot of speculative multiples. These facilities are not available to Group B shares. However, shares can be moved from Group B to Group A and *vice versa* depending upon the criteria for shifting. For instance, the Bombay Stock Exchange has laid down several criteria for shifting shares from Group B to Group A, such as, an equity base of ₹ 10 crores, a market capitalisation of ₹ 25-30 crores, a public holding of 35 to 40 per cent, a shareholding population of 15,000 to 20,000, good dividend paying status etc. Group B2 shares are again divided into B1 and B shares on the Bombay Stock Exchange. B1 shares represent well traded scrips among the B Group and they have weekly settlement.

Apart from the above, there is another group called Group C shares. Under Group C, only odd lots and permitted securities are included. A number of shares that are less than the market lot are known as odd lots. Market lot refers to the minimum number of shares of a particular security that must be transacted on a stock exchange. Odd lots have settlement once in a fortnight or once on Saturdays. Permitted securities are those that are not listed on a stock exchange but are listed on other stock exchanges in India. So, they are permitted to be traded on this stock exchange. Odd lots cannot be easily transacted on the stock exchange and so they are not liquid in nature.

## ❖ Advantages of listing

The advantages of listing may be summarised as follows:

(i) **Facilitates buying and selling of securities:** Listing paves way for easy buying and selling of securities. Constant marketing facilities are assured for listed securities.

(ii) **Ensures liquidity:** The prices of listed securities are quoted daily in the market. Hence, securities can be converted into cash readily at quoted prices and thus listing ensures liquidity.

(iii) **Offers wide publicity:** Listed securities give wide publicity to the companies concerned. It is so because the names of listed companies are frequently mentioned in stock market reports, TV, Newspapers, Radio, etc. This has an advertising effect for such companies and this will automatically widen the market for their securities. According to Hasting, 'A listed security will receive more attention from investment advisory services than an unlisted one.'

(iv) **Assures finance:** The very fact that a security is listed in a recognised stock exchange adds to the prestige of that company and it enables the company to raise the necessary finance by the issue of such securities expeditiously.

(v) **Enables borrowing:** Listed securities are preferred as collateral securities by commercial banks and other lending institutions because they are rated high in market quotations and there is a ready market for them also. Thus, borrowings are made easier against the securities of the listed companies.

(vi) **Protects investors:** Listing companies have to necessarily submit themselves to the various regulatory measures by disclosing vital informations about their assets, capital structure, profits, dividend policy, allotment procedure, bonuses, etc. Hence, listing aims at protecting the interest of investors to a greater extent.

## ❖ Drawbacks

At the same time, listing brings some bad effects also. The disadvantages of listing are as follows:

(i) **Leads to speculation:** Listed securities offer wide scope for the speculators to manipulate the values in such a way as may be detrimental to the interests of the company. In such a situation, artificial forces play a more dominant role than the free market forces. The stock market may not reflect the true picture of a listed security. Again, the managerial personnel may themselves indulge in speculative activities with regard to listed securities by misusing the inside information available to them.

(ii) **Degrades company's reputation:** Sometimes, listed securities are subject to wide fluctuations in their values. They may become a victim of depression. They are immediately reflected on the stock exchange, whereas unlisted securities escape from this misery. These wide fluctuations in their values have the effect of degrading the company's reputation and image in the eyes of the public as well as the financial intermediaries.

**(iii) Discloses vital informations to competitors:** For getting the securities listed, a company has to disclose vital informations such as, dividends and bonuses declared, a brief history of the company, sales, remuneration to managerial personnel and so on. It amounts to leaking of secrecy of the company's operations to trade rivals. Even trade unions may demand higher wages and bonus on the basis of these informations. Thus, listing may prove disadvantageous to a company.

## LISTING PROCEDURE

As stated earlier, listing enables a company to include its securities in the official list of one or more recognised stock exchanges for the purpose of trading. A company which requires its securities to be listed must comply with the following formalities:

The company concerned must apply in the prescribed form along with the following documents and details:

*(i)* Certified copies of Memorandum and Articles of Association, Prospectus or Statement in lieu of Prospectus, Underwriting agreements, agreements with vendors and promoters, etc.

*(ii)* Specimen copies of shares and debenture certificates, letter of call, allotment, acceptance and renunciation.

*(iii)* Copies of balance sheets and audited accounts for the last 5 years.

*(iv)* Copies of offers for sale and circulars or advertisements offering any securities for subscription or sale during the last 5 years.

*(v)* Certified copies of agreements with managerial personnel.

*(vi)* Particulars of dividends and bonuses paid during the last 10 years.

*(vii)* A statement showing dividends or interest in arrears if any.

*(viii)* A brief history of the company since its incorporation, giving details of its activities.

*(ix)* Particulars regarding its capital structure.

*(x)* Particulars of shares and debentures for which permission to deal is applied for and their issue.

*(xi)* A statement showing the distribution of shares along with a list of highest 10 holders of each class or kind of securities of the company stating the number of securities held by them.

*(xii)* Particulars of shares forfeited.

*(xiii)* Certified copies of agreements if any with the Industrial Finance Corporation, ICICI, etc.

*(xiv)* Listing agreement with the necessary initial and annual listing fee.

## ❖ Criteria for listing

A company which desires its securities to be listed on a recognised stock exchange must satisfy the following conditions:

(*i*) At least 60 per cent of each class of securities issued must be offered to the public for subscription and the minimum issued capital should be ₹ 3 crores.

(*ii*) The minimum public offer for subscription must be at least 25 per cent of each issue and it must be offered through advertisement in newspapers at least for a period of 2 days.

(*iii*) The company should be of a fair size having broad based capital structure and public interest in its securities.

(*iv*) There must be at least 10 public shareholders for every ₹ 1 lakh share of fresh issue of capital and it is 20 in the case of subsequent issue of shares. This criterion is different for investment companies.

(*v*) A company having more than ₹ 5 crores paid-up capital must list its securities on more than one stock exchange. Listing on the regional stock exchange is compulsory.

(*vi*) The company must pay interest on the excess application money received at the rates ranging between 4 per cent and 15 per cent depending on the delay beyond 10 weeks from the date of closure of the subscription list.

(*vii*) The Articles of Association of the company must provide for the following:

(*a*) A common form of transfer shall be used.

(*b*) Fully paid-up shares will be completely free from lien.

(*c*) Partly paid-up shares will be subject to lien only to the extent of call money due at a fixed time.

(d) Calls in advance carry only interest and not dividend rights.

(*e*) Unclaimed dividends shall not be forfeited before the claim becomes time barred.

(*f*) The right to call of shares shall be given only after the necessary sanction by the general body meeting.

(*g*) Transfer of shares shall be registered within 30 days of deposit of request and the balance certificates shall be issued within the same period.

(*viii*) The existing companies must adhere to the ceiling in expenditure of public issues.

(*ix*) A certificate to the effect that shares from promoter's quota are not sold or transferred for a period of 3 years must be submitted.

## ❖ Listing obligations

A company whose securities have been listed on a stock exchange has to perform certain obligations also. Some of the important obligations have been given here under:

The company has to compulsorily notify the stock exchange:

(*i*) The date of the board meeting at which the declaration or recommendation of dividend or the issue of right or bonus share will be considered.

(*ii*) Any change in the company's director or managerial personnel by death, resignation, removal or otherwise.

(*iii*) Any issue of new shares, rights shares or otherwise as well as the issue of any privileges or bonuses to members, even before they are intimated to shareholders.

(*iv*) Any change in the company's capital structure.

(*v*) Any material change in the general character or nature of the company's business.

(*vi*) Any reissue of forfeited securities or the issue of any other securities held in reserve for future issue.

(*vii*) Any action which will result in the redemption, cancellation or retirement of any securities listed on the stock exchange.

(*viii*) Any intention to make a drawing of listed securities.

(*ix*) Any other information necessary to enable the shareholders to appraise the company's position so as to avoid the establishment of a false market in the shares of the company.

(*x*) In addition to the above, the company has to forward to the stock exchange:

(*a*) Copies of all notices and circulars sent to the shareholders including the proceedings of ordinary and extraordinary general meetings.

(*b*) Certified copies of all resolutions passed by the company as soon as such resolutions become effective.

(*c*) Copies of statutory and annual reports and annual audited accounts as soon as they are issued as well as the director's report.

(*d*) Annual return of at least 10 principal holders of each class of security of the company.

## ❖ Additional obligations

The company must satisfy the following additional conditions:

(*i*) The company must recommend or declare all dividends/cash bonuses, at least, 5 days before the commencement of the closure of its transfer books.

(*ii*) The company must advise the stock exchange in writing of all such dividends/cash bonuses recommended or declared immediately after the Board meeting has been held.

(*iii*) The company must close the transfer books only for the purpose of declaration of dividend or for the issue of rights/bonus shares.

(*iv*) The company must grant to shareholders the right of renunciation in all cases of rights issue.

(*v*) The company must undertake to maintain all letters of allotment, regret, acceptance and rights serially and to issue letters of allotment and regret simultaneously at the same time.

(*vi*) The company must issue receipts for all securities deposited for registration/exchange/ subdivision or for any other purpose and it should not charge any fee for it.

The recognised stock exchange has power to call for such other information as may be necessary or to produce further documents in the interest of the investors. In such a case, the company concerned must comply with those requirements also.

## ❖ New listing obligations

One of the conditions for listing of securities is that any company enlisting its shares on stock exchanges must comply with Clause 49 of the new listing regulations. Under the said clause, necessary powers have been delegated to the SEBI to fix the composition of company boards with a view to achieve good governance standards. Accordingly, the SEBI has laid down the following conditions which the companies concerned will have to follow from 2006 onwards.

(*i*) The companies should have at least 50 per cent of their boards filled in by non-executive directors.

(*ii*) If the chairman of the company happens to be a non-executive director, one-third of the board should consist of independent directors.

(*iii*) If the chairman is an executive director, the number of independent directors goes up to 50 per cent.

The SEBI has been given powers to punish recalcitrant companies with large fines and even delist shares as a last resort.

## ❖ Listing agreement

The stock exchange authorities will scrutinise the application carefully and if they are satisfied with all the particulars/documents submitted, they will call upon the company to execute a listing agreement. This agreement contains a list of conditions and obligations which the company should strictly observe, failing which, the stock exchange may suspend or withdraw the listing facility. Many conditions for listing have been laid down with a view to protect the interest of investors and to ensure that applicants for large blocks of shares are not given undue preference over others.

## ❖ Delisting/suspension of companies

During the ten year period 2001-11, 786 companies have got listed in the BSE. But it is surprising to note that around 2800 companies have disappeared from the bourses during the same period as shown below:

| | |
|---|---|
| No. of companies delisted | 1,640 |
| No. of companies suspended from trading | 1,196 |
| Compulsorily delisted | 876 |

A stock may be compulsorily delisted due to any of the following reasons:

- Loss making with negative net worth.
- Suspension of securities from trading for more than 6 months.
- Infrequent trading in the preceding 3 years.
- Conviction of company/promoters/directors for violation of the SEBI Act.

- Address of company/promoters/directors not known.
- Shareholding below the minimum level according to listing agreement.

Trading suspension may be due to:

- Non-compliance with listing agreements.
- Non-submission of the corporate governance report.
- Non-payment of listing fees.

### ❖ Resources to shareholders

In the case of compulsory delisting, promoters are bound to purchase the outstanding securities from the holders if they wish to sell the stock at a fair price determined by SEBI's regulations.

In the case of suspension, an opportunity will be given to the company concerned to defend its case. If the suspension is revoked, investors will get an exit opportunity. Otherwise, they have to wait until they receive the delisting order to exit the stock, when the promoter has to make an offer to buy it.

## REGISTRATION OF STOCK BROKERS

A broker is none other than a commission agent who transacts business in securities on behalf of his clients who are non-members of a stock exchange. Thus, a non-member can purchase and sell securities only through a broker who is a member of the stock exchange. To deal in securities on recognised stock exchanges, the broker should register his name as a broker with the SEBI. A stock broker must possess the following qualifications to register as a broker:

(*i*) He must be an Indian citizen with 21 years of age.

(*ii*) He should neither be a bankrupt nor compounded with creditors.

(*iii*) He should not have been convicted for any offence, fraud, etc.

(*iv*) He should not have engaged in any other business other than that of a broker in securities.

(*v*) He should not be a defaulter of any stock exchange.

(*vi*) He should have completed 12th standard examination.

Apart from individuals, corporate and institutional members can also become brokers. Brokers will be selected by the selection committee of the stock exchange on the basis of their qualifications, experience, financial status, their performance in the written test, interview, etc.

### ❖ Registration procedure

(*i*) The prospective broker must apply to the SEBI through the stock exchange of which he is a member.

(*ii*) The stock exchange should forward the application within 30 days of receipt of the application.

*(iii)* After going through the application, the SEBI may call for additional informations or clarifications if necessary regarding the dealings in securities. The SEBI may also request the applicant to appear before it for personal representation.

*(iv)* After ascertaining whether the applicant is eligible to be admitted as a member and whether he has the necessary infrastructure facilities, the SEBI may grant a certificate to the stock broker. The stock exchanges concerned will be duly informed of the same.

*(v)* The certified stock broker must abide by the prescribed code of conduct.

*(vi)* The stock broker has to pay the prescribed registration fees as indicated below:

*(a)* ₹ 5,000 for each financial year for those brokers whose annual turnover does not exceed ₹ 1 crore during any financial year.

*(b)* ₹ 5,000 plus 1/100 of 1 per cent of the turnover in case the annual turnover exceeds ₹ 1 crore.

*(vii)* The registration of a broker will be suspended if the broker violates any provisions of the SEBI Act, rules and regulations of the exchange and if he does not follow the prescribed code of conduct.

*(viii)* The registration will be cancelled if the broker is convicted of a criminal offence or guilty or fraud or if he repeatedly violates the provisions of the SEBI Act or rules and regulations of the stock exchange or the prescribed code of conduct.

*(ix)* Every stock broker has to maintain a minimum amount of deposit called security deposit or base minimum capital with the stock exchange. It is ₹ 5 lakh for brokers in Bombay and Calcutta Stock Exchanges, ₹ 3.5 lakh for brokers in Delhi and Ahmedabad Stock Exchanges and ₹ 2 lakh for others. This deposit must be in the form of cash to the extent of 25 per cent, in the form of fixed deposit for another 25 per cent and the balance in the form of securities with a 30 per cent margin.

In addition to the above, every broker has to maintain additional capital depending upon his business volume not exceeding 8 per cent of his gross outstanding business in the exchange including the security deposit.

## ❖ Code of conduct for stock brokers

To discharge the duties in the best interest of investors and other stock brokers, a code of conduct has been prescribed for brokers in accordance with the statutory requirements. They have been briefly summarised below:

*(i)* A stock broker must honestly and promptly execute all orders for buying and selling of securities at the best possible market price. He must make prompt payment to his clients in the case of sales and prompt delivery in the case of purchases.

*(ii)* He should not discriminate small investors against big investors.

*(iii)* He must issue a contract note for all transactions as specified by the stock exchange without any delay.

*(iv)* He must maintain complete secrecy of his client's personal investments and other informations of a confidential nature.

(*v*) He should not induce or initiate purchases or sales just for the sake of his brokerage or commission.

(*vi*) He should not give any false or misleading information with a view to encouraging purchases or sales and thereby getting his commission.

(*vii*) He should not entertain those clients who have failed to carry-out their commitments in respect of securities with other stock brokers.

(*viii*) The capacity in which he is acting must be duly informed to his client. In other words, he must disclose whether he is acting as a principal or as an agent. In all cases, he must give top priority to his client's interest.

(*ix*) He is not expected to render any investment advice except under those circumstances which warrant it.

(*x*) He must possess adequate infrastructure facilities and maintain proper staff to render prompt, efficient and fair services to his clients.

(*xi*) He should not advertise his business publicly except when it is permitted by the stock exchange.

(*xii*) He should not adopt any unfair practices with a view to attract clients from other brokers.

(*xiii*) He should not knowingly and willfully deliver documents which constitute bad delivery.

(*xiv*) He should not fail to submit the necessary returns to the SEBI and the stock exchange as and when they have to be submitted as per the statutory regulations. These returns should not contain any false or misleading information.

(*xv*) He must exercise reasonable care, diligence and skill in the discharge of his functions as a broker.

(*xvi*) He must maintain high standards of integrity and honesty, promptness and fairness in the conduct of all his business.

(*xvii*) Above all, he should not indulge in fraudulent or deceptive transactions or spread rumours with a view to create a false market and making personal gains.

(*xviii*) He must abide by all the rules and regulations of the regulating authorities including the stock exchange.

(*xix*) He must maintain proper books of account, records and documents as required by the various regulating authorities.

(*xx*) He must produce the above books and records for inspection whenever an inspection is undertaken as per the provisions of the SEBI Act.

## FUNCTIONS OF BROKERS

The following are the important functions generally performed by all the brokers.

**(i) Client registration**

First of all, a trading broker has to enter into an agreement in the specified format with his client before accepting any orders on his client's behalf. The said agreement has to be executed on non-judicial stamp paper, duly signed by both the parties on all the pages. In addition to the agreement, the broker shall seek other information about the client in the client registration form. The information may relate to:

(*a*) Investors financial profile.

(*b*) Investors risk profile and risk-taking ability.

(*c*) Investor's social profile.

(*d*) Investors identification details.

(*e*) Family, income, age and employment details.

(*f*) Details of investments in other assets.

(*g*) Financial liabilities, etc.

The broker has to obtain recent passport size photos (3 copies) in the case of individual clients and of all partners in the case of partnership firms. In the case of corporate customers, he has to obtain the photos of dominant promoters. The broker should not forget to take proof of identification of the client. It is also mandatory to give an unique code for each client for easy identification. There is no limit on the maximum number of clients for a broker.

**(ii) Obtaining margin money**

It is also mandatory for the broker to collect margins from his clients in all cases where the margin in respect of the client in settlement, would work-out to be more than ₹ 50,000. The margins so collected must be kept separately in the client's bank account and it must be utilised for making payment/settlement in respect of that client.

**(iii) Execution of orders**

The important function of a broker is to execute his client's orders swiftly and carefully. Hence, he has to obtain clear-cut confirmed order instructions from the clients so that the necessary orders may be placed on the system. To execute a trade order for a client, the broker must obtain specific instructions as to:

(*a*) The name of the company whose securities have to be bought or sold.

(*b*) The precise number of shares required.

(*c*) The limit/market price conditions, etc.

**(iv) Supply of necessary slips**

On execution of the trade, the broker, *i.e.*, the trading member should inform his client the order number. He should also give copies of the trade confirmation slip, modification slip, cancellation slip, etc. to enable the client to take necessary follow-up action.

**(v) Issue of contract note**

The broker should then issue a contract note to his clients for all trades, whether for purchase or sale of securities, executed with all relevant details. This contract note should be issued within 24 hours of the execution of the contract. It should be duly signed by the broker or his authorised signatory or client attorney. Every broker is expected to maintain the duplicate copy of each contract note issued for five years.

**(vi) Statement of particulars in a contract note**

It is mandatory to mention the following particulars in a contract note issued by a stock broker.

(*a*) The name, address and SEBI registration number of the member broker.

(*b*) The name of partner/proprietor/authorised signatory.

(*c*) Dealing office address, telephone number, fax number and code number of the member given by the exchange.

(*d*) Unique identification number.

(*e*) Contract number, date of issue of contract note, settlement number and time period for settlement.

(*f*) Client's name and code number.

(*g*) Order number and order time corresponding to trades.

(*h*) Trade member and trade time.

(*i*) Quantity and kind of security bought or sold by the client.

(*j*) Purchase/sale rate and brokerage.

(*k*) Service tax rates and any other charges levied by the broker.

(*l*) Affixing of appropriate stamps on the original contract note as per the Stamp Act of the relevant state.

(*m*) Addition of a clause stating that 'the client will hold the security blank at his own risk'.

**(vii) Payment/delivery of securities**

It is the duty of every trading member (broker) to make payments to his clients (in the case of sale) or deliver the securities purchased within 24 hours of payout unless the client has requested otherwise. All brokers have to exercise great caution in accepting deliveries of securities on behalf of their clients to avoid the introduction of any fake/forged/stolen securities into the market.

**(viii) Charging of brokerage and other charges**

As per the SEBI guidelines, every broker is entitled to charge brokerage not exceeding 2.5 per cent. In addition to brokerage, the following items are charged:

(*a*) Service Tax (5 per cent of the brokerage).

(*b*) Stamp duty as per the Stamp Act of the State Government.

(*c*) SEBI turnover fee.

(*d*) Transaction tax as presented by the Central Government (₹ 1,500 per crore trade).

**(ix) Maintenance of bank accounts**

It is the function of a broker to maintain separate bank accounts for his clients' funds and also for his own funds. However, funds can be transferred from the client's account to the clearing account for the purpose of meeting pay-in obligations on behalf of the clients and *vice versa* in the case of funds payout.

**(x) Receipt of interest, dividends, rights, etc.**

In case securities are brought cum vouchers, cum coupons, cum dividend, cum cash bonus, cum bonus issues, cum rights, etc., the client is entitled to receive all vouchers, coupons, dividends, cash bonus, etc., in addition to original securities bought. In such a case, it is the duty of the broker to receive all such privileges on behalf of his client.

**(xi) Settlement of disputes**

In case any dispute arises between the broker and his client, it is the duty of the broker himself to take the initiative and resolve the dispute.

## REGISTRATION OF SUB-BROKERS

Apart from the brokers, there are other categories of persons called sub-brokers. As a matter of fact, a sub-broker is not a member of a stock exchange. But, he is a person who acts as an agent of a stock broker. He transacts the securities trading business on behalf of his clients through stock brokers. Such sub-brokers should also get a certificate of registration from the SEBI. Just like brokers, they have to satisfy the eligibility criteria, pay registration fees and follow the code of conduct and the various rules and regulations framed by the regulating authorities from time-to-time. Excepting the registration fees, other aspects are more or less similar to brokers and hence they are not repeated here.

## KINDS OF BROKERS AND THEIR ASSISTANTS

The main players in the secondary market are the brokers. They may act in different capacities – as a principal, as an agent, as a speculator and so on. Hence, it is essential to study the different kinds of brokers and their assistants. Brokers may be classified as follows:

### 1. Jobbers

A jobber is a professional independent broker who deals in securities on his own behalf. In other words, he purchases and sells securities in his own name. His main job is to earn a margin of profit due to price variations of securities. A jobber plays in the market for quick returns. He is a professional broker who carefully judges the worth of the securities and makes a good forecast of their future price movements. He buys securities as a owner, keeps them for a very short period and sells them for profit known as the 'jobber's turn'. Thus, a jobber does not work on commission basis but works for profit. So, a jobber can deal either with a broker or with another jobber. In London Stock Exchange, every member of the stock exchange has to indicate very clearly whether he would like to act as a broker or as a jobber. In India, this rigid classification is not strictly followed. Generally, a jobber specialises in a limited number of shares. When a broker wants to purchase or sell securities on behalf of his clients, he usually approaches the jobber first. A jobber will always quote a two-way price called double-barreled price. The lower one indicates the price at which he is ready to purchase and the higher one indicates the price at which he is ready to sell. If this quotation is agreeable to a broker, he may finalise the deal on behalf of his client. If the quotation is not suitable, the broker goes to another jobber.

## 2. Tarawaniwalas

A tarawaniwala is an active member in the Bombay Stock Exchange. He is very similar to a jobber in the London Stock Exchange particularly with regard to the method of transacting business. But, a tarawaniwala can act both as a broker as well as a jobber. Basically, he is a jobber. At the same time, he is not prohibited from acting as a broker. The drawback of this system is that a tarawaniwala can act against the interest of investors by purchasing securities from them in his own name at lower prices and selling the same securities to them at higher prices. Hence, many committees have pointed out the questionable practices being adopted by a tarawaniwala. Now, the Securities Contracts (Regulation) Act of 1956 provides that a member of a stock exchange can act as a principal only for a member of a recognised stock exchange. In case he wants to act as such for a non-member, he must get his consent and this fact must be disclosed in the agreement also.

## 3. Commission brokers

A commission broker is nothing but a broker. He buys and sells securities on behalf of his clients for a commission. He is permitted to deal with non-members directly. He does not purchase or sell in his own name. Generally, a broker acts for a large number of his clients, and therefore, he deals in a large variety of securities. He gets the orders from his clients and executes them through jobbers.

## 4. Sub-brokers/remisiers

As stated earlier, a sub-broker is an agent of a stock broker. He helps the clients to buy and sell securities only through the stock broker. Since he is not a member of a stock exchange, he cannot directly deal in securities. He is subject to similar restrictions as are applicable to member brokers. He is called remisier in the Bombay Stock Exchange. His commission is paid out of the commission received by the brokers for whom he is acting as an agent. Hence, remisiers are also called 'half commission men'. Generally, their commission cannot exceed 40 per cent of the commission received on the business transacted by them.

## 5. Authorised clerks

An authorised clerk is one who is appointed by a stock broker to assist him in the business of securities trading. A broker cannot be present always on the trading floor of a stock exchange, and therefore, he requires the assistance of others to carry on the trading activities on his behalf. As per the rules of the stock exchange, each broker can employ a specified number of authorised clerks to transact the securities trading business. They are called 'member assistants' in the Madras Stock Exchange. In Bombay Stock Exchange, each member broker can employ a maximum number of 5 clerks. In Calcutta Stock Exchange, it is 8 and it is 3 in Madras Stock Exchange.

Generally, authorised clerks are given power of attorney to act on behalf of brokers and hence they can sign on behalf of brokers. They cannot transact any business in their own names at any cost and the brokers are personally liable for all the dealings carried out by the authorised clerks on behalf of the brokers. Brokers have to pay entrance fee, annual subscription, etc. for each of their authorised clerks as per the rules of the stock exchange and they can be removed at any time after duly informing the stock exchange concerned.

## METHODS OF TRADING IN A STOCK EXCHANGE

The stock exchange operations at floor level are highly technical in nature. Non-members are not permitted to enter into the stock market. Hence, various stages have to be completed in executing a transaction at a stock exchange. The steps involved in the method of trading have been given below:

**(i) Choice of a broker**

The prospective investor who wants to buy shares or the investor who wants to sell his shares cannot enter into the hall of the exchange and transact business. They have to act through only member brokers. They can also appoint their bankers for this purpose, since bankers can become members of the stock exchange as per the present regulations. So, the first task in transacting business on a stock exchange is to choose a broker of repute or a banker. Such persons alone can ensure prompt and quick execution of a transaction at the best possible and profitable price.

After choosing the broker, one has to find out whether the broker is willing to transact business on his behalf. Generally, the brokers demand a letter of introduction or a reference from a respectable party like Notary Public. Only when he is satisfied with the financial position of the party, he will be willing to act on behalf of him.

**(ii) Placement of order**

The next step is the placing of order for the purchase or sale of securities with the broker. The order is usually placed by telegram, telephone, letter, fax, etc. or in person. To avoid delay, it is placed generally over the phone. To reduce the cost also, it is placed in abbreviations, *i.e.*, 'Buy 100 SBI @ ₹ 156'. It means that it is an order for the purchase of 100 shares of State Bank of India @ ₹ 156/-. The orders may take any one of the following forms:

**(a) At best order:** It is an order which does not specify any specific price. It must be executed immediately at the best possible price. The client may also fix a timeframe within which the order has to be executed, *e.g.*, 'Buy 100 Essar Oil at Best'.

**(b) Limit order:** It is an order for the purchase or sale of securities at a fixed price specified by the client, *e.g.*, 'Sell 100 DCM @ ₹ 76'.

**(c) Immediate or cancel order:** It is an order for the purchase or sale of securities immediately at the quoted prices. If the order could not be executed at the quoted prices immediately, it should be treated as cancelled, *e.g.*, 'Buy 100 DCM @ ₹ 76 immediate'.

**(d) Discretionary order:** It is an order to buy or sell shares at whatever price the broker thinks reasonable. This is possible only when the client has complete faith on the broker.

**(e) Limited discretionary order:** It is an order to buy or sell securities within a specified price range and/or within the given time period as per the best judgement of the broker.

**(f) Open order:** It is an order to buy or sell without fixing any time limit or price limit on the execution of the order. It is similar to discretionary order.

(g) **Stop loss order:** It is an order to sell as soon as the price falls up to a particular level or to buy when the price rises up to a specified level. This is mainly to protect the clients against a heavy fall or rise in prices so that they may not suffer more than the pre-specified amount.

On receiving the orders, they are first recorded in a rough memo book and then they are transferred to the 'Order Book'.

**(iii) Execution of orders**

Big brokers transact their business through their authorised clerks. Small ones carry-out their business personally. Orders are executed in the Trading ring of a stock exchange which works from 12 noon to 2 p.m. on all working days from Monday to Friday and a special one hour session on Saturday. Trading outside the trading hours are called 'Kerb dealings'.

The floor of the stock exchange is divided into a number of markets (pits) according to the nature of security dealt in. The authorised clerk/broker goes to the pit and the jobbers offer two-way quotes for the scrips they deal in. They act as market makers and provide liquidity to the market. The Bombay Stock Exchange has introduced screen-based trading from March 1995, called BOLT (BSE Online Trading). It has been designed to get the best bids and offers from the jobber's book as well as the best buy and sell orders from the order book. If the quotation is not acceptable to the broker, he may make a counter bid/offer. Ultimately, the bargain may be closed at a price mutually acceptable to both the parties. In case the quotation is not acceptable to him, the broker may go to another dealer and make a bargain. All bargains on the stock exchanges are settled by word of mouth and there is no written contract signed immediately by the parties concerned. Once the transaction is finalised, the details are recorded in a chaupri or rough notebook. Sauda Block Books or confirmation memos are provided by the stock exchange. The details are recorded in these books also. The prices at which different scrips are traded on a particular day are published on the next day in the newspapers. An authorised representative of the stock exchange is also present in the hall to supervise the trading.

**(iv) Preparation of contract notes**

Usually, the authorised clerks enter the particulars of the business transacted during a particular day in the 'Kacha Sauda Book' from the rough notebooks at the close of that working day. From Kacha Sauda Books, they are transferred to 'Pucca Sauda Books' which are maintained separately for the ready delivery contracts and forward delivery contracts. Then the broker/authorised clerk prepares a contract note. A contract note is a written agreement between the broker and his client for the transactions executed. It contains the details of the contract made for the purchase/sale of securities, the brokerage chargeable, name of the company, number of shares bought/sold, net rate, etc. It is prepared in a prescribed form and a copy of it is also sent to the client.

**(v) Settlement of transactions**

Finally, the settlement is made by means of delivering the share certificates along with the transfer deed. The transfer deed is duly signed by the transferor, *i.e.*, the seller. It bears the stamp of the selling broker. The buyer then fills up the particulars in the transfer deed. At present, the settlement can be made by any one of the following methods:

(a) **Spot delivery settlement:** Under this method, the delivery of securities and payment for them are effected on the date of the contract itself or on the next day.

(b) **Hand delivery settlement:** Under this method, the delivery of securities and payment are effected within the time stipulated in the agreement or within 14 days from the date of the contract whichever is earlier. Most of the transactions are conducted on this basis.

(c) **Clearing settlement:** Under this method, the transactions are cleared and settled through the clearing house. Usually those securities which are frequently traded and are usually in demand are cleared through the clearing house. These transactions are also referred to as the transactions for 'the account'.

(d) **Special delivery settlement:** Under this method, delivery of securities and payment may take place at any time exceeding 14 days following the date of the contract as specified in the contract and permitted by the governing board.

**(vi) Lodging for transfer and return of certificates**

Finally, the shares have to be registered in the name of the buyer. For this purpose, the share certificate along with the duly filled transfer deed must be sent to the company. The transfer deed should bear adequate share transfer stamp. After verifying the bonafide of the transfer, the company has to transfer the shares in the name of the buyer and send them back within 2 months. The share certificate should bear a new ledger folio number, transfer number, buyer's name, etc. on the reverse side of it. This completes the legal formality for transfer of shares from the seller to the buyer.

## CURRENT SETTLEMENT PROCEDURE OF TRADING TRANSACTIONS

In case any investor purchases shares, the payment for the shares is required to be done prior to the payin date for the relevant settlements. Of course, it is subject to the rules and regulations of the exchange also.

Similarly, in the case of sale of shares, the delivery of shares has to be made prior to the payin date for the relevant settlement or as otherwise provided in the rules and regulations of the exchange.

On the other hand, brokers are required to make payment or give delivery of securities within 24 hours of the payout day since T + 2 rolling settlement is being followed *w.e.f.* April 1, 2003.

There is a provision to get direct delivery of shares in investors/client's beneficiary accounts instead of getting them through their brokers. In such a case, the investor has to give details of his beneficiary account and his Depository Participant's identity number to his broker along with the standing instructions for 'Delivery-in' to his Depository Participant for accepting shares in his beneficiary account. The Clearing Corporation/House in such a case will send the payout instructions directly to the Depositors so that the securities may be credited directly to the beneficiary account when the exchange makes payment or delivers the securities to the broker. Since the settlement cycle is on T+2 basis, the exchanges have to ensure that the payout of funds and securities to the clients is done by the brokers within 24 hours of the payout.

Generally, the payin and payout day for funds and securities have been prescribed as per the settlement cycle.

A typical settlement cycle for normal (regular) market segment is given in the following table.

**TABLE 4.1: TYPICAL SETTLEMENT CYCLE FOR VARIOUS ACTIVITIES**

| *Item* | *Activity* | *Day* |
|---|---|---|
| Trading | Rolling Settlement Trading | T |
| Clearing | Custodial confirmation | T + 1 working days |
| | Delivery generation | T + 1 working days |
| Settlement | Securities and funds payin | T + 2 working days |
| | Securities and funds payout | T + 2 working days |
| Post-settlement | Valuation debit | T + 2 working days |
| | Auction | T + 3 working days |
| | Bad delivery reporting | T + 4 working days |
| | Auction settlement | T + 5 working days |
| | Close out | T + 5 working days |
| | Rectified bad delivery payin and payout | T + 6 working days |
| | Re-bad delivery reporting and pick-up | T + 8 working days |
| | Close out of re-bad delivery | T + 9 working days |

## ❖ Settlement and payment

Till January 1, 2002 an Account Period Settlement was in vogue. It has been discontinued since January 1, 2002 pursuant to SEBI directives. An account period settlement is a settlement where the trades pertaining to a period stretching over more than one day are settled on a net basis. For example, trades for the period Monday to Friday are settled together on a net basis.

## ❖ Rolling settlement

In the place of account period settlement, rolling settlement has been introduced. In a rolling settlement, trades executed during the day are settled based on the net obligations for that day. At present, the trades pertaining to the rolling settlement are settled on T + 2 day basis where T stands for the trade day. It means that trades executed on Monday have to be settled on the following Wednesday provided there are no intervening holidays. The settlement cycle is on T + 2 rolling settlement basis *w.e.f.* April 1, 2003.

## ❖ Payin day and payout day

As far as the payment is concerned, one should have an exposure to payin day and payout day. Payin day is the day when the brokers shall make payment or make delivery of securities to the exchange. On the other hand, payout day is the day when the exchange makes payment or delivery of securities to the broker.

## ❖ 'Market Trade' and 'Off Market Trade'

Any trade settled through a clearing corporation is called 'market trade'. These trades are carried out through stock brokers on a stock exchange. On the other hand if a trade is settled directly between two parties without the involvement of clearing corporation, it is termed as 'off market trade'. The same delivery instruction slip can be used for both by specifying one of the two options.

## ❖ Good delivery and bad delivery

A share certificate together with its transfer deed which meets all the requirements of title transfer from the transferor (seller) to the transferee (buyer) is called good delivery in the market. For example, if the share certificate is genuine and the transferor has good title to it, the delivery of such document together with transfer deed will be called good delivery.

On the other hand, delivery of a share certificate together with a deed of transfer which does not meet the requirements of title transfer from the seller to the buyer is called a bad delivery in the market. For example, delivery of a fake or stolen share certificate together with a deed of transfer is a clear case of bad delivery.

# ONLINE TRADING

The Information Technology has brought out revolutionary changes in the operations of stock exchanges in India. The traditional method of trading without the use of technology was time-consuming and inefficient. Further, it imposed limits on trading volumes and efficiency. To overcome those defects and to provide efficient and transparent services, the NSE has introduced a nationwide online fully automated Screen Based Trading System (SBTS). Now, other stock exchanges have been forced to adopt SBTS and today India can boast that almost 100 per cent trading take place through electronic order matching.

Under SBTS, a member can punch into the computers quantities of securities and the prices at which he likes to transact the transaction. It is executed as soon as it finds a matching sale or buy order from a counterparty. Thus, technology is used to carry the trading platform from the trading hall of the exchanges to the premises of the brokers. NSE has carried the trading platform further to the PCs at the residence of the investors through the internet and the handheld devices through WAP for the convenience of the mobile investors.

## ❖ Modus operandi of E-trading

The typical trading network is shown in the following diagram:

As shown in the picture, the NSE has a main computer which is connected through Very Small Aperture Terminal (VSAT) installed at its office. The main computer runs on a fault tolerant STRATUS main computer at the exchange. Brokers have terminals (identified as PCs in the figure) installed at their premises which are connected through VSATs/Leased Lines/ Modems.

When investors inform their brokers to place orders either for purchase or sales, the brokers enter the orders through their PCs which run under Windows NT and send signal to the satellite via VSAT/Leased Line/Modem. The signal is then directed to mainframe computer kept

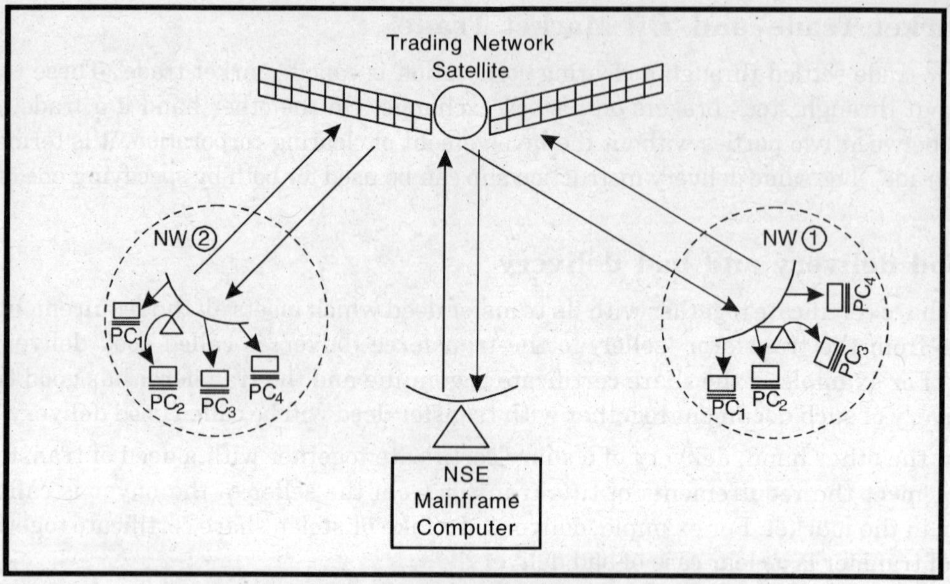


**Fig. 4.1: Trading Network**

at NSE via VSAT at NSE office. A message relating to order activity is broadcast to the respective member. The order confirmation message is immediately displayed on the PC of the broker. This order will be executed if it matches with the existing passive order(s). Otherwise, it will wait for the active orders to enter the system till it is matched.

On order matching, a message is broadcast to the respective member. The trading system operates on a Strict Price/Time priority. All orders received on the system are sorted with the best priced order getting the first priority for matching. In other words, the best buy order should match with the best sell order. If more orders are similar priced, then orders are sorted on time priority basis, *i.e.*, the first come gets the top priority.

All dealings are transparent, objective and fair since all orders are matched automatically by the computer. In case an order does not find a match, it remains in the system displaying it to the whole market till a fresh order comes in or the earlier order is cancelled or modified.

This trading system provides greater flexibility to the investors since various kinds of orders with quantity or price conditions can be placed according to the discretion of investors. Similarly, several time-related conditions can be easily built into an order.

This system also provides complete market information online. The market screens at any point of time provide complete information as to:

(*i*) Total order depth in a security.

(*ii*) The best five buys and sells in the market.

(*iii*) The quantity traded during the day in that security.

(*iv*) The high and the low price for each security.

(*v*) The last traded price for a security, etc.

## BSE-BOLT SYSTEM

Similarly, the BOLT System (Bombay Online Trading) has been introduced in the Bombay Stock Exchange. Now, all scrips on BSE are being traded through BOLT.

The brokers and their agents conduct trading under the BOLT system from their Trading Work Stations (TWS). At every TWS, the BOLT system displays 'touchline' which will share the best bid and offer prices presently available in the market. The BOLT system also displays at every TWS 'Market view' which will provide a detailed market information on each listed stock.

## MOBILE TRADING

The mobile trading was recently introduced in the Indian market to make stock market trading easier. One has to approach any mobile service provider for securing internet connectivity with adequate bandwidth on his phone. He is also required to register for an online amount offer which he is automatically entitled to services under the mobile platform.

For the mobile trading, most brokers offer two options now –

(*i*) Using the handset's browser, and

(*ii*) Using a downloadable application.

In both cases, one can reach the broker's server for trading by using internet connectivity. If one has GPRS activated in his phone, he can log on to his online trading account through his phone, just as he would with his desktop. One can follow a URL and log in with the given 'user name' and 'password' which can be subsequently changed and thereafter this new ID can be used for connecting one's trading account. Once it is connected, it is similar to an online trading account. This mobile trading platform lets one to have an easy access to live stock quotes and check on his margins, order-book status and real-time net position.

### ❖ Features

The special features of mobile trading platform are:

- Facility to create a market-watch window.
- Watching best buy/sell bids for a scrip.
- Checking the margin status and the client's buying power.
- Placing orders with options to view pending orders.
- Modifying and cancelling those orders.
- Viewing of Intra-day stock charts.
- Getting of stock advice through SMS.
- Instant transferring of funds.

The mobile-based trading has gained so much popularity that from a daily average turnover of ₹ 1.66 crores in 2010, it has zoomed to a daily average turnover of ₹ 1,780 crores in the beginning of 2014 on the NSE.

## ALGO TRADING

Algo trading refers to algorithmic. It is nothing but the use of computer programs to execute trades in the stocks, commodity or financial markets. In other words, it is a new form of computer based trading that allows investors to put through trades in milliseconds as against the time-consuming traditional form of manual trading. Algo trading makes the whole trading process faster and simpler by reducing man-hours and increasing productivity. Thus, algo trading is a programmed trading where trades are automatically triggered by computers programmed to pick into action if certain market conditions are met. These conditions are purely by the underlying code or algorithm.

Algo trading is a kind of High Frequency Trading (HFT) by shortening the execution time of a trade to a few milliseconds. Algo trading enables the execution of stock market trades in such a manner that the prices of stocks are not influenced by momentary swings in the market.

### ❖ Execution algos

There are two common types of execution algos. They are: (1) Volume Weighted Average Price (VWAP) and (2) Time Weighted Average Price (TWAP). In the case of VWAP, the algo's objective is to executive the order at a price that is as close as possible to this weighted average price. The VWAP is calculated by weighting a stock's price quotes through the trading session with volumes traded at each price. On the other hand, the TWAP strategy breaks up a large order into equal parts and then dribbles buy or sell orders into the market evenly over the session. This ensures that the price at which an investor buys or sells is not affected by momentary swings in the market.

### ❖ Alpha-generating algos

Apart from execution algos, there are also alpha-generating algos which actively try to make money exploiting minor deviations in securities or markets. They may be: (1) Arbitrage algos and (2) Trend following algos.

Arbitrage algos earn profits from trading on anomalies between securities, trading ventures or asset classes. They may earn exploiting differentials between futures and cash markets. On the other hand, trend following algos identify a reversal in trends through technical analysis and get benefits from the momentum at an early stage itself.

It is found that nearly 30 per cent of trading in the Indian equity market is algo-based. The NSE trading platform incorporates execution algos such as the VWAP or TWAP.

### ❖ SEBI guidelines

Since computer programs like algos are constantly on the hunt for money making opportunities, manual traders are edged out of such trades. Hence, SEBI has introduced some checks on algo trading. Some of these checks are:

1. To route all algorithmic trades only through broker servers.
2. To have an effective check over quantity and price of such order by the exchange concerned.

3. To switch on brokers terminal only manually after following all risk management procedures.
4. To impose economic disincentive for high daily order-to-trade ratio.
5. To monitor price, order quantity, order value and open order value of algo trades during the trading session by the stock brokers under the supervision of the exchanges.
6. To ratify the algos used by the brokers by the exchangers concerned.

If adequate precautions are not taken by the exchanges as well as brokers for algo trading they would be held liable by the SEBI.

### ❖ Broker-friendly Portal

To facilitate easy and convenient day-to-day operations, broker-friendly portals have been launched by stock exchanges. A member portal provides a Web-enabled interface between the trading members and the exchange. For instance, NSE has launched "NSE Assist" and the MCX-SX "My Exchange".

## MERITS OF ONLINE TRADING

The following are the important merits of online trading:

(i) **Faster trading:** Technology driven trading is faster than manual trading. Once the order is matched, it is executed immediately.

(ii) **Accessible to all:** It provides full anonymity by accepting orders from members irrespective of the size of the orders – whether big or small without disclosing their identity. Thus, it provides equal access to all.

(iii) **Faster incorporation of price-sensitive information:** The SBTS allows faster incorporation of price-sensitive information into the prevailing prices and thus, it increases the information efficiency of the markets.

(iv) **Widening the market:** It also widens the market by enabling the market participants to trade with one another simultaneously irrespective of their geographical locations. Thus, it improves the depth and liquidity of the market.

(v) **Saving of time and cost:** The SBTS electronically matches orders on a strict price condition as well as on time priority basis. Hence, it cuts down cost as well as time in executing orders.

(vi) **Fully transparent:** Online trading is fully automated and screen-based. Everything is transparent on the screen and hence, there is no possibility to play any hide and seek game.

(vii) **No errors and frauds:** The price conditions, quantity conditions, etc. are punched into the computers by the members themselves. So, the risk of error is very less. Moreover, the trading is fully automated and screen-based and hence, frauds cannot enter into the system.

(viii) **Perfect audit trail:** It also provides perfect audit trail which helps to resolve disputes by logging in the trade execution on entirety. Thus, online trading ensures efficiency, liquidity and transparency in the trading on stock exchanges.

# TYPES OF STOCK MARKET ORDERS (NSE-NEAT SYSTEM)

## ❖ NEAT — National Exchange for Automated Trading

The NEAT system permits the trading members, *i.e.*, the brokers to entertain orders with various conditions attached to them as per the requirements of investors. These conditions may be broadly classified into the following categories:

(*i*) Time conditions.

(*ii*) Quantity conditions.

(*iii*) Price conditions, and.

(*iv*) Quantity Freezes.

### (i) Time conditions

The time conditions may relate to the following:

**(a) Day order:** A day order is an order which is valid for the day on which it is entered. If the order is not executed during the day, the system automatically cancels the order at the end of the day.

**(b) GTC — A Good Till Cancelled:** It is an order which remains in the system until it is cancelled by the user.

**(c) GTD — A Good Till Days:** This type of order allows the user to specify the number of days/date till which the order should stay in the system if not executed.

**(d) IOC — Immediate or Cancel order:** An immediate or cancel order allows the user to buy or sell a security as soon as the order is released into the system, failing which the order stands to be cancelled from the system.

### (ii) Quantity conditions

Similarly, the quantity conditions may relate to any of the following:

**(a) DQ — Disclosed Quantity:** An order with a Disclosed Quantity condition allows the user to disclose only a portion of the total order quantity to the market. For example, if the order quantity is 20,000 and the disclosed quantity is 4,000, then 4,000 only is disclosed to the market. After the said quantity is fully matched, a subsequent quantity of 4,000 will be disclosed. Thus, totally five disclosures with the same order number are shown one after the other in the market.

**(b) MF — Minimum Fill order:** This order facilitates the user to specify the minimum quantity for which an order should be traded in the market.

**(c) AON — All or None order.** This quantity condition implies that the full order quantity of the user should be traded at a time and if not nothing should be traded in his name. For instance, a buy order of 15,000 with an AON condition is entered, then the trade has to take place for 15,000 quantity, all at one time. In other words, it means one trade of 15,000 quantity.

**(iii) Price conditions**

The price conditions attached to an order may relate to any one of the following:

(a) **STOP-LOSS order:** If a user gives stop-loss order, it is released into the market only when the last traded price for that security in the normal market reaches or surpasses the trigger price. The trigger price is the price at which an order gets triggered from the stop-loss book. Before triggering, the order does not participate in matching and hence, it cannot get traded.

(b) **MKT order:** Market orders are orders for which the price is specified on 'MKT' at the time of order entry. For such orders, the system determines the price.

(c) **ATO — At The open:** At the open market, orders are entered during pre-open stage.

(d) **ABO — At Best order:** This order does not specify any price. It implies that it must be executed immediately at the best possible price. The user may also fix a timeframe within which this order has to be executed.

(e) **DO — Discretionary order:** This is an order to buy or sell securities at whatever the price the broker thinks reasonable. This is possible only where the client has complete faith on the broker.

**(iv) Quantity price freezes**

There are certain freezing conditions attached with this system. They may relate to the following:

(a) **Quantity freeze:** There is an in-built mechanism by which an order results in a quantity freeze if the quantity ordered is greater than 10 per cent of the issue size of the security.

(b) **Price freeze:** Sometimes, a limit order may be given for the purchase or sale of securities at a fixed price specified by the client. All such limit price orders are checked for certain validations. The limit price should be in multiples of tick size and within the days minimum/maximum price range. Otherwise, the order will be rejected by the system automatically.

## CARRY OVER OR BADLA TRANSACTIONS

Carry over or badla refers to the postponement of the settlement of a transaction till the next settlement period. It is nothing but a facility to carry forward the transaction from one settlement period to another. The scrips in specified categories alone could be carried forward. In fact, it is a kind of concession given to the speculator by the other party. It involves payment of some charge known as 'Badla charge' by the speculator. Badla charges are fixed on the basis of demand and supply conditions in the market and they are fixed on a fortnightly basis. Hence, these rates could vary in different settlement periods.

To effect Badla transactions, two bargains have to be made. The first one is to cancel out the original transaction by squaring it up. The cancelling transaction is effected at making up price which is determined by the authorities of the stock exchanges concerned. The making up price is generally the closing quotation for the security in question in the current settlement.

The second one is to reopen the original bargain for settlement on the next settlement day. For example, a bull speculator wants to carry forward his purchase position to the next settlement.

(*i*) First, he has to reverse his purchase position in the current settlement by entering into a sale transaction at the making up price. He pays or receives the difference between the contract price and the making up price as the case may be.

(*ii*) Secondly, he creates a fresh purchase position for the next settlement. For allowing the bull to defer the bargain till the next settlement, the other party will make a charge. This charge is called 'Contango charge'. The bull does so in the expectation of a rise in price in the next settlement. Thus, contango charge is nothing but the amount paid by a bull speculator to the other party usually a bear for obtaining a 'carry over' (badla) of his purchase agreement to the next settlement. Sometimes, badlawalas may advance money to finance the purchase of securities by the bull. In such a case, interest has to be paid and such interest is also called 'Contango'.

In the same way, a bear speculator may like to carry forward his sale position to the next settlement. In such a case:

(*i*) First, he has to reverse his sale position in the current settlement by entering into a purchase transaction at the making up price. He pays or receives the difference between the contract price and the making up price as the case may be.

(*ii*) Secondly, he enters into a fresh contract for the resale of securities and thus creates a fresh sale position for the next settlement. This is done in expectation of a fall in the price of securities during the next settlement period. For this, the bear has to pay a certain charge called 'Backwardation charge'. Thus, backwardation refers to the amount paid by a bear to facilitate him to renew a bargain until the next settlement date. Now, badla transactions have been banned.

### ❖ Badla and short selling

Indeed, badla transactions facilitate short selling. Short sellers are those who sell shares without owning them. They create scope for more investment. Their presence is also vital for the smooth functioning of a stock exchange provided they act within their limits. Selling too heavily without owning securities is also dangerous if it exceeds a particular limit. In a falling market, short sellers have to purchase to cover their sales position and it automatically arrests a fall in security prices and *vice versa*. At present, short selling has been permitted from December 2007 onwards. The delivery of securities at the time of settlement has been made mandatory. No marked short selling is permitted.

### ❖ Badla and stock lending

Badla transactions require financing managements. Bulls and bears require finance to cover their position till the next settlement date. Moreover, stock lending is vital for effecting short selling. Hence, these speculators either borrow from the money market or approach the stock financiers for this purpose.

### ❖ SEBI guidelines

Though badla transactions have the effect of expanding the market and providing liquidity to the market, very often they lead to high speculative activity and larger volatility in the stock market. Hence, it was banned by the SEBI since December 1993. However, it has announced a modified forward trading system which is effective from October 9, 1995. The important features of the revised Forward Trading System are the following:

(*i*) Each individual broker must have a capital adequacy norm of 3 per cent and it is 6 per cent for each institutional broker. This must be complied with *w.e.f.* April 1, 1996.

(*ii*) The limit of 25 per cent of the turnover imposed on carry forward deals has been removed due to the implementation of capital adequacy norms.

(*iii*) Transactions can be carried forward for a maximum period of 90 days. But, squaring off is permitted up to a maximum of five settlements only (For each settlement, 15 days and altogether 75 days only). Beyond this stipulated period, transactions have to be settled by actual delivery or payment as the case may be.

(*iv*) The graded margin of 20 per cent to 50 per cent of carry forward position has been dispensed with. Instead, a flat margin of 15 per cent marked to market has been fixed on a weekly basis as recommended by the Patel Committee.

(*v*) This margin for carry forward transactions can vary according to market sentiments. For example, a higher margin can be insisted upon if the price of the securities goes up and *vice versa*. In the case of volatile scrips, the margin can go up to 100 per cent.

(*vi*) Brokers are allowed self-certification on their status on settlements subject to recheck by the SEBI. There is no monthly audit as recommended by the Patel Committee.

(*vii*) There is no need to publish the carry forward position of each broker scrip-wise before the commencement of each carry forward session.

(*viii*) Stock exchanges can allow carry forward transactions only after getting necessary permission from the SEBI. Permission will be generally granted only if the stock exchange concerned has screen-based trading, and other infrastructural facilities.

Meanwhile, the Government of India appointed another committee under the chairmanship of J.S. Varma to go into the question of carry forward system in July 1997. This committee has made the following recommendations:

(*i*) Capital adequacy norms and other prudential safeguards with regard to carry forwards should be strictly enforced.

(*ii*) Scrips chosen for carry forward must be having sufficient floating stock.

(*iii*) The maximum period of 90 days allowed for carry forwards shall be eliminated.

(*iv*) Similarly, the maximum period of 75 days allowed for squaring off shall be eliminated.

(*v*) The limit of ₹ 10 crores fixed on the financier funding shall be relaxed.

(*vi*) Instead of a flat margin of 5 per cent, a uniform margin of 10 per cent of the gross position with a daily marking to market prices shall be maintained.

(*vii*) The segregation of carry forward trades and delivery trades shall be abolished.

## GENUINE TRADING vs. SPECULATIVE TRADING

Investors can deal with stock exchange securities either for a genuine trading purpose or for the purpose of speculative trading. Genuine investors generally give/take delivery of shares with no intention to postpone the settlement to the next period. Their primary motive is to get long-term gains. On the other hand, speculators do not take/give delivery of shares. They deal in differences in the purchase and sale prices. Their main intention is to carry forward the transactions and get short-term gains due to price differences.

## KINDS OF SPECULATORS

As stated earlier, buyers and sellers of stock exchange securities have to act through authorised brokers only. A broker is, thus, an intermediary between buyers and sellers of securities. Brokers have to represent their clients who may be individuals, institutions like companies, banks and other financial institutions, mutual funds, trusts, etc. These clients may trade in securities either for speculative purpose or for genuine purpose. It all depends upon their intention to take/give delivery of securities or just to carry forward and gain the difference in prices.

The stock brokers are the main players in the secondary market. There are various categories of brokers as listed below:

(i) **Client brokers:** These brokers do simple brokering business by acting as intermediaries between the buyers and sellers and they earn only brokerage for their services rendered to the clients.

(ii) **Floor brokers:** Floor brokers refer to those authorised clerks and sub-brokers who enter the trading floor and execute orders for their clients or for members. They have to be physically present in the trading ring and transact the business on behalf of their clients.

(iii) **Jobbers/taravaniwallas:** Jobbers are those brokers who specialise in selected scrips. They are called taravaniwallas and they are wholesalers doing both buying and selling in selected scrips only. They are ready to buy and sell simultaneously in selected scrips by quoting both bid and offer prices to the brokers and the sub-brokers on the trading floor. They earn profit through the margin between buying and selling rates.

(iv) **Badla financiers/badliwallas:** Badliwallas are those members whose main function is to give finance for carry forward deals in specified securities in return for interest. This interest is called badla rate. They also lend securities for the brokers who have oversold at the time of settlement. Carry forward transactions are facilitated by these financiers.

(v) **Arbitrageurs:** Arbitragers are those brokers who buy securities in one market and sell them in another market to take advantage of the price differences prevailing in different markets for the same scrips. Thus, they deal in inter-market transactions and get profits through differences in prices as between different markets.

(vi) **Bulls/tejiwallas:** Bulls are those brokers of a stock exchange who are very optimistic of the rise in prices of securities. Hence, they go on buying shares in expectation of selling them at higher prices later. Thus, in a bull market, there will be excess of purchases over sales.

**(vii) Bears/mandiwallas:** On the other hand, bears are those member brokers who are always pessimistic and they expect a fall in the prices of securities. Hence, they go on selling securities. They are known as mandiwallas and they go on selling securities in expectation of a fall in prices. Therefore, a bearish market refers to a falling market and there will be excess sales over purchases.

**(viii) Other speculators**

**(a) Stags:** Stags are those members who neither buy nor sell securities in the market. They simply apply for subscription to new issues expecting to sell them at a higher price later when such issues are quoted on the stock exchange. Generally, stags buy new issues and sell them on allotments or even before allotment for a profit. Since they act fast they are referred to as stags — a fast runner.

They can do this only in the grey market. Grey market is a market for dealing in unlisted securities and new issues before listing and deals in grey market are illegal. Grey deals take place outside the trading ring of the stock exchange and outside the trading hours. Yet grey market thrives in many new issues before listing and the quotation is given as premium over the issue price.

**(b) Wolves:** These are brokers who are fast speculators called wolves. These brokers are very quick to perceive changes in the trends of the market and trade fast and make a fast-buck. They are not generally caught in the wrong foot.

**(c) Lame ducks:** These are bear brokers who sell ultimately short by making wrong moves. Hence, they will lose in the market. Generally, they sell securities without having shares and therefore, they are caught in the wrong foot.

## SPECULATIVE TRANSACTIONS

The speculative activity in a stock exchange can be carried out through any one of the following transactions:

(*i*) Option dealing.
(*ii*) Wash sales.
(*iii*) Arbitrage.
(*iv*) Cornering.
(*v*) Rigging the market.
(*vi*) Blank transfers.
(*vii*) Margin trading.

### (i) Option dealing

As the very name implies, an option contract gives the option holder an option to buy or sell securities at a predetermined price on or before a specified date in future. The price so determined is called the 'strike price' or 'exercise price'.

When the option gives the option holder a right to buy securities at a predetermined price, it is called call option. On the other hand, when the option gives the option holder a right to sell securities at a predetermined price on or before a specified date in future, it is called Put Option.

When both rights are given to an option holder, it is called Double Option. When a speculator expects the price of a security to rise in future, he may purchase a call option. In such a case, he will be able to purchase the security at a lower price and sell it at a higher price which may be prevailing in the market at a future date. Suppose the price does not rise according to his expectation, he may not exercise his option. In that case, he has to pay only the premium called 'option money' and he cannot lose more than that amount. Thus, his risk is limited to that extent only; but his gain potential is unlimited (For a detailed study, refer to the Chapter Derivatives).

### ❖ Options for hedging

Options can be used for the purpose of hedging also. Hedging is a device through which one can protect himself against losses due to price fluctuations of securities. For instance, a bull speculator may agree to purchase certain securities at a certain price. At the same time, he may hedge himself by buying a 'put option' so that any loss that he may suffer while purchasing the securities as per his original contract may be compensated by the exercise of his 'put option'.

**(ii) Wash sales**

It is a device through which a speculator is able to reap huge profits by creating a misleading picture in the market. In other words, it is a kind of fictitious transaction in which a speculator sells a security and then buys the same at a higher price through another broker. Thus, he creates a false or misleading opinion in the market about the price of the security in question. As a result of such false opinion, the price records a further rise and the speculator is now able to get good profits by selling the securities to the public. It is purely in the interest of speculators, and hence, there is severe penalty for such sales.

**(iii) Arbitrage**

Arbitrage is undertaken to make profit out of the differences in prices of a security in two different markets. It is a highly skilled speculative activity. If the price of a certain security is higher in one market than in another, the speculator will purchase that security in the cheaper market with a view to selling it at a profit in another market and thereby to reap huge profits. The speculator has to act very quickly since the prices are highly sensitive and they may get equalised within a very short period. Since arbitrage involves carrying of a security from one market to another, it is also described as 'traffic in securities'. Such a traffic may be carried on between two markets within the country or in two different countries. The former one is called 'domestic arbitrage' and the latter 'foreign arbitrage'. Ultimately, arbitraging has the effect of equalising the prices of a security at different places, and thus, it is beneficial to the market.

**(iv) Cornering**

Cornering refers to the process of holding the entire supply of a particular security by an individual or a group of individuals with a view to dictating terms to the short-sellers and earning more profits. When the entire or a major share of supply of a particular security is held by an individual or group of persons, the short-sellers (*i.e.*, bears) who have contracted to sell the security without actually possessing it, would be unable to deliver it to the buyers, who have cornered the market. In such a case, the buyers will be able to dictate terms to the short-sellers and get good profits. In a technical sense, the short-sellers will be 'squeezed' through cornering. It is also a prohibited activity.

**(v) Rigging the market**

Rigging refers to the process of creating an artificial condition in the market, whereby the market value of a particular security is pushed up. It is due to a strong bull movement as a result of which the demands of the buyers push up the price. Speculators holding bulk of such securities buy and sell to 'make a market' and finally sell their holdings gradually to get huge profits when the prices rule high in the market. It is also not a desirable activity since it prevents the free interplay of demand and supply.

**(vi) Blank transfers**

Blank transfers facilitate speculative activities through carry over or badla transactions. When the transferor (seller) simply signs the transfer form without specifying the name of the transferee (buyer) it is called 'blank transfer'. Badla transactions involve temporary purchases and sales of securities. If they have to be registered, it involves a lot of inconveniences due to registration fees, stamp duty, etc. To avoid this, blank transfers are increasingly used in carry over transactions.

Blank transfer is also an undesirable activity due to the following risks:

(*i*) If the shares are partly paid-up, the seller's liability for the uncalled portion continues even after he has actually sold them. It is not justifiable.

(*ii*) The 'blank transferee' escapes from the payment of stamp duty, transfer fees, etc. which means a loss of revenue to the government.

(*iii*) The 'blank transferees' name is not disclosed. So, he can evade income tax also.

(*iv*) It also enables the 'blank transferees' to gain control of the management of companies without actually disclosing their names.

(*v*) The blank transferee's name will not be recorded in the register of companies. So, the registers are incomplete and they give a misleading information to prospective investors.

(*vi*) Registered shares are made freely negotiable through blank transfers. So, it encourages unhealthy speculation. Due to these unhealthy consequences, blank transfers are not prohibited.

**(vii) Margin trading**

Margin trading is carried on by the clients with funds borrowed from their brokers. It is a popular method of speculative trading. Under this method, the client opens an account with his broker. He makes a deposit of cash or securities in this account. He also agrees to maintain a minimum margin of amount always in his account. When a broker purchases securities on behalf of his client, his account will be debited and *vice versa*. The debit balance, if any, is automatically secured by the client's securities lying with the broker. In case it falls short of the minimum agreed amount, the client has to deposit further amount into his account or he has to deposit further securities. If the prices are favourable, the client may instruct his broker to sell the securities. When such securities are sold, his account will be credited. The client may have a bigger margin now for further purchases. It is not an undesirable activity since it acts as a check against excessive speculation. It is so because fresh purchases have to be supported by fresh deposits unless there is excessive margin in the account. It rarely happens. Moreover, the broker's investment is safe since it is backed by client's securities.

## STOCK INDICES

A stock market index is one which indicates the pattern of movements of the prices of a group of securities which are considered to be the representative sample of the entire stock market. The stock market index is an invaluable guide to study the trend of growth patterns in the economy, to analyse as well as forecast business cycles and also to correlate stock market indices to various economic activities.

The stock market index is a convenient and effective product due to the following reasons:

(*i*) It acts as a barometer for market behaviour.

(*ii*) It is used to benchmark portfolio performance.

(*iii*) It helps to allocate scarce resources to the best performed companies reflected through best performed scrips.

(*iv*) It is used as a forecasting tool to predict the future movement of stock indices and also the business cycles.

(*v*) It is used in derivative instruments like index futures and index options.

(*vi*) It can be used for passive fund management as in the case of index funds.

### ❖ Stock indices of BSE and NSE

**Indices of BSE**

**(i) Sensex:** The stock index which is very popular in BSE is Sensex. It is otherwise called BSE Sensitive Index. The base year for this index is April 79. It was launched on 2nd January, 1986. The BSE Sensex is a value-weighted index composed of originally 30 companies representing various sectors on the exchange. At present, all scrips are selected from specified groups only. This index is available online and it is updated continuously.

**(ii) BSE national index:** This index is made up of 100 scrips with 1982-84 as the base year. The special feature of this index is that it includes prices of scrips in other major stock exchanges of Delhi, Calcutta, Ahmedabad and Madras. In such a case, the average price of the scrip is taken for the compilation of the index.

**(iii) BSE 200:** It was introduced in May 1994 with 1989-90 as the base year. This index consists of equity shares of 200 companies selected on the basis of market capitalisation, volume of turnover and strength of the companies' fundamentals. It comprises of scrips of both specified and non-specified groups.

**(iv) Dollex:** It is nothing but BSE-200 expressed in Dollar values so that it may be useful to foreign investors. In Dollex, the BSE-200 is modified by dividing the current rupee market value by Rupee-Dollar Conversion Rate.

**(v) BSE-500:** It was introduced in 1999 with the base year 1999 itself. It is treated to be a standard index covering all sections of the economy as well as the major part of capitalisation.

### ❖ 'IPO Index'

The Bombay Stock Exchange (BSE) has launched IPO Index, the first of its kind in India recently. This index aims at tracking the value of companies for two years from the date of their listing after their initial public offers. According to BSE, IPOs of companies with a free float market capitalisation of INR 100 crores and above on its first day of listing would be included in the index. Follow-on public offers would be excluded from it. Some of the internationally prominent IPO indices are Dow Jones STOXX IPO Index, FTSE Renaissance IPO Index, NYSE IPO Composite Index and Bloomberg IPO Index.

### ❖ Green index — BSE Greenex

This is the first index which is based on actual performance in the energy efficiency front. It has been co-developed with gTrade, a domestic sustainability firm working on financial innovations in energy efficiency. This index gives equal weightage to both energy efficiency and profitability. From BSE 100, 20 companies have been picked up. This index is targeted at retail as well as institutional investors who look for investments in companies with strong long-term prospects and develop green financial products. In fact companies that are able to balance energy efficiency and profitability give better returns for investors.

### ❖ Carbon index

The BSE has also launched Carbon index with the objective of offering investors expertise in analysing the risks and opportunities associated with climate change and with carbon regulation. Initially, all companies in the BSE top 100 will be eligible for inclusion in the carbon index. This index is very useful to investors to mitigate their exposure to financial risks associated with climate change.

## INDICES OF NSE

The common and popular name of the NSE index is CNX index. All NSC indices are prepared by the India Index Services and Products Ltd. (IISL) which is a joint venture of NSE, CRISIL and Standard & Poor. The CNX stands for the following:

C stands for CRISIL

N stands for NSE

X stands for Index

Addition of the letters S&P with any index indicates that it is supported by Standard and Poor also.

### ❖ Major CNX Indices

(i) **S&P CNX Nifty:** It is a popular index of NSE. It was introduced in April 96 with 96 as the base year. It comprises of a well-diversified 50 stock index accounting for 23 sectors of the economy. Of the total traded value of all stocks on the NSE, the total value of Nifty stocks is about 70 per cent and Nifty stocks represent about 59 per cent of the total market capitalisation.

(ii) **S&P CNX Diety:** It is nothing but S&P CNX Nifty expressed in dollars and hence, it is basically a dollar-dominated index. This is mainly intended for foreign investors. It is computed at Online Rupee-Dollar exchange rate.

**(iii) CNX Nifty Junior:** This index was launched in December 1996 and S&P CNX Nifty and CNX Nifty Junior together account for 100 most liquid stocks in India. The two indices are synchronised so that they will always operate as disjoint sets in the sense that a stock will never appear in both indices at the same time.

**(iv) S&P CNX 500 Equity Index:** It comprises of 500 stocks covering 79 industries. It is purely a market capitalisation weighted index. It covers 97 per cent of the total turnover in BSE and 73 per cent of the total market capitalisation.

**(v) CNX Midcap 200 Index:** As the very name implies, it is the index for the stocks of midcap companies, covering industries having market capitalisation between ₹ 150 crores and ₹ 1,000 crores.

**(vi) CNX Segment Indices:** This index reflects the stock market performance of the various segments of the Indian corporate sector like multinationals, PSUs, etc.

**(vii) NSE Government Security Index:** This index is meant for all Government of India Bonds issued after April 1992 but redeemable after 1997. The base date of the index is 1st January, 1997. This index is calculated on daily basis with the help of market capitalisation. New issues are added to the index while the old ones could be removed as soon as they are redeemed.

## ❖ Rebranding of Indices

The NSE indices have been rebranded with 'Nifty' as pre fix from November 9, 2015 onwards. For example, CNX Nifty will hereafter be called 'Nifty 50'. Similarly, Nifty Junior has become 'Nifty Next 50' and CNX IT has become 'Nifty IT' and so on. Today, the Nifty family has around 50 indices and it has become the barometer for the Indian stock market. Nifty has also become a global brand gaining high credibility.

The indices of BSE have also been rebranded with 'S&P' as pre fix. The major rebranded indices of BSE are:

- S&P BSE Sensex
- S&P BSE 100
- S&P BSE 200
- S&P BSE Midcap
- S&P BSE Smallcap

The overall performance of the Indian equity markets is displayed in the following Table 4.2.

**TABLE 4.2: OVERALL PERFORMANCE OF INDIAN SECONDARY MARKET**

*(Amount in ₹Crores)*

| *Item* | *2020-21* | | *2021-22 (P)* | |
|---|---|---|---|---|
| | *Number* | *Amount* | *Number* | *Amount* |
| 1 | 2 | 3 | 4 | 5 |
| **II. Secondary Market** | | | | |
| **BSE** | | | | |
| Sensex: End Period | 49,509.2 | | 58,568.5 | |
| Period Average | 40,826.4 | | 55,774.6 | |
| Price Earnings Ratio @ | 34.4 | | 25.8 | |
| Market Capitalisation to GDP ratio (%) | 103.2 | | 111.7 | |
| Turnover Cash Segment | | 10,45,089.5 | | 13,38,225.3 |
| Turnover Equity Derivatives Segment | | 3,50,60,169.0 | | 6,60,78,327.8 |
| **NSE** | | | | |
| Nifty 50: End Period | 14,690.7 | | 17,464.8 | |
| Period Average | 12,016.9 | | 16,662.7 | |
| Price Earnings Ratio @ | 33.2 | | 22.9 | |
| Market Capitalisation to GDP ratio (%) | 102.5 | | 110.7 | |
| Turnover Cash Segment | | 1,53,97,908.2 | | 1,65,66,257.4 |
| Turnover Equity Derivatives Segment | | 64,36,18,108.1 | | 1,69,52,33,134.5 |

.....: Nil. P: Provisional (for 2021-22). #: Net of redemptions. @: As at end of the period.
***Note:*** Figures in the columns might not add up to the total due to rounding of numbers.
***Source:*** SEBI, NSE, BSE, various merchant bankers and RBI staff calculations.
***Source:*** RBI Annual Report, 2022.

## DEFECTS OF INDIAN STOCK/CAPITAL MARKET

The Indian stock market is suffering from many limitations. Some of the important ones are the following:

**(i) Absence of genuine investors**

As it is, speculative activities outplay the genuine trading activities. Very negligible fraction of transactions represent purchases or sales by genuine investors. Most of the transactions are carry forward transactions with a speculative motive of deriving benefit from short-term price fluctuations. Speculators are only interested in taking a bet on the stock and profiting from its price swings. Hence the market is not subject to free interplay of demand and supply for securities. It is reported that approximately ₹ 3,000 crores is traded between the Bombay Stock Exchange and the National Stock Exchange every day. Investors buying and selling existing holdings contribute a very small portion of this. Almost 85 per cent is contributed by speculators.

**(ii) Presence of price rigging**

There is a tendency among companies issuing securities to artificially push up the prices before the issue of securities. This is generally done by buying and selling securities by a few group of persons among themselves and thereby pushing the prices up. There is a strong bull movement in the market.

**(iii) Prevalence of insider trading**

Insider trading has been accepted as a routine practice in India. Insiders are those who have access to unpublished price-sensitive information by virtue of their position in the company and who use such information in their best advantage. Since it is an undesirable activity, the SEBI has introduced many regulations to curb insider trading. All of them remain in paper only and it is said that controlling insider trading is similar to controlling black money.

**(iv) Lack of liquidity**

Though there are approximately 7,800 listed companies in India, the shares of only a few companies are actively traded in the market and they are liquid. It is reported that of the total turnover on the BSE and the NSE, over 60 per cent is concentrated in just 10 stocks. Again, more than 60 per cent trading is confined to five cities: Delhi Mumbai, Ahmedabad, Chennai and Kolkata. Moreover, 25 brokers account for more than 40 per cent of trading volumes. Hence, investors of many companies are on the horns of a dilemma on account of lack of liquidity. A vast majority of the shares are illiquid and hence investors of such companies' shares have to burn their hand.

A study recently points out that shares of 207 companies were traded every day; shares of 538 companies were traded once a week; shares of 396 companies were traded once a fortnight; shares of 954 companies were traded once a month; and shares of 959 companies were traded once a year. It clearly shows that the Indian stock market is suffering from poor liquidity. Another study points out that out of 8,000 and odd companies listed hardly 400 to 600 companies are well traded. It means that in nearly 90 per cent of the companies, there is no liquidity as the market is not developed in them.

**(v) Scarcity of floating securities**

To add fuel to the fire, there is scarcity of floating securities in the market. It is due to the fact that institutional investors who collectively own nearly 75 per cent of the equity capital in the private sector, retain their holdings with themselves without offering them for trading. On the other hand, the individual investors too are not exposed to wider portfolio investment. They have sticky portfolio habits. Hence, the market is highly volatile and it is subject to easy price manipulations.

Shri Paul Joseph's study reveals that nearly 75 per cent of the inadequately traded companies have a paid-up capital of less than ₹ 3 crores and their public holding is poor. Nearly 80 per cent of the thinly-traded companies have public holding of less than 60 per cent of the paid-up equity. In the bulk of these companies, there are less than 10,000 shareholders on the Registers. The holding of the promoters and financial institutions is so heavy that no public interest exists. Hence trading cannot take place.

To make matters worse, there is inadequate supply of good scrips leading to supply and demand imbalances.

**(vi) Lack of transparency**

Though many regulations have been introduced to inject transparency to the operations of stock market, they are not successful. Many brokers are violating the regulations with a view to cheat the innocent investing community. While the day's opening, high, low and closing prices are reported, no information is available to investors regarding the volume of transactions carried out at the highest and lowest prices. The time taken to execute a transaction is also not reported.

**(vii) Poor response of Indian households**

At present there is lack of confidence of genuine investors in the stock market. An analysis of the portfolio of Indian households reveals the poor response to the securities of companies.

Capital markets, including mutual funds, account for merely 3-4 per cent of total household savings reflecting a lack of investment culture in India. Even today, a very negligible percentage goes to household saving in shares and debentures as revealed in the following Table.

**TABLE 4.3: FINANCIAL SAVING OF THE HOUSEHOLD SECTOR**

*(Per cent of GNDI)*

| *Item* | *2015-16* | *2016-17* | *2017-18* | *2018-19* | *2019-20* | *2020-21* |
|---|---|---|---|---|---|---|
| 1 | 2 | 3 | 4 | 5 | 6 | 7 |
| **A. Gross Financial Saving** | **10.7** | **10.4** | **11.9** | **11.8** | **11.7** | **15.5** |
| *of which:* | | | | | | |
| 1. Currency | 1.4 | –2.1 | 2.8 | 1.4 | 1.4 | 1.9 |
| 2. Deposits | 4.6 | 6.3 | 3.0 | 4.2 | 4.2 | 6.3 |
| 3. Shares and Debentures | 0.2 | 1.1 | 1.0 | 0.4 | 0.4 | 0.5 |
| 4. Claims on Government | 0.5 | 0.7 | 0.9 | 1.1 | 1.3 | 1.6 |
| 5. Insurance Funds | 1.9 | 2.3 | 2.0 | 2.0 | 1.8 | 2.6 |
| 6. Provident and Pension Funds | 2.1 | 2.1 | 2.1 | 2.1 | 2.2 | 2.5 |
| **B. Financial Liabilities** | **2.7** | **3.0** | **4.3** | **4.0** | **3.9** | **4.0** |
| **C. Net Financial Saving (A – B)** | **7.9** | **7.3** | **7.5** | **7.8** | **7.9** | **11.5** |

GNDI: Gross National Disposable Income.
***Note:*** Figures may not add up to total due to rounding off.
***Source:*** NSO.
***Source:*** RBI Annual Report, 2022.

**(viii) High volatility of stock market**

For instance, the volatile variation in the S&P BSE Sensex is displayed in the following Table:

**TABLE 4.4: S&P BSE SENSEX DATA**

| **Year** | **Open** | **High** | **Low** | **Close** |
|---|---|---|---|---|
| 2020-21 | 29468.49 | 52516.76 | 27500.79 | 49509.15 |
| 2021-22 | 49509.15 | 62245.43 | 47204.50 | 58568.51 |
| 2022-23 | 58568.51 | 62052.57 | 50921.22 | 61418.96 |

***Source:*** www.bseindia.com

This high rate of volatility is not conducive for the smooth functioning of the stock market.

**(ix) Cumbersome procedures of settlement**

Trade transactions have to be settled by physical delivery of securities accompanied by transfer deeds. It means that securities have to move from the seller to the seller's broker and from the buyer's broker to the buyer. It makes the settlement dilatory. Again the buyer has to lodge the securities for transfer. This process takes two or three months. The irksome settlement procedures result in frequent delays in payment for shares as well.

**(x) Problem of odd lots**

Generally, the listed securities are included under Group A or Group B categories as stated earlier. The other tradable securities which are not listed are called 'odd lots' and they come under the category of Group C. This group also contains permitted securities which are listed on other exchanges and not on the particular stock exchange concerned.

Investors in India have to face the problem of odd lots. Generally, as per the existing practice, all sales of odd lots are subject to discounts varying up to 15 per cent and all purchases are subject to a premia of 15 per cent or even more. It means that the investor is a tremendous loser. It discourages investments on odd lots and thereby limiting the trading activities of odd lots.

**(xi) Dominance of financial institutions**

Few financial institutions like the UTI, LIC and GIC dominate the Indian stock market scene. Hence, the Indian stock market is significantly influenced by the actions of these few institutions. It actually reduces the level of competition in the stock market which is not a healthy trend for the growth of any stock market.

**(xii) Lack of professionalism**

On the one hand, one can find highly competent and professional brokers playing an active and positive role in the market. On the other hand, many brokers are found to be lacking in high professional standards. Brokers with little skill or experience enter into big contracts. Therefore, defaults become quite common. Kerb trading is also quite common.

The high membership fees imposed by stock exchanges stand as a hindrance to qualified professionals to participate in stock market operations. For instance, the NSE used to charge ₹ 1.3 crores for new membership and insist ₹ 1 crore for net worth. However, with the entry of MCX stock exchange, the membership fee has been reduced to ₹ 30 lakh and it is being followed by BSE.

**(xiii) High trading cost**

Transaction costs on Indian stock exchanges are found to be between two and thirty-eight times more for cash and derivative segments when compared with the average figures for leading stock exchanges in the world. High trading costs automatically discourage domestic traders apart from forcing foreign investors to migrate to cheaper trading platforms in other emerging countries.

**(xiv) Lack of developed debt market**

In India, for a common investor, capital market means equity investments only reflecting his ignorance about the role of debt market. In fact, debt instruments and debt related derivatives are major drivers of global stock markets where equities account for only 10-20 per cent of the trading activities. The development of debt markets would ease corporate financing and funding of large infrastructure projects in the country. In India, mostly, institutional investors play a significant role in the wholesale government securities and that too only for their statutory liquidity requirements.

**(xv) Unhealthy competition of merchant bankers**

At present, there are about 900 merchant bankers rendering their services in the capital market. The increase in the number of merchant bankers has led to unhealthy competition and dilution of the quality of issues. Merchant bankers tend to show a definite bias towards the issuing company instead of protecting the interest of investors. They help the unscrupulous promoters to raise funds for dubious projects at unjustifiable premium. The ultimate sufferers are the investors.

**(xvi) Other defects**

The investor's apathy to stock exchanges is clearly visible due to their loss of confidence. There are many reasons for this. There is considerable delay in refunding application money, issuing of allotment letters, posting of share certificates etc. It takes more than 6 months to effect transfer of shares. Bad deliveries, loss of certificates, etc. are quite common. No immediate action is generally taken on investor's complaints. To make matters worse, the Investors' Association in India is still a weak body.

## RECENT DEVELOPMENTS

Many steps have been taken in recent years to reform the secondary market so that it may function efficiently and effectively. Steps are also being taken to broaden the market and make it function with greater degree of transparency and in the best interest of investors. Some of the developments in this direction are the following:

**(i) Regulation of intermediaries**

To improve the functioning of intermediaries in the capital market, strict control is being exercised on them by SEBI. The intermediaries such as merchant bankers, underwriters, brokers, sub-brokers, bankers to the issue etc. must be registered with the SEBI. It is proposed that the registration should be subject to renewal from time-to-time instead of making it a permanent one. SEBI has powers to suspend them after conducting an enquiry. It is also planning to conduct examinations to them. To improve their financial adequacy, capital adequacy norms have been fixed. Brokers are expected to maintain a minimum capital of ₹ 5 lakh in major exchanges and ₹ 2 lakh in minor exchanges. Again, they have to keep a minimum net worth of 8 per cent of the annual turnover.

**(ii) Change in the management structure**

In the early periods, the boards of stock exchanges were dominated by brokers whose decisions were not fair and transparent. The SEBI now requires that 50 per cent of the directors must be non-broker directors or Government representatives. Further, it is obligatory that a non-broker professional shall be appointed as the executive director.

**(iii) Insistence of quality securities**

For efficient and active functioning of a stock exchange, quality securities are absolutely essential. Realising this fact, the SEBI has announced recently revised norms for companies accessing the capital market so that only quality securities are listed and traded in stock exchanges. For instance, dividend payment condition (dividend payment for at least 3 years out of the immediately preceding 5 years of issue) has been laid down for companies to go for public issue. Again, participation of financial institutions in the capital is essential for entry into the capital market. These measures ensure that only quality securities enter into the market.

**(iv) Prohibition of insider trading**

Insiders can easily enter into manipulative dealings against the interest of the public on the basis of any unpublished price-sensitive information available to them because of their position in the company. Now, there is a ban on insider trading and hence, an insider is prevented from dealing in securities of any listed company on the basis of any unpublished price-sensitive information.

Now, SEBI (Insider Trading) Amendment Regulations, 2002 have been formed giving more powers to SEBI to curb insider trading. The government now seems to think that defining insider trading in the SEBI Act itself will make it more strongly enforceable in a court of law.

SEBI draft regulation points out that short-term profit from any transactions made by an insider will have to be surrendered to the company. Insiders are management personnel, *i.e.*, directors and officers of the company who are beneficial owners of 10 per cent or more of any class of equity shares.

**(v) Transparency of accounting practices**

To ensure correct pricing mechanism and wider participation, all attempts are being taken to achieve transparency in trading and accounting procedures. Brokers are asked to show their prices, brokerage, service tax, etc. separately in the contract notes and their accounts. Of course, the service tax is collected from the clients and paid to the government.

**(vi) Strict supervision of stock market operations**

The Ministry of Finance and the SEBI supervise the operations in stock exchanges very strictly. The SEBI monitors the operations of stock exchanges very closely with a view to ensuring that the dealings are conducted in the best interest of the overall financial environment in the country in general and the investors in particular. Strict rules have been framed with regard to recognition of stock exchanges, membership, management, maintenance of accounts, etc. Further, stock exchanges have been asked to subject the broker accounts, to better inspection and audit. Sometimes, the SEBI itself organises such inspection of broker firms and their accounts. Again, stock exchanges are inspected by the officers of the SEBI from time-to-time. Any violation of rules and regulations involves penalties immediately.

**(vii) Prevention of price rigging**

Greater powers have been given to SEBI under SEBI (Prohibition of Fraudulent and Unfair Trade Practices Relating to Security Markets) Regulations, 1995 to curb price rigging. In fact, the SEBI exercised its powers in 1996 for the first time by issuing show-cause notices to the various parties — promoters, brokers and clients involved in price rigging. Further, certain procedural changes have been planned in the auction route to curb price rigging. Thus, all efforts are being taken to protect the interest of genuine investors.

**(viii) Encouragement of market-making**

There is greater transparency in the dealings of market-makers and the securities with market-makers command higher level of liquidity. Market-makers offer two-way quotations one for purchase price and the other for sale price in respect of the same security. They have to comply with many rules and regulations strictly with regard to minimum number of scrips for market-making, timely payment of margins, adequate financial strength, adequate turnover, etc. Hence, market-making has been made compulsory on OTCEI at least for a period of 18 months from the date of opening of the offer by the sponsors or designated member. Moreover, companies seeking listing, with paid-up capital ranging between ₹ 3 crores and ₹ 5 crores and without a track record of commercial production of at least 2 years, shall have to appoint market- makers compulsorily. Again, there is a provision for voluntary market-making on OTCEI. Market-making is also encouraged in other stock exchanges as well in order to develop healthy practices in the market.

**(ix) Discouragement of price manipulations**

The SEBI is taking all steps to prevent price manipulations in all stock exchanges. It has instructed all stock exchanges to keep special margins in addition to the normal ones on the scrips which are subject to wide price fluctuations. The SEBI itself insists upon a special margin of 25 per cent or more (in addition to the regular margin) on purchases of scrips which are subject to sharp rise in price. This margin money should be retained by the stock exchange concerned for a period of one to three months. All stock exchanges have been directed to suspend trading in a scrip in case any one of the stock exchanges suspends trading in that scrip for more than a day due to price manipulation or fluctuation. Suspension of trading in a scrip can be done indefinitely in concurrence with the SEBI.

**(x) Protection of investors' interest**

Much importance is given to protect the interest of investors by instructing the exchanges to take timely action for the redressal of their grievances. For this purpose, the SEBI issues 'Investors' Guidance Services' to guide and educate the investors about grievances and remedies available apart from giving information about various investment avenues, their merits, tax benefits available, illegal transactions, etc. Disciplinary Action Committees have been set up in each stock exchange to take up complaints against companies, brokers, etc. All efforts have been taken to make this committee function effectively and efficiently with better representation. Stock exchanges have been instructed to enlarge their panel of arbitrators so as to dispose of all the pending arbitration cases very speedily. The SEBI itself takes up complaints against companies, brokers, etc.

With a view to give more details of accounts and other related matters, the SEBI has revised the required disclosure guidelines. Accordingly, the prospectus and abridged prospectus should contain additional details on accounts such as details of public or rights issue made in the preceding 3 years, tax implication, *i.e.*, book depreciation and tax depreciation, important accounting ratios, significant accounting policies, loss of market share, other ventures promoted by the same company, etc.

Moreover, the SEBI has issued specific guidelines to deal with bad deliveries. For instance, in the case of bad deliveries on account of fake or stolen shares, the responsibility should be on the introducing broker and the exchange should file a case and take action against that broker immediately. Similarly, selling brokers are bound to rectify or replace defective share transfer deeds if they are returned under objection after book closure.

Again, each stock exchange is under a legal obligation to create an Investor Protection Fund. The main objective of this fund is to compensate the investors for losses suffered by them due to default on the part of stock exchanges. An investor can claim up to ₹ 1 lakh from major exchanges and up to ₹ 50,000 from others.

Investors have been permitted to form associations and register them under the SEBI. These associations are expected to promote the interest of investors by increasing their awareness about various investments, dealings in stock exchange, illegal transactions, etc., and also by taking timely action for the redressal of their grievances. Nearly 27 Investors' Associations have been registered with the SEBI so far.

Recently, steps are being taken to connect 14 regional stock exchanges under the name of Interconnected Stock Exchange of India. This is attempted with a view to enhancing the investor information as well as efficiency in the market.

**(xi) Free pricing of securities**

A new era in the capital market has begun with the process of liberalisation started from June 1991 onwards. In May 1992, the Capital Issues Control Act was abolished and the functions of the Controller of Capital Issues were entrusted to SEBI. Now, any company is free to enter the capital market to raise the necessary capital at any price that it wants. Thus, a new era of free capital market has ushered in.

Very recently, the SEBI has permitted companies to issue shares below the face value of ₹ 10 and liberalised the norms for initial public offerings. This is mainly to permit companies with intrinsic value of shares below ₹ 10 to tap the market at a low price. Even existing companies can split up their shares accordingly.

**(xii) Freeing of interest rates**

Interest rates on debentures and on PSU bonds were freed in August 1991 with a view to raising funds from the capital market at attractive rates depending on the credit rating. Companies can now offer any rate to the public and mobilise the savings.

**(xiii) Setting up of credit rating agencies**

Credit rating agencies have been set up for awarding credit rating to the money market instruments, debt instruments, deposits and even to equity shares also. Now, all debt instruments must be compulsorily credit rated by a credit rating agency so that the investing public may not be deceived by financially unsound companies. It is a healthy trend towards a developed capital market.

**(xiv) Introduction of electronic trading**

The OTCEI has started its trading operations through the electronic media. Similarly, BSE switched over to electronic trading system in January 1995, called BOLT. Again, NSE went over to screen-based trading with a national network. Under this system, investment counters can be spread throughout the country under the electronic network. The buyers and sellers living apart from each other can trade in corporate securities through electronic media and through telephone/teller/computer in the case of OTC. Hence, there is a national market with no physical location, no trading ring, no stock exchange building, no hustle, and bustle scenes, etc. which are commonly found in conventional stock exchanges. So, many of the defects and deficiencies found in the present stock exchange market can be rectified through this electronic trading.

**(xv) Establishment of OTC/OTCEI/NSE**

Investors have to face many ordeals in the conventional stock exchanges. Delays in refunding application money, issuing of allotment letters, posting of share certificates are quite common. Trading in new issues prior to formal listing of such issues is also prevalent. Rigging up of prices before the flotation of new issues, manipulations of high premium on new issues are also rampant. To overcome many of such defects, OTC/OTCEI, and NSE have been established. The scope for manipulations, speculations and malpractices is very less if trading is shifted to OTC/OTCEI, etc. The OTC markets are fully automated exchanges where tradings could be carried out through a network of telephone/computers/tellers spread throughout the country. It is mainly intended for small investors who are unable to get a fair price. The NSE is for bigger companies with a wide network of shareholders. They have shorter settlement periods, *i.e.*, (T+ 2) and quicker payments and deliveries within a period of 7 to 14 days. It is also meant for venturesome and risky companies. Similarly, the OTCEI and all other stock exchanges have a screen-based trading with a nationwide market. Spot deals with full transparency, daily settlement system, ringless trading and greater liquidity are the important features of these markets. Thus, the introduction of many tiers to the structure of the securities market has broadened the capital market to a greater extent and it is a boon to all genuine investors.

**(xvi) Introduction of depository system**

To avoid bad delivery, forgery, theft, delay in settlement and to speed up the transfer of securities, the depository system has been approved by the Parliament on July 23, 1996. A depository is an organisation where the securities of a shareholder are held in the electronic form through a process of dematerialisation. The investor has to simply open an account with the depository through a depository participant. The account will be credited with the purchase of securities and debited with the sale of securities. There is no physical transfer of shares. Everything is done through electronic media. The depository system facilitates investors to hold securities in the electronic form rather than in physical form. Since the operations are computer linked, they are transparent, speedier, less speculative and cost-effective.

The SEBI has directed that all offer of public/rights issue/offer for sale should only be of 'dematerialised shares' in future. So, the investor will be compulsorily required to open a depository account with a Depository Participant (DP) for making an application. All DPs will act as collection agents. Applications have to be made only with cheques or bank drafts. Cash or stock invest will not be accepted. Hence, the stock invest scheme will have a natural death.

The allotment and credit of shares to the beneficiary account will be completed within 21 days from the date of closure of the issue. If it is not done, interest at 15 per cent is payable to the investors for the period of delay beyond 21 days. It is a welcome step indeed since the investors can be completely free from the worries of loss of certificates through theft, mutilation, etc., and it would promote investment to a greater extent.

**(xvii) Buyback of shares**

With a view to heavy fluctuations in the prices of shares and to adjusting the demand and supply of shares in the market, companies have been permitted to buy back their own shares. The Companies (Amendment) Ordinance, 1999 has been promulgated:

(*i*) Restricting buyback of shares to 25 per cent of the paid-up capital,

(*ii*) Imposing a limit on the usage of funds for the purpose of buyback to 25 per cent of the paid-up capital and free reserves, and

(*iii*) Restricting the further issue of the same securities within 24 months, after the buyback.

It is hoped that idle cash in the hands of one company will be channelled of another company having a pressing need and further it will be used to correct the valuation of their stock. However, the cash employed in buyback at the cost of investment plans could turn out to be a costly affair in the long run.

**(xviii) Disinvestment of shares of public sector units**

To bring down the government holding and to push up the privatisation process, the disinvestment programme has been implemented. This would also activate the capital market by increasing the availability of number of shares in the market for trading. A disinvestment commission has been established for this purpose. In spite of the steps taken, only 10 per cent of the government's disinvestment target has been achieved in the last 3 years. To speed up the process of disinvestment, the Ministry of Finance has proposed to set up a Special Purpose Vehicle (similar to the one available in the case of mutual Funds). Its sole objective would be to hold and sell public enterprise equity until Government ownership falls to 49 per cent in each public sector enterprise. There is a proposal for cross holdings by public sector units also. The Central Government has plans to raise ₹ 40,000 crores through disinvestment during 2010-11. This is the biggest target in the history of the disinvestment programme.

**(xix) Starting of Self-Regulatory Organisations (SROs)**

The SEBI is encouraging the starting of SROs for the purpose of implementing the SCRA, SEBI Act, Rules, Regulations and Guidelines issued by the government from time-to-time. This would reduce the work of the regulatory authorities. For this purpose, the SEBI is encouraging the various market intermediaries like merchant bankers, stock brokers, underwriters, mutual funds etc. to start organising themselves into SROs and to get recognition from the SEBI. For instance, the SEBI has granted recognition to the SRO of merchant bankers registered as the Association of Merchant Bankers of India (AMBI). This is the first SRO recognised by the SEBI. It is expected that more such SROs would come up in future. With the increasing SROs, the Stock Exchanges can emerge as Public Service Institutions catering to the increasing demands of investors in the country. SROs can be a valuable component to a market regulator in achieving the objectives of securities regulation.

The following SROs have been formed in India by various market participants:

1. Association of Merchant Bankers of India.
2. Association of Mutual Funds of India.
3. Registrars of Association of India.

The SROs monitor the functioning of their members with regard to compliance of laws, statutory regulations as well as their own code of conduct. Certain SROs also establish common professional standards to ensure uniformity in the functioning of their members.

The SROs assist SEBI in formulation of policies as well as various rules and regulations. Some SROs provide arbitration in case of disputes among their members. SROs also conduct professional development and training programme for their members.

Most of the SROs have a code of conduct for their members. All codes advise their members to observe the principles of fairness, integrity and ethics in business dealings. They are advised to ensure compliance with all the laws and regulations.

**(xx) Stock watch system**

The SEBI is contemplating to introduce a New Stock Watch System to trace out the source of undesirable trading if any in the market. The Stock Watch System simply works as a mathematical model which keeps a constant watch on the market movement. When the model is activated, certain parameters are put to work at once. It would bring to light automatically the scrips which are under alert. This alert list divides the scrips into three categories such as least bothersome, bothersome and most bothersome indicating blue, yellow and red signals respectively. This process would facilitate an immediate audit of the scrips put under alert so that undesirable trading and the players who do it can be traced out. This would go a long way in developing a healthy capital market.

**(xxi) Setting up of National Market System (NMS)**

On the recommendation of the Pherwani Committee, the government has initiated steps for setting up of NMS. The committee recommended that there should be three tiers, namely:

(*i*) Principal or Big Stock Exchanges like Mumbai, Kolkata, etc. forming the first tier;

(*ii*) Regional Stock Exchanges like those in major State capitals forming the second tier;

(*iii*) Additional trading floors sponsored or managed by either Principal or Regional Stock Exchanges forming the third tier.

This NMS would facilitate electronic trading and settlement throughout the country on the basis of standard prices and a fixed margin of service charges/commission for the broker. The NMS envisages a separate set of licensed brokers all over the country and registered sub-brokers for retail booking. The government has recognised the NSE in 1993 itself for setting up of the NMS. The NMS would definitely improve the quality and efficiency of service in the capital market.

**(xxii) Trading in derivatives**

Dr. L.C. Gupta Committee which had gone into the question of introduction of derivative trading, has recommended to introduce trading in Index Futures to start with and then trading in options. Bye-laws have already been framed by the NSE and BSE based on the recommendation of the Committee. Trading in derivatives has been introduced by bringing necessary amendment to the Securities Contract Regulation Act. Recently, mutual funds have also been permitted to trade in derivatives. These measures would make the capital market active.

**(xxiii) Reserve Bank of India's measures**

The RBI is also taking measures to revive the capital market which is undergoing a period of sluggishness. It has permitted commercial banks to invest up to 5 per cent of their incremental deposits in ordinary shares of the corporate sector including PSUs. Again, banks are allowed to extend loans to corporates against shares held by them so as to enable them to meet promoters' contribution to the equity in new companies. The RBI has also increased the ceiling for bank's advances to individuals against shares and debentures. Further, financial institutions have been allowed to purchase and sell treasury bills.

**(xxiv) Stock Lending Mechanism**

To make the capital market active by putting idle stocks to work, another innovative mechanism, *viz.*, Stock Lending Scheme has been introduced by the SEBI. Though the scheme was approved in 1997, it was put into action only on February 10, 1999. The National Securities Clearing Corporation Limited (NSCCL) is the first Approved Intermediary (IA) to implement the scheme. The scheme introduced by the NSCCL is known as 'Automated Lending and Borrowing Mechanism' (ALBM).

All clearing members are eligible to participate in this scheme. All lending and borrowing transactions are backed by 100 per cent collateral. The NSCCL bears all risks attached with these transactions. The institutional/individual investors willing to lend/borrow securities approach their broker participant (also a clearing member) for putting through a securities lending transaction.

It involves a lender willing to part with his securities for a specified period and a borrower willing to accept them at market determined rates. The meeting point for the lender and borrower is the ALBM session conducted every Wednesday by the NSCCL. The lender gets the benefit of a reasonable return called lending fee for parting with the securities for a specified period. The lender is assured of getting equivalent securities by the NSCCL on the settlement date. If the borrower fails to return the equivalent securities on the settlement date, the NSCCL has power to carry-out an auction, buy the shares on behalf of the lender and return them to him. It is proposed to conduct ALBM session on Saturdays also.

It is a golden chance for the investors to make their idle shares work harder and thereby increase the trading activities of the capital market.

## SECURITIES LENDING (SLB) — RECENT REFORMS

Most borrowers resort to SLB for covering short sell or exploring arbitrage opportunities. The SLB transactions can be carried out only through authorised intermediaries and settlement failures are prevented through daily auctions of exchanges. Moreover, the SEBI has allowed a broad array of instruments such as cash, bank guarantees, Government securities, CDs, and other registered securities as collaterals.

### ❖ Recent reforms

To help SLB flourish, the following reforms have been taken place:

(*i*) In April 2008, SLB transactions were permitted for up to seven day loan tenures in securities traded in the F&O segment.

(*ii*) In October 2008, the tenure was revised to 30 days.

(*iii*) In January 2010, the SEBI has permitted the loan tenures to go up to twelve months.

## ❖ Suggestions

1. The SLB transactions can be extended to securities outside the F&O segment also to make it more attractive.
2. Now, the clearing houses of the exchanges alone can act as authorised intermediaries. The SEBI can consider to enlarge the list of authorised intermediaries by considering large custodians as intermediaries.
3. Exchange still resort to auctions to cover settlement risks. These auctions are not standard for equity markets. If these auctions are discontinued, the market participants will adopt SLB with greater openness.
4. The right to lend securities is now available only to permissible lenders like mutual funds and banks. The SEBI may enlarge the list of permissible lenders by including large insurance companies also.

### (xxv) International listing

The big event in the history of Indian capital market is the listing of an Indian company's share on an American Stock Exchange. The Bangalore based Infosys Technologies shares have been listed on the Nasdaq Exchange under the symbol of 'INFY'. It is said that 10 per cent of the business in US capital market comes from trading in stocks of non-American companies. For instance, of the 5,400 companies listed on the Nasdaq, 500 are of non-US companies. The first ever overseas listing by an Indian Software Company has opened the doors for further listing. Infosys issued 2.07 million American Depository Receipts (ADRs) at $ 34 each to rake in $ 70.38 million. One ADR is equivalent to half a share. It means that two ADRs represent the face value of an underlying share. On the first trading day itself, at one stage the quotation went as high as $ 50. On the first day, more than 2 million transactions were traded.

The Union Budget has paved the way for stock exchanges to set up terminals abroad. The Nasdaq Exchange is planning to tie-up with the local exchanges. Many Indian companies such as Wipro, Satyam Computers, Microsoft, HDFC Bank, and other pharmaceutical companies are keen to list their shares on the American Stock Exchange. Such a listing would help the Indian companies to access the US capital market and extend their shareholders base so as to achieve a dispersal of shareholders. It would also increase the 'image' of the company and the investors would get a greater degree of comfort and confidence in the company. The demand for the company's stock would go up pushing up the prices both in the domestic and global market. This would also help in giving the employees stock options which could be used for the acquisition of other companies. In fact, Infosys is the first company to contemplate stock options to its employees. No doubt, this international listing will have its positive effect on the Indian capital market.

### (xxvi) Union Budget Measures 2019-20

To activate the capital market and motivate retail participation, the following measures have been announced in the Union Budget 2019-20:

- To raise the minimum public shareholding to 35 per cent from current threshold of 25 per cent.

- To ease the liquidity crunch in NBFC sector by proposing to provide short-term partial credit guarantee for the purchase of high-rated pooled assets of NBFCs for a total amount of ₹ 1 lakh crores.
- To allow Foreign Portfolio Investors (FPIs) and NRIs to subscribe to listed debt papers of real estate investment trusts (REITs) and infrastructure investment trusts (InvITS).
- To restrict imposition of Securities Transaction Tax (STT) to the difference between settlement and strike price in the case of exercise of options.
- To create an electronic fund-raising platform for listing social enterprises and voluntary organizations – a social stock exchange – under the regulatory ambit of SEBI.

**(xxvii) Rolling settlement**

In July 2001, SEBI made rolling settlement on a T+5 cycle compulsory in 414 stocks and the rest of the stocks should follow it from January 2002. But now T+ 2 rolling settlement has been introduced for all securities. It means that transactions on a stock exchange have to be settled 2 days after the trade day. The time gap between trading and settlement gives rise to settlement risk. To overcome this risk, risk management practices are being adopted by stock exchanges and clearing corporations. Exchanges provide counterparty guarantee and exchanges not providing the above guarantee must set up trade guarantee funds as per the advice of the SEBI. This fund would honour payin liabilities in the event of default by a member. As a result, 16 out of 20 exchanges have set up trade/settlement guarantee funds. The trades are now settled irrespective of any default by a member and the exchange follows up the defaulting member subsequently for the recovery of his dues. According to the Chairman of SEBI, there is a move to adopt T+1 settlement. If T+1 is brought in, it will benefit mainly small investors immensely. They will receive money the very next day after the trade day, thus rejuvenating interest in the trading system. It is also likely to increase liquidity and turnover in the stock markets. The number of transactions increased considerably since rolling settlement was introduced. For instance, the number of debit instructions to NSDZ are also going up. From a meagre 70,000 to 80,000 transactions in October-November 2001, the figure has raced up to 1.5 lakhs per day in June 2002.

Moving to a T+1 cycle will call for stiff challenges to be met by all parties as stated below:

(*i*) The stock exchanges will have to modify their software for their clearing and settlement systems.

(*ii*) Brokers must modify and upgrade their back office processing mechanisms.

(*iii*) Investors will have to be precise and sharper while interacting with their brokers or depository participants.

(*iv*) More banks should come forward to offer electronic funds transfer facility.

These measures are expected to restore confidence in the minds of investors and reverse the present sluggishness in the capital market. All these present developments in the secondary market are expected to contribute towards the development of a vibrant capital market.

**(xxviii) Opening up of a new window for block deals**

A separate window has been created in both BSE and NSE for executing huge block deals to check intra-day volatility on this count on the bourses. Large intra-day volatility was experienced on the stock exchanges when these block deals were carried out. Keeping them outside the purview of the time after the first half-an-hour will stem this volatility. Hence, this window is opened for the prior half-an-hour from 9.35 a.m. to 10.25 a.m. on all working days.

**(xxix) Extension of trading hours**

The trading hours of stock exchanges have been increased from Jan. 2010 onwards. All stock markets are opened for trading at 9 a.m., 50 minutes earlier than the usual timing. The extended hours have improved cash volumes on the NSE as shown in the following Table:

**TABLE 4.5**

| *Months* | *Average Daily Turnover (₹ Crores)* | *No. of Trades (Crores)* | *Traded Quantity (No. of shares – Crores)* |
|---|---|---|---|
| Jan. '10 | 17812.7 | 14.03 | 1804.24 |
| Dec. '09 | 13947.6 | 12.56 | 1503.84 |
| Nov. '09 | 16223.8 | 13.17 | 1574.01 |

The above figures represent volumes in NSE's, cash segment. Again, it is expected that early trading would pave the way for news flows for further trading.

**(xxx) Passing of Government Securities Act, 2007**

Recently, the Government Securities Act and Government Securities Regulations have been passed. It came into force with effect from December 1, 2007. The main purpose of this Act is to provide investor-friendly facilities such as:

1. Automatic redemption facility for government securities.
2. Facility to create lien, pledge or mortgage on such securities so that money could be borrowed at any time without much difficulties.
3. Nomination facility to effect transfers during the death of the holder.
4. Introduction of simplified procedures for the issue of duplicates.

This would go a long way in promoting the government securities market.

**(xxxi) Corporate bond trading platforms**

Corporation bond trading platforms have been set up at the NSE and BSE with a view to developing the private corporate debt market.

**(xxxii) Investor Protection Fund under SEBI Act**

The Kania Committee has recently suggested the setting up of an investor protection fund under the SEBI Act for the purpose of investor education and awareness. Its corpus could be made up of unclaimed dividend or interest under any scheme for more than 7 years, any unclaimed monies or securities lying with an intermediary for more than 7 years, monies lying unutilised in the investor protection funds of stock exchanges and all sums realised as penalties.

Again, there is a proposal to incorporate a provision in the SEBI Act for providing nomination facilities to unit holders of mutual funds and collective investment schemes.

**(xxxiii) Setting up SME exchange**

The BSE has launched SME exchange on March 13, 2012 with the listing of the first public issue of BCB finance.

The SME exchange would promote the growth of small and medium enterprises by generating potential investors, attracting varied investor profiles, reducing information asymmetry and nourishing new markets for equity financing. SME exchanges are functioning in many countries like AIM London, KOSADQ Korea and TSX venture exchange Canada. Collectively these exchanges attract more than 450 listings every year and list more than 4,000 firms. No doubt, the new SME exchange would promote balanced development besides fostering new entrepreneurs and new investment communities.

### ❖ Concessions on regulatory requirements

- The companies that come under SME Exchange are exempted from certain regulatory requirements such as.
- The need for a track record of portfolio operational prior to listing.
- Vetting to offer documents by SEBI.
- Submission of financial statements once in 6 months instead of quarterly.
- Circulation of annual accounts in a far simple format.
- Listing process simplified which can be completed within 2-3 months against 8-9 months timeframe required for the BSE.
- Merchant bankers have been assigned the role of market-makers for which they have to hold 5 per cent of the security to be listed at the time of allotment.
- The minimum lot size in IPOs as well as in secondary market trades has been fixed at ₹ 1 lakh. This is to ensure that only high net worth individuals and institutions with greater risk bearing capacity and ability to take informed decisions.

### ❖ SEBI's market lot prescription

The SEBI has prescribed 'lot sizes' for shares in an initial public offering for SME platform as listed below:

| | | |
|---|---|---|
| For a price band of up to ₹ 14 | — | 10,000 shares |
| For a band of ₹ 14-18 | — | 8,000 shares |
| For a band of ₹ 18-25 | — | 6,000 shares |
| Previously launched | — | OTCE and BSE Indo Next were not successful due to poor market participation. |

During 2012-13, ₹ 239 crores were raised through 24 issues in the SME platform.

**(xxxiv) Dominance of Foreign Institutional Investors (FIIs)**

The Indian capital market is still dominated by FIIs. The net investment by FIIs into India during 2009-10 crossed a milestone of ₹ 1,10,000 crores ($ 24.2 billion) a record figure for a single fiscal year. Similarly, FIIs investment in Indian debt touched a new record of ₹ 27,784 crores (US $ 6.04 billion) in corporate and government papers during 2009-10.

**(xxxv) Public holding raised to 25 per cent of the issue**

Very recently, it has been made obligatory that the public holding in shares of companies must be raised from the present limit of 10 per cent to 25 per cent of the issue. All the existing companies should achieve this target within a prescribed period and the new companies should adopt it from the very inception. It will pave the way for more participation of retail investors and increased turnover with free play of market forces. Again, the capital market will be more active with transparent dealings.

## MAJOR REFORMS IN THE SECONDARY MARKET (2012-13)

*(i)* To bring more liquidity, periodic call auction for illiquid scrips has been introduced. So far, 2000 scrips on BSE and 260 on NSE have been identified as illiquid scrips.

*(ii)* The timeline for registering the transfer of equity shares has been reduced to 15 days.

*(iii)* FIIs are permitted to use their investment in corporate bonds and Government securities as collateral to meet their margin requirements towards their transactions.

*(iv)* To encourage dematerialisation, all Depository Participants have been advised to provide a Basic Services Demat Account (BSDA) for their customers with limited services. No Annual Maintenance Charge shall be levied up to ₹ 50,000. From ₹ 50,000 to 2,00,000 AMC shall be ₹ 100. Regular charges can be levied in excess of this limit.

*(v)* The Rajiv Gandhi Equity Saving Scheme 2012 has been introduced to encourage flow of savings in financial instruments.

*(vi)* A separate debt segment in stock exchanges has been created called 'Dedicated Debt Segment'.

*(vii)* Permission has been granted to use Electronic Payment modes for making cash payment to investors.

*(viii)* Top 500 listed companies have been mandated to enable e-voting facility.

## MAJOR REFORMS IN THE SECONDARY MARKET (2014-15)

*(i)* Banks and financial institutions have been permitted to convert their debt into equity at a fair price or face value whichever is higher. It would pave way for tackling bad loans and for enabling lenders to obtain control over the borrower company.

*(ii)* It has been proposed to establish International Financial Service Centres (IFSC) to create an environment for attracting domestic and global players and thereby to promote vibrant financial markets.

*(iii)* A common KYC system has been introduced by SEBI with the facility of sharing information among SEBI registered intermediaries. Now, it has been extended to all entities regulated by other financial sector regulators.

*(iv)* Strict secondary market disclosure norms have been framed by SEBI. Accordingly,

  *(a)* Every company is required to disclose the outcome of board meetings within 30 minutes of closure of the meeting to the stock exchanges.

(*b*) Other material disclosures are to be made within 24 hours of occurrence of the relevant events.

(*c*) It is obligatory on the part of the company to clarify to the stock exchangers regarding any rumours about that company.

(*d*) Similarly, it is the duty of the company to confirm or deny any reported information to the stock exchanges. The reply to queries of stock exchanges should be specific, prompt and adequate.

(*e*) The listed company must disclose on its website all events/information which are material and they must be hosted for a minimum period of 5 years.

## MAJOR REFORMS DURING 2015-16

(*i*) Annulment of trades undertaken on stock exchanges may be submitted within 30 minutes from the execution of trade. In exceptional cases, this time frame may be extended to 60 minutes.

(*ii*) The activity schedule of the Auction Session has been fixed as follows:

| | | |
|---|---|---|
| Auction session | — | By T + 2 |
| Pay-in/Pay-out of auction and close-out | — | By T + 3 |

(*iii*) A listed stock exchange should ensure holding of 51 per cent by the public at all times.

(*iv*) Sec. 133 of the Finance Act 2015 has amended the Securities Contracts (Regulation) Act, 1956 with a view to including commodity derivatives as securities.

(*v*) To have unified control and to bring convergence of regulations, the Forward Market Commission has been merged with SEBI, w.e.f. September 28, 2015.

An overview of Indian Secondary Market is shown in the Table 4.6.

## TREND OF STOCK MARKET IN 2022

The stock market in India has shown an upward trend in 2021 and 2022 after its crash in March 2022 due to an increased participation by domestic investors – According to SEBI, this has been made possible due to the following reasons:

(*i*) Higher adoption of mobile and digital investing platforms.

(*ii*) Increasing attention and interest shown in IPDs.

(*iii*) Spreading of investment culture in Tier 3 and Tier 4 cities.

(*iv*) Prominence of equity as an asset class among investors.

Again, easy and accomodative financial policy adopted by the RBI, low interest rates, stimulus financial packages announced by the Government and easing of covid-19 related restrictions have made the stock market to reach a record peak in 2021.

In the calender year as on Dec. 27, 2022 the Foreign Institutional Investors have sold equities in the cash market worth ₹ 3,054 billion while to Domestic Institutional Investors have bought equities worth ₹ 2,382 billion. As a result, about 30 million new investor accounts have been added by NSDL and 26 million by CDSL. The net inflows by retail investors has touched a peak of ₹ 1,405 billion in 2021 and over ₹ 800 billion in 2022.

On the whole, the yearly change in the closing value of BSE Sensex and Nifty for the part 10 years shows a market gain of 2.95 for NSE and 2.87 for Nifty 50 whereas it shown a negative result in most of the countries including well developed countries.

**TABLE 4.6: MAJOR INDICATORS OF INDIAN STOCK MARKETS**

| *Item* | *2018-19* | *2019-20* | *Variation over 2018-19 (per cent)* |
|---|---|---|---|
| 1 | 2 | 3 | 4 |
| **A. Indices** | | | |
| S&P BSE Sensex | | | |
| Year-end | 38,673 | 29,468 | –23.8 |
| Average | 35,972 | 38,757 | 7.7 |
| Nifty 50 | | | |
| Year-end | 11,624 | 8,598 | –26.0 |
| Average | 10,860 | 11,500 | 5.9 |
| SX40 | | | |
| Year-end | 22,743 | 17,121 | –24.7 |
| Average | 21,230 | 22,636 | 6.6 |
| **B. Annualised Volatility (per cent)** | | | |
| S&P BSE Sensex | 12.0 | 27.9 | 131.5 |
| Nifty 50 | 12.4 | 27.1 | 119.1 |
| SX40 | 12.1 | 27.5 | 127.3 |
| **C. Total Turnover (in ₹ crore)** | | | |
| Equity Cash Segment | 87,24,624 | 96,59,735 | 10.7 |
| *of which* | | | |
| BSE | 7,75,590 | 6,60,896 | –14.8 |
| NSE | 79,49,004 | 89,98,811 | 13.2 |
| MSEI | 30.29 | 27.99 | –7.6 |
| Equity Derivatives Segment | 23,76,02,955 | 34,47,95,160 | 45.1 |
| *of which* | | | |
| BSE | 2,250 | 2,62,269 | 11555.7 |
| NSE | 23,76,00,705 | 34,45,32,892 | 45.0 |
| MSEI | Na | Na | Na |
| **D. Market Capitalisation (in ₹ crore)** | | | |
| BSE | 1,51,08,711 | 1,13,48,757 | –24.9 |
| NSE | 1,49,34,227 | 1,12,43,112 | –24.7 |
| MSEI | 1,47,51,584 | 1,10,34,811 | –25.2 |
| **E. Number of Listed Companies** | | | |
| BSE | 5,262 | 5,377 | 2.2 |
| NSE | 1,931 | 1,949 | 0.9 |
| MSEI | 287 | 295 | 2.8 |
| **F. P/E Ratio** | | | |
| S&P BSE Sensex | 28.0 | 17.8 | –36.5 |
| Nifty 50 | 29.0 | 19.4 | –33.2 |
| SX40 | 27.9 | 19.6 | –29.7 |

***Source:*** National Exchanges.

## QUESTIONS

# I. Objective type questions:

## A. Fill in the blanks with suitable words:

1. __________ is a process of admitting securities for trading on a recognised stock exchange.
2. The number of shares which are less than the market lot are called __________.
3. __________ is a professional independent broker who deals in securities on his own behalf.
4. The facility to carry forward a transaction from one settlement period to another is known as __________ transaction.
5. The device adopted to make profit out of the differences in prices of a security in two different markets is called __________.

[**Key:** 1. Listing, 2. Odd lots, 3. Jobber, 4. Badla, 5. Arbitrage]

## B. Choose the best answer from the given alternatives:

1. A person appointed by a stock broker to assist him in the business of securities trading is called:
   (*a*) Sub-broker (*b*) Commission broker
   (*c*) Authorised clerk (*d*) Tarawaniwala.
2. An order for the purchase of securities at a fixed price is known as:
   (*a*) Limit order (*b*) Open order
   (*c*) Discretionary order (*d*) Stop loss order.
3. Speculators who neither buy nor sell securities in the market, but still trade on them are called:
   (*a*) Wolves (*b*) Stags
   (*c*) Lame Ducks (*d*) Bears.
4. The process of holding the entire supply of a particular security with a view to dictating terms is called:
   (*a*) Wash sales (*b*) Arbitrage
   (*c*) Rigging the market (*d*) Cornering.
5. Under depository system, the allotment and credit of shares to the beneficiary amount should be completed within how many days from the date of closure of an issue?
   (*a*) 15 days (*b*) 7 days
   (*c*) 21 days (*d*) 30 days.

[**Key:** 1. (*c*), 2. (*a*), 3. (*b*), 4. (*d*), 5. (*c*)]

## C. State whether the following statements are TRUE or FALSE:

1. Grey market is a market for dealing in unlisted securities.
2. Carry forward transactions are facilitated by badliwallas.
3. OTC is mainly intended for big investors.
4. As per the Companies (Amendment) Ordinance, 1999 buyback of shares is restricted to 20 per cent of the paid-up capital of the company concerned.
5. Insider trading is legally permitted in the capital market.

[**Key:** 1. True, 2. True, 3. False, 4. False, 5. False]

## II. Short answer type questions:

1. What do you mean by listing of securities?
2. What are Group A shares?
3. Distinguish between market lots and odd lots.
4. Who is a jobber?
5. Distinguish between a remisier and an authorised clerk.
6. What is 'At best order'?
7. Distinguish between hand delivery settlement and clearing settlement.
8. Who are Floor Brokers?
9. Who are called Lame Ducks?
10. What do you know about wash sales?
11. What is called 'Rigging the market'?
12. Who is a Depository participant?
13. What are Self-Regulatory Organisations?
14. What is international listing?
15. What is margin trading?
16. What do you mean by listing of stock exchanges?

## III. Paragraph answer type questions:

1. State the criteria for listing of securities and explain how the listed securities are classified.
2. Describe the different methods of placing an order in the secondary market.
3. Discuss the different methods of settlement of transactions in a stock exchange.
4. Write a brief note on 'Badla transactions'.
5. Describe any three types of speculative transactions that can take place on a stock exchange.
6. Explain the salient features of the depository system introduced in the capital market.
7. Describe the features of the different indices of BSE.
8. Write a brief note on major CNX indices
9. Explain in detail the stock lending mechanism.
10. What is SME exchange? Analyse the privileges given to companies that come under it.
11. Analyse the causes for delisting of companies.

## IV. Essay type questions:

1. Critically examine the role of stock exchanges in the financial system of a country.
2. What do you mean by listing of securities? Describe the listing procedure and point out its merits and demerits.
3. Describe the procedure for registration of stock brokers and bring out the code of conduct for stock brokers in India.
4. Classify the brokers and explain their functions.
5. Describe in detail the method of trading in a stock exchange.

6. Distinguish between genuine trading and speculative trading and discuss the different kinds of speculators operating in a stock exchange and their method of dealing.
7. Explain in detail the modus operandi of any 6 types of speculative transactions.
8. 'The Indian stock market is suffering from many limitations.' — What are they?
9. Discuss the various measures taken in recent times to make the capital market vibrant.
10. Describe the procedure for online trading and bring out its merits.
11. What do you mean by Algo trading? Discuss its various types and importance.

# 5 SECURITIES AND EXCHANGE BOARD OF INDIA

Stock market regulation was a pre-independence phenomenon in India. During the World War II period, in the Defence Rules of India, 1943, provisions were made to check the flow of capital into production of essential commodities. These rules, which were promulgated as a temporary measure continued after the war and culminated into the Capital Issues (Control) Act, 1947.

This legislation had the following objectives:

1. To further the growth of companies with sound capital structure.
2. To avoid undue congestion or overcrowding of public issues in a particular period.
3. To ensure that investment takes place in conformity with the objectives of Five Year Plan.
4. To ensure orderly and healthy growth of capital markets with adequate protection to investors.

## CONTROLLER OF CAPITAL ISSUES (CCI)

For the purpose of achieving the above objectives, an office of the Controller of Capital Issues was set up. It was entrusted with the responsibility of regulating the capital issues in the country. The CCI was vested with the powers to approve the kind of instruments, size, timing and premium of issue.

## SECURITIES CONTRACTS (REGULATIONS) ACT

It was proved over time that the provisions in the Capital Issues (Control) Act were totally inadequate to regulate the growing dimensions of capital market activity. The government realised the necessity of creating a broad based and a more secure environment for the business to grow. This led to the enactment of Companies Act and Securities Contracts (Regulation) Act in 1956. These legislations contained several provisions relating to the issue of prospectus, disclosure of accounting and financial information, listing of securities, etc.

During the Sixth Five Year Plan period, many major industrial policy changes like opening up of the economy to outside world and greater role to private sector were initiated. India witnessed a phenomenal growth of the securities market. For the first time, the securities market showed a potential not only to mobilise the savings of the household sector but also to allocate it with some degree of efficiency for industrial development. The corporate sector relied on the security market for meeting its long-term requirements of funds. Several companies raised large resources from the market especially through debt instruments. The changes in the capital structure of companies gave birth to new intermediaries and institutions in the security market and thereby created new investment opportunities and awareness among the investors.

## MALPRACTICES IN SECURITIES MARKET

With the growth of securities market, the number of malpractices also increased in both the primary and secondary markets. The malpractices were noticed in the case of companies, merchant bankers and brokers who are all operating in the market.

A few examples of malpractices are as follows:

1. **Manipulation of security prices:** Companies issuing securities, often, artificially push up the prices before the issue of securities. This process starts well before a company seeks permission from the government for the issue of further capital. It is not only an attempt to get a higher premium on the basis of manipulated prices but also to lure investors to subscribe to these further issues.
2. **Price rigging:** A common way of pushing up the prices is to resort to circular trading — three or four parties buy and sell stocks among themselves and push the prices up.
3. **Insider trading:** Insider trading by agents of companies or brokers caused wide fluctuations in the prices of securities. Many companies have intricate network of brokers, their clients, friends and associates. The insiders who are privy to price-sensitive information use such information to their advantage and build up large fortunes.
4. **Delay in settlement:** The delay is noticed in giving delivery of shares, making payments to clients and passing contract notes.
5. **Delay in listing:** Delay in listing and commencement of trading in shares was also prevalent.
6. **Diversion of funds:** The IPO proceeds may be used to fund net buyers who support the price on the listing day or to fund group of companies in the form of 'Inter-corporate Deposits'.
7. **Non-disclosure of loans:** Any loans taken by a company may not be disclosed in the IPO prospectus.
8. **Giving false financial results:** Some companies report false and misleading financial results by understating liabilities such as outstanding loans, interest and finance charges with a view to overstating profits and reserves.

9. **Spreading false news:** Some companies try to influence the price of its shares by spreading false and misleading news of a proposed buyback and payment of dividend.
10. **Issuing preferential allotments:** Some companies indulge in the practice of issuing preferential allotments to certain entities without receiving any consideration amounts.
11. **Creation of artificial volumes of trade:** Artificial volumes of trade in a particular scrip may be created by entering into synchronised trades, circular trades, reversal of trades, etc.
12. **Other malpractices:** Much higher buyback price than the prevailing market price may be announced signalling strong financials of the company. It is done mainly to induce the shareholders to take part in the buyback.

    Again, details with regard to encumbered shares and also invocation of shares may not be disclosed at all.

## DEFICIENCIES IN THE MARKET

Besides, the Indian stock market is said to be deficient in the following respects:

(i) **Lack of diversity in financial instruments:** Lack of variety in the financial instruments available is one of the defects of the stock market. Equity shares and convertible debentures seem to be the only instruments in the armoury of companies. Preference shares, rights debenture, etc. are not issued by the companies.

(ii) **Disclosure of financial information:** The efficiency of capital market depends upon the availability of reliable and complete information about the issues and companies. The prospectus issued by a company does not contain adequate and relevant information to enable investors to take correct investment decisions. Sometimes, the information given is misleading and deceptive. Further, the brochures and pamphlets and advertisements issued at the time of public issue tend to present a biased profile of the company.

(iii) **Preponderance of speculative trading:** A major portion of transactions in stock market are done by speculative motive. The main motive is to derive benefit from short-term price fluctuations. Only a very small fraction of transactions represent purchase/sale by genuine investors.

(iv) **Poor liquidity:** The Indian stock market suffers from poor liquidity. Only a small portion of shares are actively traded and highly liquid. Most shares are traded infrequently and hence lack liquidity. According to M.R. Mayya, the Indian stock market is a peculiar amalgam of high volatility in respect of a few scrips and low liquidity in respect of a vast majority of them. It is a fact that out of about 3,500 securities listed on the exchange about 25 per cent do not get traded at all in a year. A top ten scrips account for nearly 85 to 90 per cent of the turnover.

(v) **Lack of control over brokers:** Lack of control over the activities of brokers and jobbers is another deficiency of capital market. Significantly, few people are able to cause fluctuations in the market activity. Besides, many of them lack high professional standards.

## SECURITIES AND EXCHANGE BOARD OF INDIA (SEBI)

Under these circumstances, the Government felt the need for setting up of an apex body to develop and regulate the stock market in India. Eventually, the Securities and Exchange Board of India (SEBI) was set up on April 12, 1988. To start with, SEBI was set up as a non-statutory body.

It took almost four years for the government to bring about a separate legislation called Securities and Exchange Board of India Act, 1992. The Act conferred SEBI comprehensive powers and all aspects of capital market operations.

### ❖ Objectives

According to the Preamble of the SEBI Act, the primary objective of the SEBI is to promote healthy and orderly growth of the securities market and secure investor protection. For this purpose, the SEBI monitors the activities of not only stock exchanges but also merchant bankers, etc. The objectives of SEBI are as follows:

1. To protect the interest of investors so that there is a steady flow of savings into the capital market.
2. To regulate the securities market and ensure fair practices by the issuers of securities so that they can raise resources at minimum cost.
3. To promote efficient services by brokers, merchant bankers and other intermediaries so that they become competitive and professional.

### ❖ Functions

Section 11 of the SEBI Act specifies the functions as follows:

**1. Regulatory functions:**

(*a*) Regulation of stock exchange and self-regulatory organisations.

(*b*) Registration and regulation of stock brokers, sub-brokers, registrar to all issue, merchant bankers, underwriters, portfolio managers and such other intermediaries who are associated with securities market.

(*c*) Registration and regulation of the working of collective investment schemes including mutual funds.

(*d*) Prohibition of fraudulent and unfair trade practices relating to securities market.

(*e*) Prohibition of insider trading in securities.

(*f*) Regulating substantial acquisitions of shares and takeover of companies.

**2. Developmental functions:**

(*a*) Promoting investor's education.

(*b*) Training of intermediaries.

(*c*) Conducting research and publish information useful to all market participants.

(*d*) Promotion of fair practices and code of conduct for self-regulatory organisations.

(*e*) Promoting self-regulatory organisations.

## ❖ Powers

SEBI has been vested with the following powers:

1. To call periodical returns from recognised stock exchanges.
2. To call any information or explanation from recognised stock exchanges or their members.
3. To direct enquiries to be made in relation to affairs of stock exchanges or their members.
4. To grant approval to bye-laws of recognised stock exchanges.
5. To make or amend bye-laws of recognised stock exchanges.
6. To compel listing of securities by public companies.
7. To control and regulate stock exchanges.
8. To grant registration to market intermediaries.
9. To levy fees or other charges for carrying out the purpose of regulation.
10. To declare applicability of Section 17 of the Securities Contract (Regulation) Act in any state or area and to grant licences to dealers in securities.

## ❖ Organisation

Chapter II of the SEBI Act deals with establishment, incorporation, administration and management of the Board of Directors, etc. The SEBI Act provides for the establishment of a statutory board consisting of six members. The chairman and two members are to be appointed by the Central Government, one member to be appointed by the Reserve Bank and two members having experience of securities market to be appointed by the Central Government. Section II deals with the powers of the Board.

SEBI has divided its activities into four operational departments namely primary market department, issue management and intermediaries department, secondary market department and institutional department, each headed by an Executive Director. Apart from these, there are two other departments, *viz*., Legal Department and Investigation Department, also headed by officials of the rank of Executive Directors.

**Primary market department:** Primary market department deals with all policy matters and regulatory issues relating to primary market, market intermediaries and matters pertaining to SROs and redressal of investor grievances.

**Issue management and intermediaries department:** This department is concerned with vetting of offer documents and other things like registration, regulation and monitoring of issue related to intermediaries.

**Secondary market department:** It looks after all the policy and regulatory issues for the secondary market, administration of the major stock exchanges and other matters related to it.

**Institutional investment department:** This department is concerned with framing policy for foreign institutional investors, mutual funds and other matters like publications, membership in international organisations, etc.

SEBI has two Advisory Committees, one each for primary and secondary markets. The committees are constituted from among the market players, recognised investor associations and eminent persons associated with the capital market. They provide advisory inputs in framing policies and regulations. These committees are non-statutory in nature and SEBI is not bound by the committees.

### ❖ SEBI and the Central Government

The Central Government has the power to issue directions to the SEBI Board, to supersede the Board, if necessary and to call for returns and report, etc., as and when necessary. The Central Government has also powers to give any guidelines or to make regulations and rules for SEBI and its operations.

The activities of SEBI are financed by grants from the government in addition to fees, charges, etc., collected by SEBI. The fund called the SEBI General Fund is set up to which all grants, fees, charges, etc. are credited. The fund is used to meet the expenses of the Board and to pay salaries of staff and remuneration to officers, members of the Board, etc.

## SEBI GUIDELINES

SEBI has brought out a number of guidelines separately, from time-to-time, for primary market, secondary market, mutual funds, merchant bankers, foreign institutional investors, investor protection, etc. The guidelines are described below.

### 1. Guidelines for primary market

**New company:** A new company is one: (*a*) Which has not completed 12 months commercial production and does not have audited results and (*b*) Where the promoters do not have a track record.

These companies will have to issue shares only at par.

**New company set up by Existing company:** When a new company is being set up by existing companies with a five-year track record of consistent profitability and a contribution of at least 50 per cent in the equity of new company, it will be free to price its issue, *i.e.*, it can issue its share at premium.

**Private and closely Held companies:** The private and closely held companies having a track record of consistent profitability for at least three years shall be permitted to price their issues freely. The issue price shall be determined only by the issues in consultation with lead managers to the issue.

**Existing listed companies:** The existing listed companies will be allowed to raise fresh capital by freely pricing expanded capital provided the promoter's contribution is 50 per cent on first ₹ 100 crores of issue, 40 per cent on next ₹ 200 crores, 30 per cent on next ₹ 300 crores and 15 per cent on balance issue amount.

### ❖ Reservation of issues

Reservations under public subscription for various categories of persons are made in the following manner:

| | | |
|---|---|---|
| 1. Permanent Employees | — | 10% |
| 2. Indian Mutual Funds | — | 20% |
| 3. Foreign Institutional Investors | — | 15% |
| 4. Development Financial Institutions | — | 20% |
| 5. Shareholders of Group of Companies | — | 10% |

## ❖ Composite issues

In the case of composite issue, *i.e.*, right-cum-public issue by existing listed companies differential pricing shall be allowed. In other words, issue to the public can be priced differentially as compared to issue to rights shareholders. However, justification for the price difference should be given in the offer document.

## ❖ Lock-in period

Lock-in period is five years for promoter's contribution from the date of allotment or from the commencement of commercial production whichever is late. At present, the lock-in period has been reduced to one year.

## ❖ Guidelines for public issue

1. Abridged prospectus has to be attached with every application.
2. A company has to highlight the risk factors in the prospectus.
3. Objective of the issue and cost of project should be mentioned in the prospectus.
4. Company's management, past history and present business of the firm should be highlighted in the prospectus.
5. Particulars with regard to company and other listed companies under the same management which made any capital issues during the last three years are to be stated in the prospectus.
6. Justification for premium, in the case of premium is to be stated.
7. Subscription list for public issues should be kept open for a minimum of three days and a maximum of 10 working days.
8. The collection centres should be at least 30 which include all centres with stock exchanges.
9. Collection agents are not to collect application money in cash.
10. The quantum of issue, whether through a rights or public issue, shall not exceed the amount specified in the prospectus. No retention of oversubscription is permissible under any circumstances.
11. A compliance report in the prescribed form should be submitted to SEBI within 45 days from the date of closure of issue.
12. Minimum number of shares per application has been fixed at 500 shares of face value of ₹ 100.
13. The allotments have to be made in multiples of tradable lot of 100 shares of ₹ 10 each.

14. Issues by way of bonus, rights, etc. to be made in appropriate lots to minimise odd lots.
15. If minimum subscription of 90 per cent has not been received, the entire amount is to be refunded to investors within 120 days.
16. The capital issue should be fully paid-up within 120 days.
17. Underwriting has been made mandatory.
18. Limit of listing of companies issue in the stock exchange has been increased from ₹ 3 crores to ₹ 5 crores.
19. The gap between the closure dates of various issues, *viz.*, rights and public should not exceed 30 days.
20. Issues should make adequate disclosure regarding the terms and conditions of redemption, security conversion and other relevant features of the new instrument so that an investor can make reasonable determination of risks, returns, safety and liquidity of the instrument. The disclosure shall be vetted by SEBI in this regard.
21. SEBI has made grading of all IPO mandatory for which draft documents are filled with it after April 30, 2007.

    It shall be mandatory to obtain grading from at least one credit rating agency.

    The issues shall be required to disclose all grades obtained by it in the prospectus, abridged prospectus, issue advertisements and others places where the issues is advertising for the IPO.
22. New format for abridged prospectus

    Very recently, SEBI has come out with a new format for an abridged prospectus which should be provided in the front page of the offer document. It means that every application form for the purchase of any securities of any company must be accompanied by an abridged prospectus.

    Accordingly, the front page of this abridged prospectus should disclose the following:

    Name of the promoter, details of offer to the public, types of issue, fresh issue and offer for sale component, total size of the issue and share reservation details. Moreover, details of offer for sale, price band, the minimum price lot and the QR code have to be disclosed. This new format will be applicable for all issues opening after Feb. 4, 2022.

## 2. Secondary market

**Stock Exchange**

(*i*) Board of Directors of stock exchange has to be reconstituted so as to include non-members, public representatives, government representatives to the extent of 50 per cent of total number of members.

(*ii*) Capital adequacy norms have been laid down for members of various stock exchanges depending upon their turnover of trade and other factors.

(*iii*) Working hours for all stock exchanges have been fixed uniformly.

(iv) All the recognised stock exchanges will have to inform about the transaction within 24 hours.

(v) Guidelines have been issued for introducing the system of market making in less liquid scrips in a phased manner in all stock exchanges.

**Brokers**

(i) Registration of brokers and sub-brokers is made compulsory.

(ii) In order to ensure that brokers are professionally qualified and financially solvent, capital adequacy norms for registration of brokers have been evolved.

(iii) Compulsory audit of broker's book and filing of audit report with SEBI have been made mandatory.

(iv) To bring about greater transparency and accountability in the broker-client relationship, SEBI has made it mandatory for brokers to disclose transaction price and brokerage separately in the contract notes issued to client.

(v) No broker is allowed to underwrite more than 5 per cent of public issue.

## 3. Foreign Institutional Investors (FIIs)

(i) Foreign institutional investors have been allowed to invest in all securities traded in primary and secondary markets.

(ii) There would be no restriction on the volume of investment for the purpose of entry of FIIs.

(iii) The holding of single FII in a company will not exceed the ceiling of 5 per cent of the equity capital of a company.

(iv) Disinvestment will be allowed only through stock exchanges in India.

(v) FIIs have to pay a concessional tax rate of 10 per cent on large capital gain (more than one year) and 30 per cent on short-term capital gains. A tax rate of 20 per cent on dividend and interest is prescribed.

## 4. Bonus issue

The guidelines relating to the issue of bonus shares have undergone several changes since 1969. The latest set of guidelines announced by SEBI were made effective from April 13, 1994. At present, there are in all 10 guidelines laid down for bonus shares.

(i) There should be a provision in the Articles of Association of the company for issue of bonus shares. If not, the company should pass a resolution at the General Body Meeting, making provision for capitalisation of profits. The proposal for bonus issues is recommended by the Board of Directors and then approved in the General Body Meeting.

(ii) The bonus is made out of free reserves built out of the genuine profits or share premiums collected in cash only.

(iii) Reserves created by revaluation of fixed assets are not permitted to be capitalised.

(iv) The declaration of bonus issue in lieu of dividend is not to be made.

(*v*) Bonus issues are not permitted unless the partly paid shares existing are fully paid-up.

(*vi*) No bonus issue will be permitted if there are sufficient reasons to believe that the company has defaulted in respect of payment of statutory dues to the employees such as provident fund, gratuity, bonus, etc. Further, no bonus issue is permitted if the company defaults in payment of principal or interest on fixed deposits or on debentures.

(*vii*) No bonus issue can be made within 12 months of any public issue/rights issue.

(*viii*) A company which announces bonus issue after the approval of the Board of Directors must implement the proposals within a period of six months from the date of such proposal and shall not have the option of changing the decision.

(*ix*) Consequent to the issue of bonus shares, if the subscribed and paid-up capital exceeds the authorised share capital, a resolution shall be passed by the company at its general body meeting for increasing the authorised capital.

(*x*) Issue of bonus shares after any public/rights issue is subject to the condition that no bonus shall be made which will dilute the value or rights of holders of debenture, convertible fully or partly.

The company shall forward a certificate duly signed by the issuer and duly countersigned by its statutory auditor or by a company secretary in practice to the effect that the terms and conditions for the issue of bonus shares as laid down in these guidelines have been complied with.

## 5. Rights issue

Section 81 of the Companies Act specifies the conditions to be satisfied by a public company for issuing rights shares. SEBI has issued the following guidelines for the issue of rights share.

(i) **Composite issue:** A public and rights issue can be made at different prices where these two kinds of issues are made as a composite issue by existing listed companies. There is no restriction in charging lower premium on rights issue than on public issues. The premium must be fixed by the Board of Directors in consultation with lead manager to the issue. Differential pricing in a composite issue is not permitted in the case of existing unlisted companies making public issue for the first time.

(ii) **Appointment of merchant banker:** Appointment of merchant banker is not mandatory, if the size of rights issue by a listed company does not exceed ₹ 50 lakhs. For issues of listed companies exceeding ₹ 50 lakhs, the issue is to be managed by an authorised merchant banker.

(iii) **Minimum subscription:** If the company does not receive minimum subscription of 90 per cent of the issue amount including devolvement of underwriters within 120 days from the date of opening of issue, the company has to refund the entire subscriptions within 128 days with interest at 15 per cent p.a. for delay beyond 78 days from the date of closure of the issue.

(iv) **Preferential allotment:** No preferential allotment shall be made along with the rights issue. If a company wants to make preferential allotment, it should be made independent of rights issue by complying the provisions of the Companies Act, 1956.

(v) **Underwriting:** Underwriting of rights issue is not mandatory but as per SEBI (Underwriter's) Rules and Regulations, 1993, rights issue can be underwritten.

(vi) **Rights of FCD/PCD holders:** The proposed rights issue should not dilute the value or rights of fully or partly convertible debentureholders. If the conversion of FCDs/PCDs is due within a period of 12 months from the date of rights issue, reservation of shares out of rights issue is to be made for them in proportion to the convertible part of FCDs/PCDs.

(vii) **Oversubscription not to be retained:** The quantum rights issue should not exceed as specified in the letter of offer. The companies are not allowed to retain oversubscription under any circumstances through rights issue.

(viii) **Promoter's contribution:** If the promoter's shareholding in the equity at the time of the rights issue is more than 20 per cent of the issued capital, the promoters have to ensure that their equity holding do not fall below 20 per cent of the expanded capital.

If the promoter's holdings are less than 20 per cent of the issued capital, they shall take up the unsubscribed portion of the rights issue so that their holdings amount to 20 per cent of the expanded capital.

The lock-in period is two years for the shareholdings prior to the rights issue from the date of allotment in the rights issue.

(ix) **Vetting of letter of offer by SEBI:** The letter of offer pertaining to rights issue has to be vetted by SEBI and the concerned lead manager has to obtain SEBI clearance for the draft letter of offer before approaching stock exchange for fixing the record date for the proposed issue. A copy of letter of offer is forwarded to SEBI for information if the rights issue is less than ₹ 50 lakhs. The responsibility of vetting the rights issue is passed on to merchant bankers in 1995. Rights issue not accompanied by public issue, if made three months prior to or three months after the public issue, will not have to be vetted by SEBI.

(x) **Disclosure in the letter of offer:** The letter of offer like the prospectus should conform to the disclosure prescribed in Form 2A under Section 56(3) of the Companies Act, 1956. Full justification and parameters used for issue price should clearly be mentioned in the letter of offer.

(xi) **Advertisement in newspaper:** All listed companies making rights issue shall invariably issue an advertisement in at least two all India newspapers about the despatch of letters of offer, opening date, closing date, etc. Such advertisement should be at least one week before the date of opening of the subscription list.

(xii) **Compliance report:** Within 45 days of closure of rights issue, a report in the prescribed form along with the compliance certificate from statutory auditor/practising chartered accountant/company secretary should be forwarded to SEBI by lead managers.

(xiii) **Applicability of SEBI guidelines:** The above guidelines with regard to rights issue apply only to rights issue made by existing listed companies.

**(xiv) Revised disclosure norms for listed companies:** To enable the listed companies to raise funds easily from the primary market, the SEBI has amended its Disclosure and Investor Protection Guidelines in March 2006. These guidelines are applicable to those listed companies that are regular in filing periodic returns with stock exchanges and have comprehensive investor grievances mechanism. The following are the important guidelines:

(*a*) Listed companies going in for a rights issue can now fix and disclose the issue price any time prior to fixing the record date in consultation with the designated stock exchange.

(*b*) In the case of fixed price route, for public issues of such companies, the price can be fixed before filing of the prospectus with the Registrar of companies.

(*c*) Further, companies making rights issues are now permitted to despatch an abridged letter of offer, containing disclosures as required in the abridged prospectus. However, such companies may provide the detailed letter of offer to any shareholder upon request.

(*d*) Again, companies that have filed a draft offer document with full disclosures can now come out with further capital issues even before the shares pertaining to the document are listed on the bourses.

These guidelines do not apply to rights issue by existing private companies/closely held or other unlisted companies. They have to comply with the requirements as laid down in the Companies Act.

SEBI, on 13th August, 2008, reduced the time duration for a rights issue from 109 days to 43 days.

## 6. Debentures

(*i*) The amount of working capital debenture should not exceed 20 per cent of the gross current assets.

(*ii*) The debt-equity ratio should not exceed 2 : 1.

(*iii*) The rate of interest can be decided by the company.

(*iv*) Credit rating is compulsory for all debentures except debentures issued by public sector companies, private placement of Non-Convertible Debentures (NCDs) with financial institutions and banks.

(*v*) Debentures are to be redeemed after the expiry of seven years from the date of allotment. NCD is permitted to be redeemed at 5 per cent premium.

(*vi*) Normally, debentures above seven years cannot be issued.

(*vii*) Debentures issued to public have to be secured and registered.

(*viii*) A Debenture Redemption Reserve is to be set up out of profits of the company.

(*ix*) Debenture Trustee and Debenture Trust Deed are to be finalised within six months of the public offer.

## 7. Fully Convertible Debenture (FCD), Partly Convertible Debenture (PCD) and Non-Convertible Debentures (NCDs)

(*i*) FCD/PCD/NCD issued for a period of more than 18 months are to be compulsorily credit rated.

(*ii*) The debentures converted within 18 months are treated as equity.

(*iii*) FCDs having conversion period more than 36 months will not be permitted.

(*iv*) The terms of issue should be predetermined and stated in the prospectus.

(*v*) The interest rate can be determined by the issuer.

(*vi*) Conversion after 18 months from the date of allotment but before 36 months will be optional at the hand of the debentureholders.

(*vii*) Appointment of Debenture Trustees and Creation of Debenture Redemption Reserve are not necessary if the maturity period is 18 months or less.

(*viii*) The Debenture Trust Deed should be executed within six months of the closure of the issue.

(*ix*) The offer document should specify existing and future equity, long-term debt-equity ratio, servicing of existing debentures, payment of interest on existing loans and debentures.

(*x*) No objection for second or *pari passu* charge.

(*xi*) In the case of rollover of NCD portion of debentures, the following conditions are to be complied with:

(*a*) Six months before the date of redemption, fresh credit rating should be obtained and it should be communicated to debentureholders.

(*b*) The company must have obtained the positive consent of debentureholders.

(*c*) SEBI should vet the roll over and its terms and conditions.

## 8. Guidelines for protection of the debentureholders

### (i) Servicing of debentures

A Debenture Redemption Reserve shall be created by companies issuing debentures on the following basis:

Existing companies need not create DRR up to the date of commercial production. DRR shall be created in equal instalments for the remaining period.

For new companies, creation of DRR will commence from the year the company earns profit and it should be created in equal or in one or more instalments for the remaining life of debentures.

In the case of PCDs, DRR should be created only for NCD portion.

DRR should be created up to 50 per cent of the amount before redemption commences.

Withdrawal from DRR will be permitted only after 10 per cent of the liability is actually redeemed.

DRR will be treated as a part of general reserve for the purpose of bonus issue.

In the case of new companies, distribution of dividend shall require approval of trustees to the debenture issue and the lead institution, if any.

In the case of existing companies, prior permission of the lead institution for declaring dividend exceeding 20 per cent or as per the loan covenants is necessary if the company does not comply with institutional conditions regarding interest and debt service coverage ratio.

**(ii) Protection of interest of debentureholders**

Trustees to the debenture issue shall be vested with the requisite powers for protecting the interest of debentureholders including a right to appoint a nominee director on the Board of the Company in consultation with institutional debentureholders.

Lead institution/investment institutions will monitor the progress in respect of debentures for project finance, modernisation, diversification, etc. The lead bank for the company will monitor debentures raised for working capital funds.

The company shall file with SEBI, a certificate from their bankers that the assets on which security is to be created are free from encumbrances and necessary permissions to mortgage the assets have been obtained or a no objection certificate from the financial institutions or banks for a second or *pari passu* charge in case where assets are encumbered.

The security should be created within six months from the date of issue of debentures. It can be created within 12 months provided 2 per cent penal interest is paid to debentureholders.

If the security is not created even after 18 months, a meeting of the debentureholders shall be called within 21 days to explain the reasons thereof and the date by which the security would be created.

The trustees to the debentureholders will supervise the implementation of the conditions regarding creation of security for the debenture and debenture redemption reserve.

The trustees and institutional debentureholders should obtain a certificate from the company's auditors in respect of utilisation of funds during the implementation of period of projects and at the end of each accounting year in the case of debentures for working capital.

## 9. Underwriters

(*i*) No person can act as underwriter unless he holds certificate of registration granted by SEBI.

(*ii*) The certificate of registration is valid for a period of three years from the date of issue.

(*iii*) The total underwriting obligations should not exceed 20 times of his net worth.

(*iv*) In case of devolvement, the underwriter should subscribe to such securities within 30 days of the receipt of the intimation from the company.

(*v*) The underwriter should furnish within a period of six months from the end of the financial year a copy of the balance sheet, profit and loss account, the statement of capital adequacy requirements and such other documents as required by SEBI.

(*vi*) The books of accounts should be maintained for a period of five years.

## 10. Investor protection

Investor protection is the major responsibility of the SEBI. SEBI has taken various measures to protect the interests of investors.

### ❖ New issues

The issuing company should provide fair and correct information.

Allotment process should be transparent and not tainted by any bias.

The draft prospectus of the companies is scrutinised for full and fair disclosure.

No delay in refunds or despatch of share certificates.

Underwriting obligations is necessary to inspire confidence of investors.

Risk factors and highlights should be fairly stated without any bias in the prospectus.

Listing should be timely and transferability is ensured.

Both stock exchange and companies are responsible for investor protection in respect of free trading and transferability of shares.

The investor protection is to be ensured by not only the Director/Secretary of the company but by all the parties in the new issue process namely merchant bankers, Registrars, collecting banks, stock exchange and SEBI.

Recently, SEBI has instituted the system of appointing its representatives to supervise the allotment process to ensure that no malpractices take place in allotment process. The other measures are shown in the next chapter.

## PROHIBITION OF UNFAIR TRADE PRACTICES

### ❖ Regulation of insider trading

Insider trading takes place when insiders or any persons who by virtue of their position in office or otherwise, have access to unpublished price-sensitive information relating to the affairs of the company and deal in the securities of such companies. SEBI regulates insider trading by imposing penalty up to ₹ 5.00 lakhs for those who indulge in insider trading.

SEBI has decided to hold the company promoters responsible for violation of insider norms if they possess unpublished price-sensitive information regarding the company without any legitimate purpose. 'Legitimate purpose' means sharing of such information in the ordinary course of business by an insider with partners, collaborators, lenders, customers, suppliers, merchant bankers, legal advisors. Auditors or consultants provided that such sharing has not been carried out to evade or circumvent the prohibition of these regulations. The Board of Directors are directed to maintain a structured digital database containing the names of such persons of entities with whom the information is shared.

### ❖ Investor education

SEBI has issued a few investors guidance, advertisements and published a book on 'Investor Grievances — Rights and Remedies'. SEBI has also registered certain active Investor's Association.

SEBI has issued an Advertisement Code for the issuers to ensure that the advertisements are fair and do not contain statements to mislead the investors or vitiate their informed judgement.

### ❖ Grievance cell

An Investor Grievance Cell is set up to handle investor complaints.

### ❖ Stock invest

Stock invest was designed by the SEBI in consultation with RBI and banks as an additional facility for making applications for new issues. The stock invest facility is available to individuals who can approach the bank with whom they maintain an account for issue of stock invest of required denominations for payment of application money while making an application for shares. The stock invest scheme envisages that the investor's account gets debited only on the allotment of shares. The investor, therefore, has to part with his funds only when he is eligible to get allotment of shares. Till such time, the investor's fund remains in his account and continues to earn interest, which is normally four months.

### ❖ New measures

SEBI has taken three new measures to protect investor interests on March 21, 2007.

1. Making rating compulsory for all initial public offerings.
2. Insisting on great disclosure by real estate companies entering the market.
3. Permitting short selling by institutional investors which will minimise volatility in the market.

## 11. Book building

The normal method of offering shares at a price fixed by the issuers does not take into account the investors' demands. Hence, it is not considered as an efficient method. The book building method, on the other hand, explicitly uses investor's demand for share at various prices as an important input to arrive at an offer price. The book building is done in the following steps:

(*i*) The company wishing to issue shares, approaches its merchant banker and informs him of the number of shares it wishes to issue and other material information on the company.

(*ii*) The merchant banker now invites his known investors to bid for the company's share. The investors are generally institutional investors. These investors are asked to indicate the number of shares they would like to buy at different prices. Once the price is finalised, allocation is made on the basis of highest price bid.

(*iii*) If the company agrees with the offer price, the issue goes through and the shares are allocated based on bids. The company has the option to cancel the issue if it feels that the price is too low.

(*iv*) The trading commences from the next day.

### ❖ Book building in India

The book building method of pricing securities is becoming popular in India. During 1997-98, various issuers like IPCL, HUDCO, HAL, IOC and Hindalco Industries have used book building route to fix the coupon rate on their bond issues.

## ❖ Terms associated with book building process

### ❖ Retail investor

Retail investor refers to an investor who applies or bids for securities of a company for a value of not more than ₹ 1 lakh. If he bids for more than the value, he will be branded as non-institutional buyer.

### ❖ Qualified Institutional Buyer (QIB)

Qualified Institutional Buyer means a public financial institution or a commercial bank or a mutual fund or FII or venture capitalist or an insurance company or any other such body corporate who applies or bids for securities.

### ❖ Red Herring Prospectus (RHP)

It is nothing but a prospectus which does not have details of either price or number of shares being offered or the amount of issue. Generally, the price will not be disclosed, but the number of shares and price band will be disclosed. However, all details are made available to an investor on a day just prior to the date of issue open.

### ❖ Offer document

Offer document is nothing but a prospectus in the case of public issue or offer for sale and letter of offer in the case of rights issue. It has to be filed with the Registrar of Companies and Stock Exchanges.

### ❖ Green Shoe Option

Green Shoe Option means an option of allocating shares in excess of the shares floated in the public issue and operating a post-issue price stabilising mechanism for a period not exceeding 30 days. This permission has been granted to a company to be exercised with caution through a stabilising agent. As per this arrangement, an issue could be over allotted to the extent of a maximum of 15 per cent of the issue size.

From an investor's point of view, an issue with green shoe option provides more probability of getting shares allotted to him. It also ensures that the post-listing price will be more stable than the market price.

### ❖ Syndicate member

Syndicate member refers to a person whose work is to collect the entire bid forms in a book built issue.

### ❖ Floor Price/Cap Price/Cut-off Price

In a book building issue, the issuer is required to indicate either the price band or a floor price in the red herring prospectus. The lower end price is called the floor price and the higher end price is called cap price. The actual discovered price can be any price between the two and it is called cut-off price.

## ❖ SEBI guidelines on book building

SEBI issued guidelines for new issues through book building so as to enable issuers to reap benefits arising out of price and demand discovery. The guidelines came into operational with effect from September 1997.

1. The option of 100 per cent book building shall be available only to those issuer companies which propose to make an issue of capital of and above ₹ 100 crores.
2. Book building shall be for the portion other than the promoters contribution and allocation made to permanent employees of the issuer company and shareholders of the promoting companies in case of a new company and shareholders of group companies in case of existing companies.
3. The issuing company shall appoint Category I Merchant Banker as book runner(s) and their names shall be mentioned in the draft prospectus submitted to SEBI. The lead merchant banker shall act as the lead book runner may appoint 'Syndicate Members' who shall be from those intermediaries who are registered with SEBI who are permitted to carry on activity as the 'underwriter'.
4. The draft prospectus shall be filed with SEBI by the lead merchant bankers.
5. The issuer company, after receiving final observations, if any, on the offer document from SEBI makes an advertisement in newspapers. The information in the advertisement shall contain:
   (*i*) The date of opening and closing of the bidding.
   (*ii*) The method and process of bidding.
   (*iii*) The names and addresses of the syndicate members as well as bidding terminals for accepting bids.
6. The book runner's and the company shall determine the issue price based on the bids received through syndicate members. On determination of the price, the number of securities to be offered shall be determined.
7. Once the final price is determined, all those bidders whose bids have found to be successful shall become entitled for allotment of securities.
8. On determination of the entitlement, the information regarding the same shall be intimated immediately to the investors.
9. The offer shall remain open for subscription by the public for a period of at least three working days after completing all requirement of advertisement and despatch of issue material to stock exchanges. During the time when the offer is open, the investors who have received an intimation of entitlement of securities shall submit the application forms along with the application money.
10. Arrangement shall be made by the issuer for collection of the applications by appointing mandatory collection centres depending upon the size of the issue.
11. Allotment shall be made not later than 15 days from the closure of the issue failing to which interest at the rate of 15 per cent shall be paid to the investors.

12. A final book of demand showing the results of allocation process shall be maintained by the book runners.
13. SEBI shall have the right to carry-out an inspection of the records, books and documents relating to the book building process.

### ❖ Recent reforms

With a view to benefiting small investors and to improving liquidity in the stock market, the SEBI has recently introduced some meaningful primary market reforms. Some of the important ones applicable to 'book built' route are:

(*i*) A listed company should have a minimum public holding of 25 per cent of its share on a continuous basis. This 'Free float' of 25 per cent refers to the non-promoter holdings.

(*ii*) The merchant bank's discretionary powers to allot shares to the Qualified Institutional Buyers (QIBs) have been done away with.

(*iii*) Among the QIBs' reservation of 50 per cent, mutual funds have been given a share of 5 per cent. However, they can apply for the remaining portion too.

(*iv*) The QIBs have to bid with a margin money of 10 per cent of the application value.

These measures aim at bringing much benefits to retail investors by bringing much-needed liquidity in the market.

## 12. Buyback of shares

Buyback of shares and securities is popular in countries like USA and UK. The government recently promulgated an ordinance amending the Companies Act, 1956 to permit buyback of shares by promoters of companies. Accordingly, a company can buy back its own shares and other securities to the extent of 25 per cent of the paid-up capital and free reserves. The buyback can be transacted out of company's free reserve, securities premium account or proceeds of any earlier issues specially made for buyback purposes.

### ❖ What is buyback?

Buyback is a method of cancellation of share capital. It leads to reduction in the share capital of a company as opposed to issue of shares which results in an increase in share capital.

### ❖ Why buyback?

A company may go for buyback of its shares due to any one or more of the following reasons:

1. To reduce equity base thereby injecting much-needed flexibility.
2. To prevent takeover bids.
3. To return surplus cash to shareholders.
4. To increase the underlying share value.
5. To support the share price during periods of temporary weakness.
6. To maintain a target capital structure.

## ❖ Advantages

The major advantages of buyback of shares to investors, companies and the economy are the following:

## ❖ For the investors:

1. It is a viable proposition to investors to sell back the shares instead of going through the secondary market.
2. It will improve return on capital and net profitability, increase the earnings per share and provide higher price to investors.

## ❖ For the companies:

1. It offers flexibility to companies to reorganise their capital structure.
2. It helps to eliminate discontended shareholders, fractional share-holdings and odd lots and thereby render better service to remaining shareholders by way of sustained dividend and appreciation of share value in the long run.
3. Buyback is an instrument to ward-off hostile takeover bids.

## ❖ Economy

Buyback of shares helps to revive the capital market. The operation of demand and supply factors will boost prices of shares. It also offers liquidity to dormant shares.

## ❖ SEBI guidelines

The SEBI has been made as a regulatory authority of the licence to buy back shares by the ordinance. The regulations of SEBI contains the following:

1. The companies are permitted to buy back the shares through six moves:
   (*i*) Tender offers.
   (*ii*) Open offers.
   (*iii*) Dutch auction.
   (*iv*) Repurchase of odd lots.
   (*v*) Reverse rights issue.
   (*vi*) Employee stock option.

   Tender offers will specify the exact price and will have only one price to offer.

   In the Dutch auction, shares offered at the lowest price would be given priority over others.
2. The companies are not permitted to buy back through negotiated deals, spot transactions and private placement.
3. Promoters have been debarred from participating if the company opts to buyback shares through stock exchange route.
4. Companies buying through stock exchanges must disclose purchase details daily.
5. The companies will have to specify the maximum price payable in the resolution seeking shareholders' approval.

6. The buyback must be done only in cash and an escrow account will have to be maintained by the merchant bankers.
7. No company is allowed to withdraw the buyback offer once it is announced.
8. Companies with a post buyback debt-equity ratio of more than 2 : 1 on a consolidated basis will not be allowed to implement a buyback.

Merchant bankers must be associated in every offer for buyback, wherein they would be required to give a due diligence certificate.

The Registrar of shares or transfer agents will have to certify that the company has adhered to all regulations.

## ❖ SEBI (Amendment Bill) 2002

Parliament passed the SEBI (Amendment) Bill, 2002 giving more powers to SEBI to punish market offenders. The bill entrust SEBI wide powers including seizure of books and accounts, impose fine up to ₹ 25 crores on insider trading, slap a penalty of ₹ 1 lakh a day and up to ₹ 1 crore in cases where small investors were cheated. The SEBI is being given powers to suspend the governors of the stock exchange. It is also being empowered to impound the proceedings of the exchanges.

The SEBI's governing board itself has powers to appoint investigating agency.

## RECENT GUIDELINES

- Necessary guidelines have been issued for comprehensive risk management framework for the cash market.
- A comprehensive regulation and simplified registration practices applicable to all intermediaries have been released vide SEBI (Intermediaries) Regulations, 2008.
- Creation of e-mail id for all registered intermediaries has been made mandatory for regulatory communication.
- Every company proposing to issue new securities must deposit 1 per cent of the amount of securities offered for subscription to the public and/or to the holders of the existing securities before the opening of the subscription list.
- The equity listing agreement has been amended to enhance disclosures regarding shareholding pattern and voting rights pattern for each class of shares.
- Again the Equity Listing Agreement has been amended prohibiting listed companies from issuing shares with superior rights as to voting or dividend *vis-à-vis* the rights on equity shares that are already listed.
- The ceiling for retail investors in public issues has been increased from ₹ 1 lakh to ₹ 2 lakhs.
- The SEBI has made it mandatory for all companies to have a pre-announced fixed pay date for payment of dividends and for credit of bonus shares.
- Smart order routing has been introduced to enable investors choose execution destinations based on the best price, costs, speed, settlement size, etc. This would put an end to inter-exchange arbitrage between exchanges.

### ❖ SEBI's Norms for Foreign Investments in Stocks

As per SEBI's recent guidelines, Qualified Foreign Investors (QFIs) are permitted to directly invest in the Indian equity market. A QFI is a resident of a country Compliant with the Financial Action Task Force (FATF) standards to combat money-laundering and terrorist financing. The QFIs should be an Indian resident or registered with SEBI as Foreign Institutional Investors. QFIs are allowed to invest in equities listed on Indian stock exchange in a demat account with a SEBI registered qualified depository participant.

- The depository participant should have a minimum paid-up capital of ₹ 50 crores.
- QFIs can open only one demat account.

## NEW LISTING NORMS FOR START-UPS

The following listing norms have been laid by SEBI to enable the start-ups to have an easy access to list on the 'Innovators' Growth Platform' (IGP):

- The investors, mostly institutional investors, will be required to hold 25 per cent of the capital before the issue for a period of one year only.
- Start-ups will be allowed to allocate 60 per cent of the issue size on a discretionary basis (with a lock-in period of 30 days on such shares) prior to the opening of that issue to eligible investors.
- In an open offer mechanism, the limit for acquisition will be 49 per cent.
- For delisting on IGP, the acquirer or promoter shareholding should reach 75 per cent of the total issued shares and at least 50 per cent of public shares are acquired. On BSE and NSE, delisting is achieved only when 90 per cent or more public shares are acquired.
- To migrate from the IGP to BSE/NSE platforms, the start-ups now will be required to hold 50 per cent of its capital by institutional investors.
- SEBI has permitted Alternate Investment Funds (AIFs) and Angel investors to invest in start-ups.
- SEBI has made it mandatory for independent directors to give their seasoned opinion to shareholders during delisting process to make it transparent.
- Acquirers will be permitted to specify an 'indicate price' for delisting which should not be lower than the floor price. Promoters will be bound to accept the price discovered through 'reverse book building' process provided it is equal to the floor price.

## QUESTIONS

### I. Objective type questions:

#### A. Fill in the blanks:

1. A new company which has not completed 12 month's commercial production has to issue shares only __________.
2. SEBI has powers to grant approval to __________ of stock exchanges.

3. Minimum number of shares per application has been fixed at __________ shares.
4. Registration of brokers is made __________.
5. Normally, debentures above __________ years cannot be issued.
6. The total underwriting obligation of an underwriter should not exceed __________ of his net worth.

[**Key:** 1. at par, 2. bye-laws, 3. 500, 4. compulsory, 5. seven, 6. 20 times.]

## B. State whether the following statements are TRUE or FALSE:

1. Investor protection is the major responsibility of SEBI.
2. Book building is a device to arrive at an offer price.
3. Buyback leads to increase in share capital.
4. The existing listed companies can issue shares only at par.
5. The declaration of bonus in lieu of dividend cannot be made.

[**Key:** 1. True, 2. True, 3. False, 4. False, 5. True.]

# II. Short answer type questions:

1. Explain the functions of SEBI.
2. What is book building?
3. What is buyback of shares? State its advantages.
4. What is insider trading?
5. What is stock invest?
6. What is abridged prospectus?

# III. Essay type questions:

1. Explain in detail the SEBI guidelines for primary market.
2. What are the SEBI guidelines for Bonus Issue and listing norms for start-ups?
3. Explain the functions and powers of the Securities and Exchange Board of India.
4. How does SEBI protect the interest of investors? Explain.
5. Examine critically the new guidelines issued by SEBI for book building and buyback of shares.

# 6 INVESTORS' PROTECTION

The peculiar nature of the company form of organisation is that there is diversity of ownership and management. Though thousands of shareholders have invested their money in a company, they don't have any direct connection with the day-to-day running of the business. They have invested their small means in the company through the share market to get ample returns and also to get capital appreciation of their invested funds. At the same time, they have to shoulder many risks of different kinds. Apart from the normal risks attached to every business, there may be abnormal risks also in the form of dishonesty and impropriety of all the counterparties with whom they come into contact while investing their funds. Hence, there arises a necessity to protect them from all such risks so that their confidence in the market may be built-up and they may actively participate in the market with boosted confidence. It will go a long way in creating a healthy and vibrant capital market.

## NEED FOR INVESTORS' PROTECTION

The need for investors' protection arises due to the following reasons:

**(i) To instil confidence in investors' minds:** Investors' confidence is very essential for the smooth and successful functioning of the capital market. When their confidence is shaken or when they lose their confidence in the market, there will be a severe jolt in the market. Many investors are tempted to invest with an expectation of making good fortunes out of their investment. If it does not happen, they come away from the market. Such a situation is not at all desirable. Therefore, it is vital to build-up investors' confidence by creating a conducive atmosphere for investment through investors' protection measure.

**(ii) To create a conducive atmosphere for investment:** A proper and sound investment climate is very essential for industrial development. The corporate customers would find it easy to raise capital at affordable minimum cost only when there is efficient and secured investment climate. In fact, strong investors' protection measures would create a healthy investment climate.

**(iii) To ensure transparency in dealing:** The investors would be able to evaluate their prospective investments only when there is transparency of dealings of companies and all the intermediaries connected with the stock market. Investment decisions would be taken on the basis of full disclosures made by companies in various areas. All investors' protection measures aim at bringing the much needed transparency and disclosures in all key areas.

**(iv) To create a vibrant capital market:** Investors would freely enter into the capital market in large numbers only when their interest is fully protected from all angles. This increased participation would develop the market and once the market gets developed, it would again attract more and more investors. Thus, investors' protection would indirectly promote a vibrant capital market.

**(v) To regulate the market on sound lines:** Investors' protection measures in the form of regulations would make all market players work within the ambit of regulations. It would lead to a smooth and stable functioning of the market on desired lines.

**(vi) To create discipline in the market:** All investors' protection measures aim at minimising the unhealthy practices, undue speculation, unnecessary malpractices, etc. in the market. It would go a long way in creating a good discipline among all market players.

**(vii) To create accountability among market players:** A sense of accountability is created among all players in the market by means of laying down strict disclosure norms and taking stringent investors' protection measures. This accountability makes them comply with all requirements failing which they are answerable to the regulatory bodies.

**(viii) To create awareness among investors:** Above all, investors must be aware of their own rights and liabilities, grey areas of frauds, the type of frauds that can take place, etc. Hence, investor protection measures also aim at educating the prospective and present investors on these aspects. This would enable them to protect themselves from all unhealthy and fraudulent practices by becoming saviours of their own protection.

## FACTORS AFFECTING INVESTORS' INTEREST

There are many factors that affect investors' interest and thereby cause dissatisfaction among them. The prominent causes are:

### (i) Price rigging

Price rigging is nothing but the artificial manipulation of prices of securities by forming cartels by bulls and bears. They don't allow the market forces of demand and supply to play their due role. These artificial prices create a market wind in either directions to which innocent investors fall as victims.

**(ii) Insider trading**

Insider trading refers to the purchase or sale of securities by persons who hold price-sensitive information about the company due to their fiduciary relationship with that company. In other words, insiders get regular profits at the expense of a majority of uninformed investors.

**(iii) Excessive speculation**

Speculation, if it exceeds its limit, would affect the interest of investors to a greater extent. If brokers, in order to earn more and more profits due to a probable rise in price, may engage themselves in a buying spree far beyond their capacity. It would result in non-fulfilment of their settlement promises which may lead to market crash. Ultimately, the innocent investors suffer for no fault of theirs.

**(iv) Lack of transparency**

In order to attract investors, some companies may present a rosy picture of their financial position by manipulating their system of accounting. The accounts are not at all transparent in their disclosures. Again, the stock market dealings are not transparent.

**(v) Short selling**

Short selling refers to selling of scrips without owning them by bear cartels with the anticipation that these shares could be purchased at a much lesser price in future when delivery would be actually made. It leads to extreme volatility in the market.

**(vi) Restricted trading**

One of the serious grievances of the investors is restricted trading in stock exchanges. Though there is an increase in the turnover of stock exchanges, it is restricted to a few shares only with the top 10 shares accounting for about 80 per cent of the turnover and top 100 shares for 99 per cent of the turnover.

**(vii) Restricted trading hours and trading days**

Another factor arises from the fact that the trading hours of stock exchanges are very small and the market also remains closed on many days a week. This affects the marketability and liquidity of securities.

**(viii) Dominance of few stock exchanges**

Though many stock exchanges are functioning in India, a lion's share of the dealings are held in BSE and NSE only. The regional stock exchanges are gradually losing their importance.

**(ix) Dominance of institutional and foreign institutional investors**

The institutional investors, particularly the foreign institutional investors dominate the Indian capital market. They dictate the terms in the market. They account for nearly 80 per cent of the new issues. The ownership of equities by individuals and households is gradually coming down.

**(x) Excessive volatility**

Due to the impact of IT revolution, LPG policies, introduction of innovative instruments and adoption of flexible interest rate structure, the volatility in the capital market has been greatly increased. The small investors are not able to face such a situation with confidence.

**(xi) Grievances against listed companies**

Moreover, the investors complaints against listed companies are manifold. Some of them are:

(*i*) Non-receipt of share certificates.
(*ii*) Non-receipt of refund orders.
(*iii*) Non-receipt of duplicate securities.
(*iv*) Non-receipt of certificates after consolidation.
(*v*) Non-receipt of certificates after splitting.
(*vi*) Bad delivery of share certificates.
(*vii*) Failure to effect transfers and delay in executing transfers.
(*viii*) Non-receipt of interest on listed debentures.
(*ix*) Non-receipt of redemption proceeds of listed debentures.
(*x*) Non-receipt of allotment advice.
(*xi*) Complaints regarding revalidations.

**(xii) Grievances against members of stock exchanges**

The nature of complaints against the members of the stock exchanges are:

(*i*) Non-receipt of delivery of shares.
(*ii*) Non-receipt of dividend.
(*iii*) Non-receipt of rights shares.
(*iv*) Non-receipt of bonus shares.
(*v*) Non-receipt of sale proceeds.
(*vi*) Disputes relating to non-settlement of accounts.
(*vii*) Disputes regarding rate differences, etc.

**(xiii) Miscellaneous grievances**

Miscellaneous grievances arise due to:

(*i*) Non-repayment of fixed deposits in financial companies.
(*ii*) Non-repayment of deposits in manufacturing companies.
(*iii*) Non-redemption of mutual funds and all complaints relating to mutual funds.
(*iv*) Complaints relating to shares and debentures in unlisted companies.

## INVESTORS' PROTECTION MEASURES

In order to sustain and promote investors' confidence in the capital market, many measures have been taken by different agencies. They can be studied under the following heads:

(*i*) Measures taken by Stock Exchanges.
(*ii*) Measures taken by the Company Law Board.
(*iii*) Measures taken by SEBI.
(*iv*) Measures taken by the Court.

(*v*) Measures taken by the Central Government.

(*vi*) Measures taken by the Department of Company Affairs (DCA).

**(i) Measures taken by stock exchanges**

A number of measures have been taken by stock exchanges to protect the interest of investors. Some of the important measures taken in this direction are the following:

(*i*) An Investors' Service Cell has been established in BSE to deal with all matters involving complaints against listed companies and also against the members of the exchange. A similar cell called Investor Grievance Cell has been set up in the NSE.

(*ii*) An Investor Protection Fund has been set up in NSE as a trust to compensate investors' claims, which may arise due to non-settlement of obligations by the defaulting trading members. In BSE also, 'A Stock Exchange Customers' Protection Fund' has been created in the interest of the investors to settle their legitimate claims against defaulting members.

(*iii*) Further, a Trade Guarantee Fund has been introduced in the BSE to guarantee the settlement of trades so that there may not be any default by members in payment. It would increase confidence in the minds of secondary market participants and thus the interest of investors are protected.

(*iv*) Restricted trading hours and trading days are no more problems ever since the introduction of screen-based online trading system in all stock exchanges and also due to the implementation of extended trading hours recently.

(*v*) To remove the existence of excessive speculation, many reform measures such as introduction of strict transparency and disclosure norms, abolition of Badla system and carry forward schemes, adoption of rolling settlement, etc. have been taken and strictly implemented.

(*vi*) The SEBI has taken many positive steps to remove the various unhealthy practices that are commonly found in stock exchanges. The common unhealthy practices are insider trading, price rigging, circular trading, trading in fake shares etc. The SEBI has laid down various rules and regulations to curb such practices and these rules and regulations are subject to review and revision from time-to-time. The stock exchanges follow those rules and regulations strictly and implement them in letter and spirit.

(*vii*) Moreover, BSE and NSE conduct investor awareness programmes to educate the investor on various aspects of the working of the capital market so that they may enter into the market with confidence. These programmes cover a wide range of topics including Investors' Grievance Redressal system available to investors, the availability of Investors' Protection Fund, Trade Guarantee Fund, etc.

**(ii) Measures taken by the Company Law Board**

Wide powers have been given to the Company Law Board to protect the interest of investors as well as depositors under the Companies Act. Accordingly, many steps have been initiated in this direction. Some of such important steps are the following:

(*i*) Where a company has failed to repay any deposit as per the terms and conditions of such deposit, the Company Law Board may direct the company concerned by an order to make payment of such deposits under Section 58A(9) of the Companies Act.

(*ii*) Where a company refuses to register the transfer of any shares or debentures, an appeal can be made by the aggrieved party to the Company Law Board under Section 111 of the Companies Act within two months of the receipt of the notice of such refusal.

(*iii*) Under Section 163(6) of the Companies Act, every investor has a right to get any extract or copy of the documents of the company or inspect any documents of the company. This right should be exercised through the Company Law Board only. It facilitates complete transparency of all documents of the company.

(*iv*) Again, Section 196(4) gives a right to any person to inspect the minute book of all general meetings and further that the Company Law Board may direct that a copy of such minutes required shall be sent to the person requiring it.

(*v*) The Company Law Board may also direct the company concerned to send copies of the balance sheet and auditors, report to any investor requiring it under Section 219(4) of the Companies Act.

(*vi*) To prevent oppression and mismanagement, the Central Government may appoint such number of persons as the Board specifies on the basis of a written order of the Company Law Board to safeguard the interest of shareholders under Section 408 of the Companies Act. Such persons would hold office as directors for such a period not exceeding three years.

(*vii*) To safeguard the interest of shareholders and in public interest, the Company Law Board may prevent any change in the Board of Directors which might affect the company prejudicially as per Section 409 of the Companies Act.

(*viii*) The shareholders of a company may also request the Company Law Board to issue orders for conducting investigation of the affairs of the company by an investigator or inspectors under Section 235 of the Companies Act. Such wide powers have been given to protect the interest of shareholders who are the investors. In fact, the shareholders are the real owners of the company and the Board of Directors and the managers are the agents of the shareholders only.

**(iii) Measures taken by SEBI**

A company comes into existence only out of the shareholder's willingness to invest a part of their resources at risk. A shareholder cannot leave the company unless some other investor steps into his shoes. Thus, investors' confidence is very essential for capital formation. Realising the imperative need to ensure investors' protection, a separate regulating body, *viz.*, the Securities and Exchange Board of India (SEBI) has been set up with the main objective of protecting the investors' interest. Of course, the SEBI has taken a number of steps to safeguard the interest of investors by framing many rules and regulations then and there. Most of these guidelines have been discussed in detail in the chapter 'Securities and Exchange Board of India'. However, some of the important measures taken are discussed briefly hereunder:

(*i*) The SEBI has issued and published detailed guidelines regarding the rights and responsibilities of investors and also the various aspects of capital market dealings and operations. It enables the investors to be aware of their rights and responsibilities besides enabling them to be acquaint with the capital market operations.

(*ii*) It has formed a separate Investors' Grievances and Guidance Division at its Head office.

(*iii*) An automated complaint handling system has been introduced to deal with all types of investors' complaints.

(*iv*) All speculation prone products such as Badla trading, Carry Forward Schemes like Automatic Lending and Borrowing Mechanism (ALBM), Borrowing and Lending Securities Scheme, etc. have been either banned or allowed with much restrictions by SEBI. It has the effect of curbing speculation.

(*v*) The disclosure norms for public issues have been made more stringent. To simplify the issue process, an abridged prospectus has been permitted.

(*vi*) This abridged prospectus is vetted by SEBI before public issue or an acknowledgement card is issued to ensure complete disclosure of facts.

(*vii*) The promoters' contribution for each public issue has been fixed by SEBI. The minimum contribution should be 20 per cent of the total issue.

(*viii*) All risk factors involved in an issue should be disclosed prominently in the prospectus so that an investor can evaluate that issue before taking any investment decision.

(*ix*) A transparent and flexible pricing method through book building process has been introduced. The investors' feedback forms the basis for pricing of shares.

(*x*) To avoid all malpractices connected with allotment of shares, a representative of the SEBI supervises the allotment process. He must be present at the time of finalisation of the basis of allotment.

(*xi*) Again, it has been made mandatory for the brokers to disclose the transaction price as well as their brokerage in the Contract Notes issued by them to their clients.

(*xii*) To do away with all fraudulent practices in physical handling of shares, dematerialisation has been introduced. Separate guidelines have been issued with regard to the depository services and also for various intermediaries associated with it.

(*xiii*) To bring financial discipline in the derivative market, various guidelines have been issued for dealing with various derivative products.

(*xiv*) It has established SCORES system which enables an investor to directly lodge any complaint online. Such a complaint is considered as 'e-complaint'. Investors can log on to SCORES at any time and from anywhere and check the status of the complaints with a help of a username and password provided to them when lodging their grievances.

(*xv*) It has laid down necessary guidelines for providing exit opportunity to all dissenting shareholders of a company in accordance with the Companies Act, 2013.

*(xvi)* In Nov. 2021, it has published the 'Investor Charter' for the securities market to protect investor's interest, promote transparency in the market and to enhance awareness, trust and confidence among investors. It has been publishing the status of disposal of investors' grievance received in SCORES on its website on a monthly basis. Grievances pending for more than 3 months are also published.

**(iv) Measures taken by the Court**

Generally, all regulatory bodies like SEBI, RBI, DCA, etc. have an in-built system to redress the grievances of investors. In case the investors are not satisfied with the orders of the regulators, an appeal can be made to the Securities Appellate Tribunals against those orders. In case the Appellate Tribunals also fail to satisfy the aggrieved investor, judiciary is resorted to as a last resort. Thus, the court will interfere only as a last resort to redress the grievances of investors. The following are the instances of court's intervention under the various Acts governing the securities market.

(1) Under the SEBI Act, no civil court can entertain any suit or proceedings against the order of the Securities Appellate Tribunal. However, an appeal can be made to the Supreme Court within 60 days from the date of communication of the order of the Securities Appellate Tribunal.

(2) Under the Securities Contracts (Regulation) Act, 1956, the Securities Appellate Tribunal is vested with the powers of a civil court under the code of civil procedures. Therefore, any aggrieved person can appeal to the high court against the order within 60 days from the date of communication of the order of the Securities Appellate Tribunal.

(3) Under the Companies Act, any aggrieved person can appeal to the high court within 60 days from the date of communication of the decision or order of the National Company Law Tribunal.

**(v) Measures taken by the Central Government**

To protect the interest of investors and to promote investor education and awareness, the Central Government has established a Fund called 'Investors' 'Education and Protection Fund'. All amounts that remain unclaimed or unpaid at the hands of the companies must be transferred to this fund. This fund will be utilised to protect investors' interest and to promote investors' awareness through multimedia, publicity, seminars and conferences. This fund is administered by a trust.

**(vi) Measures taken by the Department of Company Affairs**

The investors' interest is protected by Department of Company Affairs in the following ways:

*(i)* One Investors' Grievance Officer has been appointed to handle all complaints received from investors.

*(ii)* As soon as complaints are received from investors' they are acknowledged by giving a specific number for each complaint.

*(iii)* The complaint is taken to the companies concerned for necessary adjustment.

*(iv)* The status of the complaint is also displayed on the website of DCA.

(v) In case of non-settlement of complaints, the matter will be referred to the Registrar of companies for final prosecution.

(vi) Complaints received from depositors are referred to the RBI in the case of Non-banking Financial Companies and to the Company Law Board in the case of Non-banking Non-financial Companies for redressal.

The status of investor grievances received and redressed by SEBI is shown in the following Table.

**Table 6.1: Status of Investor Grievances Received and Redressed**

| *Financial Year* | *Grievances Received Year-wise* | *Grievances Redressed Year-wise* | *Pending Actionable Grievances** |
|---|---|---|---|
| 2020-21 | 58,873 | 50,425 | 5,171 |
| 2021-22 | 42,694 | 48,883 | 2,364 |

* excludes complaints against whom regulatory actions are initiated.

***Source:*** SEBI Report 2021-22.

## QUESTIONS

## I. Objective type questions:

### A. Fill in the blanks:

1. __________ is the artificial manipulation of prices of securities.
2. Selling of securities without owning them is called __________.
3. A trade guarantee fund has been set up in __________.
4. An appeal for refusal to effect transfer of shares can be made to __________.
5. When the Securities Appellate Tribunal fails to redress investors' grievances __________ will interfere.

[**Key:** 1. Price Rigging, 2. Short Selling, 3. BSE, 4. Company Law Board, 5. Court]

### B. State whether the following statements are TRUE or FALSE:

1. 'Insider Trading' is a speculative activity.
2. An Investor Protection Fund has been set up in NSE.
3. When a company fails to repay deposits, and appeal must be made to the court immediately.
4. SEBI has a separate Investors' Grievances and Guidance Division.

[**Key:** 1. False, 2. True, 3. False, 4. True]

### C. Choose the best answer from the following:

1. Regarding bad delivery of shares, the authority to be approached for redressal is

   (a) SEBI (b) Registrar to the issue

   (c) Stock Exchange (d) Company Law Board/ Department of Company Affairs

2. The Investor Education and Protection Fund has been set up by
   (*a*) NSE (*b*) Central Government
   (*c*) BSE (*d*) SEBI
3. The aggrieved investor can appeal against the order of the Appellate Tribunal within
   (*a*) 60 days (*b*) 45 days
   (*c*) 30 days (*d*) 90 days

[**Key:** 1. (*c*), 2. (*b*), 3. (*a*)]

## II. Short answer type questions

1. List down only three possible grievances against listed companies.
2. Mention any two grievances of investors against stock exchanges.
3. What is Insider Trading?
4. What is short selling?
5. When will the Court interfere to redress investors' grievances?
6. What is investor charter?

## III. Paragraph type questions

1. State the need for and importance of investor's protection.
2. Analyse the grievances of investors against listed companies.
3. Explain the grievances of investors against the members of Stock Exchange.
4. Discuss the role of stock exchanges in dealing with investors' complaints.
5. How does the Department of Company Affairs solve investors' complaints?

## IV. Essay type questions

1. Highlight the various measures taken by the different authorities to protect the interest of investors in India.
2. List down the major grievances of investors against listed companies and members of stock exchanges and narrate the steps taken to redress them.

7

# OTCEI, NSE AND BSE

The growth of capital market and money market which constitute important components of the financial system is crucial for the economy. In recent years, these two markets are undergoing structural changes. A number of specialised institutions have been created consciously to strengthen the capital market and money market.

This chapter describes the functions and working of three such institutions, *viz.*,

1. Over The Counter Exchange of India.
2. National Stock Exchange.
3. Bombay Stock Exchange.

## OVER THE COUNTER EXCHANGE OF INDIA (OTCEI)

The market where secondhand securities are bought and sold is referred to as the stock market. Presently, the stock market consists of 22 regional stock exchanges and two national stock exchanges known as the National Stock Exchange (NSE) and the Over The Counter Exchange of India (OTCEI).

The OTCEI was incorporated in 1990 as a company under the Companies Act, 1956. It became fully operational on September 1992, with opening of a counter in Bombay. The OTCEI is recognised by the Government of India as a recognised stock exchange under Section 4 of the Securities Control Regulation Act, 1956.

### ❖ Features of the OTCEI

1. It is a national, ringless and computerised exchange.
2. As opposed to the traditional ring in the stock exchange, the trading will be 'screen based'. Transactions would take place through satellite communication telephone lines.
3. Trading on the OTCEI takes place through a network of computers of OTC dealers located at different places within the same city and even across cities. These computers allow dealers to quote, query and transact through a central OTC computer, using the telecommunication links.

4. Small and medium-sized companies with a paid-up capital between ₹ 30 lakhs and ₹ 10 crores may be enlisted on the OTCEI. The maximum limit has now been raised to ₹ 25 crores.
5. OTCEI deals in equity shares, preference shares, bonds, debentures and warrants.
6. A company which is listed on any other recognised stock exchange in India is not permitted simultaneously for listing on OTCEI.
7. The minimum offer should be 40 per cent of the issued capital or ₹ 20 lakhs worth of shares in face value, whichever is higher.

## ❖ Promoters

The OTCEI has been promoted by all India financial institutions, namely, UTI, ICICI, IDBI, IFCI, LIC, GIC, SBI Capital Markets and CanBank Financial Services Ltd.

The number of shares held and shareholding pattern of the promoters are shown in Table 7.1.

**TABLE 7.1: SHARE OF PROMOTERS IN OTCEI**

| *Institutions* | *Number of Shares held* | *Shareholding pattern (per cent)* |
|---|---|---|
| UTI | 20,00,000 | 20 |
| ICICI | 20,00,000 | 20 |
| IFCI | 8,00,000 | 8 |
| LIC | 8,00,000 | 8 |
| IDBI | 17,00,000 | 17 |
| GIC | 1,60,000 | 1.6 |
| SBI Capital Ltd. | 11,00,000 | 11 |
| CanBank Financial Service | 8,00,000 | 8 |
| New India Insurance | 1,60,000 | 1.6 |
| Oriental Insurance | 1,60,000 | 1.6 |
| United India Insurance | 1,60,000 | 1.6 |
| National Insurance | 1,60,000 | 1.6 |

The top executives of the promoters are on the Board of Directors of the OTCEI. The operations are supervised by SEBI and the Government of India.

## ❖ Participants in OTCEI market

The various participants in the OTCEI are:

### 1. Members and dealers appointed by OTCEI

These members and dealers appointed by the OTCEI may act as brokers and serve as market-makers.

Market making is a process of making two-way quotes, *i.e.*, buy as well as sell quotes for the same scrip by the sponsor. The maximum permissible spread between the buy and sell is 10 per cent. Compulsory market making has to be undertaken by the sponsor of the scrips for a minimum period of 18 months from the date of public trading. At the end of 18 months, the sponsor may withdraw from market making functions, provided an alternate compulsory market-maker has been assigned for the scrip. The sponsor will arrange one or more member/dealer to make market in the scrip sponsored by it, known as Additional Market-maker.

The compulsory and additional market-maker must hold at least 5 per cent of public offering between themselves for the purpose of market-making.

The members, in addition, carry-out the vital function of sponsorship. The sponsorship involves:

(*a*) Appraising a company at its project.

(*b*) Certifying to OTCEI the investment worthiness of the company and its project.

(*c*) Valuing the shares of the company.

(*d*) Obtaining governmental clearances for the issue of shares.

(*e*) Managing the public issue of securities.

(*f*) Servicing as a market-maker in the issued scrip for at least three years from the date of commencement of trade.

The member of OTCEI may be an institution, a banking subsidiary, a merchant bank or a finance company approved by SEBI.

**2. Companies, whose securities are listed on OTCEI**

Every company desirous of listing would have to get sponsored by a member of the OTCEI.

**3. Investors who trade in the OTCEI**

**4. Registrar who**

(*a*) Keeps custody of share certificates.

(*b*) Maintains register of members.

**5. Settlement bank**

It clears the payment between counters.

**6. SEBI and Government which exercises an overall supervision on OTCEI**

## TRADING IN OTC EXCHANGE

Every investor is required to register with OTC prior to trading. The investor registration is required to be done only once and is valid for trading on any OTC counter in the country and in any scrip. The registration is, at present, done free of cost. The purpose of investor registration is to facilitate computerised trading.

For buying and selling shares on OTC, an investor needs the INVEST OTC CARD which can be obtained from any OTC counter free of any charge just on filling the application form.

## ❖ Steps involved in buying/selling scrips

(*i*) Walk into any convenient OTC counter.

(*ii*) The PTI OTC Scan at each dealer's counter continuously displays the best buy and sell quotes offered by market-makers and also all other market-related information. All quotes and transactions are entered in the Central OTC computer which can be accessed by any dealer's computer, through telephone lines with modems.

(*iii*) See the price of shares on the PTI OTC Scan at the counter.

(*iv*) Decide to buy/sell.

(*v*) Ask counter operator to deal on your behalf.

(*vi*) Deal gets confirmed automatically at the best price.

(*vii*) In case of buying:

(*a*) Make cheques for payment.

(*b*) Get the Counter Receipt (CR). The CR is tradable and contains all information which appears on a share certificate.

(*c*) Return CR when cheque is cleared.

(*d*) Collect final CR within 7 days.

(*viii*) In case of selling:

(*a*) Give CR and Transfer Deed (TD) to counter.

(*b*) Receive sales confirmation slip.

(*c*) Return when CR and TD are cleared and collect cheque.

**BUYING AND SELLING**

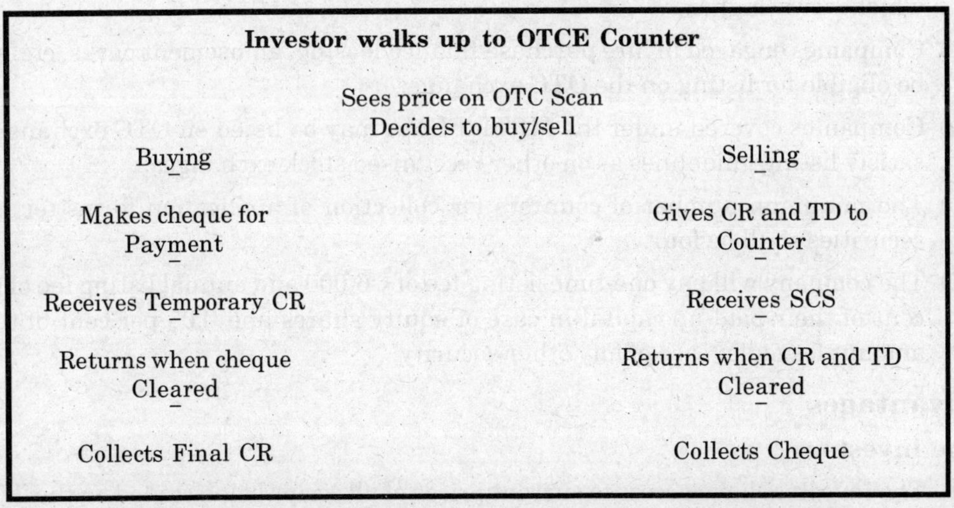


**Fig. 7.1: Steps involved in buying and selling scrips**

## ❖ Depository system

The OTCEI's unique depository system enables convenient and faster settlement for investors. The OTCEI's depositors transfer delivery electronically to the purchaser as soon as the trade is completed. Share certificates are not delivered to the purchaser. Their movement in a national market is brought with risk and operational delays. The OTCEI's depository system minimises the possibilities of bad deliveries on the exchange by ensuring the validity of the seller's transfer deed at the time of transfer as on the other exchanges. The settlement on the OTC exchange takes place on a rolling basis two days after the day of trade. This means faster payments to the seller and faster deliveries to the buyer.

The OTC exchange offers a whole lot of investor services, namely:

(*i*) Splitting/consolidation of PCRs (Counter Receipt).

(*ii*) Transfer/nomination.

(*iii*) Change in joint holder's names.

(*iv*) Exchange of PCR for share certificate and vice versa.

The OTC counter is truly a single window for investments. For each of the above services requested by investors, an Application Acknowledgement Slip (AAS) will be issued, nominal service charges may be levied and the services will be completed within reasonable time specified by OTCEI.

## ❖ Listing on OTC Exchange

The OTC exchange can list companies with issued capital from ₹ 30 lakhs up to ₹ 25 crores. The eligibility for listing are:

(*i*) The issue size should be a minimum of ₹ 20 lakhs or 25 per cent of the paid-up capital, whichever is higher.

(*ii*) Companies engaged in hire purchase/finance/leasing, amusement parks, etc. shall not be eligible for listing on the OTC exchange.

(*iii*) Companies covered under the MRTP/FEMA may be listed on OTC exchange if they satisfy listing guidelines as on other recognised stock exchanges.

(*iv*) The minimum number of counters for collection of application forms for issues of securities shall be four.

(*v*) The company will pay one-time listing fee of ₹ 6,000 and annual listing fee of 0.05 per cent of their paid-up capital in case of equity shares and 0.05 per cent of the gross amount issued in case of any other security.

## ❖ Advantages

### For the investors

1. The investors have access to current prices of all scrips being traded on the 'PTI Scan' display. This ensures transparency in trading. In a stock exchange, there is no transparency in the transaction and the investors do not know what price the scrip was bought and sold at.

2. Quick settlements and definite liquidity is ensured to investors.
3. It is a preverified trade and therefore no bad deliveries are possible.
4. Market-makers ensure price stability, liquidity and depth of the market.
5. Transaction is possible from remote location of the country on a national network exchange.
6. Automatic registration of shares lodged by an individual up to 0.5 per cent of its total paid-up equity is possible.
7. It is a foolproof system where manipulations will be minimal as deals will be matched on the computer screen on the spot.

**For the company**

1. Small and medium-sized companies would be able to raise required capital through OTCEI.
2. The cost of public issue is low.
3. The company gets high visibility at national level.
4. Dependable source of funds through structured bought out deals at reasonable prices is possible.
5. The companies listed on OTC would be subjected to low income tax.
6. The cumbersome process of obtaining the listing of the share may not be there for listing on OTC exchange.
7. Companies which require listing on OTCEI have to offer 10 per cent of the share capital for listing as against 60 per cent being the offer to the public in other stock exchanges.
8. Strong support for the share in secondary market through the presence of committed market-makers is available.

## ❖ Operational highlights

**TABLE 7.2: PERFORMANCE OF OTCEI FROM 1992-93 TO 1995-96**

| | *1992-93* | *1993-94* | *1994-95* | *1995-96* |
|---|---|---|---|---|
| No. of companies | 6 | 24 | 47 | 65 |
| No. of deals | 3568 | 25,145 | 2,27,322 | 61,130 |
| Volume (No. of shares in lakhs) | 3.66 | 69.03 | 921.57 | 287.66 |
| Value of transaction (in crores) | 1.55 | 38.74 | 365.02 | 119.86 |
| No. of members | 16 | 35 | 58 | 94 |
| No. of dealers | 89 | 167 | 225 | 235 |
| No. of investors | 35,000 | 1,05,000 | 2,85,000 | 3,00,000 |

The OTCEI has been promoted to address the problems faced by medium-sized companies and investors at large. It has set-up a modern electronic stock exchange to evolve cost-effective solution to these problems. It is now operating in 54 cities in 19 states. The OTCEI is moving towards setting higher standards to the benefit of the corporate and the investing community in India. The turnover in OTCEI during 2000-2001 was ₹ 126 crores.

## ❖ Recent trends

SEBI relaxed norms for listing on the OTCEI during March 1995.

1. Finance and leasing companies were allowed to get listed on OTCEI.
2. The minimum post-issue capital to be offered to the public to enable listing was lowered from 40 per cent to 25 per cent.

In April 1995, OTCEI modified its guidelines to allow listing of finance companies with more stringency.

1. The minimum issued capital was increased from ₹ 30 lakhs to ₹ 1 crore for finance companies.
2. A three-year track record of profitability was made compulsory before listing takes place.
3. OTCEI sponsor of these companies should hold at least 10 per cent of the public offer as market making inventory as against 5 per cent for other companies.

To facilitate offers for sale of bought out deals, OTCEI changed its guidelines in January 1996. The revised guidelines did away with the requirement of making an offer for sale of the entire bought out deal to the public, except the market-making inventory. The offerer can now offer a minimum 25 per cent of the bought out deals to the public. At the same time, the ratio of involvement of OTCEI members to non-OTCEI members has been brought down from 60 : 40 to 10 : 90.

The new guidelines issued by the SEBI stated that any company wanting to make a public issue should have a track record of dividend payment for at least three years immediately preceding five years before making the public issue.

If the companies do not satisfy this requirement, then they must at least get their project appraised by a financial institution or a nationalised bank which would participate in the public issue to the extent of at least 10 per cent of the total outlay in the form of equity or long-term debt.

With a view to reviewing the working of the OTCEI and making recommendations for its further improvement, SEBI appointed an eight-member committee under the chairmanship of Dr. S.A. Dave on April 17, 1996.

The recommendations of the Dave Committee are as follows:

1. The companies which are unable to make public issue as a consequence of the above guidelines be allowed with some checks.
2. The companies which do not satisfy the criteria should be allowed to get listed on the OTCEI provided they appoint a sponsor and two market-makers to the issue.
3. Companies which get delisted from regional stock exchanges should be allowed to list on OTCEI since shareholders of delisted companies do not have a platform to off-load their holdings. These companies should, however, be treated under a special category on the OTCEI.

4. The companies discussed above should be allowed listing on the OTCEI with a minimum lock-in period of three years. After three years, these companies may either choose to remain on the OTCEI or seek listing on other stock exchanges.
5. The ceiling of ₹ 25 crores on the equity capital of a company seeking listing on the OTCEI be removed.
6. The current rolling settlement system of three days should be increased to five years.
7. The committee stressed upon the need of increased involvement of the promoters of OTCEI.

There is no significant performance in the OTCEI nowadays.

## NATIONAL STOCK EXCHANGE (NSE) OF INDIA

The high-powered committee on the establishment of new stock exchanges headed by M.J. Pherwani, the former UTI Chairman, first mooted the idea of a National Stock Exchange in June 1991.

The committee identified the following weaknesses in the Indian stock markets.

1. Inefficient and outdated trading system resulting in non-transparent operations which has an adverse effect on investors' confidence.
2. Outdated settlement system inadequate to cater to the growing volume of business leading to delays and illiquidity in market.
3. Inability of various stock exchanges to function cohesively in terms of legal structure, regulatory framework, trading and settlement procedures, jobbing and spreads.
4. Inability to develop a debt market.

The establishment of National Stock Exchange (NSE) is a step to overcome the deficiencies of the existing stock market and to bring Indian financial markets in line with international markets.

The National Stock Exchange of India was incorporated in November 1992 with an equity capital of ₹ 25 crores and promoted by IDBI, ICICI, LIC, GIC and its subsidiaries, State Bank of India and SBI Capital Markets Limited.

### ❖ Objectives

The NSE has the following objectives:

1. To establish nationwide trading facility for equities, debts and hybrids.
2. To facilitate equal access to investors across the country.
3. To provide fairness, efficiency and transparency to the securities trading.
4. To enable shorter settlement cycles.
5. To meet international securities market standard.

## ❖ Features of NSE

1. The NSE employs a fully automated screen-based trading system.

   Investors can trade from 400 cities on a real-time basis.
2. It has three segments: the capital market segment, wholesale debt market segment and derivatives market.

   The capital market segment covers equities, convertible debentures and retail trade in debt instruments like non-convertible debentures. Securities of medium and large companies with nationwide investor base, including securities traded on other stock exchanges are traded in NSE through trading members.

   The wholesale debt market segment is a market for high value transactions in government securities, public sector bonds, commercial papers and other debt instruments.

   On the wholesale market segment, there are two types of entities, *viz.*, trading members and participants. Trading members are recognised members of the exchange selected on the basis of selection criteria laid down under the provisions of SEBI and the Securities Contract (Regulation) Act, 1956. They can trade on their own or on behalf of their clients. Participants are the organisations directly responsible for the settlement of trades.
3. The NSE market is a fully automated screen-based environment. There is no trading floor as is prevalent in the traditional stock exchanges.
4. The market operates with all participants stationed at their offices and making use of their computer terminals, to receive market information, to enter orders and to execute trade. Through 1,777 satellite dishes, there are 3,000 computer terminals connected to NSE.
5. The trading members in the capital market segment are connected to the central computer in Mumbai through a satellite link-up using VSATs and now fibre optic cables. The trading members in the wholesale debt market segment are linked, through dedicated high speed lines, to the central computer at Mumbai.
6. The NSE has opted for an order-driven system. The system provides enormous flexibility to trading members. A trading member can place various conditions on the order in terms of price, time or size. When an order is placed by a trading member, an order confirmation slip is generated. All orders received are stored in price and time priority. The computer system automatically searches for a match and no sooner to the same is found, the deal is struck. If it does not find a match immediately as may happen in the case of less liquid securities, the order is kept pending in the computer unless specified otherwise by the trading member.
7. When a trade takes place, a trade confirmation slip is printed at the trading member's workstation. It gives details like price, quantity, code number of the party and so on.
8. The identity of the trading member is not revealed to others when he places an order or when his pending orders are delayed. Hence, large order can be placed in NSE without the fear of influencing the market sentiment.

9. On the eight day of trading, each member gets a statement showing his net position, the amount of cash he has to transfer to the clearing bank and the securities he has to deliver to the clearing house.
10. Members are required to deliver securities and cash by the thirteenth and fourteenth day, respectively. The fifteenth day is the payout day.
11. The automated trade matching system secures the best price available in the market to the investor. The trading member can transact a high volume of business efficiently.
12. India Index Services and Products Ltd. (IISL) is a subsidiary of NSE Strategic Investment Corporation set up in May 1998 to provide a variety of indices and index related services and products.
13. NSE is also a part of a commodity exchange in the sense that it is a shareholder in NCDEX.

**Comparison between Stock Exchange, OTCEI and NSE**

| ***Basis*** | ***Stock Exchange*** | ***OTCEI*** | ***NSE*** |
|---|---|---|---|
| 1. Membership | Individuals, Firms and Corporates | Corporates only | Individuals, Firms and Corporates |
| 2. Method of Trading | Floor Screen-based | Screen-based | Screen-based |
| 3. System of Trading | Quote-driven Manual | Code-driven Computers linked to central OTCEI through telephone lines | Order-driven Computer linked by satellite through VSAT |
| 4. Settlement | T+ 2 | T+ 2 rolling settlement | Same day to T+ 2 in WDM Standard Delivery in Equity market |
| 5. Transparency | NIL | Ensured | Total transparency |
| 6. Intermediary | Jobber needed | Not needed | Not needed |

## NSE and Wholesale Debt Market (WDM)

Prior to the commencement of trading in WDM segment of NSE, the only trading mechanism available in the debt market was the telephone market. NSE provided for the first time in the country, an online, automated trading facility across a wide range of debt instruments.

The trading system of the exchange known as NEAT (National Exchange for Automated Trading) is fully automated, screen-based trading system that enables members across the country to trade simultaneously with enormous ease and efficiency.

WDM segment provides trading facilities for a variety of debt instruments. Initially, government securities, treasury bills and bonds issued by public sector undertakings were made available for trading. This range has been widened to include non-traditional instruments like Floating Rate Bonds, Zero Coupon Bonds, Index Bonds, Commercial Papers, Certificate of Deposits,

Corporate Debentures, State Government Loans, Bonds issued by Financial Institutions, Units of Mutual Funds and Securitised debt.

In order to enable investors like Provident Fund, Trusts, NBFCs and other high net worth investors to deal in debt instruments, the exchange has introduced a small booklet facility where an order of minimum of ₹ 1 lakh can be placed on the trading system of the exchange.

The operations of NSE in Wholesale Debt Market is shown in Table 7.3.

**TABLE 7.3: NSE TRADING IN WDM SEGMENT (2021-22)**

(₹ in crores)

| | |
|---|---|
| 1. Number of Trades | 5403 |
| 2. Trade Value (Net) | ₹ 378429.54 |
| 3. Average Daily Value | ₹ 1461.12 |

**Source:** https://www.inseindia.com/content/debt/debt_busineegrowth.htm

During the year 2014, NSE was ranked as the 2nd largest exchange in respect of contracts traded in stock futures. NSE is ranked 1st in the world in respect of contracts traded in index options. During the year 2014, NSE was ranked as the 7th largest exchange in the world in index futures.

NSE earned a net profit after tax of ₹ 779.68 crores in 2014.

During 2014, the income generated from trading was ₹ 1918.12 crores.

## ❖ National Securities Clearing Corporation

NSE has set up a wholly-owned subsidiary — National Securities Clearing Corporation that takes up the responsibility of settlement by opening guarantee. There is seamless integration of trading and settlement with full guarantee which protects the interest of investors fully. It commenced clearing operation in April 1996.

## ❖ National stock exchanges proposed system of Public Issue Offerings (PIOs)

The current process of initial offering is a lengthy one involving considerable time and costs. Considering several infirmities afflicting primary issue market for all types of securities, NSE has worked out an unique facility for achieving quantum improvement in the process of primary issues. The exchange is proposing to provide a facility for issue of securities for time-bound Initial Public Offerings (IPOs) and perpetual IPO.

Time-bound IPO includes primary issues for initial public offers and subsequent issues by companies. Perpetual IPO includes continuous offering of securities by the issues like open-ended mutual funds.

NSE PIO facility would operate through a fully automated screen-based system. Its facility can be used for all types of primary issues which are designed to meet specific requirements of issuer, investors and trading members. The system can also be used for issues which have various combinations or components of book building and fixed price issues. The software designed by the exchange provides flexibility for making issues of any security whether equity, debt or any other hybrid instrument.

## ❖ Objectives

The main objectives of starting the primary issues through a screen-based automated trading system are:

1. To provide facility to the issuer for online issue of securities.
2. To provide wide retail distribution network.
3. To reduce the cost of issue of securities.
4. To reduce delay in listing of securities.

## ❖ Time-bound PIO system

This system can be used for price/rate discovery in case of book building as well as for collecting subscription for fixed price. Issuer will announce certain number of securities in case of fixed price offerings and the total amount to be raised in case of book building. Eligible trading members will place subscription orders of investors specifying the number of shares or price as the case may be. The issue will be closed after a specified number of days after which the issuer will decide the allocation based on the offers received. The exchange proposes to provide a software which will help the issuer in finalising the basis of allotment as per the guidelines issued by SEBI.

After the allotment, the exchange will generate dummy trades for successful investors and send it to the respective members in the form of obligation. After the receipt of the obligation data, the members will initiate and expedite the process of fund collection and printing of application forms. The exchange proposes to provide a special software to trading members which will maintain a complete IPO back office system including printing of application forms, fund management and report generation.

Completed application forms and funds will be received by the exchange on a predetermined day based on which final despatch of certificates and release of funds will be done.

## ❖ Internet broking

NSE launched internet trading in early February 2000. It is the first exchange in the country to provide web-based access to investors to trade directly on the exchange. The orders originating from the PCs of the investors are routed through the internet to the trading terminals of the designated brokers with whom they are connected and further to the exchange for trade executions. Soon after these orders get matched and result into trades, the investors get confirmation about them on their PCs through the same internet route.

## ❖ Wireless Application Protocol (WAP)

SEBI has approved trading through wireless medium on WAP platform. WAP is introduced in November 2000. This provides access to its order book through the handheld devices, which use WAP technology. This serves primarily retail investors who are mobile and want to trade from any place when the market prices for stocks at their choice are attractive.

## BOMBAY STOCK EXCHANGE (BSE)

The Bombay Stock Exchange is the oldest stock exchange in Asia and it was established as early as 1875 itself. It is under the control of a Governing Body consisting of 19 directors. Among them, one is an executive director, another one is a RBI nominee. Nine are elected by brokers and the balance five are public representatives. It has more than 700 members and most of them are individual members. At present, corporate members are being admitted.

There are three segments in BSE. They are:

(*i*) Equity segment.

(*ii*) Debt segment, and.

(*iii*) Derivative segment.

### 1. Equity segment

In this segment, there are nearly 5,624 listed companies. It has market capitalisation of ₹ 51,38,015 crores during 2007-08. The cash segment turnover during 2007-08 was ₹ 15,78,856 crores. Many of the companies listed on BSE are small in size. The shares of the listed companies of this exchange are grouped into three categories in terms of their quantitative characteristics. They are:

(*i*) Group A shares, having large equity base, very high liquidity and consistency of good performance.

(*ii*) Group $B_1$ shares, having sound financial conditions, high liquidity and equity of more than ₹ 3 crores.

(*iii*) Group $B_2$ shares, having equity below ₹ 3 crores, low trading record and not sound financial conditions.

### 2. Debt segment

This segment purely deals with debt securities. It has also got two sub-segments on the basis of the different issues of debt securities. These segments are:

(*i*) F Segment, and

(*ii*) G Segment.

The F segment deals with all corporate debt securities while the G segment deals with different Government securities, treasury bills, PSU bonds, etc.

### 3. Derivative segment

This segment is meant for derivative trading only. Recently, SEBI has permitted some of the derivative products like index futures, currency futures, interest rate futures, etc,. and hence derivatives trading is picking up in BSE. The derivative segment turnover was just ₹ 9 crores in 2005-06 and it has gone up to ₹ 2,42,308 crores in 2007-08.

In 2008, Corporate Bond Trading platform has been set up in BSE to develop the private corporate debt market.

## 4. SME and Start-up Platform

The SME and Start-up Platform has completed 10 years of operations during 2021. It has helped 377 projects to raise funds to the fine of ₹ 4,011 crores. The market value of stocks listed on SME platform amounts to ₹ 47,929 crores, and for startp platform, it is ₹ 588 crores.

The key indicators of BSE and NSE are shown for three years from 2019-20 to 2020-21 in the following Table 7.4:

**TABLE 7.4: KEY INDICATORS OF BSE AND NSE**

| *Indicators* | *BSE Sensex* | | *NSE Nifty* | |
|---|---|---|---|---|
| | *2019-20* | *2020-21* | *2019-20* | *2020-21* |
| **1** | **2** | **3** | **4** | **5** |
| Sensex/Nifty | | | | |
| (*i*) End Period | 29,468.5 | 49,509.2 | 8,597.8 | 14,690.7 |
| (*ii*) Average | 38,756.7 | 40,826.4 | 11,488.0 | 12,016.9 |
| PE ratio @ | 26.40 | 26.80 | 19.38 | 38.45 |
| PB ratio @ | 2.95 | 2.83 | 2.45 | 3.96 |
| Gross Turnover (₹ in crores) | 660,896.02 | 690,843.00 | 89,98,811.07 | 1,09,22,052.89 |
| Market Capitalisation (₹ in crores) | 1,13,48,756.59 | 1,88,03,518.6 | 1,12,43,112 | 1,86,46,759 |

***Source:*** SEBI – Handbook of Statistics 2021

The total number of companies listed on BSE as on March 31, 2022 was 5,350 as against 5,477 as on March 31, 2021.

The number of listed companies in NSE during 2021-22 was 2,065 as against 1,968 in 2020-21.

## QUESTIONS

## I. Objective type questions:

### A. Fill in the blanks:

1. Companies with a paid-up capital between ₹ __________ and ₹ 25 crores can be enlisted on OTCEI.
2. NSE follows __________ driven system.
3. The umbrella brand for NSE is __________.
4. Members of OTCEI are __________ only.
5. The Bombay Stock Exchange was established in __________.

[**Key:** 1. ₹ 30 lakhs, 2. order, 3. Nifty, 4. corporates, 5. 1875]

**B. State whether the following statements are TRUE or FALSE:**

1. OTCEI is a national exchange.
2. The member of OTCEI may be individuals.
3. There is no trading floor in NSE.
4. The wholesale debt market is a market for Government securities.
5. DFHI is a specialised capital market institution.
6. BSE does not permit corporate membership.

[**Key:** 1. True, 2. False, 3. True, 4. True, 5. False, 6. False]

## II. Short answer type questions:

1. What is market making?
2. What is depository system?
3. State the features of OTCEI.
4. What is trade confirmation slip?
5. State the objectives of NSE.

## III. Essay type questions:

1. Explain the advantages of OTCEI to investors and the company.
2. Discuss the method of trading in OTCEI.
3. Make a comparison between Stock Exchange, OTCEI and NSE.
4. Explain the features of NSE and its method of trading..
5. Explain the features of BSE.

# 8 DEPOSITORY SYSTEM

## DEFINITION AND MEANING

The term depository is defined as 'a central location for keeping securities on deposit'. It is also defined as 'a facility for holding securities, either in certificated or uncertificated form to enable book entry transfer of securities'.

It is understood from the above two definitions that the depository is a place where securities are stored, recorded in the books on behalf of the investors.

In recent times, the volume of securities and the size of the business handled have increased manifold. Hence, the present-day depositories are fully automated to serve the customers faster and with accuracy.

Therefore, a depository can be defined as, 'an institution which transfers the ownership of securities in electronic mode on behalf of its members'.

A depository is a nominee who keeps the scrips on behalf of the investors. He undertakes the custodian role. The depository leads the capital market towards a scripless system through immobilisation and dematerialisation of share certificates. Immobilisation of securities means stopping the physical movement. The number physical certificates that pass between company and customers become negligible as lodged and the immobilised certificates are registered in the name of depository nominee. Dematerialisation means issue of one certificate in favour of the Depository Nominee or not issuing the certificates. The depository operates the computerised book entry transfer for the securities. This results in a speedier and more liquid trading environment. The depository also undertakes the trade and settlement processing through its subsidiary as a part of its function.

## OBJECTIVES OF A DEPOSITORY

A depository enables the capital market to achieve the following objectives:

1. Reduce the time for transfer of securities.
2. Avoid the risk of settlement of securities.
3. Enhance liquidity and efficiency.
4. Reduce cost of transaction for the investor.
5. Create a system for the central handling of all securities.
6. Promote the country's competitiveness by complying with global standards.
7. Provide service infrastructure in a capital market.

## ACTIVITIES OF THE DEPOSITORY

The main activities of the depository are as follows:

1. Accepting deposit of securities for custody.
2. Making computerised book entry deliveries of securities which are immobilised in its custody.
3. Creating computerised book entry pledges of securities in its custody.
4. Providing for withdrawal of securities.
5. Undertaking corporate actions like distribution of dividend and interest.
6. Redemption of securities on maturity.

## INTERACTING INSTITUTIONS

There are three institutions that are interacting in a depository system:

1. The Central Depository.
2. Share Registrar and Transfer Agent.
3. Clearing and Settlement Corporation.

### 1. Central depository

The central depository is a nominee who holds the securities on behalf of the investors and maintains records related to that in an electronic mode.

### 2. Share registrar and transfer agent

The registrar is an institution that controls the issuance of securities.

The transfer agent is one who retains the names and addresses of registered securities owners and re-register traded securities in the names of new owners.

### 3. Clearing and settlement corporation

It is a centre to do trade matching and settle the funds and exchange securities.

# DEPOSITORY PROCESS

## 1. Immobilisation of shares

Immobilisation of shares is the first step in the depository process. In the immobilisation process, the share certificates are submitted to the depository which converts the physical certificates into electronic data and starts issuing statement of accounts for the holdings of the investors or shareholders.

The immobilisation process is illustrated in the following figure:

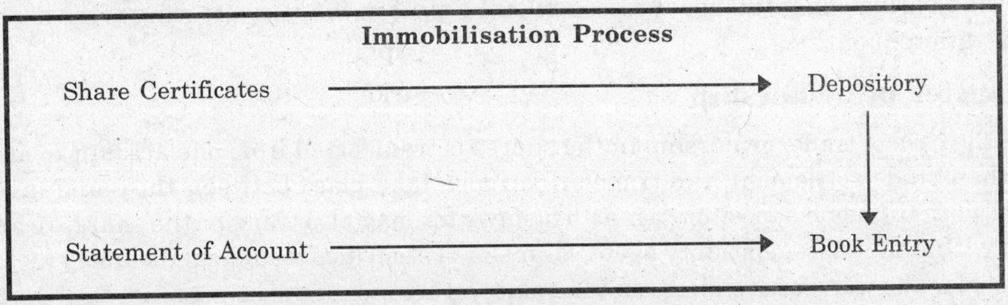


**Fig. 8.1: Immobilisation Process**

The steps involved in the process of converting the existing paper certificates into an electronic mode are as follows:

1. The stock exchange will notify through an advertisement after which the investors may deposit their shares into the Central Depository through an Authorised Depository Agent with whom the investors' account will be maintained.
2. On receipt of the share certificate, the Depository or the Depository's Agent sends the certificate to the Registrar and Transfer Agent for registering Depository Nominee's name.
3. Within a prescribed period, the Registrar will transfer the scrips, after confirming that the shares are good for disposition, in the name of the Depository Nominee and return it for safe custody with the Depository. The depository will credit the account of the investor with the number of shares deposited.

Thereafter the shares get traded through a book entry system.

In the case of fresh issues, the applicant will have to give depository account particulars in the application form. Successful applicants will have their account credited directly. Those who do not have any account will have to open an account with any of the Authorised Depository to enable the allotment and future trade.

## ❖ Withdrawal of shares

The shares which are held in the depository can be withdrawn by the investor. The withdrawn scrip takes physical form as in the case of pre-immobilised model.

## TRADING IN A DEPOSITORY SYSTEM

When the investor sells his share, the depository debits the 'Free Balance' of the seller and credits the 'Available Balance' of the buyer for the scrip traded on the settlement day. After the payment has been made by the buyer, the available balance will be converted into free balance which can be traded by the buyer. It is like, a Share Bank where the balances are in the form of different corporate entities' shares instead of currency. Confirmation statements are sent to the investors after the accounts are adjusted or at stipulated intervals. The delivery and settlement process will be the same as at present except that physical delivery will be replaced by a book entry. The clearing and settlement process will take place in the separate wing of the depository or in the different entity.

### ❖ Transfer of ownership

In the case of trade, ownership in the shares is transferred from one account to another. Other than trade settlement, the transfer can also take place between the same investor's accounts with the same depository agent. The investor may also transfer the shares to another account within the same depository agent. Transfer of securities to immediate family member is also possible. The transfer of shares can take place on account of the investor offering the shares as collateral security for a loan. In this process, the institution's lien can be marked in the accounts. In case the lien is marked, the share will not be treated as a 'Free' and could not be available for trade. When the loan is repaid, the lien is cancelled and thereafter the shares will be available for trade.

### ❖ Declaration of dividend/bonus/rights

Though the shares are in the names of the depository nominee, the real owners are individuals or institutions. When a company declares dividend/rights or bonus issues, the depository will prepare the record of investors as on the record date and submit it to the Registrar of Company. The dividend will be sent by the Registrar after calculating the dividend payable to each investor directly. When a company declares bonus shares, the Registrar will calculate the bonus entitlement and advise the depository about the number of shares to be credited to each accountholder. In the case of the rights offer, based on the record of depositories, the Registrar will prepare a letter of offer and send it to the investor. The Registrar will advise the depository the number of shares to be credited to each account on the basis of the application and allotment. Based on this advice, the investor's account will be credited by the depository reporting system.

The Depository is functioning in an advanced automated environment. So, the reporting system is fast and highly superior. The investors get the following statements regularly: (*i*) Contract statements with details of trade, (*ii*) Confirmation statements with details of trade, (*iii*) Monthly traded particulars, and (*iv*) Quarterly statements showing the security balances.

## DEPOSITORIES IN THE INTERNATIONAL MARKET

Group of thirty, a private sector group concerned with the working of International Financial System, convened a symposium in London during 1989, to discuss the state of clearance and settlement practices in the world's principal markets. This symposium formed a group to suggest:

(*i*) A set of international standards with regard to world capital markets and also (*ii*) A specified time limit for their implementation. The committee recommended, among other things, that the clearance and settlement process be improved through the usage of depositories.

The G30 recommendations, as commonly referred to, suggested that the Central Depository should perform the functions of settlement of securities and the ancillary service of safe custody and administration of securities held in its custody.

Following this, many countries have set up depositories. The concept of depositories has transformed the capital markets on account of speed and accuracy of trade settlement. They have also resulted in attracting a number of global players into the economy because the participants are confident about the genuineness of the securities and the transfer process completed within minimum timeframe.

## DEPOSITORY SYSTEM IN INDIA

The agenda for capital market reform was set in motion by the government in tandem with the policy of economic liberalisation. Modernisation of stock exchanges and related system and procedures constituted an integral part of this programme. The stock exchanges in India were characterised by lack of transparency, complex trading procedure and age-old settlement system resulting in inordinate delays and manifold risks.

The settlement system called for physical movement of share certificates in recording ownership changes in the company books. The serious risks associated with the paper-based settlement system were bad deliveries, delays in transfer and registration, mutilation, loss, forgery and theft of certificates. The share transfer in India takes place on an average about 2 months while in other countries it takes just a few days. The inadequacies of the settlement mechanism were brought into sharp focus and highlighted on several investors, forums. There was a pressing demand to modernise the infrastructure and introduce automated trading to bring Indian capital market at par with world standards.

Promulgation of the Depository Act, 1996 is one of the series of steps taken by the government for removing the shortcomings of the present system.

The depository system aims at replacing the manual system of share transfer, settlement of transactions and physical delivery of shares by a method of simple book entries. The system is envisaged to reduce the total time taken to complete a transaction and ensure greater liquidity.

## SEBI (DEPOSITORIES AND PARTICIPANTS) REGULATION ACT, 1996

The Depositories Ordinance was promulgated in September 1995. Following the issue of ordinance, the SEBI circulated a consultative paper seeking views from the public on the framework of depository system. This was followed by issue of the SEBI (Depositories and Participants) Regulations which was promulgated by the government in May 1996.

The features of the Act and the regulations are briefed hereunder:

## ❖ Scope of the Act

The scope of the legislation extends to the issue of scripless trading, transfer of ownership by means of book entries through electronic media and holding of securities through depository system as also fungibility of shares.

## ❖ Features of the Act

**Depository institutions:** The Act provides for creation of one or more depository institutions registered under the Companies Act and predominantly owned by the market participants.

The SEBI has proposed that the minimum net worth of a depository should be ₹ 100 crores.

**Depository participants:** The Act envisages that a depository will interface with the users through a set of Depository Participants (DPs). They are persons dealing directly with the depository for their clients. The DP is a crucial link between the investor and the depository. The DP will be deemed as an agent of the depository. The depository will therefore be responsible for the acts of omission and commission on the part of the depository participants.

The SEBI has proposed that the following entities could be permitted to be registered as depository participants, namely commercial banks, financial institutions, stock exchanges, financial services companies owned to the extent of 75 per cent by any of the above mentioned institutions as well as companies registered abroad providing custodial, clearing or settlement services in the securities market and approved by the Central Government.

**Investors' choice:** An investor is given the option between holding physical securities as at present and having a depository based ownership record. Such an option can be exercised by the investor either at the time of an initial offer of securities by a company indicating his choice in the application form or at any subsequent time. The investor will have also the freedom to switch from the depository mode to non-depository mode and *vice versa.*

**Free transferability:** The Act has made free transferability of shares. The Act has taken away the companies' right to use their discretion in effecting transfer of securities by deleting Sec. 22A from the Securities Contracts Regulation Act and inserting Sec. 111A in the Companies Act. This would mean that, once the agreed consideration is paid by the buyer, he is automatically entitled to all the rights associated with the security. As soon as the intimation regarding delivery of security is received, the transfer will be effected by a depository participant on delivery versus payment basis. In the depository mode, no transfer deed is required and the procedural requirements under Sec. 108 of the Companies Act have been dispensed with.

**Rights of transferee:** The Act provides that the transferee of a security will be entitled to all the rights including voting rights associated with the security. However, if any transfer is made in contravention of any provisions of SEBI Act or Sick Industrial Companies Act, the issuer company or depository or SEBI can make an application to the Company Law Board (CLB). Pending the completion of enquiry, the CLB can suspend the voting rights in respect of the securities so transferred. However, the transferee in such case will continue to enjoy the economic rights like bonus, rights and dividend attached to the security. After the enquiry if the

CLB is satisfied about the contravention, it can direct the depository to make rectification in ownership records.

**Fungibility:** Section 83 of the Companies Act requires that each share in a company shall be distinguished by an appropriate number. This section is deleted now and the Act has made that the securities held by a depository are fungible. As per the Act, share certificates need not carry distinctive numbers and all shares will form part of a fungible mess. All share certificates will become interchangeable like withdrawing money from a bank account without being concerned about the number printed on the currency notes at the time of deposit into the bank and at the time of withdrawal of money.

**No stamp duty:** The Act has done away with stamp duty on secondary market transactions in the depository mode. At the time of issue of securities, the issuer company shall pay stamp duty on the total amount of securities issued, whether through a depository or direct to investors in the form of physical certificates. Where an investor opts to exit from a depository and seeks to issue of physical certificates from the issuer, the issue of such certificates shall attract stamp duty as is payable on the issue of duplicate certificates. All transactions outside the depository made will attract stamp duty as at present.

**Depository records as legal evidence:** The ownership records maintained by the depository or the participants will be accepted as *prima facie* evidence in legal proceedings. The depository records will receive the same treatment as available to banks under the Bankers' Book Evidence Act.

**Pledge or hypothecation:** A depository shall allow for the creation of pledge or hypothecation in respect of securities left in the depository mode.

The Depositories Related Laws (Amendment) Ordinance of 1997 makes consequential changes in the Companies Act, 1956; the Industrial Development Bank of India, 1954; the State Bank of India Act, 1955; the State Bank of India (Subsidiary Banks) Act, 1959; the Banking Companies (Acquisition and Transfer of Undertaking) Act, 1970 and 1980 and the Indian Stamp Act, 1899. It enables shares of statutory bodies like the Industrial Development Bank of India, the State Bank of India, other public sector banks and the units of mutual funds including those of UTI to be traded by means of the depository system.

## DEPOSITORY PROCESS IN INDIA

The depository process can be described as under:

There are four constituents in this system. They are: (*i*) The depository, (*ii*) The depository participant, (*iii*) The beneficial owner, and (*iv*) The issuer.

**The depository:** The depository is entrusted with the securities for effecting the transfer of ownership of the securities. He is the custodian of his clients' securities. The depository has no right over the security except with the transfer of it.

**The depository participant:** The depository participant (DP) is the link between the depositors and the owner of securities. He is deemed as an agent of the depository. The depository, therefore, is responsible for the acts of omission and commission on the part of the DP. The depository and DP are registered with SEBI which regulates their functioning.

Clearing houses of recognised stock exchanges, non-banking financial companies with minimum networks and banks including foreign banks are eligible to become DP.

**The beneficial owner:** The beneficial owner is the real owner of the security. He lodges his securities with the depository in the form of book entries. He has all rights and liabilities associated with the securities.

**The issuer:** It is the company which issues the security.

The issuer first gives the investors a choice of holding their securities either in the physical form or the scripless form (through the depository). The investors make their choice and communicate to the issuing company at the time of initial offer itself. Thereafter, the issuing company intimates the depository details about the allotment of securities. The depository in turn records the names of allottees of the securities in their records as the beneficial owners. The name of the depository is entered by the issuer as the registered holder of the securities.

The investor is free to exercise his option either at the time of applying for the securities or at any time thereafter. The investor is free to alter his choice subsequently.

When the owner changes his choice to the depository system, he is required to surrender the certificates to the issuing company. The issuer cancels them and substitutes the name of the depository as the registered owner in the place of the name of the allottee. Thereafter, the depository records in the book the name of the allottee as beneficial owner. Subsequent transfer under depository system is denoted by means of book entry on receipt of intimation in the prescribed form.

An investor who wishes to avail himself of the services will have to open an account with the depository through a depository participant. The investor has to enter into an agreement with the DP after which he is issued a client number.

To convert his physical holding of securities into a dematerialised form, the investor should make an application to the DP in a Dematerialisation Request Form (DRF). The DP forwards the DRF within seven days of receipt along with share certificates to the issuer or to its Registrar and Share Transfer Agent (RTA) after electronically registering the request with the depository. The depository at the same time electronically intimates the dematerialisation request to the respective issuer company or the Registrar and Share Transfer Agent. The issuer or the RTA verifies the validity of the share certificate as well as the signature of the investor appearing in DRF. Thereupon, it intimates its authorisation to credit the shares in the name of the investor. On receipt of the intimation, the depository causes the entry to be made in the account of the client at the DP.

To withdraw his securities balance, the investor makes an application to the depository through the DP in a Rematerialisation Form Request (RFR). Upon receipt of the request, the DP verifies the balance available to the extent of the request contained in the RFR and electronically intimates the request to the depository. The depository thereupon blocks the balance of the DP and intimates the RFR to the issuer or the RTA. Upon the acceptance of the RFR, the issuer company or the RTA issues share certificates within 30 days.

## BENEFITS OF DEPOSITORY SYSTEM

The depository system confers the following benefits:

### ❖ Benefits to investors

1. This system will eliminate paperwork as the book entry system does not need physical movement of certificates for transfer process.
2. The risk of bad deliveries, fraud and misplaced, mutilated and lost share certificates will not exist.
3. The electronic media will shorten settlement time and hence the investor can save time and increase the velocity of security movement.
4. Investors will be able to change portfolio more frequently.
5. The distribution of dividends, interest and other benefits will be speedier as the ownership can be easily identifiable.
6. The cost of transfer is less as the share transfers are exempt from stamp duty.
7. Faster payment is in the ensured case of sale of shares.

The cost comparison for trading in physical and demat segments is made in the following Table 8.1.

**TABLE 8.1: A COMPARISON OF COST FOR A LONG-TERM INVESTOR WHO BUYS AND TRADES SHARES WORTH ₹ 10,000**

*(Fig. in basic points)*

| | *Without Transacting* | | | *With Transacting 10 Times* | | |
|---|---|---|---|---|---|---|
| | *Physical Shares* | *Demat Shares* | *Savings* | *Physical Shares* | *Demat Shares* | *Savings* |
| Brokerage | 75-100 | 50-75 | 25-50 | 750-1000 | 500-750 | 250-500 |
| Stamp Duty | 50 | — | 50 | — | — | — |
| Postal Charges | 10-30 | — | 10-30 | — | — | — |
| Company Objection (notarisation, etc.) | 10-30 | — | 10-30 | — | — | — |
| Settlement charges | — | 5-10 | – (5-10) | — | 50-100 | – (50-100) |
| Custody (5 years) | — | — | – (25-50) | — | 5-10 | – (5-10) |
| Total | | | 35-100 | | | 140-445 |

***Source:*** An Investor's Guide to Depository — NSDL.

### ❖ Benefits to companies

1. The companies will be able to know the particulars of beneficial owners and their holdings periodically.
2. At the time of declaration of dividends, bonus, etc., there will not be any rush for transfer related activities for the companies.

3. Investor complaints will be reduced substantially as majority of the present-day complaints relate to signature difference, time lapse during the transfer and mutilated certificates.

   The financial institutions will not have the problem of processing and storing huge volume of scrips. They can depute their team for other productive business development-oriented purposes.

4. It would be possible to send notices and annual reports without delay because all securities of the company with the participant are accumulated and held in the name of the participant in the Depository's book.

### ❖ Benefits to the capital market

1. The capital market will be more transparent as the trading, clearing and settlement mechanism have to be highly automated and interlinked with the depository among themselves.
2. The market will be highly automated and efficient due to the usage of computing and telecommunication technology for the back office activities for all the capital market players.
3. The investors' confidence will improve due to the above two aspects.
4. The foreign investors will start participating in the market resulting in a more buoyant capital market.
5. The existence of depository will result an increase in the volume of trade both by number and value.
6. It will attract more number of the Indian middle income group within the ambit of the capital market players either through direct involvement or through mutual funds.

## NATIONAL SECURITIES DEPOSITORY LTD. (NSDL)

The first depository in India — The National Securities Depository Limited (NSDL) was established in 1996. It has been promoted by the Industrial Development Bank of India, Unit Trust of India and National Stock Exchange. NSDL started operations in November 1996 and has made significant progress since then.

NSDL performs a wide range of securities related functions through the DPs:

1. Maintenance of individual investors' beneficial holdings in an electronic form.
2. Dematerialisation and rematerialisation of securities.
3. Account transfer for settlement of trade in electronic shares.
4. Allotments in the electronic form in case of initial public offerings.
5. Distribution of non-cash corporate actions.
6. Facility for freezing/locking of investor accounts.
7. Facility for pledge and hypothecation of securities.

## CENTRAL DEPOSITORY SERVICES (INDIA) LTD. (CDSL)

The CDSL has been set up by Bombay Stock Exchange and cosponsored by SBI, Bank of India, Bank of Baroda and HDFC Bank. It commenced its operation on March 22, 1999.

The depository services for listed companies are given in the following Table.

**TABLE 8.2: DEPOSITORY SERVICES FOR LISTED COMPANIES**

| *Particulars* | *NSDL* | | *CDSL* | |
|---|---|---|---|---|
| | ***2020-21*** | ***2021-22*** | ***2020-21*** | ***2021-22*** |
| 1 | 2 | 3 | 4 | 5 |
| Number of Investor Accounts (lakhs) | 217 | 267 | 334 | 630 |
| Number of Companies Signed up (Listed and Unlisted), *of which* | 34,225 | 37,478 | 16,464 | 18,268 |
| No. of Companies that are Listed | 5,681 | 5,846 | 5,764 | 5,886 |
| Quantity of Securities in Demat Form (crores) | 2,43,352 | 2,77,353 | 47,443 | 56,757 |
| Value of Securities in Demat Form (₹ crores) | 2,43,74,524 | 3,01,87,556 | 27,43,936 | 37,17,278 |
| Market Capitalisation of Listed Companies Joined in Demat (₹ crores) | 2,07,76,010 | 2,66,74,665 | 2,03,52,629 | 2,63,55,532 |
| Custody Value of Shares of Listed Companies (₹ crores) | 1,78,91,666 | 2,29,38,892 | 23,25,563 | 32,28,356 |
| Ratio of Dematerialised Equity Shares to Total Outstanding Shares Listed (per cent) | 86.1 | 86.0 | 11.5 | 12.2 |

*Source:* NSDL and CDSL
***Source:*** SEBI Annual Report, 2021-22

## DRAWBACKS

Inspite of the progress made, introduction of demat trading has not been an unqualified success. The subsequent paragraphs explain the drawbacks or issues of the existing system and the steps to be taken to make the Depository System in India an efficient one.

1. **Multiple depositories:** A depository is a service institution like any other basic infrastructural institutions. It is expected to provide service at minimum cost to customers and investors. But, it requires capital investment of about ₹ 100 crores. This cost has to be borne by the participating investors and investors attached to the depository over a period of time. In case there are more than one depository, the capital cost will have to be distributed among the investors. Thus, multiple depositories result an increased cost rather than reducing it to the depository users. In USA though there are three depositories, the Depository Trust Corporation accounts for more than 90 per cent of the trade volume. In Germany, the system has been integrated operationally into almost a single system.

A single depository structure instead of the present multidepository model will result in a number of benefits such as lower transaction cost, reduced inter-depository movements of messages and transfers, better service from depository participants and easy interaction with stock exchange.

2. **Clearing and settlement corporations:** The depository legislation and SEBI regulations have overlooked the activities of the clearing and settlement corporation which is a vital factor for the success of the depository. There has to be a centralised clearing and settlement corporation to handle the trade in all the exchanges. The clearing and settlement corporation has to be an integral part of the depository so that the back office activities related to the settlement can be executed effectively with speed. In USA, the National and Clearing Corporation acts as the centralised institution for coordinating settlement activities regardless of the market where the trade takes place.

In India, there is a need to set up a clearing and settlement corporation as a part of the depository to have interface with the various exchanges.

3. The depository regulation provides for the selection of the company for immobilisation of securities rather than making it a process to start from the companies. The choice of admitting the security is that of the depository. If the company wants to sever its relationship with depository on a future date, the investors will be put to lot of inconvenience and hardship. Similarly, the depositories will be vying with one another to garner business resulting in inter-depository competition which will affect the service industry concept in the long run.

4. In India, the retail investors hold about 30 per cent of the market capitalisation. These investors have not yet shown any interest for demat trading. This may be due to lack of awareness or old habits or the fear of being caught in the tax net.

Even in the US, where dematerialisation of shares is in practice over 25 years, many investors prefer to hold their equity in scrip form.

As long as shareholding in demat form is not made compulsory by a suitable regulation, there will be a large number of shareholders who will opt to hold their equity in scrip form.

5. There are two rates for the securities of the companies that have joined the depository, one for the immobilised shares and another one for the physical ones. The existence of different rates will be deterrent to the smooth trade and settlement process.

The depository participants act on an accountholder's written instructions to give effect to his change of address, change of signature and again rely upon matching the signature. This system is susceptible to misuse. Again it is possible that the cancelled shares are presented to the company for dematerialising, and in the absence of proper checks and controls, which will make it unique, non-duplicable and non-copyable, these get dematted. Once dematted, a share loses its individual identity and the company may not be in a position to reverse its action. Counterfeiting of shares and introducing them in the market is relatively easy in the absence of duplication proof security features. This is particularly relevant in case of companies that are old and have issued shares from time-to-time.

SEBI should issue guidelines laying down security features to make share certificate counterfeit-proof. These should be enforced on companies by suitable amendments to model listing agreements.

## REMEDIAL MEASURES

The government and the regulatory authorities have initiated a number of measures to overcome the constraints.

1. SEBI has undertaken a public awareness programme to popularise the concept of demat trading.
2. To increase the volume in demat segment, SEBI has made it compulsory for the institutional investors and banks having a minimum portfolio of securities of ₹ 10 crores to settle transaction in respect of the selected list of eight securities only through demat format with effect from January 15, 1988.
3. Due to lack of liquidity in the demat segment, SEBI has allowed delivery of demat securities in the physical trading as well from April 6, 1996. An investor purchasing shares in the physical segment may get delivery in demat shares and such shares will be good delivery. But, today, demat trading has become the order of the day.
4. Now, SEBI has introduced Basic Services Demat Account (BSDA) with limited services with a view to achieving wider financial inclusion and for encouraging the holding of demat accounts.

## QUESTIONS

### I. Objective type questions:

### A. Fill in the blanks:

1. A depository is an ________ which transfers the ownership of securities in ________ mode.
2. The central depository __________ the security on behalf of the investors.
3. __________ of shares is the first step in the depository process.
4. __________ is the link between the depository and the owner.
5. Depository system reduces time for __________ of securities.
6. __________ indemnifies the loss to the beneficial owner caused to him due to the negligence of the depository or the depository participant.

[**Key:** 1. institution - electronic, 2. holds 3. immobilisation, 4. Depository participant, 5. transfer, 6. depository.]

### B. State whether the following statements are TRUE or FALSE:

1. There are two institutions interacting in a depository system.
2. Stamp duty is not exempted in share transfer through depository.
3. Depository system leads to scripless system.
4. Immobilisation of securities means stopping the physical movement of shares.
5. To withdraw the balance of securities, the investor has to make an application in Dematerialisation Request Form.

6. The investors have the option of subscribing to securities in either physical or dematerialised form.
7. All new initial public offerings are compulsorily made in demat form.

[**Key:** 1. False, 2. False, 3. True, 4. True, 5. False, 6. True, 7. False.]

## C. Choose the best from the following:

1. In a depository system, depository refers to:
   (*a*) Share (*b*) Shareholder
   (*c*) Institution (*d*) None of these
2. The first step in the depository process is:
   (*a*) Appointment of transfer agent (*b*) Establishment of clearing corporation
   (*c*) Selection of depository participant (*d*) Immobilisation of shares
3. The vital link between the investor and the depository is:
   (*a*) A central depository (*b*) Depository Participant
   (*c*) Settlement Corporation (*d*) All of the above.

[**Key:** (*i*) (*c*), (*ii*) (*d*), (*iii*) (*b*)]

## II. Short answer type questions:

1. Define a depository.
2. State the objectives of depository.
3. What is fungibility?
4. Write a note on Depository Participant.
5. What is rematerialisation?

## III. Essay type questions:

1. Explain the immobilisation process.
2. Describe the advantages of depository system.
3. Explain the features of SEBI (Depository and Participants) Regulation Act.
4. Discuss the drawbacks of the depository system and suggest measures to make it an efficient one.

## SECTION - B

# FINANCIAL SERVICES

9. Financial Services
10. Merchant Banking
11. Hire Purchase
12. Leasing
13. Venture Capital
14. Mutual Funds
15. Discounting, Factoring and Forfaiting
16. Securitisation of Debt
17. Derivatives
18. Credit Rating
19. Credit Cards
20. Practicals in Stock Market Operations

# 9 FINANCIAL SERVICES

## MEANING, SCOPE AND INNOVATIONS

The Indian financial service industry has undergone a metamorphosis since 1990. During the late seventies and eighties, the Indian financial service industry was dominated by commercial banks and other financial institutions which cater to the requirements of the Indian industry. In fact, the capital market played a secondary role only. The economic liberalisation has brought in a complete transformation in the Indian financial services industry.

Prior to the economic liberalisation, the Indian financial service sector was characterised by so many factors which retarded the growth of this sector. Some of the significant factors were:

(*i*) Excessive controls in the form of regulations of interest rates, money rates, etc.

(*ii*) Too many control over the prices of securities under the erstwhile controller of capital issues.

(*iii*) Non-availability of financial instruments on a large-scale as well as on different varieties.

(*iv*) Absence of independent credit rating and credit research agencies.

(*v*) Strict regulation of the foreign exchange market with too many restrictions on foreign investment and foreign equity holding in Indian companies.

(*vi*) Lack of information about international developments in the financial sector.

(*vii*) Absence of a developed government securities market and the existence of stagnant capital market without any reformation.

(*viii*) Non-availability of debt instruments on a large-scale.

However, after the economic liberalisation, the entire financial sector has undergone a see-saw change and now we are witnessing the emergence of new financial products and services almost everyday. Thus, the present scenario is characterised by financial innovation and financial creativity and before going deep into it, it is imperative that one should understand the meaning and scope of financial services.

## MEANING OF FINANCIAL SERVICES

In general, all types of activities which are of a financial nature could be brought under the term 'financial services'. The term 'Financial Services' in a broad sense means 'mobilising and allocating savings'. Thus, it includes all activities involved in the transformation of saving into investment.

The 'financial service' can also be called 'financial intermediation'. Financial intermediation is a process by which funds are mobilised from a large number of savers and make them available to all those who are in need of it and particularly to corporate customers. Thus, financial service sector is a key area and it is very vital for industrial developments. A well developed financial service industry is absolutely necessary to mobilise the savings and to allocate them to various investable channels and thereby to promote industrial development in a country.

## FEATURES OF FINANCIAL SERVICES

Financial services have certain basic features as stated below:

(i) **Customer-oriented:** Like any other service industry financial service industry is also a customer-oriented one. That customer is the king and his requirements must be satisfied in full should be the basic tenant of any financial service industry. It calls for designing innovative financial products suitable to varied risk-return requirements of customers. Above all, there should be timely delivery of services.

(ii) **Intangibility:** Financial services are intangible and therefore, they cannot be standardised or reproduced in the same form. Hence, there is a need to have a track record of integrity, reputation, good corporate image and timely delivery of services.

(iii) **Simultaneous performance:** Yet another feature is that both production and supply of financial services have to be performed simultaneously. Therefore, both suppliers of services and consumers should have a good rapport, clear-cut perception and effective communication.

(iv) **Dominance of human element:** Financial services are dominated by human element and thus, they are people-intensive. It calls for competent and skilled personnel to market the quality financial products. But, quality cannot be homogenised since it varies with time, place and customer-to-customer.

(v) **Perishability:** Financial services are immediately consumed and hence inventories cannot be created. There is a greater need for balancing demand and supply properly. In other words, marketing and operations should be closely interlinked.

## IMPORTANCE OF FINANCIAL SERVICES

Financial services cater to the requirements of both individual and corporate customers. In fact, the successful functioning of any financial system depends upon the range of financial services offered by vendors of services. Financial services can be defined to include not only the provision of a financial service but also the sale of a financial product or both. The importance of financial services can be realised from the following:

(i) **Economic growth:** The financial service industry mobilises the savings of the people and channels them into productive investment by providing various services to the people. In fact, the economic development of a nation depends upon these savings and investment.

(ii) **Promotion of savings:** The financial service industry promotes savings in the country by providing transformation services. It provides liability, asset and size transformation service by providing large loans on the basis of numerous small deposits. It also provides maturity transformation services by offering short-term claim to savers on their liquid deposit and providing long-term loans to borrowers.

(iii) **Capital formation:** The financial service industry facilitates capital formation by rendering various capital market intermediary services. Capital formation is the very basis for economic growth. It is the principal mobiliser, of surplus funds to finance productive activities and thus, it promotes capital accumulation.

(iv) **Provision of liquidity:** The financial service industry promotes liquidity in the system by allocating and reallocating savings and investment into various avenues of economic activity. It facilitates easy conversion of financial assets into liquid cash at the discretion of the holder of such assets.

(v) **Financial intermediation:** The financial service industry facilitates the function of intermediation between savers and investors by providing a means and a medium of exchange and by undertaking innumerable services.

(vi) **Contribution to GNP:** The contribution of financial services to GNP has been going on increasing year-after-year in almost all countries in recent times.

(vii) **Creation of employment opportunities:** The financial service industry creates and provides employment opportunities to millions of people all over the world.

## CLASSIFICATION OF FINANCIAL SERVICE INDUSTRY

The financial intermediaries in India can be traditionally classified into two:

(*i*) Capital market intermediaries, and

(*ii*) Money market intermediaries.

The capital market intermediaries consist of term lending institutions and investing institutions which mainly provide long-term funds. On the other hand, money market intermediaries consist of commercial banks, co-operative banks and other agencies which supply only short-term funds. Hence, the term 'financial services industry' includes all kinds of organisations which intermediate and facilitate financial transactions of both individuals and corporate customers.

## SCOPE OF FINANCIAL SERVICES

Financial services cover a wide range of activities. They can be broadly classified into two namely:

(*i*) Traditional activities.

(*ii*) Modern activities.

## ❖ Traditional activities

Traditionally, the financial intermediaries have been rendering a wide range of services encompassing both capital and money market activities. They can be grouped under two heads, *viz.*;

(*i*) Fund-based activities, and

(*ii*) Non-fund-based activities.

## ❖ Fund-based activities

The traditional services which come under fund-based activities are the following:

(*i*) Underwriting of or investment in shares, debentures, bonds, etc. of new issues (primary market activities).

(*ii*) Dealing in secondary market activities.

(*iii*) Participating in money market instruments like commercial papers, certificate of deposits, treasury bills, discounting of bills, etc.

(*iv*) Involving in equipment leasing, hire purchase, venture capital, seed capital, etc.

(*v*) Dealing in foreign exchange market activities.

## ❖ Non-fund-based activities

Financial intermediaries provide services on the basis of non-fund-based activities also. This can also be called 'fee-based' activity. Today, customers whether individual or corporate are not satisfied with mere provision of finance. They expect more from financial service companies. Hence, a wide variety of services, are being provided under this head. They include the following:

(*i*) Managing the capital issues, *i.e.*, management of pre-issue and post-issue activities relating to the capital issue in accordance with the SEBI guidelines and thus enabling the promoters to market their issues.

(*ii*) Making arrangements for the placement of capital and debt instruments with investment institutions.

(*iii*) Arrangement of funds from financial institutions for the clients' project cost or his working capital requirements.

(*iv*) Assisting in the process of getting all government and other clearances.

## ❖ Modern activities

Besides the above traditional services, the financial intermediaries render innumerable services in recent times. Most of them are in the nature of non-fund-based activity. In view of the importance, these activities have been discussed in brief under the head 'New financial products and services'. However, some of the modern services provided by them are given in brief hereunder:

(*i*) Rendering project advisory services right from the preparation of the project report till the raising of funds for starting the project with necessary government approval.

(*ii*) Planning for mergers and acquisitions and assisting for their smooth carry out.

(*iii*) Guiding corporate customers in capital restructuring.

(*iv*) Acting as trustees to the debentureholders.

(*v*) Recommending suitable changes in the management structure and management style with a view to achieving better results.

(*vi*) Structuring the financial collaboration/joint ventures by identifying suitable joint venture partner and preparing joint venture agreement.

(*vii*) Rehabilitating and reconstructing sick companies through appropriate scheme of reconstruction and facilitating the implementation of the scheme.

(*viii*) Hedging of risks due to exchange rate risk, interest rate risk, economic risk and political risk by using swaps and other derivative products.

(*ix*) Managing the portfolio of large Public Sector Corporations.

(*x*) Undertaking risk management services like insurance services, buy-back options, etc.

(*xi*) Advising the clients on the question of selecting the best source of funds taking into consideration the quantum of funds required, their cost, lending period, etc.

(*xii*) Guiding the clients in the minimisation of the cost of debt and in the determination of the optimum debt-equity mix.

(*xiii*) Undertaking services relating to the capital market such as:

- (*a*) Clearing services,
- (*b*) Registration and transfers,
- (*c*) Safe custody of securities,
- (*d*) Collection of income on securities.

(*xiv*) Promoting credit rating agencies for the purpose of rating companies which want to go public by the issue of debt instruments.

## ❖ Sources of revenue

Accordingly, there are two categories of sources of income for a financial service company namely: (*i*) fund-based, and (*ii*) fee-based.

Fund-based income comes mainly from interest spread (difference between the interest paid and earned), lease rentals, income from investments in capital market and real estate. On the other hand, fee-based income has its sources in merchant banking, advisory services, custodial services, loan syndication, etc. In fact, a major part of the income is earned through fund-based activities. At the same time, it involves a large share of expenditure also in the form of interest and brokerage. In recent times, a number of private financial companies have started accepting deposits by offering a very high rate of interest. When the cost of deposit resources goes up, the lending rate should also go up. It means that such companies should have to compromise the quality of its investments.

Fee-based income, on the other hand, does not involve much risk. But, it requires a lot of expertise on the part of a financial company to offer such fee-based services.

## CAUSES FOR FINANCIAL INNOVATION

Financial intermediaries have to perform the task of financial innovation to meet the dynamically changing needs of the economy and to help the investors cope with an increasingly volatile and uncertain marketplace. There is a dire necessity for the financial intermediaries to go for innovation due to the following reasons:

(i) **Low profitability:** The profitability of the major financial intermediary, namely the banks has been very much affected in recent times. There is a decline in the profitability of traditional banking products. So, they have been compelled to seek out new products which may fetch high returns.

(ii) **Keen competition:** The entry of many financial intermediaries in the financial sector market has led to severe competition among themselves. This keen competition has paved the way for the entry of varied nature of innovative financial products so as to meet the varied requirements of the investors.

(iii) **Economic liberalisation:** Reform of the financial sector constitutes the most important component of India's programme towards economic liberalisation. The recent economic liberalisation measures have opened the door to foreign competitors to enter into our domestic market. Deregulation in the form of elimination of exchange controls and interest rate ceilings have made the market more competitive. Innovation has become a must for survival.

(iv) **Improved communication technology:** The communication technology has become so advanced that even the world's issuers can be linked with the investors in the global financial market without any difficulty by means of offering so many options and opportunities. Hence, innovative products are brought into the domestic market in no time.

(v) **Customer service:** Nowadays, the customer's expectations are very great. They want newer products at lower cost or at lower credit risk to replace the existing ones. To meet this increased customer sophistication, the financial intermediaries are constantly undertaking research in order to invent a new product which may suit to the requirement of the investing public. Innovations, thus, help them in soliciting new business.

(vi) **Global impact:** Many of the providers and users of capital have changed their roles all over the world. Financial intermediaries have come out of their traditional approach and they are ready to assume more credit risks. As a consequence, many innovations have taken place in the global financial sector which has its own impact on the domestic sector also.

(vii) **Investor awareness:** With a growing awareness amongst the investing public, there has been a distinct shift from investing the savings in physical assets like gold, silver, land, etc. to financial assets like shares, debentures, mutual funds, etc. Again, within the financial assets, they go from 'risk free' bank deposits to risky investments in shares. To meet the growing awareness of the public, innovation has become the need of the hour.

### ❖ Financial engineering

Thus, the growing need for innovation has assumed immense importance in recent times. This process is being referred to as financial engineering. Financial engineering is the lifeblood of any financial ability. 'Financial engineering is the design, the development and the implementation of innovative financial instruments and processes and the formulation of creative solutions to problems in finance'.

## FINANCIAL SERVICES AND PROMOTION OF INDUSTRIES

Financial service companies play a vital role in pooling surplus funds from the public and deploying them in an efficient manner for the growth of the economy as a whole. They channel the funds of surplus economic units to those who intend to spend on real capital investment. The efficient transformation of mobilised funds into real capital helps to promote and develop industries on a large-scale. Their role in the promotion of industries can be summarised as follows:

(i) **Industrial promotion through merchant banking services:** Most of the financial institutions function as promoters of industrial enterprises by rendering merchant banking services. As merchant bankers, they help the prospective entrepreneurs to conceive an idea, identify project, prepare feasibility reports, prepare necessary documents, get necessary licences and approvals from regulatory bodies and so on. They also arrange for tie-up loans and provide their skills and experience for the successful issue management of companies. They also render corporate advisory services for financial restructuring, merger and acquisitions, bought out deals, etc. Thus, merchant banking services are a real boon for industrial development.

(ii) **Working capital finance through factoring services:** For most of the industries, in particular small-scale and medium industries, a lot of working capital is tied up in the form of trade debts and bills. Delays in collection process lead to liquidity problems and consequently to delay in production and supplies for many industries. To speed up the cash flow and solve the problems of undue delays in collections, factoring services are provided to industries. Factoring is an arrangement whereby the factoring service provider buys trade debts and bills and pays 80 per cent of the debts taken over immediately so that quick and convenient funding is available to corporate clients. Thus, factoring converts credit bills and trade debts into cash so that industries may not suffer due lack of working capital.

(iii) **Equipment finance through leasing:** High rate of inflation, severe cost escalation, heavy taxation, meagre internal resources and paucity of funds at the disposal of financial institutions have forced many corporate bodies to go for alternative means of financing their projects. To them, a new source of financing capital assets has emerged in the form of financial lease or equipment lease. An equipment lease is also contractual arrangement whereby the financial intermediary (lessor) transfers the right to use the capital asset (equipment) to the lessee (corporate customer) for an agreed period of time, in return for the payment of rent. Thus, leasing entails companies to acquire the right to use a capital asset without the necessity of making any down payment at all. Hence, leasing serves as a hundred per cent financing tool to industries.

(iv) **Financial resources through mutual funds:** Mutual funds act as a vehicle in galvanising the savings of the people by offering various schemes suitable to various classes of investors for the development of industries. All industrial units have to raise their funds by resorting to the capital market by the issue of shares and debentures. The mutual funds not only create a demand for these capital market instruments but also supply a large source of funds to the market. Thus, the industries are assured of their capital requirements.

(v) **Long-term risk capital through venture capital:** The financial service firms promote industrial development by encouraging innovative entrepreneurs to take up high technology projects involving heavy risks by means of providing not only capital but also management skills. The venture capital company generally enters into a project as a co-promoter and shares the risks and rewards of the enterprise.

(vi) **Risk management through derivatives:** In these days of free market economy, the corporate customers are exposed to various risks such as exchange rate risk, interest rate risk, political risk and so on. There is an imperative need for them to protect their operating projects by shifting some of the uncontrollable financial risks to the financial service companies. Today, risk management becomes a must for the survival of industries. Financial service companies undertake these risks by means of offering derivative products like forwards, futures, options, swaps, etc.

(vii) **Debenture issue through credit rating:** Credit rating agencies facilitate limited companies to borrow necessary funds from the public without much difficulties by rating their debentures. These ratings are useful in instilling confidence in investors. Ratings can be used as a marketing tool to create better image of the companies. Thus, the industry as a whole benefits from ratings by direct mobilisation of savings from the public at a lesser cost than from lending institutions.

(viii) **Development finance through development banking services:** The industrial development in any country virtually depends upon the nature and talent of development financial services available to industries. Generally, these development banks extend finance for modernisation, expansion, revival and rehabilitation of industries. They also promote new industries by rendering services like underwriting, guaranteeing and refinancing.

(ix) **Industrial development through specialised services:** Financial service firms provide a number of specialised services like bill discounting, underwriting, guaranteeing, refinancing, promoting backward areas, stock lending, depository services, credit card services, stock broking services and so on. By providing these services, they also contribute for the industrial development.

## NEW FINANCIAL PRODUCTS AND SERVICES

Today, the importance of financial services is gaining momentum all over the world. In these days of complex finance, people expect a Financial Service Company to play a very dynamic role not only as a provider of finance but also as a departmental store of finance. With the injection of the economic liberalisation policy into the economy and the opening of the economy to multinationals, the free market concept has assumed much significance. As a result, the clients — both corporates and individuals are exposed to the phenomena of volatility and uncertainty and hence they expect the financial service company to innovate new products and services so as to meet their varied requirements.

As a result of innovations, new instruments and new products are emerging in the capital market. The capital market and the money market are getting widened and deepened. Moreover, there has been a structural change in the international capital market with the emergence of new products and innovative techniques of operation in the capital market. Many financial intermediaries including banks have already started expanding their activities in the financial services sector by offering a variety of new products. As a result, sophistication and innovations have appeared in the arena of financial intermediations. Some of them are briefly discussed below:

(i) **Merchant banking:** A merchant banker is a financial intermediary who helps to transfer capital from those who possess it to those who need it. Merchant banking includes a wide range of activities such as management of customers' securities, portfolio management, project counselling and appraisal, underwriting of shares and debentures, loan syndication, acting as banker for the refund orders, handling interest and dividend warrants, etc. Thus, a merchant banker renders a host of services to corporates and thus promotes industrial development in the country.

(ii) **Loan syndication:** This is more or less similar to 'consortium financing'. But, this work is taken up by the merchant banker as a lead manager. It refers to a loan arranged by a bank called lead manager for a borrower who is usually a large corporate customer or a government department. The other banks who are willing to lend can participate in the loan by contributing an amount suitable to their own lending policies. Since a single bank cannot provide such a huge sum as loan, a number of banks join together and form a syndicate. It also enables the members of the syndicate to share the credit risk associated with a particular loan among themselves.

(iii) **Leasing:** A lease is an agreement under which a company or a firm, acquires a right to make use of a capital asset like machinery, on payment of a prescribed fee called 'rental charges'. The lessee cannot acquire any ownership to the asset, but he can use it and have full control over it. He is expected to pay for all maintenance charges and repairing and operating costs. In countries like the USA, UK and Japan equipment leasing is very popular and nearly 25 per cent of plant and equipment is being financed by leasing companies. In India also, many financial companies have started equipment leasing business. Commercial banks have also been permitted to carry on this business by forming subsidiary companies.

(iv) **Mutual funds:** A mutual fund refers to a fund raised by a financial service company by pooling the savings of the public. It is invested in a diversified portfolio with a view to spreading and minimising risk. The fund provides investment avenue for small investors who cannot participate in the equities of big companies. It ensures low risks, steady returns, high liquidity and better capital appreciation in the long run.

(v) **Factoring:** Factoring refers to the process of managing the sales ledger of a client by a financial service company. In other words, it is an arrangement under which a financial intermediary assumes the credit risk in the collection of book debts for its clients. The entire responsibility of collecting the book debts passes on to the factor. His services can be compared to a del credere agent who undertakes to collect debts. But, a factor provides credit information, collects debts, monitors the sales ledger and provides finance against debts. Thus, he provides a number of services apart from financing.

(vi) **Forfaiting:** Forfaiting is a technique by which a forfaitor (financing agency) discounts an export bill and pay ready cash to the exporter who can concentrate on the export front without bothering about collection of export bills. The forfaitor does so without any recourse to the exporter and the exporter is protected against the risk of non-payment of debts by the importers.

(vii) **Venture capital:** A venture capital is another method of financing in the form of equity participation. A venture capitalist finances a project based on the potentialities of a new innovative project. It is in contrast to the conventional 'security based financing'. Much thrust is given to new ideas or technological innovations. Finance is being provided not only for 'start-up capital' but also for 'development capital' by the financial intermediary.

(viii) **Custodial services:** It is yet another line of activity which has gained importance, of late. Under this, a financial intermediary mainly provides services to clients, particularly to foreign investors, for a prescribed fee. Custodial services provide agency services like safe keeping of shares and debentures, collection of interest and dividend and reporting of matters on corporate developments and corporate securities to foreign investors.

(ix) **Corporate advisory services:** Financial intermediaries particularly banks have set up corporate advisory service branches to render services exclusively to their corporate customers. For instance, some banks have extended computer terminals to their corporate customers so that they can transact some of their important banking transactions by sitting in their own office. As new avenues of finance like Euro loans, GDRs, etc. are available to corporate customers, this service is of immense help to the customers.

(x) **Securitisation:** Securitisation is a technique whereby a financial company converts its illiquid, non-negotiable and high value financial assets into securities of small value which are made tradable and transferable. A financial institution might have a lot of its assets blocked up in assets like real estate, machinery, etc., which are long-term in nature and which are non-negotiable. In such cases, securitisation would help the financial institution to raise cash against such assets by means of issuing securities of small values to the public. Like any other security, they can be traded in the market. It is best suited to housing finance companies whose loans are always long-term in nature and their money is locked up for a considerable long period in real estates. Securitisation is the only answer to convert these illiquid assets into liquid assets.

**(xi) Reverse mortgage:** In 2007-08, the National Housing Bank and commercial banks have introduced an innovative product, *viz.*, reverse mortgage to enable the senior citizens to fetch value out of their property without selling it. In a normal mortgage, a home buyer borrows money to finance his home. In a Reverse Mortgage (RM), the owner of a house property surrenders the title of his property to a lender and raises money. Again, in a normal mortgage, the borrower gets 60-70 per cent of the money upfront. But, in a RM, generally the lender does not pay the entire amount. On the other hand, he pays out a regular sum each month for the agreed time. The owner, normally a senior citizen, can use the property and stay with his spouse for the rest of their lives. Thus, the owner can ensure a regular cash flow in times of need and enjoy the benefit of using the property. Usually, after the death of the owner, the spouse can continue to use the property. In case, both die during the period of the RM scheme, the lender will sell the property, take his share and distribute the rest among the heirs. It is called reverse mortgage because the payment stream is 'reversed'. Instead of making monthly payments to a lender, as in the case of a regular mortgage, a lender makes regular payments to a senior citizen. A RM facilitates to convert an immovable asset into an income generating one.

There are other options available to a senior citizen to payback the entire loan amount. The legal heirs have also an option to pay back the loan and take possession of the property.

The concept of RM is very popular in US/UK. But it is quite new to India. Parents in India still want their property to pass on to their children after they are no longer there, mainly due to social and emotional considerations.

**(xii) New reverse mortgage plan:** Banks have started introducing a new reverse mortgage plan along with life insurance companies. This new product is called 'Reverse Mortgage Enabled Annuity' scheme. It requires an insurance company to undertake the risk of uncertainty of life of the person availing this scheme.

Under this scheme, depending upon the age of both spouses, about 60-75 per cent of loan value of the home is transferred by the bank to the insurance company. The value as assessed by the bank will be taken into account and not the market value. This corpus is treated an investment fund by the insurance company, which would pay a monthly annuity till the last of spouses is alive.

However, there is some flexibility to withdraw 25 per cent of lump sum of the loan value for health purposes or for other contingencies. There are two options available to senior citizens under this scheme. They are:

(*a*) Return a purchase price, and

(*b*) No return of purchase price.

The purchase price is nothing but the loan amount for single senior citizen. No return of purchase price would be suitable since the monthly annuity is higher and after their demise the account will be closed. 'Return of Purchase Price' option would be suitable to couples since the annuity payments would continue even after the demise of the first spouse. Of course, the annuity payments would be comparatively less compared to the first option. Since it is a new product, it is not very popular among senior citizens.

**(xiii) Derivative security:** A derivative security is a security whose value depends upon the values of other basic variables backing the security. In most cases, these variables are nothing but the prices of traded securities. A derivative security is basically used as a risk management tool and it is resorted to cover the risks due to price fluctuations by the investments manager. Just like a forward contract which is a derivative of a spot contract, a derivative security is derived from other trading securities backing it. Naturally, the value of a derivative security depends upon the values of the backing securities. Derivative helps to break the risks into various components such as credit risk, interest rates risk, exchange rates risk and so on. It enables the various risk components to be identified precisely and priced them and even traded them if necessary. Financial intermediaries can go for derivatives since they will have greater importance in the near future. In India some forms of derivatives are in operation. Example: Forwards in forex market.

**(xiv) New products in forex market**: New products have also emerged in the forex markets of developed countries. Some of these products are yet to make full entry in Indian markets. Among them, the following are the important ones:

**(a) Forward contracts:** A forward transaction is one where the delivery of a foreign currency takes place at a specified future date for a specified price. It may have a fixed maturity for, *e.g.*, 31st May or a flexible maturity for, *e.g.*, 1st to 31st May. There is an obligation to honour this contract at any cost, failing which, there will be some penalty. Forward contracts are permitted only for genuine business transactions. It can be extended to other transactions like interest payments.

**(b) Options:** As the very name implies, it is a contract wherein, the buyer of the option has a right to buy or sell a fixed amount of currency against another currency at a fixed rate on a future date according to his option. There is no obligation to buy or sell, but it is completely left to his option. Options may be of two types namely call options and put options. Under call options, the customer has an option to buy and it is the option to sell under put options. Options trading would lead to speculation and hence there are much restrictions in India.

**(c) Futures:** It is a contract wherein, there is an agreement to buy or sell a stated quantity of foreign currency at a future date at a price agreed to between the parties on the stated exchange. Unlike options, there is an obligation to buy or sell foreign exchange on a future date at a specified rate. It can be dealt only in a stock exchange.

**(d) Swaps:** A swap refers to a transaction wherein a financial intermediary buys and sells a specified foreign currency simultaneously for different maturity dates — say, for instance, purchase of spot and sale of forward or *vice versa* with different maturities. Thus, swaps would result in simultaneous buying and selling of the same foreign currency of the same value for different maturities to eliminate exposure risk. It can also be used as a tool to enter arbitrage operations, if any, between two countries. It can also be used in the interest rate market also. It is explained in detail under the chapter derivatives.

(xv) **Letter Of Credit (LOC):** It is an innovative funding mechanism for the import of goods and services on deferred payment terms. LOC is an arrangement of a financing institution/bank of one country with another institution/bank/agent to support the export of goods and services so as to enable the importers to import no deferred payment terms. This may be backed by a guarantee furnished by the institution/bank in the importing country. The LOC helps the exporters to get payment immediately as soon as the goods are shipped, since the funds would be paid out of the pool account with the financing agency and it would be debited to the account of the borrower agency/importer whose contract for availing the facility is already approved by the financing agency on the recommendation of the overseas institution. It acts as tool of financing which is for a certain period and on certain terms for the required goods to be imported. The greatest advantage is that it saves a lot of time and money on mutual verification of bonafides, source of finance, etc. It serves as a source of forex.

## INNOVATIVE FINANCIAL INSTRUMENTS

In recent years, innovation has been the keyword behind the phenomenal success of many of the financial service companies and it forms an integral part of all planning and policy decisions. This has helped them to keep in tune with the changing times and changing customer needs. Accordingly, many innovative financial instruments have come into the financial market in recent times. Some of them have been briefly discussed here under:

(i) **Commercial paper:** A commercial paper is a short-term negotiable money market instrument. It has the character of an unsecured promissory note with a fixed maturity. It can be issued for a period of not less than 7 days and up to one year for a minimum denomination lot of ₹ 5 lakhs and multiples thereof. Banking and non-banking companies can issue this for raising their short-term debt. It also carries an attractive rate of interest. Commercial papers are sold at a discount from their face value and redeemed at their face value. Since its denomination is very high, it is suitable only to institutional investors and companies.

(ii) **Treasury bill:** A treasury bill is also a money market instrument issued by the Central Government. It is also issued at a discount and redeemed at par. Recently, the Government has come out with short-term treasury bills of 182-days bills and 364 days bills.

(iii) **Certificates of deposit:** The scheduled commercial banks have been permitted to issue certificate of deposit without any regulation on interest rates. This is also a money market instrument and unlike a fixed deposit receipt, it is a negotiable instrument and hence it offers maximum liquidity. As such, it has a secondary market too. Since the denomination is very high, it is suitable to mainly institutional investors and companies.

(iv) **Inter-Bank Participations (IBPs):** The scheme of inter-bank participation is confined to scheduled banks only for a period ranging between 91 days and 180 days. This may be 'with risk' participation or 'without risk' participation. However, only a few banks have so far issued IBPs carrying an interest rate ranging between 14 and 17 per cent per annum. This is also a money market instrument.

(v) **Zero interest convertible debenture/bonds:** As the very name suggests, these instruments carry no interest till the time of conversion. These instruments are converted into equity shares after a period of time.

(vi) **Deep discount bonds:** There will be no interest payments in the case of deep discount bonds also. Hence, they are sold at a large discount to their nominal value. For example, the Industrial Development Bank of India issued in February 1996 deep discount bonds. Each bond having a face value of ₹ 2,00,000 was issued at a deep discounted price of ₹ 5,300 with a maturity period of 25 years. Of course, provisions are there for early withdrawal or redemption in which case the deemed face value of the bond would be reduced proportionately. This bond could be gifted to any person.

(vii) **Index-linked gilt bonds:** These are instruments having a fixed maturity. Their maturity value is linked to the index prevailing as on the date of maturity. Hence, they are inflation-free instruments.

(viii) **Option bonds:** These bonds may be cumulative or non-cumulative as per the option of the holder of the bonds. In the case of cumulative bonds, interest is accumulated and is payable only on maturity. But, in the case of non-cumulative bond, the interest is paid periodically. This option has to be exercised by the prospective investor at the time of investment.

(ix) **Secured premium notes:** These are instruments which carry no interest for three years. In other words, their interest will be paid only after 3 years, and hence, companies with high capital-intensive investments can resort to this type of financing.

(x) **Medium-term debentures:** Generally, debentures are repayable only after a long period. But, these debentures have a medium-term maturity. Since they are secured and negotiable, they are highly liquid. These types of debt instruments are very popular in Germany.

(xi) **Variable rate debentures:** Variable rate debentures are debt instruments. They carry a compound rate of interest, but this rate of interest is not a fixed one. It varies from time-to-time in accordance with some pre-determined formula as we adopt in the case of Dearness Allowance calculations.

(xii) **Non-convertible debentures with equity warrants:** Generally, debentures are redeemed on the date of maturity. But, these debentures are redeemed in full at a premium in installments as in the case of anticipated insurance policies. The installments may be paid at the end of 5th, 6th, 7th and 8th year from the date of allotment.

(xiii) **Equity with 100 per cent safety net:** Some companies make '100 per cent safety net' offer to the public. It means that they give a guarantee to the issue price. Suppose, the issue price is ₹ 40/- per share (nominal value of ₹ 10/- per share), the company is ready to get it back at ₹ 40/- at any time, irrespective of the market price. That is, even if the market price comes down to ₹ 30/- there is 100 per cent safety net and hence the company will get it back at ₹ 40/-.

**(xiv) Cumulative convertible preference shares:** These instruments along with capital and accumulated dividend must be compulsorily converted into equity shares in a period of 3 to 5 years from the date of their issue, according to the discretion of the issuing company. The main object of introducing it is to offer the investor an assured minimum return together with the prospect of equity appreciation. This instrument is not popular in India.

**(xv) Convertible bonds:** A convertible bond is one which can be converted into equity shares at a predetermined timing either fully or partially. There are compulsory convertible bonds which provide for conversion within 18 months of their issue. There are optionally convertible bonds which provide for conversion within 36 months. There are also bonds which provide for conversion after 36 months and they carry 'call' and 'put' features.

***Example:*** In June 1989, the Tata Iron and Steel Company issued 30 lakh partly convertible debentures of ₹ 1,200 each for cash at par with the following terms:

(*a*) Conversion of ₹ 600 par value into one equity share of ₹ 100 at a premium of ₹ 500 on Feb 1, 1990,

(*b*) Interest rate of 12 per cent per annum, and

(*c*) Redemption of the non-convertible portion at the end of 8 years.

**(xvi) Debentures with 'Call' and 'Put' feature:** Sometimes, debentures may be issued with 'Call' and 'Put' feature. In the case of debentures with 'Call feature', the issuing company has the option to redeem the debentures at a certain price before the maturity date. In the case of debentures with 'Put feature', the company gives the holder the right to seek redemption at specified times at predetermined prices.

**(xvii) Easy Exit bond:** As the name indicates, this bond enables the small investors to encash the bond at any time after 18 months of its issue and thereby paving a way for an easy exit. It has a maturity period of 10 years with a call option any time after 5 years. Recently, the IDBI has issued this type of bond with a face value of ₹ 5,000 per bond. Interest is payable half-yearly at the rate of at least 2.5 per cent p.a. over the State Bank of India's 3-year fixed deposit rate at any time or 1.5 per cent p.a. above the interest rate on 10-year government bonds.

**(xviii) Retirement bond:** This type of bond enables an investor to get an assured monthly income for a fixed period after the expiry of the 'wait period' chosen by him. No payment will be made during the 'wait period.' The longer the wait period, the higher will be the monthly income. Besides these, the investor will also get a lump sum amount on maturity. For example, the IDBI has issued Retirement Bond '96 assuring a fixed monthly income for 10 years after the expiry of the wait period. This bond can be gifted to any person.

**(xix) Regular income bond:** This bond offers an attractive rate of interest payable half-yearly with the facility of early redemption. The investor is assured of regular and fixed income. For example, the IDBI has issued Regular Income Bond '96 carrying 16 per cent interest p.a. It is redeemable at the end of every year from the expiry of 3 years from the date of allotment.

**(xx) Infrastructure bond:** It is a kind of debt instrument issued with a view of giving tax shelter to investors. The resources raised through this bond will be used for promoting investment in the field of certain infrastructure industries. Tax concessions are available under Sec. 88, Sec. 54 EA and Sec. 54 EB of the Income Tax Act. HUDCO has issued for the first time such bonds. Its face value is ₹ 1,000 each carrying an interest rate of 15 per cent per annum payable semi-annually. This bond will also be listed in important stock exchanges.

**(xxi) Carrot and stick bonds:** Carrot bonds have a low conversion premium to encourage early conversion, and sticks allow the issuer to call the bond at a specified premium if the common stock is trading at a specified percentage above the strike price.

**(xxii) Convertible bonds with a premium put:** These are bonds issued at face value with a put, which means that the bondholder can redeem the bonds for more than their face value.

**(xxiii) Debt with equity warrant:** Sometimes bonds are issued with warrants for the purchase of shares. These warrants are separately tradable.

**(xxiv) Dual currency bonds:** Bonds that are denominated and pay interest in one currency and are redeemable in another currency come under this category. They facilitate interest rate arbitrage between two markets.

**(xxv) ECU Bonds (European Currency Unit Bonds):** These bonds are denominated in a basket of currencies of the 10 countries that constitute the European community. They pay principal and interest in ECUs or in any of the 10 currencies at the option of the holder.

**(xxvi) Yankee bonds:** If bonds are raised in USA, they are called Yankee bonds and if they are raised in Japan, they are called Samurai Bonds.

**(xxvii) Flip-flop notes:** It is a kind of debt instrument which permits investors to switch between two types of securities — *e.g.*, to switch over from a long-term bond to a short-term fixed-rate note.

**(xxviii) Floating Rate Notes (FRNs):** These are debt instruments which facilitate periodic interest rate adjustments.

**(xxix) Loyalty coupons:** These are entitlements to the holder of debt for two to three years to exchange into equity shares at discount prices. To get this facility, the original subscriber must hold the debt instruments for the said period.

**(xxx) Global Depository Receipt (GDR):** A global depository receipt is a dollar-denominated instrument traded on a stock exchange in Europe or the USA or both. It represents a certain number of underlying equity shares. Though the GDR is quoted and traded in dollar terms, the underlying equity shares are denominated in rupees. The shares are issued by the company to an intermediary called depository in whose name the shares are registered. It is the depository which subsequently issues the GDRs.

**(xxxi) Green Bonds:** Those bonds whose proceeds are deployed in eco-friendly projects are called green bonds. In other words, those bonds are issued to raise funds for a 'green' project like climate change, renewable energy, sustainable water, waste management, clean transport, etc.

**(xxxii) Market Linked Debenture:** Market Linked Debentures are those debentures/bonds where the interest payout or coupon is not mentioned as in usual debentures or bonds. Instead, the return is made contingent upon the movement in another market which is referred to as underlying market. The underlying market may be an index of a stock such as the Nifty or Sensex or Government Security or Gold. The greatest advantage of this debenture is that the investor gets the advantage of investing in another market.

## CLASSIFICATION OF EQUITY SHARES

On the basis of the nature of shares, the nature of industry to which they belong and the nature of trading, equity shares can be called by different names. The popular classification is as follows:

**(i) Blue chip shares:** Shares of well known and established companies are called Blue Chip Shares. They must show consistent growth over the years. These shares have bright future prospects and they are expected to contribute sustained growth in the future also.

**(ii) Defensive shares:** These shares tend to fall less in a bear market when compared with other shares and they provide a safe return for the investor's money. In other words, these shares are more stable than other shares. Naturally, Blue Chips fall under this category also.

**(iii) Growth shares:** Growth shares represent the shares of fast growing companies. They show increasing and higher than average earnings per share than the industry. They are good for long-term investment, although the current yield of such shares can be insignificant because of their higher P/E ratios.

**(iv) Cyclical vs. non-cyclical shares:** Cyclical shares are those which rise and fall in price with the state of the national economy of the industries to which they belong like construction, automobiles, cement, engineering, etc. They may also be affected by international economy of industries such as shipping, aviation and tourism. They also include shares which are affected by natural phenomena like fertilisers, tea, etc.

If the shares are not affected by such cyclical changes either due to the state of the national economy or the international economy, they are called non-cyclical shares. Shares of drug companies, insurance companies and basic foodstuffs of many consumer products companies come under this category.

**(v) Turnaround shares:** Turnaround shares are those which either rise or fall all in a sudden due to turnaround situations prevailing in companies. They offer opportunities to investors to pick-up the shares when their price is low.

**(vi) Active shares:** Active shares are those in which there are frequent and day-to-day dealings. They must be bought and sold at least three times a week. Investors can buy or sell these shares quite easily in the market.

**(vii) Alpha shares:** Alpha shares are those which are most frequently traded in the market. They are also called specified shares or cleared securities. They are included under Group A shares while listing on a stock exchange.

**(viii) Sweat shares:** Sweat shares refer to those shares which are issued to employees or workers who contribute for the development of a company by providing necessary know how using their intellectual property. There must be value addition to the company because of their active involvement in the company and they contribute their might for the progress of the company. Sweat shares are indeed a reward for hard, active and dedicated work for the development of a company.

The emergence of various financial products and instruments have transformed the financial service sector from being a conservative industry to a very dynamic one. These innovations have enlarged the menu of assets available to the investors and borrowers so as to meet their varied requirements. The introduction of new borrowing instruments have facilitated capital formation which is very vital for the economic development of any country. Above all, the development of new financial instruments will in turn improve the capacity of financial intermediaries to manage risks. Better risk management will ultimately lead to the improved allocation of resources in the best interest of the economy as a whole.

To enable the financial service industry to play a dynamic role and to face the global competition in an effective way, the Government of India has recently taken the following steps:

(*i*) Privatisation of public sector undertaking.

(*ii*) Shifting of pricing issues from the controller of capital issues to free pricing.

(*iii*) Full convertibility of Indian rupee on current account.

(*iv*) Permitting private sector to participate in banking and mutual funds.

(*v*) Deregulation of interest rates.

(*vi*) Allowing corporate sector to raise debt/equity in international markets.

(*vii*) Signing of the GATT agreement and the affirmation of the WTO financial services sector agreement.

It is time for the financial service agencies to exploit the opportunities that lie ahead in tune with the developing pace of the economy. It requires them to adopt new instruments and innovative means of financing to meet the growing financial requirements of the various segments of the economy.

## CHALLENGES FACING THE FINANCIAL SERVICE SECTOR

However, the financial service sector has to face many challenges in its attempt to fulfil the ever-growing financial demands of the economy. Some of the important challenges are briefly reported hereunder:

(i) **Lack of qualified personnel:** The financial service sector is fully geared to the task of 'financial creativity'. However, this sector has to face many challenges. In fact, the dearth of qualified and trained personnel is an important impediment in its growth. Hence, it is very vital that a proper and a comprehensive training must be given to the various financial intermediaries.

(ii) **Lack of investor awareness:** The introduction of new financial products and instruments will be of no use unless the investor is aware of the advantages and uses of the new and innovative products and instruments. Hence, the financial intermediaries should educate the prospective investors/users of the advantages of the innovative instruments through literature, seminars, workshops, advertisements and even through audio-visual aids.

(iii) **Lack of transparency:** The whole financial system is undergoing a phenomenal change in accordance with the requirements of the national and global environments. It is high time that this sector gave up their orthodox attitude of keeping accounts in a highly secret manner. Hence, this sector should opt for better levels of transparency. In other words, the disclosure requirements and the accounting practices have to be in line with the international standards.

(iv) **Lack of specialisation:** In the Indian scene, each financial intermediary seems to deal in different financial service lines without specialising in one or two areas. In other words, each intermediary is acting as a financial supermarket delivering so many financial products and dealing in different varieties of instruments. In other countries, financial intermediaries like Newtons, Solomon Brothers, etc., specialise in one or two areas only. This helps them to achieve high levels of efficiency and excellence. Hence, in India also, financial intermediaries can go for specialisation.

(v) **Lack of recent data:** Most of the intermediaries do not spend more on research. It is very vital that one should build-up a proper database on the basis of which one could embark upon 'financial creativity'. Moreover, a proper database would keep oneself abreast of the recent developments in other parts of the whole world and above all, it would enable the fund managers to take sound financial decisions.

(vi) **Lack of efficient risk management system:** With the opening of the economy to multinationals and the exposure of Indian companies to international competition, much importance is given to foreign portfolio flows. It involves the utilisation of multicurrency transactions which exposes the client to exchange rate risk, interest rate risk and economic and political risk. Unless a proper risk management system is developed by the financial intermediaries as in the West, they would not be in a position to fulfil the growing requirements of their customers. Hence, it is absolutely essential that they should introduce Futures, Options, Swaps and other derivative products which are necessary for an efficient risk management system.

The above challenges are likely to increase in number with the growing requirements of the customers. The financial service sector should rise up to the occasion to meet these challenges by adopting new instruments and innovative means of financing so that it could play a very dynamic role in the economy.

## PRESENT SCENARIO

**(i) Conservatism to dynamism**

At present, the financial system in India is in a process of rapid transformation, particularly after the introduction of reforms in the financial sector. The main objective of the financial sector reforms is to promote an efficient, competitive and diversified financial system in the country. This is essential to raise the allocative efficiency of available savings, increase the return on investment and thus to promote the accelerated growth of the economy as a whole. As a result, we have recently witnessed phenomenal changes in the money market, securities market, capital market, debt market and the foreign exchange market. In this changed context, the role of financial services has assumed greater significance in our country. At present, numerous new financial intermediaries have started functioning with a view to extending multifarious services to the investing public in the area of financial services. The emergence of various financial institutions and regulatory bodies have transformed the financial services sector from being a conservative industry to a very dynamic one.

**(ii) Emergence of primary equity market**

Now, we are also witnessing the emergence of many private sector financial services. The capital markets which were very sluggish, have become a popular source of raising finance. The number of stock exchanges in the country has gone up from 9 in 1980 to 22 in 2010. The aggregate funds raised by the industries in the primary markets have gone from ₹ 5,976 crores in 1991-92 to ₹ 69,192 crores in 2010. The number of companies listed on the stock exchange have also gone up from 2,265 in 1980 to 9,000 in 2006-07. Thus, the primary equity market has emerged as an important vehicle to channelise the savings of the individuals and corporates for productive purposes and thus to promote the industrial and economic growth of our nation.

**(iii) Concept of credit rating**

There is every possibility of introducing equity grading. Hitherto, the investment decisions of the investors have been based on factors like name recognition of the company, operations of the group, market sentiments, reputation of the promoters, etc. Now, grading from an independent agency would help the investor in his portfolio management and thus, equity grading is going to play a significant role in investment decision-making. From the company point of view, equity grading would help to broaden the market for their public offer, to replace the name recognition by objective opinion and to have a wider investor base. Thus, grading would give further fillip to the primary market. Moreover, the concept of credit rating would play a significant role in identifying the risk level of the corporate entity in which the investor wants to take part.

Now, it is mandatory for the non-banking financial companies to get credit rating for their debt instruments. The four major credit rating agencies functioning in India are:

1. Credit Rating Information Services of India Ltd. (CRISIL),
2. Credit Analysis and Research Ltd. (CARE),
3. Investment Information and Credit Rating Agency (ICRA), and
4. Duff Phelps Credit Rating Pvt. Ltd. (DCR India).

Their activities have been mainly confined to debt instruments only.

**(iv) Process of globalisation**

Again, the process of globalisation has paved the way for the entry of innovative and sophisticated financial products into our country. Since the government is very keen in removing all obstacles that stand in the way of inflow of foreign capital, the potentialities for the introduction of innovative international financial products in India are very great. Moreover, India is likely to enter the full convertibility era soon. Hence, there is every possibility of introduction of more and more innovative and sophisticated financial services in our country.

**(v) Process of liberalisation**

Realising all these factors, the Government of India has initiated many steps to reform the financial service industry. The government has already switched over to free pricing of issues from pricing issues by the controller of capital issues. The interest rates have been deregulated. The private sector has been permitted to participate in banking and mutual funds and the public sector undertakings are being privatised. The Finance Act, 1992 has brought into effect large-scale amendments in the tax structure of long-term capital gains. The Finance Act, 1994 has given a further boost by lowering the lock-in period from 3 years to 1 year, in order to get the entitlement as a long-term capital asset. The Securities Exchange Board of India has liberalised many stringent conditions so as to boost the capital and money markets. In this changed context, the financial service industry in India has to play a positive and dynamic role in the years to come by offering many innovative products to suit to the varied requirements of the millions of prospective investors spread throughout the country.

## QUESTIONS

### I. Objective type questions:

#### A. Fill in the blanks:

1. The important goal of the financial service industry is to mobilise and allocate ________.
2. Underwriting of shares by a financial intermediary is a kind of ________activity.
3. ________ services are mainly provided to foreign investors.
4. ________ bonds are sold at a large discount to their nominal value.
5. To regulate the securities market and to protect the investor's interest. ________ has been created by the Government of India.
6. Term lending institutions are ________ market intermediaries.

[**Key:** 1. savings, 2. fund based, 3. Custodial, 4. Deep discount, 5. SEBI, 6. capital]

#### B. Choose the best answer from the following:

1. The following one is a kind of fee-based activity of a financial intermediary

   (*a*) Hire purchase financing (*b*) Leasing

   (*c*) Capital issue management (*d*) Underwriting of shares.

2. Find the odd man out:

   (*a*) Commercial paper (*b*) Share certificate

   (*c*) Certificate of deposit (*d*) Treasury bill

3. The process of managing the sales ledger of a client by a financial service company is called:
   (*a*) Forfaiting (*b*) Factoring
   (*c*) Leasing (*d*) Securitisation of debt
4. The inflation-free instrument is:
   (*a*) Option bond (*b*) Index-linked gilt bond
   (*c*) Variable rate debenture (*d*) Deep discount bond
5. Non-banking companies should compulsorily get credit rating for their:
   (*a*) Capital market instruments (*b*) Money market instruments
   (*c*) Debt market instruments (*d*) All of the above

[**Key:** 1. (*c*), 2. (*b*), 3. (*b*), 4. (*b*), 5. (*c*)]

## C. State whether the following statements are TRUE or FALSE:

1. Financial service companies earn a major part of their income through fee-based activities.
2. Loan syndication is a kind of consortium advance.
3. A derivative security is resorted to earn huge profits due to price fluctuations and hence it is basically a speculative security.
4. A forward contract is a derivative of a spot contract.
5. In the case of debentures with 'put feature', the company can redeem the debenture at any time according to its discretion before the maturity date.

[**Key:** 1. False, 2. True, 3. False, 4. True, 5. False]

## II. Short answer type questions:

1. What do you mean by financial service?
2. List down any four fund-based activities of a financial service company.
3. State the causes for financial innovation in the financial service sector.
4. Distinguish between loan syndication and venture capital.
5. What is factoring? Is it similar to forfaiting?
6. Discuss any three new products available in the forex market.
7. What is a convertible bond? Give an example.
8. As between medium-term debentures and variable rate debentures, which one do you prefer and why?
9. Discuss the special features of a cumulative convertible preference share.
10. What do you understand by the term 'financial engineering'?

## III. Essay type questions:

1. Define a financial service industry and discuss the various services rendered by it.
2. 'Financial intermediaries have to perform the task of financial innovation to meet the dynamically changing needs of the economy'— Discuss the above statement in the light of the various innovative products introduced in recent times in the financial service sector.
3. Discuss briefly some of the innovative financial instruments introduced in recent times in the financial service sector.
4. Critically analyse the present position of the financial service sector in India and state the challenges it has to face in the years to come.
5. What factors have retarded the growth of the financial service sector during the period of pre-economic liberalisation? Discuss its position during the post-economic liberalisation period.

# 10 MERCHANT BANKING

## INTRODUCTION

The term merchant banking is used differently in different countries and so there is no precise definition for it. In London, merchant banker refers to those who are members of British Merchant Banking and Securities House Association who carry on consultation, leasing, portfolio services, assets management, euro credit, loan syndication, etc. In America, merchant banking is concerned with mobilising savings of people and directing the funds to business enterprise.

## DEFINITION

There is no universal definition for merchant banking. It assumes diverse functions in different countries. So, merchant banking may be defined as, 'an institution which covers a wide range of activities such as management of customer services, portfolio management, credit syndication, acceptance credit, counselling, insurance, etc.'

The Notification of the Ministry of Finance defines a merchant banker as, 'any person who is engaged in the business of issue management either by making arrangements regarding selling, buying or subscribing to the securities as manager, consultant, advisor or rendering corporate advisory service in relation to such issue management.'

## ORIGIN

Merchant banking originated through the entering of London merchants in financing foreign trade through acceptance of bill. Later, the merchants assisted the government of underdeveloped countries in raising long-term funds through flotation of bonds in London money market. Over a period, they extended their activities to domestic business of syndication of long-term and short-term finance, underwriting of new issues, acting as registrars and share transfer agents, debenture trustees, portfolio managers, negotiating agents for mergers, takeover, etc. The post-war period witnessed the rapid growth of merchant banking through the innovative instrument like Euro, Dollar and the growth of various financial centres like Singapore, Hong Kong, Bahrain, Kuwait, Dubai, etc.

## MERCHANT BANKING IN INDIA

In India prior to the enactment of Indian Companies Act, 1956, managing agents acted as issue houses for securities, evaluated project reports, planned capital structure and to some extent provided venture capital for new firms. Few share broking firms also functioned as merchant bankers.

The need for specialised merchant banking service was felt in India with the rapid growth in the number and size of the issues made in the primary market. The merchant banking services were started by foreign banks, namely the National Grindlays Bank in 1967 and the Citibank in 1970. The Banking Commission in its report in 1972 recommended the setting up of merchant banking institutions by commercial banks and financial institutions. This marked the beginning of specialised merchant banking in India.

To begin with, merchant banking services were offered along with other traditional banking services. In the mid-eighties, the Banking Regulations Act was amended permitting commercial banks to offer a wide range of financial services through the subsidiary route. The State Bank of India was the first Indian Bank to set up Merchant Banking Division in 1972. Later ICICI set up its Merchant Banking Division followed by Bank of India, Bank of Baroda, Canara Bank, Punjab National Bank and UCO Bank. The merchant banking gained prominence during 1983-84 due to new issue boom.

## MERCHANT BANKS AND COMMERCIAL BANKS

There are differences in approach, attitude and areas of operations between commercial banks and merchant banks. The differences between merchant banks and commercial banks are summarised below:

1. Commercial banks basically deal in debt and debt-related finance and their activities are appropriately arrayed around credit proposals, credit appraisal and loan sanctions. On the other hand, the area of activity of merchant bankers is 'equity and equity-related finance'. They deal with mainly funds raised through money market and capital market.
2. Commercial banks are asset-oriented and their lending decisions are based on detailed credit analysis of loan proposals and the value of security offered against loans. They generally avoid risks. The merchant bankers are management-oriented. They are willing to accept risks of business.
3. Commercial bankers are merely financiers. The activities of merchant bankers include project counselling, corporate counselling in areas of capital restructuring, amalgamations, mergers, takeover, etc., discounting and rediscounting of short-term paper in money markets, managing, underwriting and supporting public issues in new issue market and acting as brokers and advisors on portfolio management in stock exchange. Merchant banking activities have impact on growth, stability and liquidity of money markets.

## SERVICES OF MERCHANT BANKS

The financial institutions in India could not meet the demand for long-term funds required by the ever expanding industry and trade. The corporate sector enterprises, therefore, meet their requirements through issue of shares and debentures in the capital market. To raise money from capital market, promoters bank upon merchant bankers who manage the whole show by rendering multifarious services. The merchant bankers also advise the investors regarding incentives available in the form of tax reliefs and other statutory obligations.

The services of merchant bankers are described in detail in the following section.

### 1. Corporate counselling

Corporate counselling covers the entire field of merchant banking activities, *viz.*, project counselling, capital restructuring, project management, public issue management, loan syndication, working capital, fixed deposit, lease financing, acceptance credit, etc. The scope of corporate counselling is limited to giving suggestions and opinions to the clients and help taking actions to solve their problems. It is provided to a corporate unit with a view to ensure better performance, maintain steady growth and create better image among investors.

### 2. Project counselling

Project counselling includes preparation of project reports, deciding upon the financing pattern to finance the cost of the project and appraising project report with the financial institutions or banks. Project reports are prepared to obtain government approval, get financial assistance from institutions and plan for the public issue. The financing mix is to be decided keeping in view the rules, regulations and norms prescribed by the government or followed by financial institutions. The projects are appraised, as to the location, technical, commercial and financial viability of the project. Project counselling also includes filling up of application forms with relevant information for obtaining funds from financial institutions.

### 3. Loan syndication

Loan syndication refers to assistance rendered by merchant banks to get mainly term loans for projects. Such loans may be obtained from a single development finance institution or a syndicate or consortium. Merchant Bankers help corporate clients to raise syndicated loans from commercial banks.

Merchant banks help clients approach financial institutions for term loans. The decision as to which financial institution should be approached depends on industry, location of the unit and size of project cost. The Merchant Bankers, first, make an appraisal of the project to satisfy that it is viable. The next step is designing capital structure, determining the promoter's contribution and arriving at a figure of approximate amount of term loan to be raised. The merchant banker has to ensure that the project adheres to the guidelines for financing industrial projects. After verifications that the project would be eligible for term loan, a preliminary meeting is fixed with financial institution. If the financial institution agrees to consider the proposal, the application is filled in and submitted along with other documents. The Merchant Bankers involvement enables the company to state that it has exercised due diligence in the exercise of obligations under various regulations.

## 4. Issue management

Management of issue involves marketing of corporate securities, *viz.*, equity shares, preference shares and debentures or bonds by offering them to public. Merchant banks act as intermediary whose main job is to transfer capital from those who own it to those who need it.

The issue function may be broadly divided into pre-issue management and post-issue management. In both the stages, legal requirements have to be complied with and several activities connected with the issue have to be coordinated.

The pre-issue management is divided into:

(*i*) Issue through prospectus, offer for sale and private placement.

(*ii*) Marketing and underwriting.

(*iii*) Pricing of Issues.

**(i) Public issue through prospectus**

(*a*) The most common method of public issue is through prospectus.

(*b*) Offers for sale are offers through the intermediary of issue house or firm of stock broker. The company sells the entire issue of shares or debentures to the issue house at an agreed price which is generally below the par value.

(*c*) The direct sale of securities by a company to investors is called private placement. The investors include LIC, UTI, GIC, SFC, etc.

To bring out a public issue, merchant bankers have to coordinate the activities relating to issue with different government and public bodies, professionals and private agencies. They have to ensure that the information required by the Companies Act and SEBI are furnished in the prospectus and get it vetted by reputed solicitor.

The copies of consent of experts, legal advisor, attorney, solicitor, bankers, bankers to the issue, brokers and underwriters are to be obtained from the company making the issue, to be filed along with prospectus to the Registrar of Companies. After the prospectus is ready, it has to be sent to SEBI for vetting. It is only after clearance by SEBI, the prospectus can be filed with the Registrar of Companies.

Brokers to the issue canvass subscription by mailing the literature to the clients and undertaking wide publicity. Members of stock exchange are appointed as brokers to the issue.

Principal brokers, in addition to the functions of brokers assist merchant bankers to devise strategy for success of the public issue, keep liaison between merchant banker and stock exchanges and canvass support for the issue among stock brokers. Sometimes, they undertake centralised mailing of prospectus, application forms and other publicity material at the instant of the merchant banker.

Bankers to the issue accept applications along with subscriptions tendered at their designated branches and forward them to the Registrar.

The brokers to the issue, principal agent and bankers to the issue are appointed by merchant bankers.

**(ii) Marketing**

After despatch of prospectus to SEBI, the merchant bankers arrange a meeting with company representatives and advertising agents to finalise arrangements relating to date of opening and closing of issue, registration of prospectus, launching publicity campaign and fixing date of board meeting to approve and sign prospectus and pass the necessary resolutions.

Publicity campaign covers the preparation of all publicity material and brochures, prospectus, announcement, advertisement in the press, radio, TV, investors' conference, etc. The merchant bankers help choosing the media, determining the size and publications in which the advertisement should appear.

The merchant banker's role is limited to deciding the number of copies to be printed, checking accuracy of statements made and ensure that the size of the application form and prospectus conform to the standard prescribed by the stock exchange. The merchant banker has to ensure that the material is delivered to the stock exchange at least 21 days before the issue opens and to brokers to the issue, branches of brokers to the issue and underwriters on time.

Security issues are underwritten to ensure that in case of under-subscription the issues are taken up by the underwriters. SEBI has made underwriting mandatory for issues to the public. The underwriting arrangement should be filed with the stock exchange. Particulars of underwriting arrangement should be mentioned in the prospectus.

The various activities connected with pre-issue management are a time- bound programme which has to be promptly attended to. The execution of the activities with clockwork efficiency would lead to a successful issue.

**(iii) Pricing of issues**

The SEBI Guidelines 1992 for capital issues have opened the capital market to free pricing of issues. Pricing of issues is done by companies themselves in consultation with the merchant bankers. Pricing of issue is part of pre-issue management.

An existing listed company and a new company set up by an existing company with five-year track record and existing private closely held company and existing unlisted company going in for public issues for the first time with two-and-a-half years track record of constant profitability can freely price the issue. The premium has to be decided after taking into account net asset value, profit earning capacity and market price. Justification of price has to be stated and included in the prospectus.

**(iv) Post-issue management**

The post-issue management consists of collection of application forms and statement of account received from bankers, screening applications, deciding allotment procedure, mailing of allotment letters, share certificates and refund orders.

Registrars to the issue play a major role in post-issue management. They receive the applications, verify them and submit the basis of allotment to the stock exchange. After the basis of allotment is approved by the stock exchange and allotted by the board, the auditor/company secretary has to certify that the allotment has been made by the company as per the basis of allotment approved by the exchange. Registrars have to ensure that the applications are processed and allotment/refund orders are sent within 70 days of the close of the issue. The time limit of 70 days has proved difficult to adhere and applicants have to wait for anytime between 90 to 180 days. Merchant bankers assist the company by coordinating the above activities.

**(v) Underwriting of public issue**

Underwriting is a guarantee given by the underwriter that in the event of undersubscription, the amount underwritten, would be subscribed by him. It is an insurance to the company which proposes to make public offer against risk of undersubscription. The issues packed by well-known underwriters generally receive a high premium from the public. This enables the issuing company to sell securities quickly.

All public issues have to be fully underwritten. Only Category I, II and III merchant bankers are permitted to underwrite an issue subject to the limit that the outstanding commitments of any such individual merchant banker at any point of time do not exceed five times of his net worth (paid-up capital and free reserves excluding revaluation reserves). This criteria is applicable to brokers also. Lead managers have to underwrite mandatorily 5 per cent of the issue or ₹ 2.5 lakhs whichever is less. Banks/merchant banking subsidiaries cannot underwrite more than 15 per cent of any issue.

By ensuring a direct stake in the underwriting, the merchant bankers make raising of external resources easy.

**(vi) Managers, consultants or advisors to the issue**

The managers to the issue assist in the drafting of prospectus, application forms and completion of formalities under the Companies Act, appointment of Registrar for dealing with share applications and transfer and listing of shares of the company on the stock exchange. Companies are free to appoint one or more agencies as managers to the issue. SEBI guidelines insist that all issues should be managed by at least one authorised merchant banker. Ordinarily, not more than two merchant bankers should be associated as lead managers, advisers and consultants to a public issue. In issues of over ₹ 100 crores, up to a maximum of four merchant bankers could be associated as managers.

## 5. Portfolio management

Portfolio refers to investment in different kinds of securities such as shares, debentures or bonds issued by different companies and securities issued by the government. It is not merely a collection of unrelated assets but a carefully blended asset combination within a unified framework. Portfolio management refers to maintaining proper combination of securities in a manner that they give maximum return with minimum risk.

Merchant bankers provide portfolio management service to their clients. Today, the investor is very prudent. Every investor is interested in safety, liquidity and profitability of his investment. But investors cannot study and choose the appropriate securities. They need expert guidance. Merchant bankers have a role to play in this regard. They have to conduct regular market and economic surveys to know:

(*i*) Monetary and fiscal policies of the government.

(*ii*) Financial statements of various corporate sectors in which the investments have to be made by the investors.

(*iii*) Secondary market position, *i.e.*, how the share market is moving.

(*iv*) Changing pattern of the industry.

(*v*) The competition faced by the industry with similar type of industries.

The merchant bankers have to analyse the surveys and help the prospective investors in choosing the shares. The portfolio managers generally will have to classify the investors based on capacity and risk; they can take and arrange appropriate investment. Thus, portfolio management plans successful investment strategies for investors.

The portfolio management service is very important need of the day since one-eighth of our investment at present comes from rural areas. Even though there are 23 stock exchanges in our country, 28 nationalised banks with network of about 50,000 branches, only one-eighth of the savings is mobilised from the rural areas. By establishing portfolio management centres at various areas, more investments can be augmented from villages. Instead of concentrating on large investors, there is immediate need to develop small investors which could be done through portfolio management.

The role which can be played by non-resident Indians in the economic development of a country is not small. With their technical skill and foreign exchange and also with their knowledge of foreign market, they can contribute much for the country. In order to utilise this opportunity, government is offering number of facilities and incentives. But the NRI investment is not showing any signs of substantial improvement for corporate sector. This is due to the NRI accounts being scattered with various branches of banks throughout the country and no institution is taking action to pool these resources. The non-resident themselves for investment will have to follow many rules and regulations which are complicated. In this regard, merchant bankers should help the NRI in selecting right type of securities and offering expertise guidance in fulfilling government regulations. By this service to NRI accountholders, merchant bankers can mobilise more resources for the corporate sector.

### 6. Advisory service relating to mergers and takeovers

A merger is a combination of two or more companies into a single company where one survives and others lose their corporate existence. A takeover is the purchase by one company acquiring controlling interest in the share capital of another existing company. Merchant bankers are the middlemen in setting negotiation between the offeree and offeror. Being a professional expert, they are apt to safeguard the interest of the shareholders in both the companies. Once the merger partner is proposed, the merchant banker appraises merger/takeover proposal with respect to financial viability and technical feasibility. He negotiates purchase consideration and mode of payment. He gets approval from the government/RBI, drafts scheme of amalgamation and obtains approval from financial institutions.

### 7. Offshore finance

The merchant bankers help their clients in the following areas involving foreign currency.

(*i*) Long-term foreign currency loans,

(*ii*) Joint venture abroad,

(*iii*) Financing exports and imports, and

(*iv*) Foreign collaboration arrangements.

The bankers render other financial services such as appraisal, negotiations and compliance with procedural and legal aspects.

### 8. Non-resident investment

The services of merchant bankers include investment advisory services to NRI in terms of identification of investment opportunities, selection of securities, investment management, etc. They also take care of the operational details like purchase and sale of securities, securing necessary clearance from RBI for repatriation of interest and dividend.

## MERCHANT BANKERS AS LEAD MANAGERS

As per SEBI guidelines, it is mandatory that all public issues should be managed by merchant bankers in the capacity of lead managers. Only in the case of right issues not exceeding ₹ 50 lakhs, such an obligation is not necessary. The number of lead managers to be appointed by a company depends upon the size of the issue as shown below in the Table 10.1.

**TABLE 10.1: APPOINTMENT OF LEAD MANAGERS**

| *Sl. No.* | *Size of the Issue* | *Maximum Number of Lead Managers* |
|---|---|---|
| 1 | Less than ₹ 50 crores | 2 |
| 2 | ₹ 50 crores to ₹ 100 crores | 3 |
| 3 | ₹ 100 crores to ₹ 200 crores | 4 |
| 4 | ₹ 200 crores to ₹ 400 crores | 5 |
| 5 | Above ₹ 400 crores | 5 or more as prescribed by SEBI |

### ❖ Duties and responsibilities of lead managers

The most important aspect of merchant banking business is to function as lead managers to the issue management. As lead managers, they have to exercise reasonable care and diligence in issue management by paying attention to the following:

(*i*) It is the duty of every lead manager to enter into an agreement with the issuing companies stating the details regarding their responsibilities, liabilities, mutual rights, functions, disclosures, refund, allotment, etc. A copy of this agreement should be submitted to the SEBI at least one month before the opening of the issue for subscription.

(*ii*) One merchant banker cannot have association with another merchant banker who does not hold a certificate of registration with the SEBI.

(*iii*) Similarly, a lead manager cannot undertake the work of issue management if the issuing company is its associate.

(*iv*) In case there are more than one lead managers to an issue, the responsibilities of each of them should be clearly defined in the agreement.

(*v*) A lead manager is under an obligation to accept a minimum underwriting obligation of 5 per cent of the total underwriting commission or ₹ 25 lakhs whichever is less. If he is not able to comply with the above provision, it is his duty to make managements with another merchant banker associated with that issue to underwrite the said amount. Of course, it must be duly intimated to the SEBI.

(*vi*) A lead manager has to exercise due care and diligence in the verification of prospectus or letter of offer.

(*vii*) He has to submit due diligence certificate rating that the prospectus or letter of offer is in conformity with the documents relevant to the issue, the disclosures are true, fair and adequate and all legal requirements connected with the issue have been duly complied with.

(*viii*) Every lead manager has to submit all the particulars of an issue, draft prospectus or letter of offer, etc. to the SEBI at least two weeks before the date of filing with the Registrar of Companies or regional stock exchanges or both.

(*ix*) In case of any suggestions or modifications given by the SEBI, he has to ensure that they are properly incorporated in the appropriate areas.

(*x*) In the case of development, the lead manager has to ensure the collection of the specified amount from the underwriters.

(*xi*) Every lead manager is responsible for ensuring timely refund of excess application money received from the applicants.

(*xii*) It is his duty to mail the share/debenture certificate immediately on allotment or inform it to the depository participant.

## QUALITIES REQUIRED FOR MERCHANT BANKERS

Merchant bankers play a significant role as a catalyst to transform the project ideas into industrial ventures. They help promotion of the enterprise by undertaking various activities such as market surveys, choice of suitable location and its size, preparation of documents and obtaining consent from various authorities. They help in taking important decisions such as financing mix, management of public issues, credit syndication, etc. The success of the merchant bankers depends on the quality of service and soundness of advice to clients. To perform these services effectively, the merchant bankers are expected to possess certain qualities which are described below:

1. Ability to analyse various aspects such as technical, financial and economic aspects concerning the formation of an industrial project.
2. Knowledge about the various aspects of capital markets, trends in stock exchange, psychology of investing public, change in the economic and technological environment in the country.
3. Ability to build-up the bank-client relationship and live up to the clients' expectations with total involvement in the project assigned to them.
4. Innovative approach in developing capital market instruments to satisfy the ever-changing needs of investing public.

5. Integrity and maintenance of high professional standards are the essential requisites for the success of merchant bankers in the present scenario.

## GUIDELINES FOR MERCHANT BANKERS

Merchant banking has been statutorily brought within the framework of the Securities and Exchange Board of India under SEBI (Merchant Bankers) Regulations, 1992.

1. In terms of the guidelines issued during April 1990, all merchant bankers will require authorisation by SEBI to carry-out business.

The criteria for authorisation include:

(*i*) Professional qualification in finance, law or business management;

(*ii*) Infrastructure like adequate office space, equipment and manpower;

(*iii*) Employment of two persons who have the experience to conduct business of merchant bankers;

(*iv*) Capital adequacy;

(*v*) Past track record, experience, general reputation and fairness in all transactions.

2. SEBI issued further guidelines classifying the merchant bankers into four categories based on the nature and range of activities and their responsibilities to SEBI investors and issuers of securities. SEBI has issued revised guidelines on December 22, 1992 classifying the activities of merchant bankers as follows:

The first category consists of merchant bankers who carry on any activity of issue management which will *inter alia* consists of preparation of prospectus and other information relating to the issue, determining financial structure, tie-up of financiers and final allotment and refund of subscription and to act in the capacity of managers, advisor or consultant to an issue, portfolio manager and underwriter.

The second category consists of those authorised to act in the capacity of comanager/advisor, consultant, underwriter to an issue or portfolio manager.

The third category consists of those authorised to act as underwriter, advisor or consultant to an issue.

The fourth category consists of merchant bankers who act as advisor or consultant to an issue.

Minimum net worth for first category is ₹ 1 crore, second category ₹ 50 lakhs, third category ₹ 20 lakhs and fourth category is nil.

The above classification was valid up to December 1997 only.

3. An initial authorisation fee, an annual fee and renewal fee may be collected by SEBI.

4. All issues must be managed at least by one authorised banker, functioning as the sole manager or the lead manager. Ordinarily, not more than two merchant bankers should be associated as lead managers. But, for issues over ₹ 100 crores and above, the number of lead managers may go up to a maximum of four. The specific responsibilities of each lead manager must be submitted to SEBI prior to the issue.

5. The lead merchant banker holding a certificate under Category I shall accept a minimum underwriting obligation of 5 per cent of the total underwriting commitment or ₹ 25 lakhs whichever is less.

6. Each merchant banker is required to furnish to the SEBI half-yearly unaudited financial results when required by it with a view to monitor the capital adequacy of the merchant banker.

7. SEBI has prescribed a code of conduct to the merchant bankers. The banker must perform his duties with highest standards of integrity and fairness in all his dealings. He will render at all times high standards of service, exercise due diligence, ensure proper care and exercise independent professional judgement. The merchant banker and his personnel will act in an ethical manner in all his dealings with the investors, clients and fellow bankers. All merchant bankers must adhere to the code of conduct.

8. The above guidelines will be administered by SEBI and it will supervise the activities of merchant bankers.

9. SEBI has been vested with power to suspend or cancel the authorisation in case of violation of the guidelines.

10. To ensure transparency and accountability in the operation of merchant bankers and to protect the investors, a number of obligations and responsibilities have been imposed on them. It has been decided to ask merchant bankers to enter into an agreement with corporate body setting out their mutual rights, liabilities and obligations relating to an issue particularly on disclosure, allotment and refund, maintenance of books of accounts and submission of half-yearly reports to SEBI.

11. Inspections will be conducted by SEBI to ensure that provisions of the regulations are properly complied with and to investigate the complaints from customers. It is obligatory on the part of merchant bankers to furnish all the details sought by the investigating team. The regulations, however, indicate that the board would give reasonable notice to merchant bankers before undertaking inspection. On the basis of inspection report, the board will communicate the contents of the report to the concerned merchant banker to give him/her an opportunity to put forth his/her submissions. On receipt of the explanations, if any, of the merchant bankers, the SEBI would advise merchant bankers to take any measures that it may deem fit, and to comply with the provisions of the regulations.

The notification procedure relating to action to be initiated against merchant banks in case of default has been detailed out. The regulations empower SEBI to take action against defaulting banker such as suspension/cancellation of registration. In case of deliberate manipulation, or price rigging or cornering activities or deterioration in the financial position, the board is empowered to cancel the registration of the merchant banker. Under the regulation, the SEBI is empowered to suspend a registration of a member banker in case the merchant banker furnishes wrong or false information, fails to resolve the complaints of the investors, etc. The penalty or suspensation or cancellation of registration can be imposed by SEBI only after holding an enquiry and giving sufficient opportunity to the merchant banker of being heard. Any merchant banker aggrieved by an order of SEBI, can, however, appeal to the Union Government.

In September 1997, SEBI brought about some major changes in SEBI (Merchant Bankers) Rules and Regulations, 1992. Accordingly, only corporate bodies will be allowed to function as merchant bankers. Moreover, the multiple categories of merchant bankers shall be abolished and there will be just one entity, *viz.*, Merchant Banker. The merchant bankers presently functioning as Merchant Bankers Category II, III and IV shall have an option to either upgrade themselves as Merchant Bankers (presently Merchant Banker Category I) or seek separate registration as Underwriters or Portfolio Managers under the respective regulations. The merchant bankers will be prohibited from carrying out fund-based activity other than those related exclusively to the capital markets. In effect, the activities undertaken by NBFCs such as accepting deposits, leasing and bill discounting would not be allowed to be undertaken by a merchant banker.

## MERCHANT BANKERS' COMMISSION

As determined by the Finance Ministry, Government of India, merchant bankers are eligible to charge commission/fee from their clients as detailed below:

(*i*) A merchant banker can charge 0.5 per cent as the maximum commission for whole of the issue.

(*ii*) They can charge project appraisal fees.

(*iii*) A lead manager can claim a commission of 0.5 per cent up to ₹ 25 crores and 0.2 per cent in excess of ₹ 25 crores.

(*iv*) Underwriting Commission.

*(Per cent)*

| *Type of Security* | *On amount devolving on Underwriters* | *On amount subscribed by public* |
|---|---|---|
| 1. Equity shares | 2.50 | 2.50 |
| 2. Preference shares/debentures | | |
| (*a*) Up to ₹ 5 lakhs | 2.50 | 1.50 |
| (*b*) Excess of ₹ 5 lakhs | 2.00 | 1.00 |

(*v*) Brokerage commission 1.5 per cent.

(*vi*) Other expenses like advertising, printing, Registrar's expenses, stamp duty, etc. in connection with the issue can be reimbursed from its clients.

## MERCHANT BANKERS IN THE MARKET-MAKING PROCESS

The Securities and Exchange Board of India (SEBI) has stated that merchant bankers must be involved more closely in the market-making process as share brokers do not have the requisite expertise to evaluate the fundamentals of the scrips before taking over the role of market-makers. Further, share brokers, generally being partnership firms, do not have the financial clout which is necessary for market-making activity. Resultantly, the SEBI has suggested that any member of the stock exchange, along with one merchant banker registered with SEBI could act as a market-maker.

The SEBI has felt that to ensure liquidity of scrips, it was necessary to facilitate greater movement, which could only be achieved through the institution of market-makers. Market-makers would also create a market for the scrips by offering two-way quotes to the investors. A minimum of ten scrips have been proposed by SEBI for the market-makers.

## PROGRESS OF MERCHANT BANKING IN INDIA

Up to 1970, there were only two foreign banks which performed merchant banking operations in the country. SBI was the first Indian commercial bank and ICICI the first financial institution to take up the activities in 1972 and 1973 respectively. As a result of buoyancy in the capital market in 1980s some commercial banks set up their subsidiaries to operate exclusively in merchant banking industry. In addition, a number of large stock broking firms and financial consultants also entered into business. Thus, by the end of the 1980s, there were 33 merchant bankers belonging to three major segments, *viz.*, commercial banks, all India financial institutions, and private firms. Merchant banking functions of these institutions was related only to management of new capital issues.

Merchant banking industry which remained almost stagnant and stereotyped for over two decades, witnessed an astonishing growth after the process of economic reforms and deregulation of Indian economy in 1991. The number of merchant banks increased to 115 by the end of 1992-93, 300 by the end of 1993-94 and 501 by end of August 1994. All merchant bankers registered with SEBI under four different categories include 50 commercial banks, 6 all India financial institutions — ICICI, IFCI, IDBI, IRBI, Tourism Finance Corporation of India, Infrastructure Leasing and Financial Services Ltd. and private merchant bankers.

The number of registered intermediaries operating in India is shown in the following Table.

**TABLE 10.2: REGISTERED INTERMEDIARIES OTHER THAN STOCK BROKERS AND SUB-BROKERS**

| *Type of Intermediary* | *No. of Registered Intermediaries as on March 31, 2019* | *No. of Registered Intermediaries as on March 31, 2020* |
|---|---|---|
| Registrar to Issue and Share Transfer Agents | 77 | 80 |
| Merchant Bankers | 209 | 215 |
| Underwriters | 2 | 2 |
| Depository Participants – NSDL | 277 | 285 |
| Depository Participants – CDSL | 598 | 614 |
| Credit Rating Agencies | 7 | 7 |
| Bankers-to-an-Issue | 65 | 66 |
| Debenture Trustees | 32 | 31 |
| KYC (Know Your Client) Registration Agency (KRA) | 5 | 5 |
| FPIs (including deemed FPIs) | 9,556 | 9,823 |
| Custodians | 19 | 19 |
| Designated Depository Participants | 16 | 16 |

| | | |
|---|---|---|
| Alternative Investment Funds | 547 | 649 |
| Venture Capital Funds | 195 | 189 |
| Foreign Venture Capital Investors | 250 | 251 |
| Portfolio Managers | 321 | 351 |
| Investment Advisers | 1,149 | 1,291 |
| Research Analysis | 625 | 680 |
| **Total** | **13,950** | **14,576** |

***Source:*** SEBI Annual Report, 2020.

In addition to Indian merchant bankers, a large number of reputed international merchant bankers like Merrill Lynch, Morgan Stanley, Goldman Sachs, Jardie Fleming, Kleinwort Benson, etc. are operating in India under authorisation of SEBI. As a result of proliferation, Indian merchant bankers are faced with severe competition not only among themselves but also with the well-developed global players.

## PROBLEMS OF MERCHANT BANKERS

1. SEBI guidelines have authorised merchant bankers to undertake issue-related activities only with an exception of portfolio management. These guidelines have made the merchant bankers either to restrict their activities or think of separating these activities from the present one and float new subsidiary and enlarge the scope of its activities.
2. SEBI guidelines stipulate a minimum net worth of ₹ 1 crore for authorisation of merchant bankers. Small but professional and specialised merchant bankers who do not have a net worth of ₹ 1 crore may have to close down their business. The entry is denied to young, specialised professionals into merchant banking business.
3. Non-cooperation of the issuing companies in timely allotment of securities and refund of application money is another problem of merchant bankers. The guidelines have put the responsibility on the merchant bankers. They have to seek the cooperation of the issuing company to shoulder the responsibility.

## SCOPE FOR MERCHANT BANKING IN INDIA

In the present-day capital market scenario, the merchant banks play the role of an encouraging and supporting force to the entrepreneurs, corporate sectors and the investors. There is vast scope for merchant bankers to enlarge their operations both in domestic and international market.

**(i) Growth of new issues market:** The growth of new issue market is unprecedented since 1990-91. The amount of annual average of capital issues by non-government public companies was only about ₹ 90 crores in the 70s, the same rose to over ₹ 1,000 crores in the 80s and further to ₹ 22,232.69 crores in 2009-10. The number of capital issues has also increased from 516 in 1991-92 to 1,211 in 2005-06. The trend is expected to continue in future.

**(ii) Entry of foreign investors:** An outstanding development in the history of Indian capital market was its opening up in 1992 by allowing foreign institutional investors to invest in primary and secondary market and also permitting Indian companies to directly tap foreign capital through euro issues. Within two years to March 1994, the total inflow of foreign capital through these routes reached to about $ 5 billion. It is estimated that this figure may go up to $ 35-40 billion by the turn of this century. Further, foreign direct investment a investment by NRIs have risen considerably due to number of incentives offered to them. They need the services of merchant bankers to advise them for their investment in India. The increasing number of joint ventures abroad by Indian companies also require expert services of merchant bankers.

**(iii) Changing policy of financial institutions:** With the changing emphasis in the lending policies of financial institutions from security orientation to project orientation, corporate enterprises would require the expert services of merchant bankers for project appraisal, financial management, etc. The policy of decentralisation and encouragement of small and medium industries will further increase the demand for technical and financial services which can be provided by merchant bankers.

**(iv) Development of debt market:** The concept of debt market has set to work through National Stock Exchange and the Over The Counter Exchange of India. The total amount mobilised through privately placed debt securities in 2009-10 was ₹ 67,790.46 crores. The development of debt market will offer tremendous opportunity to merchant bankers.

**(v) Innovations in financial instruments:** The Indian capital market has witnessed innovations in the introduction of financial instruments such as non-convertible debentures with detachable warrants, cumulative convertible preference shares, zero coupon bonds, deep discount bonds, triple option bonds, secured premium notes, floating rate bonds, auction-rated debentures, etc. This has further extended the rôle of merchant bankers as market-makers for these instruments.

**(vi) Corporate restructuring:** As a result of liberalisation and globalisation, the competition in the corporate sector is becoming intense. To survive in the competition, companies are reviewing their strategies, structure and functioning. This had led to corporate restructuring including mergers, acquisitions, splits, disinvestments and financial restructuring. This offers good opportunity to merchant bankers to extend the area of their operations.

**(vii) Disinvestment:** The government raised ₹ 2,000 crores through disinvestment of equity shares of selected public sector undertakings in 1993-94. The government proposes to shift the present method of periodic sale of public sector shares to round the year off-loading of shares directly on the stock exchange from the year 1995-96. The government will sell the shares of identified public sector at any time during the year when they get a good price above minimum stipulated level. This is likely to provide good business to merchant bankers in future.

The above discussion highlights that the scope of merchant banking is vast and there lies immense opportunities ahead of merchant bankers. They should develop adequate infrastructure including expertise in order to provide full range of merchant banking services to corporate sector.

### ❖ SEBI guidelines for merchant bankers

To protect the investors interest, the SEBI has made it mandatory for merchant bankers to disclose on their websites the following:

For each issue the matters to be disclosed are:

- Three year track record of companies whose IPOs/FPOs were managed by them for each issue the matters to be disclosed are:
- Issue size.
- Extent of over/under subscription.
- The shareholding of the QIBs at the end of each of the three subsequent financial years.
- Financials of the company for three years.
- Earnings per share and price-earning multiple at the end of the each three financial years.
- Post-listing *vis-à-vis* the peer as well the industry average.

The extent of trading of shares whether active or thin.

## QUESTIONS

### I. Objective type questions:

### A. Fill in the blanks:

1. The minimum net worth for the first category of merchant banker is ₹ ________.
2. A merchant banker can claim a charge ________ per cent as the commission for the whole issue.
3. The direct sale of securities to investors is called ________.
4. Merchant banks deal with funds raised through ________ and ________.
5. The lead merchant banker under Category I shall accept a minimum underwriting of ________ per cent of total underwriting commitment or ₹ ________ whichever is less.

[**Key:** 1. ₹ 1 crore, 2. 0.5 per cent, 3. private placement, 4. money market and capital market, 5.5 per cent - ₹ 25 lakhs.]

### B. State whether the following statements are TRUE or FALSE:

1. Loan syndication refers to getting term loans for projects from consortium.
2. The most common method of public issue is through private placement.
3. Bankers to the Issue accept applications along with subscriptions through their designated branches.
4. A new company can freely price the issue.
5. Brokers to the issue canvass subscription and undertake publicity.

[**Key:** 1. True, 2. False, 3. True, 4. False, 5. True]

## II. Short answer questions:

1. What is portfolio management?
2. Define merchant banker.
3. State the qualities required for a merchant banker.
4. Discuss the problems of merchant bankers in India.
5. Write a note on 'Project counselling'.

## III. Essay type questions:

1. Distinguish between a commercial bank and a merchant bank.
2. 'The scope for merchant banking is great in India'. Discuss.
3. Explain the services of merchant bankers.
4. Explain in detail the 'pre-issue management'.
5. Discuss the guidelines issued for merchant bankers by SEBI and discuss their progress and problems.

# 11 HIRE PURCHASE

Hire purchase is a method of selling goods. In a hire purchase transaction, the goods are let out on hire by a finance company (creditor) to the hire purchase customer (hirer). The buyer is required to pay an agreed amount in periodical installments during a given period. The ownership of the property remains with creditor and passes on to hirer on the payment of last installment.

## FEATURES OF HIRE PURCHASE AGREEMENT

1. Under hire purchase system, the buyer takes possession of goods immediately and agrees to pay the total hire purchase price in installments.
2. Each installment is treated as hire charges.
3. The ownership of the goods passes from buyer to seller on the payment of the installment.
4. In case the buyer makes any default in the payment of any installment, the seller has right to repossess the goods from the buyer and forfeit the amount already received treating it as hire charge.
5. The hirer has the right to terminate the agreement any time before the property passes. That is, he has the option to return the goods in which case he need not pay installments falling due thereafter. However, he cannot recover the sums already paid as such sums legally represent hire charge on the goods in question.

## LEGAL POSITION

The Hire Purchase Act, 1972 defines a hire purchase agreement as, an agreement under which goods are let on hire and under which the hirer has an option to purchase them in accordance with the terms of agreement under which:

1. Payment is to be made in installments over a specified period.
2. The possession is delivered to the purchaser at the time of entering into a contract.

3. The property in the goods passes to the purchaser on payment of the last installment.
4. Each installment is treated as hire charge so that if default is made in payment of any one installment, the seller is entitled to take away the goods.
5. The hirer/purchaser is free to return the goods without being required to pay any further installments falling due after the return.

## HIRE PURCHASE AGREEMENT

There is no prescribed form for a hire purchase agreement, but it has to be in writing and signed by both parties to the agreement.

A hire purchase agreement must contain the following particulars:

*(i)* The description of goods in a manner sufficient to identify them.

*(ii)* The hire purchase price of the goods.

*(iii)* The date of commencement of the agreement.

*(iv)* The number of installments in which hire purchase price is to be paid, the amount, and due date.

## HIRE PURCHASE AND CREDIT SALE

Higher purchase transaction is different from credit sale.

In case of actual sale, the title in the property, *i.e.*, ownership and possession is transferred to the purchase simultaneously, in hire purchase, the ownership remains with the seller until last instalment is paid.

## HIRE PURCHASE AND INSTALLMENT SALE

Hire purchase transaction is different from installment system. In case of installment system, it is not only the possession but also the ownership of goods which is transferred to the buyer immediately at the time of agreement. Further, when the buyer stops payment of dues, the seller has no right to repossess the goods. He has the only right to sue the buyer for the non-payment by returning the goods but has the right of disposing of the goods in any manner as he likes. Any loss of goods should be borne only by the buyer as risk lies with the ownership.

## HIRE PURCHASE AND LEASING

Hire purchase is also different from leasing.

(i) **Ownership:** In a contract of lease, the ownership rests with the lessor throughout and the lessee (hirer) has no option to purchase the goods.

(ii) **Method of financing:** Leasing is a method of financing business assets whereas hire purchase is a method of financing both business assets and consumer articles.

(iii) **Depreciation:** In leasing, depreciation and investment allowance cannot be claimed by the lessee. In hire purchase, depreciation and investment allowance can be claimed by the hirer.

(iv) **Tax benefits:** The entire lease rental is tax deductible expense. Only the interest component of the hire purchase installment is tax deductible.

(v) **Salvage value:** The lessee, not being the owner of the asset, does not enjoy the salvage value of the asset. The hirer, in purchase, being the owner of the asset, enjoys salvage value of the asset.

(vi) **Deposit:** Lessee is not required to make any deposit, whereas 20 per cent deposit is required in hire purchase.

(vii) **Rent-purchase:** With lease, we rent and with hire purchase we buy the goods.

(viii) **Extent of finance:** Lease financing is invariably 100 per cent financing. It requires no immediate down payment or margin money by the lessee. In hire purchase, a margin equal to 20-25 per cent of the cost of the asset is to be paid by the hirer.

(ix) **Maintenance:** The cost of maintenance of the hired asset is to be borne by the hirer himself. In case of finance lease only, the maintenance of leased asset is the responsibility of the lessee.

(x) **Reporting:** The asset on hire purchase is shown in the balance sheet of the hirer. The leased assets are shown by way of footnote only.

**DIFFERENCES BETWEEN LOAN, HIRE PURCHASE AND LEASING**

| ***Criteria*** | ***Loan*** | ***Hire Purchase*** | ***Leasing*** |
|---|---|---|---|
| Ownership | Borrower | Financier | Lessor |
| Relationship | Lender-borrower | Owner-hirer | Lessor-lessee |
| Buying | Borrower buys the equipment | Owner purchases and supplies to the hirer | Lessor purchases and supplies to Lessee |
| Compensation | Interest | Hire Charges | Lease rent |
| Repayment | Principal and interest paid in installments | Hire charges paid along with installments | Lease rent paid periodically |
| Insurance | At borrower's cost | At owner's cost | At lessor's cost |

## ORIGIN AND DEVELOPMENT

The growth and development of hire purchase system can be traced back to the advent of industrial development in UK. Henry Moore, a Bishogate piano-maker introduced the system of hire purchase in 1846 in UK. Cowperwait & Sons, a furniture dealer introduced the hire purchase system in the US in 1807. The singer manufacturing company started selling sewing machine under hire purchase agreement. The idea was developed by Wagon Companies which were formed to finance the purchase of wagons by collieries. The Wagon Companies bought the wagons and then let them out collieries under hire purchase agreement.

All early hire purchase transactions were financed by manufacturers or dealers themselves. Subsequently, independent finance house came into existence to offer hire purchase of wide variety of consumer articles, automobiles and industrial machinery on hire purchase.

In India, hire purchase finance started only after World War I. However, it was only after World War II that its growth assumed visible dimension. The concept of hire purchase was not quite popular in the pre-independence period though a few were endeavouring to increase the volume of their business with the provision of extending credit to intending buyers. With the increase in economic activity, many non-banking financing companies entered the scene in the fifties and sixties.

The pioneers in the field were Commercial Credit Corporation Limited, Motor and General Finance Limited, and Investments Supply Limited. These companies were set up predominantly to finance road transport sector. The volume of hire purchase business was around ₹ 635 crores in 1987-88, out of which automobiles accounted for 55 per cent. Today, about 25 per cent of sale of commercial vehicles is accounted by hire purchase. It is estimated by the Federation Hire Purchase Association that the stock-on-hire of hire purchase companies comprising corporate and non-corporate entities would be approximately ₹ 3,000 crores now.

In addition to commercial vehicles, purchase of consumer articles like household appliances, air-conditioners, refrigerators, office furniture and equipment are financed through hire purchase. In recent years, the consumer durable goods market is experiencing an unprecedented boom. The growing Indian middle class — 100 to 150 million, growing at a rate of 20 per cent per annum and their willingness to mortgage the future for today's enjoyment have led to spectacular growth in hire purchase business.

The institutions engaged in the hire purchase business in organised sector include commercial banks, cooperatives banks, State Finance Corporations, National Small Industries Corporations and in the unorganised sector they comprise a large number of partnership firms and individuals.

The National Small Industries Corporation supplies machineries to small-scale industries under hire purchase. The Industrial Development Bank of India indirectly participates in financing hire purchase business by way of rediscounting usance bills/promotes arising out of sale of indigenous machinery on hire purchase basis. The Industrial Credit and Investment Corporation also has a discounting scheme of usance bills under hire purchase scheme.

## BANKS AND HIRE PURCHASE BUSINESS

Through a recent notification issued on 7.9.1990 under Clause (0) of Sub-section (1) of Section 6 of the Banking Regulation Act, 1949 the Government of India has permitted banks to engage in 'hire purchase' business. Though the statutory framework now enables the banks to carry on hire purchase business and to set up subsidiaries for undertaking such business, the Reserve Bank of India is of the view that in the public interest and in the interest of banking policy, the following guidelines should be made applicable to banks so far as hire purchase business is concerned:

(*i*) At present, banks shall not themselves undertake directly (*i.e.*, departmentally) the business of hire purchase.

(*ii*) Banks which have set up subsidiaries, (*i.e.*, a company in which it holds not less than 51 per cent of the shares) for the business of equipment leasing, merchant banking, etc., may undertake the hire purchase business either through such a subsidiary or through a separate subsidiary. Other banks may set up subsidiaries to transact hire purchase business either exclusively or together with the business of equipment leasing. Banks desirous of undertaking hire purchase business through an existing or new subsidiary as above, will require prior approval of the Reserve Bank of India.

*(iii)* An existing bank subsidiary that may hereafter transact hire purchase business or a new subsidiary set up to transact such business, as provided in Clause (ii) above, shall engage itself in the financing of other companies or concerns engaged in hire purchase business.

*(iv)* Investment of a bank in the shares of its subsidiary set up for undertaking equipment leasing and/or hire purchase business together with investment of the bank in shares of other companies carrying on equipment leasing and/or hire purchase business, shall not in the aggregate exceed 10 per cent of the paid-up capital and reserves of the bank.

*(v)* While banks may invest in shares of other hire purchase companies within the limits specified in Section 19(2) of the Banking Regulation Act, 1949 with the Reserve Bank's prior approval they shall not act as promoters of such companies.

*(vi)* Any application to be made to the controller of capital issues in connection with the setting up of a new subsidiary or for subsequent issue of capital, shall need prior clearance form the Reserve Bank of India.

*(vii)* Banks setting up a subsidiary for the purpose of carrying hire purchase business or through the existing subsidiaries should furnish such information in such form and at such time as the Reserve Bank may required from time-to-time.

## BANK CREDIT FOR HIRE PURCHASE BUSINESS

The subsidiary of commercial banks lend to the dealer or to finance intermediary who has already financed articles sold by the dealer to the hirer under a hire purchase contract. While considering proposals from dealers or hire purchase financing companies, the bank subsidiary has to take extra precautions, looking to the particular nature of transaction under hire purchase contract.

When offered this type of business, the bank subsidiary would make an assessment of the standing and financial position of the dealer or of the hire purchase company, and take into consideration the principles of good lending and carry-out the procedure below:

**(i) Customer:** When approached for hire purchase facility, the subsidiary should take care to make the assessment of the standing and financial position of the business customer.

**(ii) Purpose:** The type of goods being used to finance in the hire purchase transaction is of great importance. In the event of default, the bank may reconsider repossessing the goods and selling them to clear the advance. Thus, if the goods can be readily sold elsewhere (*e.g.*, a relatively new car), then these agreements are better security than those for (say) cameras which will have a lower resale value.

**(iii) Amount:** Bank subsidiaries taking up hire purchase business would do well to discourage small individual loans. In order to ensure proper servicing and monitoring, it is also essential to a have floor limit in the amount of individual hire purchase transactions. While it may be about ₹ 50,000 for automobile sector, it may be about ₹ 10,000 for consumer durables.

**(iv) Period:** The facility will normally be extended over to three years.

**(v) Repayment:** Repayment are spread evenly, or agreed, over the loan period. The repayment should be adaptable to the hirer's needs. The repayment can usually be tailor-made to suit the income generated from the use of asset so that it is self-financing. Sometimes, repayment holidays can be allowed and repayment is delayed until the asset is operational or producing profit. To ensure timely recovery in the case of car two-wheeler, and consumer durable financing, it would be preferable to have institutional tie-ups with employers'/employees' cooperative societies for which the eligibility criteria can be laid down.

**(vi) Security:** Technically, hire purchase advance is against hypothecation of equipment/ vehicles and pledge of hundis/pronotes and lodgements of hire purchase agreements. The bank subsidiary will ask the borrower to complete the bank's form of security to charge the security under an equitable/hypothecation charge. If the borrower is a limited company which is not of sufficient strength to allow equitable/hypothecation facility and if suitable security is not available, it is normal to obtain a debenture over the assets of the company under which a floating charge is obtained.

If necessary, the bank subsidiary will ask the hirer to furnish a guarantor of means and the bank would in such a case insist that the guarantor should also accept the hundies. It is a practice with some banks to insist for insurance policy to indemnify the bank against the default of the hirer. The premiums will be charged to the hirer.

In view of the cost and difficulty of the repossession of a fast depreciating asset, the customer's ability to repay is vital and no reliance is placed on security.

**(vii) Monitoring and control:** The bank needs to exercise control over the ongoing situation. A periodical certificate should be obtained from the finance company at the monthly intervals, stating the total amount of outstanding but excluding those hire purchase agreements which have become in arrears and are, therefore, suspects. One or two months in arrears may be acceptable but more than that suggest that the particular hirer is in permanent default. The bank will keep a running total of these amounts, returning agreements which have become lapsed to their customers.

## QUESTIONS

### I. Objective type questions:

#### A. Fill in the blanks:

1. In hire purchase, the ownership remains with the ____________ until last installment paid.
2. In hire purchase, depreciation can be claimed by the ____________.

3. NSIC supplies __________ on hire purchase to __________.
4. With __________ we rent and with __________ we buy the goods.

[**Key:** 1. Seller, 2. hirer, 3. machine - small-scale industry, 4. lease-hire purchase.]

## B. State whether the following statements are TRUE or FALSE:

1. The hirer has the option to terminate the agreement before the property passes on to him.
2. In installment sale, the buyers has right of repossession.
3. The hirer enjoys salvage value.
4. Banks can undertake hire purchase directly.

[**Key:** 1. True, 2. False, 3. True, 4. False.]

## II. Short answer type questions:

1. Distinguish between hire purchase and installment sale.
2. Distinguish between hire purchase and lease.
3. Explain the features of hire purchase.

## III. Essay type questions:

1. Discuss the legal position of 'hire purchase' and distinguish it from leasing.
2. Distinguish between 'loan' and 'hire purchase' and analyse the factors to be considered by a banker while granting credit for hire purchase business.

# 12 LEASING

Traditionally, firms acquire productive assets and use them as owners. The sources of finance to a firm for procuring assets may be internal or external. Over the years, there has been a declining trend in the internally generated resources of Indian companies due to low profitability. The financial institutions experience paucity of funds at their disposal to meet the increasing needs of borrowers. Further, modern business environment is becoming more and more complex. To succeed in the situation, the firms aim at growth with stability. To accomplish this objective, firms are required to go for massive expansion, diversification and modernisation. Essentially, such projects involve a huge amount of investment. High rate of inflation, severe cost escalation, heavy taxation and meagre internal resources forced many companies to look for alternative means of financing the projects. Leasing has emerged as a new source of financing capital assets.

## CONCEPT OF LEASING

Leasing, as a financing concept, is an arrangement between two parties, the leasing company or lessor and the user or lessee, whereby the former arranges to buy capital equipment for the use of the latter for an agreed period of time in return for the payment of rent. The rentals are predetermined and payable at fixed intervals of time, according to the mutual convenience of both the parties. However, the lessor remains the owner of the equipment over the primary period.

By resorting to leasing, the lessee company is able to exploit the economic value of the equipment by using it as if he owned it without having to pay for its capital cost. Lease rentals can be conveniently paid over the lease period out of profits earned from the use of the equipment and the rent is cent per cent tax deductible.

**A Lease is defined as follows:**

'Lease is a form of contract transferring the use or occupancy of land, space, structure or equipment, in consideration of a payment, usually in the form of a rent'.

**— Dictionary of Business and Management**

'Lease is a contract whereby the owner of an asset (lessor) grants to another party (lessee) the exclusive right to use the asset usually for an agreed period of time in return for the payment of rent'.

**— James C. Van Horne**

'A contract between lessor and lessee for the hire of a specific asset selected from a manufacturer or vendor of such assets by the lessee. The lessor retains the ownership of the asset. The lessee has possession and use of the asset on payment of specified retain over the period'.

**— Equipment Leasing Association of UK**

Thus, in a contract of lease, there are two parties involved: (*i*) lessor and (*ii*) the lessee. The lessor can be a company, a cooperative society, a partnership firm or an individual in manufacturing or allied activities. The lessee can be even a doctor or any other specialists who use costly equipment for the practice of his profession.

### ❖ Leasing as a source of finance

Leasing is an important source of finance for the lessee. Leasing companies finance for:

1. Modernisation of business.
2. Balancing equipment.
3. Cars, scooters and other vehicles and durables.
4. Items entitled to 100 per cent or 50 per cent depreciation.
5. Assets which are not being financed by banks/institutions.

## STEPS INVOLVED IN LEASING TRANSACTION

The steps involved in a leasing transaction are summarised as follows:

1. First, the lessee has to decide the asset required and select the supplier. He has to decide about the design specifications, the price, warranties, terms of delivery, servicing, etc.

2. The lessee, then enters into a lease agreement with the lessor. The lease agreement contains the terms and conditions of the lease such as,

(*a*) The basic lease period during which the lease is irrecoverable.

(*b*) The timing and amount of periodical rental payments during the lease period.

(*c*) Details of any option to renew the lease or to purchase the asset at the end of the period.

(*d*) Details regarding payment of cost of maintenance and repairs, taxes, insurance and other expenses.

3. After the lease agreement is signed, the lessor contacts the manufacturer and requests him to supply the asset to the lessee. The lessor makes payment to the manufacturer after the asset has been delivered and accepted by the lessee.

## TYPES OF LEASE

The lease agreement can be classified broadly into four categories:

### 1. Financial lease

A financial lease is also known as capital lease, long-term lease, net lease and close lease. In a financial lease, the lessee selects the equipment, settles the price and terms of sale and arranges with a leasing company to buy it. He enters into an irrevocable and non-cancellable contractual agreement with the leasing company. The lessee uses the equipment exclusively, maintains it, insures and avails of the after-sales service and warranty backing it. He also bears the risk of obsolescence as it stands committed to pay the rental for the entire lease period.

The financial lease could also be with purchase option, where at the end of the predetermined period, the lessee has the option to buy the equipment at a predetermined value or at a nominal value or at fair market price. The financial lease may also contain a non-cancellable clause which means that the lessor transfers the title to the lessee at the end of the lease period.

Under a financial lease, the rate of lease would be fixed based on the kind of lease, the period of lease, periodicity of rent payment, and the rate of depreciation and other tax benefits available. The leasing company also charges nominal service charges to cover legal and other costs. The leasing company may also insist on collaterals or bank's guarantee in individual cases. In a large number of cases, the financial leases are used as financing-cum-tax planning tool.

The financial lease is very popular in India as in other countries like USA, UK and Japan. On an all India basis, at present, approximately a lease worth ₹ 75 crores to ₹ 100 crores is transacted as a tax planning device. The high cost of equipment such as office equipment, diesel generators, machine tools, textile machinery, containers, locomotives, etc. are leased under financial lease.

### 2. Operating lease

An operating lease is also known as service lease, short-term lease or true lease. In this lease, the contractual period between lessor and lessee is less than the full expected economic life of equipment. This means that the lease is for a limited period, may be a month, six months, a year or few years. The lease is terminable by giving stipulated notice as per the agreement. Normally, the lease rentals will be higher as compared to other leases on account of short period of primary lease. The risk of obsolescence is enforced on the lessor who will also bear the cost of maintenance and other relevant expenditure. The lessor also does the services like handling warranty claims, paying taxes, scheduling and performing maintenance and keeping complete records lease suitable for,

(*i*) Computers, copy machines and other office equipments, vehicles, material handling equipments, etc. which are sensitive to obsolescence, and

(*ii*) Where the lessee is interested in tiding over temporary problem.

**DISTINCTION BETWEEN A FINANCIAL LEASE AND OPERATING LEASE**

| *Financial Lease* | *Operating Lease* |
|---|---|
| 1. A financial lease is like an installment loan. It is a legal commitment to pay for the entire cost of the equipment plus interest over a specified period of time. The lessee commits to a series of payment which in total exceed the cost of the equipment. | 1. An operating lease is a rental agreement. The lessee is not committed to paying more than the original cost of equipment during contractual period. |
| 2. It excludes provisions for maintenance or taxes which are paid separately by the lessee. | 2. Operating lease provides for maintenance expenses and taxes of the lessor. |
| 3. The risk of obsolescence is assumed by the lessee. | 3. Leasing company assumes risk of obsolescence. |
| 4. Contract period ranges from medium to long term. | 4. Contract period ranges from intermediate to short-term. |
| 5. Contracts are usually non-cancellable. | 5. Contracts are usually cancellable either by the lessor or by the lessee. |
| 6. Aircrafts, land and building, heavy machinery are leased. | 6. Computers, office equipments, automobiles, truck, etc., are leased. |
| 7. The lease involves a financial commitment similar to a loan by a leasing company. It places the lessee in a position of borrow. | 7. The financial commitment is restricted to regular rental payment. The rentals find a place in the P&L A/c of the lessee. |
| 8. The lessor fulfils financial function. | 8. The lessor fulfils service function. |

## 3. Leverage lease

A leverage lease is used for financing those assets which require huge capital outlay. The outlay for purchase cost of the asset generally varies from ₹ 50 lakhs to ₹ 2 crores and has economic life of 10 years or more. The leverage lease agreement involves three parties — the lessee, the lessor and the lender. The lessor acquires the assets as per the terms of the lease agreement but finances only a part of the total investment, say 20 per cent to 50 per cent. The balance is provided by a person or a group of persons in the form of loan to the lessor. The loan is generally secured by mortgage of the asset besides assignment of the leased rental payments. The position of the lessee under a leveraged leasing agreement is the same as in the case of any other type of lease. In leveraged lease, a wide range of equipments such as railroad, rolling stock, coal mining, electricity generating plants, pipelines, ships, etc. are acquired.

Under a leverage lease, there are some attractive investment features in the form of after-tax consequences for the owner of the equipment. By investing 20 per cent or 25 per cent of the cost of an asset, the lessor is entitled to 100 per cent allowance for depreciation plus the investment allowance. In addition, interest expenses related to his borrowings are also tax deductible. From the point of view of lessee, lease rentals are deductible in full as an operating expense.

### 4. Sale and lease back

Under this type of lease, a firm which has an asset sells it to the leasing company and gets it back on lease. The asset is generally sold at its market value. The firm receives the sale price in cash and gets the right to use the asset during the lease period. The firm makes periodical rental payment to the lessor. The title to the asset vests with the lessor. Most of the lease back agreements are on a net-net basis which means that the lessee pays all maintenance expenses, property taxes and insurance. In some cases, the lease agreement allows the lease to repurchase the property at the termination of lease.

The sale and lease back agreement is beneficial to both lessor and lessee. The lessor gets immediate cash which becomes available for working capital or for further expansion and lessor gets tax benefits. Retail stores, office buildings, multipurpose industrial building and shopping centres are financed under this method.

### 5. Cross-border lease

Cross-border lease is international leasing and is known as transnational leasing. It relates to a lease transaction between a lessor and lessee domiciled in different countries and includes exports leasing. In other words, the lessor may be of one country and the lessee may be of another country. To illustrate, if a leasing company in USA makes available an air bus on lease to air India, there would be a cross-border lease.

Indian leasing industry is unlikely to deal in export border leases for big ticket items such as aircraft but it is well placed to contribute to India's export earnings by offering the lease option. First leasing company has initiated discussions with Bulgar Leasing of Bulgaria to export bull dozers and shovels in significant number of an export lease to that country.

### 6. Wet lease and dry lease

A wet lease is one where the lessor is responsible for full control and maintenance of leased asset. For instance, the Jet Airways has entered into a wet lease agreement with Oman Airways for two air buses for 6 months from May 2009.

On the other hand, a dry lease involves the payment of insurance and maintenance costs by the lessee.

### 7. Vendor leasing

A vendor leasing is one where the retail vendors tie up with the lease finance companies which give financing option to the customers of the vendors to purchase a product. This type of lease is popular in auto finance.

## INSTALLMENT BUYING, HIRE PURCHASE AND LEASING

In installment buying, the property passes on to the buyer immediately as soon as the first installment is made. The balance amount is payable in installments. Under the contract of installment, the buyer has no right to return the goods. In case of default, the seller has the right to file a suit in the court of law to recover his dues.

Hire purchase is an agreement under which the owner delivers the goods to the buyer who agrees to make periodical payment as hire charges. The possession of goods vests with the hirer but the ownership remains with the seller. On full payment of hire charges, the buyer gets the option of purchasing the goods. On default, the seller can reclaim the goods, subject to certain provisions of Hire Purchase Act.

Hire purchase resembles leasing in certain ways. In both the cases, the right to use the equipment is transferred to the hirer/lessee.

In leasing, the entire lease rentals represent a hire charge and it is treated as expense and hence tax deductible. Under hire purchase, a part of installment represents capital payment and hence it is not an expense. A part of the installment is interest on the loan which is considered as revenue expenditure and hence it is tax deductible.

In leasing, rental charges are debited to Profit and Loss Account and the leased asset is not shown in the Balance Sheet of the lessee. As against this, the hire purchaser capitalises the asset brought under hire purchaser contract. The liability for future hire purchase installments not yet due is shown separately in the balance sheet.

## ADVANTAGES OF LEASING

The following are the advantages of leasing:

1. **Permit alternative use of funds:** A leasing arrangement provides a firm with the use and control over asset without incurring huge capital expenditure. The firm is required only to make periodical rental payments. It saves considerable funds for alternative uses which would otherwise be tied up in fixed capital.
2. **Faster and cheaper credit:** Depending on tax structure of the lessee, it costs less than other methods of acquiring assets. It permits firms to acquire new equipment without going through formal scrutiny procedure. Hence, acquisition of assets under leasing agreement is cheaper and faster than any other source of finance.
3. **Flexibility:** Leasing arrangements may be tailored to the lessee's needs more easily than ordinary financing. Lease rentals can be structured to match the lessee's cash flows. It can be skipped during the months when the cash flows are expected to be low.
4. **Facilitates additional borrowings:** Leasing may increase long-term ability to acquire funds. The lessee can utilise more funds for working capital needs. Moreover, acquisition of assets under the lease agreement does not alter debt-equity ratio. Hence, the lessee can go for additional borrowings in case need arises.
5. **Protection against obsolescence:** A firm can avoid risk of obsolescence by entering into operating lease agreement. This is highly useful in respect of assets which become obsolete at a faster rate.
6. **No restrictive covenants:** The restrictive covenants such as debt-equity ratio, declaration of dividend, etc. which are usually imposed under debenture or loan agreement are absolutely absent in a lease agreement.

7. **Hundred per cent financing:** Lease financing enables a firm to acquire the use of an asset without having to make a down payment. So, hundred per cent financing is assured to the lessee.
8. **Boon to small firm:** The firms which are either small or have uncertain records of earning are able to obtain the use of asset through lease financing. It is a boon to small firms and technocrats who are able to make promoter's contribution as required by financial institutions.

## DISADVANTAGES OF LEASING

1. Lease is not a suitable mode of project finance. This is because rentals are repayable soon after entering into lease agreement while in new projects cash generations may start only after a long gestation period.
2. Certain tax benefits/incentives such as subsidy may not be available on leased equipment.
3. The value of real assets such as land and building may increase during lease period. In such a case, the lessee loses the advantage of a potential capital gain.
4. The cost of financing is generally higher than that of debt financing.
5. A manufacturer who wants to discontinue a particular line of business will be not in a position to terminate the contract except by paying heavy penalties. If it is a owned asset, the manufacturer can sell the equipment at his will.
6. If the lessee is not able to pay rentals regularly, the lessor would suffer a loss particularly when the asset is a sophisticated one and less liquid.
7. In case of lease agreement, it is lessor who has purchased the asset from the supplier and not the lessee. Hence, the lessee by himself is not entitled to any protection in case the supplier commits breach of warranties in respect of the leased assets.
8. In the absence of exclusive laws dealing with the lease transaction, several problems crop up between lessor and lessee resulting in unnecessary complications and avoidable tension.

## HISTORY AND DEVELOPMENT OF LEASING

The history of leasing dates back to 200 B.C. when Sumerians leased goods. Romans had developed a full body law relating to lease for movable and immovable property. However, the modern concept of leasing appeared for the first time in 1877 when the Bell Telephone Company began renting telephones in the USA. In 1832, Cottrell and Leonard leased academic caps, gowns and hoods. Subsequently, during 1930s, the Railway Industry used leasing service for its rolling stock needs. In the post-war period, the American Airlines leased their jet engines for most of the new aircrafts. This development ignited immediate popularity for the lease and generated growth of leasing industry.

Since World War II, the use of leasing has been greatly expanded and is constantly used for new products and new industries. In May 1952, Henry Scholfeld set up a separate Corporation in the USA to handle lease transaction. He founded the US Leasing Corporation with a capital of

$ 20,000. Since 1963, commercial banks have been allowed to engage themselves in direct leasing. In the early 1960s, leasing entered the United Kingdom following its successful and rapid development in the USA.

The concept of financial leasing was pioneered in India during 1973. The first company was set up by the Chidambaram Group in 1973 in Madras. The company undertook leasing of industrial equipment as its main activity. The Twentieth Century Leasing Company Limited was established in 1979. By 1981, four finance companies joined the fray. The performance of First Leasing Company Limited and the Twentieth Century Leasing Company Limited motivated others to enter the leasing industry. In 1980s, financial institutions made entry into leasing business. Industrial Credit and Investment Corporation was the first of all India financial institution to offer leasing in 1983. Entry of commercial banks into leasing was facilitated by an amendment of Banking Regulation Act, 1949. State Bank of India was the first commercial bank to set up a leasing subsidiary, SBI capital market, in October 1986. Canbank Financial Services Ltd., BOB Financial Service Ltd., and PNB Financial Services Limited followed suit. Industrial Finance Corporation's Merchant Banking division started financing leasing companies as well as equipment leasing and financial services. There was thus virtual explosion in the number of leasing companies rising to about 400 companies in 1990.

In the subsequent years, the adverse trends in capital market and other factors led to a situation where apart from the institutional lessors, there were hardly 20 to 25 private leasing companies who were active in the field. The total volume of leasing business transacted by both private and public sector leasing companies was ₹ 5,000 crores in 1993 and it is expected to cross ₹ 10,000 crores by March 1995.

## LEGAL ASPECTS OF LEASING

As there is no separate statute for equipment leasing in India, the provisions relating to bailment in the Indian Contract Act govern equipment leasing agreements as well. Section 148 of the Indian Contract Act defines bailment as:

'The delivery of goods by one person to another, for some purpose, upon a contract that they shall, when the purpose is accomplished, be returned or otherwise disposed of according to the directions of the person delivering them. The person delivering the goods is called the 'bailor' and the person to whom they are delivered is called the 'bailee'.

Since an equipment lease transaction is regarded as a contract of bailment, the obligations of the lessor and the lessee are similar to those of the bailor and the bailee (other than those expressly specified in the lease contract) as defined by the provisions of Sections 150 and 168 of the Indian Contract Act. Essentially, these provisions have the following implications for the lessor and the lessee.

1. The lessor has the duty to deliver the asset to the lessee, to legally authorise the lessee to use the asset, and to leave the asset in peaceful possession of the lessee during the currency of the agreement.
2. The lessee has the obligation to pay the lease rentals as specified in the lease agreement, to protect the lessor's title, to take reasonable care of the asset, and to return the leased asset on the expiry of the lease period.

## CONTENTS OF A LEASE AGREEMENT

The lease agreement specifies the legal rights and obligations of the lessor and the lessee. It typically contains terms relating to the following:

1. Description of the lessor, the lessee, and the equipment.
2. Amount, time, and place of lease rental payments.
3. Time and place of equipment delivery.
4. Lessee's responsibility for taking delivery and possession of the leased equipment.
5. Lessee's responsibility for maintenance, repairs, registration, etc., and the lessor's right in case of default by the lessee.
6. Lessee's right to enjoy the benefits of the warranties provided by the equipment manufacturer/supplier.
7. Insurance to be taken by the lessee on behalf of the lessor.
8. Variation in lease rentals if there is a change in certain external factors like bank interest rates, depreciation rates, and fiscal incentives.
9. Option of lease renewal for the lessee.
10. Return of equipment on expiry of the lease period.
11. Arbitration procedure in the event of dispute.

## INCOME TAX PROVISIONS RELATING TO LEASING

The principal income tax provisions relating to leasing are as follows:

1. The lessee can claim lease rentals as tax-deductible expenses.
2. The lease rentals received by the lessor are taxable under the head of 'Profits and Gains of Business or Profession'.
3. The lessor can claim investment allowance (this may be doubtful) and depreciation on the investment made in leased assets.

## SALES TAX PROVISIONS PERTAINING TO LEASING

The major sales tax provisions relevant for leasing are as follows:

1. The lessor is not entitled for the concessional rate of central sales tax because the asset purchased for leasing is meant neither for resale nor for use in manufacture. (It may be noted that if a firm buys an asset for resale or for use in manufacture, it is entitled for the concessional rate of sales tax).
2. The 46th Amendment Act has brought lease transactions under the purview of 'sale' and has empowered the Central and State Government to levy sales tax on lease transactions. While the Central Sales Tax Act has yet to be amended in this respect, several State Governments have amended their sales tax laws to impose sales tax on lease transactions.

## ACCOUNTING TREATMENT OF LEASE

All particulars generally required as per legal requirements specified in Schedule VI of the Companies Act will also apply to leasing. The accounting treatment in the books of the lessor will be as follows:

### ❖ Books of lessor

*(i)* The lessor has to disclose the asset given under lease agreement as an asset in his balance sheet as per the method adopted for other fixed assets.

*(ii)* The lease rentals received under financial lease should be shown in the income statement on the credit side under the head 'Gross Income'.

*(iii)* The lease rentals received should be shown on actual basis and not on accrual basis.

*(iv)* A minimum statutory depreciation on leased asset should be charged to income statement separately.

*(v)* Generally, a fair value of the leased asset to be recovered every year is ascertained and it is called 'annual lease charge'.

*(vi)* When the annual lease charge is more than the statutory depreciation, the difference is called lease equalisation charge. It is also charged to income statement.

*(vii)* When the annual lease charge is less than the statutory depreciation, the difference is again called lease equalisation charge. But, it is credited in the income statement.

*(viii)* For adjusting the annual lease charge stated above, a Lease Equalisation Account and a Lease Adjustment Account will be opened as follows:

**(a) When the Annual Lease Charge is more than the Minimum Statutory Depreciation. The Entry to be Passed is:**

Lease Equalisation A/c Dr.

To Lease Adjustment A/c

**(b) When the Annual Lease Charge is less than the Minimum Statutory Depreciation**

Lease Adjustment A/c Dr.

To Lease Equalisation A/c

***Note:*** Balance in Lease Adjustment A/c will appear in the Balance Sheet, whereas the Lease Equalisation A/c will go to the Income Statement as shown below:

Dr. **Profit and Loss Account** Cr.

| | | | |
|---|---|---|---|
| To Statutory Depreciation | xxxxx | By Gross Income<br>Lease rental<br>*Add:* Lease Equalisation<br>(or)<br>*Less:* Lease Equalisation | <br>xxxxx<br><br><br>xxxxx |

**Balance Sheet**

| | | | | |
|---|---|---|---|---|
| | | Assets<br>Fixed Assets<br>Leasehold Asset<br>*Less:* Accumulated<br>Depreciation<br>*Less:* Lease Adjustment | <br><br>xxxxx<br><br>xxx<br>xxx | <br><br><br><br><br>xxxxx |

## ❖ Books of lessee

For the financial lease, no special treatment is necessary in the books of the lessee since it is a off-balance sheet financing. Hence, the following treatment is necessary:

(*i*) The assets taken under lease agreement should be shown by way of a footnote in the Balance Sheet.

(*ii*) However, the lease rentals paid should be charged to the Income Statement.

(*iii*) The lease rentals should be shown on accrual basis. Hence, necessary adjustments should be made for any outstanding or prepaid lease rent in the income statement as well as in the balance sheet.

(*iv*) It is also desirable to disclose the future obligations of the lease as per lease agreement by way of a footnote.

# METHOD OF ASCERTAINING LEASE RENTALS

From the lessee's point of view, as seen already, he has to make an important financial decision — whether to buy a capital equipment or take it on a lease basis. Similarly, from the lessor's point of view, he has to be very careful in computing the lease rentals so that he may not suffer due to any loss at a later stage. Generally, the following method is adopted for determining the lease rentals:

## ❖ Determination of lease rentals

The following steps may be adopted for determining the lease rentals:

**Step 1:** First, find out the total cost of the asset.

Total cost = Cost of the asset + Freight charges + Insurance + Taxes + Installation charges, etc.

**Step 2:** Then, ascertain the cash flows to the lessor on account of ownership of the asset. While ascertaining the cash flows, the tax advantage on depreciation, investment allowance, if any, etc. should be taken into account. The cash flows should be computed for each year separately as follows:

Cash flow = Amount of depreciation – Tax advantage on depreciation – Tax advantage on investment allowance + *Salvage value

* ***Note:*** It should be considered only in the last year of the life of the asset.

**Step 3:** The new step is to calculate the present value of already computed cash flows (as stated in Step 2) year-wise with the help of PV factor. Generally, the present value factor at a certain percentage discount rate will be given. So, it is easy to calculate the PV of cash flows as follows:

For example: PV factor @ 10 per cent discount

Year I = 0.813, Year II = 0.717, Year III = 0.697, Year IV = 0.606, Year V = 0.517

PV of cash flows = Cash flow for each year × PV factor at a given discount rate

**Step 4:** The fourth step is to ascertain the minimum required net recovery through lease rentals with the help of the following formula:

Minimum required net recovery through Lease Rental (MRLR) = Cost of the asset (Step 1) – The present value of cash flow (Step 3)

**Step 5:** From this MRLR, it is easy to find out the post-tax lease rentals with the help of the present value factor of annuity. This annuity discount factor at the specified discount rate for a specified period will also be given, *e.g.*, Annuity Discount factor at 10 per cent. Discount for 5 years = 3.105.

$$\text{Post-Tax Lease Rental (PTLR)} = \frac{\text{MRLR}}{\text{PV Factor of Annuity}}$$

**Step 6:** Finally, the pre-tax lease rentals can be ascertained by adjusting the PTLR for the tax factor as follows:

$$\text{Pre-Tax Lease Rental (LR)} = \text{PTLR} \times \frac{100}{\text{Tax Rate}}$$

From this, lease rental for each month can be computed. Usually, this rent will be expressed in terms of per thousand and per month.

Therefore,

$$\text{the rate per month} = \text{Pre-tax lease rental (CR)} \times \frac{10{,}000}{\text{Total cost of the asset}} \times \frac{1}{12}$$

## ❖ Buy or lease decision

Successful financial management requires taking sound financial decisions at the appropriate time. One such decision is to decide whether to buy a capital asset or to take it on a lease basis. These two alternate proposals should be carefully studied before taking any final decision. The financial viability of both the proposals should be evaluated by adopting the normal technique of capital budgeting. Generally, the NPV (Net Present Value) technique is used for this purpose. The present values of net cash outflows after tax from these two options should be compared and the one with lower present value of cash outflows is to be selected.

## ❖ Decision-making process

For taking a final decision, the following factors should be taken into account:

(*i*) As usual calculate depreciation on the capital asset to be bought by applying the formula:

$$\text{Depreciation} = \frac{\text{Cost of Asset} - \text{Salvage Value}}{\text{No. of Years of Life}}$$

*(ii)* Then, ascertain savings in tax on depreciation with the help of the tax rate.

Saving in tax on depreciation = Depreciation × Tax rate

*(iii)* Similarly, find out savings in tax on interest paid with the help of the tax rate for the given period.

*(iv)* Then, calculate the Present Value of After-tax cash outflows under purchase option with the help of the appropriate discount rate (minimum required rate of return).

Generally, the present value of rupee one due for the given period (any number of years) can be found with the help of the following formula:

$$PV = \frac{1}{(1+r)^n}$$

where, PV means present value

r refers to rate of interest/discount

n means number of years.

*(v)* For buy or lease decisions, the present value is found out by multiplying the net cash outflow with the PV factor at the discount rate.

*(vi)* Similarly, calculate the present value of after-tax cash outflows under lease option.

*(vii)* Finally, see which proposal has the lower present value of cash outflows. For example, after discounting all the after-tax cash outflows to the present value, over the life of the asset say 10 years, we get

NPV of buying = X

PPV of leasing = Y

If Y is lesser leasing option, it has to be preferred and if X is lesser buying option it has to be chosen.

## OTHER FACTORS INFLUENCING BUY/BORROW OR LEASE DECISION

A firm may propose to acquire a certain asset either with equity funds or with a financial lease. The firm's management, in such a case, should take into consideration certain factors while evaluating the above financial proposals. These factors are:

1. **Capital adequacy:** If the firm has adequate shareholders' equity, it is better to go for buying the asset rather than taking it out on a lease basis. In the absence of sufficient capital, raising new capital or retaining a greater proportion of earnings should be considered rather than assuming further debt obligations through leasing.
2. **Liquidity considerations:** A firm has to maintain sufficient liquidity for meeting any sudden shortfall in cash inflows or for meeting any capital expenditures. If sufficient liquidity is not available, leasing is the solution.

3. **Flexibility considerations:** Buying an asset involves one-time payment which cannot be flexible. If the asset is bought through borrowed funds, that will be rigid repayment schedule. On the other hand, leasing arrangements may be tailored to the lessee's needs more easily and lease rentals can be structured to match the lessee's cash flows.
4. **Nature of asset:** For those assets which become obsolete at a faster rate, 'buying' that asset is not preferable. The best solution is to go for operating leasing which serves as a protection against obsolescence.
5. **Availability of finance:** In the absence of adequate owned funds, one has to go for borrowed funds to buy an asset. There is no guarantee for the continuous availability of borrowed funds and there is a fear of repayment on demand stipulated by some lending institutions. On the other hand, fixed rate finance may be available by leasing the equipment and there is also a guaranteed continuous availability of finance. Again, there may not be any restrictive covenants under leasing which are normally found in all loan agreements.
6. **Debt Capacity:** From the lessee's point of view leasing is off-balance sheet financing and hence it increases the overall debt capacity of a firm. Leasing plays a vital role in a firm's overall financing strategy to the extent to which it enables the firm to increase its overall debt raising capacity. Hence, buy or lease decision depends upon the financing strategy of a firm also.
7. **Grants and incentives consideration:** Government grants, incentives and other benefits are available for purchased equipment as well as leased equipment depending upon the government's policy. Therefore, the method of finance either to buy or lease should take into account the eligibility conditions to avail of such grants and incentives.
8. **Borrowing restrictions:** Borrowings for the purpose of acquiring an asset may not be permitted due to some restrictive covenants and government regulations. Sometimes, the memorandum may restrict the borrowing powers of the company. In such cases, leasing is the only answer to acquire such assets.
9. **Administrative considerations:** Buy or lease decision depends on administrative conveniences like simplicity of book-keeping procedures, easy cash flow forecasting, etc. Generally, firms prefer those methods of finance which facilitate easy administration.

## STRUCTURE OF LEASING INDUSTRY

The present structure of leasing industry in India consists of: (*i*) Private Sector Leasing and (*ii*) Public Sector Leasing.

The private sector leasing consists of:

(*i*) Pure Leasing Companies,

(*ii*) Hire Purchase and Finance Companies, and

(*iii*) Subsidiaries of Manufacturing Group Companies.

The public sector leasing organisations are divided into:

(*i*) Leasing Divisions of Financial Institutions,

(*ii*) Subsidiaries of Public Sector Banks, and

(*iii*) Other Public Sector Leasing Organisations.

## ❖ Private sector leasing

**(i) Pure leasing companies:** These companies operate independently without any link or association with any other organisation or group of organisation. The First Leasing Company of India Limited, The Twentieth Century Finance Corporation Limited, and the Grover Leasing Limited, fall under this category.

**(ii) Hire purchase and finance companies:** The companies started prior to 1980 to do hire purchase and finance business especially for vehicles added leasing to their activities during 1980. Some of them do leasing as major activity and some others do leasing on a small-scale as a tax planning device. Sundaram Finance Limited and Motor and General Finance Limited belong to this group.

**(iii) Subsidiaries of manufacturing group companies:** These companies consist of two categories,

(*a*) Vendor leasing.

(*b*) In-house leasing.

**(a) Vendor leasing:** These types of companies are formed to boost and promote the sale of its parent companies' products through offering leasing facilities.

**(b) In-house leasing:** In-house leasing or capture leasing companies are set up to meet the fund requirements or to avoid the income tax liabilities of the group companies.

## ❖ Public sector leasing

**(i) Financial institutions:** The financial institutions such as IFCI, ICICI, IRBI and NSIC have set up their leasing divisions or subsidiaries to do leasing business. The Shipping Credit and Investment Company of India offers leasing facilities in foreign currencies for ships, deep seas' fishing vehicles and related equipments to its clients.

**(ii) Subsidiaries of banks:** The commercial banks in India can, under Section 19(1) of the Banking Regulation Act, 1949, set up subsidiaries for undertaking leasing activities. The SBI was the first bank to start a subsidiary for leasing business in 1986.

Leasing in SBI is transacted through, Strategic Business Unit (SBU) of the bank. Each SBU is manned by specially trained staff and is equipped with the latest technological aids to meet the needs of top corporate clients. For the bank as a whole, leasing is considered as a high growth area. Now, the bank is concentrating only on 'Big Ticket Leasing' which is generally of ₹ 5 crores and above. So far, SBI has disbursed more than ₹ 300 crores by way of leasing with the average size of deal being ₹ 25 crores.

**(iii) Other public sector organisations:** A few public sector manufacturing companies such as Bharat Electronics Limited, Hindustan Packaging Company Limited, Electronic Corporation of India Limited have started to sell their equipment through leasing.

## PROBLEMS OF LEASING

Leasing has great potential in India. However, leasing in India faces serious handicaps which may mar its growth in future. The following are some of the problems.

(i) **Unhealthy competition:** The market for leasing has not grown with the same pace as the number of lessors. As a result, there is over supply of lessors leading to competition. With the leasing business becoming more competitive, the margin of profit for lessors has dropped from four to five per cent to the present 2.5 to 3 per cent. Bank subsidiaries and financial institutions have the competitive edge over the private sector concerns because of cheap source of finance.

(ii) **Lack of qualified personnel:** Leasing requires qualified and experienced people at the helm of its affairs. Leasing is a specialised business and persons constituting its top management should have expertise in accounting, finance, legal and decision areas. In India, the concept of leasing business is of recent one and hence it is difficult to get right man to deal with leasing business. On account of this, operations of leasing business are bound to suffer.

(iii) **Tax considerations:** Most people believe that lessees prefer leasing because of the tax benefits it offers. In reality, it only transfers the benefit, *i.e.*, the lessee's tax shelter is lessor's burden. The lease becomes economically viable only when the transfer's effective tax rate is low. In addition, taxes like sales tax, wealth tax, additional tax, surcharge, etc. add to the cost of leasing. Thus, leasing becomes more expensive form of financing than conventional mode of finance such as hire purchase.

(iv) **Stamp duty:** The States treat a leasing transaction as a sale for the purpose of making them eligible to sales tax. On the contrary, for stamp duty, the transaction is treated as a pure lease transaction. Accordingly, a heavy stamp duty is levied on lease documents. This adds to the burden of leasing industry.

(v) **Delayed payment and bad debts:** The problem of delayed payment of rents and bad debts add to the costs of lease. The lessor does not take into consideration this aspect while fixing the rentals at the time of lease agreement. These problems would disturb the prospects of leasing business.

## PROSPECTS

The world leasing industry grew at a rate of about 10 per cent. As the economy is opened up, there will be substantial demand for a variety of leasing products such as foreign currency leases, cross-border leases, leverage leases, etc. Leasing companies are bound to go for substantial growth in line with international trends.

Leasing has great prospects in India. It is on the threshold of a major breakthrough in the industrial development due to liberalised economic policy measures initiated by the government. Leasing as a convenient and flexible financing option can play a vital role in the process of industrial development. The leasing industry has taken the centre stage with the Government and public sector undertakings are looking to industry to finance railway, telecommunication, transport, power and infrastructure sectors. The infrastructure financing so crucial for an economic growth cannot be accelerated without leasing industry. The Government has indicated that it is open to suggestions for reviewing the existing policies. Such conduciveness and the willingness to prevent bottlenecks in the area of taxation and other areas will go a long way in speeding up the growth of the industry.

## QUESTIONS

### I. Objective type questions:

### A. Fill in the blanks:

1. In financial lease, __________ bears the risk of obsolescence.
2. __________ lease is for a limited period.
3. The leased asset is shown on the Balance sheet of the __________.
4. An equipment lease transaction is regarded as a contract of __________.
5. The entire lease rental is treated as __________ in the books of lessor.

[**Key:** 1. lessee, 2. Operating lease, 3. lessor, 4. bailment, 5. income]

### B. State whether the following statement are TRUE or FALSE:

1. In financial lease, the contracts are cancellable either by the lessor or by the lessee.
2. The average lease agreement involves three parties.
3. Vendor leasing companies are formed to promote the sale of its parent companies.
4. In-house leasing companies are set up to avoid income tax liabilities of the group companies.
5. The lessee can claim investment allowance.

[**Key:** 1. False, 2. True, 3. True, 4. True, 5. False]

### II. Short answer questions:

1. What is cross-border lease?
2. Write a note on 'Sale and Lease Back'.
3. What is vendor leasing?
4. Define leasing.
5. What is leverage lease?

### III. Essay type questions:

1. Discuss the advantages and disadvantages of leasing.
2. Explain the different kinds of leasing.
3. Explain the structure of leasing industry in India.
4. What are the problems of leasing in India? Analyse the factors that influence buy or lease decision.

# 13 VENTURE CAPITAL

Venture capital is a growing business of recent origin in the area of industrial financing in India. The various financial institutions set up in India to promote industries have done commendable work. However, these institutions do not come up to the benefit of risky ventures when they are undertaken by new or relatively unknown entrepreneurs. They contend to give debt finance, mostly in the form of term loans to the promoters and their functioning has been more akin to that of commercial banks. The financial institutions have devised schemes such as seed capital scheme, risk capital fund, etc. to help new entrepreneurs. However, to evaluate the projects and extend financial assistance, they follow the criteria such as safety, security, liquidity and profitability and not potentiality. The capital market with its conventional financial instruments/schemes does not come much to the benefit or risky venture. New institutions such as mutual funds, leasing and hire purchase companies have been established as another source of finance to industries. These institutions also do not mitigate the problems of new entrepreneurs who undertake risky and innovative ventures.

India is poised for a technological revolution with the emergence of new breed of entrepreneurs with required professional temperament and technical know-how. To make the innovative technology of the entrepreneurs a successful business venture, support in all respects and more particularly in the form of financial assistance is all the more essential. This has necessitated the setting up of venture capital financing division/companies during the later part of eighties.

## CONCEPT OF VENTURE CAPITAL

The term 'Venture Capital' is understood in many ways. In a narrow sense, it refers to, investment in new and tried enterprises that are lacking a stable record of growth.

In a broader sense, venture capital refers to the commitment of capital as shareholding, for the formulation and setting up of small firms specialising in new ideas or new technologies. It is not merely an injection of funds into a new firm, it is a simultaneous input of skill needed to set up the firm, design its marketing strategy and organise and manage it. It is an association with successive stages of firm's development with distinctive types of financing appropriate to each stage of development.

### ❖ Meaning of venture capital

Venture capital is long-term risk capital to finance high technology projects which involve risk but at the same time has strong potential for growth. Venture capitalists pool their resources including managerial abilities to assist new entrepreneurs in the early years of the project. Once the project reaches the stage of profitability, they sell their equity holdings at a high premium.

### ❖ Definition of a venture capital company

A venture capital company is defined as 'a financing institution which joins an entrepreneur as a copromoter in a project and shares the risks and rewards of the enterprise'.

## FEATURES OF VENTURE CAPITAL

Some of the features of venture capital financing are as under:

1. Venture capital is usually in the form of an equity participation. It may also take the form of convertible debt or long-term loan.
2. Investment is made only in high risk but high growth potential projects.
3. Venture capital is available only for commercialisation of new ideas or new technologies and not for enterprises which are engaged in trading, booking, financial services, agency, liaison work or research and development.
4. Venture capitalist joins the entrepreneur as a copromoter in projects and shares the risks and rewards of the enterprise.
5. There is continuous involvement in business after making an investment by the investor.
6. Once the venture has reached the full potential, the venture capitalist disinvests his holdings either to the promoters or in the market. The basic objective of investment is not profit but capital appreciation at the time of disinvestment.
7. Venture capital is not just injection of money but also an input needed to set up the firm, design its marketing strategy and organise and manage it.
8. Investment is usually made in small and medium-scale enterprises.

### ❖ Disinvestment mechanism

The basic objective of a venture capitalist is to sell off the investment made by him to get substantial capital gains. This process is called disinvestment mechanism. Generally, when the project reaches the stage of profitability, the venture capitalists try to make an exit from the business. Various disinvestment options are available and some of the important methods are briefly explained below:

1. **IPO method:** Under this method, a venture capital company makes an exit through public issue of capital by listing on a stock exchange. This listing of shares facilitates higher price of securities, adds prestige to the company, and ensures better credibility with the investors and the public.

2. **Sale of shares method or promoter's buyback:** Under this method, the shares are sold to the entrepreneurs who promoted the project. The promoters can even form a trust for this purpose by getting contributions from employees and borrowings from financial institutions.
3. **Put and call method:** Under this method, the venture capitalist enters into a formal exit agreement with an entrepreneur at a price based on a predetermined formula with put and call options. The put option is the right to sell and call option is the right to buy the shares by that entrepreneur.
4. **Trade sales or sale to other venture capital funds:** Under this method, the entire stake of the company is sold to another venture capitalist or a corporate body at an agreed price.
5. **Liquidation:** When a project fails, the venture capital company automatically exits by liquidation. The project may fail due to competition, use of obsolete technology, poor management, etc.

### ❖ Activities of VC funds

- Provide seed capital for industries and support a concept or idea.
- Provide additional capital to new business at various stages of growth.
- Bridge finance/project financing.
- Equity financing to management groups for taking over other companies.
- Capital to new entrepreneurs in foreign operations.
- Capital to mature enterprises for expansion, diversification and restructuring.
- Research and development financing for product development.
- Start-up capital for initial production and marketing.
- Development financing for facilitating public issues.
- Acquisition or buyout financing for acquiring another firm.
- Turnaround financing for turning around a sick unit.

## SCOPE OF VENTURE CAPITAL

Venture capital may take various forms at different stages of the project. There are four successive stages of development of a project, *viz.*, development of a project idea, implementation of the idea, commercial production and marketing and finally large-scale investment to exploit the economies of scale and achieve stability. Financial institutions and banks usually start financing the project only at the second or third stage but rarely from the first stage. But venture capitalists provide finance even from the first stage of idea formulation. The various stages in the financing of venture capital are described below:

1. **Development of an idea — seed finance:** In the initial stage, venture capitalists provide seed capital for translating an idea into business proposition. At this stage, investigation is made in depth which normally takes a year or more.
2. **Implementation stage — start-up finance:** When the firm is set up to manufacture a product or provide a service, start-up finance is provided by the venture capitalists.

The first and second stage capital is used for full scale manufacturing and further business growth.

3. **Fledging stage — additional finance:** In the third stage, the firm has made some headway and entered the stage of manufacturing a product but faces teething problems. It may not be able to generate adequate funds and so additional round of financing is provided to develop the marketing infrastructure.
4. **Establishment stage — establishment finance:** At this stage, the firm is established in the market and expected to expand at a rapid pace. It needs further financing for expansion and diversification so that it can reap economies of scale and attain stability. At the end of the establishment stage, the firm is listed on the stock exchange and at this point the venture capitalist disinvests their shareholdings through available exit routes.

Before investing in small, new or young hi-tech enterprises, the venture capitalists look for percentage of key success factors of a venture capital project. They prefer projects that address these problems. An idea developed for these success factors has been presented in Table 13.1.

After assessing the viability of projects, the investors decide for what stage they should provide venture capital so that it leads to greater capital appreciation.

**TABLE 13.1: KEY SUCCESS FACTORS OF VENTURE CAPITAL PROJECTS**

| *Sl. No.* | *Key Factors* | *Developed Country* | | | | *Developing Country* | | | |
|---|---|---|---|---|---|---|---|---|---|
| | | **VI** | **I** | **LI** | **NI** | **VI** | **I** | **LI** | **NI** |
| 1 | Management skill of entrepreneurs | 100 | — | — | — | 100 | — | — | — |
| 2 | Management skills of venture capitalists | 14 | 72 | 14 | — | 40 | 40 | 20 | — |
| 3 | Affinity of interests between both parties | 57 | 20 | 14 | — | 40 | 40 | 20 | — |
| 4 | Financial commitment of entrepreneurs | 57 | 29 | — | 14 | 60 | 40 | — | — |
| 5 | Projects potential for rapid growth | 57 | 14 | 29 | — | 80 | — | 20 | — |
| 6 | Project's potential to generate above average capital appreciation | 72 | 28 | — | — | 60 | 40 | — | — |
| 7 | Project's potential to generate current income | 14 | 43 | 29 | 14 | 40 | 60 | — | — |
| 8 | Availability of tech expertise | 14 | 72 | 14 | — | 60 | 20 | 20 | — |
| 9 | Possibility of exit offered by project | 14 | 72 | 14 | — | 40 | 60 | — | — |
| 10 | Value of underlying assets | — | 43 | 29 | 28 | — | 80 | 20 | — |
| 11 | Strength of credit backing | 14 | 43 | 14 | 29 | 40 | 60 | — | — |
| 12 | Involvement of a multilateral institution (*e.g.*, IFC) | — | — | — | — | — | 60 | 20 | 20 |

**Keys**

VI Absence of this constitutes an insurmountable obstacle for an institution to develop venture capital activities in the country.

I The presence of this factor constitutes a clear to an incentive to an institution for developing venture capital activities in the country.

LI The presence of this factor may influence the favourable decision of an institution for, but does not constitute a decisive factor.

NI Not Important.

All the above stages of finance involve varying degrees of risks and the venture capital industry, only after analysing such risks, invests in one or more. Hence, they specialise in one or more but rarely all.

## IMPORTANCE OF VENTURE CAPITAL

Venture capital is of great practical value to every corporate enterprise in modern times.

### I. Advantages to investing public

1. The investing public will be able to reduce risk significantly against unscrupulous management, if the public invest in venture fund who in turn will invest in equity of new business. With their expertise in the field and continuous involvement in the business, they would be able to stop malpractices by management.
2. Investors have no means to vouch for the reasonableness of the claims made by the promoters about profitability of the business. The venture funds equipped with necessary skills will be able to analyse the prospects of the business.
3. The investors do not have any means to ensure that the affairs of the business are conducted prudently. The venture fund having representatives on the Board of Directors of the company would overcome it.

### II. Advantages to promoters

1. The entrepreneur for the success of public issue is required to convince the underwriters, brokers and thousands of investors. But to obtain venture capital assistance, he will be required to sell his idea to justify the officials of the venture fund. Venture capital provides a solid capital base for future growth by injecting long-term equity financing.
2. Public issue of equity shares has to be preceded by a lot of efforts, *viz.*, necessary statutory sanctions, underwriting and broker's arrangement, publicity of issue, etc. The new entrepreneurs find it very difficult to make underwriting arrangements which require a great deal of effort. Venture fund assistance would eliminate those efforts by leaving entrepreneur to concentrate upon bread and butter activities of business.
3. Costs of public issues of equity share often range between 10 per cent to 15 per cent of nominal value of issue of moderate size, which are often even higher for small issues. The company is required, in addition to above, to incur recurring costs for maintenance of share registry cell, stock exchange listing fee, expenditure on printing and posting

of annual reports, etc. These items of expenditure can be ill-afforded by the business when it is new. Assistance from venture fund does not require such expenditure.

**Business partner:** The venture capitalists act as business partners who share the rewards as well as the risks.

**Mentoring:** Venture capitalists provide strategic, operational, tactical and financial advice based on past experience with other companies in similar situations.

**Alliances:** The venture capitalists help in recruitment of key personnel, improving relationship with international markets, coinvestment with other VC firms and in decision making.

## III. General

1. A developed venture capital institutional set-up reduces the time-lag between a technological innovation and its commercial exploitation.
2. It helps in developing new processes/products in conducive atmosphere, free from the dead weight of corporate bureaucracy, which helps in exploiting full potential.
3. Venture capital acts as a cushion to support business borrowings, as bankers and investors will not lend money with inadequate margin of equity capital.
4. Once venture capital funds start earning profits, it will be very easy for them to raise resources from primary capital market in the form of equity and debts. Therefore, the investors would be able to invest in new business through venture funds and, at the same time, they can directly invest in existing business when venture fund disposes its own holding. This mechanism will help to channelise investment in new hi-tech business or the existing sick business. These businesses will take-off with the help of finance from venture funds and this would help in increasing productivity, better capacity utilisation, etc.
5. The economy with well-developed venture capital network induces the entry of large number of technocrats in industry, helps in stabilising industries and in creating a new set of trained technocrats to build and manage medium and large industries, resulting in faster industrial development.
6. A venture capital firm serves as an intermediary between investors looking for high returns for their money and entrepreneurs in search of needed capital for their start-ups.
7. It also paves the way for private sector to share the responsibility with public sector.

## ORIGIN

Venture capital as a new phenomenon originated in the US and developed spectacularly worldwide since the second half of the seventies. American Research and Development Corporation, founded by Gen. Doriot soon after the Second World War, is believed to have heralded the institutionalisation of venture capital in the USA. Since then, the industry has developed in many other countries in Europe, North America and Asia. The real development of VC took place in 1958 when the Business Administration Act was passed by the US Congress. In the US alone, there are 800 venture capital firms managing around $ 40 billion of capital with annual accretions of between $ 1 billion and $ 5 billion. It is reported that some of the present-day giants like Apple, Microsoft, Xerox, etc. are the beneficiaries of venture capital.

UK occupies a second place after US in terms of investment in VC. The concept became popular in late sixties in UK. The Government's Business Expansion Scheme which permitted individuals to claim tax reliefs for investment in companies not listed in stock exchange led to the success of VC in UK. The CHARTER House Development Limited is the oldest venture capital company established in 1934 in UK. The Bank of England established its venture capital company in late 40s. The UK witnessed a massive growth of industry during 70s and 80s. During 1988, there were over 1,000 venture capital companies in UK which provided ₹ 3,700 crores to over 1,500 firms.

The success of venture capital in these countries prompted other countries to design and implement measures to promote venture capital and their total commitment have been rising.

## INITIATIVE IN INDIA

Indian tradition of VC for industry goes back more than 150 years when many of the managing agency houses acted as venture capitalists providing both finance and management skill to risky projects. It was the managing agency system through which Tata Iron and Steels and Empress Mills were able to raise equity capital from the investing public. The Tatas also initiated a managing agency house, named Investment Corporation of India in 1937 which by acting as venture capitalist, successfully promoted hi-tech enterprises such as CEAT Tyres, Associated Bearings, National Rayon, etc. The early form of venture capital enabled the entrepreneurs to raise large amount of funds and yet retain management control. After the abolition of managing agency system, the public sector term lending institutions met a part of venture capital requirements through seed capital and risk capital for hi-tech industries which were not able to meet promoter's contribution. However, all these institutions supported only proven and sound technology while technology development remained largely confined to government labs and academic institutions. Many hi-tech industries, thus, found it impossible to obtain financial assistance from banks and other financial institutions due to unproven technology, conservative attitude, risk awareness and rigid security parameters.

Venture capital's growth in India passed through various stages. In 1973, R.S. Bhatt Committee recommended formation of ₹ 100 crore venture capital fund. The Seventh Five Year Plan emphasised the need for developing a system of funding venture capital. The Research and Development Cess Act was enacted in May 1986 which introduced a cess of 5 per cent on all payments made for purchase of technology from abroad. The levy provides the source for the venture capital fund.

United Nations Development Programme in 1987 on behalf of Government examined the possibility of developing venture capital in private sector. Technology Policy Implementation Committee in the same year also recommended the same provisions. Formalised venture capital took roots when venture capital guidelines were issued by Comptroller of Capital Issues in November 1988.

## GUIDELINES

The following are the guidelines issued by the Government of India:

1. The public sector financial institutions, State Bank of India, scheduled banks, foreign banks and their subsidiaries are eligible for setting the venture capital funds with a minimum size of ₹ 10 crores and a debt-equity ratio of 1 : 1.5. If they desire to raise funds from the public, promoters will be required to contribute a minimum of 40 per cent of capital. Foreign equity up to 25 per cent subject to certain conditions would be permitted.

   The guidelines provide for non-resident Indians investment up to 74 per cent on a repatriable basis and 25 per cent to 40 per cent on a non-repatriable basis. It should invest 60 per cent of its funds in venture capital activity. The balance amount can be invested in new issue of any existing or new company in equity, cumulative convertible preference shares, debentures, bonds or any other security approved by Comptroller of Capital Issues.
2. The venture capital companies and venture capital funds can be set up as joint venture between stipulated agencies and non-institutional promoters but the equity holding of such promoters should not exceed 20 per cent and should not be largest single holder.
3. Venture capital assistance should go to enterprises with a total investment of not more than ₹ 10 crores.
4. The Venture Capital Company (VCC)/Venture Capital Fund (VCF) should be managed by professionals and should be independent of the parent organisation.
5. The VCC/VCF will not be allowed to undertake activities such as trading, broking, money market operations, bills discounting, inter-corporate lending. They will be allowed to invest in leasing to the extent of 15 per cent of the total funds developed. The investment on revival of risk units will be treated as a part of venture capital activity.
6. Listing of VCCs/VCF can be according to the prescribed norms and underwriting of issues at the promoter's discretion.
7. A person holding a position or full-time chairman/president, chief executive, managing director or executive director/whole-time director in a company will not be allowed to hold the same position simultaneously in the VCC/VCF.
8. The Venture Capital assistance should be extended to:
   (*i*) The enterprise having investment up to ₹ 10 crores in the project.
   (*ii*) The technology involved should be new and untried or it should incorporate significant improvement over the existing technologies in India.
   (*iii*) The promoters should be new, professionally or technically qualified with inadequate resources.
   (*iv*) The enterprise should be established in the company form employing professionally qualified person for maintenance of accounts.

9. Share pricing at the time of disinvestment by a public issue or general sale offer by the company or fund may be done subject to this being calculated an objective criteria and the basis disclosed adequately to the public.

## THE INDIAN SCENARIO

### ❖ Methods of venture financing

Venture capital is available in four forms in India:

1. Equity participation.
2. Conventional loan.
3. Conditional loan.
4. Income notes.

1. **Equity participation:** Venture capital firms participate in equity through direct purchase of shares but their stake does not exceed 49 per cent. These shares are retained by them till the assisted projects making profit. These shares are sold either to the promoter at negotiated price under buyback agreement or to the public in the secondary market at a profit.
2. **Conventional loan:** Under this form of assistance, a lower fixed rate of interest is charged till the assisted units become commercially operational, after which the loan carries normal or higher rate of interest. The loan has to be repaid according to a predetermined schedule of repayment as per terms of loan agreement.
3. **Conditional loan:** Under this form of finance, an interest-free loan is provided during the implementation period but it has to pay royalty on sales. The loan has to be repaid according to a predetermined schedule as soon as the company is able to generate sales and income.
4. **Income notes:** It is a combination of conventional and conditional loans. Both interest and royalty are payable at much lower rates than in case of conditional loans.

At present, several venture capital firms are incorporated in India and they are promoted either by All India Financial Institutions like IDBI, ICICI, IFCI, State level financial institutions, public sector banks or promoted by foreign banks/private sector or financial institutions like Indus Venture Capital Fund. The present venture capital players can be broadly classified into the following four categories:

### (i) Companies promoted by all India FIs

- Venture Capital Division of IDBI.
- Risk Capital and Technology Finance Corporation Ltd. (RCTC) (Subsidiary of IFCI).
- Technology Development and Information Company of India Ltd. (TDICI), (Promoted by ICICI and UTI).

### (ii) Companies promoted by state FI

- Gujarat Venture Finance Ltd. (Promoted by GUC).
- Andhra Pradesh Industrial Development Corporation Venture Capital Ltd. (Promoted by APIDC).

### (iii) Companies promoted by banks

- Canbank Venture Capital Fund (Promoted by Canfina and Canara Bank).
- SBI Venture Capital Fund (Promoted by SBI Caps).
- Indian Investment Fund (Promoted by Grindlays Bank).
- Infrastructure Leasing (Promoted by Central Bank of India).

### (iv) Companies in private sector

- Indus Venture Capital Fund (Promoted by Mafatlals and Hindustan Lever).
- Credit Capital Venture Fund (India) Ltd.,
- 20th Century Venture Capital Corporation Ltd.,
- Venture Capital Fund (Promoted by V.B. Desai & Co.)

A brief account of major ingredients of Indian venture capital industry is presented here.

## 1. IDBI venture capital fund

The initial impetus was given by IDBI's Technology Division when venture capital fund was set up in 1986 for encouraging commercial application of indigenously developed technology and adopting imported technology for wider domestic applications.

The salient features of the scheme are:

1. Financial assistance under the scheme is available to projects whose requirements range between ₹ 5 lakhs and ₹ 2.5 crores. The promoter's stake should be at least 10 per cent for the ventures below ₹ 50 lakhs and 15 per cent for those above ₹ 50 lakhs.
2. Assistance was extended in the form of unsecured loan involving minimum legal formalities. Interest at a concessional rate of 9 per cent is charged during technology development and trial run production and 17 per cent once the product is introduced in the market.
3. The fund extends financial assistance to ventures such as chemicals, computer softwares, electronics, biotechnology, non-conventional energy, food processing, medical equipment, etc.
4. If the project does not succeed, IDBI can insist on transfer of technology to some other promoter designated by it on mutually agreed terms and conditions. The fund finances in start-up stage and the next priority is seed stage fund.

## 2. The Risk Capital and Technology Finance Corporation (RCTC)

The Risk Capital and Technology Finance Corporation Ltd. (RCTC), the subsidiary of IFCI provides venture capital through technology — finance and development scheme to meet the specific needs of such technology development. The RCTC, apart from providing assistance in the form of risk capital, is expected to finance hi-tech projects in the form of venture capital for technology upgradation and development. The assistance is provided in the form of short-term conventional loan or interest-free conditional loans allowing profit and risk sharing with the project sponsors or equity participation.

## 3. Technology Development and Information Company of India Limited (TDICI – 1998)

The venture capital fund was jointly created by Industrial Credit and Investment Corporation of India (ICICI) and Unit Trust of India (UTI) to finance projects of professional technocrats in the small and medium-size industries who take initiative in designing and developing indigenous technology in the country. TDICI's first venture capital fund of ₹ 20 crores was subscribed equally by ICICI and UTI under the new Venture Capital Unit Scheme I of UTI. Under the scheme TDICI sanctioned financial support of ₹ 20 crores to 40 projects which include computer hardware, computer integrated manufacturing system, tissue culture, chemicals, food and feed technology, environmental engineering, etc.

The TDICI's second venture fund of ₹ 100 crores has been contributed by UTI, ICICI, other financial institutions, banks, corporate sector, etc. By March 31, 1993, TDICI has disbursed ₹ 25.81 crores to 42 companies under scheme I and ₹ 79.29 crores to 79 companies under scheme II in a variety of industries such as computer, electronics, biotechnology, medical, non-conventional energy, etc. Many of these projects are set up by first generation entrepreneurs:

(*i*) TDICI invests in companies with attractive growth and earnings potential with a view of achieving long-term capital gain. TDICI involves in seed, start-up, and growth stage companies in a wide spectrum of industrial subsectors.

(*ii*) The scheme seeks to assist technocrats involved in developing commercially viable technologies or products, implementing indigenously developed yet untested technologies on a commercial scale, and adapting innovative technologies for domestic applications.

(*iii*) The assistance per project may be up to ₹ 2 crores in the form of equity and/or conditional loan (with flexible interest rates and repayment period).

(*iv*) The equity in the project would be held for a period of 5-8 years and thereafter sold to the promoter (at a mutually price) or disposed in the secondary market.

(*v*) During the development phase, the conditional loan would carry no interest; during the post-development phase the interest rate on it would depend on the commercial viability of the project.

## 4. Gujarat Venture Finance Ltd. (GVFL)

The Gujarat Industrial Investment Corporation promoted Gujarat Venture Finance Ltd., the first state-level venture finance company to begin venture finance activities since 1990. It provides financial support to the ventures whose requirements range between ₹ 25 lakhs and ₹ 2 crores. GVFL provides finance through equity participation and quasi-equity instruments. The firms engaged in biotechnology, surgical instruments, conservation of energy and food processing industries are covered by GVFL. Total corpus of ₹ 24 crores of the fund was cofinanced by GIIC, IDBI, state-level finance corporations, some private corporate and the World Bank.

## 5. Andhra Pradesh Industrial Development Corporation's Venture Capital Ltd. (APIDC-VCL)

The APIDC-VCL was launched in June 1990 with a fund of ₹ 13.50 crores of which ₹ 4.5 crores was contributed by the World Bank, ₹ 3 crores by IDBI and ₹ 1.5 crores was committed by Andhra Bank. APIDC-VCL has a few proposal for venture capital financing in the sphere of biotechnology and computer software applications. Assistance to each venture is in the range of ₹ 25 lakhs to ₹ 1 crores and does not exceed 49 per cent of the total equity of a project. Assistance is normally in the form of equity but depending on the circumstances loans may also be provided.

## 6. Canara Bank

Canara Bank has set up a venture capital fund called Canbank Venture Capital Fund worth ₹ 10 crores. It sanctions funds to diverse fields like chemicals, machines, foodstuffs, etc.

## 7. State Bank of India Capital Markets Ltd. (SBI CAP)

The State Bank of India's subsidiary SBI Capital Markets Ltd. extend venture capital assistance to technical entrepreneurs who have good technique ability but lack financial strength. The support is by way of either direct subscription or by way of underwriting support to the company. In any case, direct participation will not be in excess of 49 per cent of the total paid-up capital of the assisted unit. The projects in high priority thrust areas such as import substitute, high export potential, hi-tech options are preferred. The equity holdings of assisted companies are generally disinvested in a period of three years either by way of sale to public, sale in the OTC exchange of India, sale by private treaty or by buyback arrangements with promoters or their nominees.

## 8. Indus venture capital fund

Indus venture capital fund is one of the noteworthy private sector venture companies. It has been promoted with a starting corpus of ₹ 21 crores contributed by several Indian and international institutions and companies. Indus venture management limited has been entrusted to manage the fund of Indus venture capital fund. It provides equity and management support to the firms. Financial assistance is given to those firms who confine their commercial operations in areas of health care products, electronics and computer technology. Investment strategy of the funds is not to invest more than 10 per cent of its corpus in one project and equity stake in a company may be up to 50 per cent. The basic objective is to earn capital gains through equity liquidation after a certain reasonable time span.

The leading leasing company, 20th Century Finance Corporation has launched venture capital fund worth ₹ 20 crores to cater to the needs of small businessmen.

## 9. Credit capital venture fund limited

The first private sector venture capital fund called, Credit Capital Venture Fund Ltd. (CVF) was set up by Credit Capital Corporation Limited (CVF) in April 1989 with an authorised capital of ₹ 10 lakhs. ₹ 6.5 crores was subscribed by International financial agencies. The CVF went to public in January 1990 to raise ₹ 3.5 crores. It provides entrepreneurs who have ideas and ability, but no finance, with equity capital for new greenfield projects. Its main thrust area would be export-oriented industries and technology-oriented projects. The present portfolio of the fund consists of investment in six units worth ₹ 25 lakhs. CVF launched a new venture fund of ₹ 10 crores called 'The Information Technology Fund, to provide direct equity support to projects in the technology information field.

## 10. ICICI Venture Funds Management Co. Ltd.

It was founded in 1988 as a joint venture with the Unit Trust of India. Subsequently, the UTI's share was bought by the ICICI and thus, it became a fully owned subsidiary of the ICICI. Initially, this fund shows interest in start-up stage of any venture and its next priority is to concentrate on later stage capital.

## 11. SIDBI Venture Capital Ltd.

The SIDBI Venture Capital Ltd. is a wholly-owned subsidiary of SIDBI incorporated in July, 1999. It is interested in the start-up stage of ventures.

## 12. The Indian Venture Capital Association (IVCA)

The IVCA is a non-profit organisation set up to facilitate the growth of VC and private equity in India. The main objective of the ICVA is to encourage and assist creation of more VC funds and foster a platform for VC and PE funds to interact with each other. It has at present 80 members.

# PRESENT POSITION

There were 20 venture capital companies in India both in private and public sector in 1994.

In the year 2000, SEBI registered 13 more VC funds and their number increased to 32.

The details of Venture Capital Funds in India are shown below:

**TABLE 13.2: REGISTERED VENTURE CAPITAL FUNDS AND ALTERNATIVE INVESTMENT FUNDS**

| *Particulars* | *No. of Registered Intermediaries 2019* | *No. of Registered Intermediaries 2020* |
|---|---|---|
| 1 | 2 | 3 |
| Venture Capital Funds | 195 | 189 |
| Foreign Venture Capital Funds | 250 | 251 |
| Alternative Investment Funds | 547 | 649 |

***Source:*** SEBI Annual Report, 2021-22.

The SEBI has permitted VC funds to invest in real estate. This has opened the doors for organised debt and equity instruments in the real estate sector. Alternate Investment Funds (AIFs) are basically funds established or incorporated in India for the purpose of pooling in capital from Indian and foreign investors for investing. Category 1 of AIFs may include venture capital fund.

## SUGGESTIONS FOR THE GROWTH OF VENTURE CAPITAL FUNDS

Venture capital industry is at the take-off stage in India. It can play a catalytic role in the development of entrepreneurship skill that remains unexploited among the young and energetic technocrats and other professionally qualified talents. It can help promote new technology and hi-tech industries, which involve high risk but promises attractive rate of return. In order to ensure success of venture capital in India, the following suggestions are offered:

### 1. Exemption/concession for capital gains

Capital gains law represents a hurdle to the success of venture capital financing. The earnings of the funds depend primarily on the appreciation in stock values. Further, the capital gains may arise only after 3 to 4 years of investment and that the projects, being in new risky areas, may not even succeed. Capital gains by corporate bodies in India are taxed at a much higher rate than gains of individual investors. Taking into account the high investment risk and long gestation period this is a deterrent to the development of VCFs.

The benefit of capital gains, under Section 48 of the Act is not significant. Hence, it would be advisable that all long-term capital gains earned by VCFs should be exempted from tax or subjected to concessional flat rate. Further, capital gains reinvested in new ventures should also be exempted from tax. Section 52(E) of the Act should be amended to give effect to this.

### 2. Development of stock markets

Guidelines issued by Finance Ministry provides for the sale of investment by way of public issue at the price to be decided on the basis of book value and earning capacity. However, this method may not give the best available prices to venture fund as it will not be able to consider the future growth potential of the invested company.

One of the major factors which contributed to the success of venture funds in the West is development of secondary and tertiary stock markets. These markets do not have listing requirements and are spread over all important cities and towns in the country. These stock markets provide excellent disinvestment mechanism for venture funds. In India, however, stock market is not developed beyond a few important cities.

Success of venture capital fund depends very much upon profitable disinvestment of the capital contributed by it. In the US and UK, secondary and tertiary markets helped in accomplishing the above. However, in India, promotion of such markets is not feasible in the prevailing circumstances as such laissez-faire policy may attack persons with ulterior motives in the business to the detrimental of the general public. However, stock market operations may be started at many more big cities where, say, the number of stock exchanges can be increased to 50. Further, permission to transact in unlisted securities with suitable regulation will ensure firsthand contact between venture fund and investors.

### 3. Fiscal incentives

Fiscal incentives may be given in the form of lowering the rate of income tax. It can be accomplished by:

(*i*) Application of provisions applicable to non-corporate entities for taxing long-term capital gains.

(*ii*) An allowance to funds similar to Section 80-CC of Income Tax Act, say 20 per cent of the investment in new venture which can be allowed as deduction from the income.

### 4. Private sector participation

In the US and UK where the economy is dominated by private sector, development of venture fund market was possible due to very significant role played by private sector which is often willing to put money in high risk business provided higher returns are expected. The guidelines by Finance Ministry provide that non-institutional promoter's share in the capital of venture fund cannot exceed 20 per cent of total capital; further they cannot be the single largest equityholders. The private sector, because of this provision, may not like to promote venture fund business.

Promotion of venture funds by private sector, in addition to public financial institution and banks, is recommended as:

(*a*) Private sector is in advantageous position as compared to financial institutions and banks to provide managerial support to new ventures as leading industrial houses have a pool of experienced professional managers in all fields of management, *viz.*, marketing, production and finance.

(*b*) The leading business houses will be able to raise funds from the investing public with relative ease.

### 5. Review the existing laws

Today's need is to review the constraints under various laws of the country and resolve the issues that could come in the way of growth of the innovative mode of financing. Suitable exemption should be given from Section 43A of the Companies Act to venture capital finance companies so that they are not required to comply with several provisions of the Act applicable to public limited companies.

Amendment of Section 77 of the Companies Act is required to enable the new venture capital companies to buy back their shares at the time of disinvestments by VC Finance Companies.

Ceiling on inter-corporate loans and investments as specified in Sections 370 and 372 of the Companies Act should be relaxed in case of VC Finance Companies and Venture Capital Companies to enable them to invest suitably in newly promoted companies.

The only investment available to a VC Finance Company for investment is equity shares. This restriction should be relaxed so that a VC Finance Company can finance through preferential issues and conditional loans.

The scope of VC should not only be confined to start-up finance but also be broadened to development finance, expansion and growth, buyouts, mergers and amalgamations.

The restriction on investment of 80 per cent of the entire funds within a period of 3 years should be removed.

### 6. Limited partnership

The practice of limited partnership as in vogue in UK should be permitted in order to promote integration of objects between the managers and contributories for the success of venture capital projects

### 7. Public issue through OTCEI

The suggestion of Malegam Committee regarding making the public issue through OTCEI should be implemented in case of certain specified industries.

The initiative on the part of the government in the direction would see rapid growth of a new breed of venture capital assisted entrepreneurs.

## NITIN DESAI COMMITTEE'S RECOMMENDATIONS

A committee on Technology Innovation and Venture Capital headed by the former finance secretary Nitin Desai was appointed by the Planning Commission in 2006 to suggest measures to increase the flow of VC funds for commercialisation of technology ventures. The above committee has made the following suggestions:

(*i*) To set up an Early Stage Venture Fund (ESVF) through Public-Private Partnership (PPP) under the auspices of the DSIR (Department of Scientific and Industrial Research) and the major non-commercial research organisations of the government.

(*ii*) To provide fiscal incentive by way of a set-off against taxable income for those individuals who invest in start-ups which emanate from incubation facilities in research institutions.

(*iii*) To extend the same fiscal incentive to those who invest in domestic venture capital funds with a corpus less than ₹ 250 crores provided such VCFs would be investing mainly in seed stage companies.

(*iv*) To create Limited Liability Corporations (LLCs) through an amendment on redeemability under the Companies Act.

(*v*) To extend the applicability of such LLCs and the proposed Limited Liability Partnership (LLP) structure to venture capital funds.

(*vi*) To grant tax exemption of capital gains for registered VCFs on exit from unlisted companies.

(*vii*) To remove the restriction on investment of 25 per cent in a single VC undertaking by domestic and foreign VCFs.

(*viii*) To remove the minimum capitalisation requirement of Indian subsidiaries of SEBI-registered foreign VC investors.

## QUESTIONS

### I. Objective type questions:

#### A. State whether the following statements are TRUE or FALSE:

1. Venture capital is only in the form of equity participation.
2. Venture capital is available for trading concern also.
3. The basic objective of investment is capital appreciation.
4. Venture capitalists share the risk in the business.
5. Non-resident Indians can invest up to 100 per cent on repatriable basis in VC Fund.

[**Key:** 1. False, 2. False, 3. True, 4. True, 5. False]

#### B. Fill in the blanks:

1. The minimum size of VC Fund is ₹ __________.
2. Venture capital originated in __________.
3. In the implementation stage of a project, venture capital firms provide __________ finance.
4. VC firms are allowed to invest in leasing up to __________ of the total funds deployed.
5. VC firms usually invest in __________ and __________ scale industries.

[**Key:** 1. ₹ 10 crores, 2. USA, 3. Start-up, 4. 15 per cent, 5. small and medium]

### II. Short answer questions:

1. What is Venture Capital?
2. State the features of Venture Capital.
3. Explain the various stages of Venture Capital Financing.
4. Discuss the importance of Venture Capital.
5. Write note on 'SBI CAP'.
6. What are the disinvestment options available in India?

### III. Essay type questions:

1. Explain the scope and importance of venture capital.
2. Explain the performance of various venture capital firms functioning in India.
3. Discuss the scope of Venture Capital in India.
4. What is the strategic role of Venture Capital in the development of a country?
5. Make suggestions for the success of venture capital in India.
6. Describe the different methods of venture financing and discuss the various disinvestment mechanisms available to a venture capitalist.

# 14 MUTUAL FUNDS

In the financial industry, the talk of the day is 'mutual funds'.

## INTRODUCTION

Of late, mutual funds have become a hot favourite of millions of people all over the world. The driving force of mutual funds is the 'safety of the principal' guaranteed, plus the added advantage of capital appreciation together with the income earned in the form of interest or dividend. People prefer mutual funds to bank deposits, life insurance and even bonds because with a little money, they can get into the investment game. One can own a string of blue chips like ITC, TISCO, Reliance, etc., through mutual funds. Thus, mutual funds act as a gateway to enter into big companies hitherto inaccessible to an ordinary investor with his small investment.

### ❖ What is a Mutual Fund?

To state in simple words, a mutual fund collects the savings from small investors, invest them in government and other corporate securities and earn income through interest and dividends, besides capital gains. It works on the principle of 'small drops of water make a big ocean'. For instance, if one has ₹ 1,000 to invest, it may not fetch very much on its own. But, when it is pooled with ₹ 1,000 each from a lot of other people, then, one could create a 'big fund' large enough to invest in a wide varieties of shares and debentures on a commanding scale and thus, to enjoy the economies of large-scale operations. Hence, a mutual fund is nothing but a form of collective investment. It is formed by the coming together of a number of investors who transfer their surplus funds to a professionally qualified organisation to manage it. To get the surplus funds from investors, the fund adopts a simple technique. Each fund is divided into a small fraction called 'units' of equal value. Each investor is allocated units in proportion to the size of his investment. Thus, every investor, whether big or small, will have a stake in the fund and can enjoy the wide portfolio of the investment held by the fund. Hence, mutual funds enable millions of small and large investors to participate in and derive the benefit of the capital market growth. It has emerged as a popular vehicle of creation of wealth due to high return, lower cost and diversified risk.

## SCOPE OF MUTUAL FUND

As stated earlier, a mutual fund is nothing but a pool of the investors' funds. The special feature of a mutual fund is that the contributors and the beneficiaries of the fund are one and the same class of people, *i.e.,* investors. Nobody else can claim that fund. Since the investors themselves contribute to the pool of fund and enjoy it and its fruits, the term 'Mutual' has been employed.

The important features of a mutual fund are the following:

(*i*) A mutual fund belongs to those who have contributed to that fund and thus, the ownership of the fund lies in the hands of the investors.

(*ii*) Since all investors cannot take part in the management of the fund, it is left in the hands of investment professionals who earn a fee for their services.

(*iii*) The pool of funds collected is invested in a portfolio of marketable securities.

(*iv*) The investors' share in the fund is represented by 'units' just like shares in the case of share capital of a company. The unit value depends upon the value of the portfolio held by the fund. Hence, the value changes almost every day and it is called Net Asset Value.

(*v*) Generally, the investment portfolio of the mutual fund is created according to the objective of the fund. For example, a sectoral mutual fund invests its funds in a specific sector like IT sector, oil sector, etc.

## DEFINITION

The Securities and Exchange Board of India (Mutual Funds) Regulations, 1993 defines a mutual fund as 'a fund established in the form of a trust by a sponsor, to raise monies by the trustees through the sale of units to the public, under one or more schemes, for investing in securities in accordance with these regulations'.

These mutual funds are referred to as Unit Trusts in the UK and as open-ended investment companies in the USA. Therefore, Kamm, J.O. defines an open-ended investment company as 'an organisation formed for the investment of funds obtained from individuals and institutional investors who in exchange for the funds receive shares which can be redeemed at any time at their underlying asset values'.

According to Weston J. Fred and Brigham, Eugene, F., Unit Trusts are 'Corporations which accept dollars from savers and then use these dollars to buy stocks, long-term bonds, short-term debt instruments issued by business or government units; these corporations pool funds and thus reduce risk by diversification'.

Thus, mutual funds are corporations which pool funds by selling their own shares and reduce risk by diversification.

### ❖ Fund unit vs. share

Just like shares, the price of units of a fund is also quoted in the market. This price is governed basically by the value of the underlying investments held by that fund. At this juncture, one should not confuse a mutual fund investment on units with that of an investment on equity shares. Investment on equity share represents investment in a particular company alone. On the other hand, investment on an unit of a fund represents investment in the parts of shares of a large number of companies. This itself gives an idea how safe the units are. If a particular company fails, the shareholders of that company are affected very much, whereas the unitholders of that company are able to withstand that risk by means of their profitable holdings in other companies' shares.

Again, investment on equity shares can be used as a tool by speculators and inveterate stock market enthusiasts with a view of gaining abnormal profits. These people play an investment game in the stock market on the basis of daily movement of prices. But, mutual funds cannot be invested for such purposes and the mutual fund is not at all concerned with the daily ebbs and flows of the market. In short, mutual fund is not the right investment vehicle for speculators. Mutual funds are, therefore, suitable only to genuine investors, whereas shares are suitable to both the genuine investors and the speculators.

## ORIGIN OF THE FUND

The origin of the concept of mutual fund dates back to the dawn of commercial history. It is said that Egyptians and Phoenicians sold their shares in vessels and caravans with a view of spreading the risk attached with these risky ventures. However, the real credit of introducing the modern concept of mutual fund goes to the Foreign and Colonial Government Trust of London established in 1868. Thereafter, a large number of close-ended mutual funds were formed in the USA in 1930s followed by many countries in Europe, the Far East and Latin America. In most of the countries, both open-ended and close-ended types were popular. In India, it gained momentum only in 1980, though it began in the year 1964 with the Unit Trust of India launching its first fund, the Unit Scheme 1964.

## TYPES OF FUNDS/CLASSIFICATION OF FUNDS

In the investment market, one can find a variety of investors with different needs, objectives and risk-taking capacities. For instance, a young businessman would like to get more capital appreciation for his funds and he would be prepared to take greater risks than a person who is just on the verge of his retiring age. So, it is very difficult to offer one fund to satisfy all the requirements of investors. Just as one shoe is not suitable for all legs, one fund is not suitable to meet the vast requirements of all investors. Therefore, many types of funds are available to the investor. It is completely left to the discretion of the investor to choose any one of them depending upon his requirement and his risk-taking capacity.

Mutual fund schemes can broadly be classified into many types as given in the chart given below:

**CHART 14.1**
**SCHEMES OF MUTUAL FUNDS**

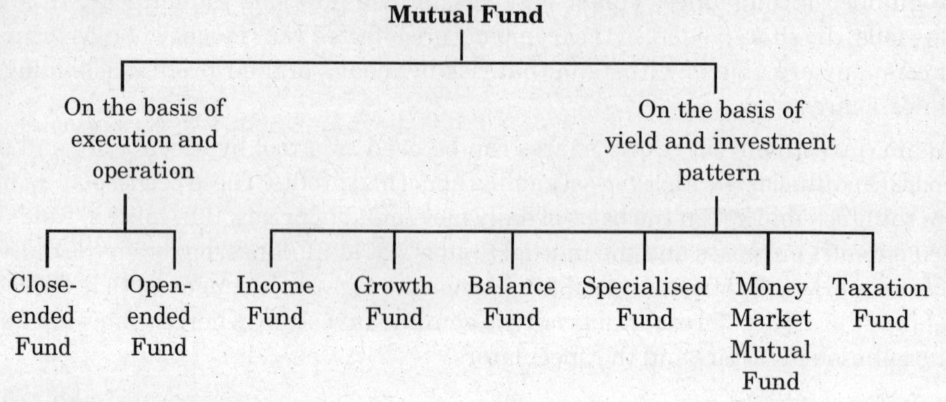


## ❖ On the basis of execution and operation

### (A) Close-ended funds

Under this scheme, the corpus of the fund and its duration are prefixed. In other words, the corpus of the fund and the number of units are determined in advance. Once the subscription reaches the predetermined level, the entry of investors is closed. After the expiry of the fixed period, the entire corpus is disinvested and the proceeds are distributed to the various unitholders in proportion to their holding. Thus, the fund ceases to be a fund, after the final distribution.

**Features:** The main features of the close-ended funds are:

(*i*) The period and/or the target amount of the fund is definite and fixed beforehand.

(*ii*) Once the period is over and/or the target is reached, the door is closed for the investors. They cannot purchase any more units.

(*iii*) These units are publicly traded through stock exchange and generally, there is no repurchase facility by the fund.

(*iv*) The main objective of this fund is capital appreciation.

(*v*) The whole fund is available for the entire duration of the scheme and there will not be any redemption demands before its maturity. Hence, the fund manager can manage the investments efficiently and profitably without the necessity of maintaining any liquidity.

(*vi*) At the time of redemption, the entire investment pertaining to a close-ended scheme is liquidated and the proceeds are distributed among the unitholders.

(*vii*) From the investor's point of view, it may attract more tax since the entire capital appreciation is realised in at one stage itself.

(*viii*) If the market condition is not favourable, it may also affect the investor since he may not get the full benefit of capital appreciation in the value of the investment.

(*ix*) Generally, the prices of close-ended scheme units are quoted at a discount of up to 40 per cent below their Net Asset Value (NAV).

## (B) Open-ended funds

It is just the opposite of close-ended funds. Under this scheme, the size of the fund and/or the period of the fund is not predetermined. The investors are free to buy and sell any number of units at any point of time. For instance, the Unit Scheme (1964) of the Unit Trust of India is an open ended one, both in terms of period and target amount. Anybody can buy this unit at any time and sell it also at any time at his discretion.

The main features of the open-ended funds are:

(*i*) There is complete flexibility with regard to one's investment or disinvestment. In other words, there is free entry and exit of investors in an open-ended fund. There is no time limit. The investor can join in and come out from the fund as and when he desires.

(*ii*) These units are not publicly traded but, the fund is ready to repurchase them and resell them at any time.

(*iii*) The investor is offered instant liquidity in the sense that the units can be sold on any working day. In fact, the fund operates just like a bank account, wherein one can get cash across the counter for any number of units sold.

(*iv*) The main objective of this fund is income generation. The investors get dividend, rights or bonuses as rewards for their investment.

(*v*) Since the units are not listed on the stock market, their prices are linked to the Net Asset Value (NAV) of the units. The NAV is determined by the fund and it varies from time-to-time.

(*vi*) Generally, the listed prices are very close to their Net Asset Value. The fund fixes a different price for their purchases and sales.

(*vii*) The fund manager has to be very careful in managing the investments because he has to meet the redemption demands at any time made during the life of the scheme.

To put it in a nutshell, the open ended funds have a perpetual existence and their corpus is ever-changing depending upon the entry and exit of members.

## ❖ On the basis of yield and investment pattern

### (A) Income funds

As the name suggests, this fund aims at generating and distributing regular income to the members on a periodical basis. It concentrates more on the distribution of regular income and it also sees that the average return is higher than that of the income from bank deposits.

The main features of the Income funds are:

(*i*) The investor is assured of regular income at periodic intervals, say half-yearly or yearly and so on.

(*ii*) The main objective of this type of fund is to declare regular dividends and not capital appreciation.

(*iii*) The pattern of investment is oriented towards high and fixed income yielding securities like debentures, bonds, etc.

(*iv*) This is best suited to the old and retired people who may not have any regular income.

(*v*) It concerns itself with short-run gains only.

## (B) Pure growth funds (growth-oriented funds)

Unlike the income funds, growth funds concentrate mainly on long run gains, *i.e.,* capital appreciation. They do not offer regular income and they aim at capital appreciation in the long run. Hence, they have been described as 'Nest Eggs' investments.

The main features of the growth funds are:

(*i*) The growth-oriented fund aims at meeting the investors' need for capital appreciation.

(*ii*) The investment strategy, therefore, conforms to the fund objective by investing the funds predominantly on equities with high growth potential.

(*iii*) The fund tries to get capital appreciation by taking much risks and investing on risk-bearing equities and high growth equity shares.

(*iv*) The fund may declare dividend, but its principal objective is only capital appreciation.

(*v*) This is best suited to salaried and business people who have high risk-bearing capacity and ability to defer liquidity. They can accumulate wealth for future needs.

## (C) Balanced funds

This is otherwise called "income-cum-growth" fund. It is nothing but a combination of both income and growth funds. It aims at distributing regular income as well as capital appreciation. This is achieved by balancing the investments between the high growth equity shares and also the fixed income earning securities.

## (D) Specialised funds

Besides the above, a large number of specialised funds are in existence abroad. They offer special schemes so as to meet the specific needs of specific categories of people like pensioners, widows, etc. There are also funds for investments in securities of specified areas, *e.g.*, Japan Fund, South Korea Fund, etc. In fact, these funds open the door for foreign investors to invest on the domestic securities of these countries.

Again, certain Funds may be confined to one particular sector or industry like fertilisers, automobiles, petroleum, etc. These funds carry heavy risks since the entire investment is in one industry. But, there are high risk-taking investors who prefer this type of fund. Of course, in such cases, the rewards may commensurate with the risk taken. At times, it may be erratic. The best example of this type is the Petroleum Industry Funds in the USA.

## (E) Money Market Mutual Funds (MMMFs)

These funds are basically open-ended mutual funds and as such they have all the features of the open-ended fund. But, they invest in highly liquid and safe securities like commercial paper, banker's acceptances, certificates of deposits, treasury bills, etc. These instruments are called money market instruments. They take the place of shares, debentures and bonds in a capital market. They pay money market rates of interest. These funds are called 'money funds' in USA and they have been functioning since 1972. Investors generally use it as a 'parking place' or 'stop-gap arrangement' for their cash resources till they finally decide about the proper avenue for their investment, *i.e.*, long-term financial assets like bonds and stocks.

Since MMMFs are a new concept in India, the RBI has laid down certain stringent regulations. For instance, the entry to MMMFs is restricted only to scheduled commercial banks and their subsidiaries. MMMFs can invest only in specified short-term money market instruments like Certificate of Deposits, Commercial Papers and 182-day Treasury Bills. They can also lend to call market. These funds go for safe and liquid investment. Frequent realisation of interest and redemption of fund at short notice are the special features of this fund. The funds will not be subject to reserve requirements. The repurchase could be subject to a minimum lock-in period of 3 months.

Since the RBI has fixed the minimum amount of investment as ₹ 1 lakh, it is out of the reach of many small investors. In the USA, the minimum amount is only $ 100. Recently, the private sector funds have been permitted to deal in money market mutual funds. Generally, it is best suited only to institutional investors like banks and other financial institutions.

### (F) Taxation funds

A taxation fund is basically a growth-oriented fund. But, it offers tax rebates to the investors either in the domestic or foreign capital market. It is suitable to salaried people who want to enjoy tax rebates particularly during the month of February and March. In India, at present, the law relating to tax rebates is covered under Sec. 88 of the Income Tax Act, 1961. An investor is entitled to get 20 per cent rebate in Income Tax for investments made under this fund subject to a maximum investment of ₹ 10,000 per annum. The Tax Saving Magnum of SBI Capital Market Limited is the best example for the domestic type. UTI's US $ 60 million India Fund, based in the USA, is an example for the foreign type.

## ❖ Other Classification

### (G) Leveraged funds

These funds are also called borrowed funds since they are used primarily to increase the size of the value of portfolio of a mutual fund. When the value increases, the earning capacity of the fund also increases. The gains are distributed to the unitholders. This is resorted to only when the gains from the borrowed funds are more than the cost of borrowed funds.

### (H) Dual funds

This is a special kind of close-ended fund. It provides a single investment opportunity for two different types of investors. For this purpose, it sells two types of investment stocks, *viz.*, income shares and capital shares. Those investors who seek current investment income can purchase income shares. They receive all the interest and dividends earned from the entire investment portfolio. However, they are guaranteed a minimum annual dividend payment. The holders of capital shares receive all the capital gains earned on those shares and they are not entitled to receive any dividend of any type. In this respect, the dual fund is different from a balanced fund.

### (I) Index funds

Index funds refer to those funds where the portfolios are designed in such a way that they reflect the composition of some broad-based market index. This is done by holding securities in the same proportion as the index itself. The value of these index-linked funds will automatically go up whenever the market index goes up and *vice versa*. Since the construction of portfolio is entirely based upon maintaining proper proportions of the index being followed, it involves less administrative expenses, lower transaction costs, less number of portfolio managers, etc. It is so because only fewer purchases and sales of securities would take place.

### (J) Bond funds

These funds have portfolios consisting mainly of fixed income securities like bonds. The main thrust of these funds is mostly on income rather than capital gains. They differ from income funds in the sense income funds offer an average returns higher than that from bank deposits and also capital gains lesser than that in equity shares.

### (K) Aggressive growth funds

These funds are just the opposite of bond funds. These funds are capital gains oriented and thus the thrust area of these funds is 'capital gains'. Hence, these funds are generally invested in speculative stocks. They may also use specialised investment techniques like short-term trading, option writing, etc. Naturally, these funds tend to be volatile in nature.

### (L) Offshore mutual funds

Offshore mutual funds are those funds which are meant for non-residential investors. In other words, the sources of investments for these funds are from abroad. So, they are regulated by the provisions of the foreign countries where those funds are registered. These funds facilitate flow of funds across different countries, with free and efficient movement of capital for investment and repatriation. Offshore funds are preferred to direct foreign investment, since, it does not allow foreign domination over host country's corporate sector. However, these funds involve much currency and country risk and hence they generally yield higher return.

### (M) Property fund

It is a real estate mutual fund. It is an investment vehicle which buys, develops, manages and sells real estate assets. Its investment also includes shares/bonds of companies involved in real estate and mortgage-backed companies.

In India, these funds are subject to the approval of the Department of Economic Affairs, Ministry of Finance and the RBI monitors such funds by issuing directions then and there. In India, a number of offshore funds exist. 'India Fund' and 'India Growth Fund' were floated by the UTI in UK and USA respectively. The State Bank of India floated the India Magnum Fund in Netherlands. 'The Indo-Suez Himalayan Fund NV' was launched by Canbank Mutual Fund in collaboration with Indo-Suez Asia Investment Services Ltd. It also floated 'Commonwealth Equity Fund'.

## (N) Fund-of-funds

A fund-of-funds scheme is a mutual fund scheme that invests in other mutual fund schemes. The concept is widely prevalent abroad. Mutual funds in India are being allowed to launch fund-of-funds.

## (O) Real Estate Mutual Fund (REMF)

The REMF scheme is a mutual fund scheme with the investment objective of direct or indirect investment in real estate property.

For instance, HDFC properly fund has been promoted as a joint venture of HDFC and SBI. This fund has floated two schemes, *viz.,* HDFC Real Estate Fund with a corpus of ₹ 1,000 crores to invest in commercial, residential, hospitality and integrated projects all over India.

Another scheme HDFC IT corridor fund with a corpus of ₹ 464 crores to focus on IT infrastructure spread across major towns in India.

## (P) Gold Exchange Traded Fund (ETF)

A gold exchange traded fund is nothing but exchange listed mutual fund representing some units of gold. Each unit represents one gram of gold generally and in the case of quantum gold ETF, it is 0.5 gram. This ETF can be traded on the floor of a stock exchange for which one must have a Demat and trading account. The demat for stock transaction can be used for dealing in ETF also. ETFs are listed both in NSE and BSE. Interested investors can buy units of a gold ETF from the open market. One can enjoy the benefit of price appreciation in gold without any regard to its safety and storing charges. Moreover, physical investment on gold eats into price appreciation in the form of making charges and wastage charges. At present, there are 12 exchange listed gold ETFs in India, the largest and the most liquid being benchmark mutual funds GoldBEES. The intra-day volume in this ETF is around 1.5 and 2 lakh units.

Recently, some mutual funds have come forward to invest in gold ETF schemes under fund-of-funds option. Investors who do not intend to open a Demat account can choose this option. The demand for gold ETF is on the increase in recent years due to run-up in gold prices. There were 4.89 Gold ETF retail folios as on 31st March, 2014 occupying the largest group of investors under this category.

## (Q) Exchange Traded Funds (ETFs)

As the very name implies, these funds are traded only on stock exchange, *viz.*, BSE and NSE. These are passively managed funds and the investors have to keep demat and broker accounts to buy and sell ETFs. Systematic Investment Plan is not allowed in ETF.

## (R) Liquid Funds

Liquid funds are those funds which are invested in liquid instruments such as treasury bills, repos, commercial papers and certificate of deposits. They may be invested in short-term debts also which are also very liquid in nature.

## (S) Arbitrage Funds

Arbitrage funds are basically short-term funds like Liquid Funds. Since the returns are lower in Liquid Funds, Arbitrage Funds have come into spotlight. The main aim of these funds is to generate returns from the mispricing opportunities that arise in cash and futures market. Profits arise by buying a stock at a cheaper rate in cash market and selling the same in futures market. The discretional risk (rise or fall in market price) is minimum since these funds take both long (buy) and short (sell) positions and *vice versa* at the same time in respect of the same asset.

## IMPORTANCE OF MUTUAL FUNDS

The mutual fund industry has grown at a phenomenal rate in the recent past. One can witness a revolution in the mutual fund industry in view of its importance to the investors in general and the country's economy at large. The following are some of the important advantages of mutual funds:

(i) **Channelising savings for investment:** Mutual funds act as a vehicle in galvanising the savings of the people by offering various schemes suitable to the various classes of customers for the development of the economy as a whole. A number of schemes are being offered by MFs so as to meet the varied requirements of the masses, and thus, savings are directed towards capital investments directly. In the absence of MFs, these savings would have remained idle. Thus, the whole economy benefits due to the cost-efficient and optimum use and allocation of scarce financial and real resources in the economy for its speedy development.

(ii) **Offering wide portfolio investment:** Small and medium investors used to burn their fingers in stock exchange operations with a relatively modest outlay. If they invest in a few shares, some may even sink without a trace never to rise again. Now, these investors can enjoy the wide portfolio of the investment held by the mutual fund. The fund diversifies its risks by investing on a large varieties of shares and bonds which cannot be done by small and medium investors. This is in accordance with the maxim 'Not to lay all eggs in one basket'. These funds have large amounts at their disposal, and so, they carry a clout in respect of stock exchange transactions. They are in a position to have a balanced portfolio which is free from risks. Thus, MFs provide instantaneous portfolio diversification.

(iii) **Providing better yields:** The pooling of funds from a large number of customers enables the fund to have large funds at its disposal. Due to these large funds, mutual funds are able to buy cheaper and sell dearer than the small and medium investors. Thus, they are able to command better market rates and lower rates of brokerage. So, they provide better yields to their customers. They also enjoy the economies of large-scale and can reduce the cost of capital market participation. The transaction costs of large investments are definitely lower than that of small investments. In fact, all the profits of a mutual fund are passed on to the investors by way of dividends and capital appreciation. The expenses pertaining to a particular scheme alone are charged to the respective scheme. Most of the mutual funds so far floated have given a dividend at the rate ranging between 12 per cent p.a. and 17 per cent p.a. It is fairly a good yield. It is an ideal vehicle for those who look for long-term capital appreciation.

(iv) **Rendering expertised investment service at low cost:** The management of the fund is generally assigned to professionals who are well trained and have adequate experience in the field of investment. The investment decisions of these professionals are always backed by informed judgement and experience. Thus, investors are assured of quality services in their best interest. Due to the complex nature of the securities market, a single investor cannot do all these works by himself or he cannot go to a professional manager who manages individual portfolios. In such a case, he may charge hefty management fee. The intermediation fee is the lowest being 1 per cent in the case of a mutual fund.

(v) **Providing research service:** A mutual fund is able to command vast resources and hence it is possible for it to have an in-depth study and carry-out research on corporate securities. Each fund maintains a large research team which constantly analyses the companies and the industries and recommends the fund to buy or sell a particular share. Thus, investments are made purely on the basis of a thorough research. Since research involves a lot of time, efforts and expenditure, an individual investor cannot take up this work. By investing in a mutual fund, the investor gets the benefit of the research done by the fund.

(vi) **Offering tax benefits:** Certain funds offer tax benefits to its customers. Thus, apart from dividends, interest and capital appreciation, investors also stand to get the benefit of tax concession.

For instance, under Section 80L of the Income Tax Act, a sum of ₹ 10,000 received as dividend (₹ 13,000 to UTI) from a MF is deductible from the gross total income. Under Section 88A, 20 per cent of the amount invested is allowed to be deducted from the tax payable. Under the Wealth Tax Act, investments in MF are exempted up to ₹ 5 lakhs.

The mutual funds themselves are totally exempt from tax on all income on their investments. But all other companies have to pay taxes and they can declare dividends only from the profits after tax. But, mutual funds do not deduct tax at source from dividends. This is really a boon to investors.

(vii) **Introducing flexible investment schedule:** Some mutual funds have permitted the investors to exchange their units from one scheme to another and this flexibility is a great boon to investors. Income units can be exchanged for growth units depending upon the performance of the funds. One cannot derive such a flexibility in any other investments.

(viii) **Providing greater affordability and liquidity:** Even a very small investor can afford to invest in mutual funds. They provide an attractive and cost-effective alternative to direct purchase of shares. In the absence of MFs, small investors cannot think of participating in a number of investments with such a meagre sum. Again, there is greater liquidity. Units can be sold to the fund at any time at the Net Asset Value and thus quick access to liquid cash is assured. Besides, branches of the sponsoring bank is always ready to provide loan facility against the unit certificates.

(ix) **Simplified record keeping:** An investor with just an investment in 500 shares or so in 3 or 4 companies has to keep proper records of dividend payments, bonus issues, price movements, purchase or sale instruction, brokerage and other related items. It is tedious and it consumes a lot of time. One may even forget to record the rights issue and may have to forfeit the same. Thus, record keeping is the biggest problem for small and medium investors. Now, a mutual fund offers a single investment source facility, i.e., a single buy order of 100 units from a mutual fund is equivalent to investment in more than 100 companies. The investor has to keep a record of only one deal with the mutual fund. Even if he does not keep a record, the MF sends statements very often to the investor. Thus, by investing in MFs, the record keeping work is also passed on to the fund.

(x) **Supporting capital market:** Mutual funds play a vital role in supporting the development of capital markets. The mutual funds make the capital market active by means of providing a sustainable domestic source of demand for capital market instruments. In other words, the savings of the people are directed towards investments in capital markets through these mutual funds. Thus, funds serve as a conduit for disintermediating bank deposits into stocks, shares and bonds. Mutual funds also provide a valuable liquidity to the capital market, and thus, the market is made very active and stable. When foreign investors and speculators exit and re-enter the markets *en masse*, mutual funds keep the market stable and liquid. In the absence of mutual funds, the prices of shares would be subject to wide price fluctuation due to the exit and re-entry of speculators into the capital market *en masse*. Thus, it is rendering an excellent support to the capital market and helping in the process of institutionalisation of the market.

(xi) **Promoting industrial development:** The economic development of any nation depends upon its industrial advancement and agricultural development. All industrial units have to raise their funds by resorting to the capital market by the issue of shares and debentures. The mutual funds not only create a demand for these capital market instruments but also supply a large source of funds to the market, and thus, the industries are assured of their capital requirements. In fact, the entry of mutual funds has enhanced the demand for India's stocks and bonds. Thus, mutual funds provide financial resources to the industries at market rates.

(xii) **Acting as substitute for Initial Public Offerings (IPOs):** In most cases, investors are not able to get allotment in IPOs of companies because they are often oversubscribed many time. Moreover, they have to apply for a minimum of 500 shares which is very difficult particularly for small investors. But, in mutual funds, allotment is more or less guaranteed. Mutual funds are also guaranteed a certain percentage of IPOs by companies. Thus, by participating in MFs, investors are able to get the satisfaction of participating in hundreds of varieties of companies.

(xiii) **Reducing the marketing cost of new issues:** The mutual funds help to reduce the marketing cost of the new issues. The promoters used to allot a major share of the initial public offering to the mutual funds and thus they are saved from the marketing cost of such issues.

(xiv) **Keeping the money market active:** An individual investor cannot have any access to money market instruments since the minimum amount of investment is out of his reach. On the other hand, mutual funds keep the money market active by investing money on the money market instruments. In fact, the availability of more money market instruments itself is a good sign for a developed money market which is essential for the successful functioning of the Central Bank in a country.

Thus, mutual funds provide stability to share prices, safety to investors and resources to prospective entrepreneurs.

## RISKS

Mutual funds are not free from risks. It is so because basically the mutual funds also invest their funds in the stock market on shares which are volatile in nature and are not risk-free. Hence, the following risks are inherent in their dealings:

(i) **Market risks:** In general, there are certain risks associated with every kind of investment on shares. They are called market risks. These market risks can be reduced, but cannot be completely eliminated even by a good investment management. The prices of shares are subject to wide price fluctuations depending upon market conditions over which nobody has a control. Moreover, every economy has to pass through a cycle — Boom, Recession, Slump and Recovery. The phase of the business cycle affects the market conditions to a larger extent.

(ii) **Scheme risks:** There are certain risks inherent in the scheme itself. It all depends upon the nature of the scheme. For instance, in a pure growth scheme, risks are greater. It is obvious because if one expects more returns as in the case of a growth scheme, one has to take more risks.

(iii) **Investment risks:** Whether the mutual fund makes money in shares or loses depends upon the investment expertise of the Asset Management Company (AMC). If the investment advice goes wrong, the fund has to suffer a lot. The investment expertise of various funds are different and it is reflected on the returns which they offer to investors.

(iv) **Business risks:** The corpus of a mutual fund might have been invested in a company's shares. If the business of that company suffers any setback, it cannot declare any dividend. It may even go to the extent of winding up its business. Though the mutual fund can withstand such a risk, its income paying capacity is affected.

(v) **Political risks:** Successive governments bring with them new economic ideologies and policies. It is often said that many economic decisions are politically motivated. Changes in Government bring in the risk of uncertainty which every player in the financial service industry has to face. So, mutual funds are no exception to it.

## ORGANISATION OF THE FUND

The structure of mutual fund operations in India envisages a three-tier establishment namely:

(*i*) A sponsor institution to promote the fund,

(*ii*) A team of trustees to oversee the operations and to provide checks for the efficient, profitable and transparent operations of the fund, and,

(*iii*) An Asset Management Company (AMC) to actually deal with the funds.

**(i) Sponsoring institutions:** The company which sets up the mutual fund is called the sponsor. The SEBI has laid down certain criteria to be met by the sponsor. These criteria mainly deal with adequate experience, good past track record, net worth, etc.

**(ii) Trustees:** Trustees are people with long experience and good integrity in their respective fields. They carry the crucial responsibility of safeguarding the interest of investors. For this purpose, they monitor the operations of the different schemes. They have wide ranging powers and they can even dismiss Asset Management Companies with the approval of the SEBI.

**(iii) Asset Management Company (AMC):** The AMC actually manages the funds of the various schemes. The AMC employs a large number of professionals to make investments, carry-out research and to do agent and investor servicing. In fact, the success of any mutual fund depends upon the efficiency of this AMC. The AMC submits a quarterly report on the functioning of the mutual fund to the trustees who will guide and control the AMC.

## OPERATION OF THE FUND

A mutual fund invites the prospective investors to join the fund by offering various schemes so as to suit to the requirements of different categories of investors. The resources of individual investors are pooled together and the investors are issued units/shares for the money invested. The amount so collected is invested in capital market instruments like shares and debentures and money market instruments like treasury bills, commercial papers, etc.

For managing this fund, a mutual fund gets an annual fee of 1.25 per cent of funds managed at the maximum as fixed by the SEBI (MF) Regulations, 1993 and if the funds exceed ₹ 100 crores, it is only 1 per cent. It cannot take more than that. Of course, regular expenses like custodial fee, cost of dividend warrants, fee for registration, the asset management fee, etc., are debited to the respective schemes. These expenses cannot exceed 3 per cent of the assets in the respective schemes each year. The remaining amount is given back to the investors in full.

## FACILITIES AVAILABLE TO INVESTORS

**Repurchase facilities:** The units of close-ended schemes must be compulsorily listed in recognised stock exchanges. Such units can be sold or bought at market prices. But, units of open-ended schemes are not at all listed and hence they have to be bought only from the fund. So, the fund reserves the right to buy back the units from its members. This process of buying back the units from the investors by the fund is called repurchase facility. This is available in both schemes so as to provide liquidity to investors. The price fixed for this purpose is called repurchase price.

**Reissue facilities:** In the case of open-ended schemes, units can be bought only from the fund and not in the open market. The units bought from the investors are again reissued to those who are interested in purchasing them. The price fixed for this purpose is called reissue price.

**Rollover facilities:** At the time of redemption, the investor is given an option to reinvest his entire investment once again for another term. An investor can overcome an adverse market condition prevailing at the time of redemption by resorting to this rollover facility. This is applicable in the case of close-ended funds.

**Lateral shifting facilities:** Some mutual funds permit the investors to shift from one scheme to another on the basis of the Net Asset Values with a view of providing total flexibility in their operation. This is done without any discount on the fund and without any additional charges. This is a great privilege given to the investors. This shifting is called 'lateral shifting'.

**Dividend Sweep Facility (DSF):** Dividend sweep facility is one where an unit holder is given an option to sweep or invest the dividend earned in a scheme into any other open-ended scheme. This is different from dividend reinvestment scheme where the dividend earned is invested in the same scheme in which dividend was declared.

**Systematic Withdrawal Plan (SWP):** This is a facility wherein investors can opt to systematically withdraw money on predetermined dates either weekly, monthly or quarterly. It is nothing but redemption at predetermined regular intervals at the option of an unitholder.

**Trigger Facility (TF):** It is a facility where a transaction is automatically triggered in the investor folio on the occurrence of a certain event. For example, an investor can opt to trigger a redemption or a switch to another scheme if a certain appreciation level is attained say 25 per cent gain. Similarly, an investor can opt to trigger a redemption or switch over to a debt scheme when investments in equity fund have significantly appreciated so that capital may be conserved. Triggers really serve as financial planning tools and investors can book timely profits using triggers.

## NET ASSET VALUE

The repurchase price is always linked to the Net Asset Value (NAV). The NAV is nothing but the market price of each unit of a particular scheme in relation to all the assets of the scheme. It can otherwise be called 'the intrinsic value' of each unit. This value is a true indicator of the performance of the fund. If the NAV is more than the face value of the unit, it clearly indicates that the money invested on that unit has appreciated and the fund has performed well.

### ❖ Illustration

For instance, Fortune Mutual Fund has introduced a scheme called Millionaire Scheme. The scheme size is ₹ 100 crores. The value of each unit is ₹ 10. It has invested all the funds in shares and debentures and the market value of the investment comes to ₹ 200 crores.

Now, $\text{NAV} = \dfrac{200 \text{ crore}}{100 \text{ crore}} \times \text{value of each unit}$

$= 2 \times 10 = 20$

Thus, the value of each unit of ₹ 10 is worth ₹ 20.

Hence, the NAV = ₹ 20.

This NAV forms the basis for fixing the repurchase price and reissue price.

The investor can call up the fund any time to find out the NAV. Some MFs publish the NAV weekly in two or three leading daily newspapers.

## PERFORMANCE EVALUATION OF MUTUAL FUNDS

A fund manager's performance can be assessed with the help of certain benchmarks. Benchmarks are nothing but independent portfolios that are not managed by any fund manager. They are purely representative of the behaviour in market returns of selected securities. For instance, the S&P CNX Nifty is a portfolio of 50 securities traded on the National Stock Exchange. Similarly, the BSE Sensitive Index is a portfolio of 30 securities traded on the Bombay Stock Exchange. These indices and their movement to a large extent represent the movement in prices as well as returns, of large, actively traded stocks in the equity market. These independent portfolios can be used to measure the performance of a fund manager.

### ❖ Qualities of an ideal benchmark

To have a meaningful performance evaluation of a fund manager, his fund performance should be compared with the benchmarks. For fruitful comparison, the benchmark should have the following qualities:

(*i*) The benchmark should be completely independent.

(*ii*) The fund manager should not have any influence over it nor should he manage it.

(*iii*) The benchmark should comprise of market securities and it should be representative of the risk and return of the underlying market.

(*iv*) The benchmark value should be publicly available everyday for the purposes of computing returns and comparison.

(*v*) As far as possible, the benchmark should represent the investment objective of the fund with which a comparison has to be made. In other words, the benchmark portfolio should match the mutual fund portfolio in objectives.

### ❖ Benchmarks Used in the Mutual Fund Industry

The same benchmark cannot be used for all the schemes of a mutual fund. It differs from scheme-to-scheme and from fund-to-fund depending upon the objective of its portfolio. Generally, the following benchmarks are used in the mutual fund industry:

(*i*) For actively managed all equity portfolios, the BSE Sensex and the S&P CNX Nifty are used as benchmarks.

(*ii*) For broad based equity portfolios, S&P CNX 500 is used as benchmark since this index tracks the returns on the equity shares of 500 companies.

(*iii*) For sectoral funds, sectoral indices are used to evaluate the performance of those funds. For instance, if the fund's portfolio consists of only bank stocks, the appropriate benchmark is nothing but the index of bank stocks rather than the broad general market index.

(*iv*) For short-term liquid funds and money market funds, the Treasury Bill Rates and the NSE Mibor are used as benchmarks.

(*v*) For bond funds, I-Bex, an index of government bonds is used as a benchmark.

(*vi*) For a combination of both equity funds and debt funds, the benchmark should also be a combination of an equity index and a debt market index in the same proportion of the fund investments.

### ❖ Benchmark as a tool for performance evaluation

Once the benchmark is decided, then one should know how to evaluate the performance of a mutual fund with the help of the chosen benchmark. One has to simply compare the behaviour of the returns of the benchmark and the NAV of the mutual fund over the same period of time. It clearly indicates to what extent the mutual fund portfolio has tracked the underlying benchmark. If a fund performs better than the benchmark, it is said to have outperformed. On the other hand, if the performance is worse when compared to the benchmark, it is said to have underperformed. A common size graph can be used for an effective and fruitful comparison of NAV and the benchmark.

### ❖ SEBI guidelines on benchmark

The SEBI has laid down the following conditions for the use of benchmark:

(*i*) Mutual funds should use only those benchmarks that reflect the asset allocation of the fund.

(*ii*) The period of comparison of returns should be identical for the fund and the benchmark.

(*iii*) If the scheme's offer document indicates a benchmark for return comparisons, the same should be used by the scheme.

(*iv*) Growth funds with more than 60 per cent in equity should always use any of the standard indices like Sensex, NSE Nifty, BSE 100 and CRISIL 500. These indices should be used consistently throughout. Changes can happen only when asset allocation of the fund has changed significantly, and trustees approve the change.

(*v*) Income funds with more than 60 per cent in debt should use a bond market index on benchmark.

(*vi*) Balanced funds can make use of tailored benchmarks that combine equity and bond index returns in the same proportion as in the asset allocation of the fund.

(*vii*) Money market funds can make use of a money market instrument or a combination of such instruments as benchmarks.

### ❖ Risk-return evaluation

There is no justification in evaluating a fund's performance by comparing only the returns of the fund with the benchmark. It is better to study the returns along with the risk. Therefore, it is necessary to compare funds returns with benchmarks, on a risk-adjusted basis. For this, the return and risk for both the fund and the benchmark should be computed and from this the return earned per unit of risk should be found out for both.

***Example:***

| ***BENCHMARK*** | | ***FUND*** | |
|---|---|---|---|
| ***Return*** | ***Risk (Standard Deviation)*** | ***Return*** | ***Risk*** |
| 15% | 10% | 18% | 11% |

The above table clearly shows that the fund has outperformed the benchmark in terms of return. But at the same time, it is accompanied by a higher level of risk. Therefore, the return per unit of risk is ascertained as follows:

**For the benchmark**

The return per unit of risk = 15/10 = 1.5.

**For the fund**

The return per unit of risk = 18/11 = 1.63.

It is noted that the return per unit of risk for the fund is higher. It means that the fund has performed better on a risk-adjusted basis also.

## SHARPE'S MODEL FOR EVALUATION

William Sharpe has given a model for evaluating the fund's performance on a risk-adjusted basis. His model is based on the comparison of 'excess return' per unit of risk for both the fund and the benchmark. The risk is measured by the standard deviation. The excess return is ascertained with the help of risk-free rate.

Excess return = Actual return of the fund – Risk-free rate

Generally, the return on the 90-day treasury bill of the government is taken on the risk-free rate. Let us assume the risk-free rate is 7 per cent. Using the same figures given in the example above, performance can be evaluated by applying Sharpe's Model as follows:

### For the benchmark

Excess return = 15 – 7 = 8

Risk-free rate = 7

Sharpe ratio = 8/10 = 0.8

### For the fund

Excess return = 18 – 7 = 11

Risk-free rate = 7

Sharpe ratio = 11/11 = 1

The fund is ranked as an outperformer since it is giving a superior return on a risk-adjusted basis when compared to the benchmark.

## TREYNOR'S MODEL FOR EVALUATION

In Sharpe's model, the return per unit of risk is measured with the help of standard deviation (risk). But in Jack Treynor's model, we measure return per unit of Beta (risk).

Treynor's Ratio (Ti) = (Ri – Rf)/βi

where Ri represents return on fund, Rf is risk-free rate of return and βi is beta of the fund. A high and positive Treynor's ratio shows a superior risk-adjusted performance of a fund and *vice versa*.

## JENSON MODEL

Michael Jenson has developed another model to measure the performance of a fund on the basis of risk-adjusted factor. It is called Differential Return Method. It measures the performance of a fund by comparing the actual returns of the fund with the returns actually expected out of it over a given period at the given level of its systematic risk. The surplus between the two returns is called Alpha.

The expected return of a fund can be calculated by means of the following formula:

Expected rate (Ri) = Rf + βi(Rm – Rf)

where βi is the given level of risk and Rm the average market return during the given period.

Then Alpha = Actual return – Expected or required return.

Higher the Alpha, superior is the performance of the fund and *vice versa*.

## OTHER PARAMETERS OF PERFORMANCE

Apart from risk and return parameters, other parameters are also employed to evaluate the performance of mutual funds. Some of them are given below:

(*i*) Credit quality of the portfolio by looking at the credit ratings of the investments in the portfolio.

(*ii*) Portfolio turnover rate — a high turnover rate indicates high profitability from most market turns but at the cost of higher transaction cost.

(*iii*) The liquidity of the portfolio — liquid funds having a large turnover ratio indicate good performance.

(*iv*) Performance in relation to market indices.

(*v*) Performance in relation to peer group comparisons in the same category.

(*vi*) Performance in relation to investment options available to the investor.

(*vii*) The expense ratio of the fund — the ratio of total expenses of the fund to the average net assets of the fund. Higher the expense ratio, lesser its efficiency. But it depends upon the size and type of the fund also.

## INVESTOR'S RIGHTS

The SEBI (MF) Regulations, 1993 contains specific provisions with regard to investor servicing. Certain rights have been guaranteed to the investors as per the above regulations. They are as follows:

**(i) Unit certificates:** An investor has a right to receive his unit certificates on allotment within a period of 10 weeks from the date of closure of subscription lists in the case of a close-ended scheme and 6 weeks from the date of closure of the initial offer in the case of an open-ended scheme.

**(ii) Transfer of units:** An investor is entitled to get the unit certificates transferred within a period of 30 days from the date of lodgement of the certificates along with the relevant transfer forms.

**(iii) Refund of application money:** If a mutual fund is not able to collect the statutory minimum amount (close-ended funds — ₹ 20 crores, open-ended funds — ₹ 50 crores or 60 per cent of the targeted amounts whichever is higher), it has to return the application money as refund within a period of 6 weeks from the date of closure of subscription lists. If the refund is delayed beyond this period, each applicant is entitled to get the refund with interest at the rate of 15 per cent p.a. for the period of delay.

**(iv) Audited annual report:** Every mutual fund is under an obligation to its investors to publish the audited annual report and unaudited half-yearly report through prominent newspapers in respect of each of its schemes within 6 months and 3 months respectively of the date of closure of accounts.

**(v) Net asset value:** Again, every investor has the right to receive information about the NAV at intervals not exceeding 3 months in the case of open-ended scheme and one month in the case of close-ended funds. It must also be published at least in two daily newspapers.

## GENERAL GUIDELINES

For proper functioning of mutual funds and for ensuring investor protection, the following important guidelines have been framed by the Government of India:

### (A) General

(*i*) Money market mutual funds would be regulated by the RBI while other mutual funds would be regulated by the Securities and Exchange Board of India (SEBI).

(*ii*) Mutual fund shall be established in the form of trusts under the Indian Trust Act and be authorised for business by the SEBI.

(*iii*) Mutual funds shall be operated only by separately established Asset Management Companies (AMCs).

(*iv*) At least 50 per cent of the Board of AMC must be independent directors who have no connections with the sponsoring organisation. The directors must have professional experience of at least 10 years in the relevant fields such as portfolio management, financial administration, etc.

(*v*) The AMC should have a minimum net worth of ₹ 5 crores at all times.

(*vi*) The SEBI is given the power to withdraw the authorisation given to any AMC if it is found to be not serving the best interest of investors as well as the capital market. It is not applicable to bank-sponsored AMCs.

## (B) Business activities

(*i*) Both AMCs and trustees should be treated as two separate legal entities.

(*ii*) AMCs should not be permitted to undertake any other business activity except mutual funds.

(*iii*) One AMC cannot act as the AMC for another mutual fund.

## (C) Schemes

(*i*) Each scheme of a mutual fund must be compulsorily registered with the SEBI before it is floated in the market.

(*ii*) The minimum size of the fund should be ₹ 20 crores in the case of each close-ended scheme and it is ₹ 50 crores for each open-ended scheme.

(*iii*) Close-ended schemes should not be kept opened for subscription for more than 45 days. For open-ended schemes, the first 45 days should be considered for determining the target figure or the minimum size.

(*iv*) If the minimum amount or 60 per cent of the targeted amount, whichever is higher, is not raised, then the entire subscription has to be refunded to the investors.

(*v*) To provide continuous liquidity, close-ended schemes should be listed on stock exchanges. In the case of open-ended schemes, mutual funds shall sell and repurchase units at predetermined prices based on the Net Asset Value and such prices should be published at least once in a week.

(*vi*) For each scheme, there should be a separate and responsible fund manager.

## (D) Investment norms

(*i*) Mutual funds should invest only in transferable securities either in the capital market or money market or securitised debt. It cannot exceed 10 per cent in the case of growth funds and 40 per cent in the case of income funds.

(*ii*) The mutual fund should not invest more than 5 per cent of its corpus of any scheme in any one company's shares.

(*iii*) This list of 5 per cent can be extended to 10 per cent if all the schemes of a mutual fund are taken together.

(*iv*) No scheme should invest in any other scheme under the same AMC.

(*v*) No mutual fund under all its schemes taken together can invest more than 15 per cent of the funds in the shares and debentures of any specific industry, except in the case of those schemes which are specifically floated for investment in one or more specified industries.

### (E) Expenses

(*i*) The AMC may charge the mutual fund with investment management and advisory fees. Such fees should have been disclosed in the prospectus.

(*ii*) The initial issue expenses should not exceed 6 per cent of the funds raised under each scheme.

(*iii*) Excepting the initial issue expenses, all other expenses to be charged to the fund should not exceed 3 per cent of the weekly average net assets outstanding during the current year. It must be disclosed through advertisements, accounts, etc.

### (F) Income distribution

All mutual funds must distribute a minimum of 90 per cent of their profits in any given year.

### (G) Disclosure and reporting

(*i*) The SEBI is given wide powers to call for any information regarding the operation of mutual funds and any of its schemes from the mutual fund or any person associated with it like the AMC, Trustee, Sponsor, etc.

(*ii*) Every mutual fund is required to send its copies of duly audited annual statements of accounts, six-monthly unaudited accounts, quarterly statements of movements in net assets for each of its schemes to the SEBI.

(*iii*) The SEBI can lay down the accounting policies, the format and contents of financial statements and other reports.

(*iv*) The SEBI shall also lay down a common advertising code for all mutual funds to comply with.

### (H) Accounting norms

(*i*) All mutual funds should segregate their earnings as current income, short-term capital gains and long-term capital gains.

(*ii*) Accounting for all the schemes must be done for the same year ending.

### (I) Winding up

(*i*) Each close-ended scheme should be wound up or extended with the permission of the SEBI as soon as the predetermined period is over.

(*ii*) An open-ended scheme shall be wound up, if the total number of units outstanding after repurchases at a point of time falls below 50 per cent of the originally issued number of units.

### (J) Violation of guidelines

The SEBI can, after due investigation, impose penalties on mutual funds for violating the guidelines as may be necessary.

## SELECTION OF A FUND

Mutual funds are not magic institutions which can bring treasure to the millions of their investors within a short span of time. All funds are equal to start with. But in due course of time, some excel the other. It all depends upon the efficiency with which the fund is being managed by the professionals of the fund. Hence, the investor has to be very careful in selecting a fund. He must take into account the following factors for evaluating the performance of any fund and then finally decide the one he has to choose:

(i) **Objective of the fund:** First of all, he must see the objective of the fund — whether income-oriented or growth-oriented. Income-oriented are backed mainly by fixed interest yielding securities like debentures and bonds, whereas growth-oriented are backed by equities. It is obvious that growth-oriented schemes are more risky than income-oriented schemes, and hence, the returns from such schemes are not comparable with each other. The investor should compare the particular scheme of one fund with the same scheme of another fund and make a comparative analysis. His objective should also coincide with the objective of the scheme which he proposes to choose.

(ii) **Consistency of performance:** A mutual fund is always intended to give steady long-term returns, and hence, the investor should measure the performance of a fund over a period of at least three years. Investors are satisfied with a fund that shows a steady and consistent performance than a fund which performs superbly in one year and then fails in the next year. Consistency in performance is a good indicator of its investment expertise.

(iii) **Historical background:** The success of any fund depends upon the competence of the management, its integrity, periodicity and experience. The fund's integrity should be above suspicion. A good historical record could be a better horse to bet on than new funds. It is in accordance with the maxim 'A known devil is better than an unknown angel'.

(iv) **Cost of operation:** Mutual funds seek to do a better job of the investible funds at a lower cost than the individuals could do for themselves. Hence, the prospective investor should scrutinise the expense ratio of the fund and compare it with others. Higher the ratio, lower will be the actual returns to the investor.

(v) **Capacity for innovation:** The efficiency of a fund manager can be tested by means of the innovative schemes he has introduced in the market so as to meet the diverse needs of investors. An innovator will be always a successful man. It is quite natural that an investor will look for funds which are capable of introducing innovations in the financial market.

(vi) **Investor servicing:** The most important factor to be considered is prompt and efficient servicing. Services like quick response to investor's queries, prompt despatch of unit certificates, quick transfer of units, immediate encashment of units, etc., will go a long way in creating a lasting impression in the minds of investors.

**(vii) Market trends:** Traditionally, it has been found that the stock market index and the inflation rate tend to move in the same direction, whereas the interest rates and the stock market index tend to move in the opposite direction. This sets the time for the investor to enter into the fund and come out of it. A prudent investor must keep his eyes on the stock market index, interest rate and the inflation rate. Of course, there is no scientific reasoning behind it.

**(viii) Transparency of the fund management:** Again, the success of a mutual fund depends to a large extent on the transparency of the fund management. In these days of investor awareness, it is very vital that the fund should disclose the complete details regarding the operation of the fund. It will go a long way in creating a lasting impression in the minds of the investors to patronise the fund for ever.

In fact, the wider range of products/services offered by the different funds, have made the investor quality-conscious. He is now in a position to assess the quality of the products offered by MFs in the financial market. MFs cannot simply attract savings by mere lucrative advertisements. The cult of the equity has spread to many small investors who have become very discerning in selecting mutual funds.

## COMMERCIAL BANKS AND MUTUAL FUNDS

With a view to providing wider choice to small investors, the Government of India has permitted the banks to launch mutual funds as subsidiaries. There has been an urgent need for the banks to enter into the field of mutual funds due to the following reasons:

(*i*) Banks are not able to provide better yields to the investing public with their savings and fixed deposit interest rates, whereas many financial intermediaries, with innovative market instruments offering very attractive returns, have entered the financial market. So, banks are not able to compete with them in tapping the savings. Hence, there is a necessity to enter into the field of MFs.

(*ii*) The gross domestic savings has risen from 10 per cent in fifties to 20 per cent in eighties, thanks to the massive branch expansion programme of banks and their growing deposit mobilisation. Since the banks have branches in the rural as well as urban sectors, they can reach out to everyone in the country. Hence, a MF backed by a bank will be in a better position to tap the savings effectively and vigorously for the capital market.

(*iii*) Indian investors, particularly small and medium ones, are not very keen in investing any substantial amount directly in capital market instruments. They may also hesitate to invest in an indirect way through private financial intermediaries. On the other hand, if such intermediary has the backing of a bank, investors may have confidence and come forward to invest. Thus, banks have the advantage of 'public confidence' which is very essential for the success of mutual funds.

(*iv*) Earlier, banks were not permitted to tap the capital market for funds or to invest their funds in the market. Now, a green signal has been given to them to enter into this market and reap the maximum benefits.

(*v*) Banks can provide a wider range of products/services in mutual funds by introducing innovative schemes and extend their professionalism to the mutual funds industry.

(*vi*) Banks, as merchant banks, have wide experience in the capital market and hence managing a mutual fund may not be a big problem for them.

(*vii*) The entry of banks would provide much needed competition in the mutual fund industry which has been hitherto monopolised by the UTI. This competition will improve customer service and widen customer choice also.

(*viii*) In the Indian economy, the eighties witnessed the operation of both the process of intermediation and disintermediation. The disintermediation process can be easily harnessed by commercial banks through mutual funds. The process of disintermediation of time deposits into mutual funds would benefit the capital market because it would provide a sustainable domestic source of demand.

(*ix*) Above all the, investor servicing can be effectively done by banks through their network of branches spread throughout the country. Hence, the commercial banks have entered into the mutual fund market without any hesitancy.

(*x*) Moreover, the profitability of banks has been very much affected due to too many restrictions on their lending policies. They have been compelled to seek some other alternatives to increase their profits by means of diversifying their activities. Mutual funds offer an excellent outlet for diversification.

## MUTUAL FUNDS ABROAD

The mutual funds have been growing at an unprecedented pace throughout the world. In the USA, mutual funds have been labelled as the 'bank deposits of 1990s'. Mutual funds have changed the American financial landscape by offering a menu of investment choice and some companies like Fidelity Investments, Vanguard and Merrill Lynch are very popular among them. The Americans have been pouring in over $ 1 billion every day into these funds. According to a study, the industry was expected to have $ 2 trillion in assets by 1995 or 1996 and touch the $ 3 trillion mark by 2000. But, in 1993 itself the fund touched the $ 2 trillion mark. In the US today, nearly 83 million investors forming 27 per cent of the households save in 4,558 funds. In fact, the number of mutual funds outnumber the number of listed companies on the New York Stock Exchange. This industry has an annual growth of about 20 to 25 per cent.

The funds in UK have already crossed the 1,000 mark by the end of 1987. The top 25 funds in terms of performance come from Japan and the Far East growth sectors. Some of them have doubled their money within a period of just one year. In Australia also, these funds have been very successful particularly on account of 46.8 per cent rise to Australian All Shares Index. MFs are growing in size and importance in countries like Hong Kong, Singapore, Philippines, Thailand, South Korea etc.

## MUTUAL FUNDS IN INDIA

In India, the mutual fund industry has been monopolised by the Unit Trust of India ever since 1963. Now, the commercial banks like the State Bank of India, Canara Bank, Indian Bank, Bank of India and the Punjab National Bank have entered into the field. To add to the list are the LIC of India and the private sector banks and other financial institutions. These institutions have successfully launched a variety of schemes to meet the diverse needs of millions of small investors. The Unit Trust of India has introduced huge portfolio of schemes like Unit 64, Mastergain, Mastershare, etc. It is the country's largest mutual fund company with over 25 million investors and a corpus exceeding ₹ 55,000 crores, accounting for nearly 10 per cent of the country's stock market capitalisation. The total corpus of the 13 other mutual funds in the country is less than ₹ 15,000 crores. The SBI fund has a corpus of ₹ 2,925 crores deployed in its 16 schemes servicing over 2.5 million shareholders.

There are also mutual funds with investments sourced abroad called 'Offshore Funds'. They have been established for attracting NRI investments to the capital market in India. The India Fund Unit Scheme 1986 traded in the London Stock Exchange and the India Fund Unit Scheme 1988 traded in the New York Stock Exchange were floated by the Unit Trust of India and 'The India Magnum Fund' was floated by the State Bank of India. At present, there are 16 different offshore Indian funds which have brought about $ 2.7 billion to the Indian market.

Besides the above, the LIC and the GIC have also entered into the market. Again, many private organisations have entered into the field. Most of the schemes have declared a dividend ranging between 13.5 per cent and 17 per cent. In most of the cases, it is around 14 per cent only.

The recent trend in the mutual fund industry is to go for tie-up arrangements with foreign collaborators. We find Tatas tying up with Kleinworth Benson; GIC with George Soros; Credit Capital with Lazard Brothers; Kothari with Pioneer; ICICI with JP Morgan; 20th Century with Morgan and so on. Of course, these tie-ups would bring in new perspective, systems and technology and this very foreign tag may add credit to the institution.

The private sector which entered the arena in 1993 is concentrating on the primary market. It is so because investments in new shares fetch appreciation between 30 and 1500 per cent in a very short period. Promoters too give preferential treatment to mutual funds because it reduces their marketing cost. Again, they go for fund participation in a venture even before it goes public. They see potential for immense appreciation in unlisted securities which intend to go to public with a short period of one year.

Today, mutual funds have started playing a positive role in the country's saving revolution.

The funds mobilised by mutual funds under various schemes as on March 29, 2016 are displayed in the following Table.

**TABLE 14.1: SCHEME-WISE RESOURCE MOBILISATION AND ASSETS UNDER MANAGEMENT BY MUTUAL FUNDS AND AUM AS ON MARCH 31, 2022**

| *Sr. No.* | *Schemes* | *Number of Schemes* | *Number of Folios* | *Funds Mobilised for the Period (₹crores)* | *Repurchase/ Redemption for the Period (₹crores)* | *Net Inflow/(+ve)/ Outflow(–ve)/ for the Period (₹crores)* | *Net Assets under Management (₹crores)* |
|---|---|---|---|---|---|---|---|
| | | *(As on March 31, 2022)* | | *(From April 01, 2021 to March 31, 2022)* | | | *As on March 31, 2022* |
| A | **Open-ended Schemes** | **1,120** | **12,88,53,769** | **93,11,181** | **89,79,812** | **3,31,370** | **36,95,800** |
| I | Income/Debt Oriented Schemes | 312 | 73,86,732 | 8,24,634 | 84,92,989 | –68,354 | 12,98,961 |
| II | Growth/Equity Oriented Schemes | 365 | 8,59,30,228 | 4,01,035 | 2,36,630 | 1,64,405 | 13,65,456 |
| III | Hybrid Schemes | 135 | 1,14,50,510 | 2,66,567 | 1,71,347 | 95,220 | 4,79,918 |
| IV | Solution Oriented Schemes | 35 | 55,78,745 | 3,400 | 2,135 | 1,265 | 29,537 |
| V | Other Schemes | 273 | 1,85,07,554 | 2,15,545 | 76,711 | 1,38,834 | 5,21,928 |

*Source:* SEBI Annual Report, 2021-22.

As on March 31, 2020, there were 44 active mutual funds of which 36 were in the private sector and the remaining 8 were in the public sector. The assets managed by the mutual fund industry were ₹ 22.3 lakh crores as on March 31, 2020.

## Dominance of small investors

No doubt, mutual funds have become a very popular investment vehicle for small investors. The dominance of retail investors in the mutual fund industry can be seen from the following analysis of folios of mutual funds.

**TABLE 14.2: NUMBER OF FOLIOS OF MUTUAL FUNDS**

| *Investor Classification* | *Number of Folios* | |
|---|---|---|
| | ***2020-21*** | ***2021-22*** |
| Individuals | 9,48,75,160 (96.9) | 12,57,54,565 (97.1) |
| NRIs/OCBs | 18,67,922 (1.9) | 23,44,636 (1.8) |
| FPIs | 3,014 (0%) | 199 (0%) |
| Corporates/Institutions/Others | 11,19,433 (1.1) | 14,05,252 (1.1) |
| **Total** | **9,78,65,529** | **12,95,04,652** |

***Source:*** SEBI Annual Report, 2021-22

## REASONS FOR SLOW GROWTH

Of late, mutual funds find their going very tough. Most of the funds are not able to collect the targeted amount from small investors. Investors tend to keep out of the new issue mutual funds and they prefer to buy units from the secondary market even by paying a brokerage fee of 3 per cent. The mutual fund industry has to face many problems also. Some of them are:

(i) **Disparity between NAV and listed price:** Small investors are really bewildered at the lack of proper pricing for their units. Though the NAV seems to be good, the listed prices are awfully poor. Of course, the NAV is used as a parameter to rate the performance of the mutual funds. However, in practice, almost all the mutual fund schemes are deeply discounted to their NAV by as much as 30 to 40 per cent. Thus, the real dilemma for the investor is this disparity between the NAV and the listed price. Due to this factor, investors are not able to dispose of their units in the market and hence there is no liquidity at all. As on 30.9.95, nearly 23 funds were traded at a discount to their NAV ranging from 5 per cent to 35 per cent.

(ii) **No uniformity in the calculation of NAV:** It is interesting to note that there is no standard formula for the calculation of the NAV. With the result, different companies apply different formula, and hence, any fruitful comparison of one fund with another is not at all possible. Hence, small investors cannot form a concrete opinion on the performance of different funds.

(iii) **Lack of transparency:** Mutual funds in India are not providing adequate information and materials to the investors. It was expected that they would provide a detailed investment pattern of their various schemes. They would also have frequent and continuing communications with the unit-holders. Unfortunately, most of the funds are not able to send even quarterly report to their members. For the success of mutual funds, it is very essential that they should create a good rapport with the investors by declaring their entire holdings to them.

(iv) **Poor investor servicing:** Mutual funds have failed to build up investor confidence by rendering poor services. Due to the recurring transfer problems and non-receipt of dividend in time, people are hesitant to touch the mutual fund scrip. Instances are there where people have to wait for more than six months to get their unit certificates. Again, the percentage of units under objection with the funds is also very high ranging between 3 per cent and 10 per cent. It is also said that the fake certificates are also very high. This deteriorated after-sales service to the investors has positively affected the growth of this industry. Many investors have been driven out of this mutual fund industry due to this poor servicing. In the case of a company, there is a statutory obligation to convene the meeting of the shareholders and place before them important matters for discussion. There is no such meeting in the case of a mutual fund company.

(v) **Too much dependence on outside agencies:** In India, most of the funds depend upon outside agencies to collect data and to do research. There is no doubt that research-driven funds can ensure good returns to its members. But, one should not rely on borrowed research. Since research involves a lot of money, mutual funds think that their overhead cost will go up and thereby their administrative expenses will go beyond the 3 per cent level fixed by the SEBI. In practice, it may not be so. In fact, they have to pay more for borrowed research and even that cannot be fully relied upon. Unless they set up their own research cell, they cannot succeed in the business.

(vi) **Investor's psychology:** Investors often compare units with that of shares and expect a high listing price. They don't realise that unit is a low-risk long-term instrument. Indeed, mutual funds are only for those who have the patience to wait for a long period say 3 to 5 years. But, in practice, people don't have the patience. Hence, units are not popular among the public.

(vii) **Absence of qualified sales force:** Efficient management of a fund requires expertised knowledge in portfolio management and skill in execution. Without professional agents and intermediaries, it cannot be managed efficiently. Unfortunately, such professional people are rare. One can find a network of qualified brokers to deal in shares and stocks. Such persons are conspicuously absent in the mutual fund industry and this absence of large and qualified sales force makes the industry suffer a setback.

(viii) **Other reasons:** Few funds which have not performed well have actually demoralised the investing public. Moreover, the listing of close-ended funds on the stock exchanges has compelled the medium and small investors to go back to the stock market and face the hassles and headaches of its dealing. Above all, there is a lack of investor education in the country. Most of the investors are not aware of the mutual fund industry and the various products offered by it.

## FUTURE OF MUTUAL FUND INDUSTRY

In spite of the above bottlenecks, the mutual fund industry is having a good prospect in our country. It is likely to show a good progress in the coming years due to a variety of factors:

1. The Securities and Exchange Board of India is lending its full support for the promotion of the mutual fund industry directly as well as indirectly. For instance, it has allowed the promoters of a company to retain 75 per cent holding. It has raised the minimum subscription amount to ₹ 5,000 for an individual investor for direct investment. It has also introduced the proportionate allotment scheme. All these factors stand in the way of small investors from entering into the capital market directly and they favour only big investors. So, a small investor has to necessarily seek the services of a mutual fund industry with his meagre savings.
2. Moreover, ever since the disbanding of the Comptroller of Capital Issues Office, many companies have entered into the market with a petty premium on their shares. Naturally, the small investors find them out of their reach, and hence, they have to seek the blessings of the mutual fund industry. One can easily subscribe to mutual funds shares at par with one's little investment.
3. In recent times, the interest rates on bank deposits have been declining. The household savers are looking for alternative avenues which could bring higher returns. The returns on the mutual fund schemes compare favourably with the returns on bank deposits.

4. The trend of rising P/E ratio, the entry of large domestic institutional investors, the opening of the market to the foreign investors, etc., would make stock market inaccessible to the small investors. Hence, they have to necessarily go to the mutual fund industry.
5. Mutual funds provide a wider range of products so as to meet the diverse needs of the investing public. The investors have a good choice to meet their different expectations like security, growth and liquidity.
6. The Government has also given the necessary impetus by providing tax concessions and tax exemptions. When the mutual fund industry is receiving a preferential treatment at the hands of the Government, it is bound to grow in future.
7. The Department of Company Affairs has agreed to amend the Companies Act to grant voting rights in companies for mutual funds.
8. Again mutual funds have been permitted to underwrite shares also.
9. The Union Budget 2009-10 contains many measures to encourage the mutual fund industry. These measures include:
   (*i*) Permission to launch real estate mutual funds.
   (*ii*) Adoption of revised norms for the valuation of debt securities.
   (*iii*) Mandatory listing of all close-ended schemes (except equity-linked savings schemes).
   (*iv*) Granting of permission to invest in Indian Depository Receipts.
10. The entry load for all direct applicants in mutual funds has been waived.
11. Recently, SEBI has recommended some measures to make it popular and to bring in more transparency in the working of mutual funds industry. They are:
   (*i*) Doubling of saving limits for mutual fund products such as equity linked savings schemes, mutual fund linked Retirement Plans etc. so that investors can avail tax benefits under Sec. 80C.
   (*ii*) Treating MF pension products on par with insurance so that final maturity amount may be tax exempt
   (*iii*) Introduction of Mutual Fund Retirement Plan which will carry an additional tax exempt limit of ₹ 50,000 so that they can compete with insurance and National Pension schemes.
   (*iv*) Permitting MFs to invest their seed capital in their own schemes with a view to driving greater accountability on their performance.
   (*v*) Increasing the net worth of the MF from ₹ 10 crores to ₹ 50 crores.
   (*vi*) Reducing the single issuer limit to 10 per cent of the NAV of the scheme and the sector-specific exposure limit from 30 per cent to 25 per cent to mitigate risks arising on account of high levels of exposure.
12. SEBI has made it mandatory for all mutual funds to display a coloured label depending upon the risk of investment since colours are a powerful mode of communication to stakeholders especially for the financially illiterate. Accordingly, it is mandatory to

use BLUE colour for low risk, YELLOW colour for medium risk and BROWN colour for high risk.

13. The level of risk in mutual fund schemes has been increased from three to five as low, moderately low, moderate, moderately high and high.
14. The single sector exposure limit has been reduced from 30 per cent of NAV to 25 per cent of NAV.
15. The total exposure of the debt schemes of mutual funds to a group shall not exceed 20 per cent of the net assets of the scheme.
16. Now, Gold Monetisation Scheme (GMS) 2015 has been introduced to replace Gold Deposit Schemes (GDS). This GMS has been designated as gold related instrument in line with banks' GDS.
17. Each mutual fund is required to disclose on its website details regarding the performance of each scheme managed by the AMC.

All these factors would go a long way in making mutual funds an increasingly popular, lucrative and cost-efficient vehicle for investment. The advent of mutual funds has augured well for genuine and good entrepreneurs too. The promoters suffered grievously during 1987 and early 1988 due to the failure of their new issues. Now 'mutual funds' are able to cycle the saver's resources productively for equity capital in the industry and thus, new entrepreneurs are guaranteed of their new issues.

If mutual funds ensure good returns, quick liquidity and safety and create a good rapport with the investors, their future will be very bright. They act as a media between bank deposit and share in the sense it involves a higher risk than a bank deposit and hence a better return, but a lower risk than a share and hence more safety. Hence, soon it would become and ideal vehicle for investment in India. It is time for the mutual funds to act as 'mutual friends' by creating a good rapport with the investors by rendering efficient and prompt services. No doubt, there is a bright future for mutual funds in India.

## QUESTIONS

### I. Objective type questions:

#### A. Fill in the blanks:

1. The corpus of the fund and its duration are prefixed under __________ funds.
2. __________ Fund invests in highly liquid securities like commercial paper.
3. The company which sets up a mutual fund is called __________.
4. The __________ is nothing but the intrinsic value of each unit of a mutual fund.
5. The small investor's gateway to enter into big companies is __________.

[**Key:** 1. close-ended, 2. Money market-mutual, 3. sponsor, 4. net asset value, 5. mutual fund.]

## B. Choose the best answer from the following:

1. The best suited fund to the business people is:

   (*a*) Income fund (*b*) Balanced fund

   (*c*) Growth fund (*d*) Taxation fund

2. The facility offered to investors to shift from one scheme to another under the same fund is called:

   (*a*) Rollover facility (*b*) Repurchase facility

   (*c*) Reissue facility (*d*) Lateral shifting facility

3. Mutual funds are very popular in:

   (*a*) USA (*b*) UK

   (*c*) Japan (*d*) India

4. The pattern of investment of a mutual fund is oriented towards fixed income yielding securities under:

   (*a*) Growth fund scheme (*b*) Income fund scheme

   (*c*) Balanced fund scheme (*d*) Money market mutual fund scheme

5. In India, the company which actually deals with the corpus of the mutual fund is called:

   (*a*) Sponsor company (*b*) Trustee company

   (*c*) Asset management company (*d*) Mutual fund company

[**Key:** 1. (*c*), 2. (*d*), 3 (*a*), 4. (*b*), 5. (*c*).]

## C. State whether the following statements are TRUE or FALSE:

1. The units of the open-ended funds cannot be publicly traded.
2. Rollover facility is available only in the case of close-ended funds.
3. Commercial banks can take up mutual funds business directly.
4. In India, the RBI regulates the functioning of the mutual funds.
5. Mutual funds can underwrite shares of public limited companies.

[**Key:** 1. True, 2. True, 3. False, 4. False, 5. True]

## II. Short answer type questions:

1. What is a mutual fund? Give an example.
2. Discuss any two schemes that can be offered by a mutual fund.
3. Distinguish between a share and a mutual fund unit.
4. What are the special features of an open-ended fund?
5. Distinguish between an income fund and a growth fund.
6. What is a specialised fund? Give an example.
7. What are the risk associated with mutual funds?
8. Describe the structure of the mutual fund operations in India.
9. What do you mean by Rollover facility? When is it available to an investor?

10. What is Net Asset Value? How is it computed?
11. What do you mean by Gold ETF? State its importance

## III. Essay type questions:

1. Define a mutual fund and describe the various schemes that can be offered by it.
2. 'Mutual funds provide stability to share prices, safety to investors and resources to prospective entrepreneurs'. Discuss.
3. What rights and facilities are available to an investor of a mutual fund? What factors should be considered before selecting a mutual fund?
4. To what extent commercial banks in India are better fitted to take up the mutual fund business? What problems do they encounter in this direction?
5. Discuss the present state of the mutual funds in India and outline the causes for their slow growth.

# 15 DISCOUNTING, FACTORING AND FORFAITING

## INTRODUCTION

In India, the financial services sector is developing at a faster rate so as to meet the emerging needs of the economy. Many innovative schemes have been introduced by this sector and one such area wherein it has been introduced is book debt financing. Financial institutions try to extend their financial assistance to a larger cross-section of the trading community through book debt financing. A kind of book debt financing is already practised in India by the commercial banks. It is nothing but bill financing. This type of financing is done either by way of direct purchase of bills of customers or discounting them.

## DISCOUNTING

Generally, a trade bill arises out of a genuine credit trade transaction. The supplier of goods draws a bill on the purchaser for the invoice price of the goods sold on credit. It is drawn for a short period of 3 to 6 months and in some cases for 9 months. The buyer of goods accepts the same and binds himself liable to pay the amount on the due date. In such a case, the supplier of goods has to wait for the expiry of the bill to get back the cost of the goods sold. It involves locking up of his working capital which is very much needed for the smooth running of the business or for carrying on the normal production process. It is where the commercial banks enter into as a financier.

The commercial banks provide immediate cash by discounting genuine trade bills. They deduct a certain charge as discount charges from the amount of the bill and the balance is credited to the customer's account and thus, the customer is able to enjoy credit facilities against the discounting of bills. Of course, this discount charges include interest for the unexpired period of the bill plus some service charges. Bill financing is the most liquid one from the banker's point of view since, in time of emergencies, they can take those bills to the Reserve Bank of India for rediscounting purposes. In fact, it was viewed primarily as a scheme of accommodation for banks. Now, the situation is completely changed. Today, it is viewed as a kind of loan backed by the security of bills.

Bill financing is superior to the conventional and traditional system of cash credit in many ways.

(*i*) First of all, it offers high liquidity, in the sense, funds could be recycled promptly and quickly through rediscounting.

(*ii*) It offers quick and high yield. The banker gets income in the form of discount charges at the time of discounting the bills.

(*iii*) Again, there is every opportunity to earn the spread between the rates of discount and rediscount.

(*iv*) Moreover, bills drawn by business people would never be dishonoured and they are not subject to any fluctuations in their values.

(*v*) Cumbersome procedures to create the security and the positive obligations to maintain it are comparatively very fewer.

(*vi*) Even if the bill is dishonoured, there is a simple legal remedy. The banker has to simply note and protest the bill and debit the customer's account. Bills are always drawn with recourse and hence, all the parties on the instrument are liable till the bill is finally discharged.

(*vii*) Above all, these bills would be very much useful as a base for the maintenance of reserve requirements like CRR and SLR.

It is for these reasons, the Reserve Bank of India has been trying its best to develop a good bill market in India. The Reserve Bank of India introduced a Bill Market Scheme as early as 1952 itself and thereafter, with some modifications. It has lowered the effective rate of interest on bill finance by 1 per cent below the cash credit rate. Despite many efforts of the Reserve Bank of India to promote and develop a good bill market, bill financing forms barely 5 per cent of the total credit extended by banks. The latest step of the Reserve Bank of India to promote the bill market is the launching of the factoring service organisations.

## FACTORING

As stated earlier, a lot of working capital is tied up in the form of trade debts. Collection of debts, especially for the small-scale and medium-scale companies is the biggest problem. The average collection period has been on the increase. Delays in collection process, in turn, lead to liquidity problems and consequently to delay in production and supplies. The peculiar situation in India is that a number of small-scale units are catering to the requirements of a single large buyer. This large buyer is always known for his procrastination in paying his small suppliers. The crux of the problem is not so much the failure to pay altogether as the failure to pay on time. As a result, the interest cost of financing book debts is quite heavy. This increase in cost of capital reduces profit and competitiveness of a company particularly the small ones in the market. Ultimately, the small unit may become even sick. To overcome this situation, the factoring service has been conceived.

## MEANING

The word 'Factor' has been derived from the Latin word 'Facere' which means 'to make or to do'. In other words, it means 'to get things done'. According to the Webster Dictionary, 'Factor' is an agent, as a banking or insurance company, engaged in financing the operations of certain companies or in financing wholesale or retail trade sales, through the purchase of account receivables. As the dictionary rightly points out, factoring is nothing but financing through purchase of accounts receivables.

Thus, factoring is a method of financing whereby a company sells its trade debts at a discount to a financial institution. In other words, factoring is a continuous arrangement between a financial institution, (namely the factor) and a company (namely the client) which sells goods and services to trade customers on credit. As per this arrangement, the factor purchases the client's trade debts including accounts receivables either with or without recourse to the client, and thus, exercises control over the credit extended to the customers and administers the sales ledger of his client. The client is immediately paid 80 per cent of the trade debts taken over and when the trade customers repay their dues, the factor will make the remaining 20 per cent payment. To put it in a layman's language, a factor is an agent who collects the dues of his client for a certain fee.

## DEFINITION

Robert W. Johnson in his book 'Financial Management' states, 'factoring is a service involving the purchase by a financial organisation, called a factor, of receivables owed to manufacturers and distributors by their customers, with the factor assuming full credit and collection responsibilities'.

According to V.A. Avadhani, 'factoring is a service of financial nature involving the conversion of credit bills into cash'.

In the words of Kohok, 'factoring is an asset-based means of financing by which the factor buys up the book debts of a company on a regular basis, paying cash down against receivables, and then collects the amounts from the customers to whom the company has supplied goods'.

Prof. S.P. Singh, a member of the study group appointed by the RBI to examine the feasibility of introducing factoring services in India feels that 'factoring which traditionally meant buying of book debts for cash is not merely invoice discounting or credit insurance'.

## MODUS OPERANDI

A factor provides finance to his client up to a certain percentage of the unpaid invoices which represent the sale of goods or services to approved customers. The modus operandi of the factoring scheme is as follows:

(*i*) There should be a factoring arrangement (invoice purchasing arrangement) between the client (which sells goods and services to trade customers on credit) and the factor, which is the financing organisation.

(*ii*) Whenever the client sells goods to trade customers on credit, he prepares invoices in the usual way.

(*iii*) The goods are sent to the buyers without raising a bill of exchange but accompanied by an invoice.

(*iv*) The debt due by the purchaser to the client is assigned to the factor by advising the trade customers, to pay the amount due to the client, to the factor.

(*v*) The client hands over the invoices to the factor under cover of a schedule of offer along with the copies of invoices and receipted delivery challans or copies of R/R or L/R.

(*vi*) The factor makes an immediate payment up to 80 per cent of the assigned invoices and the balance 20 per cent will be paid on realisation of the debt.

## TERMS AND CONDITIONS

The existence of an agreement between the factor and the client is central to the function of factoring. The main terms and conditions generally included in a factoring agreement are the following:

(*i*) Assignment of debt in favour of the factor,

(*ii*) Selling limits for the client,

(*iii*) Conditions within which the factor will have recourse to the client in case of non-payment by the trade customer,

(*iv*) Circumstances under which the factor will have recourse in case of non-payment,

(*v*) Details regarding the payment to the factor for his services, say for instance, as a certain percentage on turnover,

(*vi*) Interest to be allowed to the factor on the account where credit has been sanctioned to the supplier, and

(*vii*) Limit of any overdraft facility and the rate of interest to be charged by the factor.

## FUNCTIONS

As stated earlier, the term 'factoring' simply refers to the process of selling trade debts of a company to a financial institution. But, in practice, it is more than that. Factoring involves the following functions:

(*i*) Purchase and collection of debts,

(*ii*) Sales ledger management,

(*iii*) Credit investigation and undertaking of credit risk,

(*iv*) Provision of finance against debts, and

(*v*) Rendering consultancy services.

**(i) Purchase and collection of debts:** Factoring envisages the sale of trade debts to the factor by the company, *i.e.*, the client. It is where factoring differs from discounting. Under discounting, the financier simply discounts the debts backed by account receivables of the client.

He does so as an agent of the client. But, under factoring, the factor purchases the entire trade debts and thus, he becomes a holder for value and not an agent. Once the debts are purchased by the factor, collection of those debts becomes his duty automatically.

**(ii) Sales ledger management:** Sales ledger management function is an important one in factoring. Once the factoring relationship is established, it becomes the factor's responsibility to take care of all the functions relating to the maintenance of sales ledger. The factor has to credit the customer's account whenever payment is received, send monthly statements to the customers and to maintain liaison with the client and the customer to resolve all possible disputes. He has to inform the client about the balances in the account, the overdue period, the financial standing of the customers, etc. Thus, the factor takes up the work of monthly sales analysis, overdue invoice analysis and credit analysis.

**(iii) Credit investigation and undertaking of credit risk:** The factor has to monitor the financial position of the customer carefully, since, he assumes the risk of default in payment by customers due to their financial inability to pay. This assumption of credit risk is one of the most important functions which the factor accepts. Hence, before accepting the risk, he must be fully aware of the financial viability of the customer, his past financial performance record, his future ability, his honesty and integrity in the business world, etc. For this purpose, the factor also undertakes credit investigation work.

**(iv) Provision of finance:** After the finalisation of the agreement and sale of goods by the client, the factor provides 80 per cent of the credit sales as prepayment to the client. Hence, the client can go ahead with his business plans or production schedule without any interruption. This payment is generally made without any recourse to the client. That is, in the event of non-payment, the factor has to bear the loss of payment.

**(v) Rendering consultancy services:** Apart from the above, the factor also provides management services to the client. He informs the client about the additional business opportunities available, the changing business and financial profiles of the customers, the likelihood of coming recession, etc.

## TYPES OF FACTORING

The type of factoring services varies on the basis of the nature of transactions between the client and the factor, the nature and volume of client's business, the nature of factor's security, etc. In general, the factoring services can be classified as follows:

(*i*) Full service factoring or without recourse factoring.

(*ii*) With recourse factoring.

(*iii*) Maturity Factoring.

(*iv*) Bulk factoring.

(*v*) Invoice factoring.

(*vi*) Agency factoring.

(*vii*) International factoring.

(*viii*) Suppliers' guarantee factoring.

(*ix*) Limited factoring.

(*x*) Buyer based factoring.

(*xi*) Seller based factoring.

**(i) Full service factoring or without recourse factoring:** Under this type, a factor provides all kinds of services discussed above. Thus, a factor provides finance, administers the sales ledger, collects the debts at his risk and renders consultancy service. This type of factoring is a standard one. If the debtors fail to repay the debts, the entire responsibility falls on the shoulders of the factor since he assumes the credit risk also. He cannot pass on this responsibility to his client and, hence, this type of factoring is also called 'Without Recourse' factoring.

**(ii) With recourse factoring:** As the very name suggests, under this type, the factor does not assume the credit risk. In other words, if the debtors do not repay their dues in time and if their debts are outstanding beyond a fixed period, say 60 to 90 days from the due date, such debts are automatically assigned back to the client. The client has to take up the work of collection of overdue account by himself. If the client wants the factor to go on with the collection work of overdue accounts, the client has to pay extra charges called 'Refactoring Charges'.

**(iii) Maturity factoring:** Under this type, the factor does not provide immediate cash payment to the client at the time of assignment of debts. He undertakes to pay cash as and when collections are made from the debtors. The entire amount collected less factoring fees is paid to the client immediately. Hence, it is also called 'Collection Factoring'. In fact, under this type, no financing is involved. But all other services are available.

**(iv) Bulk factoring:** Under this type, the factor provides finance after disclosing the fact of assignment of debts to the debtors concerned. This type of factoring is resorted to when the factor is not fully satisfied with the financial condition of the client. The work relating to sales ledger administration, credit control, collection work, etc., has to be done by the client himself. Since the notification has been made, the factor simply collects the debts on behalf of the client. This is otherwise called as 'Disclosed Factoring' or 'Notified Factoring'.

**(v) Invoice factoring:** Under this type, the factor simply provides finance against invoices without undertaking any other functions. All works connected with sales administration, collection of dues, etc., have to be done by the client himself. The debtors are not at all notified and hence they are not aware of the financing arrangement. This type of factoring is very confidential in nature and hence it is called 'Confidential Invoice Discounting' or 'Undisclosed Factoring'.

**(vi) Agency factoring:** The word agency has no meaning as far as factoring is concerned. Under this type, the factor and the client share the work between themselves as follows:

(*a*) The client has to look after the sales ledger administration and collection work, and.

(*b*) The factor has to provide finance and assume the credit risk.

**(vii) International factoring:** Under this type, the services of a factor in a domestic business are simply extended to international business. Factoring is done purely on the basis of the invoice prepared by the exporter. Thus, the exporter is able to get immediate cash to the extent of 80 per cent of the export invoice under international factoring. International factoring is facilitated with the help of export factors and import factors.

**(viii) Suppliers' guarantee factoring:** This type of factoring is suitable for business establishments which sell goods through middlemen. Generally, goods are sold through wholesalers, retailers or through middlemen. In such cases, the factor guarantees the supplier of goods against invoices raised by the supplier upon another supplier. The bills are assigned in favour of the factor who guarantees payment of those bills. This enables the supplier to earn profits without much financial involvement.

**(ix) Limited factoring:** Under this type, the factor does not take up all the invoices of a client. He discounts only selected invoices on merit basis and converts credit bills into cash in respect of those bills only.

**(x) Buyer based factoring:** In most cases, the factor is acting as an agent of the seller. But under this type, the buyer approaches a factor to discount his bills. Thus, the initiative for factoring comes from the buyers' end. The approved buyers of a company approach a factor for discounting their bills to the company in question. In such cases, the claims on such buyers are paid by discounting the bills without recourse to the seller and the seller also gets ready cash. This facility is available only to reputed creditworthy buyers and hence it is also called 'Selected Buyer Based Factoring'.

**(xi) Seller based factoring:** Under this type, the seller, instead of discounting his bills, sells all his accounts receivables to the factor, after invoicing the customers. The seller's job is over as soon as he prepares the invoices. Thereafter, all the documents connected with the sale are handed over to the factor who takes over the remaining functions. This facility is extended to reputed and creditworthy sellers and hence it is also called 'Selected Seller Based Factoring'.

## FACTORING VS. DISCOUNTING

Factoring differs from discounting in many respects. They are:

(*i*) Factoring is a broader term covering the entire trade debts of a client whereas discounting covers only those trade debts which are backed by accounts receivables.

(*ii*) Under factoring, the factor purchases the trade debt and thus becomes a holder for value. But, under discounting the financier acts simply as an agent of his customer and he does not become the owner. In other words, discounting is a kind of advance against bills, whereas factoring is an outright purchase of trade debts.

(*iii*) The factors may extend credit without any recourse to the client in the event of non-payment by customers. But, discounting is always made with recourse to the client.

(*iv*) Accounts receivables under discount are subject to rediscounting, whereas it is not possible under factoring.

(*v*) Factoring involves purchase and collection of debts, management of sales ledger, assumption of credit risk, provision of finance and rendering of consultancy services. But, discounting involves simply the provision of finance alone.

(*vi*) Bill discounting finance is a specific one in the sense that it is based on an individual bill arising out of an individual transaction only. On the other hand, factoring is based on the 'whole turnover', *i.e.,* a bulk finance is provided against a number of unpaid invoices.

(*vii*) Under discounting, the drawee is always aware of the bank's charge on receivables. But, under undisclosed factoring, everything is kept highly confidential.

(*viii*) Bill financing through discounting requires registration of charges with the Registrar of Companies. In fact, factoring does not require such registration.

(*ix*) Discounting is always a kind of 'in-balance sheet financing'. That is, both the amount of receivables and bank credit are shown in the balance sheet itself due to its `with recourse' nature. But, factoring is always 'off-balance sheet financing'.

## COST OF FACTORING

The cost of factoring comprises of two aspects namely finance charges and service fees. Since the factor provides 80 per cent of the invoice as credit, he levies finance charges. This charge is normally the same interest rates which are in vogue in the banking system. Factoring is a cheap source because the interest is charged only on the amount actually provided to the client as repayment of his supplies. Apart from this financial charge, a service charge is also levied. This service fees is charged in proportion to the gross value of the invoice factored based on sales volume, number of invoices, work involved in collections, etc. Generally, the factor charges a service fee on the total turnover of the bills. It is around 1 per cent. If the bills get paid earlier, service charges could be reduced depending upon the volume of work involved.

### Pricing of factoring services

While pricing factoring services, the following components should be taken into account:

(*i*) Factoring fees or administrative charges.

(*ii*) Discount charges.

### Factoring fees

This is charged mainly as administrative expenses for providing various services to the clients namely:

(*i*) Sales ledger administration.

(*ii*) Credit control administration.

(*iii*) Bad debts administration.

This fees is normally computed with reference to the projected sales turnover of the client during the next twelve months. It is always quoted as a per cent of projected sales turnover. Generally, this charge varies between 1 per cent and 2.5 per cent of the projected turnover. In fact, the quantum of levy actually depends on several factors as given below:

(*a*) Reputation of the client as well as the debtors.

(*b*) Nature of the industry to which the client belongs.

(*c*) Volume of sales per annum.

(*d*) Terms of sales.

(*e*) Average invoice value.

(*f*) Security available to the factor.

(*g*) Type of factoring service offered.

(*h*) Profit margin.

Usually, a minimum handling/administrative charge is stipulated to which a certain per cent of the projected turnover is added.

### ❖ Discount charges

For providing instant credit to the client by way of prepayment, some charges have to be levied and they are called discount charges. This charge is normally linked with the base rate.

## COSTING AND PRICING TECHNIQUE

Generally, cost-plus pricing strategy is adopted for fixing the price for factoring services. Therefore, factoring charge = cost + profit.

While arriving at the cost, one should take into account the fixed cost which remains fixed irrespective of volume of business and the variable cost which varies directly with the volume of business transacted.

Again, the pricing strategy depends on the costing technique that is being adopted, *i.e.*, either absorption costing or marginal costing. Absorption costing is based on the principle that the client would be required to pay for the entire fixed cost as well as the variable cost while in the case of marginal costing, the entire variable cost and a part of fixed cost only would be recovered.

Normally, the factoring cost involves both direct cost as well as administrative cost as shown below:

**Cost Sheet for Factoring Service**

| | | | |
|---|---|---|---|
| (A) | Direct Cost | | |
| | Per invoice amount | ......... | |
| | Per active account | ......... | |
| | Per debtor account | ......... | |
| | Per client | ......... | % of turnover |
| | Bad debt provision | ......... | % of turnover |
| | Total direct cost | ......... | |
| (B) | Administrative Cost | ......... | % of turnover |
| (C) | Total Factoring Cost | = A + B | |
| (D) | Profit | = ......... | % of turnover |

∴ (E) Required Factoring Charge $= \dfrac{C + D}{\text{Total Turnover}} \times 100$

= % of turnover

### *Example: Illustration*

X has a turnover of ₹ 20 lakhs during the last 12 months. The computation of costing and the resultant pricing for X will be as follows:

| *Description* | *No. of Instruments* | *Cost per Instrument* ₹ | *Total Cost* ₹ |
|---|---|---|---|
| Invoices | 1,800 | 1.50 | 2,700.00 |
| Active accounts | 80 | 50.00 | 4,000.00 |
| No. of customers | 120 | 4.00 | 480.00 |
| Per client - 1 per cent of turnover (20 lakhs) | | | 2,000.00 |
| Transmission cost | | 10 per cent of turnover | 200.00 |
| Total direct cost (A) | | | 9,380.00 |
| Administrative cost (B) | | 15 per cent of turnover | 3,000.00 |
| Total operative cost (C = A + B) | | | 12,380.00 |
| Profit required | | 1 per cent of turnover | 20,000.00 |
| Hence, total required income | | | 32,380.00 |
| ∴ Factoring charge would be | | = 1.62 | |

## ❖ Accounting system

Generally, a factoring company keeps the following accounts to record the factoring transactions:

**(i) Sales ledger control account:** It contains the main asset account of various debtors of clients. It is nothing but the client's debtors accounts.

**(ii) Debt purchase account:** It is a replica account of sales ledger control account. In other words, it is a copy account of sales ledger control account and hence the sales ledger control account and debt purchased account would depict the same balance at a given period. It is also called Master Control Account.

**(iii) Client current account:** It is nothing but a statement of account of a client showing all debits and credits.

**(iv) Bank account:** It is used to record all cash received from debtors of clients and cash paid to the client.

Sales Ledger Control Account and Debt Purchased Account must be maintained separately for each customer.

## ❖ Accounting procedure

The following journal entries have to be passed at different stages:

**1. When invoices are assigned**

Sales Ledger Control A/c Dr.

To Debt Purchased A/c

(Being debtors assigned)

**2. When payment (80 per cent of invoice) is made to client**

Client Current A/c Dr.

To Bank A/c

(Being cash paid to client)

**3. When payment is made by debtors**

(*a*) Bank A/c Dr.

To Client Current A/c

(Being cash received)

(*b*) Debt Purchased A/c Dr.

To Sales Ledger Control A/c

(Being debtors' account cancelled)

**4. When credit notes (if any) are assigned**

Debt Purchased A/c Dr.

To Sales Ledger Control A/c

(Being credit notes adjusted)

At the end of each month, a copy of the debt purchased account and the clients current account would be sent to the client. From these accounts, the client would be able to know the extent of collections made, outstanding amount, etc.

## BENEFITS

Factoring offers a number of benefits to the clients. Some of the important benefits are:

**(i) Financial service:** Many of the manufacturers and traders find their working capital being locked up in the form of trade debts. This has been a great handicap to the small-scale and medium-scale manufacturers because they have to wait for 3 months to 9 months to realise their debts. In the mean time, the business may suffer due to want of funds. In fact, many business concerns fail more as a result of inadequate cash flow than anything else. The key to successful working capital management lies in the ability of an enterprise to convert sales into cash flow and the speed at which it is done. The major benefit of the factoring service is that the clients will be able to convert their trade debts into cash up to 80 per cent immediately as soon as the credit sales are over. They need not wait for months together to get cash for recycling.

Another major advantage is that there are no constraints by way of fixed limits as in the case of cash credit or O.D. As sales grow, the financial assistance also grows and both are directly proportional to each other.

The greatest advantage is that factoring assures immediate cash flow. When the cash position improves, the client is able to make his purchases on cash basis and thus, he can avail of cash discount facilities also.

**(ii) Collection service:** Collection of debts is another problematic area for many concerns. It is found that over 60 per cent of the total sales of the SSI sector and over 50 per cent of total sales of the medium-scale and large-scale sector are made on "On Account Terms of Payment", *i.e.,* credit sales. It means that collection of debts becomes an important internal credit management and it requires more and more time. So, industrialists cannot concentrate on production. Delay in collection process often leads to delay in production and supplies. Moreover, the interest cost of financing book debts is also on the increase. Ultimately, it affects the profitability of the company. Now, this collection work is completely taken up by the factoring organisation, leaving the client to concentrate on production alone. This is an important service rendered by a factor to his client. The cost of collection is also cut down as a result of the professional expertise of a factor.

**(iii) Credit risk service:** In the absence of a factor, the entire credit risk has to be borne by the client himself. Bad debts eat away the profits of a concern and in some cases, it may lead to the closure of a business. But, once the factoring relationship is established, the client need not bother about the loss due to bad debts. The factor assumes the risk of default in payment by customers and thus, the client is assured of complete realisation of his book debts. Even if the customer fails to pay the debt, it becomes the responsibility of the factor to pay that amount to the client. It is the greatest advantage of factoring.

**(iv) Provision of expertised 'Sales Ledger Management' service:** Administration of sales ledger is purely an accounting function which can be performed efficiently only by a few. In fact, the success of any organisation depends upon the efficiency with which the sales ledger is managed. It requires a specialised knowledge which the client may not possess. But, the client can receive services like maintenance of accounting records, monthly sales analysis, overdue invoice analysis and customer payment statement from the factor. Besides, he maintains contact with customers to ensure that they repay their dues promptly. Thus, it becomes the factor's responsibility to take care of all the functions relating to the maintenance of sales ledger. Thus, factoring offers an excellent credit control for the client.

**(v) Consultancy service:** Factors are professionals in offering management services like consultancy. They collect information regarding the creditworthiness of the customers of their clients, ascertain their track record, quality of portfolio turnover, average size of inventory, etc., and pass on the same to their clients. It helps the clients avoid poor quality and risky customers. They also advise their clients on important financial matters. Generally, no time is available to the client for investigating his customer's credit standing. Now, the factor takes up this work on behalf of his client.

**(vi) Economy in servicing:** Factors are able to render very economic service to their clients because their overhead cost is spread over a number of clients. Moreover, their service charges are also reasonable. Factoring is a cheap source of finance to the client because the interest rate is charged only on the amount actually provided to the client, say, for instance, 80 per cent of his total invoices and not on the total amount of the invoices. Thus, clients are able to get factoring services at economic rates.

**(vii) Off-balance sheet financing:** Factoring is an off-balance sheet means of financing. When the factor purchases the book debts of the client, these debts no longer exist on the current asset side of the balance sheet. It leads to reduction in debts and less collection problems. The client can utilise the money so received to reduce his current liabilities. It means an improved current ratio.

This can be better understood by means of an illustration.

Given below is the Balance Sheet of X Co. Ltd.

**Balance Sheet before Factoring Arrangement**

| ***Liabilities*** | ₹ | ***Assets*** | ₹ |
|---|---|---|---|
| Current Liabilities | | Current Assets | |
| Bank loan — against stock | 5,00,000 | Stock | 8,00,000 |
| Bank loan — against bills | 4,00,000 | Receivables | 6,00,000 |
| Others | 2,00,000 | Others | 2,00,000 |
| Net working capital | 5,00,000 | | |
| | 16,00,000 | | 16,00,000 |

Now, the current ratio comes to 16,00,000 : 11,00,000 = 1.45 : 1

Now, receivables of ₹ 6,00,000 are purchased by the factoring agent. The factor pays 80 per cent cash immediately. So, the company gets ₹ 4,80,000 which is used for paying some liabilities like bank loan and others. The amount due from the factor comes to ₹ 1,20,000 being 20 per cent of the balance of receivables.

**The New Balance Sheet after Factoring Arrangement**

| ***Liabilities*** | ₹ | ***Assets*** | ₹ |
|---|---|---|---|
| Current Liabilities | | Current Assets | |
| Bank loan against stock | 5,00,000 | Stock | 8,00,000 |
| Others | 1,20,000* | Receivables | |
| | | (Due from factor) | 1,20,000 |
| Networking capital | 5,00,000 | Others | 2,00,000 |
| | 11,20,000 | | 11,20,000 |

Now the current ratio comes to 11,20,000 : 6,20,000 = 1.8 : 1

****Note:*** Bank loan against bills is paid out of ₹ 4,80,000 received from the factor. The balance ₹ 80,000 is paid to other liabilities. Hence, other liabilities appear as ₹ 1,20,000 in the new balance sheet.

**(viii) Trade benefits:** Availability of ready cash against bills enables the supplier to negotiate better prices for the inputs and also offer finer terms to customers. It ensures a steady flow of inputs on the one hand and better market prospects on the other. Again, factoring enables the supplier to concentrate on production and materials management without bothering about the financial management. Factoring enables clients to offer longer credit facilities to their customers and thus to attract more business. Thus, many trade benefits are available under factoring.

**(ix) Miscellaneous service:** Generally, factors are able to computerise their operations fully. So, they are able to render prompt service at reasonable rates. They spend more on MIS analysis. They also build bigger credit library of debtors by means of collecting information about new debtors.

Thus, improved cash flow through realisation of trade debts by factoring, efficient follow-up of collections, computerised sales ledger maintenance and the competitive rates are the main benefits of factoring.

## FACTORING IN INDIA

In India, the idea of providing factoring services was first thought of by the Vaghul Working Group. It had recommended that banks and private non-banking financial companies should be encouraged to provide factoring services with a view to helping the industrialists and traders to tide over their financial crunch arising out of delays in the realisation of their book debts. The RBI subsequently constituted a study group in January 1988 under the chairmanship of Mr. C.S. Kalyanasundaram, former Managing Director of the SBI, to examine the feasibility of starting factoring services. On the recommendation of the committee, the Banking Regulations Act was amended in July 1990 with a view of enabling commercial banks to take up factoring services by forming separate subsidiaries.

In the public interest and in the interest of banking policy, the RBI is of the view that:

(*i*) The banks should not directly undertake the business of factoring.

(*ii*) The banks may set up separate subsidiaries or invest in factoring companies jointly with other banks.

(*iii*) A factoring subsidiary or a joint venture factoring company may undertake the factoring business. But, they should not finance other factoring companies.

(*iv*) The banks can invest in the shares of factoring companies not exceeding 10 per cent of the paid-up capital and reserves of the bank concerned.

But, recently in February 1994, the RBI has permitted all banks to enter into factoring business departmentally. Perhaps, this step would have been taken with a view of giving further impetus to the factoring system. Since factoring requires special skills and infrastructure, the RBI has further stipulated that:

(*i*) Factoring activities should be treated on par with loans and advances and should accordingly be given risk weight of 100 per cent for calculation of capital to risk asset ratio.

(*ii*) A bank's exposure shall not exceed 25 per cent of the bank's capital funds to an individual borrower and 50 per cent to a group of borrowers. Factoring would also be covered within the above exposure ceiling along with equipment leasing and hire purchase finance.

(*iii*) Factoring services should be provided only in respect of those invoices which represent genuine trade transactions.

In India, the factoring service was first started by the State Bank of India in association with the Small Industries Development Bank of India, Union Bank of India, State Bank of

Saurashtra and State Bank of Indore. The pioneering factoring company founded by the SBI is called 'SBI-Factors and Commercial Services Pvt. Ltd., (SBI-FACS)'. It was started in July 1991 with a subscribed capital of ₹ 25 crores. It has been allotted the Western Zone composing of Maharashtra, Gujarat, Goa, Madhya Pradesh, The Union Territories of Dadra and Nagar HAVELI, Daman and Diu. Similarly, the RBI has allotted the Southern Region to the Canara Bank, the Northern Region to the Punjab National Bank and the Eastern Region to the Allahabad Bank for providing necessary factoring services to the clients of those regions. This zonal restriction has been removed by the RBI in 1993. In South, Canara Bank has already established Can Factors Ltd. Now, these two factoring companies can operate in the centres outside their given zones. Besides the above, some non-banking companies also have started entering into factoring services. Now, seven NBFC factors do the majority of factoring. They are Canbank Factors, India Factoring and Finance, Siemens Factoring, Billy Financial Services, IFC Factors and Pinnacle Capital Solutions. Recently, all existing non-deposit-taking non-banking finance companies and non-banking investment and credit companies with an asset size of ₹ 1,000 crores and above have been permitted to undertake factoring business. Thus, factoring service has got a very bright future in India due to its superiority over other forms of financing.

## ❖ Regulation of Factors (Assignment of Receivables) Bill 2011

The Government is in the process of enacting the above bill which seeks to provide for and regulate the assignment of receivables by making provisions for registration and rights and obligations of parties. The bill empowers the RBI to issue directions, call for information from the factors and prohibit financial institutions from undertaking business if the factor fails to comply with the directions given by the RBI. The bill also provides for the establishments of a central registry which would maintain details regarding all transactions carried out by factors. It makes registration of all factor transactions mandatory. Besides, factors would be entitled to take legal resource for recovering assigned debt and receivables from buyers of goods and services.

## ❖ Factoring Regulation (Amendment) Bill 2020

The above Bill has been passed by taking into account all the recommendations of the Standing Committee on Finance submitted on Feb. 2020. The main features are:

(*i*) Integration of Trade Receivable Discounting System (TReDS) with GSTN e-invoicing portal leading to automatic uploading of all GST invoices on the TReDS platform to enable real-time sharing of data that will allow buyers and sellers to have a single window access to invoices.

(*ii*) Bringing invoices arising from Central and State Governments compulsorily under the ambit of TReDS so that payments pending from the Government which are approved for MSMEs are made available to them on a timely basis.

(*iii*) Extension of credit insurance for domestic factoring so that additional protection may be provided to the factor.

(*iv*) Introducing credit rating mechanism for receivables.

(*v*) Granting a special status of specialised MSMEs Funding Agency to factoring companies so that a major portion of their corpus is earmarked for the benefit of MSMEs.

# INTERNATIONAL FACTORING

Generally, factoring services are very popular for domestic business. They are gradually entering into export business also.

Just as domestic suppliers, the exporters also find that there is a considerable delay in receiving payments from the importers. As a result, they are hard pressed for money to ensure their profitability as well as to maintain and expand their export business. In this situation, international factoring comes really handy to them to find the required resources.

## ❖ Definition

The International Institute for the Unification of Private Law in 1988 has defined international factoring as follows:

'Factoring means an arrangement between a factor and his client which includes at least two of the following services to be provided by the factor: (*i*) Finance, (*ii*) Maintenance of accounts, (*iii*) Collection of Debts and (*iv*) Protection against credit risks'.

As the definition points out, the services of a factor in a domestic business are simply extended to international trade. However, the functioning of this scheme is different depending upon the type of export factoring and the arrangement made by the exporter and the factor.

## ❖ Types of export factoring

Generally, in the absence of factoring, all export finance transactions are backed by Letters of Credit. But, factoring relates purely to 'Open Account Transactions' with no promissory notes and collaterals. Factoring is done entirely on the basis of the invoice prepared by the exporter and so it is purely an 'invoice-based export finance' technique.

In an international factoring transaction, there are four parties namely:

(*i*) The exporter who is taking the place of a client in a domestic transaction.

(*ii*) The importer who is taking the role of a customer in a domestic transaction.

(*iii*) Export Factor (EF).

(*iv*) Import Factor (IF).

The exporter (client) and the factor enter into an agreement for export factoring which may take any one of the following types:

(*i*) Two factor system.

(*ii*) Single factor system.

(*iii*) Direct export factor system.

(*iv*) Direct import factor system.

## ❖ Two factor system

There are two factors under this system — one in the export's country and the other in the importer's country. When the exporter wants to do business with some importer or importers, he approaches the factor in his country and informs him of his business proposal, the likely size of the business, the number of invoices likely to be raised, the value of the consignment and the currency involved.

This export factor in turn informs the same to his counterpart, *i.e.*, import factor in the importing country. The import factor makes enquiries regarding the financial position of the importer and his dealings and, if satisfied, he conveys the message to the export factor. He also indicates the limit for factoring and his commission for undertaking this work. Then, the export factor contacts the exporter and conveys the positive findings and his readiness to cover the credit risk through factoring. If the rates are acceptable to the exporter, he signs an agreement with the export factor.

Once this factoring relationship is established, the exporter sends the goods to the importer along with the invoice with a condition that the payments should be made to the import factor. Two copies of the invoices are sent to the export factor along with a notification that the debts have been assigned to the import factor. At this stage, the export factor makes payment immediately to the extent of 80 per cent of the invoice amount to the exporter.

Thereafter, the export factor informs the import factor about the financial deal by sending a copy of the invoice. Now, it becomes the responsibility of the import factor to monitor and maintain the account and take all possible efforts to collect the amount at the due date. When the amount is collected, it is sent to the export factor. In case of any default, the import factor has to pay the amount to the export factor from his own sources.

When the amount is realised from the import factor, the export factor pays the balance of 20 per cent of the invoice amount to the exporter. The cost of factoring is debited to the exporter's account and the commission due to the import factor is also sent. Thus, the financial dealing has to be carried out with the help of two factors and hence it is called 'Two factor system'.

### ❖ Single factor system

Under this system also, two factoring companies, as stated earlier, are involved. However, the responsibility of making the payment, maintenance of books of accounts, its administration, etc., initially rest with the export factor. But, just to cover the credit risk, the export factor enters into an agreement with the import factor to collect the debt from the importer, in case the export factor is not able to realise the amount. If such a contingency arises, the export factor has to assign the debt in favour of the import factor. Thus, the import factor is called upon to assist the export factor only during the times of difficulties in realising the debt. Otherwise, the export factor himself will do all the work. So, it is called 'Single factor system'.

### ❖ Direct export factor system

Under the system, there is a factoring agreement directly between the exporter and this export factor and no other party is involved. The entire export credit risk, the administration of the account, the advance payments, etc. have to be done only by the export factor. Hence, it is called 'direct' export factor system'.

### ❖ Direct import factor system

It is just the opposite of direct export factor system. The agreement is between the exporter and the import factor in the importer's country. The import factor assumes all responsibilities for the collection of the debt from the importer.

## FACTORING IN OTHER COUNTRIES

In European countries, factoring organisations have an option to finance both domestic and export business. The tough business conditions and continued recession across Europe have affected the factoring business of late. Hence, some factoring organisations had to wind up their business in UK as well as in the USA. Again, there has been merger of factoring companies. Now, more than 700 factoring companies are operating in some forty countries. Nine out of ten of the world's strongest banks now have their own foothold in the factoring industry.

In the USA, the Fuji Bank's Chicago-based Heller financial has taken over the CIT Group factoring. It has become the biggest US factor. Similarly, BNY Financial acquired BT Factors in 1990. Again, Citizen's and Southern Commercial acquired the Security Pacific in 1989 and it is now called 'National Bank Commercial'. In all, there were 17 big factors and the total US factoring business volume was more than $ 51 billion in 1991. In the USA, the factoring organisations specialise in financing the apparel business which accounts for nearly 75 per cent of the total volume of factoring business.

Italy occupies the first position in terms of factoring business volume, followed by the USA. The UK occupies the third position. In Japan, the first specialised factoring company was established only in 1972 when Sanwa Bank started the Sanwa Business Credit Co. The special feature of the Japanese factoring business is that they focus on discounting of promissory notes in contrast to cash financing of accounts receivables.

Factoring is also becoming popular in North America, Asia, Singapore, Malaysia and South Korea. It is said that factoring in Singapore and Malaysia is growing at a faster rate of 40 per cent a year.

However, export factoring is popular in countries like Germany, Belgium and Netherlands where the export factoring business accounts for nearly 30 per cent of the total factoring business. In India also, the ECGC is thinking of introducing such a scheme very shortly. The latest country to take up the business of factoring is China, which is giving importance to export factoring.

## ACCOUNTING TREATMENT IN THE BOOKS OF FACTOR AND FIRM

Factor, being an intermediate between the customers and client, should be responsible to record all and sundry transactions, maintain ledger accounts and record for allied matters. The accounting entries are:

**Accounting entries in the books of factor**

(*i*) On payment of advance to seller

| | | | |
|---|---|---|---|
| Seller's Personal A/c | Dr. | ... | |
| To Bank A/c | | | ... |

(*ii*) Sending invoice to buyer

| | | | |
|---|---|---|---|
| Buyer's Personal A/c (debtor) | Dr. | ... | |
| To Sales A/c | | | ... |

(*iii*) On due date, when amount is received

| | | | |
|---|---|---|---|
| Bank A/c | Dr. | ... | |
| To Debtor's Personal A/c | | | ... |

(*iv*) Payment of balance of money to client (seller)

| | | | |
|---|---|---|---|
| Seller's Personal A/c | Dr. | ... | |
| To Bank A/c | | | ... |

(*v*) He pays the balance payment only after deducting factoring commission and interest.

(*vi*) Transferring factoring commission and interest to Profit and Loss account.

| | | | |
|---|---|---|---|
| Factoring Commission A/c | Dr. | ... | |
| Interest A/c | Dr. | ... | |
| To Profit and Loss A/c | | | ... |

(*vii*) When a buyer refuses to pay/pays part amount and the rest become bad debts, such bad debt is a loss to the factor.

| | | | |
|---|---|---|---|
| Bad Debts A/c | Dr. | ... | |
| Bank A/c | Dr. | ... | |
| To Debtor's Account | | | ... |

(*viii*) Such bad debt is adjusted in factoring commission.

| | | | |
|---|---|---|---|
| Factoring Commission A/c | Dr. | ... | |
| To Bad Debts A/c | | | ... |

(*ix*) The amount of factoring commission is transferred to Profit and Loss account.

**Accounting entries in the books of firm**

(*i*) When advance is received from factors

| | | | |
|---|---|---|---|
| Bank A/c | Dr. | ... | |
| To Factor's A/c | | | ... |

(*ii*) When factoring commission is paid

| | | | |
|---|---|---|---|
| Factoring Commission A/c | Dr. | ... | |
| To Bank A/c | | | ... |

(*iii*) When interest on advance is paid

| | | | |
|---|---|---|---|
| Interest on Factoring Advance A/c | Dr. | ... | |
| To Bank A/c | | | ... |

(*iv*) On transfer of factoring commission and interest to Profit and Loss account.

| | | | |
|---|---|---|---|
| Profit and Loss A/c | Dr. | ... | |
| To Factoring Commission A/c | | | ... |
| To Interest on Factoring Advance A/c | | ... | |

## ❖ Costs and benefits of factoring

There are two types of cost involved in factoring, *viz.*, (*i*) Factoring commission, and (*ii*) Interest on advances given to the factor.

Factoring commission is charged for credit evaluation, collection and other services and also to cover bad debt losses. It is charged as a percentage of full net face value of receivables factored. In advanced countries like USA and UK, Factoring Commission ranges from 1 to 3 per cent. In India, a charge around 2.5 to 3 per cent is made. The interest on advances ranges between 18 and 22 per cent.

The benefits of factoring to the business are savings in cost of credit administration and cost of bad debt.

A business concern has to evaluate the cost and benefit to arrive at a decision before using the factoring service.

### *Illustration*

A manufacturing concern has a total sales of ₹ 16,00,000 and its average collection period is 90 days. The past experience indicates a bad debt loss around 1.5 per cent of credit sales. The company spends ₹ 25,000 on credit administration and collection. A factor is prepared to buy the firm's receivables by charging 2 per cent commission. The factor will pay advance receivable at an interest of 18 per cent after withholding 10 per cent as reserve.

Calculate the cost and benefit to the company and also effective rate of annual cost of factoring.

## ❖ Cost and benefit

Credit Sales = ₹ 16,00,000

Average Collection Period = 90 days

Average Receivables = ₹ 4,00,000

Factoring Commission $= \frac{4,00,000}{100} \times 2$

= ₹ 8,000

Reserve $= \frac{4,00,000}{100} \times 10$

= ₹ 40,000

Amount available for advance = 4,00,000 – 8,000 – 40,000

= ₹ 3,52,000

Interest on advance $= \frac{3,52,000 \times 18 \times 90}{100 \times 360} \times 18 \times 90$

= ₹ 15,840

= 3,52,000 – 15,840

Advance to be paid = ₹ 3,36,160

**Savings (Annual)**

Cost of credit administration $= ₹\,25{,}000$

Cost of bad debts $= \dfrac{3{,}52{,}000 \times 1.5}{100} = ₹\,24{,}000$

Total saving $= ₹\,49{,}000$

**Cost (Annual)**

Factoring commission $= \dfrac{8{,}000 \times 360}{90} = ₹\,32{,}000$

Interest charge $= \dfrac{15{,}840 \times 360}{90} = ₹\,63{,}360$

Total cost $= 32{,}000 + 63{,}360 = ₹\,95{,}360$

Net cost of factoring $= 95{,}360 - 49{,}000 = ₹\,46{,}360$

Rate of annual cost $= \dfrac{46{,}360 \times 100}{3{,}36{,}000} = 13.79$ per cent

## EDI FACTORING

To assist international factoring, the FCI has developed a special communication system for its members called Electronic Data Interchange Factoring. This is mainly to speed up the business communications so that factoring becomes more effective. EDI factoring facilitates paperless trading. The sellers and debtors can exchange their communications relating to purchase order, invoice, payment, etc. through EDIFACT message. Thus, factoring can be done efficiently and speedily.

There is a good scope for factoring business in India. However, to succeed in the business, the factor has to take into account the following:

(*i*) A factor has to adopt credit appraisal skills of a very high order in India.

(*ii*) He has to develop a very strong MIS on the basis of day-to-day transactions of debtors.

(*iii*) He should follow an efficient monitoring mechanism for receivables and debtors.

(*iv*) He should computerise all his operations, maintain incisive record of collection experience and build a good credit library of debtors.

(*v*) Above all, he must pay attention to the commercial viability of the deal, and the balanced book of assets of his client.

(*vi*) He must ascertain whether his client is a man of high integrity and his debtors command good respect in the financial market.

## FORFAITING

Forfaiting is another source of financing against receivables like factoring. This technique is mostly employed to help an exporter for financing goods exported on a medium-term deferred basis.

The term 'a forfait' is a French word denoting 'to give something' or 'give up one's rights' or 'relinquish rights to something'. In fact, under forfaiting scheme, the exporter gives up his right to receive payments in future under an export bill for immediate cash payments by the forfaitor. This right to receive payment on the due date passes on to the forfaitor, since, the exporter has already surrendered his right to the forfaitor. Thus, the exporter is able to get 100 per cent of the amount of the bill minus discount charges immediately and get the benefits of cash sale. Thus, it is a unique medium which can convert a credit sale into a cash sale for an exporter. The entire responsibility of recovering the amount from the importer rests with the forfaitor. Forfaiting is done without any recourse to the exporter, *i.e.*, in case the importer makes a default, the forfaitor cannot go back to the exporter for the recovery of the money.

### ❖ Definition

Forfaiting has been defined as 'the non-recourse purchase by a bank or any other financial institution, of receivables arising from an export of goods and services'.

### ❖ Factoring vs. Forfaiting

Both factoring and forfaiting are used as tools of financing. But there are some differences:

(*i*) Factoring is always used as a tool for short-term financing, whereas forfaiting is for medium-term financing at a fixed rate of interest.

(*ii*) Factoring is generally employed to finance both the domestic and export business. But, forfaiting is invariably employed in export business only.

(*iii*) The central theme of factoring is the purchase of the invoice of the client, whereas it is only the purchase of the export bill under forfaiting.

(*iv*) Factoring is much broader in the sense. It includes the administration of the sales ledger, assumption of credit risk, recovery of debts and rendering of consultancy services. On the other hand, forfaiting mainly concentrates on financing aspects only and that too in respect of a particular export bill.

(*v*) Under factoring, the client is able to get only 80 per cent of the total invoice as 'credit facility', whereas the 100 per cent of the value of the export bill (of course deducting service charges) is given as credit under forfaiting.

(*vi*) Forfaiting is done without recourse to the client, whereas it may or may not be so under factoring.

(*vii*) The bills under forfaiting may be held by the forfaitor till the due date or they can be sold in the secondary market or to any investor for cash. Such a possibility does not exist under factoring.

(*viii*) Forfaiting is a specific one in the sense that it is based on a single export bill arising out of an individual transaction only. But, factoring is based on the 'whole turnover', *i.e.*, a bulk finance is provided against a number of unpaid invoices.

## WORKING OF FORFAITING

In a forfaiting transaction, the exporter is 'the client' and the financial institution is called 'the forfaitor' and the importer is 'the debtor'. When an exporter intends to export goods and services, he approaches a forfaitor and gives him the full details of his likely export dealing such as the name of the importer, the country to which he belongs, the currency in which the export of goods would be invoiced, the price of the goods and services, etc. He discusses with him the terms and conditions of finance. If it is acceptable, a sale contract is signed between the exporter and the importer on condition that the payment should be made by the importer to the forfaitor.

As usual, bills or promissory notes are signed by the importer. Such notes are guaranteed by the importer's bank and forwarded to the exporter's bank. Generally, such notes would be released to the exporter only against shipping documents. When goods are exported, the shipping documents are handed over to the exporter's bank. The exporter's bank, then forwards the shipping documents to the importer's bank after releasing the notes/bills to the exporter. These documents finally reach the hands of the importer through his bank.

Thereafter, the exporter takes these notes to the forfaitor who purchases them and gives ready cash after deducting discount charges.

### ❖ Cost of forfaiting

The cost of forfaiting finance is always at a fixed rate of interest which is usually included in the face value of the bills or notes. Of course, it varies depending upon the arrangements duration, creditworthiness of the party, the country where the importer is staying, the denomination of the currency in which the export deal is to be done and the overall political, economic and monetary conditions prevailing in the importer's country. Since the forfaitor has to assume currency fluctuation risk, interest rate fluctuation risk and the country's risk, he charges a fee and obviously it varies according to the risk factor involved in the deal.

## BENEFITS OF FORFAITING

(i) **Profitable and liquid:** From the forfaitor's point of view, it is advantageous because he not only gets immediate income in the form of discount charges, but also, can sell them in the secondary market or to any investor for cash.

(ii) **Simple and flexible:** It is also beneficial to the exporter. All the benefits that are available to a client under factoring are automatically available under forfaiting also. However, the greatest advantage is its simplicity and flexibility. It can be adopted to any export transaction and the exact structure of finance can also be determined according to the needs of the exporter, importer and the forfaitor.

(iii) **Avoids export credit risks:** The exporter is completely free from many export credit risks that may arise due to the possibility of interest rate fluctuations or exchange rates fluctuations or any political upheaval that may affect the collection of bills. Forfaiting acts as an insurance against all these risks.

(iv) **Avoids export credit insurance:** In the absence of forfaiting, the exporter has to go for export credit insurance. It is very costly and at the same time it involves very cumbersome procedures. Hence, if an exporter goes for forfaiting, he need not purchase any export credit insurance.

(v) **Confidential and speedy:** International trade transactions can be carried out very quickly through a forfaitor. It does not involve much documentary procedures. Above all, it is confidential. The speed and confidentiality with which deals are made beneficial for both the parties namely the exporter and the importer. No banking relationship with the forfaitor is necessary, since, it is a one-time transaction only.

(vi) **Suitable to all kinds of export deal:** It is suitable to any kind of goods — whether capital goods exports or commodity exports. Any export deal can be subject to forfaiting.

(vii) **Cent per cent finance:** The exporter is able to convert his deferred transaction into cash transaction through a forfaitor. He is able to get 100 per cent finance against export receivables.

(viii) **Fixed rate finance:** Forfaiting provides finance always at a fixed rate only. So, there is no need to enter into any hedging transactions to protect against interest rate and exchange rate risks.

## ❖ Drawbacks

(i) **Non-availability for short and long periods:** Forfaiting is highly suitable to only medium-term deferred payments. Forfaitors do not come forward to undertake forfeit financing for long periods, since, it involves much credit risks. Similarly, it cannot be used for availing short-term credit or contracts involving small amounts because they do not give rise to any bills or notes. Hence, exporters who require short-term and long-term credit have to seek some other alternative source.

(ii) **Non-availability for financially weak countries:** Similarly, forfaitors generally do not come forward to undertake any forfeit financing deal involving an importer from a financially weak country. Generally, the forfaitor has a full grasp of the financial and political situation prevailing in different countries, and hence, he would not accept a deal if the importer stays in a risky country. In exceptional cases, it can be undertaken at a higher price.

(iii) **Dominance of western currencies:** In International forfaiting, transactions are dominated in leading western currencies like Dollar, Pound Sterling, Deutshe Mark and French and Swiss Francs. Hence, our trade contracts have to be in foreign currencies rather than in Indian rupees.

(iv) **Difficulty in procuring international bank's guarantee:** Forfaitors do not normally finance an export deal unless it is supported by an unconditional and irrevocable guarantee from an international bank known to the forfaitor. Generally, it is the duty of the exporter to procure a guarantee of this kind and it is a stupendous task for an exporter to do so.

# FORFAITING IN INDIA

Forfaiting, as a source of finance, has gained substantial momentum abroad. Though it had its origin in 'Zurich', it has been well established in all the financial centres of the world. Some of the important forfaiting centres are London, Zurich, Hong Kong, Singapore and Frankfurt. It has become a popular source of finance among Europeans.

In India, forfaiting is slowly emerging as a new product in the liberalised financial market. It was approved by the Union Government only in January, 1994. The existing scheme available for exporters like concessional finance by commercial banks, insurance cover against export credit risks by ECGC, etc. are available mainly to large and well established exporters. In this context, forfaiting may be a real boon to the small, as well as, new exporters.

In India, forfaiting is done by the EXIM Bank. The minimum value of a forfaiting transaction is ₹ 5,00,000. A special form of pronote/bill has to be used for forfaiting transactions. An Indian exporter who wants to avail of this service has to approach the EXIM bank through his bank. The EXIM Bank would obtain the forfaiting quotation from the forfaiting agency abroad. Based on this, the exporter would workout his price to be quoted to the importer. If the importer accepts the price and the payment terms, the contract would be finalised and executed. The exporter would then get cash through forfaiting arrangements for which he has to enter into a separate contract with the forfaitor through the EXIM Bank.

However, in order to encourage forfaiting finance business, it is necessary to designate export contracts in leading international currencies. In the wake of economic liberalisation and opening of our economy to the global market, there are good prospects for forfaiting business in India. To promote forfaiting business, it is essential that we should denominate our trade contracts in foreign currencies rather than in Indian rupees. Now, since the rupee has gained strength, it is time for us to denominate our trade obligations in foreign currencies so that the pace of forfaiting business may be accelerated mainly to boost our export trade.

## QUESTIONS

### I. Objective type questions:

### A. Fill in the blanks with suitable word or words:

1. The process of selling trade debts of a client to a financial intermediary is called __________.
2. If a factor provides finance after disclosing the fact of assignment of debts to the debtors concerned, it is called __________.
3. The idea of providing factoring services was first thought of in India by __________.
4. The central theme of forfaiting is the purchase of __________ by a financial service company.
5. In India, forfaiting is done by __________ bank.

[**Key:** 1. factoring, 2. Bulk factoring or Disclosed factoring, 3. Vaghul Working Group, 4. export bill, 5. EXIM]

### B. Choose the best answer:

1. Trade debts have to be assigned in favour of the financing company under:

   (*a*) Discounting (*b*) Forfaiting

   (*c*) Factoring (*d*) All of the above

2. Refactoring charges have to be paid in the case of:

   (*a*) Maturity factoring (*b*) With recourse factoring

   (*c*) Invoice factoring (*d*) Full service factoring

3. Under forfaiting, the client is able to get credit facility to the extent of:

   (*a*) 100 per cent of the value of the export bill

   (*b*) 80 per cent of the value of the export bill

(*c*) 75 per cent of the value of the export bill

(*d*) 90 per cent of the value of the export bill

4. Under factoring, the factor acts in the capacity of:

(*a*) An agent of his client (*b*) A trustee

(*c*) A holder for value (*d*) An administrator

5. The first bank in India to start factoring business is:

(*a*) Canara Bank (*b*) State Bank of India

(*c*) Punjab National Bank (*d*) Allahabad Bank

[**Key:** 1. (*c*), 2. (*b*), 3. (*a*), 4. (*c*), 5. (*b*)]

## C. State whether the following statements are TRUE or FALSE:

1. Factoring does not require any registration of charges with the Registrar of companies.
2. Forfaiting is nothing but international factoring.
3. Forfaiting is always done without any recourse to the client.
4. Discounting a bill is much broader than factoring.
5. Under the single factor system, the import factor takes up all work connected with the international financial dealing by himself.

[**Key:** 1. True, 2. False, 3.True, 4. False, 5. False]

## II. Short answer type questions:

1. Distinguish between discounting and factoring.
2. What is factoring? Discuss its modus operandi.
3. Explain clearly the various functions involved in factoring.
4. What do you mean by Invoice factoring? Is it similar to full service factoring?
5. What are Refactoring Charges?
6. Distinguish between 'with recourse factoring' and 'without recourse factoring'.
7. Explain briefly any two types of export factoring.
8. What is Edifactoring? Discuss its importance.
9. Define Forfaiting. Is it similar to international factoring?
10. What is international factoring? Who are the parties involved in it?
11. State the main features of the Factoring Regulation (Amendment) Bill 2020.

## III. Essay type questions:

1. Define factoring and state how is it superior to Bill financing.
2. Discuss in detail the various services rendered by factoring intermediaries.
3. Explain the different types of factoring and their significance.
4. Critically assess the role of forfaiting as a source of financing.
5. Distinguish between factoring and forfaiting and state the scope for the introduction of such service in India.

# 16

# SECURITISATION OF DEBT

The financial system all over the world is in the process of rapid transformation. As a result, the capital market, money market and the debt market are getting widened and deepened. It is interesting to note that new instruments and new products are emerging in the debt market too. In fact, the development of a debt market increases the efficiency of a capital market to a greater extent. Again, along with the equity market, there is bound to be a natural growth in the debt market also. Thus, it is obvious that a debt market should also have both primary and secondary markets. In this context, debt or asset securitisation assumes a significant role and it is one of the most innovative techniques introduced in the debt market to achieve the above objective. Moreover, it is the debt market which has provided more impetus for capital formation than the equity market in the economically advanced countries.

## WHAT IS SECURITISATION?

Securitisation of debt or asset refers to the process of liquidating the illiquid and long-term assets like loans and receivables of financial institutions like banks by issuing marketable securities against them. In other words, it is a technique by which a long-term, non-negotiable and high-valued financial asset like hire purchase is converted into securities of small values which can be tradable in the market just like shares.

Thus, it is nothing but a process of removing long-term assets from the balance sheet of a lending financial institution and replacing them with liquid cash through the issue of securities against them. Under securitisation, a financial institution pools its illiquid, non-negotiable and long-term assets, creates securities against them, gets them rated and sells them to investors. It is an ongoing process in the sense that assets are converted into securities, securities into cash, cash into assets and assets into securities and so on.

Generally, extension of credit by banks and other financial institutions in the form of bills purchase or discounting or hire purchase financing appears as an asset on their balance sheets. Some of these assets are long-term in nature and it implies that funds are locked up unnecessarily for an undue long period. So, to carry on their lending operations without much interruptions, they have to rely upon various other sources of finance which are not only costly but also not available easily. Again, they have to bear the risk of the credit outstandings. Now, securitisation is a ready-made solution for them. Securitisation helps them to recycle funds at a reasonable cost and with less credit risk. In other words, securitisation helps to remove these assets from the balance sheets of financial institutions by providing liquidity through tradable financial instruments.

Again from another angle also, securitisation is a boon to financial institutions. From the risk management point of view, the lending financial institutions have to absorb the entire credit risk by holding the credit outstandings in their own portfolio. Securitisation offers a good scope for risk diversification.

It is worthwhile to note that the entire transaction relating to securitisation is carried out on the asset side of the balance sheet. That is one asset (illiquid) is converted into another asset (cash).

## ❖ Definition

As stated earlier, securitisation helps to liquefy assets mainly of medium and long-term loans and receivables of financial institutions. The concept of securitisation can be defined as follows:

'A carefully structured process whereby loans and other receivables are packaged, underwritten and sold in the form of asset backed securities'.

Yet another simple definition is as follows:

'Securitisation is nothing but liquefying assets comprising loans and receivables of an institution through systematic issuance of financial instruments'.

According to Hendersen, J. and Scott, J.P., 'Securitisation is the process which takes when a lending institution's assets are removed in one way or another from the balance sheet of that lending institution and are funded instead, by investors who purchase a negotiable financial instrument evidencing this indebtedness without recourse, or in some cases with limited recourse, to the original lender'.

Thus, financial assets can be made liquid through securitisation, *i.e.,* through packaging loans and selling them in the market. It is very clear from the above definitions that securitisation is nothing but the packaging of a pool of financial assets into marketable securities. In brief, illiquid assets are converted into tradable securities.

## ❖ Structured securities vs. conventional securities

Securitisation is basically a structured financial transaction. It envisages the issue of securities against illiquid assets and such securities are really structured securities. It is so because, they are backed by the value of the underlying financial asset and the credit support of a third party also. At this stage, one should not confuse such structured securities with conventional securities like bonds, debentures, etc. They differ from each other in the following respects.

1. **Source of repayment:** In the case of conventional securities, the primary source of repayment is the earning power and cash flow of the issuing company. But, under

securitisation, the issuing company is completely free from this botheration since the burden of repayment is shifted to a pool of assets or to a third party.

2. **Structure:** Under securitisation, the securities may be structured in such a way so as to achieve a desired level of risk and a desired level of rating depending upon the type and amount of assets pooled. Such a choice is not available in the case of conventional securities.
3. **Nature:** In fact, these structured securities are basically derivatives of the traditional debt instruments. Of course, the credit standing of these securities is well supported by a pool of assets or by a guarantee or by both.

## SECURITISATION VS. FACTORING

At this stage, one should not confuse the term 'securitisation' with that of 'factoring'. Since both deal with the assets, *viz.,* book debts and receivables, it is very essential that the differences between them must be clearly understood. The main differences are:

(*i*) Factoring is mainly associated with the assets (book debts and receivables) of manufacturing and trading companies whereas securitisation is mainly associated with the assets of financial companies.

(*ii*) Factoring mainly deals with trade debts and trade receivables of clients. On the other hand, securitisation deals with loans and receivables arising out of loans like hire purchase finance receivables, receivables from Government departments, etc.

(*iii*) In the case of factoring, the trade debts and receivables in questions are short-term in nature whereas they are medium term or long-term in nature in the case of securitisation.

(*iv*) The question of issuing securities against book debts does not arise at all in the case of factoring whereas it forms the very basis of securitisation.

(*v*) The factor himself takes up the 'collection work' whereas it can be done either by the originator or by a separate servicing agency under securitisation.

(*vi*) Under factoring, the entire credit risk is passed on to the factor. But under securitisation, a part of the credit risk can be absorbed by the originator by transferring the assets at a discount.

## MODUS OPERANDI

For the operational mechanics of securitisation, the following parties are required:

(*i*) The originator.

(*ii*) A Special Purpose Vehicle (SPV) or a trust.

(*iii*) A merchant or investment banker.

(*iv*) A credit rating agency.

(*v*) A servicing agent — Receiving and Paying Agent (RPA).

(*vi*) The original borrowers or obligors.

(*vii*) The prospective investors, *i.e.,* the buyers of securities.

The various stages involved in the working of securitisation are as follows:

1. Identification stage/process.
2. Transfer stage/process.
3. Issue stage/process.
4. Redemption stage/process.
5. Credit rating stage/process.

**1. Identification process:** The lending financial institution either a bank or any other institution for that matter which decides to go in for securitisation of its assets is called the 'originator'. The originator might have got assets comprising of a variety of receivables like commercial mortgages, lease receivables, hire purchase receivables, etc. The originator has to pick-up a pool of assets of homogeneous nature, considering the maturities, interest rates involved, frequency of repayments and marketability. This process of selecting a pool of loans and receivables from the asset portfolios for securitisation is called 'identification process'.

**2. Transfer process:** After the identification process is over, the selected pool of assets are then 'passed through' to another institution which is ready to help the originator to convert those pools of assets into securities. This institution is called the Special Purpose Vehicle (SPV) or the trust. The pass through transaction between the originator and the SPV is either by way of outright sale, *i.e.,* full transfer of assets in question for valuable consideration or by passing them for a collateralised loan. Generally, it is done on an outright sale basis. This process of passing through the selected pool of assets by the originator to a SPV is called transfer process and once this transfer process is over, the assets are removed from the balance sheet of the originator.

**3. Issue process:** After this transfer process is over, the SPV takes up the onerous task of converting these assets of various types of different maturities. It is on this basis, the SPV issues securities to investors. The SPV actually splits the package into individual securities of smaller values and they are sold to the investing public. The SPV gets itself reimbursed out of the sale proceeds. The securities issued by the SPV is called by different names like 'Pay through Certificates', 'Pass through Certificates'. Interest only Certificates, Principal only Certificates, etc. The securities are structured in such a way that the maturity of these securities may synchronise with the maturities of the securitised loans or receivables.

**4. Redemption process:** The redemption and payments of interest on these securities are facilitated by the collections received by the SPV from the securitised assets. The task of collection of dues is generally entrusted to the originator or a special servicing agent can be appointed for this purpose. This agency is paid a certain percentage of commission for the collection services rendered. The servicing agent is responsible for collecting the principal and interest payments on assets pooled when due and he must pay a special attention to delinquent accounts. Usually, the originator is appointed as the servicer. Thus, under securitisation, the role of the originator gets reduced to that of a collection agent on behalf of the SPV, in case he is appointed as a collection agent. A pass through certificate may be either 'with recourse' to the originator or 'without recourse'. The usual practice is to make it 'without recourse'. Hence, the holder of a pass through certificate has to look to the SPV for payment of the principal and interest on the certificates held by him. Thus, the main task of the SPV is to structure the deal, raise proceeds by issuing pass through certificates and arrange for payment of interest and principal to the investors.

**5. Credit rating process:** Since the pass through certificates have to be publicly issued, they require credit rating by a good credit rating agency so that they become more attractive and easily acceptable. Hence, these certificates are rated at least by one credit rating agency on the eve of the securitisation. The issues could also be guaranteed by external guarantor institutions like merchant bankers which would enhance the creditworthiness of the certificates and would be readily acceptable to investors. Of course, this rating guarantee provides a sense of confidence to the investor with regard to the timely payment of principal and interest by the SPV.

Pass through certificates, like debentures, directly reflect the ownership rights in the assets securitised, their repayment schedule, interest rate, etc. These certificates, before maturity, are tradable in a secondary market to ensure liquidity for the investors. They are negotiable securities and hence they can be easily tradable in the market.

### ❖ Role of merchant bankers

Merchant or investment bankers can play a big role in asset securitisation. They generally act as Special Purpose Vehicle. There are many issues involved in securitisation namely the timing of the issue of pass through certificates, pricing of these certificates for marketing and above all underwriting of these issues. In private placement, they act as agents for the issuer connecting the sellers and buyers. They can also involve in structuring the issue to see that the issue meets all legal, regulatory, accounting, tax and other requirements. In all these aspects, merchant bankers have a definite role to play. The mere fact that an issue has been underwritten by a popular merchant banker will add credit to that issue and it would become more attractive from the investor's point of view. Thus, securitisation enlarges the activities of the merchant bankers too.

### ❖ Role of other parties

The other parties in the game of securitisation are the original borrowers and the prospective investors. The original borrowers refer to those who have availed of the loan facilities from the lending institution, i.e., the originator. They are also called obligors. In fact, the success of the securitisation process depends upon these original borrowers. If they fail to meet their commitments on the due dates, the securitisation process will be at danger. In fact, the receipts of cash flows from the original borrowers are passed through to the investors. The prospective investors are nothing but the public at large who are willing to purchase the pass through certificates.

## STRUCTURE FOR SECURITISATION/TYPES OF SECURITIES

Securitisation is a structured transaction, whereby the originator transfers or sells some of its assets to a SPV which breaks these assets into tradable securities of smaller values which could be sold to the investing public. The appropriate structure for securitisation depends on a variety of factors like quality of assets securitised, default experience of original borrowers, amount of amortisation at maturity, financial reputation and soundness of the originator, etc.

The general principle is that the securities must be structured in such a way that the maturity of these securities may coincide with the maturity of the securitised loans. However, there are three important types of securities as listed below:

(*i*) Pass through and pay through certificates,

(*ii*) Preferred stock certificates, and

(*iii*) Asset-based commercial papers.

## ❖ Pass through and pay through certificates

In the case of pass through certificates, payments to investors depend upon the cash flow from the assets backing such certificates. In other words, as and when cash (principal and interest) is received from the original borrower by the SPV, it is passed on to the holders of certificates at regular intervals and the entire principal is returned with the retirement of the assets packed in the pool. Thus, pass through certificates have a single maturity structure and the tenure of these certificates is matched with the life of the securitised assets.

On the other hand, pay through certificates have a multiple maturity structure depending upon the maturity pattern of underlying assets. Thus, two or three types of securities with different maturity patterns like short- term, medium, term and long-term may be issued. The greatest advantage is that they can be issued depending upon the investor's demand for varying maturity patterns. This type is more attractive from the investor's point of view because the yield is often inbuilt in the price of the securities themselves, i.e., they are offered at a discount to face value as in the case of deep discount bonds.

## ❖ Preferred stock certificates

Preferred stocks are instruments issued by a subsidiary company against the trade debts and consumer receivables of its parent company. In other words, subsidiary companies buy the trade debts and receivables of parent companies, convert them into short-term securities, and help the parent companies to enjoy liquidity. Thus, trade debts can also be securitised through the issue of preferred stocks. Generally, these stocks are backed by guarantees given by highly rated merchant banks and hence they are also attractive from the investor's point of view. These instruments are mostly short-term in nature.

## ❖ Asset-based commercial papers

This type of structure is mostly prevalent in mortgage-backed securities. Under this type, the SPV purchases portfolio of mortgages from different sources (various lending institutions) and they are combined into a single group on the basis of interest rates, maturity dates and underlying collaterals. They are, then, transferred to a trust which, in turn, issues mortgage-backed certificates to the investors. These certificates are issued against the combined principal value of the mortgages and they are also short-term instruments. Each certificate holder is entitled to participate in the cash flow from underlying mortgages to the extent of his investments in the certificates.

### ❖ Other types

Apart from the above, there are also other types of certificates namely:

(*i*) Interest only certificates, and

(*ii*) Principal only certificates.

In the case of interest only certificates, payments are made to investors only from the interest incomes earned from the assets securitised. As the very name suggests, payments are made to investors only from the repayment of principal by the original borrowers, in the case of principal only certificates. These certificates enable speculative dealings since the speculators know well that the interest rate movements would affect the bond values immediately. For instance, the principal only certificates would increase in value when interest rates go down. It is so because, it becomes advantageous to repay the existing debts and resort to fresh borrowings at lower cost. This early redemption of securities would benefit the investors to a greater extent. Similarly, when the interest rates go up, interest only certificate holders stand to gain since more interest would be available from the underlying assets. One cannot exactly predict the future movements of interest, and hence, these certificates give much scope for speculators to play their game.

Thus, securitisation offers much scope for the introduction of newer and newer instruments so as to meet the varying requirements of investors. Debt securitisation offers a variety of investment instruments to the investing public at large as well as to the financial intermediaries like mutual funds, insurance companies, etc.

## SECURITISABLE ASSETS

As stated earlier, all assets are not suitable for securitisation. For instance, trade debts and receivables are not generally suitable for securitisation, whereas they are readily acceptable to a factor. Only in rare cases, they are securitised. Example: Preferred Stock Certificates.

The following assets are generally securitised by financial institutions:

(*i*) Term loans to financially reputed companies.

(*ii*) Receivables from Government Departments and Companies.

(*iii*) Credit card receivables.

(*iv*) Hire purchase loans like vehicle loans.

(*v*) Lease finance.

(*vi*) Mortgage loans, etc.

## BENEFITS OF SECURITISATION

Debt securitisation provides many benefits to all the parties, such as, the originator, investors and the regulatory authorities. Some of the important benefits are the following:

**(i) Additional source of fund:** The originator, (i.e., the lending institution) is much benefitted because securitisation provides an additional source of funds by converting an otherwise illiquid asset into ready liquidity. As a result, there is an immediate improvement in the cash flow of the originator. Thus, it acts as a source of liquidity.

**(ii) Greater profitability:** Securitisation helps financial institutions to get liquid cash from medium-term and long-term assets immediately rather than over a longer period. It leads to greater recycling of funds which, in turn, leads to higher business turnover and profitability. Again, the cash flow could be recycled for investment in higher yielding assets. This means greater profitability. Moreover, economies of scale can be achieved since securitisation offers scope for the fuller utilisation of the existing capabilities by providing liquid cash immediately. It results in additional business turnover.

Again, the originator can also act as the receiving and paying agent. If so, it gets additional income in the form of servicing fee.

**(iii) Enhancement of capital adequacy ratio:** Securitisation enables financial institutions to enhance their capital adequacy ratio by reducing their assets volume. The process of securitisation necessitates the selection of a pool of assets by the financial institutions to be sold or transferred to another institution called SPV. Once the assets are transferred, they are removed from the balance sheet of the originator. It results in the reduction of assets volume, thereby increasing the capital adequacy ratio. Capital adequacy ratio can also be improved by replacing the loan assets with the lesser risk-weighted assets. Thus, the removal of assets from the Balance Sheet under a true sale improves the capital adequacy norms.

**(iv) Spreading of credit risk:** Securitisation facilities the spreading of credit risk to different parties involved in the process of securitisation. In the absence of securitisation, the entire credit risk associated with a particular financial transaction has to be borne by the originator himself. Now, the originator is able to diversify the risk factors among the various parties involved in securitisation. Thus, securitisation helps to achieve diversification of credit risks which are greater in the case of medium-term and long-term loans. Thus, it is used as tool for risk management.

**(v) Lower cost of funding:** In view of enhancement of cash flows and diversification of risk factors, securitisation enables the originator to have an easy access to the securities market at debt ratings higher than its overall corporate rating. It means that companies with low credit rating can issue asset-backed securities at lower interest cost due to high credit rating on such securities. This helps it to secure funds at lower cost. Moreover, the criteria for choosing the pool of assets ensures an efficient cost of funds. In the present context of scarcity of funds and higher interest rates, securitisation provides a good scope for cheap funding.

**(vi) Provision of multiple instruments:** From the investor's point of view, securitisation provides multiple new investment instruments so as to meet the varying requirements of the investing public. It also offers varieties of instruments for other financial intermediaries like mutual funds, insurance companies, pension funds, etc., giving them many choices.

**(vii) Higher rate of return:** When compared to traditional debt securities like bonds and debentures, securitised securities offer better rate of return along with better liquidity. These instruments are rated by good credit rating agencies and hence more attractive. Being structured asset-based securities, they offer more protection and yield a good return. The bankruptcy/winding up of the originator does not affect the investors since the payment is guaranteed by the SPV.

**(viii) Prevention of idle capital:** In the absence of securitisation, capital would remain idle in the form of illiquid assets like mortgages, term loans, etc., in many of the lending institutions. Now, securitisation helps recycling of funds by converting these assets into liquidity, liquidity into assets, assets into liquidity and so on by means of issuing tradable and transferable securities against these assets. Thus, it provides impetus for capital formation.

**(ix) Better than traditional instruments:** Certificates are issued to investors against the backing of assets securitised. The underlying assets are used not only as a collateral to the certificates but also to generate the income to pay the principal and interest to the investors. It does not entail any servicing needs and hence does not require much costs. It is better that even mutual fund units because it is issued against the backing of collateral securities, whereas there is no such backing for mutual fund certificates. Thus, these instruments, being structured asset-backed securities, afford a greater protection to investors.

Again, there is much transparency from the investor's point of view. They can very well see the collateral pool that a particular issue represents and this transparency reduces uncertainty as to the risk element.

**(x) Other benefits:** Securitisation, if carried out in true spirit, leads to greater economy in the use of capital with efficiency and cost-effectiveness in both funding and lending. This is a great boon to the regulating authorities as well since their primary objective is to prevent the accumulation of capital where it is not needed.

In the long run, it is beneficial to the borrowers also. They will be able to get funds at cheaper rates since the originators are likely to pass on the benefit to the ultimate borrowers. There is no doubt that securitisation is a low-cost and innovative funding source ensuring economy in the use of capital.

## SECURITISATION AND BANKS

There is a vast scope for commercial banks to go in for securitisation due to the following factors:

**(i) Innovative and low cost source of fund:** Traditionally, deposit has been the only dependable source of funds for banks over the years. But, in recent times, banks have to face severe competition from other non-banking institutions in deposit mobilisation. Now, securitisation offers an excellent source of funds at cheaper rates. Unlike deposits, it will not entail any servicing needs and the consequent increase in costs.

**(ii) Better capital adequacy norms:** Securitisation has the effect of improving the capital adequacy norms of banks. Generally, commercial firms utilise the cash flow from securitisation for repayment of their borrowings, and thus, they can achieve a good debt-equity ratio. But, in the case of banks, borrowings are limited. So, they can better utilise the cash flow to create lower risk-weighted assets. Hence, high risk-weighted assets can be easily converted into lower risk-weighted assets. Thus, it helps banks to achieve better capital adequacy norms.

**(iii) Creation of more credit:** In India, banks are subject to high statutory pre-emptions for which more liquid cash is essential now and then. This has necessarily impaired the capacity of banks to create credit. In fact, securitisation is not at all affected by these factors. The cash flow from securitisation could be very well used for further expansion of credit without any statutory restrictions.

**(iv) Increased profitability:** The profitability of banks has been very much affected to a greater extent in these days due to many factors. In this context, securitisation has a salutary impact on the profitability of banks. It provides for more liquidity, quicker recycling of funds and greater economy in the use of capital. This has the effect of improving the profitability of banks. Besides, they can also earn income in the form of service fee by acting as receiving and paying agent.

**(v) Tool for asset-liability management and risk management:** Securitisation can be better used as a tool to avoid mismatch in the asset-liability management. It would reduce the overdependence of banks on the market for money at call and short notice as well as the refinancing agencies for recycling of funds. Again, it can be used as a risk management tool also. It completely eliminates the interest risks and thus it provides a hedge to banks against interest risks which are inherent in the free interest rate market.

## CONDITIONS FOR SUCCESSFUL SECURITISATION

If securitisation of debt has to be successful, the following conditions must have been fulfilled.

*(i)* Ultimately, the success of securitisation depends upon the ability of the original borrower to repay his loan. Therefore, selection of assets to be securitised requires utmost care. The assets should be ranked and selected on the basis of least losses and to provide for maximum protection to the investor.

*(ii)* The credit rating is an integral part of securitisation. Hence, credit rating must be done by credit rating agencies on a scientific basis and the ratings should be unquestionable. Then only, the prospective investor's confidence can be built. The credit rating agencies should take into account the various types of risks such as credit risk, interest risk, liquidity risk, etc., along with other usual factors.

*(iii)* The SPV should be a separate organisation from that of the originator. It should be completely insulated from the parent corporate entity so that SPV could be protected from the danger of bankruptcy.

*(iv)* The pass through certificates or any other similar instruments arising out of securitisation must be listed in stock exchanges so that they may be readily acceptable to investors. It would provide instant liquidity and moreover, its price could also be easily ascertained.

(*v*) Alternatively, it is also advisable to provide two-way quotations for facilitating the buying and selling of the pass through certificates in the market as in the case of mutual fund units.

(*vi*) There must be standardised loan documentation for similar loans so that there may be uniformity between different financial institutions. It must carry a right to assign debts to third parties, so that, it could be sold or transferred to the SPV.

(*vii*) There should be a proper accounting treatment for the various transactions involved in asset securitisation. Suitable accounting norms for the recognition of the trust created for securitised debt should be evolved. The accounting system should provide for the removal of the securitised assets from the balance sheet of the originator. Only then, the real benefit will go to the originator.

(*viii*) Above all, there should be proper and adequate guidelines given by the regulatory authorities dealing with the various aspects of the process of securitisation.

## SECURITISATION ABROAD

The credit of introducing the concept of securitisation goes to America where the first structured asset securitised financing came into being in 1970. In 1970, the newly created Government National Mortgage Association (Ginnie Mae) began its operations by publicly trading in securities, backed by a pool of mortgage loans. It was followed by Federal National Mortgage Association and similar organisations. These organisations bought residential mortgage loans, made pools out of them and issued mortgage-backed securities against them. The payment of principal and interest of these instruments was also guaranteed. The securities issued by it were called 'Mortgage pass through securities'. A pool of mortgages was created by putting together assets that had similar characteristics in terms of duration, interest rate and quality. The pool was then placed with a trust which actually sold the certificates drawn against such mortgages to the investors either directly or through private placement. Thus, the concept of securitisation was confined to mortgages only.

However, in March 1985, non-mortgage collaterals started getting securitised in the USA. For instance, the first offering of 192 million of lease backed certificates for Sperry Lease Finance Corporation was underwritten by The First Boston. Now, it has become a popular mode of financing in America. It is slowly becoming a global phenomenon covering transactions relating to various modes of finance.

Securitisation is gaining popularity in UK also in recent years only. Like America, this concept started with mortgage securitisation. The Bank America Finance Ltd., UK issued mortgage securities in January 1985 against the residential property mortgages as underlying assets. The first mortgage securitisation issue for the international market arranged was MINI in London in 1985. Now, clearing banks and building societies have entered into this market under the supervision of the Bank of England. Securitisation of debt and the consequent debt instruments are now popular in countries like Italy, Australia, Canada, France, Spain, and Japan. In many of these countries, the process of securitisation has been encouraged by passing suitable legislations.

## SECURITISATION IN INDIAN CONTEXT

Generally, securitisation of auto loans has been popular in India. Now, the securitisation market has spread into several asset classes, viz., housing loans, corporate loans, commercial mortgage receivables, project receivables, toll revenues, gold loans, and recently microfinance loans too. The Asset- Backed Securitisation (ABS) is very popular in India due to the growing retail loan portfolio of banks, short-term maturity of these loans, and above all, the investors familiarity with the underlying assets.

The Mortgage-Backed Securitisation (MBS) has been rather slow in India due to the long maturity periods, lack of secondary market liquidity and the risk arising from prepayments/ repricing of the underlying loan.

Very recently, Single Loan Sell-off (LSO) of corporate loans of banks and other financial institutions is gaining momentum in the Indian Securitisation market. On the other side of the coin, direct assignment of single loan or retail loan pools, as against securitisation, has also been gaining importance in India. It does not require any issuance of instruments like PTCs.

## NEW GUIDELINES ON SECURITISATION

Recently, the RBI has issued guidelines allowing commercial banks to finance Special Purpose Vehicles (SPVs) which have been formed to transfer securitised assets separated from them. Some of the important guidelines are:

(*i*) All banks, term lending institutions and NBFCs have to securitise only standard assets.

(*ii*) Banks can finance SPVs which are engaged in transferring securitised assets.

(*iii*) While financing SPVs, an independent third party, other than the orginator's (banks) group entities, should provide at least 25 per cent of the liquidity facility. It means that every bank should locate a third party for financing SPVs.

(*iv*) The liquidity facility provided by banks should not be available for:

  (*a*) Meeting recurring lapses of securitisation,

  (*b*) Funding acquisition of additional assets by SPVs,

  (*c*) Funding the financial scheduled repayment of investors, and

  (*d*) Funding breach of warranties.

## LEGAL FRAMEWORK FOR SECURITISATION

The Securities Contracts (Regulation) Act, 1956 has been amended in 2007 with a view to providing a legal framework for trading in securitised debt. The important amendments are:

(*i*) The term 'securities' as mentioned in the Act includes securitisation instruments.

(*ii*) The SEBI's permission is necessary to issue securitisation instruments.

(*iii*) A legal framework has been provided for trading in securitised debt, mortgage-backed debt, etc.

### ❖ New regulations

The SEBI has recently released SEBI (Public Offer and Listing of Securitised Debt Instruments) Regulations 2008, continuity rules and regulations governing the issue and listing of securitised debt instruments.

### ❖ Guidelines 2010

In April 2010, draft guidelines have been issued in respect of securitisation transactions. These include:

(*i*) A Minimum Holding Period (MHP) of 9 months and 12 months respectively by the originators for loans with maturity of less than 24 months and more than 24 months.

(*ii*) A Minimum Retention Requirement (MRR) of 5 per cent and 10 per cent by the originators has been proposed for loans with a maturity of less than 24 months and more than 24 months respectively.

(*iii*) The total exposure of banks to the: (*a*) Special Purpose Vehicle, (*b*) Securitised assets, and (*c*) Credit enhancements not to exceed 20 per cent.

(*iv*) Resecuritisation, synthetic securitisation and securitisation with revolving structures to be prohibited.

## CAUSES FOR THE UNPOPULARITY OF SECURITISATION IN INDIA

Though securitisation brings many benefits, it is not firmly rooted in Indian soil due to the following reasons:

(i) **New concept:** Securitisation itself is a new concept in debt market. There is much unawareness not only among the investors but also among the various financial intermediaries. Though securitisation brings immediate benefits to the lending institutions, most of them neither aware of this concept nor its advantages.

(ii) **Heavy stamp duty and registration fees:** Basically, securitisation requires the transfer of various illiquid and non-performing assets to a central agency called Special Purpose Vehicle. This transfer involves heavy stamp duty and registration fees. These costs are so exorbitant that people are automatically discouraged to go in for this innovative technique of financing.

(iii) **Cumbersome transfer procedures:** Again, the transfer of assets involves very complicated and cumbersome legal procedures which stand as a real impediment in the way of securitisation.

(iv) **Difficulty in assignment of debts:** The right to assign debts to third parties has been permitted only under certain circumstances under the Transfer of Property Act and in fact, this transfer/sale of debts forms the central theme of securitisation. Hence, the Transfer of Property Act should be suitably amended so as to facilitate securitisation in India.

(v) **Absence of standardised loan documentation:** As it is, there is no standardised loan documentation procedure in India. There is no uniformity between different financial institutions regarding the loan documentation even for the same type of loans. In such a case, it becomes very difficult for an agency like the Special Purpose Vehicle to pool the similar assets of the various financial institutions for securitisation.

**(vi) Inadequate credit rating facilities:** Credit rating is an integral part of securitisation. Unfortunately, credit rating in India is at its infancy level. Now only, it becomes obligatory to get credit rating for all debt instruments issued by non-banking companies. The credit rating agencies are not adequately available in India at present to take up the stupendous task of credit rating instruments for securitisation purposes. However, a good progress has been made in this direction in recent times.

**(vii) Absence of proper accounting procedures:** Proper accounting procedure should be evolved for securitisation. Creation of a Trust or Special Purpose Vehicle is a must for securitisation and as such there is no accounting procedure for the recognition of this trust. Again, securitisation paves way for the removal of the securitised assets from the balance sheet of the originator. How should one account for it? It is a challenge to the accounting professionals in the country to evolve suitable accounting procedures for securitisation.

**(viii) Absence of proper guidelines:** One can find a lot of guidelines issued by the regulatory authorities to deal with mutual funds, non-banking companies, etc. But, they are conspicuously absent in the field of securitisation. There are various processes involved in securitisation right from the identification process to the redemption process. Again, various types of structures are available. Hence, proper guidelines must be issued covering all these aspects so that financial intermediaries can go for securitisation without any hesitation and thus securitisation becomes a smooth affair.

**(ix) Casual approach to prudent approach:** Securitisation gives room to adopt a casual approach as against a prudent approach in traditional risk management of the loan portfolios of financial institutions. It leads to 'disowning of the risks' rather than 'managing the risks'.

**(x) Principal/agent problems:** The growing complexity as well as lengthening of the chain involving multiple intermediaries have resulted in increased distance from the originator. This longer chain obviously gives rise to several principal/agent problems.

**(xi) Modelling issues:** The fundamental modelling issues have resulted in incorrect estimation of riskiness and default correlations of the underlying assets.

## PROSPECTS OF SECURITISATION

There is a bright future for securitisation in India due to the following factors:

(*i*) With the liberalisation of the financial markets, there is bound to be more demand for capital.

(*ii*) There has been an explosive growth of capital market and a vast increase in the investor base in recent times.

(*iii*) The entry of newer financial intermediaries like mutual funds, money market, pension funds, etc., has paved the way for floating debt instruments easily in the market.

(*iv*) Debt instruments have become popular in recent times since corporate customers are not willing to take recourse to the equity route as a major source of financing their projects.

(*v*) There is a proposal to establish Asset Reconstruction Fund as per the Narasimhan Committee recommendations for the purpose of securitisation of non-performing assets.

(*vi*) Since the financial institutions and banks have to follow the capital adequacy norms as recommended by the Narasimhan Committee, they have to necessarily go for securitisation.

The above factors clearly indicate that there is a vast scope for the introduction of the concept of securitisation of assets on a large-scale as an innovative step for resource mobilisation. More than that, it is used as a tool to improve the balance sheets by bringing out changes in the critical financial ratios like debt-equity ratio, return on assets ratio, asset turnover ratio, capital adequacy ratio, etc.

There is much scope for securitisation in respects of loans under: (*i*) Mortgage, (*ii*) housing loans, (*iii*) other term loans, and (*iv*) credit and receivables.

In the case of non-banking financial companies also, lease receivables and vehicle loans could be readily securitised. With nearly ₹ 70,000 crore outstanding corporate debts of financial institutions, at least ₹ 50,000 crore could be securitised and thereby the financial institutions could raise their liquidity for greater profitability.

While most of the innovations in the financial service industry directly benefit the customers, these innovations like factoring and securitisation directly bring benefits to the financial institutions themselves first and then to the public at large. It is high time that the Government came forward with all positive help to encourage securitisation in India. The immediate need of the hour is to amend the various relevant Acts like the Transfer of Property Act, 1882; the Registration Act, 1908; Stamp Laws Act, 1809, etc., to make asset securitisation a smooth affair. Proper accounting procedures should be evolved besides appropriate guidelines by the regulatory authorities. Securitisation would facilitate the transfer of capital from non-performing and idle assets to more efficient assets. Creation of new debt instruments would further deepen the financial market. On the whole, the economy would be developed at a faster rate than what it is, if securitisation becomes a popular technique of financing. Since the stamp duties have been considerably reduced in States like Maharashtra and the National Stock Exchange has decided to list securitised assets, securitisation is expected to have a very bright future in India and the debt market is expected to become very active in the days to come.

## QUESTIONS

### I. Objective type questions:

#### A. Fill in the blanks:

1. The process by which a financial intermediary liquify its illiquid assets through systematic issuance of financial instruments is called __________.
2. Securitisation is mainly associated with the assets of __________ companies.

3. The lending financial institution which decides to go in for securitisation is called ________.
4. ________ instruments are issued by a subsidiary company against the trade debt of its parent company.
5. In India, securitisation has been pioneered by ________ bank.

[**Key:** 1. Securitisation, 2. financial, 3. originator, 4. Preferred stock certificates, 5. Citibank]

## B. Choose the best answer from the following:

1. The concept of securitisation is associated with:
   (*a*) Capital Market (*b*) Money Market
   (*c*) Debt Market (*d*) Foreign Exchange Market.
2. In the case of securitisation, the trade debts and receivables are mostly in the nature of:
   (*a*) Short-term (*b*) Medium-term
   (*c*) Long-term (*d*) Both medium-term and long-term.
3. Under securitisation, selected pool of assets are 'passed through', for converting them into securities, to another institution called:
   (*a*) Originator (*b*) Special Purpose Vehicle
   (*c*) Credit Rating Company (*d*) Servicing agent.
4. Which one of the following is a short-term debt instrument?
   (*a*) Preferred stock certificate
   (*b*) Pass through certificate
   (*c*) Asset-based commercial paper
   (*d*) Principal only certificate.
5. The asset generally not suitable for securitisation is:
   (*a*) Receivables from Government Department
   (*b*) Trade receivables
   (*c*) Hire Purchase finance receivables
   (*d*) Mortgage loans.

[**Key:** 1. (*c*), 2. (*d*), 3. (*b*), 4. (*a*), 5. (*b*)]

## C. State whether the following statements are TRUE or FALSE:

1. Securitisation can be used as a tool to improve the balance sheet by bringing out necessary changes in the capital adequacy norms.
2. Pass through and pay through certificates have a multiple maturity structure.
3. As between a pass through certificate and a mutual fund unit, the mutual fund unit is preferable to an investor.
4. Securitisation is mainly associated with the assets of financial companies.
5. Securities issued against the assets securitised are not negotiable and hence they cannot be traded in the market.

[**Key :** 1. True, 2. False, 3. False, 4. True, 5. False]

## II. Short answer type questions:

1. What is securitisation?
2. Distinguish between securitisation and factoring.
3. Discuss the modus operandi of securitisation.
4. Discuss the role of merchant bankers in securitisation.
5. Explain the special features of pass through certificates. Are they similar to pay through certificates?
6. 'Asset-based commercial paper structure is mostly prevalent in mortgaged backed securities'. Discuss.
7. What are the assets suitable for securitisations?
8. 'Securitisation is a financial boon to commercial banks'. Do you agree? Support your answer with valid points.
9. Analyse the causes for the unpopularity of the concept of securitisation in India.
10. Discuss briefly the role of Special Purpose Vehicle in securitisation.

## III. Essay type questions:

1. Define securitisation and discuss its modus operandi.
2. Explain in detail the various structures available for securitisation. Which structure is suitable to Indian conditions at present?
3. Bring out clearly the various benefits of securitisation.
4. Analyse the causes for the unpopularity of the concept of securitisation in India. What suggestions do you offer to make it popular?
5. Trace out the development in the field of securitisation in abroad and in India and discuss its future prospects in India.

# 17 DERIVATIVES

With the opening of the economy to multinationals and the adoption of the liberalised economic policies, the economy is driven more towards the free market economy. The complex nature of the financial structuring itself involves the utilisation of multicurrency transactions. It exposes the clients, particularly corporate clients to various risks such as exchange rate risk, interest rate risk, economic risk and political risk.

With the integration of the financial markets and free mobility of capital, risks also multiplied. For instance, when countries adopt floating exchange rates, they have to face risks due to fluctuations in exchange rates. Deregulation of interest rates cause interest risks. Again, securitisation has brought with it the risk of default or counterparty risk. Apart from it, every asset — whether commodity or metal or share or currency — is subject to depreciation in its value. It may be due to certain inherent factors and external factors like the market conditions, Government's policy, economic and political conditions prevailing in a country and so on.

In the present state of the economy, there is an imperative need for the corporate clients to protect their operating profits by shifting some of the uncontrollable financial risks to those who are able to bear and manage them. Thus, risk management becomes a must for survival since there is a high volatility in the present financial markets.

In this context, derivatives occupy an important place as a risk-reducing machinery. Derivatives are useful to reduce many of the risks discussed above. In fact, the financial service companies can play a very dynamic role in dealing with such risks. They can ensure that the above risks are hedged by using derivatives like forwards, futures, options, swaps, etc. Derivatives, thus, enable the clients to transfer their financial risks to the financial service companies. This really protects the clients from unforeseen risks and helps them to get their due operating profits or to keep the project well within the budgeted costs. To hedge the various risks that one faces in the financial market today, derivatives are absolutely essential.

## ❖ Meaning

In a broad sense, many commonly used instruments can be called derivatives since they derive their value from an underlying asset. For instance, equity share itself is a derivative, since, it derives its value from the firm's underlying assets. Similarly, one takes an insurance against his house covering all risks. This insurance is also a derivative instruments on the house. Again, if one signs a contract with a building contractor stipulating a condition, that, if the cost of materials goes up by 15 per cent, the contract price will also go up by 10 per cent. This is also a kind of derivative contract. Thus, derivatives cover a lot of common transactions.

In a strict sense, derivatives are based upon all those major financial instruments which are explicitly traded like equities, debt instruments, forex instruments and commodity based contracts. Thus, when we talk about derivatives, we usually mean only financial derivatives, namely, forwards, futures, options, swaps, etc. The peculiar features of these instruments are that:

*(i)* They can be designed in such a way so as to cater to the varied requirements of the users either by simply using any one of the above instruments or by using a combination of two or more such instruments.

*(ii)* They can be designed and traded on the basis of the expectations regarding the future price movements of underlying assets.

*(iii)* They are all off-balance sheet instruments.

*(iv)* They are used as a device for reducing the risks of fluctuations in asset values.

As the word implies, a derivative instrument is derived from 'something' backing it. This something may be a loan, an asset, an interest rate, a currency flow, a stock trade, a commodity transaction, a trade flow, etc. Derivatives enable a company to hedge 'this something' without changing the flow associated with the business operation.

## ❖ Definition

It is very difficult to define the term derivatives in a comprehensive way since many developments have taken place in this field in recent years. Moreover, many innovative instruments have been created by combining two or more of these financial derivatives so as to cater to the specific requirements of users, depending upon the circumstances. In spite of this, some attempts have been made to define the term 'derivatives'.

One such definition is, 'Derivatives involve payment/receipt of income generated by the underlying asset on a notional principal'.

According to another definition, 'Derivatives are a special type of off-balance sheet instruments in which no principal is ever paid'.

Yet another definition runs as follows: 'Derivatives are instruments which make payments calculated using price of interest rates derived from on balance sheet or cash instruments, but do not actually employ those cash instruments to fund payments'.

All these definitions point out the fact that transactions are carried out on a notional principal, transferring only the income generated by the underlying asset.

## KINDS OF FINANCIAL DERIVATIVES

As already discussed, the important financial derivatives are the following:

(*i*) Forwards,

(*ii*) Futures,

(*iii*) Options, and

(*iv*) Swaps.

**Forwards:** Forwards are the oldest of all the derivatives. A forward contract refers to an agreement between two parties to exchange an agreed quantity of an asset for cash at a certain date in future at a predetermined price specified in that agreement. The promised asset may be currency, commodity, instrument, etc.

**Example:** On June 1, X enters into an agreement to buy 50 bales of cotton on December 1 at ₹ 1,000 per bale from Y, a cotton dealer. It is a case of a forward contract where X has to pay ₹ 50,000 on December 1 to Y and Y has to supply 50 bales of cotton.

In a forward contract, a user (holder) who promises to buy the specified asset at an agreed price at a fixed future date is said to be in the 'Long position'. On the other hand, the user (holder) who promises to sell at an agreed price at a future date is said to be in 'Short position'. Thus, 'long position' and 'short position' take the form of 'buy' and 'sell' in a forward contract.

## FEATURES OF FORWARD CONTRACTS

In a forward contract, the supply of an asset is promised at a future date. This contract is usually referred to as 'Forward Rate Contract' (FRC).

**(i) Over The Counter Trading (OTC):** These contracts are purely privately arranged agreements and hence, they are not at all standardised ones. They are traded 'Over The Counter' (OTC) and not in exchanges. There is much flexibility since the contract can be modified according to the requirements of the parties to the contract. Parties enter into this kind of contract on the basis of the custom, and hence, it is also called 'customised contract'.

**(ii) No down payment:** There must be a promise to supply or receive a specified asset at an agreed price at a future date. The contracting parties need not pay any down payment at the time of agreement.

**(iii) Settlement at maturity:** The important feature of a forward contract is that no money or commodity changes hand when the contract is signed. Invariably, it takes place on the date of maturity only as given in the contract.

**(iv) Linearity:** Another special feature of a forward rate contract is linearity. It means symmetrical gains or losses due to price fluctuation of the underlying asset. When the spot price in future exceeds the contract price, the forward buyer stands to gain. The gain will be equal to spot price minus contract price. If the spot price in future falls below the contract price, he incurs a loss. The gain which one can get when the price moves in one direction will be exactly equal to the loss when the price moves in the other direction by the same amount. It means that the loss of the forward buyer is the gain of the forward seller and *vice versa*.

**(v) No secondary market:** A forward rate contract is a purely private contract, and hence, it cannot be traded on an organised stock exchange. So, there is no secondary market for it.

**(vi) Necessity of a third party:** There is a need for an intermediary to enable the parties to enter into a forward rate contract. This intermediary may be any financial institution like bank or any other third party.

**(vii) Delivery:** The delivery of the asset which is the subject matter of the contract is essential on the date of the maturity of the contract.

## FINANCIAL FORWARDS

Forward rate contracts for commodities are commonly found in India. But, the use of this instrument in the financial market is a new phenomenon. The popular type of financial forward rate contract is the forward rate currency contract.

### ❖ Forward Rate currency contract

It is a contract where exchange of currencies is promised at an agreed exchange rate at a specified future date. The important feature of this contract is that the pay-off is proportional to the difference between the rate specified in the Forward Rate Contract and the price of the currency prevailing in the market at the time of settlement.

The following table shows the position of net pay-off to the holder of a forward rate contract:

**TABLE 17.1: NET PAY-OFF TO A HOLDER OF A FORWARD CONTRACT TO BUY 1 LAKH UNITS OF A COMMODITY**

| | | | | | |
|---|---|---|---|---|---|
| Forward rate (₹/Unit) | | 2.75 | | | |
| Spot rate on maturity (₹) | 2.65 | 2.70 | 2.75 | 2.80 | 2.85 |
| Net payoff (₹ lakhs) | –10 | –0.05 | 0.0 | +0.05 | +10 |

***Source:*** Journal of the Indian Institute of Bankers.

The above table clearly shows that the net pay-off is exactly equal to the difference between the forward rate and the spot rate at the time of settlement.

### ❖ Forward rate contract on interest rate

The extension of the forwards to the interest market is an important innovation. This type of contract is called Forward Rate Agreement (FRA). It is a contract where parties enter into a forward interest rate agreement at a specified future date. On the date of maturity, the difference between the forward interest rate as mentioned in the agreement and the interest rate prevailing in the market at that time (Spot rate) is paid/received (as the case may be) on a notional principal

### Diagram showing Forward Rate Agreement

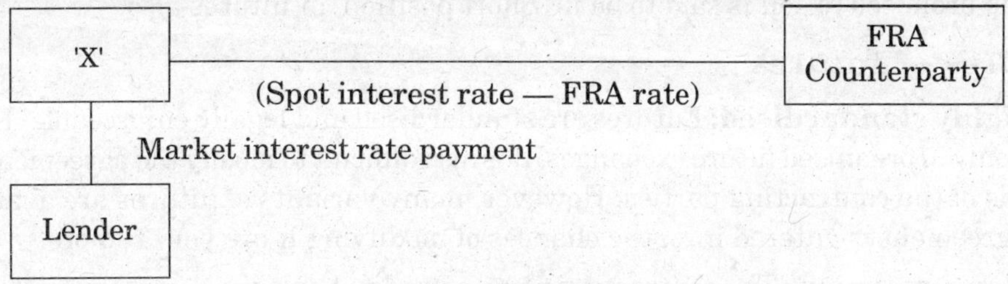


Pay-off Table

| | | |
|---|---|---|
| Interest paid by 'X' | = | Market interest rate |
| Interest received by 'X' from FRA counterparty | = | Difference between FRA interest rate and market interest rate |
| Net interest paid by 'X' | = | FRA interest rate |

***Source:*** Journal of the Indian Institute of Bankers.

The special feature of this contract is that the holder or user of this forward is protected against future rise in interest rates. It is so because, on the due date, the interest which he has to pay will be exactly equal to the Forward Rate Agreement rate. For example, a financial intermediary expects a good demand for funds after 4 months. So, he enters into a Forward Rate Agreement after 4 months at a specified interest rate. After 4 months, he has to pay or receive the difference between the FRA interest rate and the market interest rate. As a result, his net payment of interest on the funds borrowed after 4 months will be equal to the FRA rate only.

The diagram and the pay-off table explains the position clearly.

This type of agreement is confined to short period only and due to risk of default, long dated forward rate contracts are not popular. Thus, forwards are becoming popular in financial markets in recent times.

## FUTURES

A futures contract is very similar to a forward contract in all respects excepting the fact that it is completely a standardised one. Hence, it is rightly said that a futures contract is nothing but a standardised forward contract. It is legally enforceable and it is always traded on an organised exchange.

Clark has defined future trading 'as a special type of futures contract bought and sold under the rules of organised exchanges'. The term 'future trading' includes both speculative transactions where futures are bought and sold with the objective of making profits from the price changes and also the hedging or protective transactions where futures are bought and sold with a view to avoiding unforeseen losses resulting from price fluctuations.

A futures contract is one where there is an agreement between two parties to exchange any asset or currency or commodity for cash at a certain future date, at an agreed price. Both the parties to the contract must have mutual trust in each other. It takes place only in organised futures markets and according to well established standards.

As in a forward contract, the trader who promises to buy is said to be in 'Long position' and the one who promises to sell is said to be in 'Short position' in futures also.

## ❖ Features of futures

**(i) Highly standardised:** Futures are standardised and legally enforceable. Hence, they are traded only in organised future exchanges. It is also difficult to modify the agreement according to the needs of the contracting parties. However, many variants of futures are available. But, once the agreement is entered into, the chances of modifying it are very remote.

**(ii) Down payment:** The contracting parties need not pay any down payment at the time of agreement. However, they deposit a certain percentage of the contract price with the exchange and it is called initial margin. This gives a guarantee that the contract will be honoured.

**(iii) Settlements:** Though future contracts can be held till maturity, they are not so in actual practice. Futures instruments are 'marked to the market' and the exchange records profit and loss on them on daily basis. That is, once a futures contract is entered into, profits or losses to both the parties are calculated on a daily basis. The difference between the futures price and the spot price on that day constitutes either profit or loss depending upon the prevailing spot prices. The spot price is nothing but the market price prevailing then.

For example, on Monday morning, X enters into a futures agreement with Y to buy 50 bales of cotton at ₹ 100 per bale on Friday afternoon. At the close of trading on Monday, the futures price goes up by ₹ 10 per bale. Now, X will get a cash profit of ₹ 500 for 50 bales at the rate of ₹ 10 per bale. X can also cancel the existing futures contract with the price ₹ 100 per bale or he can enter into a new futures contract at ₹ 110 per bale.

Generally, these profits or losses are accumulated in the margin accounts of the parties. But, if there are continuous losses and if the initial margin falls below a minimum level called 'maintenance margin', then the exchange authorities will interfere. In such a situation, the contract automatically lapses. The default risk due to such a lapse is limited to the profit or loss booked during that day. Since the exchange guarantees the performance of the contract by both the counterparties, the default risk is borne by the exchange.

**(iv) Hedging of price risks:** The main feature of a futures contract is to hedge against price fluctuations. The buyers of a futures contract hope to protect themselves from future spot price increases and the sellers from future spot price decreases. Parties enter into futures agreements on the basis of their expectations of the future price in the spot market for the assets in question.

**(v) Linearity:** As stated earlier, futures contract is nothing but a standardised forward contract. Therefore, it also possesses the property of linearity. Parties to the contract get symmetrical gains or losses due to price fluctuation of the underlying asset on either direction

**(vi) Secondary market:** Futures are dealt in organised exchanges, and as such, they have secondary market too.

**(vii) Non-delivery of the asset:** The delivery of the asset in question is not essential on the date of maturity of the contract in the case of a futures contract. Generally, parties simply exchange the difference between the future and spot prices on the date of maturity.

## TYPES OF FUTURES

Like forwards, futures may also be broadly divided into two types namely:

(*i*) Commodity futures.

(*ii*) Financial futures.

### ❖ Commodity futures

A commodity future is a futures contract in commodities like agricultural products, metals and minerals, etc. In organised commodity future markets, contracts are standardised with standard quantities. Of course, this standard varies from commodity-to-commodity. They also have fixed delivery dates in each month or a few months in a year. In India, commodity futures in agricultural products are popular.

Some of the well established commodity exchanges are as follows:

(*i*) London Metal Exchange (LME) to deal in gold.

(*ii*) Chicago Board of Trade (CBT) to deal in soyabean oil.

(*iii*) New York Cotton Exchange (CTN) to deal in cotton.

(*iv*) Commodity Exchange, New York (COMEX) to deal in agricultural products.

(*v*) International Petroleum Exchange of London (IPE) to deal in crude oil.

### ❖ Financial futures

Financial futures refer to a futures contract in foreign exchange or financial instruments like treasury bill, commercial paper, stock market index or interest rate. It is an area where financial service companies can play a very dynamic role. Financial futures are very popular in Western countries as hedging instruments to protect against exchange rate/interest rate fluctuations and for ensuring future interest rates on loans.

Just like forward rate currency contracts and forward rate contracts on interest rates, we have futures contracts on currency and interest rates. But, the primary objective of futures markets is to enable individuals and companies to hedge against price fluctuations. For example, risks due to interest rate fluctuations and exchange rate fluctuations are very common. These risks cannot be eliminated but transferred to a counterparty. This counterparty may have a hedging motive with opposite requirements.

The stock index futures contract is a futures contract on major stock market indices. This type of contract is very much useful for speculators, investors and especially portfolio managers. They can hedge against future decline or increase in prices of portfolios depending upon the situation. Generally, the asset will not be delivered on the maturity of the contract. The parties simply exchange the difference between the future and spot prices on the date of maturity. But, these kinds of financial futures are relatively new in India.

Some of the well established financial futures exchanges are the following:

(*i*) International Monetary Market (IMM) to deal in US treasury bills, Euro-dollar deposits, Sterling, etc.

(*ii*) London International Financial Futures Exchange (LIFFE) to deal in Euro-dollar deposits.

(*iii*) New York Futures Exchange (NYFE) to deal in Sterling, Euro-dollar deposits, etc.

## FORWARDS VS. FUTURES CONTRACT

For all practical purposes, when a forward contract is standardised and dealt in an organised exchange, it becomes a futures contract. Basically, they both seem to be one and the same. However, they differ from each other in the following respects.

**(i) Nature of the contract:** A forward contract is not at all a standardised one. It is a tailor-made contract in the sense that the terms of the contract like quantity, price, period, date, delivery conditions, etc. can be negotiated between the parties according to their convenience. On the other hand, a futures contract is a highly standardised one where all the terms of the contract are standardised and they cannot be altered to the requirements of the parties to the contract.

**(ii) Existence of secondary market:** Since forward contract is a customised contract, it is not a standard one. So, it cannot be traded on an organised exchange. With a result, there is no secondary market for a forward contract. But, futures contract can be traded on organised exchanges. Hence, it has a secondary market.

**(iii) Settlement:** A forward contract is always settled only on the date of maturity. But, a futures contract is always settled daily, irrespective of the maturity date, in the sense that, it is 'marked-to-market' on a daily basis.

**(iv) Modus operandi:** Generally, parties enter into a forward agreement with the help of some financial intermediary like a bank. But, it is not so in the case of a futures contract. It is mainly facilitated through organised exchanges and the question of a third party does not arise.

**(v) Down payment:** In the case of a forward contract, the contracting parties need not pay any down payment at the time of agreement. However, in the case of a futures contract, the contracting parties have to deposit a certain percentage of the contract price as 'Margin money' with the exchange. It acts as a collateral to support the contract.

**(vi) Delivery of the asset:** The delivery of the asset in question is essential on the date of maturity of the contract in the case of a forward contract, whereas a futures contract does not end with the delivery of the asset. The parties merely exchange the difference between the future and spot prices on the date of maturity.

## ADVANTAGES

One can derive the following advantages from a forward as well as futures contract:

**(i) Protection against price fluctuations:** Parties to these contracts can protect themselves against the risk of adverse fluctuations in the price of assets in question. For instance, the buyer of a forward rate currency contract can avoid the risk of a possible adverse hike in the exchange rate in future. Similarly, the buyer of a commodity future contract can avoid the risk of a possible price escalation in future. Thus, risks can be overcome.

(ii) **Avoidance of carrying costs:** The buyer of this contract can avoid paying carrying costs on the asset bought in advance since he need not take delivery of the asset in advance of the time it is required.

(iii) **Proper planning for buying/selling:** These contracts enable the parties to buy or sell assets at the time when they are most required and thus they prevent the need to purchase or sell assets in advance of future requirements. Thus, they facilitate proper planning for buying and selling.

(iv) **Proper portfolio management:** Portfolio managers, investors or even speculators can use these contracts to hedge against future declines in portfolios or against adverse future fluctuations in prices. Thus, they act as boon to portfolio managers in portfolio management.

(v) **Proper cash management:** These contracts avoid the payment of the purchase price immediately. In the absence of these contracts, liquid cash must have been paid at the time of the contract itself. Now, the purchaser can make use of this fund to earn further income till the maturity of the contract. Thus, efficient cash management is made possible with the help of these contracts.

(vi) **Purchases and sales in bulk:** These contracts facilitate bulk purchases and sales of assets at short notice in advance of delivery and even in advance of production.

(vii) **Highly flexible:** These contracts are highly flexible and if the parties to the contract prefer to close out their positions, they can do so by exchanging the net difference between the positions. They need not take the trouble of exchanging the assets physically.

(viii) **Boon to financial intermediaries:** These contracts give a very good scope for the financial companies to play a dynamic role. They can act as intermediaries between the parties. They can diversify their activities by innovating new instruments in this field and taking up new lines of financial activities in the best interest of their customers.

## OPTIONS

In the volatile environment, risk of heavy fluctuations in the prices of assets is very heavy. Option is yet another tool to manage such risks.

As the very name implies, an option contract gives the buyer an option to buy or sell an underlying asset (stock, bond, currency, commodity, etc.), at a predetermined price on or before a specified date in future. The price so predetermined is called the 'strike price' or 'exercise price'.

### ❖ Writer

In an options contract, the seller is usually referred to as a 'writer' since he is said to write the contract. It is similar to the seller who is said to be in 'Short position' in a forward contract. However, in a put option, the writer is in a different position. He is obliged to buy shares. In an option contract, the buyer has to pay a certain amount at the time of writing the contract for enjoying the right to buy or sell.

### ❖ American option vs. European option

In an option contract, if the option can be exercised at any time between the writing of the contract and its expiration, it is called as an American option. On the other hand, if it can be exercised only at the time of maturity, it is termed as European option.

## TYPES OF OPTIONS

Options may fall under any one of the following main categories:

(*i*) Call option.

(*ii*) Put option.

(*iii*) Double option.

(*iv*) In the Money option (ITM).

(*v*) At the Money option (ATM).

(*vi*) Out of the Money option (OTM).

**(i) Call option:** A call option is one which gives the option holder the right to buy an underlying asset (commodities, foreign exchange, stocks, shares, etc.) at a predetermined price called 'exercise price' or strike price on or before a specified date in future. In such a case, the writer of a call option is under an obligation to sell the asset at the specified price, in case the buyer exercises his option to buy. Thus, the obligation to sell arises only when the option is exercised.

**(ii) Put option:** A put option is one which gives the option holder the right to sell an underlying asset at a predetermined price on or before a specified date in future. It means that the writer of a put option is under an obligation to buy the asset at the exercise price provided the option holder exercises his option to sell.

**(iii) Double option:** A double option is one which gives the option holder both the rights — either to buy or to sell an underlying asset at a predetermined price on or before a specified date in future.

**(iv) In The Money (ITM) option:** An ITM is an option which gives a positive cash flow to the holder if it were exercised immediately. This can happen only when the current index is higher than the strike price in the case of a call option. In other words, a call option on the index is said to be ITM when the spot price, *i.e.*, the current index is higher than the strike price. Suppose the current index is much higher than the strike price, the call is said be deep ITM.

The opposite is the case of put option. The put is said to be ITM if the current index is lower than the strike price.

**(v) At The Money (ATM) option:** An ATM is one which gives a zero cash flow to its holder if it were exercised immediately. An option on the index is deemed to be ATM when the current index is equal to the strike price.

**(vi) Out of The Money option (OTM):** If the immediate exercise of an option gives a negative cash flow to its holder, that option is said to be an OTM. Thus, a call option on the index is OTM when the current index is lower than the strike price. If the index is much lower than the strike price, the call option is said to the deep OTM.

The reverse is the case of put option. The put is said to be OTM if the current index is higher than the strike price.

## ❖ Option premium

In an option contract, the option writer agrees to buy or sell an underlying asset at a future date for an agreed price from/to the option buyer/seller at his option. This contract, like any other contract, must be supported by consideration. The consideration for this contract is a sum of money called 'premium'. The premium is nothing but the price which is required to be paid for the purchase of 'right to buy or sell'.

The premium, one pays, is the maximum amount to which he is exposed in the market, since, in any case he cannot lose more than that amount. Thus, his risk is limited to that extent only. However, his gain potential is unlimited. In the case of a double option, this premium money is also double.

## ❖ Options market

Options market refers to the market where option contracts are bought and sold. Once an option contract is written, it can be bought or sold on the options market. The first option market namely the Chicago Board of Options Exchange was set up in 1973. Thereafter, several options markets have been established.

## FEATURES OF OPTION CONTRACT

(i) **Highly flexible:** On one hand, option contracts are highly standardised and so they can be traded only in organised exchanges. Such option instruments cannot be made flexible according to the requirements of the writer as well as the user. On the other hand, there are also privately arranged options which can be traded 'over the counter'. These instruments can be made according to the requirements of the writer and user. Thus, it combines the features of 'futures' as well as 'forward' contracts.

(ii) **Down payment:** The option holder must pay a certain amount called 'premium' for holding the right of exercising the option. This is considered to be the consideration for the contract. If the option holder does not exercise his option, he has to forego this premium. Otherwise, this premium will be deducted from the total pay-off in calculating the net pay-off due to the option holder.

(iii) **Settlement:** No money or commodity or share is exchanged when the contract is written. Generally, this option contract terminates either at the time of exercising the option by the option holder or maturity whichever is earlier. So, settlement is made only when the option holder exercises his option. Suppose the option is not exercised till maturity, then the agreement automatically lapses and no settlement is required.

(iv) **Non-linearity:** Unlike futures and forward, an option contract does not possess the property of linearity. It means that the option holder's profit, when the value of the underlying asset moves in one direction is not equal to his loss when its value moves in the opposite direction by the same amount. In short, profits and losses are not symmetrical under an option contract. This can be illustrated by means of an illustration:

Mr. X purchases a two-month call option on rupee at ₹ 100 = $ 3.35. Suppose, the rupee appreciates within two months by $ 0.05 per one hundred rupees, then the market price would be ₹ 100 = $ 3.40. If the option holder Mr. X exercises his option, he can purchase at the rate mentioned in the option, *i.e.*, ₹ 100 = $ 3.35. He gets a pay-off at the rate of $ 0.05 per every one hundred rupees. On the other hand, if the exchange rate moves in the opposite direction by the same amount and reaches a level of ₹ 100 = $ 3.30, the option holder will not exercise his option. Then, his loss will be zero. Thus, in an option contract, the gain is not equal to the loss.

(v) **No obligation to buy or sell:** In all option contracts, the option holder has a right to buy or sell an underlying asset. He can exercise this right at any time during the currency of the contract. But, in no case, he is under an obligation to buy or sell. If he does not buy or sell, the contract will be simply lapsed.

## ❖ Option trading in shares and stocks

When an option contract is entered into with an option to buy or sell shares or stocks, it is known as 'share option'. Share option transactions are generally index-based. All calculations are based on the change in index value. For example, the present value of an index is 300. A person Mr. X buys a 3-month call option for an index value of 350 by paying 10 per cent of the present index value in points at the rate of ₹ 10 per point. Now, the option price is taken as ₹ 300 and the strike price or exercise price is ₹ 350.

So long as the index remains below 350, the option holder will not exercise his option since he will be incurring losses. Now, the loss will be limited to the premium paid at the rate of ₹ 10 per point. As the spot price increases beyond the strike price level, exercise of the option becomes profitable. Suppose the spot rate reaches 360, option may be exercised. The option holder gets a profit of ₹ 100 (10 points × 10). However, his net position will be ₹ 100 – 300 (premium 10 per cent on 300 × 10). He incurs a net loss of ₹ 200. When the spot rate reaches 380, the break-even point is reached. Beyond this index value, the option holder starts making a profit.

A person with more money can trade the index at a higher price of ₹ 100 or ₹ 200 per index point. However, this kind of game can be played by speculators only. Genuine portfolio managers can use this instrument to hedge their risks due to heavy fluctuations in the prices of shares and stocks.

## ❖ Currency options

Suppose an option contract is entered into between parties to purchase or sell foreign exchange, it is called 'currency option'. This can be illustrated by an example. An option holder buys in September, dollar at the exchange rate of £1= $ 1.900 maturing in November. The spot rate then was £1 = $ 1.875. The strike price therefore is £1 = $ 1.900. Suppose the purchaser also pays a premium of 7.04 cents per £ 1 as long as the price of pound in the market remains below

$ 1.900, the option will not be exercised. Of course, the option holder suffers a loss, but his loss is limited to the premium paid at the rate of 7.04 cents per £ 1. When the spot price increases beyond the strike price, it is profitable to exercise the option. For instance, the spot rate becomes $ 1.9200 per £ 1, if the option holder exercises his option now, he will get a profit of $ .200 per £ 1. However, his net position will be .0200 – 0704 (premium) = – $ .0504 (loss). If the spot rate goes up to £ 1 = $ 1.9704, the break-even point is reached. Beyond this level, the option holder gets profit by exercising his option.

On the other hand, the writer of the option gets profit as long as the option is not exercised. His profit is limited to the premium received, *i.e.*, 7.04 cents per £ 1. When the spot rate goes beyond the strike price, the option holder will exercise his option. At the rate 1 £ = $ 1.9704, the writer of the option is also at the break-even point. If spot rate goes beyond this level, the option writer will suffer a net loss.

## BENEFITS

Option trading is beneficial to the parties. For instance, index-based options help the investment managers to insure the whole portfolio against fall in prices rather than hedging each and every security individually.

Again, option writing is a source of additional income for the portfolio managers with a large portfolio of securities. In fact, large portfolio managers can guess the future movement of stock prices accurately and enter into option trading. Generally, the option writers are the most sophisticated participants in the option market and the option premiums are simply an additional source of income.

Options trading is also quite flexible and simple. For instance, option transactions are index-based and so all calculations are made on the change in index value. The value at which the index points are contracted forms the basis for the calculation of profit or loss, fixing of option price, etc.

In an option contract, the loss is pegged to the minimum of amount, *i.e.*, to the extent of the option premium alone. Hence, the players in the option market know that their losses can be quantified and limited to the amount of premium paid. This may also lead to high speculation. Therefore, it is very essential that options trading must be encouraged for the purpose of hedging risks and not for speculation.

## SWAPS

Swap is yet another exciting trading instrument. In fact, it is a combination of forwards by two counterparties. It is arranged to reap the benefits arising from the fluctuations in the market — either currency market or interest rate market or any other market for that matter.

### ❖ Features

The following are the important features of swap:

**(i) Basically a forward:** A swap is nothing but a combination of forwards. So, it has all the properties of a forward contract discussed above.

**(ii) Double coincidence of wants:** Swap requires that two parties with equal and opposite needs must come into contact with each other. As stated earlier, it is a combination of forwards by two counterparties with opposite but matching needs. For instance, the rate of interest differs from market-to-market and within the market itself. It varies from borrowers-to-borrowers due to the relative creditworthiness of borrowers.

Therefore, borrowers enjoying comparative credit advantage in floating rate debts will enter into a swap agreement to exchange floating rate interest with the borrowers enjoying comparative advantage in fixed interest rate debt, like bonds.

In a bond market, lending is done at a fixed rate for a long duration, and therefore, the lenders do not have the opportunity to adjust the interest rate according to the situation prevailing in the market. So, the lenders are very much concerned with the creditworthiness of borrowers and they expect a premium for the risk involved. This premium is rather high in the case of less creditworthy borrowers.

On the other hand, in the short-term market, the lenders have the flexibility to adjust the floating interest rate (short-term rate) according to the conditions prevailing in the market as well as the current financial position of the borrower. Hence, the short-term floating interest rate is cheaper to the borrower with low credit rating when compared with fixed rate of interest. But, for borrowers with high credit rating, both these rates are cheaper. But, their advantage is comparatively higher in the case of fixed rate debt instruments. Naturally, a borrower with high credit rating will go for long-term funds while a borrower with low credit rating will opt for short-term funds at floating rates. In such a situation, if the borrower with low credit rating wants long-term funds at fixed rates, he has to swap the floating rate interest with fixed rate interest with another counterparty (borrower with high credit rating). Thus, two borrowers must have opposite and matching needs.

**(iii) Necessity of an Intermediary:** Swap requires the existence of two counterparties with opposite but matching needs. This has created a necessity for an intermediary to connect both the parties. By arranging swaps, these intermediaries can earn income also. Financial companies, particularly banks, can play a key role in this innovative field by virtue of their special position in the financial market and their knowledge of the diverse needs of the customers.

**(iv) Settlement:** Though a specified principal amount is mentioned in the swap agreement, there is no exchange of principal. On the other hand, a stream of fixed rate interest is exchanged for a floating rate of interest, and thus, there are streams of cash flows rather than single payment. For instance, one party agrees to pay a fixed rate interest to another party, and, at the same time, he agrees to receive a floating rate of interest from the same party. Both these rates are calculated on a notional principal and there is a continuous exchange of interest rates during the currency of the agreement. There is no such thing as single payment on the due date.

**(v) Long-term agreement:** Generally, forwards are arranged for short period only. Long dated forward rate contracts are not preferred because they involve more risks like risk of default, risk of interest rate fluctuations, etc. But, swaps are in the nature of long-term agreement and they are just like long dated forward rate contracts. The exchange of a fixed rate for a floating rate requires a comparatively longer period.

### ❖ Kinds of swap

A swap can be arranged for the exchange of currencies, interest rates, etc. A swap in which two currencies are exchanged is called cross-currency swap. A swap in which a fixed rate of interest is exchanged for a floating rate is called interest rate swap. This interest rate swap can also be arranged in multi-currencies. A swap in which one stream of floating interest rate is exchanged for another stream of floating interest rate is called 'Basis swap'. Thus, swap can be arranged according to the requirements of the parties concerned and many innovative swap instruments can be evolved like this.

## CREDIT DEFAULT SWAP (CDS)

### ❖ Parties to CDS

Before analysing the various parties involved in CDS, it is very vital that one should have an exposure to certain technical terms used in CDS contacts. The risk of default committed by a particular company is called credit event and the company is called reference entity. Thus, credit events may relate to bankruptcy, failure to pay, repudiation/moratorium, restructuring, obligation default, etc. The buyer the right to sell particular bond issued by the company for its per value when a credit event occurs, and this bond is known as reference obligation. The total par value of the bonds which can be sold is known as the CDS notional principal.

Anticipating some credit risk, the lender may purchase a CDS on the money lent to a borrower.

He is called the protection buyer. He agrees to pay premium to the party from whom CDS is purchased over a period of time in return for compensation if a credit event occurs to a reference entity. The party is called protection seller. Thus, the lender uses default as a credit event to swap it in exchange for repayment from the protection seller.

## CREDIT DEFAULT SWAP VS. INSURANCE

A Credit Default Swap (CDS) appears to be an insurance contract since the protection buyer pays a premium and in return receives a sum of money if credit event occurs. But, in actual practice, there are lot of differences between the two. They are as follows:

1. In case of CDS, the protection buyer need not own the underlying security or other form of credit exposure. But, in the case of insurance, to purchase an insurance, the insured should have an insurable interest like owning a debt obligation.
2. The protection buyer is not expected to suffer any loss in order to recover on the CDS. But, suffering of loss is a must to claim under insurance.
3. The CDS provides an equal payout to all holders according to market wide method. But, insurance provides an indemnity against losses actually suffered by the policyholder.
4. There is no need for the protection seller to be a regulated entity in CDS, whereas the insurer must be a regulated body.

5. Similarly, the protection seller is not required to maintain any reserves to pay-off buyers, whereas such reserves are obligatory under insurance.
6. From pricing angle, the cost of insurance is determined by the actuarial analysis. On the other hand, CDS are derivatives whose cost is determined by financial model and by arbitrage relationships with other credit market instruments like loans and bonds.
7. Insurance contracts require the disclosure of all kinds known risks involved which is not generally required under CDS.
8. A majority of insurance contracts are not tradable whereas CDS is traded on the OTC market.
9. CDS differs from insurance with regard to tax, accounting and in regulatory jurisdictions.
10. In insurance, there are basically two parties, *viz.*, insurer and the insured while in the case of CDS there are three parties, *viz.*, reference entity, protection buyer and protection seller.

## TYPES OF CREDIT DEFAULT SWAP

As seen earlier, CDS is a kind of counterparty agreement by which a third party credit risk is transferred from one party to another. Thus, lender who faces credit risk from a third party can transfer it to a counterparty who agrees to insure the risk in exchange of regular installments. In the event of any default by the third party, the insurer will have to purchase the defaulted asset (debt obligation) from the insured party and in turn insure will pay the remaining interest and the principal to the insured. The CDS has various forms depending on the underlying reference entity and other varying contractual obligations. Some of these types are given below:

### ❖ Single name CDS

As the very name implies, under this type the reference entity is an individual corporation or a bank or a Government.

### ❖ Multi-name CDS or Indexed CDS

This type of CDS is issued on a multiple reference entity linked to an index or a tranche of indices. For example, (1) CDX Index which is consisting of 125 North American investment grade firms. (2) TraXX Index has an equal share of the notional amount of the debt outstanding.

### ❖ Basket CDS

Like Indexed CDS, it is related to portfolios of reference entities which may vary from 3 to 100. Thus, it is a group of reference entities and pay-off follows when the first of these reference entities defaults. This is more customised than indexed CDS.

### ❖ Contingent CDS

Under this type, the pay-off requires both a credit event and an additional trigger which can be a credit event with respect to another reference entity or a specified movement in some market variable.

### ❖ Loan CDS

It is very similar to regular CDS except that the underlying reference entity is limited strictly to the syndicated secured loans rather than any other loan.

### ❖ Funded CDS

Under this type the protection buyer is not exposed to the counter party risk of the protection seller since the protection seller makes an initial payment which is used to settle events.

### ❖ Dynamic CDS

Under this type, the notional amount determines the pay-off linked to the mark to market value of a portfolio of swaps.

### ❖ Binary CDS

Under this type, in the event of a default the pay-off is a specific dollar amount.

## ADVANTAGES

The following advantages can be derived by a systematic use of swap:

(i) **Borrowing at lower cost:** Swap facilitates borrowing at lower cost. It works on the principle of the theory of comparative cost as propounded by Ricardo. One borrower exchanges the comparative advantage possessed by him with the comparative advantage possessed by the other borrower. The net result is that both the parties are able to get funds at cheaper rates.

(ii) **Access to new financial markets:** Swap is used to have access to new financial markets for funds by exploring the comparative advantage possessed by the other party in that market. Thus, the comparative advantage possessed by parties is fully exploited through swap. Hence, funds can be obtained from the best possible source at cheaper rates.

(iii) **Hedging of risk:** Swap can also be used to hedge risk. For instance, a company has issued fixed rate bonds. It strongly feels that the interest rate will decline in future due to some changes in the economic scene. So, to get the benefit in future from the fall in interest rate, it has to exchange the fixed rate obligation with floating rate obligation. That is to say, the company has to enter into a swap agreement with a counterparty, whereby, it has to receive fixed rate interest and pay floating rate interest. The net result is that the company will have to pay only floating rate of interest. The fixed rate it has to pay is compensated by the fixed rate it receives from the counterparty. Thus, risks due to fluctuations in interest rate can be overcome through swap agreements. Similar agreements can be entered into for currencies also.

(iv) **Tool to correct asset-liability mismatch:** Swap can be profitably used to manage asset-liability mismatch. For example, a bank has acquired a fixed rate interest bearing asset on the one hand and a floating rate interest bearing liability on the other hand. In case the interest rate goes up, the bank would be much affected because with the increase in interest rate, the bank has to pay more interest. This is so because, the interest payment is based on the floating rate. But, the interest receipt will not go up, since the receipt is based on the fixed rate. Now, the asset-liability mismatch emerges. This can be conveniently managed by swap. If the bank feels that the interest rate would go up, it has to simply swap the fixed rate with the floating rate of interest. It means that the bank should find a counterparty who is willing to receive a fixed rate interest in exchange for a floating rate. Now, the receipt of fixed rate of interest by the bank is exactly matched with the payment of fixed rate interest to swap counterparty. Similarly, the receipt of floating rate of interest from the swap counterparty is exactly matched with the payment of floating interest rate on liabilities. Thus, swap is used as a tool to correct any asset-liability mismatch in interest rates in future.

(v) **Additional income:** By arranging swaps, financial intermediaries can earn additional income in the form of brokerage.

## IMPORTANCE OF DERIVATIVES

Thus, derivatives are becoming increasingly important in world markets as a tool for risk management. Derivative instruments can be used to minimise risk. Derivatives are used to separate the risks and transfer them to parties willing to bear these risks. The kind of hedging that can be obtained by using derivatives is cheaper and more convenient than what could be obtained by using cash instruments. It is so because, when we use derivatives for hedging, actual delivery of the underlying asset is not at all essential for settlement purposes. The profit or loss on derivative deal alone is adjusted in the derivative market.

Moreover, derivatives do not create any new risk. They simply manipulate risks and transfer them to those who are willing to bear these risks. To cite a common example, let us assume that Mr. X owns a car. If he does not take an insurance, he runs a big risk. Suppose he buys an insurance (a derivative instrument on the car), he reduces his risk. Thus, having an insurance policy reduces the risk of owing a car. Similarly, hedging through derivatives reduces the risk of owning a specified asset which may be a share, currency, etc.

Hedging risk through derivatives is not similar to speculation. The gain or loss on a derivative deal is likely to be offset by an equivalent loss or gain in the values of underlying assets. 'Offsetting of risks' is an important property of hedging transactions. But, in speculation, one deliberately takes up a risk openly. When companies know well that they have to face risk in possessing assets, it is better to transfer these risks to those who are ready to bear them. So, they have to necessarily go for derivative instruments.

All derivative instruments are very simple to operate. Treasury managers and portfolio managers can hedge all risks without going through the tedious process of hedging each day and amount/share separately.

Till recently, it may not have been possible for companies to hedge their long-term risk, say 10-15 year risk. But with the rapid development of the derivative markets, now, it is possible to cover such risks through derivative instruments like swap. Thus, the availability of advanced derivatives market enables companies to concentrate on those management decisions other than funding decisions.

Further, all derivative products are low-cost products. Companies can hedge a substantial portion of their balance sheet exposure, with a low margin requirement.

Derivatives also offer high liquidity. Just as derivatives can be contracted easily, it is also possible for companies to get out of positions in case that market reacts otherwise. This also does not involve much cost.

Thus, derivatives are not only desirable but also necessary to hedge the complex exposures and volatilities that the companies generally face in the financial markets today.

## INHIBITING FACTORS

Though derivatives are very useful for managing various risks, there are certain inhibiting factors which stand in their way. They are as follows:

(i) **Misconception of derivatives:** There is a wrong feeling that derivatives would bring in financial collapse. There is an enormous negative publicity in the wake of a few incidents of financial misadventure. For instance, Barings had its entire net worth wiped out as a result of its trading and options writing on the Nikkei index futures. There are some other similar incidents like this. To quote a few: Procter and Gamble, Indah Kiat, Showa Shell, etc. However, it must be understood that derivatives are not the root cause for all these troubles. Derivatives themselves cannot cause such mishaps. But, the improper handling of these instruments is the main cause for this and one cannot simply blame derivatives for all these mishappenings.

(ii) **Leveraging:** One of the important characteristic features of derivatives is that they lend themselves to leveraging. That is, they are 'high risk-high reward vehicles'. There is a prospect of either high return or huge loss in all derivative instruments. So, there is a feeling that only a few can play this game. There is no doubt that derivatives create leverage and leverage creates increased risk or return. At the same time, one should keep in mind that the very same derivatives, if properly handled, could be used as an efficient tool to minimise risks.

(iii) **Off-balance sheet items:** Invariably, derivatives are off-balance sheet items. For instance, swap agreements for substituting fixed interest rate bonds by floating rate bonds or for substituting fixed rate interest bearing asset by floating rate interest paying liability. Hence, accountants, regulators and others look down upon derivatives.

(iv) **Absence of proper accounting system:** To achieve the desired results, derivatives must be strongly supported by proper accounting systems, efficient internal control and strict supervision. Unfortunately, they are all at infancy level as far as derivatives are concerned.

(v) **In-built speculative mechanism:** In fact, all derivative contracts are structured basically on the basis of the future price movements over which the speculators have an upper hand. Indirectly, derivatives make one accept the fact that speculation is beneficial. It may not be so always. Thus, derivatives possess an inbuilt speculative mechanism.

(vi) **Absence of proper infrastructure:** An important requirement for using derivative instrument like options, futures, etc. is the existence of proper infrastructure. Hence, the institutional infrastructure has to be developed. There has to be effective surveillance, price dissemination and regulation of derivative transactions. The terms of the derivative contracts have to be uniform and standardised.

## RECENT DEVELOPMENTS

At present, Derivative Trading has been permitted by the SEBI on the derivative segment of the BSE and the F&O segment of the NSE. The nature of derivative contracts permitted are:

(*i*) Interest rate swaps (IRS) introduced in July 1999.

(*ii*) Index Futures contracts introduced in June 2000.

(*iii*) Index options introduced in June 2001.

(*iv*) Stock options introduced in July 2001.

(*v*) Currency Futures and options introduced in 2008.

(*vi*) Interest rate futures introduced in August 2009.

(*vii*) Credit Default Swap (CDS) of corporate lenders introduced in October 2011.

(*viii*) Volatility Index Futures introduced in February 2014.

The minimum contract size for a derivative contract in ₹ 2 lakhs. Besides the minimum contract size, there is a stipulation for the lot size of a derivative contract. The lot size refers to number of underlying securities in one contract. The lot size of the underlying individual security should be in multiples of 100 and fractions, if any should be rounded off to the next higher multiple of 100. This requirement along with the requirement of minimum contract size forms the basis for arriving at the lot size of a contract.

Apart from the above, there are market wide limits also. The market wide limit for index products is NIL. For stock-specific products, it is of open positions. But, for option and futures the following wide limits have been fixed:

(*i*) 30 times the average number of shares traded daily, during the previous calendar month in the cash segment of the exchange.

Or

(*ii*) 10 per cent of the number of shares held by non-promoters, *i.e.*, 10 per cent of the free float in terms of number of shares of a company.

### ❖ Eligibility conditions

The SEBI has laid down some eligibility conditions for Derivative Exchange/Segment and its Clearing Corporation/House. They are as follows:

- The Derivatives Exchange/Segment shall have online surveillance capability to monitor positions, prices, and volumes on a real-time basis so as to deter market manipulation.
- The Derivatives Exchange/Segment should have arrangements for dissemination of information about trades, quantities and quotes on a real-time basis through at least

two information vending networks, which are easily accessible to investors across the country.

- The Derivatives Exchange/Segment should have arbitration and investor grievances redressal mechanism operative from all the four areas/regions of the country.
- The Derivatives Exchange/Segment should have satisfactory system of monitoring investor complaints and preventing irregularities in trading.
- The Derivative Segment of the Exchange would have a separate Investor Protection Fund.
- The Clearing Corporation/House shall perform full novation, *i.e.*, the Clearing Corporation/House shall interpose itself between both legs of every trade, becoming the legal counterparty to both or alternatively should provide an unconditional guarantee for settlement of all trades.
- The Clearing Corporation/House shall have the capacity to monitor the overall position of members across both derivatives market and the underlying securities market for those members who are participating in both.
- The level of initial margin on Index Futures Contracts shall be related to the risk of loss on the position. The concept of value-at-risk shall be used in calculating required level of initial margins. The initial margins should be large enough to cover the one-day loss that can be encountered on the position on 99 per cent of the days.
- The Clearing Corporation/House shall establish facilities for Electronic Funds Transfer (EFT) for swift movement of margin payments.
- In the event of a member defaulting in meeting its liabilities, the Clearing Corporation/House shall transfer client positions and assets to another solvent member or close-out all open positions.
- The Clearing Corporation/House should have capabilities to segregate initial margins deposited by Clearing Members for trades on their own account and on account of his client. The Clearing Corporation/House shall hold the clients' margin money in trust for the client purposes only and should not allow its diversion for any other purpose.
- The Clearing Corporation/House shall have a separate Trade Guarantee Fund for the trades executed on Derivative Exchange/Segment.

## ❖ Investors' protection

The SEBI has taken the following measures to protect the money and interest of investors in the derivative market. They are as follows:

- Investor's money has to be kept separate at all levels and is permitted to be used only against the liability of the investor and is not available to the trading member or clearing member or even any other investor.
- The trading member is required to provide every investor with a risk disclosure document which will disclose the risks associated with the derivatives trading so that investors can take a conscious decision to trade in derivatives.

- Investor would get the contract note duly time stamped for receipt of the order and execution of the order. The order will be executed with the identity of the client and without client ID order will not be accepted by the system. The investor could also demand the trade confirmation slip with his ID in support of the contract note. This will protect him from the risk of price favour, if any, extended by the member.
- In the derivative markets, all money paid by the investor towards margins on all open positions is kept in trust with the Clearing House/Clearing Corporation and in the event of default of the Trading or Clearing Member the amounts paid by the client towards margins are segregated and not utilised towards the default of the member. However, in the event of a default of a member, losses suffered by the investor, if any, on settled/closed out position are compensated from the Investor Protection Fund, as per the rules, bye-laws and regulations of the derivative segment of the exchanges.

## ❖ Physical delivery in equity derivatives segment

The absence of physical delivery in the derivatives market is one of the reasons for the high volatility in the market. Hence, the SEBI has decided to allow stock exchanges to introduce physical settlement of equity derivatives so as to bring greater stability and depth to the stock market. Again, SEBI has permitted the introduction of equity derivatives contracts with tenures of up to five years and also derivative products based on the volatility indices.

## ❖ Standard lot size for equity derivatives

Lot size refers to the number of underlying securities in one contract. Recently, the SEBI has standardised the lot size for derivative contracts on individual securities. The lot size as determined by SEBI is given below in Table 17.2.

**TABLE 17.2**

| *Sl. No.* | *Price Band* | *Lot Size* |
|---|---|---|
| 1 | Price of ₹ 1,601 and above | 125 |
| 2 | Between ₹ 801 and ₹ 1,600 | 250 |
| 3 | Between ₹ 401 and ₹ 800 | 500 |
| 4 | Between ₹ 201 and ₹ 400 | 1,000 |
| 5 | Between ₹ 101 and ₹ 200 | 2,000 |
| 6 | Between ₹ 51 and ₹ 100 | 4,000 |
| 7 | Between ₹ 25 and ₹ 50 | 8,000 |
| 8 | Below ₹ 25 | Multiples of 1,000 |

## ❖ Currency derivatives

The SEBI is planning to introduce more currency derivative products in India. To begin with, currency option has been introduced in India in August 2008. A currency option is a derivative instrument which gives the owner the right, but not the obligation to exchange money denominated in one currency into another currency at a predetermined exchange rate on a specified date. The currency volumes on any given day are in the range of $ 6-7 billion.

Recently, the RBI has given permission to the country's newest stock exchange called the United Stock Exchange of India Ltd. (USE) for dealing in currency derivatives. All the 21 Indian public sector banks, leading private sector banks, public sector undertakings and corporates are shareholders of the exchange.

The currency future market is active in India. The average daily turnover in currency futures on the three active exchanges (NSE, MCX-SX and USE) stood at US $ 8.0 billion in March 2011 as against US $ 7.1 billion in March 2010.

## INDIAN SCENARIO

Though exchange-traded derivative instruments were launched in India recently, the popularity of these instruments has grown at a greater pace than the expected level. A recent survey conducted by the World Federation of Exchanges reveals that Indian exchanges have now evolved as significant players in the global derivatives arena.

### ❖ Currency derivatives

Currency futures dominate in the currency derivatives since currency options were introduced only in October 2010. While trading is allowed in four currency pairs of dollar-rupee, euro-rupee, pound-rupee and yen-rupee, it is the dollar-rupee pair that is most widely traded and accounted for almost 90 per cent of the turnover in 2010. The topmost exchange, globally, in terms of the number of contracts traded in currency futures in 2010 was MCS-SX with 885 million contracts, notional value being $ 908 billion. The NSE was second with 726 million contracts. However, in terms of the notional value of the contract traded, the Chicago Mercantile Exchange group gets the top place with $ 29,979 billion.

### ❖ Stock futures

Indian exchanges also dominate in single stock futures. According to WFE Report, the NSE tops the list when the notional value of contracts traded is considered with contracts worth $ 1,210 billion. However, in recent times, traders tend to move towards index options due to higher outlay, lower liquidity and greater risk in single stock futures.

### ❖ Index options

In the index option segment also, Indian exchanges play a dominant role. The NSE is the second largest in this segment in terms of the number of contracts traded. In fact, the BSE has registered a phenomenal growth in this segment in 2010, growing at 918 per cent. Regarding the option premium collected, the NSE collected option premiums worth $ 33 billion in 2010, being 1 per cent of the notional value of contracts traded on NSE.

The Nifty is the second largest traded index option globally with 530 million contracts. However, it is far below the top, the Kospi 200 which accounted for 3,526 million contracts traded in 2010.

## ❖ S&P and Dow Index Futures on NSE

Recently, the NSE got permission from SEBI to start trading S&P 500 and Dow Index Futures. This would give an opportunity to Indian investors to trade vs. equities during Indian trading tours on Indian rupee. It means that there is neither currency risk on account of adverse dollar-rupee movements nor the requirement of having to wait for the US markets to open to place traders.

## ❖ Credit Default Swap (CDS)

In India, recently, the following measures have been taken to encourage increased participation in CDS:

(*i*) Previously only listed corporate bonds were eligible for CDS. Now, CDS has been permitted on unlisted but rated corporate bonds also. It has been extended even to issues other than infrastructure companies.

(*ii*) Users can unwind their CDS bought position with the original protection seller at mutually agreeable or Fixed Income Money Market and Derivatives Association (FIMMDA) price.

(*iii*) CDS has been permitted on securities with original maturity up to one year as reference/deliverable obligations.

## ❖ Standardisation of Interest Rate Swap (IRS) Contracts

All IRS contracts have been standardised in India with a view to improving tradability and facilitating centralised cleaning and settlement of IRS contracts. This standardisation has been set in terms of minimum national principal amount, tenors, trading hours, settlement calculations etc.

# NON-DELIVERABLE FORWARD (NDF) MARKET

A non-deliverable forward refers to an OTC forward transaction that is settled not by delivery but by exchange of the difference between the contracted rate and some reference rate. This contract is for a fixed amount (of the non-convertible currency), on a specific due date and at an agreed forward rate. At maturity, the prevailing spot rate (reference rate) is compared with the contracted NDF rate. The difference is usually paid in the convertible currency rate on the maturity date. Usually the reference rate is determined on the basis of daily rate fixed by the central bank in question or an average rate published by several banks. This NDF market exists mostly in non-convertible or in currencies with limited onshore hedging options. It offers a convenient hedging mechanism for foreign investors who may not have full access to the onshore market of the currency concerned due to restrictions. In India, the linkage between the NDF market and the domestic financial markets remain weak.

# TRADING IN VOLATILITY INDEX FUTURES

The NSE has computed a Volatility Index called India VIX. It is the indicator of an investor's expectation of market volatility over the next 30 days. Volatility is nothing but the rate and quantum by which prices of equity/debt/currency fluctuate which is considered a measure of risk. Higher the volatility, higher is the risk. Future contracts on India VIX can be traded from Feb. 26, 2014. For example, this index would help traders to hedge volatility risk on equity investments. In fact, Nifty and India VIX are negatively correlated. So, a trader who expects prices of his stocks to fall can go long on India VIX futures contracts and cover his risk. Traders must have a demat account and a broking account to enjoy this facility.

## ❖ Performance of Derivatives Segment during 2015-16

The equity derivatives segment is the most active and dominant segment in the Indian securities market. The trends in turnover and open interest in the Equity Derivatives segment are shown in the following table.

**TABLE 17.3: TRENDS IN TURNOVER AND OPEN INTEREST IN THE EQUITY DERIVATIVES SEGMENT**

| *Year* | *No. of Contracts Traded (₹ in crores)* | | *Turnover (₹ in lakh crores)* | | *Open Interest at the end of the Year* | | | |
|---|---|---|---|---|---|---|---|---|
| | | | | | *No. of Contracts* | | *Value (₹ in crores)* | |
| | *NSE* | *BSE* | *NSE* | *BSE* | *NSE* | *BSE* | *NSE* | *BSE* |
| 1 | 2 | 3 | 4 | 5 | 6 | 7 | 8 | 9 |
| 2020-21 | 853 | 34 | 6,436 | 351 | 61,06,951 | 1,895 | 5,80,514 | 218 |
| 2021-22 | 1,866 | 67 | 16,952 | 661 | 73,59,094 | 1,888 | 5,88,567 | 173 |

***Source:*** SEBI Annual Report, 2021-22.

In India, currency derivatives are traded on BSE, NSE and MSEI. The United Stock Exchange has merged with the BSE. The trends in the currency derivatives segment are displayed in the following table.

**TABLE 17.4: TRENDS IN THE CURRENCY DERIVATIVES MANAGEMENT**

| *Year* | *No. of Contracts Traded (in lakhs)* | | *Turnover (₹ in crores)* | | *Open Interest at the End of Year (₹ in crores)* | |
|---|---|---|---|---|---|---|
| | *2020-21* | *2021-22* | *2020-21* | *2021-22* | *2020-21* | *2021-22* |
| 1 | 2 | 3 | 4 | 5 | 6 | 7 |
| BSE | 6,905 | 8,645 | 51,23,763 | 64,54,526 | 24,962 | 22,209 |
| MSEI | 133 | 120 | 98,395 | 90,270 | 526 | 357 |
| NSE | 15,957 | 27,919 | 1,21,05,978 | 2,11,75,555 | 83,133 | 1,01,038 |
| **Total** | **22,994** | **36,684** | **1,73,28,136** | **2,77,20,351** | **1,08,621** | **1,23,603** |
| | | | **Percentage Share** | | | |
| BSE | 30.0 | 23.6 | 29.6 | 23.3 | 23.0 | 18.0 |
| MSEI | 0.6 | 0.3 | 0.6 | 0.3 | 0.5 | 0.3 |
| NSE | 69.4 | 76.1 | 69.9 | 76.4 | 76.5 | 81.7 |
| **Total** | **100.0** | **100.0** | **100.0** | **100.0** | **100.0** | **100.0** |

***Source:*** SEBI Annual Report, 2021-22.

## IMPORTANT RECENT REFORMS

(*i*) On the basis of the recommendations of the Committee on Financial Benchmarks, a new company, *viz.*, Financial Benchmarks India Pvt. Ltd. (FBIL) has started functioning from Feb. 2015 onwards. It is jointly promoted by the Fixed Income Money Market and Derivative Association of India, the Foreign Exchange Dealers Association of India and the Indian Banks Association. Towards benchmarking, it has launched the FBIL Overnight Mumbai Inter-bank Offer Rate (FBIL-Overnight MIBOR) on July 22, 2015 as a first step.

(*ii*) A public dissemination system has been introduced at the Clearing Corporation of India (CCI) Ltd. for disclosing price and volume information on major inter-bank Over-the-Counter (OTC) foreign exchange derivatives. This has improved transparency and enhanced the resilience of OTC derivatives markets.

(*iii*) All IRS contracts have been already standardised. Attempts are being made to standardise interest rate swaps and foreign exchange derivatives.

(*iv*) All OTC derivatives have been brought under the reporting framework and accordingly all client transactions have to be reported to trade repositories.

(*v*) The CCIL gas been given powers to provide central counterparty (CCP) based clearing for all IRS trades. However, in the case of forex derivatives, CCPs clearing of forex forwards is mandatory.

## QUESTIONS

### I. Objective type questions:

### A. Fill in the blanks with suitable word/words:

1. An instrument which derives its value from an asset backing it is called __________.
2. __________ contracts are not at all standardised.
3. The trader who promises to buy in a forward contract is said to be in __________.
4. In an options contracts, the seller is referred to as a __________.
5. Under financial derivatives, __________ are in the nature of long-term agreements.

[**Key:** 1. derivative, 2. forward, 3. long-position, 4. writer, 5. swaps.]

### B. Choose the best answer from the following

1. Financial derivatives are mainly used for:
   (*a*) Speculative activities (*b*) Creating more risks
   (*c*) Hedging risks (*d*) Earning income
2. The instruments that are 'marked to the market' are:
   (*a*) Forwards (*b*) Futures
   (*c*) Swaps (*d*) Options
3. In an option contract, if the option can be exercised only at the time of maturity, it is called:
   (*a*) Double option (*b*) American option
   (*c*) Put option (*d*) European option

4. The predetermined price at which an underlying asset has to be bought or sold in an option contract is called:

   (*a*) Option price (*b*) Exercise price
   (*c*) Spot price (*d*) Future price

5. A combination of forwards by two counterparties with opposite but matching needs is called:

   (*a*) Swap (*b*) Option
   (*c*) Forward (*d*) Future

[**Key:** 1. hedging risks, 2. Futures, 3. European option, 4. exercise price, 5. swap.]

## C. State whether the following statements are TRUE or FALSE:

1. Forward contracts can be traded only in organised exchanges.
2. The trader who promises to sell in a futures contract is said to be in 'short position'.
3. A put option gives the option holder a right to buy an underlying asset at an exercise price in future.
4. Share option transactions are mostly index-based.
5. Swaps are nothing but long date forward rate contracts.

[**Key:** 1. False, 2. True, 3. False, 4. True, 5. True]

# II. Short answer type questions:

1. Discuss in brief the peculiar features of derivative instruments.
2. Distinguish between a forward contract and a futures contract.
3. What are the features of a forward contract?
4. What do you mean by financial forwards? Explain any one of such a contract.
5. Discuss the features of a futures contract.
6. Describe the different types of options.
7. Bring out clearly the features of an option contract.
8. Explain with a suitable illustration the options trading in shares.
9. Discuss the features of swap.
10. What is non-deliverable forwards market?

# III. Essay type questions:

1. Discuss the various kinds of financial derivatives and bring out their features briefly.
2. Distinguish between forwards and futures contract. In your opinion, which one is more beneficial as a hedging instrument?
3. State the features of options contract and explain the modus operandi of share option and currency option with suitable illustrations.
4. Define the term 'derivatives' and bring out its importance. What are the causes for the meagre use of derivative instruments in India?
5. What do you mean by credit default swap? Distinguish it from insurance. Discuss its various parties and types.

# 18 CREDIT RATING

## MEANING OF CREDIT RATING

To understand the meaning of credit rating, let us look at some definitions offered by well-known rating agencies.

**Moody's:** 'Ratings are designed exclusively for the purpose of grading bonds according to their investment qualities'.

**Australian Ratings:** 'A corporate credit rating provides lenders with a simple system of gradation by which the relative capacities of companies to make timely repayment of interest and principal on a particular type of debt can be noted'.

According to **CRISIL**, 'Credit rating is an unbiased and independent opinion as to issuer's capacity to meet its financial obligations. It does not constitute a recommendation to buy/sell or hold a particular security'.

According to **ICRA**, 'Ratings are opinions on the relative capability of timely servicing of corporate debt and obligations. These are not recommendations to buy or sell....neither the accuracy nor the completeness of the information is guaranteed'.

From the above definitions, it is understood that:

(*i*) Credit rating is an assessment of the capacity of an issuer of debt security, by an independent agency, to pay interest and repay the principal as per the terms of issue of debt. A rating agency collects the qualitative as well as quantitative data from a company which has to be rated and assesses the relative strength and capacity of company to honour its obligations contained in the debt instrument throughout the duration of the instrument. The rating given is based on an objective judgement of a team of experts from the rating agency.

(*ii*) The ratings are expressed in code number which can be easily comprehended even by the lay investors. The ratings are the quickest way of understanding a company's financial standing without going into the complicated financial reports. Credit rating is only a guidance to the investors and not a recommendation to a particular debt instrument. The important element for investment decision making in debt security are: (*a*) yield to maturity, (*b*) risk tolerance to investor, and (*c*) credit risk of the security. Clearly the focus of credit rating is on any one of these three elements, *viz.*, credit risk of the security and hence it cannot by itself be a basis for investment decision making. It is only a current opinion on the relative capacity of firms to repay debt in time.

(*iii*) Credit rating, as it exists in India, is done for a specific debt security and not for a company as a whole. No rating agency tells that it is an indicator of the financial status of the company. All that a rating agency claims is that the rating symbols indicate the capacity of the company to honour the terms of contract of a debt instrument.

(*iv*) A debt rating is not a one-time evaluation of credit risk, which can be regarded as valid for the entire life of the security. It is an ongoing appraisal. Changes in dynamic world of business may imply a change in the risk characteristics of the security. Hence, debt rating agencies monitor the business and financial conditions of the issuer to determine whether modification in rating is warranted.

(*v*) A credit rating does not create a fiduciary relationship between the rating agency and the users of rating since there is no legal basis for such relationships.

## FUNCTIONS OF CREDIT RATINGS

The credit rating firms are supposed to do the following functions:

1. **Superior information:** Rating by an independent and professional firm offers a superior and more reliable source of information on credit risk for three inter-related risks:
   (*a*) It provides unbiased opinion.
   (*b*) Due to professional resources, a rating firm has greater ability to assess risks.
   (*c*) It has access to lot of information which may not be publicly available.
2. **Low-cost information:** A rating firm which gathers, analyses, interprets and summarises complex information in a simple and readily understood format for wide public consumption represents a cost-effective arrangement.
3. **Basis for a proper risk-return trade-off:** If debt securities are rated professionally and if such ratings enjoy widespread investor acceptance and confidence, a more rational risk-return trade-off would be established in the capital market.
4. **Healthy discipline on corporate borrowers:** Public exposure has healthy influence over the management of issuer because of its desire to have a clear image.
5. **Formulation of public policy guidelines on institutional Investment:** The public policy on the kinds of securities that are eligible for inclusion in different kinds of institutional portfolios can be developed with great confidence if securities are rated professionally by independent agencies.

## ORIGIN

The credit rating concept originated in the USA. In 1860, Henry Vannum Poor started publishing financial statistics of Railroad companies. In 1909, Moody's Investors Agencies started rating railroad giving more thrust to the concept. Since then, the importance has grown extensively in the global market. System of ratings got institutionalised following the great depression. In 1933, the US Controller of Currency enacted a rule that banks could purchase securities rated only BBB/BAA or above. In 1970, Penn Central, the then largest railroad company in the world went bankrupt with just under $ 100 million in outstanding commercial paper. This forced the investors to ask for rating for commercial paper. Consequently, today, almost 100 per cent of the commercial paper volume and 99 per cent of the corporate bond volume are rated in the USA.

## CREDIT RATING IN INDIA

The environment that prevailed in America when first ratings were assigned, prevails in many developing countries today. The Indian capital market has witnessed a tremendous growth in the past few years. Companies are relying on capital markets for financing existing operations as well as for new projects rather than on institutions. In this process, the average size of debenture issued by companies, the number of companies issuing debentures and the number of investors have grown substantially.

As the number of companies borrowings directly from capital market increases, investors find that the company's size or name is no longer a sufficient assurance of the timely payment of interest and principal. Default by large and well-known companies recently in payment of interest on fixed deposits or debentures has reinforced this belief among investors. They felt the need for an independent and credible agency which judges the quality of debt obligations of different companies and assists individual and institutional investors in making investment decisions.

In this context, the Credit Rating Information Services of India Limited was set up in 1987. Following this, Investment Information and Credit Rating Agency of India was promoted in 1991 and Credit Analysis and Research Limited was floated in 1993. All the three credit rating agencies have been approved by the Reserve Bank of India.

## BENEFITS OF CREDIT RATING

**(i) Low-cost information:** Credit rating is a source of low-cost information to investors. The collection, processing and analysis of relevant information is done by a specialised agency which a group of investors can trust.

**(ii) Quick investment decision:** In the present-day complex world, ratings enable investors to take quickest possible decisions based on associated ratings.

**(iii) Independent investment decision:** For rated instruments, investors need not depend upon the advice of the financial intermediaries. As the rating symbol suggests, the creditworthiness of the instrument and indicates the degree of risk involved in it, the investors can make direct investment decisions.

**(iv) Investors' protection:** Hiring of credit agency implies that the management of the company is ready to show its operations for independent scrutiny. So, the investors who are not provided with confidential information can have overall assessment based on ratings. The creditable and objective rating agency can provide increased disclosure, better accounting standard and improved investor protection.

## BENEFITS TO RATED COMPANIES

**(i) Sources of additional certification:** Credit rating agency provides additional information to the issuers of debt/financial instruments. A highly rated firm can enter the market with great confidence. Indian experience shows that use of rating, benefit a great deal by getting larger amount of money from a wider audience at a lower cost.

**(ii) Increase the investors' population:** A sound credit rating system gives an alternative method to name recognition as a determining factor in making investment and helps increase the population of those investing in debt obligations of the company.

**(iii) Forewarns risks:** Credit rating acts as a guide to companies which get a lower rating. It forewarns the management of the perception of risk in the market and prompts to take steps on their operating and marketing risks and thereby changes the perception in the market.

**(iv) Encourages financial discipline:** Ratings also encourage discipline among corporate borrowers to improve their financial structure and performance to obtain better rating for their debt obligations.

**(v) Merchant banker's job made easy:** Merchant bankers and brokers will be relieved of the responsibility of guiding investors as to the risk of a particular investment. Merchant bankers and brokers, in the absence of objective information, go on the basis of name recognition in guiding their clients. With the advent of credit rating, what they would be required to do is to bring to the attention of their clients the ratings of debt obligations.

**(vi) Foreign collaborations made easy:** The foreign collaborators always ask for credit rating while negotiating with an Indian company. Credit rating enables to identify instantly the relative credit standing of the company. The importance of credit rating is being increasingly recognised in the Euro-markets.

**(vii) Benefits the industry as a whole:** Relatively small and unknown companies use ratings to instill confidence in investors. Higher rate companies get larger amount of money at a lower cost. Thus, the industry as a whole can benefit from ratings by direct mobilisation of savings from individuals rather than from intermediary lending institutions.

**(viii) Low cost of borrowing:** A company with highly rated instrument has the opportunity to reduce the cost of borrowing by quoting lesser interest rate on fixed deposits or debentures as the investors with low risk preference would invest in safe securities though yielding low rate of return.

(ix) **Rating as a marketing tool:** Companies with rated instruments, use rating as a marketing tool to create better image in dealing with their customers, lenders and creditors.

## CREDIT RATING AGENCIES IN INDIA

Currently, the credit rating agencies functioning in India are the following:

1. Credit Rating Information Service Limited (CRISIL).
2. Investment Information and Credit Rating Agency of India (IICRA).
3. Credit Analysis and Research (CARE).
4. Duff Phelps Credit Rating Pvt. Ltd. (DCR India).
5. Onida Individual Credit Rating Agency Ltd. (ONICRA).
6. Acwite Ratings and Research.
7. Brickwork Ratings India Pvt. Ltd.
8. India Ratings and Research Pvt. Ltd.
9. Infometrics Valuation and Rating Pvt. Ltd.

### 1. Credit Rating Information Services Limited (CRISIL)

Credit Rating Information Services Limited (CRISIL) the first credit agency was floated on January 1, 1988. It was started jointly by ICICI and UTI with an equity capital of ₹ 4 crores. Each of them holds 18 per cent of the capital. The other promoters are Asian Development Bank (15 per cent), the LIC and General Insurance Corporation and its subsidiaries and the SBI (5 per cent each), the Housing Finance Development Corporation (6.2 per cent), nine public sector and private sector banks (19.25 per cent) and 10 foreign banks (7.55 per cent).

The principal objective of CRISIL is to rate the debt obligations of Indian companies. Its rating guides investors about the risk of timely payment of interest and principal on a particular debt instrument.

#### ❖ Objectives of CRISIL

- To assist both individual and institutional investors in making investment decisions in fixed income securities.
- To enable corporates to raise large amounts at fair cost from a wide spectrum of investors.
- To enable intermediaries in placing their debt instruments with investors by providing them with an effective marketing tool.

CRISIL has five offices one each in Mumbai, Delhi, Kolkata, Chennai and Bengaluru.

#### ❖ Rating methodology

CRISIL commences a rating exercise at the request of a company. In accordance with industry practice all over the world, the methodology involves an analysis of the past performance of the company and assessment of its prospects.

The first analysis relates to the past performance of the company. However, the past is viewed not as a guide, but to understand why the company performed in the way it did, what problems it faced and what the management's response to these problems was.

To assess the future prospects, CRISIL studies the industry or industries in which the company operates and the company's position within the industry. It also makes an evaluation of the management and cash flow projections of the company and identifies the key issues concerning the company.

The industry is studied by analysing demand and supply growth, nature and basis of competition, Government policy for the company and the effect of change in Government policy on the future of the company. The position of the company within the industry is studied to understand how the company would fare in the future.

CRISIL, therefore, looks at the operating efficiency in terms of locational advantage, raw material, power and labour situation; its cost structure as compared to that of its nearest competitors and the company's market position in terms of its market share, product strength, selling and distribution arrangements, competitive advantage, customer delivery, etc.

CRISIL evaluates the management of the company with reference to its track record, the recruitment and training system, planning and control system, depth of managerial talents and succession plans, goals for the company, the philosophy of doing business, attitudes towards taking business risks and the strategies for the company. The tenacity, determination and drive of the management to overcome problems as they arise in the company is yet another factor assessed by the CRISIL.

Then, CRISIL makes its own assessment of cash flows and decides the degree of comfort available from the cash flows to meet cash needs of the company for capital expenditure, working capital growth and debt servicing obligations. In addition, it assesses the company's ability to raise funds quickly in various ways in times of necessity to meet the requirements of servicing debt.

The rating process seeks to identify the key issues concerning the company. For instance, if a company is putting up a new project, the key issue in the rating is the likelihood of timely completion of the project. The rating is a composite assessment of all these factors with the key issue getting greater attention from the rating agency.

In evaluating the ratings, CRISIL employs both qualitative and quantitative criteria. The judgement made by the CRISIL is necessarily subjective and the quantitative analysis is meant to assist in making best possible overall qualitative judgement.

CRISIL employs a multi layered decision making process in assigning ratings. When it receives a request for rating, it assigns two teams on the job. The first team meets the officials and makes an assessment of the industry, company and management. The second team is also required to make its own study of the industry. Then the first team interacts with the back-up team. The findings of the interactions are presented simultaneously in a detailed note to the Branch Internal Committee comprising at least three senior analysts of CRISIL and an Internal Committee of six senior executives and thereafter the note is presented with the recommended ratings to the Rating Committee comprising six directors of the company who are not connected with any shareholders of CRISIL. The rating committee members are chosen carefully so that they do not have any links with industries or investment agencies connected with the units being rated. This multi-layered process ensures that no individual decides on rating and that prejudices and biases are eliminated.

The evaluation of the company is made on a confidential basis. The rating process ensures complete confidentiality of information that may be provided by the company.

## ❖ Credit rating symbols

CRISIL uses the conventional rating symbols used in the USA and widely accepted in many other countries.

The following table shows the investment-wise rating symbols assigned by CRISIL and the meaning of each rating from the angle of safety to the investors.

**TABLE 18.1: CRISIL DEBENTURE RATING SYMBOLS**

| | | |
|---|---|---|
| High Investment Grades | | |
| AAA (Triple A) | : | Highest Safety |
| AA (Double A) | : | High Safety |
| Investment Grades | | |
| A | : | Adequate Safety |
| BBB (Triple B) | : | Moderate Safety |
| Speculative Grades | | |
| BB (Double B) | : | Inadequate Safety |
| B | : | High Risk |
| C | : | Substantial Risk |
| D | : | Default |

***Notes:*** 1. CRISIL may apply '+' (plus) or '–' (minus) sign for ratings from AA to C to reflect comparative standing within the category.

2. The contents within parenthesis are a guide to the pronunciation of the rating symbols.

3. Preference shares rating symbols are identical to debenture rating symbols except the letters 'pf' are prefixed to the rating symbols, *e.g.*, pf AAA ("pf Triple A").

**TABLE 18.2: CRISIL FIXED DEPOSIT RATING SYMBOLS**

| | | |
|---|---|---|
| Investment Grades | | |
| FAAA (F-Triple A) | : | Highest Safety |
| FAA (F-Double A) | : | High Safety |
| FA | : | Adequate Safety |
| Speculative Grades | | |
| FB | : | Inadequate Safety |
| FC | : | High Risk |
| FD | : | Default |

***Notes:*** 1. CRISIL may apply '+' (plus) or '–' (minus) sign for ratings from FAAA to FC to indicate the relative position within the rating category.

2. The contents within parenthesis are a guide to the pronunciation of the rating symbols.

CRISIL monitors the ratings it assigns constantly. The ratings may be upgraded, downgraded or withdrawn depending upon new information or developments concerning the company whose debt obligation is rated. It has the right to widely disseminate the ratings through the media, through its own publications or through any other methods.

**TABLE 18.3: CREDIT RATING FOR SHORT-TERM INSTRUMENTS**

| *Rating Symbol* | *Indication* |
|---|---|
| | (Each rating indicates that the degree of safety regarding timely payment on the instrument is shown against the symbol) |
| $P_{-1}$ | Very Strong |
| $P_{-2}$ | Strong |
| $P_{-3}$ | Adequate |
| $P_{-4}$ | Minimal |
| $P_{-5}$ | Expected to be in default on maturity or in default |

***Note:*** CRISIL may apply "+" signs for ratings from $P_{-1}$ to $P_{-3}$ to reflect a comparatively higher standing within the category.

## ❖ Operations of CRISIL

During 1994-95, CRISIL rated 379 instruments covering a debt volume of ₹ 34,544 crores. The cumulative number of instruments rated by CRISIL since its inception in January 1988, till the end of March 1995 has been 1,305 and the value of instruments covered has been ₹ 78,151 crores.

In 1994-95, CRISIL forged alliance with Standard & Poor's Rating Group, New York.

In 1996-97, CRISIL introduced ratings on mutual funds, bank loan ratings, and public finance ratings. Standard & Poor's acquired 9.68 per cent of the shareholdings in the company in the same year.

CRISIL secured the Certificate of Registration under SEBI (Credit Rating Agencies) Regulations in 1999.

The mutual fund ranking service for the domestic mutual fund market was introduced in the year 2000-2001. Evaluation services for firm and TV software producers and rating of personal loan securitisation transactions were introduced in 2002-03.

The name of the company was changed from the Credit Rating Information Services of India Ltd. to 'CRISIL Ltd. in 2003-04. During 2006, CRISIL launched 180 gradings to analyse the fundamental strength of IPO issues. During this year, CRISIL Small and Medium Enterprise ratings received 570 requests and assigned 490 ratings and it assigned over 1,000 SME ratings in the year 2007.

At present, Standard & Poor's acquired a majority shareholdings in CRISIL.

CRISIL has so far rated a cumulative debt volume exceeding $ 30 billion covering 1,500 debt instruments covering 1,000 companies.

## 2. Investment Information and Credit Rating Agency of India (IICRA)

The IICRA was set up by Industrial Finance Corporation of India on January 16, 1991. It is a public limited company with an authorised share capital of ₹ 101 crores. The initial paid-up capital of ₹ 3.50 crores is subscribed by IFC, UTI, LIC, GIC, SBI and 17 other banks. IICRA started its operations from 15th March, 1991.

**TABLE 18.4: IICRA RATING SCALE**

**Long-term including Debentures, Bonds and Preference Shares**

| | | |
|---|---|---|
| LAAA | : | Highest Safety |
| LAA | : | High Safety |
| LA | : | Adequate Safety |
| LBBB | : | Moderate Safety |
| LBB | : | Inadequate Safety |
| LB | : | Risk Prone |
| LC | : | Substantial Risk |
| LD | : | Default, Extremely Speculative |

**Medium-term including Fixed Deposits**

| | | |
|---|---|---|
| MAAA | : | Highest Safety |
| MAA | : | High Safety |
| MA | : | Adequate Safety |
| MB | : | Inadequate Safety |
| MC | : | Risk Prone |
| MD | : | Default |

**Short-term including Commercial Paper**

| | |
|---|---|
| A-1 | Highest Safety |
| A-2 | High Safety |
| A-3 | Adequate Safety |
| A-4 | Risk Prone |
| A-5 | Default |

***Notes:*** (*i*) The rating symbols group together similar (but not necessarily identical) concerns in terms of their relative capability of timely servicing of debts/obligations, as per terms of contracts, *i.e.*, the relative degree of safety risk.

(*ii*) The sign (+) or (–) may be used after the rating symbol to indicate the comparative position of the company within the group covered by the symbol.

(*iii*) The letter 'P' in parenthesis after the rating symbol indicates that the debt instrument is being used to raise resources by a new company for financing a new project and the rating assumes successful completion of the project.

(*iv*) The rating symbols for different instruments of the same company need not necessarily be the same.

**TABLE 18.5: IICRA RATING SYMBOLS**

| IICRA FIXED DEPOSIT RATING SYMBOLS | | IICRA CREDIT ASSESSMENT SYMBOLS | |
|---|---|---|---|
| MAAA | Highest Safety | 01. | Very Strong Capacity |
| MAA+ | | 02. | |
| MAA | High Safety | 03. | Strong Capacity |
| MAA– | | 04. | |
| MA+ | | 05. | |

| | | | |
|---|---|---|---|
| MA | Adequate Safety | 06. | Adequate Capacity |
| MA– | | 07. | |
| MB+ | | 08. | |
| MB | Inadequate Safety | 09. | Inadequate Capacity |
| MB– | | 10. | |
| MC+ | High Risk | 11. | Poor Capacity |
| MC | | 12. | |
| MC– | | 13. | |
| MD | Default | 14. | Default |

## 3. Credit Analysis and Research Limited (CARE)

The CARE was promoted in 1993 jointly with investment companies, banks and finance companies. Services offered by CARE are: (*i*) credit rating, (*ii*) Information service, (*iii*) Equity research and (*iv*) Rating of paralleled market of LPG and kerosene. Since its inception till the end of December 2007, CARE has rated 3,850 debt instruments covering a total debt volume of ₹ 80,716 crores.

### ❖ CARE

### ❖ Rating Services

CARE provides rating services to the following debt instruments.

- Debentures.
- Certificate of Deposits.
- Commercial Paper.
- Fixed Deposits.

CARE also undertakes Credit Analysis Rating of Companies for the use of bankers, other lenders and business enterprises.

**TABLE 18.6: CARE CREDIT RATING**

| *Sl. No.* | *Investment Grade* | *CARE* |
|---|---|---|
| | **For Long-term Debt Instruments** | |
| 1 | Highest Safety | CARE AAA |
| 2 | High Safety | CARE AA |
| 3 | Adequate Safety | CARE A |
| 4 | Inadequate Safety | CARE BB |
| 5 | High Risk | CARE B |
| | **For Medium-term Debt Instruments** | |
| 1 | Highest Safety | CARE AAA |
| 2 | High Safety | CARE AA |
| 3 | Adequate Safety | CARE A |
| 4 | Inadequate Safety | CARE BB |
| 5 | High Risk | CARE C |

| | For Short-term Debt Instruments | |
|---|---|---|
| 1 | Highest Safety | PR1 |
| 2 | High Safety | PR2 |
| 3 | Adequate Safety | PR3 |
| 4 | Inadequate Safety | PR4 |
| 5 | High Risk | |

The rating division of CARE has over a decade long experience in rating debt instruments/ enterprise ratings covering the full spectrum of universe comprising:

- Industrial companies.
- Service companies.
- Infrastructure companies.
- Banks.
- Financial Institutions (FIs).
- Non-bank Finance Companies (NBFCs).
- Public Sector Undertakings (PSUs).
- State government undertakings.
- Municipal Corporations.
- Structured finance transactions.
- Securitisation transactions.
- SMEs.
- SSI.
- Microfinance institutions.

In addition to debt ratings, CARE Ratings has experience in providing the following specialised grading/rating services:

- Corporate governance ratings.
- IPO Grading.
- Mutual Fund credit quality ratings.
- Insurance claims paying ability rating.
- Issuer Ratings.
- Grading of construction entities.
- Grading of maritime training institutes.
- LPG/SKO ratings.

CARE ratings is well equipped to rate all types of debt instruments like Commercial Paper, Fixed Deposit, Bonds, Debentures, Hybrid Instruments, Structured Obligations, Preference Shares, Loans, Asset-backed Securities (ABS), Residential Mortgage-backed Securities (RMBS), etc.

CARE ratings has significant presence in all sectors including Banks/FIs, Corporate and Public Finance. Coverage of CARE ratings has extended to more than 1,075 entities over the past decade and is widely accepted by investors, issuers and other market participants. CARE ratings have evolved into a valuable tool for credit risk assessment for institutional and other investors, and over the years CARE has increasingly become a preferred rating agency.

### 4. Duffs & Phelps Credit Rating India Private Ltd. (DCR)

The Duffs & Phelps is a leading international credit rating agency. The J.M. Financial and Alliance Group in joint venture with Duffs & Phelps has now set up DCR in India. Its main objective is to give credit rating to debt instruments. On special request, it may undertake rating of companies and countries as well. The popular symbol employed by DCR is D1, D2, D3, etc. depending upon the credit status. For example, the RBI has stipulated a minimum credit rating of D-2 DCR India for the purpose of issuing commercial papers by institutions.

### 5. Onida Individual Credit Rating Agency Ltd. (ONICRA)

Almost all credit rating agencies established in India undertake credit analysis work of corporate bodies only. Unlike these agencies, the ONICRA Ltd. has taken up the individual borrowers. It has been sponsored by the Onida Finance Ltd. In all credit transactions relating to credit cards, Housing Finance, Rental/HP agreements, personal loan, etc., it becomes imperative that one should know the quantum of default risk associated with such transactions before entering into those transactions. It is where the ONICRA comes into picture. It does not rate the individual as such but the risk associated with entering into those credit transactions with that individual at a certain period. Thus, it helps the users of this rating to know risks associated with credit transactions while dealing with individuals. It is gaining popularity among financial institutions.

### 6. Acwite Ratings and Research

It was formerly known as SMERA Ratings Ltd. It was established in 2011 to do bond rating and ratings of Small and Medium Enterprises. It evaluates the credibility of the existing SMEs.

### 7. Brickwork Ratings India Pvt. Ltd.

The main task of this rating agency is to assign credit ratings to bank loans, capital market instruments and SMEs. It also grades real estate investments, NGOs, hospitals and mutual fund institutions. It has Canara Bank as its leading promoter and strategic partner.

### 8. India Ratings and Research Pvt. Ltd.

It was formerly known as Fitch Ratings India Ltd. It assigns credit ratings to corporate issuers, financial institutions, project finance companies and local bodies.

### 9. Infometrics Valuation and Ratings Pvt. Ltd.

It is a RBI accredited and SEBI registered agency. This rating agency is founded by financial professionals, bankers and administrative service personnels. It evaluates and gives ratings to banks, NBFCs, SMEs and large corporates.

## SEBI GUIDELINES 1999

1. No credit rating agencies shall rate a security issued by its promoters.
2. It has barred rating agencies from rating securities issued by any borrower, subsidiary or associate of the promoter if it has a chairman, director, employee of any such firm.
3. Dual rating is compulsory for public and rights issue of debt instruments of ₹ 100 crores or more.
4. SEBI has decided to incorporate a clause in the listing agreement of stock exchanges requiring companies to co-operate with agencies by providing correct information. Refusal to do so may lead to breach of contract between rating agencies and client.
5. The issues would be required to incorporate an undertaking in their offer documents promising necessary co-operation with the rating agency in providing factual information.
6. It is also suggested that a penal clause be introduced in the listing agreement of the information provided is proved to be incorrect at a later stage, to protect investors' interest.
7. The net worth of rating agencies has been fixed at ₹ 5 crores.
8. Rating agencies can choose their methodology of operation but self-regulatory mechanism will give a better maturity status for agencies.
9. No chairman, director or employee of the promoters shall be a chairman, director or employee of the CRA or its rating committee. Promoter of a CRA is a person who holds more than 107 of holdings of the CRA.
10. Period of validity of registration shall be 3 years.

## SEBI's NEW NORMS FOR CREDIT RATING AGENCIES

New guidelines have been laid down by SEBI so that the ratings given by credit rating agencies may be based more on current and future risks rather than on historical data. These norms are as follows:

(*i*) While reviewing ratings, the agencies are directed to analyse the deterioration in the liquidity conditions and take into account any asset-liability mismatch.

(*ii*) Rating agencies are required to disclose any linkage to external support for meeting year-term maturity obligations. A specific section has been introduced on liquidity to highlight parameters such as liquid investments or cash balances, access to unutilised credit lines, liquidity coverage ratio, adequacy of cash flows for serving maturity debt obligations.

(*iii*) The rating agencies have to review their rating criteria with regard to assessment of their holding companies and subsidiaries in terms of their interlinkages, holding company's liquidity, financial flexibility and support to subsidiaries.

(*iv*) The sharp deviation in bond spreads of debt instruments *vis-á-vis* relevant benchmark yield should be treated as a 'material event' while reviewing 'the material events'.

(*v*) In case a subsidiary company gets support from the parent group or government, the rating agencies have to specify it so that timely debt servicing is guaranteed. Moreover, the rating agencies have to provide the rationale for this expectation.

(*vi*) Rating agencies need to publish their average one-year rating transition rate over a five-year period on their respective websites.

(*vii*) Each rating agency has to furnish data on sharp rating actions in investment grade rating category in a specified format to stock exchanges and depositories for disclosure on its websites on a half-yearly basis within 15 days from the end of the half year.

(*viii*) The Rating symbols should have the Credit Rating Agency's first name as prefix with effect from January 2023.

## NEW SYMBOLS OF CREDIT RATING

With a view to achieving light standards of integrity and fairness in ratings and to help the investors to easily understand credit ratings, the SEBI has very recently devised standardised symbols to rate three different long-term and short-term instruments – debt, structured finance and mutual fund schemes. These new symbols are displayed in the following Table 18.7.

**TABLE 18.7: NEW SYMBOLS OF CREDIT RATING**

| ***Degree of Risk*** | ***Rating of Long-term*** | | |
|---|---|---|---|
| | ***Debt Instruments*** | ***Debt MF Schemes*** | ***Structured Finance Instruments*** |
| Highest safety | AAA | AAAmfs | AAA(SO) |
| High safety | AA | AAmfs | AA(SO) |
| Adequate safety | A | Amfs | A(SO) |
| Moderate safety | BBB | BBBmfs | BBB(SO) |
| Moderate risk | BB | BBmfs | BB (SO) |
| High risk | B | Bmfs | B(SO) |
| Very high risk | C | Cmfs | C(SO) |
| Can default any time | D | Not applicable | D(SO) |

| ***Degree of Risk*** | ***Rating of Short-term*** | | |
|---|---|---|---|
| | ***Debt Instruments*** | ***Debt MF Schemes*** | ***Structured Finance Instruments*** |
| Very safe | A1 | A1mfs | A1(SO) |
| Safe | A2 | A2mfs | A2(SO) |
| Moderately safe | A3 | A3mfs | A3(SO) |
| Minimal safety | A4 | A4mfs | A4(SO) |
| Default expected | D | Not applicable | D(SO) |

## PRACTICAL PROBLEMS

1. The absence of widespread branch network of the rating agency may limit its skills in rating.
2. Inexperienced, unskilled or overloaded staff may not do justice to their job and the resulting ratings may not be perfect.
3. Since rating exercise involves a number of factors, a rigid mathematical formula cannot be applied to finalise rating and some element of subjectivity creeps in, thereby giving scope for bias.
4. The time factor greatly affects rating and gives misleading conclusions. A company which experiences adverse conditions temporarily will be given a low rating judged on the basis of temporary phenomenon.
5. Since the rating agencies receive a sizable fee from the companies for awarding ratings, a tendency to inflate the ratings may develop.
6. The rating is not permanent but subject to changes and moreover the agencies cannot give any guarantee for the investors.
7. Investments which have the same rating may not have identical investment quality because the number of rating categories is limited and hence cannot reflect small but meaningful differences in the degree of risk.
8. Borrowing entities give misleading advertisements about the rating symbols of their instruments. For example, 'X' Co. Ltd. which has got AAX for its debenture may mobilise fixed deposits instead of revealing the low rating for fixed deposits. Such kind of window dressing should be curtailed.

## FUTURE OF CREDIT RATING IN INDIA

At present, commercial paper, bonds and debentures with maturities exceeding 18 months and fixed deposits of large non-banking companies registered with RBI are required to be compulsorily rated. There are moves to make rating compulsory for other types of borrowings such as the fixed deposit programme of manufacturing companies. In addition, the rating agencies are expected to be called upon to enlarge volumes of securitisation of debt and structuring of customised instruments to meet the needs of issuers or different class of investors. There are number of areas where rating agencies will have to cover new ground in the coming years. The rating of municipal bonds, state government borrowings, commercial banks and public sector undertakings, etc. will be covered in the near future. So, the outlook for the credit rating industry is positive.

The experience of Indian rating agencies so far is that about 30 per cent of their ratings are not accepted or used. Instances are there when companies with poor ratings assigned by one company have gone to another for better rating. These raise doubts about the efficacy of credit rating agencies in serving the investors.

Various constraints are faced by the credit rating agencies. The major constraint is the low level of disclosure by Indian companies. Rating agencies have complained of inadequate access to information, poor quality of audit and long time-lags in the availability of data. The companies often do not cooperate whenever they feel that disclosure of a particular piece of information might not be in their interest. All these act as systematic constraint on the rating service.

The Indian credit rating agencies have made strategic alliance with reputed international agencies. They adopt, to a large extent, the rating methodologies adopted by their Western counterparts. The suitability of rating methods and models formulated in well developed markets in the West is highly doubtful in Indian conditions. The rating agencies in India have to evolve their own methodologies within the context of macroeconomic environment.

## QUESTIONS

### I. Objective type questions:

#### A. Fill in the blanks:

1. Ratings are expressed in __________.
2. AAA refers to __________.
3. Rating is only a guidance and not __________ to a debt instrument.
4. Ratings indicate the __________ status of a company.
5. Credit rating is a one-time evaluation out __________ appraisal.

[**Key:** 1. code numbers, 2. highest security, 3. recommendation, 4. financial, 5. ongoing.]

#### B. State whether the following statements are True or False:

1. Credit rating is only a current opinion on the firm's capacity to repay debt in time.
2. Ratings are done in India for a company as a whole.
3. IICRA is a public limited company.
4. Rating is compulsory for all instruments in India.
5. CRISIL commences rating exercise at the request of the Government.

[**Key:** 1. True, 2. False, 3. True, 4. False, 5. False]

### II. Short answer questions:

1. What is meant by credit rating?
2. What are the objectives of credit rating?
3. State the limitations of credit rating.
4. State the objectives of CRISIL.

### III. Essay type questions:

1. Explain the benefits of credit rating.
2. Explain the methodology followed by CRISIL in rating credit instruments.
3. Discuss the organisation and working of CRISIL.
4. Explain the working of various credit rating agencies in India.

# 19 CREDIT CARDS

Credit cards are innovative ones in the line of financial services offered by commercial banks. The idea of credit card was first developed by a Bavarian Farmer, Franz Nesbitum McNamara, an American businessman who found himself without cash at a weekend resort founded Diner's Card in 1950. Right from that time, the commercial banks and non-banking companies in the US adopted the idea of credit card to develop their business. Barclays Bank was the first bank to introduce credit card in 1966 in Britain. The credit card business got momentum in sixties and a number of banks entered the field in a big way.

Credit card culture is an old hat in Western countries. In India, it is relatively a new concept that is fast catching on. The present trend indicates that the coming years will witness a burgeoning growth of credit cards which will lead to a cashless society.

## WHAT IS A CREDIT CARD?

A credit card is a card or mechanism which enables cardholders to purchase goods, travel and dine in a hotel without making immediate payments. The holders can use the cards to get credit from banks up to 45 days. The credit card relieves the consumers from the botheration of carrying cash and ensures safety. It is a convenience of extended credit without formality. Thus, credit card is a passport to, 'safety, convenience, prestige and credit'.

## WHO CAN BE A CREDIT CARDHOLDER?

The general criteria applied is a person's spending capacity and not merely his income or wealth. The other criteria is the worthiness of the client and his average monthly balance. Most of the banks have clear out norms for giving credit cards.

1. A person who earns a salary of ₹ 60,000 per annum is eligible for a card.
2. A reference from a banker and the employers of the applicant is insisted upon.
3. In recent times, with the advent of credit bureaus and the widespread use of their credit scoring mechanism, a healthy credit score of above 750 is considered as a threshold for issuing credit cards.

4. In the absence of a minimum annual income or the desired credit score, some banks issue credit cards against a lien on their deposits.

Generally, the bank's criteria for issuing credit cards vary from bank to bank.

## TYPES OF CREDIT CARD

According to the purpose for which the credit cards are used, they can be classified into three main categories:

**1. Credit card:** It is a normal card, whereby a holder is able to purchase without having to pay cash immediately. This credit card is built around revolving credit principle. Generally, a limit is set to the amount of money a cardholder can spend a month using the card. At the end of every month, the holder has to pay a percentage of outstanding. Interest is charged for the outstanding amount which varies from 30 to 36 per cent per annum. An average consumer prefers this type of card for his personal purchase as he is able to defer payment over several months.

**2. Charge card:** A charge card is intended to serve as a convenient means of payment for goods purchased at member establishments rather than a credit facility. Instead of paying cash or cheque every time, the credit cardholder makes a purchase, this facility gives a consolidated bill for a specified period, usually one month. Bills are payable in full on presentation. There are no interest charges and no preset spending limits either. The charge card is useful during business trips and for entertainment expenses which are usually borne by the company. Andhra Bank card, BOB cards, Can card, Diner's Club card, etc. belong to this category.

**3. In-store card:** The in-store cards are issued by retailers or companies. These cards have currency only at the issuer's outlets for purchasing products of the issuer company. Payment can be on monthly or extended credit basis. For extended credit facility, interest is charged. In India, such cards are normally issued by Five Star Hotels, resorts and big hotels.

## NEW TYPES OF CREDIT CARDS

**1. Corporate credit cards:** Corporate cards are issued to private and public limited companies and public sector units. Depending upon the requirements of each company, operative Add-on cards will be issued to persons authorised by the company, *i.e.*, directors, secretary of the company. The name of the company will be embossed on Add-on cards along with the name of the Add-on cardholder. The main card is only a dummy card number in the name of the company for the purpose of billing all the charges of the Add-on cards. The transactions made by Add-on cardholders are billed to the main card and debits are made to the Company's Account.

**2. Business cards:** A business card is similar to a corporate card. It is meant for the use of proprietary concerns, firms, firms of Chartered Accountant, etc. This card helps to avail of certain facilities for reimbursement and makes their business trips convenient. An overall ceiling fixed for this card is also based on the status of the firm.

**3. Smart cards:** It is a new generation card. Embedded in the smart card, a microchip will store a monetary value. When a transaction is made using the card, the value is debited and the balance comes down automatically. Once the monetary value comes down to nil, the balance is to be restored all over again for the card to become operational. The primary feature of smart card is security. It prevents card-related frauds and crimes. It provides communication security as it verifies whether the signature is genuine or not. The card also recognises different voices and compares with the recorded original voice. It is used for making purchases without necessarily requiring the authorisation of Personal Identification Number as in a debit card. Smart card is an electronic purse which attempts to prove to be a panacea for all problems associated with traditional currency. In India, the Dena Bank launched the Smart Card in Mumbai.

**4. Debit cards:** Credit cards have proliferated during the last couple of years in all countries and have became an acceptable alternative to paper currency. The developed countries like USA has moved a step further. Debit card, an electronic product, has become more and more popular in these countries.

The number of cardholders as at the end of March 2014 stood at 394 million.

Just like credit card, the debit cardholder can present the card to the merchant, sign sales slip and forget about it. The purchase amount is automatically deducted or debited to the account of cardholder electronically and would appear in the monthly statement of account.

The debit card programme requires the customer to open an account with the bank which is not generally required in case of a credit card. This system requires a terminal known as the Point of Sale Terminal at every point of purchase. The customer, on making the purchase, inserts the card which has a magnetic strip at the back, into the slot of the machine, while the merchant enters the value of the transaction. The customer meanwhile, keys in the Personal Identification Number which is known only to the cardholder and the bank. The machine places an automatic call, checks the balance in the account and reduces the balance to the extent of the transaction value. The merchant's account, in turn, is credited for all his transactions on the next day.

## ❖ Differences between credit card and debit card

(*i*) The credit card is a 'pay later product', whereas a debit card is a 'pay now product'.

(*ii*) In the case of credit card, the holder can avail of credit for 30 to 45 days whereas, in a debit card the customer's account is debited immediately.

(*iii*) No sophisticated telecommunication system is required in credit card business. The debit card programme requires installation of sophisticated communication network.

(*iv*) Opening a bank account and maintaining a required amount are not essential in a credit card. A bank account and keeping a required amount to the extent of transaction are essential in a debit card system.

(*v*) Possibility of risk of fraud is high in a credit card. The risk is minimised through Personal Identification Number in debit card programme.

**5. ATM card:** An ATM (Automatic Teller Machine) card is useful to a cardholder as it helps him to withdraw cash from banks even when they are closed. This can be done by inserting the card in the ATM installed at various bank location.

**6. Virtual card:** There is always a fear in the minds of credit cardholders that their credit card numbers might get into the hands of some unscrupulous persons who could siphon away whatever they can. For those who do not want to part with their credit card number to the merchant website, the solution is to go for a Virtual Card.

A virtual card is nothing but a card that can be generated by anybody at any time provided he has already registered his name in the Bank's website. What is even better, one can also set monetary limits for each card— usually limited to the value of the item he intends to purchase. Of course, this value should be limited to his bank balance or the credit limit.

The greatest of all, this card simply lapses after use. It cannot be revised. Again, it cannot be used beyond 24 to 48 hours, as the case may be, after its generation. This completely prevents misuse. It is a kind of facility offered to existing cardholders at free of cost. For example, the HDFC Bank has introduced its 'Net Safe' card for its credit/debit cardholders at free of cost. They can generate a virtual card by registering at the HDFC Bank website.

**7. E-Wallet card:** For online payments, apart from debit and credit cards, new type of card has been introduced by the Axis Bank. A E-Wallet card is one which can be created instantly as and when needed by using the internet banking facility and it can be used only once. For example, in Axis Bank, to get a card one has to log on to the bank's internet banking portal, select the E-Wallet card option under the cards menu and then choose source account from which the funds would be debited. The minimum amount that can be loaded on the card is ₹ 10 and the maximum is ₹ 50,000. The validity period of the card is 48 hours. In case of partial usage or zero usage, the unutilised amount will be credited back to the user bank account within 4 days. This card can be used for making payments on all websites that accept Visa cards.

**8. E-commerce Credit Card/Co-branded Credit Card:** Recently, some banks have come forward to issue credit cards in partnership with e-commerce companies to attract more customers. This type of credit card is called co-branded credit card or e-commerce credit card. These cards offer rewards in the form of cashbacks, discounts and reward points. The 'Amazon Pay ICICI Bank Credit Card' and 'Flipkart Axis Bank Credit Card' are two such cards. Any registered Amazon Pay user can apply for ICICI Co-branded Credit Card without being a customer of that bank at that time. But, for Flipkart Axis Co-branded Credit Card, one must have a bank account either current or savings in that bank apart from being a registered Flipkart user.

## PARTIES TO A CREDIT CARD

There are three parties to a credit card — the cardholder, the issuer and the member establishments:

1. **Issuer:** The banks or other card issuing organisations.
2. **Cardholders:** Individuals, corporate bodies and non-individual and non-corporate bodies such as firms.
3. **Member establishments:** Shops and service organisations enlisted by credit card issuer who accept credit cards. The member establishments may be a business enterprise dealing in goods and services such as retail outlets, departmental stores, restaurants, hotels, hospitals, travel agencies, petrol bunks, etc.

Member establishments have to pay a certain percentage of discount on the credit card transactions to the issuer. Some organisations charge a specified sum as service charge. For instance, Indian Railways levy a service charge in addition to the fare.

### ❖ Member affiliate

There is one more party to the credit card, in the case of tie-up arrangement, called member affiliate.

The issuer, may sometimes, enter a tie-up arrangement for issuance of credit cards with other organisations. Such organisations are called member affiliates. In such cases, the organisations which have tie-up arrangements also issue cards of the issuer to their clients. Credit cards issued by member affiliates contain the name and logo of the member affiliate on the face of the card, besides name and logo of the issuer. This arrangement enlarges the scope and operations of the credit card.

Many banks have tie-up arrangement with Master Card International and Visa International. These organisations allow cardholders of one bank to use their cards in member establishment of another bank. The bank in whose fold the member establishment falls, called the Acquiring Bank, pay the amount to the merchant less his discount and the transaction is routed through either Master Card or VISA who act as the clearing agencies. Master Card or VISA route the transaction through their network to the issuing bank which in turn makes payment to the acquiring bank. The issuing bank gets a percentage of the merchant discount as stipulated by the either Master Card or VISA.

## PROCEDURE AT THE TIME OF PURCHASE AT MEMBER ESTABLISHMENTS

When a cardholder intends to make purchases, he presents his credit card for payment. The member establishment scrutinises the card with reference to the following:

1. The validity period of the card has not expired.
2. The card has not been hot listed as per the latest 'hot list'/warning bulletin.

   Whenever bank receives information about card lost/withdrawn/cancelled, it issues a warning letter. The hot list gives the latest list of invalid cards and supersedes all warning bulletin.
3. The signature of the cardholder tallies with the specimen signature on the credit card.
4. The card has not been tampered within any manner.

On being satisfied with the validity of the credit card, the merchant proceeds in the following way:

1. Obtain the impression of the card with the help of the imprinter.
2. Obtain cardholder's signature in the space provided and check whether signature tallies with the signature on the card.
3. Prepare a chargeslip in triplicate giving all details. Give one copy to the consumer, keep one copy for records and forward one copy to the bank.

## PROCEDURE FOR REIMBURSEMENT

The following procedure is followed for reimbursement to member establishments:

1. The merchant can claim reimbursement from the designated branches of bank.
2. All transactions emanating during the day are consolidated in the Summation Sheet cum BAR in triplicate.
3. The summation sheet cum BAR in duplicate along with the Bank's copy of the chargeslip should be submitted to the designated branch for reimbursement.
4. Reimbursement should be obtained within 30 days from the date of chargeslips.
5. The banks after deducting commission credit the amount of claim to the member establishment's account or pay by D/D as earlier agreed.

## FACILITIES OFFERED TO CARDHOLDERS

The various facilities offered to cardholders are described below:

1. Making purchase/availing of services at any of the member establishments.
2. Cash withdrawals at any of the branches of the issuer/member affiliate of the issuer to meet emergent requirements.
3. Add-on facility for family members. The spouse or children are entitled to use the card for making purchases.
4. Free credit period ranging from 15 to 45 days.
5. ATM facility at selected centres.
6. Wide range of insurance facilities are available which include personal accident insurance, cover for accidental death, baggage insurance, purchase protection cover against risk of fire, riot, strike, theft, etc. during transportation and concessional premium rates for personal accident insurance and mediclaim.

### ❖ New innovative services available

Nowadays, many new services are available to credit cardholders. Some of them are:

(i) **Balance transfer facility:** Under this facility, any outstanding balance of one credit card can be transferred to another.

(ii) **Cash advance facility:** Under this, in case of any emergency, a credit cardholder can go to the nearest ATM and withdraw card up to the prescribed limit.

(iii) **Dial a draft facility:** This facility enables a cardholder to put a request for a loan by calling a call centre of a credit card company. The amount will be delivered in 4 or 5 days in the form of a draft.

(iv) **Reward points facility:** A cardholder can earn reward points for all purchases made using the credit card. Finally, those reward points could be redeemed to purchase any gifts offered by the credit card company.

## BENEFITS OF CREDIT CARDS

Credit cards confer a number of advantages on cardholders, issuers and member establishments. The benefits of credit cards to various parties are given below:

### ❖ Cardholders

1. Credit cards are simple to operate and easy to carry. The holders are relieved from the risk of carrying cash or cheque book with them.
2. A card is a convenient method of payment for goods and services. The holders have the option to purchase goods and services and pay conveniently at a later date in manageable instalments compatible with their household budgets.
3. Owing to revolving nature of credit, the customer can take advantage of it as and when he pleases within the overall limit.
4. Cash can be obtained at any branch of the issuer. The ATM facility is extended to cardholders who need not stand in queues and spend time unnecessarily at banks. By just inserting a card into an ATM, the holder can withdraw crisp new notes at any time of day or night.
5. Overdraft facility is given to cardholders who are entitled to spend more than their actual limit. The amount of overdraft depends on the holder's past credit rating.
6. The purchasing power of the cardholder increases to the extent of credit limit given in the card. If wisely used by consumers, credit cards can provide them extra money interest free. All that one has to do is to settle the bill in time.
7. Credit cards provide a certain degree of prestige to the holder. The status which one gets is not only because of his membership in a credit card organisation but because the card at once makes him great in a part of wider phenomenon. Visa, American Express and Master Card are all prestigious international organisations spread over 50 to 60 countries and their affiliated cards being acceptable in thousands of establishments all over the world.

### ❖ Issuers

1. Credit cards offer high profit for the banks. They get commission or discount, usually 2.5 per cent, on sale through credit cards. An interest charge of 1.5 per cent is made on all outstandings. Thus, a single transaction through credit card, assuming the customer does not repay within the stipulated period will fetch income of 5 per cent to the bank which works out as much as 60 per cent per annum; miles ahead of the prime lending rate of many banks. As more and more take advantage of the credit facility, the credit card service becomes more profitable.
2. Where the card is issued to non-accountholders, it may help to get new customers.
3. A credit card system helps control bank cost as it reduces the number of cheques issued by the customers.

### ❖ Member establishment

1. The merchant has guarantee of payment and his account is credited immediately on submitting the charge slip into his bank. No bad debt arises in credit card transactions.
2. A good cash flow is established because of the speedy settlement of bills by banks.
3. The acceptance of card in lieu of cash reduces security risk.
4. Member establishments are able to offer credit facility to their customers without setting up their own credit arrangements.
5. More and more people accept the practical advantage of credit cards and turn to suppliers who accept the cards in settlement. This helps increase the volume of business to member establishments.

## DEMERITS OF CREDIT CARDS

The credit card is not risk-free and all players associated with it have to face an element of risk associated with it.

### ❖ Cardholders

1. The cardholders are burdened with service charge, annual fee, membership fee, etc. A high rate of interest is charged for delayed payment. A minimum of 5-10 per cent on monthly purchases apart from the additional charges are to be paid in case the consumers postpone the payment beyond the stipulated credit period. According to a recent survey, 65 per cent of cardholders are ignorant about the high interest charged on outstanding balance.
2. Credit cards tempt the holders for more purchases beyond their income and repaying capacity.

### ❖ Issuers

1. The cost involved in the credit card business is high which include cost of plastic card to be imported, cost of information, cost of placing and marketing cards, cost on staff to monitor processing of applications and to carry-out credit checks on applicants, etc. Unless the number of cardholders and the volume of business is high, the credit card business will not be a profitable one.
2. The menace of frauds perpetuated by holders of bogus cards and sometimes in collusion with the member establishments is the major problem for the issuers.
3. The average utilisation of credit card is only 20 per cent to 30 per cent in India. The underutilisation of this facility erodes the profitability of banks.

### ❖ Member establishment

1. The commission to be paid to the issuing banks/credit card organisation is heavy.
2. Some banks make delay in payment due to lack of adequate system and trained personnel which affect the cash flow of the member establishments.

## PREPAID INSTRUMENTS

Apart from debit cards and credit cards, Prepaid payment instruments (PPIs) have become popular for the purchase of goods and services and also for fund transfers. Among PPIs, PPI cards are the most popular mode used by the customers followed by mobile wallets. PPI cards include mobile prepaid instruments, gift cards, social benefit cards, foreign travel cards and corporate cards. During 2015-16, the value of transactions through PPI cards and mobile wallets have increased significantly to ₹ 254 billion and ₹ 206 billion respectively on against ₹ 105 billion and ₹ 82 billion respectively in the previous year.

## FUTURE PROSPECTS

There are 1 billion cardholders worldover. These cards have a turnover of $ 1,500 million.

There are around 19 million credit cardholders and 394 million debit cardholders in India. Over 75,000 establishments in the country accept credit cards. The credit card market is worth about ₹ 1,500 crores. The credit card industry is growing at an average rate of 35 per cent per year. The total demand for credit card and debit card is expected to increase at an alarming rate. The total number of credit cards issued stood at 5.86 crores as on September 30, 2020. Of this, the HDFC Bank has issued 1.49 crore cards and the SBI 1.1 crore cards. As on February 2021, the number of credit cards issued by the ICICI Bank stood at 1.03 crores. The ICICI Bank, SBI and HDFC Bank are the largest credit card acquirers in India. Despite the impressive pattern of growth, India as a market is in a fairly nascent stage with credit card penetration amounting to just 15 per cent of the customers. Compared to other countries in the region, India's cardholders' base is relatively small.

With the economic growth gradually outpacing population growth and with a large number of affluent middle-class, the potential market that India holds is immense. It is estimated that in the next ten years India will have a credit card population second to USA. According to few top banking professionals, the credit card business will grow by over 100 per cent every year for the next five years.

Recently, NBFCs registered with the RBI including non-deposit-taking companies are permitted to enter into credit/debit card business after getting a certificate of registration and permission to enter into that business. However, the minimum net owned funds should be ₹ 100 crores.

To realise the potential in the credit card market, the following suggestions are made:

1. Reduce the membership and annual subscription fees.
2. Encourage member establishments to accept credit cards for routine items also.
3. Make the features of cards convenient to middle-class people.
4. Enhance the cash withdrawal limits.
5. 80 per cent of the cardholders are in metropolitan areas. So, workout strategies to popularise the credit card among people in semi-urban and rural areas.

# QUESTIONS

## I. Objective type questions:

### A. Fill in the blanks:

1. A credit card enables cardholders to make purchase without making ______ payment.
2. ________ card is a convenient means of payment rather than credit facility.
3. In case the issuer of credit card enters into tie-up arrangement with another party, the party is called ________
4. Corporate credit cards are issued to ________.
5. ________ card provides communication security.

**[Key :** 1. immediate, 2. charge, 3. member affiliate,, 4. companies, 5. Smart]

### B. State whether the following statements are TRUE or FALSE:

1. The debit card programme requires the customer to open an account.
2. Insurance facilities are available to credit cardholders.
3. Bad debts arise in credit card transactions.
4. Overdraft facility is not given to cardholders.
5. Credit cards tempt the holders for more purchases.

**[Key:** 1. True, 2. True, 3. False, 4. False, 5. True.]

## II. Short answer type questions:

1. What is a credit card?
2. Who can become a cardholder?
3. Write a note on smart card.
4. What is a debit card?
5. Who are the parties to a credit card?
6. Who is a member affiliate?
7. What is a prepaid card?
8. What is co-branded credit card?

## III. Essay type questions:

1. Discuss the advantages and disadvantages of credit card to its members and banks.
2. Describe the facilities offered to credit cardholders.
3. Explain the various types of credit cards and their merits and demerits.

20

# PRACTICALS IN STOCK MARKET OPERATIONS

To enable students to gain some practical knowledge in stock market operations, specimen of some important forms that are used in day-to-day operations have been given here under. Students are advised to fill up these forms and acquire necessary practical skills in the subject.

A. Specimen of Primary Share Application Form.

B. Specimen of Share Certificate.

C. Specimen of Share Transfer Form.

D. Specimen of Proxy Form.

E. Specimen of Dematerialisation Request Form.

F. Graphs and Diagrams Showing Price Movements of Shares.

## A. SPECIMEN OF PRIMARY SHARE APPLICATION FORM

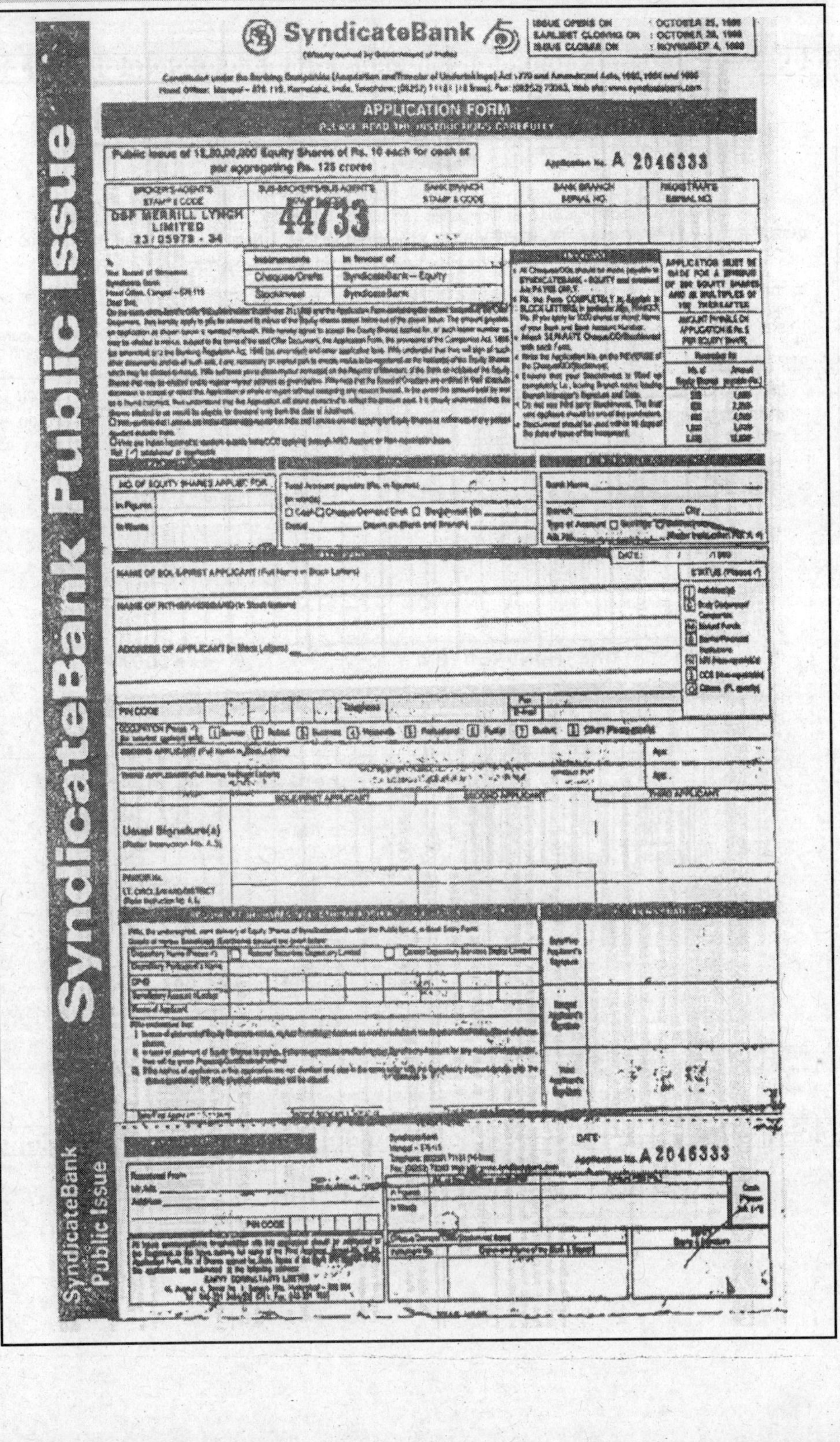

SyndicateBank Public Issue

SyndicateBank

ISSUE OPENS ON : OCTOBER 25, 1999
EARLIEST CLOSING ON : OCTOBER 28, 1999
ISSUE CLOSES ON : NOVEMBER 4, 1999

APPLICATION FORM

PLEASE READ THE INSTRUCTIONS CAREFULLY

Public Issue of 12,50,00,000 Equity Shares of Rs. 10 each for cash at par aggregating Rs. 125 crores

Application No. A 2046333

| BROKER'S/AGENT'S STAMP & CODE | SUB-BROKER'S/SUB AGENT'S STAMP & CODE | BANK BRANCH STAMP & CODE | BANK BRANCH SERIAL NO. | REGISTRAR'S SERIAL NO. |
| --- | --- | --- | --- | --- |
| DSP MERRILL LYNCH LIMITED 23/05978 - 34 | 44733 | | | |

| Instruments | In favour of |
| --- | --- |
| Cheque/Drafts | SyndicateBank — Equity |
| Stockinvest | SyndicateBank |

APPLICATION MUST BE MADE FOR A MINIMUM OF 200 EQUITY SHARES AND IN MULTIPLES OF 100 THEREAFTER

NO. OF EQUITY SHARES APPLIED FOR

In Figures

In Words

NAME OF SOLE/FIRST APPLICANT (Full Name in Block Letters)

NAME OF FATHER/HUSBAND (in Block letters)

ADDRESS OF APPLICANT (in Block Letters)

PIN CODE

STATUS (Please ✓)

SECOND APPLICANT (Full Name in Block Letters)

Age

THIRD APPLICANT (Full Name in Block Letters)

Age

| | SOLE/FIRST APPLICANT | SECOND APPLICANT | THIRD APPLICANT |
| --- | --- | --- | --- |
| Usual Signature(s) | | | |
| PAN/GIR No. | | | |
| I.T. CIRCLE/WARD/DISTRICT | | | |

SyndicateBank Public Issue

DATE

Application No. A 2046333

Received From

PIN CODE

## B. SPECIMEN OF SHARE CERTIFICATE

**इलाहाबाद बैंक** **ALLAHABAD BANK**

(भारत सरकार का उपक्रम) (A Government of India Undertaking)

[बैंककारी कंपनी (उपक्रमों का अर्जन और अंतरण) अधिनियम 1970 के अंतर्गत गठित]

[Constituted under the Banking Companies (Acquisition & Transfer of Undertakings) Act, 1970]

**प्रधान कार्यालय : 2 नेताजी सुभाष रोड, कोलकाता-700 001. Head Office : 2 Netaji Subhas Road, Kolkata-700 001.**

**शेयर प्रमाण पत्र SHARE CERTIFICATE**

यह प्रमाणित किया जाता है कि इस प्रमाण पत्र में नामित व्यक्ति, इसमें दी गई सुस्पष्ट संख्या के शेयर/(शेयरों) के, विधि के लागू प्रावधानों के अधीन पंजीकृत धारक है/हैं एवं इस प्रत्येक शेयर पर पराांकित राशि प्रदत्त कर दी गई है.

THIS IS TO CERTIFY that the person(s) named in this Certificate is/are the Registered Holder(s) of the within mentioned share(s) bearing the distinctive Number(s) herein specified subject to applicable provisions of law and that the amount endorsed herein has been paid-up on each such share.

| | | | | |
|---|---|---|---|---|
| **इक्विटी शेयर का मूल्य** | रू. 10.00 | **EQUITY SHARES EACH OF** | **Rs.** | **10.00** |
| **प्रति शेयर प्रदत्त राशि** | रू. 10.00 | **AMOUNT PAID-UP PER SHARE** | **Rs.** | **10.00** |

रजि. फोलियो सं.
Regd. Folio No. ALB042369 242219

प्रमाण पत्र क्रमांक
Certificate Number 127795

धारक का/धारकों के नाम
Name(s) of Holder(s) GORDON E

शेयरों की संख्या
No. of Shares held ONE HUNDRED ONLY ***100***

विशेषक संख्या/संख्याएँ
Distinctive No.(s) 0259507101-0259507200

Given under the Common Seal of the Bank this 23rd November, 2002 at Hyderabad

Chairman & Managing Director — Executive Director

General Manager — General Manager — Authorised Signatory

CONSOLIDATED STAMP DUTY PAID VIDE G.O. Rt. No.

टिप्पणी : इस प्रमाण पत्र में दिए गए उपर्युक्त किसी भी शेयर का अंतरण तब तक पंजीकृत नहीं होगा जब तक यह प्रमाण पत्र उसके साथ नहीं लगाया गया है।

Notes : No transfer of any of the above mentioned Shares comprised in this Certificate will be registered unless accompanied by this Certificate.

548772

# C. SPECIMEN OF SHARE TRANSFER FORM

**THIS DOCUMENT IS IMPORTANT AND REQUIRES YOUR IMMEDIATE ATTENTION**

- *Please submit this Form with enclosures to the Registrar to the Offer at their address given overleaf.*
- *Please read the enclosed Letter of Offer dated January 19, 2007 carefully before filling this Acceptance Form.*
- *All terms and expressions used herein shall have the same meaning as ascribed thereto in the Letter of Offer.*
- *Each shareholder of PLL to whom this Offer is being made, is free to offer his shareholding in PLL in whole or in part while accepting the Offer.*

| OFFER |
|---|
| **OPENS ON**: Monday - February 5, 2007 |
| **CLOSES ON**: Saturday - February 24, 2007 |

**FORM OF ACCEPTANCE-CUM-ACKNOWLEDGEMENT**

From:

Folio No./DP ID No./ Client ID No.:

To,

Alankit Assignments Limited

[Unit: **Phoenix Lamps Limited**] Alankit House, 2E/21, Jhandewalan Extension, New Delhi 110 055

Dear Sir,

Sub: Open Offer for purchase of up to 56,03,860 equity shares of Phoenix Lamps Limited [PLL] representing 20.00% of the paid up equity share capital at an offer price of Rs.190/- per fully paid-up equity share by Argon India Limited and Argon South Asia Limited ["Acquirers"] and Actis India Fund 2 LP, Actis South Asia Fund 2 LP, Actis Executive Co-Investment Plan LP and Actis Capital LLP ["Persons Acting in Concert"]

I/We refer to the Letter of Offer dated January 19, 2007 for acquiring the equity shares held by me/us in PLL.

I/We, the undersigned, have read the Letter of Offer and understood the contents including the terms and conditions mentioned therein.

☐ **FOR SHARES IN PHYSICAL FORM**

I/We accept the Offer and enclose the original share certificate (s) and duly signed transfer deed(s) in respect of my/ our shares as detailed below:

| Sr. No | Ledger Folio No | Certificate No | Distinctive Nos | | No of fully paid-up Shares |
|---|---|---|---|---|---|
| | | | From | To | |
| | | | | | |
| | | | | | |
| | | | | | |
| | | | | | |
| | | | | | |
| | | | | Total number of Shares | |

*Note: Please attach an additional sheet of paper if the above space is insufficient and authenticate the same.*

I/ We note and understand that the original share certificate (s) and valid share transfer deed(s) will be held in trust for me/ us by Registrar to the Offer until the time the acquirers pay the purchase consideration as mentioned in the Letter of Offer. I/ We also note and understand that the Acquirers will pay the purchase consideration only after verification of the documents and signatures.

☐ **SHARES IN DEMATERIALIZED FORM**

I/We holding shares in the dematerialized form, accept the Offer and enclose the photocopy of the Delivery Instruction in "Off-market" mode, duly acknowledged by the Depository Participant ("DP") in respect of my/our shares as detailed below:

| DP Name | DP ID | Client ID | Beneficiary Name | No of fully paid-up Shares |
|---|---|---|---|---|
| | | | | |

I/ We have executed an off-market transaction for crediting the shares to the escrow demat/ depository account with Alankit Assignments styled **"Argon-Phoenix Lamps-Escrow Demat Account"** with the following particulars:

| DP Name | DP ID | Client ID | ISIN |
|---|---|---|---|
| Alankit Assignments Ltd. | IN300118 | 10977858 | INE 455 B 01016 |

☐ via a delivery instruction from my account with NSDL ☐ via inter-depository delivery instruction from my account with CDSL

I/ We note and understand that the shares would reside in the Escrow Demat/ Depository Account until the time the Acquirers make payment of purchase consideration as mentioned in the Letter of Offer

# D. SPECIMEN OF PROXY FORM

**STERLITE INDUSTRIES (INDIA) LIMITED**

Registered Office: SIPCOT Industrial Complex, Madurai Byepass Road, T V Puram PO,
Tuticorin - 628 002, Tamil Nadu, India

**ATTENDANCE SLIP**

Members Folio/Client & DP - ID No. ____________________

No. of Shares ____________________

____________________

I hereby record my presence at the 34th Annual General Meeting held on Saturday, September 19, 2009, at 2.00 p.m. at Tamira Club, Tamira Niketan, SIPCOT Industrial Complex, Madurai Byepass Road, T. V. Puram P.O., Tuticorin - 628 002, Tamil Nadu, India.

(Name of Member/Proxy ____________________ Signature of Member/Proxy ____________________

**Notes:**

1. Member/Proxy holder must bring the admission slip to the Meeting and hand-over at the entrance duly signed.

---

**STERLITE INDUSTRIES (INDIA) LIMITED**

Registered Office: SIPCOT Industrial Complex, Madurai Byepass Road, T. V. Puram PO,
Tuticorin - 628 002, Tamil Nadu, India

**PROXY FORM**

I/We ________________________________________

of ________________________________________

being a member/members of the above named Company, hereby appoint ____________

____________________ of ____________________

or failing him/her ________________________________________

of ________________________________________

as my/our proxy to attend and vote for me/us on my/our behalf at the 34th Annual General Meeting of the Company to be held on Saturday, September 19, 2009, at 2.00 p.m. at Tamira Club, Tamira Niketan, SIPCOT Industrial Complex, Madurai Byepass Road, T. V. Puram P.O., Tuticorin - 628 002, Tamil Nadu, India.

Signed ____________________

Date ____________________

Affix Re. 1 Revenue Stamp

Members Folio/Client & DP - ID No. ____________________

No. of Shares ____________________

____________________

**Notes:**

1. The instrument of Proxy form shall be deposited at the Registered Office of the Company, not less than 48 hours before the time fixed for holding the Meeting.
2. The form should be signed across the stamp as per speçimen signature registered with the Company.
3. A proxy need not to be member.

# E. SPECIMEN OF DEMATERIALISATION REQUEST FORM

**ICICI Bank Demat Services**

## Sample-filled Dematerialisation Request Form (DRF)

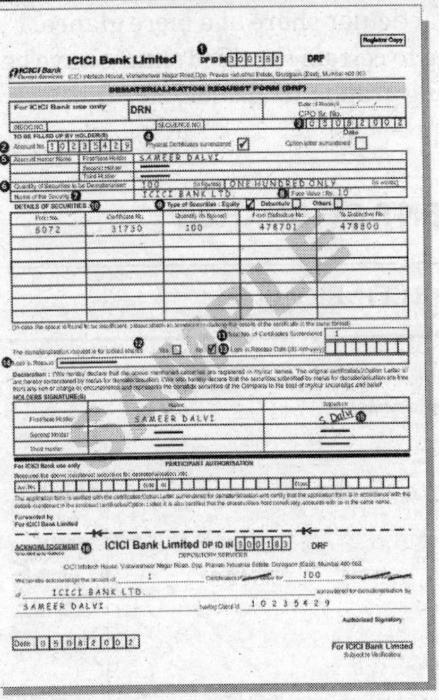
ICICI Bank Limited DRF
DEMATERIALISATION REQUEST FORM (DRF)
For ICICI Bank use only DRN
SAMEER DALVI
100 ONE HUNDRED ONLY
ICICI BANK LTD.
6072 31730 100 478701 478800
SAMPLE
SAMEER DALVI
ICICI Bank Limited DRF
ICICI BANK LTD.
SAMEER DALVI 10235429

Submit a completely filled up Demat Request Form (DRF) in triplicate for each ISIN along with defaced physical securities.

1. ***DP-ID:*** Specify your DPID here.
2. ***Account No.:*** Specify your account no. here
3. ***Date:*** Specify the date of submitting the DRF.
4. ***Physical Certificates/Option letter Surrendered:*** Put a tick against the box for 'Physical Certificates surrendered' if you are submitting defaced physical certificates. Put a tick against the box for 'Option letter surrendered' if you are submitting an option letter.

   The option letter is sent to you by the Registrar when you lodged the shares for transfer in your name along with a transfer-cum-demat request. Ensure that the time limit mentioned in the option letter is not expired.
5. ***Account Holder Name:*** Specify the name of the holders in their order in the demat account.
6. ***Quantity of Securities to be Dematerialised (in figures and in words):*** Specify the quantity in figures and in words. Mention the no. of shares/debentures/etc represented by the surrendered certificates.
7. ***Name of the Security:*** Specify the name of the security to be dematerialised from the physical certificate. Ensure that security is eligible for Demat from www.icicibank.com/Branch. Use a separate DRF for each security having a unique ISIN. However, securities for the same ISIN with the same pattern of holders but under different folio nos. can be dematerialised with a single DRF.
8. ***Face Value:*** Specify the face value of the security from the physical certificate.
9. ***Type of Securities:*** Put a tick against the box for Equity/Debenture/Others depending on the type of securities being submitted for dematerialisation.
10. ***Details of Securities:*** The details of certificates such as the folio no., certificate no., & distinctive no. must be filled up correctly on the DRF. Attach an annexure of the same format if there are more details than can be specified in the space provided. The combination and the order of holders' names on DRF and as printed on the Certificates should be identical with that in the DP account. This is subject to two exceptions:
    - The name on the demat account and that on the certificate are different merely on account of initials not being spelt out fully or put after or prior to the surname.
    - The combination of holders on the demat account and that on the certificate are the same and the difference is only in the order in which the names of the holders appear at the two places. Here, you have to submit a Transposition Request Form also along with the DRF.

    You must deface the certificates by putting a stamp or by writing "SURRENDERED FOR DEMATERIALISATION". However defacing should be done only after checking the eligibility of security, as defaced securities cannot be sold in physical form. If defacing has been done by mistake then you should send the same to registrar for replacement.

    Ensure that the certificates are attached in the same order as mentioned in the DRF.
11. ***Total No. of certificates surrendered:*** Specify the total no. of certificates surrendered. In case of an option letter, this is to be specified as 1.
12. ***Locked Shares:*** Put a tick against the box for 'Yes' if the shares are under lock-in, i.e., there are restrictions on their disposal before a specified date. Use a separate DRF for certificates under lock-in.
13. ***Lock-in Release Date:*** Specify the date on which the lock-in is getting released, i.e., restrictions on disposal of the securities are off. Use separate DRFs for securities with different lock-in release dates.
14. ***Lock-in reason:*** Specify the reason for the lock-in. Amongst lock-in securities belonging to the same ISIN but having different lock-in reason, use separate DRFs.
15. ***Signature:*** The holders should sign in the order of their names in the account. The signature should match with the specimen signature with the Registrar (If you have a doubt on this, you can get the signature on the DRF attested by your banker) as well as with ICICI Bank (If the signature differs from that with ICICI Bank, you should sign the DRF in the presence of the Branch Officer). Authenticate all alterations on the form with your full signature.
16. ***Acknowledgement:*** Fill up the acknowledgement portion of the form also. Take the tear-off portion of the first copy (Registrar copy) on submission as an acknowledgement.

The shares and DRF are sent to the registrar who then confirms the request for credit in the demat account. The normal time taken for credit is about 30 days which can vary from Registrar to Registrar.

**This sheet is only for reference. Kindly hand it over to the concerned Bank representative after use.**

# F. GRAPHS AND DIAGRAMS SHOWING PRICE MOVEMENTS OF SHARES

The price movements of individual stock over a period of time, the earnings per share, dividend per share, etc., can be better represented in the form of graphs, charts and diagrams so that one can easily find out the price trend of a particular share at a mere glance. For the benefit of students, some graphs and diagrams pertaining to certain specified shares have been presented hereunder. Students can develop the art of drawing graphs, diagrams, etc., themselves by looking at these graphs.

## I. PRICE MOVEMENT OF SHARES

SHIRPUR GOLD REFINERY Ltd.

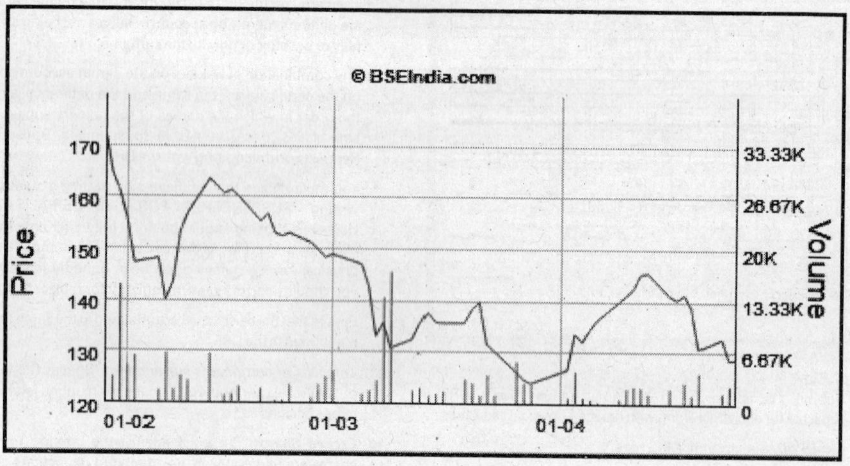


RELIANCE COMMUNICATIONS Ltd.

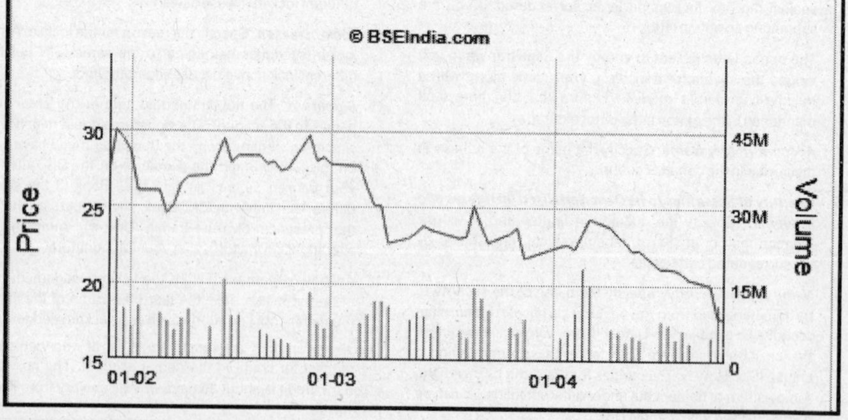

## SUN PHARMACEUTICAL INDUSTRIES Ltd.

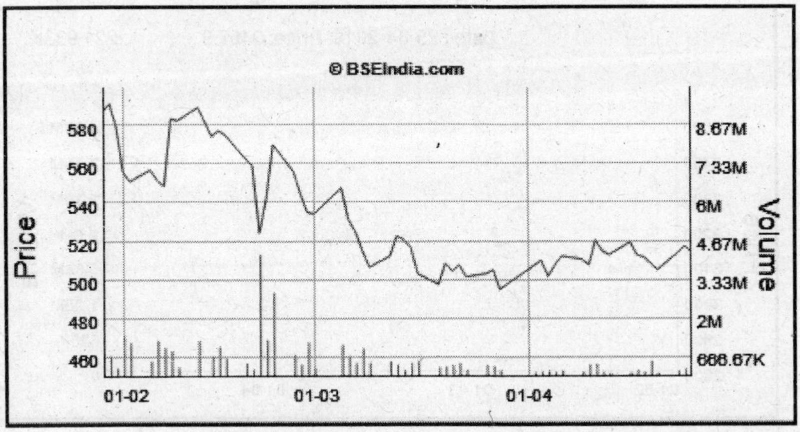


## KOTAK MAHINDRA BANK Ltd.

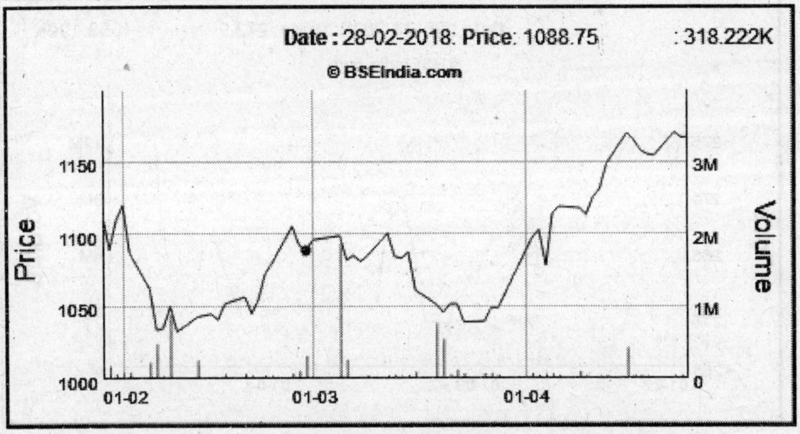


## HOUSING DEVELOPMENT FINANCE CORP. Ltd.

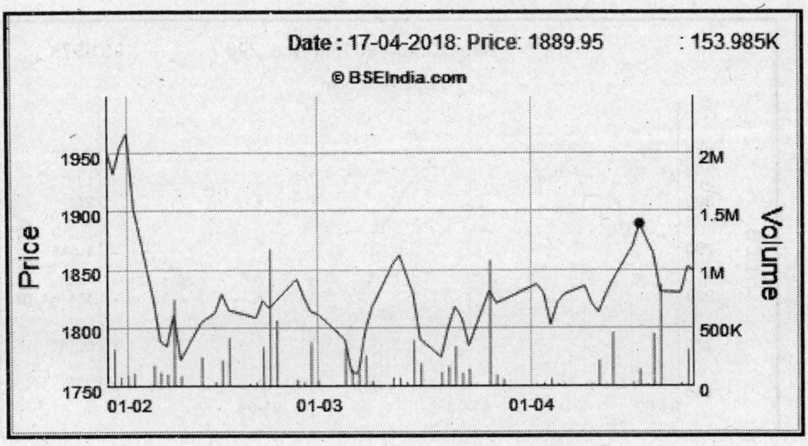

## TATA CONSULTANCY SERVICES Ltd.

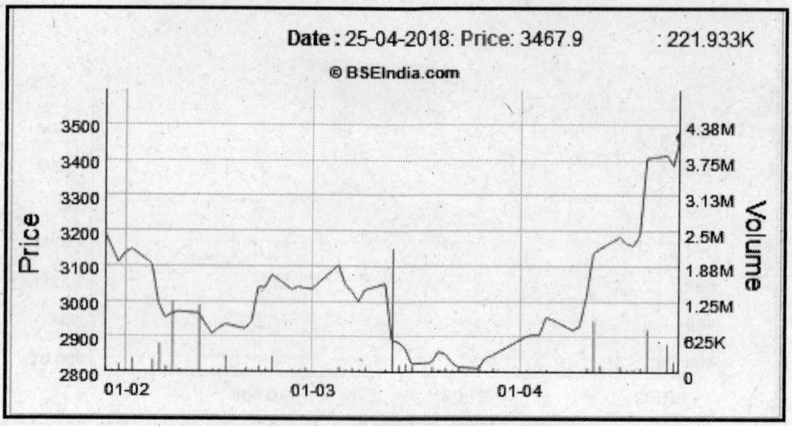


## ITC Ltd.

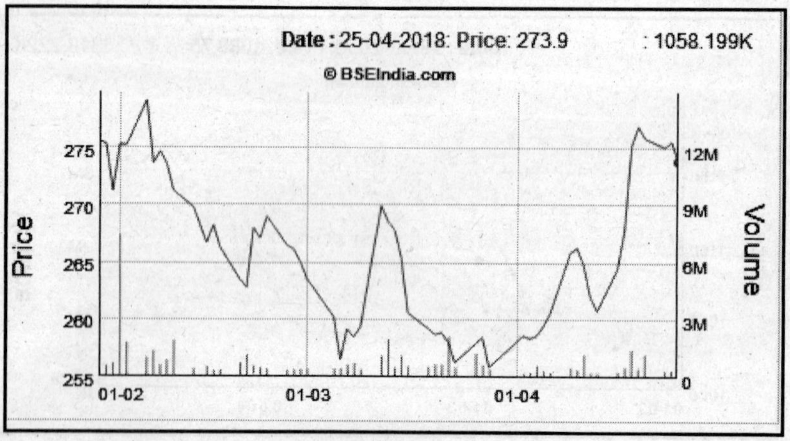


## COAL INDIA Ltd.

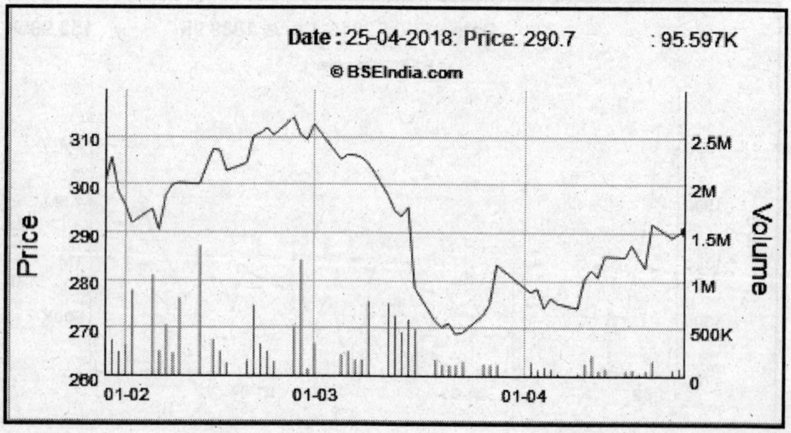

**LARSEN & TOUBRO LTD.**

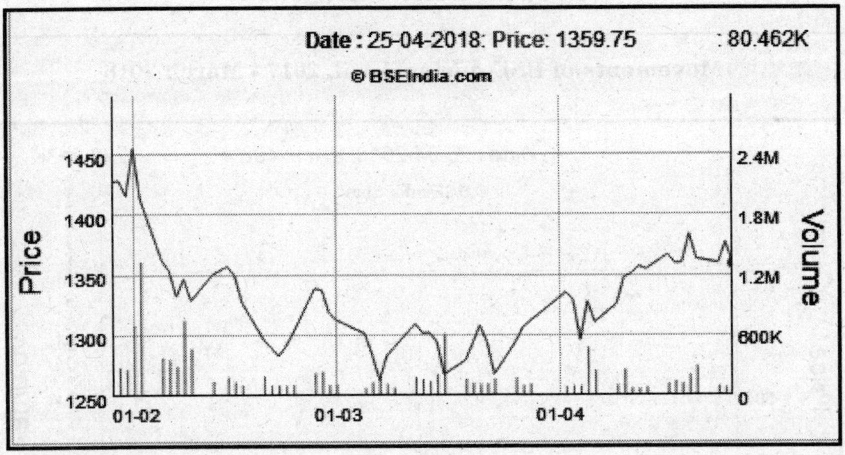


***Source:*** www.bseindia.com

## II. AXIS BANK SHARES

**Movements of BSE during April, 2017 - March 2018**

**Movements of NSE during January, 2018 - April, 2018**

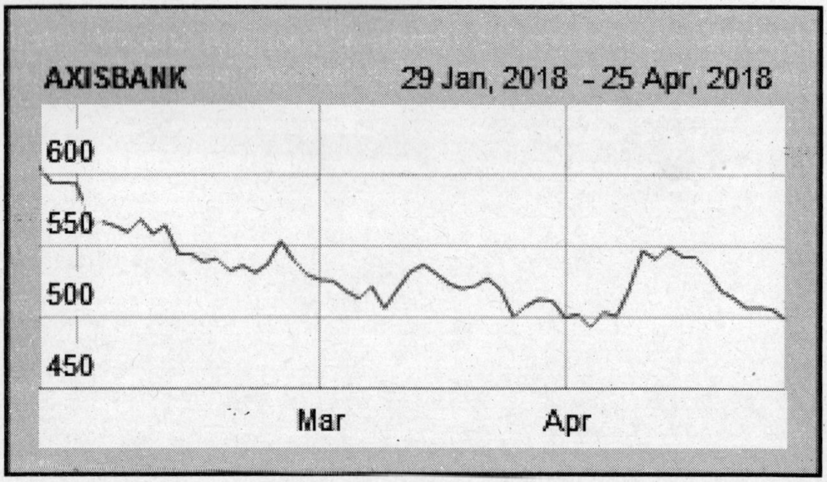


***Source:*** www.bseindia.com; www.nseindia.com